HUMANITARIAN INTERNATIONALISM
UNDER EMPIRE

HUMANITARIAN INTERNATIONALISM UNDER EMPIRE

THE GLOBAL EVOLUTION

of the

JAPANESE RED CROSS

MOVEMENT, 1877–1945

MICHIKO SUZUKI

Columbia University Press
New York

Columbia University Press
Publishers Since 1893
New York   Chichester, West Sussex
cup.columbia.edu

Copyright © 2024 Columbia University Press
All rights reserved

Library of Congress Cataloging-in-Publication Data:
Names: Suzuki, Michiko, author.
Title: Humanitarian internationalism under empire : the global evolution of the Japanese Red Cross movement, 1877–1945 / Michiko Suzuki.
Description: New York : Columbia University Press, [2024] | Includes bibliographical references and index.
Identifiers: LCCN 2023059453 (print) | LCCN 2023059454 (ebook) | ISBN 9780231211642 (hardback) | ISBN 9780231211659 (trade paperback) | ISBN 9780231559010 (ebook)
Subjects: LCSH: Nihon Sekijūjisha. | Humanitarianism—Japan—History—20th century. | Japan—History—1868- | Japan—History—1926–1945.
Classification: LCC HV580.J33 S89 2024 (print) | LCC HV580.J33 (ebook) | DDC 361.7/6340952—dc23/eng/20240202
LC record available at https://lccn.loc.gov/2023059453
LC ebook record available at https://lccn.loc.gov/2023059454

Cover design: Milenda Nan Ok Lee
Cover photo: Young nurse, photo by Ken Domon, 1938.
Domon (1909–1990) was a leading Japanese photojournalist
and photo artist in interwar and postwar Japan.
Ken Domon Museum of Photography.

FOR MOMOKO, GONTARŌ, YUMEKO,
SHIMAKO, AND RYŌTA

I pray, I will not
Will not spend my life in vain
Following the path before me, I
Walk on, walk on with resolve
With a heart so pure and clear

我が生命　おろそかにならず　示し給ふ
道こそ践まめ　心清めて

Tochigi Kimi, Dōhō-kadan *[Dōhō Poetry Society]*

CONTENTS

Acknowledgments xi
Note on Transliteration and Translation xvii
Abbreviations xix

INTRODUCTION 1

1. RESPONDING TO CRISES: A PEOPLE'S HUMANITARIAN MOVEMENT 11

2. INTERNATIONALISM IN CRISIS: THE FIFTEENTH INTERNATIONAL CONFERENCE OF THE RED CROSS IN TOKYO, 1934 36

3. TRANSNATIONAL HUMANITARIAN MOVEMENT: THE JAPANESE RED CROSS SOCIETY AND OVERSEAS EMPIRE 68

4. BEYOND EMPIRE: THE JAPANESE RED CROSS SOCIETY IN HAWAI'I AND BRAZIL 91

5. THE JAPANESE RED CROSS SOCIETY AND WORLD WAR II: CIVILIAN CASUALTIES, INTERNEES, AND PRISONERS OF WAR   108

6. NUCLEAR EMERGENCY: JAPANESE RED CROSS SOCIETY NURSES IN HIROSHIMA AND NAGASAKI, AUGUST 1945   137

CONCLUSION   165

Appendix 1. Resolutions of the XVth International Red Cross Conference   171
Appendix 2. Draft International Convention on the Condition and Protection of Civilians, Tokyo, 1934   181
Note on Sources   189
Notes   193
Bibliography   251
Index   307

ACKNOWLEDGMENTS

This book represents the completion of a nearly twenty-year journey that began when I chanced upon the testimony of a Japanese Red Cross medical doctor stationed at the Japanese Red Cross Society's (JRCS) Hiroshima Hospital in the aftermath of the Hiroshima nuclear bombing. I was profoundly struck by his ceaseless dedication to medical treatment for *hibakusha*, which continued into the postwar period. His story filled me with admiration and piqued my intellectual curiosity. In 2007, as a graduate student at SOAS University of London, I studied Japanese narratives of the atomic bomb experience under the direction of Professor Stephen Dodd. His guidance opened my mind to the cultural aspects of Japan's historical experiences. After receiving my master's degree from SOAS, I returned to Japan and joined the International Committee of the Red Cross's Tokyo staff. When the 2011 great earthquake and tsunami struck the Tohoku region in northern Japan, I was unexpectedly involved in the ICRC's response to the Fukushima nuclear crisis. While many international organizations and foreign embassies closed their offices, the JRCS immediately mobilized to cope with the emergency, and Red Cross aid workers were thrown into action. Their bravery and devotion to duty at great personal risk prompted me to ask a fundamental question: "What motivates Red Cross workers to save lives and provide relief to victims amidst extreme risk?" I decided to go back to SOAS University of London and pursue this research question.

This book grew out of my course of study at SOAS under the expert supervision of Dr. Christopher Gerteis, who with his wife Jennifer Anderson have provided intellectual guidance, friendship, and support ever since. At this time I received valued support and guidance from Stephen Dodd, Barak Kushner, Pajyashree Pandey, Janet Hunter, John Breen, Andrew Gerstle, Timon Screech, Helen McNaughton, and Griseldis Kirsch.

I owe a great debt of gratitude to the University of Tokyo's Institute of Social Science, which provided me with an institutional home when I returned to Japan and whose faculty and affiliated scholars shared their deep knowledge of Japanese, Chinese, and Korean archival sources. The Japan History Group organized by Nakamura Naofumi and Iokibe Kaoru at the Institute of Social Science was especially helpful in providing guidance in how to combine Japanese and English-language primary sources and historiography. Gregory Noble, chief editor of *Social Science Japan Journal*, supervised the writing of my first journal article, "The Japanese Red Cross Society's Emergency Responses in Hiroshima and Nagasaki, 1945," which served as the foundation for chapter 6 of this book. Satō Iwao, Genda Yūji, Uno Shigeki, Arita Shin, Fujitani Takeshi, Kenneth McElwain, Meredith Show, and scholars from the University of Tokyo International Publishing Initiative (UT-IPI) team welcomed my participation in their project. The project of the Institute of Social Science, "The Social Science of Crisis Thinking," provided me the opportunity to visit Kamaishi City in Tohoku Japan, which was a cathartic experience. I am grateful to the University of Tokyo's Global Japan Studies (GJS) group at the Institute of Advanced Studies on Asia (IASA) and the Center for Contemporary Japanese Studies (TCJS) for giving me the opportunity as a junior scholar to present my research. I have received valuable comments and advice from the University of Tokyo's Center for Pacific and American Studies, Rikkyo University's Global Liberal Arts Program, Tokyo University of Foreign Studies' Institute of Japan Studies, and Waseda University's Organization for Regional and Interregional Studies.

Among Japan-based modern Japan scholars, Nakamura Naofumi, Iokibe Kaoru, Katō Yōko, Tanimoto Masayuki, and Yijian Zhong at the University of Tokyo; Kita Yoshito and Kawai Toshinobu at Nihon University; Aoki Toshiyuki at Saga University; and Yamashita Mai at Doshisha University shared insights and advice on developing my book manuscript at a number of workshops and conferences. In the United States, Sarah Kovner provided particularly useful comments when I presented my research on the 1934 Tokyo Fifteen International Red Cross Conference at Columbia University's Twenty-sixth Annual Graduate Student Conference on East Asia in 2017. I have continued to seek her advice. I received especially useful feedback on my project from Carol Gluck when she visited Tokyo for a conference at the Tokyo University of Foreign Studies in 2016. John J. Stephan of the University of Hawai'i provided a number of references, including a glossary of prewar Japanese-Hawaiian colloquialisms, and expert advice on topics related to Japanese in Hawai'i and Russia. Melanie Oppenheimer at Australian National University, an organizer of the Conference on the Histories of the Red Cross Red Crescent Movement since 1919, provided a profound opportunity for me to present my paper at the headquarters of the IFRC in Geneva in 2019. Numerous other scholars in other countries aided this project: Julia Irwin at Louisiana State University; Maria Framke at Erfurt University; and affiliated faculty of the Global Humanitarian Research Academy of 2019 of the Leibniz Institute of European Studies, the University of Tübingen, and the University of Geneva. At key moments, I received invaluable advice from international law scholars in both Japan and Europe. I am particularly grateful to Fujita Hisakazu of Kyoto University for his insights into the development of the International Law of War relating to nuclear weapons. I am no less indebted to scholars Kobayashi Yōko and Yamazaki Yūji, at the Japanese Red Cross Toyota College of Nursing and the Japanese Red Cross College of Nursing in Tokyo.

Most of all, I want to express from the bottom of my heart my gratitude to Professor Emeritus Stephen Vlastos, University of Iowa, who for the past three years has mentored the completion of this book. His insights and attentive eye to the uses and misuses of sources deepened my understanding of history and the humanistic disciplines. I am truly grateful for his patience and generosity in nurturing my English skills and understanding of how to combine and develop historical arguments with narrative. My conversations with Professor Vlastos will long stand among the most precious experiences of my professional life.

There is no doubt that without the unstinting support of the officers of the Japanese Red Cross Society (JRCS), I would not have been able to accomplish this research. Ōtsuka Yoshiharu, Yamada Fumito, Kokawa

Naoki, Hattori Ryōichi, Hori Otohiko, Noguchi Yoshiki, Okamoto Ryūta, Yokoyama Mizufumi, Karube Masakazu, Tanaka Yasuo, Sugai Satoshi, Nagazumi Kentarō, Ōyama Hiroto, Igarashi Rena, Ōya Takamitsu, Ikai Munetoshi, and Yamada Yūsuke secured access to JRCS archives, responded to my many questions precisely, assisted my research at each step, and provided opportunities to develop my ideas in discussion groups, lectures at conferences, and workshops. In addition, on innumerable occasions, I was the beneficiary of backroom support from many anonymous JRCS officials in the International Department, the Internal Affairs Department, and the Disaster Relief Division of the Disaster Management and Social Welfare Department. I would also like to show my gratitude to retired JRCS officials Masui Takashi, Higashiura Hiroshi, Tajima Hiroshi, Satō Masanori, and Horino Masanori. They shared their personal remembrances of events and even documents they had collected during their many years of service to the JRCS. I am especially grateful to retired JRCS officials, some now deceased, who shared their experiences and insights gained from years of service that helped me to contextualize many documents I retrieved from the JRCS archives. I also received valuable assistance from Wakitani Kōichi of the JRCS Hiroshima Chapter and a number of officials at the JRCS Nagasaki Chapter. I also have to express my gratitude to Christine Beerli at the ICRC, who warmly encouraged me to pursue my research when my studies were still at a preliminary stage. Her long-term experience within humanitarian diplomacy stimulated the conceptualization of humanitarianism in my studies.

Throughout the writing of this book, I was the recipient of invaluable assistance from archivists and librarians around the world. Among them I want to give special mention to JRCS archivist Yoshikawa Ryūko, who for many decades has tirelessly catalogued JRCS documents; Ikegami Kenji and Mizuno Mariko at JRCS Toyota College of Nursing Library; Nakano Yūko at Museum Meiji-mura Archive; Fabrizio Bensi at the ICRC Archive and Grant Michell at the IFRC Archive in Geneva; Susan Watson, Alison Polivka, and Annie Werbitzky at the American Red Cross Archives in Washington, DC; Jodie Mattos at the American Red Cross of Hawaii; and staff of the British Red Cross Archives. I am also grateful to the International Red Cross and Red Crescent Movement, which in 2017 provided the opportunity to present my research at its Conference on the Prohibition and Elimination of Nuclear Weapons in Nagasaki.

Thanks is also due to the staffs of the Hiroshima Peace Memorial Museum; the Nagasaki Atomic Bomb Museum; the Nagasaki Foundation for the Promotion of Peace; the University of Tokyo Meiji Shinbun Zasshi Bunko; Diplomatic Archives of the Ministry of Foreign Affairs of Japan; National Diet Library of Japan; National Institute for Defense Studies Archives of Japan; Ikachi Lonsomelady Peace Memorial Museum; Hawaii Emigration Museum Nihojima Village; the Center for Japanese-Brazilian Studies; the Historical Museum of Japanese Immigration in Brazil; the Imperial War Museum; the British National Archives; the Hawaiian Historical Society Library; the Hawaii Times Photo Archives; the Japanese American National Museum; the Hoover Institution on War, Revolution, and Peace at Stanford University, California; and many other institutions, libraries, and archives, who provided valuables sources and materials. I also want to express my appreciation to the curators of photographic and fine arts collections: to Dennis M. Ogawa of the Nippu Jiji Photograph Collection, Kaoru Ueda of Japanese Diaspora Collections at the Hoover Institution, Julia Knight at Poster House in New York, Tanaka Kōtarō at the Ken Domon Museum of Photography, and Yamashita Natsuko at Wakayama City Museum.

Without the generous financial support of many institutions and foundations, none of this would have been possible. I want to record my heartfelt gratitude to the University of Tokyo Edge Capital (UTEC) and the University of Tokyo Future Society Initiative (FSI) Research Grant Program, the Mitsubishi Foundation, the JFE 21st Century Foundation, the Nippon Foundation, the Great Britain Sasakawa Foundation, the Japan Foundation Endowment Committee, Meiji Jingu Intercultural Research Institute Scholarships, the Institute of Social Science Research Grants of the University of Tokyo, the Japan Research Centre Grants of SOAS University of London, and travel funds from the International Committee of the Red Cross and the International Federation of Red Cross and Red Crescent Societies.

I am deeply appreciative of the team at Columbia University Press for helping me through the process of editing and publishing this book. The two anonymous reader reports were exemplary in their insight, depth, and thoroughness. The final product would have been much poorer without their input. I am also grateful to my Japanese, Chinese, Korean, English, American, and Canadian friends' assistance with English translations and wish specifically to credit Ono Hisako and Carroll Misono for the translation of the Japanese tanka poem that serves as the epigraph for this book.

The long journey to the publication of this book made me realize how much I owe to friends, colleagues, mentors, and advisors where I have lived and studied. Although too numerous to attempt to name for fear of omission, I much give special mention of the debt I owe my piano teacher, Ishiwata Hideo, and his wife Ishiwata Hiroko, who taught me perhaps the most important lesson of all: follow your passions, dedicate yourself body and soul to improvement, and never give up. They introduced me to the great German Jewish composer Sir Klaus Pringsheim, who relocated from Germany to Tokyo after the Nazi Party's rise to power and conducted the Tokyo Academy of Music Orchestra during the Fifteenth International Conference of the Red Cross at Hibiya Public Hall, Tokyo in 1934. I am also grateful for the wonderful friendship of the Japanese Red Cross Choir, for whom I played the piano accompaniment.

Most importantly, I thank my parents, Suzuki Toshio and Kyoko; my sister Ikuko and her family; grandparents on both the Suzuki and Kishino sides of the family; Suzuki Shigeomi, the Suzuki family patriarch; Kishino Masaaki and his entire family; Kuwahata Kagenobu and Noriko and their daughters; Sano Kenzō and Harumi and their entire family; Hirota Atsuko and Yoshikazu; Ono Hisako; Osanai Kōzō; Kitayama Michiko; and Rachel and Howard Freedman of London and their family. Last of all, I thank Momoko and Gontarō, my cheerful four-footed companions whose affectionate companionship as I labored over the manuscript brightened my days. I dedicate this book to all of them.

NOTE ON TRANSLITERATION AND TRANSLATION

I used the Modified Hepburn (*romaji*) system for Japanese terms, names, and titles. As is the custom in East Asia, I followed the standard order of Asian names, in which family names precede first names, except in the case of contemporary Japanese scholars who publish mainly in Western languages.

I used widely accepted English place names, including Tokyo, Osaka, Seoul (*Keijō*), Korea (*Chōsen*), Nanjing (Nanking), Nanshi District, São Paulo, and Lourenço Marques (Maputo).

Unless otherwise noted, translations into English are those of the author.

ABBREVIATIONS

AJS	America-Japan Society
ARC	American Red Cross
BRC	British Red Cross
GGK	Governor-General of Korea
GKRCS	Great Korean Red Cross Society
ICN	International Council of Nurses
ICRC	International Committee of the Red Cross
IFRC	International Federation of Red Cross and Red Crescent Societies
IJA	Imperial Japanese Army
IJN	Imperial Japanese Navy
JRCS	Japanese Red Cross Society
LORCS	League of Red Cross Societies
MOFA	Ministry of Foreign Affairs of Japan
MRCS	Manchukuo Red Cross Society
NAK	Nurses' Association of Korea
NIRK	Dutch East Indies Red Cross
NYK	Nippon Yusen Kabushiki Kaisha
PPU	Pan-Pacific Union
RCSC	Red Cross Society of China
RCRC	Red Cross and Red Crescent
RRC	Russian Red Cross

SCAP	Supreme Commander for the Allied Powers
SRCS	Shimane Red Cross Society
SSERC	JRCS Shanghai Special Expeditionary Relief Corps
WPRCD	JRCS War Prisoners' Relief Committee Department
YRCS	Yamaguchi Red Cross Society

HUMANITARIAN INTERNATIONALISM
UNDER EMPIRE

INTRODUCTION

This book recovers the history of the Japanese Red Cross Society (JRCS), and with it, the indigenous humanitarian movement in modern Japan, from a reductionist historiography that misrepresents the JRCS as a top-down organization, wholly subordinate to the government and the imperial family, and derivative of Western values and institutional models. It relocates the JRCS within a transnational discourse of peacetime and wartime international humanitarianism to which the JRCS contributed as much as it borrowed. Informed by exhaustive mining of JRCS archives and multiarchive research outside Japan, the book develops five research findings: the melding of Western and Japanese humanitarian traditions and organizational forms; the strong grassroots vector in the JRCS's steady growth to become Japan's largest international organization by World War I;[1] the society's pioneering role in Red Cross disaster relief and inclusion of non-Western national societies in the International Red Cross and Red Crescent Movement;[2] advocacy of comprehensive legal protections of civilians in wartime at the 1934 Tokyo International Red Cross Conference; and the evolution of the JRCS from a national into a transnational organization with scores of branch societies in Japan's overseas empire, in the Asia-Pacific region, and in North and South America.

The theoretical point of departure of this study is the proposition that in the period between the founding of the Geneva-based International

Committee of the Red Cross (ICRC) in 1863 and the conclusion of World War II, national Red Cross societies in Japan as well as in the West are properly conceptualized as semi-governmental organizations, chartered by governments, headed by prominent political figures, and funded by socially exclusive charities. Parallels between the American Red Cross (ARC) and the JRCS are instructive. Established in 1881, the ARC initially operated as a privately funded relief organization primarily dependent on volunteers. But when America acquired an overseas empire in 1898, the ARC soon transformed into a "quasi-official organization" operating under a U.S. Congressional charter.[3] The 1900 charter, according to historian Julia Irwin, "created a unique private-public partnership." Revised in 1905 when Secretary of War William Howard Taft assumed the presidency, the new charter "gave the U.S. Government far more authority over the ARC. Henceforth, the ARC was required to submit to an annual audit by the War Department which appointed six of the eighteen-member Central Committee."[4] In other words, even in the United States, with its centuries-old traditions of voluntarism and civil society activism, the Red Cross acted in partnership with the government, and its overseas chapters helped to secure its empire by instituting public health programs and modern medical practices that were intended to gain Filipinos' acquiescence to colonial rule.

In Japan as in the West, early twentieth-century wars provided the impetus for explosive growth in membership and revenue. With the founding of the League of Red Cross Societies (LORCS)[5] in 1919, nationally and internationally, disaster relief and development aid increasingly occupied national Red Cross societies. In evaluating the historic role of the JRCS in relationship to Japanese imperialism, it is important to keep in mind that national Red Cross societies of the period of this study were not nongovernmental organizations in the contemporary sense, and they worked closely with colonial authorities in advancing modern medical care and public health.[6] The misrepresentation of the JRCS as an outlier among pre-1945 Red Cross societies in the only English-language monograph on the JRCS, authored by British Empire historian Olive Checkland, who cited not a single Japanese-language source, arises in part from this presentist fallacy and in part from the profound Western centrism endemic of the historiography of modern humanitarianism.[7]

EUROCENTRISM IN RED CROSS HISTORIOGRAPHY

This study participates in a growing historiography on non-Western humanitarianism in the pre–World War II period that is deconstructing the binary between humanitarianism in "the West" and "the rest" of the world. Within the past two decades, histories of the Red Cross movement, exemplified by John F. Hutchinson's and Caroline Moorehead's important studies, have exposed the ICRC's founders' profound Eurocentric chauvinism, which bordered on racism. In *Champions of Charity: War and the Rise of the Red Cross*, Hutchinson observes that "the founders of the Red Cross initially conceived of its role in the world in ways that reflected the religious and moral assumptions of the nineteenth-century European bourgeoises. . . . The first task for the Red Cross, they believed, was to propagate these virtues more widely within Christendom itself, especially among the common people whose weak moral sense seemed to them to need careful nurture."[8] Hutchinson sharply comments on the condescension implicit in Red Cross cofounder Gustave Moynier's (1826–1910) concession that as "heathens," non-European peoples might still be attracted to the Red Cross's mission.[9] Caroline Moorehead's history, *Dunant's Dream: War, Switzerland and the History of the Red Cross*, advances Hutchinson's critique of ICRC Eurocentrism, showing how deeply assumptions of Western civilization's superiority permeated the leadership's thinking on the inclusion of non-Western countries. Moorehead writes, "With twenty European countries now enrolled, America falling into line and ten imperial or royal families professed supporters of Red Cross matters, the question facing the Committee was how wise it would be to extend the fellowship further, how far it would be possible to inject this 'new blood' of Red Cross humanitarian ideas into the 'veins' of other 'civilized races'?"[10] Viewed from Geneva, apparently, Japan was not yet fully "civilized." Moorehead cites Moynier's belief that "a country like Japan was simply not ready for such a progressive idea," which was Moynier's thought when he greeted the Iwakura Mission that arrived in Geneva in 1873.[11] Nor was Moynier's view exceptional, as Moorehead cites the Swiss ambassador's remark to Moynier that "the Japanese people believed it right to kill anyone who set foot on their sacred soil."[12] When Japan ratified the Geneva Conventions, Moynier condescendingly marked the occasion with a speech celebrating the advancement of the "fruit of Christian civilisation."[13]

Critical of the ICRC's founders' Eurocentrism, Hutchinson and Moorehead nevertheless represent the Turkish Red Crescent Society and the Japanese Red Cross Society, the most influential non-Western, non-Christian national societies, as dependent, imitative, and incomplete. Hutchinson downplays the significance of the Ottoman Empire as a non-European people and non-Christian state ratifying the Geneva Convention in July 1865: "It is not at all clear why the sultan's government took this decision; in all probability, it meant little more than appearing to keep up with the other powers."[14] Hutchinson's discussion of the Red Cross movement in Japan is similarly narrow. Unaware of humanitarian discourses in Japan that predated the ICRC, he interprets the appeal of the Red Cross's creed to a national striving for moral uplift and the cachet of inclusion in the ranks of fully "civilized" nations that membership signified.[15] The JRCS took root and flourished, Hutchinson contends, because JRCS was a government-controlled, top-down organization and Japanese society was "highly centralised, hierarchically organised, and very closely tied to the imperial regime."[16] Japanese society in the late nineteenth century was indeed hierarchical; however, a core argument of this book is that salient features of the JRCS's organizational development and programs, particularly pioneering programs of natural disaster relief and poverty mitigation, were bottom-up, local initiatives that succeeded because they responded to local needs and built on community values.

Moorehead follows Hutchinson in attributing Japan's Red Cross movement to utilitarian cultural borrowing from the West to compensate for civilizational backwardness. Citing the "Japanese fashion for imitating western ideas" and "tak[ing] what is long in another, and amend[ing] it with what is short in yourself," Moorehead concludes, "Into all this the Red Cross fitted perfectly. It was an obvious, unthreatening commitment, a perfect vehicle for closer relations with the West." Further, Moorehead anachronistically attributed the Japanese public embrace of the Red Cross movement to the 1890 "Imperial Rescript on Education."[17] The hollowness of such representations of the JRCS parallels these authors' condescension and undercuts their contribution in exposing the ICRC founders' biases.

THE JRCS IN JAPANESE HISTORIOGRAPHY

This study both builds on and revises Japanese scholarship on the JRCS. Writing in English, the UK-based modern Japan historian Sho Konishi conclusively demonstrates that Japan possessed a native humanitarian discourse derived from Confucianism that predated the founding of the ICRC and that the immediate predecessor of the JRCS, the Philanthropic Society, initiated the practice of administering impartial medical aid to the wounded a full decade and a half before the ICRC was founded.[18] The most recent monographic study of the JRCS by a Japan-based scholar, Nobuko Kosuge, usefully focuses on the tension between internationalism and nationalism in the JRCS and the patronage of the imperial family.[19] While agreeing with Kosuge that nationalist pride in the JRCS's high profile on the international stage enhanced its public appeal, this book highlights factors that Kosuge overlooks, namely, the salient role of local actors and the critical role of the society in responding to local needs, including alleviation of poverty, disaster relief, and public health. In making this argument, I build on Mai Yamashita's study of JRCS leader Ninagawa Arata (1873–1959) and his role in globalizing Japanese peacetime relief activities, membership, and finances.[20] Yamashita credits the steady growth in membership between the Russo-Japanese War and World War II to the JRCS's rootedness in local society and the organization's responsiveness to local needs. Membership growth, in turn, generated an income stream independent of elite charities.[21] Finally, Shimosawa Takashi shows that World War II, which in Asia began in 1937, created a period of increased government direction from prefectural governors down to municipal and village associations (*chōnaikai*) and inaugurated a final phase in JRCS's growth when families' enrollment became customary, an act of civic duty.[22]

Data on JRCS membership show sharp increases with the outbreak of war, but in contrast to the experience of the ARC and European national societies membership did not decline during peacetime.[23] Few families relinquished their membership. Several factors appear to account for this phenomenon. Because the leadership of local JRCS chapters overlapped with officeholding, families' Red Cross membership demonstrated good citizenship. A second factor was the JRCS's role in mobilizing resources to address local needs, whether material assistance in the wake of natural disasters, medical interventions during epidemics, or a form of mutual aid in the alleviation of poverty. By responding to local humanitarian crises as well as assisting the nation in Japan's foreign wars, the JRCS tapped into ordinary Japanese people's communitarianism and patriotism, and the society experienced dramatic growth in membership, which exceeded more than 2 million members in 1920, making the JRCS in the interwar period the world's largest national Red Cross society.[24]

JRCS AND JAPANESE PREWAR INTERNATIONALISM

Historians of international relations have increasingly recognized the importance of civic and semi-official organizations as vectors of internationalism's ideals and practices outside of formal diplomacy among nation-states.[25] The call to action was sounded by the distinguished diplomatic historian Akira Iriye two decades ago in the Thomas Jefferson Memorial Lecture delivered at the University of California, Berkeley, where he challenged students of international relations to expand the conceptual boundaries of their discipline through the incorporation of the study of international nongovernmental organizations. International organizations, Iriye suggested, contribute to globalization in multiple ways. By promoting shared values, mobilizing like-minded citizens, influencing governments, and deploying resources across borders, international nongovernmental organizations act as forces of globalization as much as military alliances, multinational corporations, or missionary societies.[26] In the case of Japan in the period between World War I and World War II, Thomas Burkman argues that while Japanese internationalism reached its high watermark in the 1920s, it did not grind to a halt after the Manchurian Incident in 1931–1932 and withdrawal from the League of Nations in 1933. Although Japan no longer sent representatives to the League Council and Assembly meetings, Japanese officials "continued to work within and support such organizations as the International Committee on Intellectual Cooperation and the Health Organization."[27] Similarly, Michael Auslin's study of cultural exchanges between Japan and the United States examines efforts by Prince Tokugawa Iesato, who simultaneously served as president of the JRCS and the America-Japan Society (AJS) of Tokyo, to counter diplomatic tensions with the United States. In February 1934 Prince Tokugawa Iesato created an advisory committee to the AJS that promoted public outreach through activities that ranged from welcoming American tourists to hosting a fair honoring Abraham Lincoln to arranging exhibition games by an eighteen-man, all-star baseball team that included Babe Ruth.[28]

NEW PERSPECTIVES ON RED CROSS MOVEMENTS IN ASIA, THE MIDDLE EAST, AND AFRICA

The embrace of the Red Cross across broad sectors of Japanese society and the JRCS's dynamism on the world stage, this book argues, challenges the Eurocentric narrative of the rise of modern humanitarianism that privileges the role of the ICRC, a Christian-based charity, over the contributions of national societies in general and especially those outside the West. It is, of course, a fact that the Red Cross's mission of impartially administering medical aid to wounded soldiers originated as a humanitarian response, inflected by Christianity, to the carnage of Europe's mid-nineteenth-century wars. That story is inspiring and often told. This book takes issue not with the origin story but with the accompanying narrative of the Red Cross's global expansion. The still-dominant narrative frames the Red Cross's global expansion as a process of Westernization whereby the civilizing force of Christian humanitarianism's altruism, compassion, and volunteerism emanated outward from its Swiss home base through a process of transplantation and emulation. The adoption of the Red Cross emblem by Japan and other non-Western national Red Cross societies is not, however, evidence of a specifically Christian-based humanitarian ideology. Michael Barnett notes that delegates to the inaugural Red Cross conference "treated the [Red Cross] symbol as nonsectarian," and Sho Konishi, cited earlier, argues that the use of the emblem by the JRCS had "nothing to do with Christianity."[29] It is a narrative that marginalizes not only the JRCS but also the Red Cross and Red Crescent Societies of the Ottoman Empire, Iran, India, the Qing Dynasty, and Siam among others; leaves out of history the local, non-Christian, humanitarian traditions; and devalues the institution-building capacities of non-Western peoples. What Western-centric narratives have overlooked are the agency, professionalism, and adaptive strategies that enabled Red Cross and Red Crescent Societies to take root and flourish in their national contexts.[30]

There is a growing body of scholarship on humanitarian organizations outside the West in the period preceding World War II, when the international Red Cross and Red Crescent movement was the largest humanitarian network in the world, and RCRC societies in Asia were at the forefront of modern humanitarian activities. For example, Adrian Ruprecht's study of the Red Cross movement in British India and the role of the Indian Red Cross Society contests the standard narrative of a "one-way road" relief activity from the West to the East and the South.[31] Maria Framke's research reframes the Indian Red Cross movement by arguing that the Indian Red Cross Society became the driving force in the development of Indian nationalism and anticolonial emancipation.[32] In a coauthored study, Framke and Esther Moeller show how local charitable and philanthropic traditions influenced the Egyptian Red Crescent and the Hindu Mahasabhain in South Asia through an analysis of *zakat* (obligatory almsgiving) and *ṣadaqa* (voluntary almsgiving) in Muslim tradition, and *dana* (charitable giving), *seva* (service), and *dharma* (religious duty) in the ancient discourse of Hinduism.[33] Alexandra Preiff studies the Chinese Red Swastika Society, which originated in the Chinese religious society *Daoyuan* and significantly impacted the Chinese Red Cross movement, concluding that the Red Cross Society of China (RCSC) was rooted in both existing local philanthropic activities in China and the newly arrived Western Red Cross movement.[34] In some cases, Red Cross Societies transported to Asia narrowly served the metropole. Leo van Bergen's research on the Dutch East Indies Red Cross (NIRK) describes a top-down movement fully controlled by Dutch colonial authorities. Founded in 1870, the NIRK was dominated by Dutch nationals, and the society's mission included administering medical aid to the Dutch army not only in wartime but also in military engagements to suppress "rebellions" on the grounds that armed resistance violated "our [Dutch] rights." Van Bergen also shows that the NIRK supported Dutch armed forces after World War II during the war of Indonesian independence in violation of the Red Cross's commitment to neutrality in administering humanitarian aid.[35]

CHAPTER OVERVIEW

Chapter 1 sets the stage by revising the standard historiography of the origins and development of the Red Cross movement in Japan, emphasizing its ideological and organizational melding of native and Western forms. It follows the society's evolution in the early twentieth century, with reference to wartime and peacetime relief activities: Mt. Bandai volcano relief (1888), the First Sino-Japanese War (1894–1895), the Russo-Japanese War (1904–1905); World War I (1914–1918); the Spanish flu pandemic (1918–1920); the foundation of the League of Red Cross Societies (1919); and the Great Kantō Earthquake (1923). Chapter 2 explores the JRCS's humanitarian diplomacy during the Fifteenth International Conference of the Red Cross, which convened in Tokyo in 1934, under the leadership of JRCS President Tokugawa Iesato, the sixteenth head of the Tokugawa family. The Great Depression, the 1931–1932 Manchurian Incident, the rise of National Socialism in Germany, Japan's withdrawal from the League of Nations in 1933, and the resurgence of political and economic nationalism worldwide created an atmosphere of great global uncertainty. Amid rising international tensions, the conference unanimously adopted the Tokyo Declaration of 1934, which greatly expanded both wartime and peacetime protection of civilians. Although not ratified by the Great Powers, it became the foundation of the Fourth Geneva Convention of 1949.

Chapters 3 and 4 illuminate the JRCS's development from a national to a transnational humanitarian movement through case studies of overseas branch organizations in Korea, Manchuria, Hawai'i, and Brazil. The JRCS expanded its presence overseas in tandem with Japanese emigration, which created a Japanese diaspora in the Asia Pacific region, and imperial expansion on the Asian continent. In Korea and Manchuria, the JRCS played a vital role, through the development of local medical facilities and public health, in advancing colonial modernity. JRCS Hawai'i served as an organizational bridge between local Japanese and American elites and facilitated diplomatic relations with the United States before and after strains in relations developed in the 1930s. JRCS's Brazil office acted as a vehicle for reinforcing Japanese identity among the Japanese immigrant community, which was facing coercive assimilation policies. Together, the case studies show that the overseas Japanese humanitarian movement embodied in the JRCS took the form of a multiethnic and multinational humanitarian organization that mobilized the Japanese immigrant community, engaged with local governing authorities, and enlisted the local populations in the humanitarian movement.

Chapter 5 analyzes what the JRCS was able and unable to do in fulfilment of its Red Cross mandate during the Pacific War to provide humanitarian assistance both to Allied and Japanese POWs and Allied and Japanese civilian internees. JRCS activities were more nuanced, numerous, and varied than previously understood. Chapter 6 brings to light the personal sacrifices and professional labors of the Red Cross battlefield nurses during the aftermath of the Hiroshima and Nagasaki atomic bombings in the context of the development of JRCS nursing. It shows how principles of "humanitarian professionalism" guided JRCS nurses in the midst of a truly living hell as they rendered medical aid to civilians, soldiers, and Allied POWs without discrimination. Their emergency responses demonstrate the extent to which they had internalized their professional mission as medical aid givers and eventually emerged as exemplars of the humanitarian relief ideal.

1

RESPONDING TO CRISES

A People's Humanitarian Movement

The history of the founding and growth of the Japanese Red Cross Society (JRCS) revises the conventional and reductionist view of the Red Cross movement in Japan as simply a cultural import from the West and a top-down movement directed by the Meiji government. This chapter develops three themes: native antecedents, early aristocratic leadership and imperial family patronage, and the rapid expansion and professionalization of the organization on both the national and international stages.

THE PHILANTHROPIC SOCIETY AND THE FOUNDING OF THE JRCS

The Philanthropic Society (*Hakuai-sha*), the antecedent to the JRCS, was founded in 1877 by Count Sano Tsunetami (1823–1902), who became the first president of the JRCS following Japan's ratification of the Geneva Convention in 1886, and Count Matsudaira Norikata (1839–1910).[1] Sano was born in the late Tokugawa period into a low-ranking samurai family in Saga domain and studied surgery at a Dutch school in Osaka under Ogata Kōan (1810–1863);[2] Matsudaira[3] was a high-ranking former Tokugawa official and member of the Meiji titled nobility who served in the Chamber of Elders. Sano first encountered the Red Cross organization during his visit to the 1867 Paris International Exposition. He had been sent to Paris by Saga domain to research Western-style steam-powered warships and the technology for their manufacture.[4] Six years later, he attended the 1873 Vienna International Exposition, where Japan, now a nation-state, introduced Japanese products. During this visit, Sano had a further chance to familiarize himself with the international RCRC movement.[5]

A decade after Sano first encountered the Red Cross Society in Paris, the outbreak of the 1877 Satsuma Rebellion served as the impetus to put into practice core principles of the International Committee of the Red Cross (ICRC). At the time, Japan was not a signatory to the 1864 Geneva Convention, a requirement for ICRC membership, but Sano petitioned the Meiji government asking to set up an independent organization, the Philanthropic Society, in Kumamoto, where the Meiji and Satsuma armies were locked in fierce combat. When the government declined to authorize his plan, Sano successfully appealed to the Japanese imperial family for assistance. Prince Arisugawa Taruhito (1835–1895), the acting commander of the Meiji government's army during the rebellion, endorsed Sano's proposal to allow medical relief workers of the Philanthropic Society to treat the wounded of both armies.

It appears that Prince Arisugawa approved the operations of the Philanthropic Society on his own authority without consultation with the ruling oligarchy, who viewed the idea of impartial medical aid negatively. Not only had the Meiji government not yet ratified the 1864 Geneva Convention, it applied only to international armed conflict, and the Satsuma Rebellion was a civil war. Nevertheless, Sano was determined to put into practice the Red Cross's ideal of the neutrality of humanitarian aid workers in all armed conflicts. As he expounded five years later in an address to the General Assembly of the Philanthropic Society, the Red Cross was driven by "absolute faith" in humanity.[6] Reminding his audience that, "On battlefields, the Red Cross treats the wounded without discrimination as to which side they're fighting on," he implored them to "imagine warriors who, having desperately and valiantly fought for their county, are now injured and unarmed. At this stage, they are no longer soldiers but simply human beings. We should treat them as we would our own countrymen."[7] To Sano, rendering impartial aid to wounded soldiers was nothing less than a hallmark of modern civilization: "Civilized nations not only embrace constitutional government and advanced technology but also the development of civil society, which includes providing impartial medical relief on battlefields."[8]

The Meiji government initially reacted with skepticism to the very concept of a neutral civil humanitarian organization operating in Japan. In fact, following the conclusion of the Satsuma Rebellion, it moved to dissolve the Philanthropic Society. Once again, Sano sought the support of the imperial family, this time appealing to Prince Komatsu Akihito (1846–1903), who held the rank of Lieutenant General during the Satsuma Rebellion and in later years served as nominal commander of the Japanese expeditionary forces in the First Sino-Japanese War (1894–1895). Prince Komatsu acknowledged the valuable services the Red Cross Societies performed in wartime; citing the need to be prepared for future international conflicts, he supported Sano. In the end, the Philanthropic Society survived.[9]

The Philanthropic Society used the emblem of a red circle over a red horizontal line on a white background. (See figure 1.1.) The society could not use the Red Cross emblem because it was not yet an ICRC member. It appears the Philanthropic Society was also wary of being identified too closely with the avowedly Christian ICRC.[10] An editorial published in the JRCS monthly review in 1899 argued,

> The mission of the Red Cross Society is based on benevolence.[11] The Red Cross Society embodies the ideal of superior moral character.[12] Westerners who do not believe there are also true gentlemen in Asia, presumptuously assume the Red Cross ideal to be the unique product of Christiandom. When they saw the rapid development of the Red Cross movement in Japan, they expressed skepticism, questioned its rootedness and authenticity, and dismissed our motivation to present Japan as a civilized nation, and even worse, they denied our humanitarianism.... We, however, insist that the Red Cross activities embody the indigenous civilization of each member nation.[13]

In 1879, to blunt distrust among Japan's powerful Buddhist and Shinto religious communities, the Philanthropic Society elected several Shinto priests and Buddhist monks, including Hirayama Seisai (1815–1890)[14] and

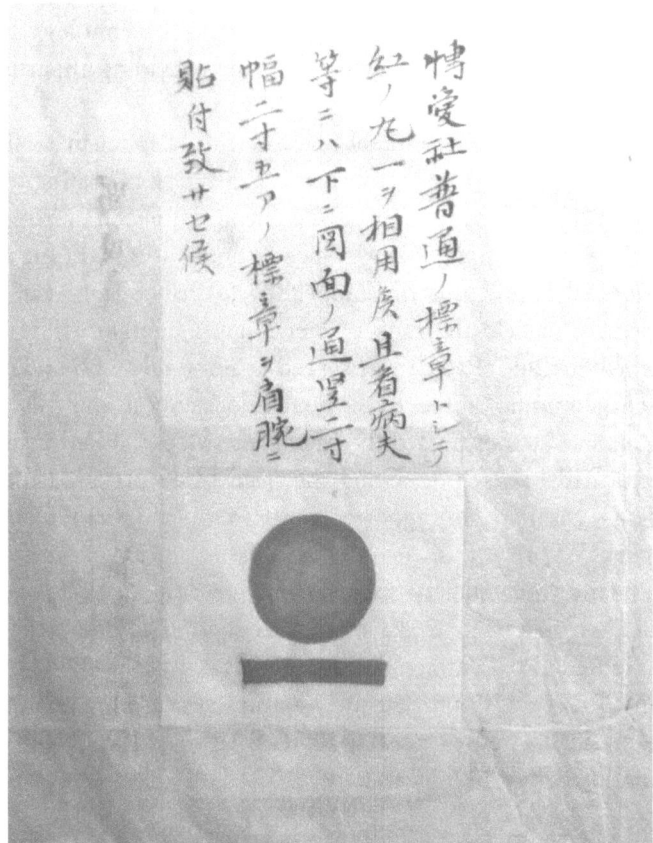

FIGURE 1.1 The emblem of the Philanthropic Society (*Hakuai-sha*), adopted in 1870, was a variation on Japan's new national flag.

Photo by author. Archival collection of the Red Cross Information Plaza, the Japanese Red Cross Society.

Shimaji Mokurai (1838–1911),[15] to the JRCS's executive committee. Japanese Christians were noticeably absent.[16] Moreover, strong support of the imperial family provided the Philanthropic Society an additional layer of protection from potential nativist opposition.

Following Japan's signing of the Geneva Convention in 1886, the Philanthropic Society was officially recognized by the ICRC as a national society and was renamed the Japanese Red Cross Society the following year.

The first Red Cross hospital was established in Tokyo shortly thereafter. The JRCS adopted the international Red Cross emblem of a red cross against a white background, which at that time was used by all national societies except the Ottoman Empire, and the society aimed to present itself as an international humanitarian organization. In keeping with its origins as the Philanthropic Society, the JRCS was not affiliated with any religious organization. Prince Komatsu assumed the position of honorary president of the JRCS, and the Meiji Emperor and Empress Shōken became major donors to the Society.[17] Other members of Japan's imperial family, as well as royalty of Great Britain, Germany, Denmark, Italy, and Thailand, received honorary memberships.[18] The JRCS's close relationship with the Japanese imperial family and association with foreign royal families enhanced its legitimacy and solidified the foundations of the JRCS in Japanese society.

NATIVE HUMANITARIANISM

As historian Sho Konishi has shown, the ICRC mission of rendering medical assistance to all wounded soldiers resonated with native Japanese ethical traditions of philanthropy and humanitarianism.[19] The classical Japanese term *hakuai*[20] that Sano adopted connoted not charity in the sense of almsgiving, but rather universal love of humanity. More precisely, *hakuai* conveyed a commitment to further the well-being of all people, without discrimination as to race, nationality, religious belief, or ideology, and embodied the Buddhist injunction to overcome egoism. Kūkai (774–835), the renowned Buddhist monk of the early Heian period, deployed the term in his celebrated work *Shōryō-shū*, to convey an all-encompassing love of nature, humanity, and the universe.[21]

Not long after the founding of the JRCS, Meiji- and Taishō-period scholars and public intellectuals espoused the idea that conceptions of humanitarianism parallel to those in the West but native to Japan accounted for the remarkable growth of the Red Cross movement in Japan. For example, in an essay published in 1910, Yumoto Fumihiko (1843–1921) contested the idea that the JRCS represented cultural borrowing from the West. Yumoto was a historian of Heian Japan. He served in a variety of positions, such as a curator of the Imperial Court Museum and the director of the Historiographical Institute of the University of Tokyo in the early twentieth century. Pointing to the influence of the Japanese ethical concept of *chūai*,[22] "faith and love," he argued that in Japan, Red Cross humanitarianism was rooted in ethical beliefs that originated in the ancient Japanese imperial court and subsequently permeated to all strata of Japanese society, from rich to poor and from samurai to merchant. As part of the praxis of native Japanese humanitarianism, he highlighted the "public" response to poverty, hunger, and famine in the Edo period, when both feudal lords and wealthy commoners responded to humanitarian crises by donating rice, soliciting donations, and providing medical treatment. According to Yumoto, traditional Japanese humanitarianism differed from nineteenth-century Western humanitarianism, which he contended was intertwined with empire, nationalism, diplomacy, and wartime relief activities.[23] Within the Japanese traditional humanitarian discourse, even farming has been considered an expression of sustainable humanitarianism, as it produced the food to feed the hungry.[24] He further argued that the Meiji imperial family's patronage of the JRCS was not modeled on Western monarchies but the revival of ancient Japanese tradition. As evidence, he cited the Yaku-in and Hiden-in[25] founded by Empress Kōmyō in 730 as examples of social welfare projects initiated by the Japanese imperial court and multiple Heian-period social welfare institutions and imperial charities.[26]

In the 1930s, the nationalist historian Tsuji Zen'nosuke (1877–1955) located the origin of native Japanese humanitarianism in significant historical events from the Heian through the Kamakura and Muromachi periods and up to the Tokugawa era. Tsuji was a leading historian on Japanese Buddhism and Japanese culture in the prewar period. He served as the first head of the Historiographical Institute of the University of Tokyo in the 1930s. He contested West-centered narratives of the Red Cross by citing a number of medieval traditions, such as humane treatment of prisoners of war and commemoration ceremonies for the war dead of enemies in the aftermath of battles.[27] In the post-war period, Enomoto Shigeharu (1890–1979), a former international law scholar at the Naval War College of Imperial Japan, argued that *jin'ai*[28] in the modern period incorporated many traditions of ethical thought, including Japanese myth, Shinto, Confucianism, Buddhism, Christianity, and Bushidō.[29]

GRASSROOTS MOVEMENTS OF THE RED CROSS IN JAPAN

While the JRCS was founded by elite officials like Sano and developed a close institutional relationship with the Japanese imperial family, its dynamic grassroots development is key to understanding its broad popular acceptance, rapid growth in membership, and early orientation toward disaster relief and community improvement. In fact, from early on, the Red Cross movement in Japan was communitarian at the local level in addition to being hierarchical and bureaucratic at the national level. The character of the JRCS as a civil society organization is evident both in its mass membership of over 700,000, which in 1900 made it the largest of any national Red Cross society,[30] and in its commitment to address social welfare issues such as poverty, hunger, orphans, epidemics, medical services, and public health in local communities struggling to survive the tumult of rapid industrialization and social change. From its earlier days, the JRCS built upon local self-improvement initiatives.

The local Red Cross movement in Shimane Prefecture illustrates the JRCS's increasingly bottom-up character. The abolition of feudal domains in 1871 caused severe social disruption in many localities, especially where conflict between factions supporting[31] and opposing the Imperial Restoration[32] still divided the community. In early Meiji Shimane, poverty was widespread, and as late as 1885 a prefectural government survey reported that approximately 54,700 people lived in extreme poverty, which was 7.4 percent of the entire population of the prefecture.[33] In order to provide a lifeline to the poorest members of the community, mostly comprised of widows and invalids, community leaders established a civil society charity in 1882, the Matsue Benevolent Love Society (*Matsue keiaisha*), which raised donations and distributed both cash and foodstuffs.[34] The society subsequently organized emergency disaster assistance following the Onoze fire of 1884 and the great flood that hit in the prefecture in 1887, which lasted for twelve days and killed seventy people. In 1888, when a great fire occurred in the Oki Islands, the society, aided by a local newspaper agency, collected over 10,000 yen in donations. In 1889, a year without major natural disasters, the Matsue Benevolent Love Society collected ninety-two yen and seventy sen to distribute to 335 needy households.[35]

Here we see how raising cash donations to address community needs built upon Tokugawa village practices of mutual aid.

In 1887, Koteda Yasusada (1840–1899), governor of Shimane Prefecture, founded the Shimane Red Cross Society (SRCS) soon after the Japanese government ratified the Geneva Convention in one example of how civil society and local government worked together to institutionalize the Red Cross movement in Japan. More than 10,000 citizens in Shimane became dues-paying members of the SRCS.[36] The society, which later became the JRCS Shimane Chapter, adopted an expansive agenda that addressed local needs. For example, to provide emotional support to families bereaved by the Satsuma Rebellion, it raised funds to establish a war memorial and hold memorial services for the 114 people killed in the Satsuma Rebellion.[37]

Local initiates to provide medical care also preceded the establishment of Red Cross hospitals. Nagase Tokihira (1836–1901), an army surgeon in the Hiroshima garrison of the Imperial Japanese Army who had previously studied under Ogata Kōan in Osaka, founded a hospital in Hiroshima Prefecture in 1876, the Philanthropic (*Hakuai*) Hospital, to provide community medical care. It is noteworthy that this hospital, the predecessor to the Hiroshima Red Cross Hospital, was originally founded to provide medical care to civilians rather than military casualties, which at the time was the exclusive mission of the ICRC.

In 1877, acting on its own initiative, the Philanthropic Hospital treated soldiers wounded in the Satsuma Rebellion. Nine years later, in 1886, the Hiroshima Philanthropic Society initiated the training of medics in anticipation of future wartime medical service. One year later, Hiroshima residents organized the Hiroshima Philanthropic Women's Association to provide nursing education to treat the war wounded. Within its first year of operations, the membership rose from 573 to 2,706. In 1888, the Hiroshima Philanthropic Society was integrated into Sano's Japanese National Philanthropic Society and became the JRCS Hiroshima Chapter.[38]

Hiroshima was not the only prefecture where Red Cross movements sprung up; elsewhere in Japan citizens and local officials formed independent, nongovernmental, nonprofit humanitarian organizations to provide medical aid in peacetime as well as war. In 1887, the year after Japan signed the Geneva Convention, Hara Yasutarō (1847–1936), the governor of Yamaguchi Prefecture, together with five community leaders, drew up plans for organizing a Red Cross Society in Yamaguchi.[39] Samurai from

Chōshū had led the movement to overthrow the Tokugawa shogun and after 1868 dominated the top ranks of the new Meiji army. It was fitting, therefore, that the manifesto of the Yamaguchi Red Cross Society (YRCS), unlike that of Shimane, stressed the value of the Red Cross in times of war: "What is the Red Cross? The Red Cross is an organization consisting of civilians who contribute to treating the wounded and sick soldiers on the battlefield."[40] The YRCS campaign was integrated into the national movement when it was reorganized as the JRCS Yamaguchi Chapter in 1888.[41]

The significance of these developments should not be underestimated. In the examples from Shimane, Hiroshima, and Yamaguchi, we see a symbiotic relationship between local and national humanitarian missions as ordinary Japanese envisioned their communities' survival as complementary to that of Japan's emergence on the world stage as a modern nation-state in the era of global imperialism.

Even before Sano's establishment of the Philanthropic Society, we find examples in Japan where doctors employed the Red Cross principle of exercising impartiality and neutrality on the battlefield. The Battle of Hakodate (1868–1869) was the final battle between loyalists of the Tokugawa shogun and the supporters of the Meiji government. During the clash, a thirty-three-year-old doctor named Takamatsu Ryōun (1837–1916), who was in charge of the Hakodate battlefield hospital, treated sick and wounded soldiers on both sides of the conflict. Takamatsu was born in Fukuoka, Kyūshū, into a prominent farm family. Like Sano Tsunetami, he studied at a Dutch medical school under Ogata Kōan in Osaka and became acquainted with the Red Cross movement during his visit to the 1867 Paris International Exposition. After returning from Europe, Takamatsu joined the medical corps of the Tokugawa army as a doctor and was sent to Hokkaido, where he put into practice the Red Cross principle of rendering medical assistance to all wounded soldiers during the battle.[42]

The depth of Takamatsu's humanitarian commitment is illustrated in the following incident. When the Tokugawa army ordered him to evacuate Hakodate and relocate the hospital to Muroran, further north, he refused to interrupt life-saving operations at the field hospital and won the support of the Russian consul to keep the hospital in operation. When the Meiji governmental forces burst into the hospital, he asked them to allow continued treatment of wounded Tokugawa soldiers, declaring that he would accept any punishment. According to the records of the

JRCS Hokkaido Chapter, Takamatsu treated approximately 1,340 sick and wounded soldiers. After the battle, Takamatsu was suspended from his duties and was detained for a period of time in Tokyo by the Meiji government.[43]

Sano subsequently invited Takamatsu to join the Philanthropic Society, but Takamatsu rejected the proposal.[44] Instead, Takamatsu dedicated the rest of his life to ameliorating the suffering of the poor. He founded the *Dōaisha*, an independent benevolent society whose mission was to provide medical care to the poor. Takamatsu never got involved in wartime relief operations, choosing instead to devote himself to Meiji social welfare programs.[45]

SERVICE IN WARTIME

After the official founding of the JRCS in 1887, the society accelerated its activities and geographically expanded its operations. The society developed a central bureaucracy and established prefectural chapters throughout Japan, in Japan's expanding empire, and overseas where Japanese formed immigrant communities. As Japan became involved in international armed conflicts, the JRCS scaled up its operations and deployed medical relief parties during the First Sino-Japanese War and the Boxer Rebellion (1900) that provided impartial treatment of the wounded.[46]

At the outbreak of the First Sino-Japanese War, Sano, president of the JRCS, reminded JRCS workers of the society's mission: "The foundation of the Red Cross Society is patriotic service (*hōkoku jippei*); our duty is to assist the provision of medical relief on the battlefield and treat sick and wounded without discrimination."[47] For the JRCS members, patriotism and Red Cross international humanitarianism were two sides of the same coin. In the First Sino-Japanese War, JRCS relief activities lasted seventeen months,[48] while the fighting itself concluded in nine months. The society operated two medical ships[49] and sent relief parties to Korea, Manchuria and Shanghai, as well as to Japanese military hospitals in Taipei, Taiwan, and Hiroshima, Tokyo, Matsuyama, Nagoya, and Kokura in Japan.[50] During the war, medical aid workers treated 100,675 sick and wounded soldiers in total,[51] including 1,484 Chinese POWs.[52] The ICRC provided funding to the JRCS to support its activities, and many national Red Cross societies such as Austria, Russia, Germany, France and the Dutch East Indies provided financial support and medical equipment.[53]

At the time of the First Sino-Japanese War, the JRCS was the only Red Cross society operating in East Asia, and it won international praise for its professionalism and impartial treatment of the war wounded, even from a number of high-ranking Chinese officials. For example, Sano received a personal letter from Li Hongzhang (1823–1901), a leading Chinese statesman, after sending a message of sympathy to Li who had been injured in an attempt on his life during peace negotiations in Shimonoseki. In addition to expressing admiration for Japan's "expertise in medicine and international law," Li attributed his recovery to the expert medical care he received from JRCS doctors. Praising the "generosity and virtue" of the JRCS, he promised to promote its "good laws and virtues" upon his return to China.[54]

A decade later during the 1904–1905 Russo-Japanese War, the JRCS became the first Red Cross society to extend its operations to maritime warfare, which became the model for the 1906 Amelioration of the Condition of the Wounded and Sick in Armies in the Field, adopted in 1906 at the Second Geneva Convention and by the Second Hague Conference in 1907. The Russo-Japanese War was the first international conflict of the twentieth century in which the International Law of War was observed by both sides.[55] The Japanese Army even attached two international law scholars to its army commands.[56] According to Dr. Ariga Nagao (1860–1921),[57] a Japanese scholar in international law, the Japanese Army's medical corps treated 21,730 Russian wounded in total, of which 1,158 died, including deaths from scurvy.[58]

The fact that both countries respected the Geneva Conventions in the Russo-Japanese War facilitated the provision of medical relief and led the JRCS to expand and improve its operations.[59] The JRCS deployed 5,170 relief workers, including officials, doctors, nurses, and trained personnel, to transport sick and injured soldiers. According to the JRCS's records, thirty-two medical relief parties were sent to battlefields in Korea and Manchuria, seventy-four to army hospitals, and four to naval hospitals in Japan. Thirty-eight medical teams served on twenty medical ships.[60] During and after the siege of Port Arthur, in which Russian and Japanese forces together sustained casualties over 80,000, 1,088 Japanese medical workers, including the JRCS relief teams, worked with 136 Russian Navy and Army medics and Russian Red Cross (RRC) doctors and nurses, and 2,790 Russian medical orderlies.[61] The JRCS donated 2,000 blankets and 1,500 sets of undershirts, nightclothes, and obi to the RRC stationed in Lushun.[62] JRCS teams in Manchuria provided emergency medical aid to 10,434 patients in JRCS field hospitals, the great majority of whom were Chinese.[63]

The JRCS's treatment of Russian POWs impacted the revision of the Geneva Conventions in later years. Over 72,000 of the 79,367 Russian POWs were sent to Japan for medical treatment. Seventeen medical ships transported sick and wounded Russian POWs to facilities in Lüshunkou, China, and Incheon, Korea, in addition to Matsuyama and Shimane in Japan.[64] In general, Russian POWs had positive opinions of the treatment they received. For instance, one POW wrote about JRCS nurses in his memoir, remembering them as charming, smiling, never giving in to exhaustion, and always carrying out their duties in a disciplined and professional manner.[65] Another POW wrote that nurses entertained them by reading newspapers in both Russian and Japanese.[66]

There were some cultural clashes; for instance, there were times when Russian patients would not eat rice and demanded bread instead.[67] The Imperial Japanese Army's relief workers also suffered from a lack of interpreters.[68] However, overall, humanitarian relief activities went well. There were a number of reports of fraternization among Japanese and Russian patients who exchanged language lessons and articles of clothing, and even lit each other's cigarettes.[69]

During World War I, the JRCS expanded its services to POWs in accordance with the 1912 Washington Declaration of the Tenth International Conference of the Red Cross, although this declaration was not adopted by the Geneva Conventions until 1929.[70] The JRCS welcomed inspection of its operations by the ICRC.[71] Dr. Ariga Nagao, an international law scholar who advised the Imperial Japanese Army during the Russo-Japanese War, became a committee member of the JRCS War Prisoner's Relief Committee when it was established in 1914.[72] During the Russo-Japanese War, treatment of POWs had been limited to general medical treatment. During World War I, however, the JRCS started to transmit Red Cross messages and delivered letters and goods from families and friends of POWs.[73] The ICRC reported to Geneva that the JRCS Shizuoka Chapter organized excursions to historical places in the vicinity of the camps,[74] whereas POWs in Europe were known to have been put to work as forced laborers.

A number of rural Japanese communities, including the JRCS chapters in Fukuoka, Ōita, and Shizuoka, hosted arriving POWs, even treating them as guests from overseas.[75] One of the best examples was the Bandō POW Camp in Tokushima, which has become iconic. Approximately 1,000 German POWs were detained in this camp, where they created their own community in Tokushima and enjoyed good relations with the local population. POWs opened a local market and established a range of facilities in the community, such as a modern printing press, bakery, bowling center, library, and even a classical music concert hall. The Bandō POW Camp hosted the inaugural performance of Beethoven's Ninth Symphony in Japan, an event publicized nationwide.[76] The participation of local JRCS chapters in these programs exhibits continuity with the native grassroots humanitarian movement of the early Meiji period.

In addition to the well-publicized exemplary treatment accorded German POWs, the JRCS raised its profile as a global humanitarian organization through its overseas medical missions, which delivered much-needed assistance to its European allies. The JRCS deployed medical workers and nurses to Russia, France, and the United Kingdom between 1914 and 1916. In 1914, the JRCS, building on cooperation with the RRC during the Russo-Japanese War, initially dispatched twenty-seven medical personnel to St. Petersburg via the Trans-Siberian Railway. They worked for a year and five months at a JRCS relief hospital, which was built and staffed by the JRCS and was singled out for praise by Tsar Nicholas II. As the war dragged on, the JRCS sent additional medical teams and twice extended the mission at the request of the Russian government. The Russian Empress Dowager, Maria Fyodorovna (1847–1928), the honorary president of the RRC, Grand Duchess Xenia Alexandrovna (1875–1960), and Grand Duchess Maria Pavlovna (1890–1958) made well-publicized visits to the JRCS hospital. In total, the JRCS treated 43,531 patients during the Russian deployment.[77]

The fiercest fighting in World War I occurred in northern France, where between 1914 and 1918 the French army alone sustained several million casualties. In response, the JRCS sent a team of twenty-nine medical workers, including twenty-two nurses, to France. Traveling by sea via the

Suez Canal, they staffed the JRCS Relief Party Hospital attached to the Minister of War and National Defense.[78] Although located in Paris, the hospital served as a frontline emergency medical care facility, and the nurses tended to an unending stream of seriously wounded Allied soldiers from the Battles of Arras, Champagne, and Verdun between 1915 and 1916. They treated 54,831 patients in total.[79] At the hospital, JRCS nurses worked with French volunteer nurses. Because the French volunteers were high society ladies who lacked medical training, it was left to JRCS nurses to perform medical procedures while French nurses carried out menial tasks such as serving meals to patients.[80] According to the working record of the JRCS, Japanese and French nurses cooperated well and respected each under very demanding conditions.[81] The Japanese press helped publicize the mission by running stories that featured biographical sketches[82] and celebrated the Japanese nurses as "Flowers of Champs-Élysées."[83] The favorable press coverage and the Japanese public's pride in Japan's status as an Allied Power aided the JRCS's membership drives and fundraising. The JRCS initially planned to mount a five-month operation in France; however, at the earnest request of the French government, the society extended operations twice, and it lasted nearly two years. The French government even asked for an additional extension. However, due to the extreme exhaustion of the JRCS workers, several of whom fell ill from overwork, it was impossible to continue their activities in Paris any longer. In September of 1916, the JRCS handed over their operations to the British Red Cross (BRC), and the JRCS nurses withdrew, returning to Japan via Cape Town.[84] Before their departure, France's president, Raymond Poincaré (1860–1934), publicly lauded the mission and expressed his great gratitude for the contributions of the JRCS.[85]

The JRCS's medical operations in the United Kingdom were no less important in adding to its prestige and world recognition. Representatives of the American Red Cross (ARC) officially welcomed JRCS nurses during the mission's stopover in Honolulu, and after arriving in the United Kingdom, they coordinated with the BRC. Dispatched to London's Netley Hospital, they worked alongside BRC nurses and tended to 70,800 patients. In recognition of their service and Japan's strong diplomatic relationship with the United Kingdom dating back to the 1902

FIGURE 1.2 JRCS nurses dispatched to the England during World War I are seen posing side by side with British Red Cross nurses. The professionalism of Japanese nurses serving in France and England during the war in Europe elevated the international status of the JRCS.

Archival collection of the Museum Meiji-mura held by the Japanese Red Cross Toyota College of Nursing, ID: C-0930A.

Anglo-Japanese Alliance, the JRCS's head doctor and chief nurse were accorded the singular honor of an audience with King George V at Buckingham Palace.[86] (See figure 1.2.)

After World War I and the eruption of the Polish-Soviet War (1919–1920), the Society provided care to Polish orphans and their guardians, who as refugees from the fighting had been stranded in Siberia.[87] In 1920 and 1921, the JRCS provided housing and administered care to 765 Polish children and seventy-nine guardians transported from Vladivostok to Tokyo and Osaka. The plight of the Polish children aroused the sympathy of not only ordinary Japanese but also the imperial family, which contributed to the relief fund. Their repatriation to Poland via London in 1922 further added to the JRCS stature as an actor on the international humanitarian stage.[88]

NATURAL DISASTERS, PANDEMICS, AND PUBLIC HEALTH

Natural disaster relief and medical aid missions were the core projects of the JRCS from its founding to the 1930s. Peacetime relief activities included a range of operations such as poverty relief, epidemic disease treatment, care of orphans, and public health services, which were not the original mandates of the ICRC. As we have seen, the JRCS initiated disaster relief decades before the founding of the League of Red Cross Societies in 1919. The JRCS's relief mission in the aftermath of the eruption of Mount Bandai in Fukushima in 1888,[89] which preceded Clara Barton's celebrated 1889 Johnstown Flood mission by one year, was among the earliest disaster relief operations by an International Red Cross-affiliated organization.[90] Following the eruption, which killed 105 people, JRCS Headquarters dispatched medical relief parties to assist local relief teams. The society also distributed food and financial aid to victims, which were brought by volunteers from Tokyo.[91] As recorded in the official history of the JRCS, "the ideal of humanitarianism (*jindō*), . . . presumes that human suffering is universal—disaster can strike any race and social class at any time and place without discrimination. . . . People of the world over celebrate universal sympathy and benevolence."[92]

On the national level, the JRCS adopted the mandate for natural disaster relief during the JRCS general assembly in 1892 and introduced the Natural Disaster Relief Regulations in 1900.[93] It was the first official Red Cross mandate for disaster relief adopted by any national Red Cross society. Subsequently, the JRCS was involved in relief operations in the wake of numerous disasters such as earthquakes, tsunamis, floods, great fires, and typhoons that struck Japan. For instance, they deployed medical workers and treated victims of the Mino-Owari (Nōbi) earthquake in 1891, the Sanriku earthquake in Tohoku in 1896, the great fire of Fukui City in 1902,[94] the Kita Tango earthquake in 1927,[95] and the 1923 Great Kantō earthquake.[96]

From this point on, peacetime relief activities became the principal focus of the JRCS until World War II, when medical aid to the wounded took center stage in Japan, as it did in every combatant country. JRCS chapters became the principal agencies to operate both professional and volunteer activities. The society was involved in social sanitation control in addition to epidemic and public health operations on the ground. It responded to nine major epidemics in the Meiji period, including the treatment of cholera in Nagasaki in 1907.[97] In 1913, the JRCS headquarters started a tuberculosis (TB) eradication campaign,[98] funded in part by donations from the imperial family. In 1912, the JRCS headquarters was moved to a new building in Shiba district, Tokyo,[99] which previously housed the government's Serum Institute, headed by Baron Kitasato Shibasaburō.[100]

The response of the JRCS to the Spanish flu pandemic provides another example of the JRCS's peacetime humanitarian operations in the interwar period. It is generally believed that 500 million were infected worldwide and between 25 to 50 million people died. The pandemic lasted from January 1918 to December 1920. According to records of the Statistics Bureau of the imperial Japanese government, in 1920 the total population of the home islands of Japan was 55,963,053.[101] Among them, a total of 23,804,637 people were infected, almost half of the entire population, and 388,727 people died.[102] The low mortality rate in Japan compared to Europe, estimated to be 1.1 percent, can be attributed in part to the vigorous response of the JRCS.[103]

JRCS local chapters, including in Taiwan, took the initiative in launching public health campaigns and providing medical care to patients. They deployed professional nurses and medical workers to the Japanese Army and Navy, public venues, and individual households to administer medical treatment; donated face masks; distributed public health campaign leaflets; and gave vaccinations to the poor free of charge. For example, mobile medical workers of the JRCS Tochigi Chapter administered vaccinations to 7,879 people, while the JRCS Fukushima Chapter distributed 11,000 face masks and vaccinated 3,000 people against Spanish flu.[104]

The scale and rapidity of the JRCS's response to the Spanish flu pandemic and other public health crises were possible only because the vast, grassroots network of Red Cross chapters, whose volunteer members rose to the challenge. In addition, medical care was directed to the most socially vulnerable people. During this period JRCS membership continued to climb and reached 2 million in 1920, to become second only to the American Red Cross.[105] Furthermore, while some chapters focused on the poor, the JRCS Iwate Chapter prioritized support to frontline civil servants. They distributed more than 2,000 handmade face masks to town offices, police, banks, schools, and newspaper agencies. The Iwate Chapter worked with the local Volunteer Nursing Association and the Patriotic Women's Association.[106]

Some local chapters were able to provide professional medical treatment. For example, the JRCS Saitama Chapter sent medical staff to treat 374 patients quarantined in their homes who were not able to gain admission to hospitals; nurses alone logged 569 service days.[107] In addition, local JRCS chapters deployed 592 medical workers to Imperial Army and Navy hospitals throughout Japan and in Taiwan from 1919 to 1921. They treated 12,735 patients in total, incurring costs totaling 48,213 yen and ninety-six sen.[108] During the pandemics, few JRCS nurses were infected or died in the line of duty.[109]

In 1924, the JRCS expanded its public health campaigns to primary schools. The Society designed seventeen posters promoting daily hygiene and distributed them to JRCS Chapters Junior Red Cross Societies to be posted in primary schools throughout Japan. (See figure 1.3.) The League of Red Cross Societies (LORCS) subsequently requested copies to promote worldwide.[110] An article reviewing the posters published in 1925 in LORCS's monthly magazine, *The World's Health*, commented, "In complete harmony with the views of the leading students of child psychology, . . . it is interesting that the health habits advocated by these posters, though depicted in so distinctly Japanese a setting, have a universal application."[111] The displaying of posters prominently bearing the the JRCS's name and symbol enhanced its reputation worldwide.

The JRCS expanded public health and disaster relief programs in the interwar period. For example, the society launched a nationwide program to promote maternity and child healthcare. Local JRCS chapters sent Red Cross nurses to schools to hold public health education sessions. When the Tohoku region suffered famine caused by frost damage in 1934, the JRCS Iwate Chapter founded an orphanage.[112]

Evidence of the JRCS's commitment to international humanitarianism in the early twentieth century is demonstrated in its donations to international disaster relief operations. The society donated 315,567 yen, 14 sen, and 9 rin to victims of the 1906 San Francisco earthquake through the ARC. It was the largest foreign donation at that time.[113] The society collected money from chapters in Japan and its colonies and from branch offices elsewhere in Asia. When China experienced the 1931 Yellow River

FIGURE 1.3 The JRCS was a major sponsor of the international Junior Red Cross. The caption reads, "Don't forget to wash your hands before mealtime and chew your food well."

Poster by the Japanese Red Cross Society. Courtesy of Poster House, accessed March 25, 2022, https://posterhouse.org/blog/posters-of-the-japan-red-cross-society/.

floods, in which approximately 40 million people were affected and 10 million people lost their homes, the JRCS donated 30,000 yuan to the Chinese Relief Flood Disaster Committee and sent a JRCS officer to Shanghai to express sympathy to victims.[114] From 1911 to 1923, the JRCS sent contributions and aid to a wide range of Red Cross and Red Crescent societies, including Italy, Greece, Bulgaria, Montenegro, Turkey, Germany, and Russia. Donations to international relief funds and operations totaled 2,554,906 yen and 516 sen in this period.[115]

The 1923 Great Kantō earthquake was the largest natural disaster relief operation of the Red Cross and Red Crescent until the 2004 Indian Ocean earthquake and tsunami. The operation lasted ten months. On September 1, 1923, a magnitude 7.9 earthquake hit the Tokyo and Yokohama region, followed by a great fire; several million people were affected and more than 100,000 lost their lives.[116] The quake destroyed Japan's capital city and delivered a great shock to the nation. The scale of destruction was so vast that for the first time, local JRCS chapters sent their own medical relief teams to the site of the disaster. The Tokyo Headquarters and staff of the JRCS were severely impacted by the great disaster. One hundred and thirty-two hospitals in Tokyo were destroyed, and the main building and warehouses of the headquarters burned to the ground. As a result, the headquarters lost all aid kits, which were worth 500,000 yen at that time.[117] The society set up emergency aid stations in many places, mobilized ambulances, provided aid for infants and children, managed sanitary control, established infectious disease hospitals, and administered emergency medical aid. The JRCS deployed 3,561 aid workers, excluding administrative staff, and treated 2,067,500 people in total.[118]

The relief operations in the aftermath of the Great Kantō earthquake were the first large-scale international aid operations of the international Red Cross and Red Crescent movement and became a model for disaster relief activities around the world. The ICRC, the LORCS,[119] and twenty-seven national chapters, including the ARC,[120] the Red Cross Society of China (RCSC), the Canadian Red Cross (CRC), the French Red Cross (FRC), the Italian Red Cross (IRC), the BRC, the Soviet Red Cross, the Chilean Red Cross, and the Colombian Red Cross all made contributions. The ARC mobilized its 3,600 chapters and the Chinese Red Cross movement mounted major campaigns. (See figure 1.4.) Responding to an appeal from President Calvin Coolidge to provide $5 million in aid, the

FIGURE 1.4 The photo shows women in Chicago dressed in kimonos and holding Japanese paper lanterns. The American public contributed generously to support earthquake relief in Japan following the 1923 Great Kantō earthquake.

Osaka Mainichi, "Kantō Shinsai Gahō, Dai San shū" [Earthquake Pictorial Edition, Part Three] (Tokyo: Osaka Mainichi, 1923).

ARC's Japanese relief fund ultimately reached $11,631,302.63. The biggest donation, $1.17 million, came from California, the state with the largest number of Japanese residents, where the JRCS had overseas chapters. As noted in its annual report, the ARC recognized "the efficiency of the Japanese government and people and particularly of the Japanese Red Cross," and did not send its own personnel to oversee the relief operation. Foodstuffs, clothing, and material for shelter totaling $5 million were delivered on U.S. government ships and private lines.[121]

Participation of the Red Cross Society of China in the Great Kantō earthquake relief operation despite ongoing tensions between the two governments is evidence of the strong spirit of international humanitarianism that characterized the Red Cross movement in Asia in the interwar period. (See figure 1.5.) The Red Cross Society of China (Beijing), headed by Tang

FIGURE 1.5 The medical relief team of the Red Cross Society of China (Shanghai) sent to Yokohama in the aftermath of the Great Kantō earthquake, September 1923.

Archival collection of the Red Cross Information Plaza, the Japanese Red Cross Society, *Beikoku Sekijūji Dokutoru Piitā Satsuei: Nihon Shinsai Shashin (Zen Hyaku Sanjū-nana yō)*, ID: PH-000005-044 (Tokyo: Nihon Sekijūjisha, 1923).

Erho (1878–1940), sent a condolence party to Tokyo, which was welcomed by Prince Kan'in Kotohito (1865–1945), honorary president of the JRCS, and donated 20,000 Chinese yuan. The Shanghai branch sent a relief party consisting of twenty-six medical workers that assisted operations at JRCS Headquarters Hospital. The Chinese relief team arrived in Tokyo on September 14 and was also welcomed by Prince Kan'in Kotohito. The Shanghai branch donated medical kits, clothing, and 4,000 Japanese yen in cash.[122] Subsequently, worldwide natural disaster relief activities became as a top priority in the International Red Cross and Red Crescent community. The budget of the JRCS allocated to natural disaster relief, 5,000,000 yen, was almost equivalent to its wartime relief activities during the Russo-Japanese War.[123] The Great Kantō earthquake opened a window to global cooperative relief operations unrestricted by national boundaries.

The JRCS's international disaster relief operations are evidence of a growing commitment to a global conception of humanitarianism and transition from bilateral assistance to multilateral international humanitarian cooperation. As a result, ordinary people became more conscious about strangers in need. As we have seen, from early on the JRCS conceived of its mandate as extending beyond aid to the victims of military conflicts, which remained the focus of the ICRC and many national Red Cross societies. One can even say that the JRCS took the lead in international disaster relief. Ultimately, the movement established a system of international cooperation in worldwide disaster relief.

THE FOUNDING OF THE LEAGUE OF RED CROSS SOCIETIES (LORCS)

One of the most momentous events in the history of modern humanitarianism was the foundation of the LORCS in 1919, currently known as the International Federation of Red Cross and Red Crescent Societies (IFRC) as a companion institution to the ICRC. While ICRC's officers were Swiss nationals and its mission concerned medical and humanitarian relief operations during wartime, LORCS's executive committee was multinational and its mission was to coordinate relief operations wherever people faced natural disasters and social crises.[124]

It is generally assumed that the ARC initiated the foundation of the LORCS at the behest of U.S. President Woodrow Wilson.[125] As we have seen, however, grassroots humanitarian relief movements not related to wartime activities developed early in Japan and were central to the JRCS's humanitarian mission. In fact, Dr. Ninagawa Arata (1873–1959), an international scholar and JRCS delegate in Europe, began advocating for the formation of a peacetime humanitarian relief organization before the conclusion of World War I when Western national Red Cross societies were consumed with wartime medical exigencies.[126] To drum up support in Japan, Ninagawa published a number of essays expounding on Japanese national identity and its premodern traditions of humanitarianism embraced by ordinary Japanese people.[127]

From June 1918 to March 1919, Ninagawa accompanied the JRCS's special commission on a tour of the United States, Britain, and Europe. Tokugawa Yoshihisa (1884–1922) headed the commission, and Ninagawa served as his deputy.[128] On July 19, 1918, Ninagawa, accompanied by Henry P. Davison, chairman of the War Council of the ARC, met with President Wilson at the White House to present his proposal and subsequently traveled to Oyster Bay, Long Island, to meet with former U.S. President, Theodore Roosevelt (1858–1919). After expressing condolences over the death of Roosevelt's son Quentin in World War I, the delegation presented the plan, to which Roosevelt responded warmly: "When Japan and the United States work together, world peace is secure."[129] Discussions with President Wilson also must have gone well. In a telegraph to Emperor Taishō three weeks later, Wilson warmly praised the JRCS mission as "an inspiring evidence" of U.S.-Japan cooperation and as "enduring evidence of the humanitarian principles which guide them in their relations with their fellowmen."[130]

Shortly after, Tokugawa Yoshihisa and Ninagawa left New York to tour European capitals, where Ninagawa lobbied the highest ranks of Red Cross officials in France, Britain, Italy, Switzerland, and Belgium to support his plan for a new organization dedicated to peacetime humanitarian relief. Not surprisingly, he did not immediately win converts at a time when the war in Europe was approaching its climax and national Red Cross societies were still focusing on wartime activities. In fact, fully occupied with rendering medical aid to tens of thousands wounded soldiers, initially the ICRC, the ARC, and the BRC all responded coolly to Ninagawa's proposal.[131]

The JRCS was something of an outlier among national Red Cross movements in that it did not limit its focus to armed conflicts. Moreover, the society was not comfortable with its movement being cast within the framework of Western-centered humanitarian enlightenment. In an article written in 1919, titled "Discussion on Humanitarian Duty and Its Technologies," later published in a collection of essays, Ninagawa argued that the charter of the League of Nations did not go far enough in addressing the problems facing humanity and that political and humanitarian agendas should be separated, describing the League of Nations as "the political league of peoples," and the League of Red Cross Societies as "the humanitarian league of peoples."[132] Ninagawa expressed pride in the JRCS's role in the establishment of the

LORCS in his essay "The Japanese as a Humanitarian People."¹³³ Writing in 1928, Ninagawa stated, "Japan's involvement in the Red Cross is not a shallow attempt to copy the West. In fact, Japan today is playing a large part in the global humanitarian movement of the Red Cross." He went on to boast that, "In reality, the JRCS stands at the top of the Red Cross movement in the world. . . . Japanese people should be proud of the fact that Japan takes first place in terms of its global humanitarian efforts in the world, today. It is such a great honor."¹³⁴

Here we see articulated both the idealism of Japanese internationalism in the age of Taishō democracy and the maturing of the JRCS ethos of patriotic humanitarianism. Rather than ranking countries by military or economic power, Ninagawa proposed that humanitarian contributions should be the central measure of the standing of nations in the global community of nation-states whose development was the vital task of all civilized people.

From early on, the JRCS's principal focus was on saving lives and alleviating suffering in humanitarian crises rather than medical aid on the battlefield, which was the original mission of Red Cross societies in Europe. With the largest membership of any humanitarian organization in Japan and among the largest in the world in the early twentieth century, the JRCS mobilized an enormous number of volunteers, from common citizens to members of the imperial family, as well as professionals such as doctors, nurses, international law scholars, interpreters, and disaster relief coordinators. Volunteers outnumbered salaried employees, and ordinary people embraced the JRCS's mission to devote themselves to humanitarianism (*jindō*), literally "the way of humanity."

2

INTERNATIONALISM IN CRISIS

The Fifteenth International Conference of
the Red Cross in Tokyo, 1934

The Japanese Red Cross Society's international prestige reached an apogee in October 1934, when it hosted the Fifteenth International Conference of the Red Cross in Tokyo. The conference was the largest international humanitarian congress of the interwar period; invited guests came from five continents, representing both nation-states and colonial possessions in the Middle East, Asia, Africa, and North and South America (figure 2.1).[1] In 1934, the world community stood at a forked road, one road leading to continued multilateral international cooperation and the other to the unraveling of the international treaties and institutions constructed after World War I, the "Great War to end all wars." In East Asia, the unraveling had already begun. The Japanese army occupied Manchuria in September 1931, which became the puppet state of Manchukuo in March 1932. Two months later, right-wing military officers assassinated Prime Minister Inukai Tsuyoshi (1855–1932), the last civilian head of the cabinet prior to the Pacific War.[2] The following year, Japan withdrew from the League of Nations over criticism of its seizure of Manchuria. In Europe, Adolf Hitler and the Nazi Party were consolidating control over the German state, and in 1935, Italy invaded Ethiopia, Africa's last sovereign nation. Everywhere, it seemed the Great Powers were showing diminished commitment to world peace and international law, including protections afforded to prisoners of war under the 1906 and

FIGURE 2.1 Official photograph of delegates to the 1934 Tokyo Conference, the largest and most geographically diverse International Red Cross and Red Crescent Conference of the interwar period.

Archival collection of the Red Cross Information Plaza, the Japanese Red Cross Society, Nihon Sekijūjisha, ed., *Dai Jūgo-kai Sekijūji Kokusai Kaigishi* (Tokyo: Nihon Sekijūjisha, 1937), introduction.

1929 Geneva Conventions and the 1925 Geneva Protocol prohibitions on the use of chemical and biological weapons.

This chapter argues that despite rising militarism at home and abroad, the JRCS capitalized on its role as the host country to advance the international Red Cross and Red Crescent movement's humanitarian agenda. Under the leadership of JRCS President Tokugawa Iesato (1863–1940), the sixteenth head of the Tokugawa Family, the JRCS opened a new chapter in the history of the Red Cross movement by bringing the conference to Asia and obtaining the unanimous agreement of delegates to the Tokyo Declaration of 1934.[3] In the process, the JRCS successfully coordinated its activities with numerous national Red Cross societies, including those of nations at odds with Japan's foreign policy, notably the Red Cross Society of China (RCSC) and the American Red Cross (ARC).

The chapter concludes by exploring the Tokyo Declaration of 1934 from the perspective of international law, peacetime humanitarian relief, international cooperation, and the movement for world peace. The principles enunciated in the 1934 Tokyo Declaration would become the foundation of the 1949 Fourth Geneva Convention's provisions on the Protection of Civilian Persons in Time of War. The standard narrative of the advance of international law of war celebrates the adoption of the 1949 Geneva Conventions as the historic milestone in the protection of civilians during wartime, which indeed it was. The fact that the Tokyo Conference was the site of the first iteration of these principles testifies to the JRCS's idealism and expansive vision of humanitarianism even as Japan's leaders pursued the war in China.[4]

TOKUGAWA IESATO AND JRCS INTERNATIONAL HUMANITARIANISM

Several factors influenced the historic decision at the 1930 Brussels International Red Cross Conference to appoint Tokyo as the host city of the 1934 Conference. After World War I, new Red Cross societies were founded in countries on every inhabited continent, and in 1934, the JRCS had already become the largest national society outside the West, with a membership of 2,810,185, including volunteers.[5] The decision also reflected confidence in the JRCS's leader, Tokugawa Iesato, a member of the League of Red Cross Societies' (LORCS) standing committee since 1930, and recognition of his deep commitment to internationalism.[6]

Born into the Tayasu branch of the Tokugawa clan in 1863, Iesato witnessed the end of the shogunate and the swift disappearance of feudal society. Educated in England, where he graduated from Eton College, he returned to Japan in 1882 and served as honorary chair of the House of Peers from 1903 to 1933.[7] Iesato avoided partisan politics, and in 1914 during the Taishō political crisis,[8] he declined an invitation from senior government leaders to succeed Yamamoto Gombei (1852–1933) as premier of the cabinet. Content to project the public image of a noble gentleman, an aristocrat from old times, he was at ease among world leaders and circulated seamlessly in high political circles in Japan, both in the era of Taishō democracy and after 1932 under military-headed cabinets. He preferred to wield influence behind the scenes. When he attended the Washington Naval Treaty Conference in 1922 as plenipotentiary together with Navy Minister Katō Tomosaburō[9] and lead negotiator Shidehara Kijūrō, Iesato maintained a low profile.[10] His experience at the Washington conference, where the first international treaties limiting armaments were signed, heightened his commitment to international cooperation and his belief world peace was possible. Prior to becoming head of the JRCS in 1929, he had become the target of the left-wing Levelers Association, which vehemently opposed the titled nobility, held the Tokugawa government responsible for discrimination against Burakumin, and set fire to his official residence as a protest.[11] Two years later in 1931, after assuming the JRCS presidency, he became the target of ultranationalists of the Blood-Pledge Corps, who denounced him as a liberal internationalist close to the United Kingdom and United States.[12] A prominent philanthropist, Iesato served as the chair of social welfare organizations such as the Tokyo Jikei Association and the Saiseikai Imperial Gift Foundation, and promoted social welfare, medical advancement, education, and cultural activities in general.[13]

When the Great Kantō earthquake of 1923 struck Tokyo and Yokohama, killing more than 100,000 people, Iesato led a successful fundraising campaign in Japan and rallied support from the International Red Cross community. The relief activities mounted after the earthquake became the largest natural disaster relief operation in the history of the international Red Cross and Red Crescent movement prior to the 2004 Indian Ocean earthquake and tsunami. The destruction of vast areas of Tokyo, the former capital of the Tokugawa shogunate, and massive loss of life affected Iesato deeply, and he used his social prestige to solicit donations. He founded the Disaster Charity Association and collected donations through the Nobleman Association supported by Crown Prince Hirohito.[14] At the 1930 Brussels Conference, Iesato, as the president of the JRCS, appealed to delegates to select Tokyo to host the 1934 conference by presenting Tokyo's rapid recovery as an inspiring example of what international humanitarian cooperation could accomplish: "At the time of the Great Earthquake of 1923, which laid waste the cities of Tokyo and Yokohama, you helped us in various ways, promptly and substantially. I am happy to say that these cities which lay as a desert of ashes and debris, have been almost entirely rehabilitated. We, therefore, most earnestly desire the next world conference be held in Tokyo so that we may show you these cities that have been so miraculously reconstructed."[15]

Tokugawa Iesato's career as a nonpartisan political figure, deep involvement in social welfare, and diplomatic experience made him the ideal leader of the JRCS during the turbulent decade of the 1930s. His fundraising success in the aftermath of the Great Kantō earthquake and aloofness from partisan politics made him a good fit with the Red Cross's commitment to political neutrality. Furthermore, his great popularity among ordinary Japanese people as *Shōgun-sama* and his strong traditional network that extended from local authorities to former *daimyō* families throughout Japan helped to make JRCS local chapters the driving force in the development of Japan's nationwide humanitarian movement.

JRCS PATRIOTIC HUMANITARIANISM IN AN AGE OF GLOBAL UNCERTAINTY

The JRCS invited eighty-one state representatives from nations around the world to the 1934 Tokyo Conference, including the recently decolonized countries of Afghanistan, Iran, and Cuba, making it the largest and most diverse international gathering of civil society organizations prior to World War II. A total of 199 officials of the Red Cross and Red Crescent societies in Europe, North and South America, Asia, Africa, the Middle East, and Oceania attended, in addition to representatives of major international organizations such as the League of Nations and the Boy Scouts.[16] The total number of participants was 319.[17]

The Tokyo Conference convened in the shadows of the carnage of World War I, which many Red Cross personnel saw as the harbinger of the age of total war, in which civilians would be indiscriminately killed by artillery and aerial bombing. Inoue Enji, the director general of the JRCS Investigation Department, predicted in an essay published in 1924 in the JRCS's monthly magazine *Hakuai*: "If war occurs in future, it will be much more cruel and brutal than the European Great War."[18] The vice-director of the LORCS, Lewis E. de Gielgud, expressed similar fears in a letter to Inoue, reporting: "The atmosphere of political tension I find prevailing in Europe is both discouraging and disquieting. We can only hope the skies will soon clear."[19] Aid workers shared the same critical sentiment that internationalism was in crisis and humankind was living on the verge of another Great War, one that would put them at tremendous risk as frontline humanitarian aid workers.

The development of military technology was making it increasingly difficult for humanitarian aid workers to render medical aid in wartime. The JRCS expressed concern that the modernization of weapons, and chemical and bacteriological weapons in particular, would imperil relief operations.[20] In the 1930s, the Geneva Conventions became the focus of intense scholarly discussion in Japan.[21] The JRCS itself published the latest edition of *The Geneva Conventions* in 1933 to train and educate Red Cross members and field aid workers.[22] Furthermore, the JRCS monthly magazine regularly carried scholarly articles on chemical warfare and the international law of war. All these works emphasized the increasing dangers posed by modern warfare to civilians and aid workers. Air raids could kill civilians indiscriminately, while chemical warfare would put at risk not only civilians but those carrying out relief activities in the aftermath of such attacks. This growing body of scholarship provided the groundwork for drawing up the Tokyo Declaration of 1934.

As an organization, the JRCS and its members were committed to humanitarian aid both at home and abroad and participated in the JRCS as patriotic Japanese. In this respect, Japanese responded much like the citizens of other nations who rushed to join the Red Cross in wartime.

The rapid growth of the JRCS's membership in the 1930s was driven in part by the surge in nationalism following the Manchurian Incident of 1931 and military expansion in northeast China.[23] (See table 2.1 and figure 2.2.) Both the JRCS leaders and the membership wanted to serve their country through the humanitarian movement, a mentality I call "humanitarian patriotism." For instance, Inoue Enji, a leading JRCS official with extensive international experience, argued in an essay published in the JRCS monthly magazine that the global mandate of the Red Cross had expanded beyond its original mission of impartial medical aid in wartime to include the advancement of public welfare worldwide by providing humanitarian aid that individual states could not accomplish on their own. He quoted from the mission statement of the LORCS in arguing that the mission of the Red Cross was to "support and supplement the mission of the nation state, not just through relief operations in wartime but in peacetime by initiating social welfare campaigns, prevention of infectious diseases, medical care during epidemics."[24] He believed that vulnerable people the world over tended to be ignored by modern states both in wartime and peacetime. Recognizing the limits of governments in addressing humanitarian issues, he argued that citizens had a patriotic duty to support the Red Cross in order to enable their countries to fulfill their humanitarian and social welfare mandates. His argument was premised on the compatibility of international humanitarianism and patriotic duty. In minimizing battlefield deaths not only of Japanese soldiers but wounded civilians and enemy combatants without discrimination, JRCS personnel could contribute to international humanitarianism while acting as loyal Japanese subjects.

As spokesman for the JRCS, Tokugawa Iesato argued that nationalism did not contradict internationalism. In a speech broadcast live nationwide, "National Aspirations (*Minzoku no Bokkō*)," to the Silver Anniversary Convention of Rotary International held in June in Chicago in 1930, he argued, "I have done so for the reason that the mutual recognition of national aspirations among the peoples of the world is not only consistent with the spirit of international cooperation and good will, but forms, in my opinion, the very foundation of what really constitutes good understanding between nations. While all the nations of the world are bound together in social, economic, and political interdependence, it is essential for each of them to cultivate a clear vision of national ideals and

TABLE 2.1 JRCS membership, 1877–1945

Year	Number of members	Year	Number of members	Year	Number of members
1877	38	1900	728,507	1923	2,232,269
1878	46	1901	784,876	1924	2,300,049
1879	63	1902	851,918	1925	2,421,776
1880	161	1903	894,760	1926	2,485,971
1881	172	1904	986,852	1927	2,470,371
1882	226	1905	1,127,711	1928	2,508,578
1883	241	1906	1,275,512	1929	2,534,721
1884	248	1907	1,397,344	1930	2,540,406
1885	268	1908	1,443,420	1931	2,554,595
1886	609	1909	1,525,822	1932	2,588,282
1887	2,179	1910	1,528,140	1933	2,638,046
1888	11,973	1911	1,552,649	1934	2,810,185
1889	20,238	1912	1,590,328	1935	2,858,744
1890	23,569	1913	1,632,752	1936	*2,885,101
1891	28,169	1914	1,694,796	1937	*2,947,559
1892	32,615	1915	1,737,449	1938	*3,256,675
1893	45,317	1916	1,758,051	1939	*3,647,377
1894	117,022	1917	1,798,832	1940	*4,031,252
1895	182,414	1918	1,853,170	1941	*4,790,835
1896	324,579	1919	1,922,056	1942	*5,868,055
1897	455,638	1920	2,003,238	1943	*8,821,002
1898	570,000	1921	2,064,200	1944	*13,374,220
1899	645,295	1922	2,185,672	1945	*15,238,429

*Includes honorary members.

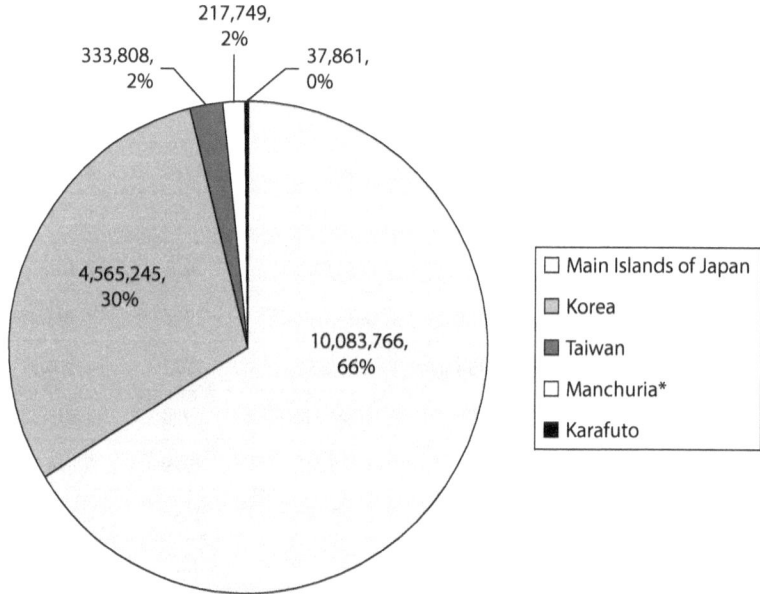

FIGURE 2.2 Imperial Japan JCRS membership by region in 1945. Note that no data are available on JRCS overseas and South Sea Mandate (Nan'yō) memberships.

*Manchukuo Red Cross Society memberships are not included.

Nihon Sekijūjisha, ed., *Nihon Sekijūjisha Shashikō, Dai Go-kan, Shōwa jūichi nen kara Shōwa nijū nen* (Tokyo: Nihon Sekijūjisha, 1969), 362–64.

aspirations, and thus appreciate the important role played by each nation in their realization."[25]

Iesato believed that nationalism, pride in progress of the nation-state, and internationalism, whose mission was to advance the well-being of people everywhere, were two sides of the same coin. In fact, Iesato went further in suggesting that healthy nationalism required a global commitment to the well-being of people everywhere. In this idealistic formulation of the Red Cross movement's mission, humanitarian service made a vital contribution to world peace.

Tensions in state-to-state relations between Japan and the United States after 1931 did not impair the close relationship between the JRCS and the ARC. When the JRCS stood as a candidate to host the Fifteenth Congress, the ARC, which had also put itself forward, withdrew its bid, choosing instead to throw its support to the JRCS.[26] The two Red Cross Societies corresponded frequently in the leadup to the 1934 conference, indicative of their special relationship in the interwar years as partners working to ameliorate the growing tension between their countries. When John Barton Payne, the chairman of the ARC and the president of the LORCS, died in the year following the conference, the JRCS held a commemoration service in Tokyo and paid special tribute to his memory, extolling his contributions to the movement. The JRCS invited the U.S. ambassador, foreign minister of Japan, and mayor of Tokyo to the service. In his memorial address, Iesato expressed the shock and grief in Japan upon learning of Payne's death and commended his role in mobilizing the international relief effort following the 1923 earthquake. "When the Great Earthquake of 1923 destroyed Tokyo, and its environs so pitilessly," he continued, Payne showed the world a "magnificent example of disaster relief that other Red Cross institutions should emulate in times of natural calamities." He praised Payne, whom the Emperor Taishō had awarded the Grand Cordon of the Order of the Rising Sun, as "the most distinguished delegate" to attend the Tokyo Fifteenth International Red Cross Conference and credited his astute stewardship to the conference's success.[27] With Payne's death, the JRCS lost its most trusted international partner.

THE JUNIOR RED CROSS AND VOICES OF CHILDREN

In the 1930s, the international Red Cross and Red Crescent movement committed itself to realizing politically obtainable humanitarian goals achieved through negotiations among civil society organizations, state agencies, armed forces, and political leaders. The 1934 conference provided an unrivaled opportunity to maintain the initiative in sustaining internationalism and advancing the humanitarian project. It is significant in this regard that the conference was the first occasion where the international Red Cross and Red Crescent humanitarian movement moved closer to the global pacifist movement. The term "peace" entered in the rhetoric of JRCS officials. It is telling that the great majority of the articles of the Tokyo Declaration of 1934 addressed peacetime Red Cross activities.

After the foundation of the LORCS in 1919, the international Red Cross and Red Crescent movement rapidly developed humanitarian activities such as social welfare, public health, nursing education, the Junior Red Cross, and natural disaster relief. Transnational activities and cooperation expanded and correspondence amongst the national Red Cross and Red Crescent societies increased worldwide. As revealed in the archive of the International Federation of Red Cross and Red Crescent Societies (IFRC),[28] national societies frequently sent funds and material aid on a bilateral basis throughout the 1920s.[29] Furthermore, the pen pal exchanges organized by the Junior Red Cross expanded to include children from Asia, South America, and the Middle East.[30] It was the period when, with the support of the LORCS, Red Cross activities became transnational, and donors and recipients were linked together globally through the national societies.

The Fifteenth International Conference of the Red Cross in Tokyo represented two global phenomena. One involved negotiations and cooperation among the directors of member national Red Cross societies, the drafting of protocols and policies by ICRC's and LORCS's executive committees, and coordination of aid operations, often in consultation with their respective governments. There was extensive correspondence amongst the heads of world national Red Cross societies in drawing up the agenda for the international meetings that convened every four years. This was the top-down movement whose deliberations were influenced by relations among the member nation status. The other movement was the civil society transnational movement, exemplified by the Junior Red Cross. The Junior Red Cross was a bottom-up grassroots movement, whose projects included encouraging children to adopt a pen pal in another country and exchange letters and essays to further understanding of world cultures and civilizations, which was believed would ameliorate tensions between nation-states in future generations.

The JRCS was a leading promoter of the Junior Red Cross worldwide, and it featured prominently in events during the Tokyo conference. (See figure 2.3.) The JRCS Junior Red Cross had enrolled 2,365,710 members by August 1934, second only to the United States.[31] During the conference, 5,068 children belonging to the Japanese Junior Red Cross participated in the congress and assisted operations and logistics.[32] They welcomed

FIGURE 2.3 Leaflet promoting the international pen pal project, distributed to delegations during the conference. The JRCS promoted person-to-person communication, underscoring their belief that children hold the key to world peace.

Archival collection of the Red Cross Information Plaza, the Japanese Red Cross Society. *Dai Jūgokai Kokusai Kaigi ni Okeru Kiroku narabini Insatsubutsu San.*

participants, delivered speeches, and accompanied guests to ceremonies and social events (figure 2.4).[33]

The Tokyo Fifteenth International Conference of the Red Cross was the first international conference where children played a prominent role. In an essay published in 1925, Inoue Enji explained that the three missions of the Junior Red Cross were the worldwide promotion of children's health, intellectual advancement, and citizenship. He extolled the Junior Red Cross as "the core of the world peace project. Because children make friends easily, person to person communication amongst children will be the way to provide for the future of friendly international relations amongst nation states."[34] Organized by the JRCS, the International Junior Red Cross Exhibition showcased the cultural, ethnic, and religious diversity of the world, which included colonial subjects, minorities, and local indigenous traditions. The exhibition featured a wide range of arts and

FIGURE 2.4 Japanese children welcoming the delegations to the Tokyo International Red Cross Conference.

"Soirée des Juniors: Zenkoku Shōnen Sekijūji Sawakai," in the archival collection of the Red Cross Information Plaza, the Japanese Red Cross Society. *Dai Jūgo-kai Sekijūji Kokusai Kaigi Kinen Shashin-chō, Shōwa Jūgo nen, Nihon Sekijūjish.*

crafts by children from around the world. For example, the JRCS Junior Red Cross exhibited Japanese handicrafts such as traditional Japanese dolls and games, while JRCS colonial branches introduced traditional arts and crafts from Korea and Manchuria. The twenty-nine national Red Cross societies that participated in the exhibition included the United States, Canada, Australia, New Zealand, India, Argentina, Chile, Lithuania, Poland, the Soviet Union, the Netherlands, the United Kingdom, France, and Germany. The Canadian Red Cross featured traditional arts of Canada's indigenous people; the Greek Red Cross displayed children's clothes from Crete; the Indian Red Cross Society exhibited Zoroastrian children's clothes; and the Peruvian Red Cross presented traditional needlework.[35] Japanese children visited the exhibition and learned about the cultural, ethnic, and religious diversity of the world. Inoue played a key leadership role in promoting the International Junior Red Cross Movement, and the society subsequently regarded children's activities as one of its most important humanitarian projects.[36] Even during World War II, Japanese children sent aid packages, including school supplies, to Chinese children through the Junior Red Cross activities of the JRCS.[37]

The broadening of international humanitarianism represented in advocacy of world peace carried with it perils for national Red Cross societies, especially in countries whose governments were increasingly committed to authoritarianism at home and militarism abroad. The founding principle of the Red Cross was absolute political neutrality, which enabled it to carry out its humanitarian mission even during wartime. When Ninagawa Arata (1873–1959), a Japanese scholar in international law who had played an instrumental role in the foundation of the LORCS in 1919, strongly criticized Japan's withdrawal from the League of Nations, describing it in print as "incredibly deplorable," and asserted that Japan as a nation had abandoned its legal responsibilities for humanitarian activities on the international stage, he was forced to retire from active service in the JRCS.[38] However, Ninagawa was the exception in the JRCS leadership group. More representative was Inoue Enji, who sought to steer a middle course between affirming international humanitarianism without jeopardizing the JRCS's political neutrality. Writing in 1934 about imperial Japan and the world crisis in *Dōhō*, the JRCS monthly bulletin for medical workers and nurses, he avoided direct criticism of Japan's withdrawal from the League of Nations and its military expansion in northeast China with this oblique and ambiguous observation: "An unprecedented Great Depression has swept the world for the last few years, and we already recognize that the people of Japan have been undergoing historic trials."[39] Inoue's pragmatic stance, which entailed avoidance of public statements critical of Japan's foreign policy, became a core attitude and policy for the JRCS from this time forward. It did not, however, dissuade the JRCS from cooperating with its counterpart in China during the Shanghai Incident.

THE 1932 SHANGHAI INCIDENT AND JRCS HUMANITARIAN DIPLOMACY

The 1932 Shanghai Incident, where division-strength Japanese and Chinese military units engaged in heavy fighting in a densely populated warzone over a six-week period, exposed the tensions between the JRCS's ideology of patriotic humanitarianism and its equally strong commitment to cooperation among all nations to advance international humanitarianism goals. In its role as Japan's Red Cross Society, it mobilized medical personnel to administer aid to wounded soldiers during the fighting. It formed seventeen medical support parties in total, of which seven teams were sent to naval hospitals on the main islands of Japan, while the remaining ten parties were deployed to medical ships and military hospitals in the war theater, with the exception of the Shanghai Military Logistics Hospital in Shanghai.[40] Notably, the JRCS Extra Relief Party No. 13 worked in Shanghai for two months and treated a total of 14,427 patients.[41]

The 1932 Shanghai Incident put unprecedented pressure on the JRCS not only because of the intensity of the battle, but also because the Imperial Japanese Army violated the Geneva Conventions in using illegal weapons and causing the death of aid workers from the RCSC.[42] (See figure 2.5.) These incidents shocked the JRCS as well as the international Red Cross and Red Crescent movement. In February 1932, the RCSC informed the JRCS about the incident through Sydney H. Brown, a specialist in international law dispatched as an ICRC observer to Shanghai and subsequently to Japan by Max Huber, president of the ICRC. According to the report sent by Brown to the JRCS on February 16, 1932, the Japanese Army used illegal weapons—dumdum bullets—and had attacked and killed one Chinese aid worker while he was conducting humanitarian relief activity with his Red Cross emblem clearly displayed. The RCSC attached a number of photos to its report, which showed the RCSC official who had fallen victim. Some of the photographs captured large bullet wounds covered in blood and the others showed a wounded official undergoing an operation at the Chinese Red Cross General Hospital in Shanghai and his dead body in a coffin surrounding by flowers during his funeral. The RCSC precisely reported to the JRCS the size of the bullet, its direction to the target, and a section of the damaged internal organs. Due to the wide opening of the bullet wound, which the Chinese Red Cross General Hospital Shanghai reported as "a defect [sic] of about two inches through which the collapsed lung could perfectly be discerned," the hospital concluded that the wound was caused by dumdum bullets.[43]

The RCSC subsequently reported to the JRCS other violations committed by the Japanese forces against aid workers. The report of

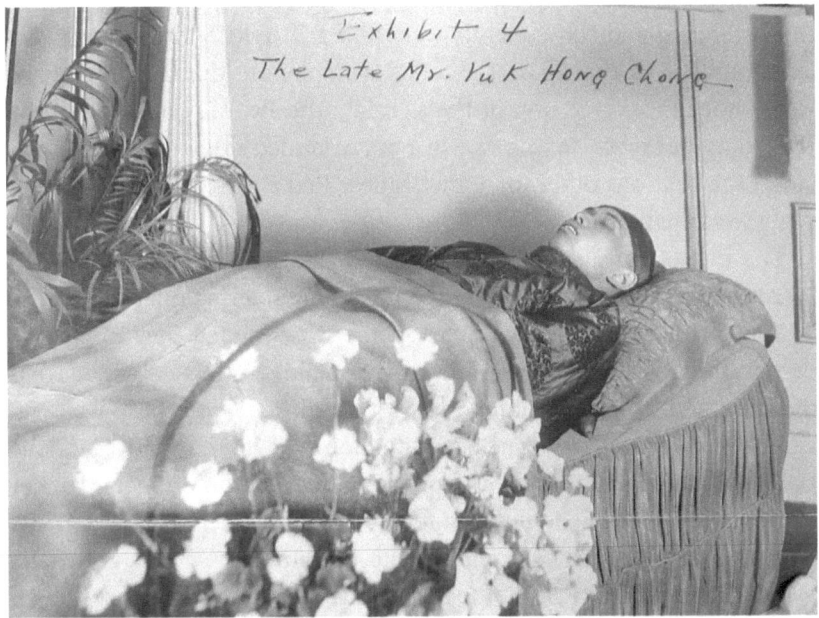

FIGURE 2.5 The JRCS SSERC report on alleged Japanese violations of the Geneva Conventions during the First Shanghai Incident contained a photograph of a Chinese Red Cross aid worker who was killed during the fighting.

Archival collection of the Museum Meiji-mura held by the Japanese Red Cross Toyota College of Nursing, *Dai Jūgo-kai Sekijūji Kokusai-kaigi, Shōwa Shichi-nen Itaru dō Kyū nen: Buraun Girugud-do Kankei*, ID: B1099-4384.

March 16, 1932, detailed eleven further alleged cases of illegal acts and offenses, some of which resulted in the death of RCSC relief workers. For example, it reported that on the afternoon of March 2, 1932, two Chinese Red Cross ambulances, dispatched to Chapei (currently Zhabei), were attacked by Japanese air strikes and set afire. In another incident, thirty-nine Red Cross rescue party trucks were conscripted by the Japanese army, which the RCSC received notification of on March 12, 1932. The report included the license plate number of each truck and ambulance and detailed the resulting damage. In another case, on January 31, 1932, four Boy Scouts working under the RCSC, wearing Red Cross armlets, had gone missing and perhaps had been illegally detained.[44] Furthermore, the report alleged that on March 3, 1932, three RCSC workers were arrested by the Japanese in the Kaiding District in a bamboo garden near Mo Lo Shiang and subsequently were killed. The RCSC also reported a large number of civilian victims. For example, on March 16, 1932, two weeks after the conclusion of the fighting, the RCSC confirmed to the JRCS that they were "taking care of 4,323 wounded soldiers and 337 civilians; organizations other than the Chinese Red Cross, are taking care of 2,447 wounded soldiers."[45]

The RCSC appealed for the support of the JRCS and pressured it to take action as the host society of the upcoming international conference in Tokyo. Indeed, the RCSC letter to the JRCS hinted they might not participate in the conference unless they obtained some assistance from the JRCS and the international Red Cross and Red Crescent movement. Extensive media coverage made the situation even more sensitive, and the JRCS was concerned that adverse publicity could become a major barrier to the success of the upcoming conference. The JRCS sent copies of RCSC reports in confidential communiques to the Ministry of Foreign Affairs (MOFA) and the Ministries of the Imperial Army and Navy, urging them to decrease illegal military operations. This warning by the JRCS to the Japanese military has remained confidential to this day. Subsequent correspondence between the JRCS, the RCSC, and the ICRC reveal the pressure the JRCS was under and the need to demonstrate its independence, not only to gain RCSC participation but also to retain credibility in eyes of the ICRC and the ARC.

It is significant that Japan's Ministry of Foreign Affairs closely followed developments in the period leading up to the convening of the conference.[46] For example, it informed the JRCS a few weeks before the conference that the Shanghai English-language newspaper, the *Evening Post*, had reported that the RCSC would submit a report on illegal acts committed by the Japanese forces in Shanghai to the forthcoming conference.[47] The uncertainty of the political situation in the aftermath of the Shanghai Incident prompted the JRCS to carry out a wide range of confidential investigations. For example, in a report it shared with the MOFA, the JRCS analyzed developments in the anti-Japanese boycott movement and the Japanese Association in China in order to anticipate the potential political impact of their activities on the conference.[48] At the same time the JRCS made a special effort to secure the participation of the RCSC. The invitation sent to the Ministry of Foreign Affairs of the Republic of China in

Nanjing read, "Japan welcomes you."[49] These efforts bore fruit on July 14, 1934, when a director general of the RCSC replied to the invitation stating, "I beg to say that it is a great honor coupled with the highest pleasure to be able to participate in the coming conference and am looking forward with great expectation to have honor to meet you all."[50] In the end, Ma Tianzhe,[51] an official of the Republic of China's Ministry of Foreign Affairs, attended as representative of the RCSC.[52] During the conference, the RCSC China Headquarters sent a second goodwill telegram expressing "deepest and hearty congratulations" and wishes for its "phenomenal success" to the chair of the congress and vice-director of the LORCS, Lewis E. de Gielgud.[53]

DIPLOMACY IN THE PLANNING OF THE TOKYO CONFERENCE

The process of preparing for the Fifteenth International Conference reveals the high priority the JRCS placed on maximizing the participation of Red Cross representatives and government officials from all corners of the globe. It also shows that the JRCS exercised a degree of political autonomy despite the ascendancy of militarism following the May 15, 1932, Incident. To rally support, Iesato held a reception in April 1934 at his private residence for twenty-nine prominent officials representing all Japanese government ministries, where he presented the JRCS's role in hosting the conference as an opportunity to exercise soft power. He boasted that "today, the Japanese Red Cross Society is accorded the highest respect among Red Cross societies around the word" at the same time that it enjoyed a long-standing close association with the Japanese imperial family.[54] He discretely suggested to the assembled officials that the Tokyo Conference was a unique opportunity to regain international standing: "Due to Japan's departure from the League of Nations, the significance of the Fifteenth International Red Cross Conference will become even more momentous for Japan as great world powers would be paying close attention to the proceedings."[55]

One month later, Iesato invited representatives of foreign embassies and consulates, including ambassadors, to his private residence to request their active participation and assistance. On a practical level, he sought support for translation, interpretation, and logistics and sought advice on matters of protocol, such as hosting receptions for wives of foreign delegates.[56] In his welcoming remarks, Iesato emphasized the international mission and visibility of the JRCS, as "not only a humanitarian organization that works in a national framework in wartime; it is also a society that undertakes natural disaster relief activities everywhere irrespective of national borders—both in Japan as well as overseas—in order to ameliorate the suffering of human beings in need" around the world.[57]

That the JRCS spared no effort to maximize participation in the Tokyo Conference is evident in its extensive correspondence with foreign Red Cross and Red Crescent societies, governments, and civic organizations around the globe.[58] The JRCS even provided discount travel tickets with the support of Japanese businesses such as the South Manchuria Railway Co., Ltd., and Nippon Yusen Kabushiki Kaisha (NYK).[59] In fact, the JRCS had previously twice failed in bids to host the conference due to objections to Japan's geographical remoteness.[60] Moreover, at a time when Japanese militarism had strained Japan's relations with the United States and Great Britain, the announcement that JRCS headquarters in Tokyo would serve as the official conference site was meant to signal to the international community the JRCS's institutional independence.

The Tokyo Conference was the first International Red Cross conference to adopt English as an official language, alongside French, in a challenge to the French-speaking, Switzerland-based ICRC movement. Although initially fiercely opposed, the Geneva leadership eventually agreed.[61] Using English as a lingua franca made the conference more independent from the ICRC. There were practical reasons as well, as delegates attending the conference were more likely to be English than French speakers. It is also possible that promoting English to official language status was a welcoming gesture to Anglo-American nations intended to ameliorate geopolitical tensions in the Asia-Pacific region.

The Red Cross eschewed taking political positions in accordance with its avowed stance of complete neutrality. This does not mean, however, that the JRCS's planning for the conference did not involve diplomatic balancing acts. A case in point was Manchukuo. Because the international community refused to recognize Manchukuo as an independent nation-state, deciding whether or not to invite delegations from the Manchukuo government tested the JRCS's political autonomy. In October 1933,

Inoue Enji and Shimazu Tadatsugu (1903–1990), a JRCS official,[62] visited the MOFA to discuss this sensitive issue with senior officials from the MOFA, Home Affairs, Imperial Army, and Imperial Navy—a year prior to the conference. The only official summary of the meeting stated, "due to the sensitivity, we agreed to defer decision-making to a higher level."[63] However, we can infer that Inoue and Shimazu prevailed, because no invitation was issued to the Manchukuo government.

The JRCS attempted to steer a middle course on the politically-charged issue of representation of colonized peoples, sending invitations to the Iraqi Red Crescent Society, the Haiti Red Cross Society, and the Nicaraguan Red Cross, which had not yet been recognized as official International RCRC members by the ICRC.[64] The Red Crescent Society of Iraq, a British protectorate, initially declined the invitation to attend, explaining, "It is impossible for the Administrative Committee to delegate any deputy owing to it being newly organized and fully occupied by its internal affairs."[65] Undeterred by the initial rejection, the JRCS persisted and in the end, the Executive Committee of the Red Crescent Alliance attended, in addition to the Turkish Red Crescent Society and the Red Lion and Sun Society of Persia.[66] One difficult issue was who was to represent British India. The JRCS invited the Indian Red Cross Society, which was founded as an independent national society,[67] whereupon Ambassador Sir Robert Clive informed the JRCS that he would be attending representing both Great Britain and "on behalf of the Government of India." This prompted the JRCS to consult with both the British government and the Indian Red Cross Society.[68] It was a delicate balancing act. In the end, the Indian Red Cross Society sent a delegation, and during the conference, the JRCS distributed reports from the Indian Red Cross Society to conference delegates, a matter of protocol that implied official recognition; at the same time, the JRCS made special provision for observer status of the British Raj.[69] In fact, Great Britain sent several representatives from their colonial territories to Tokyo,[70] while the JRCS issued invitations to the Red Lion and Sun Society of Persia. The ARC Philippines chapter, whose delegation included Americans and Filipinos, received special recognition during the conference by being seated with the representatives of the world powers.[71] In perhaps the most dramatic demonstration of the JRCS's commitment to international inclusiveness, the JRCS sponsored the Union of Red Cross and Red Crescent Societies of the USSR (Soviet RCRC) to be a member of the international Red Cross and Red Crescent movement, even though the United States refused diplomatic representation of the USSR until 1933. The LORCS accepted Soviet membership by unanimous consent just prior to the conference in early October 1934, which was publicized in the Japanese press.[72] To reciprocate, the Soviet RCRC donated 100,000 yen to the JRCS, and the USSR embassy in Tokyo held a welcome reception for delegations during the conference.[73]

To raise the visibility of the 1934 Conference, Iesato embarked on an eight-month tour of foreign capitals from August 1933 to April 1934. Although he was officially traveling in a private capacity, the purpose was to reassure the international community delegates they would receive a hospitable reception in Japan after the turbulent events of 1931 and 1932. At the LORCS headquarters in Paris, Iesato, in an inspirational address to the executive committee, cited growing international tensions as lending urgency of the promotion of cooperation among national Red Cross societies and volunteers around the world. Because the world community was "facing an age of estrangement," he argued, "more than in peacetime, this conference can provide the momentum to accomplish our high humanitarian mission. I believe that we can do it. Let's get Red Cross personnel from the world together, deepen mutual understanding, and keep hope for the future alive. We must all work together."[74] The warm reception he received gave reason for optimism. In the United States, Iesato was welcomed as a state guest in Washington, DC, and had a lunch reception with President Franklin Delano Roosevelt at the White House. He also visited the ARC headquarters to discuss a range of issues. In the United Kingdom, Iesato was granted an audience with Prince Edward VIII at Buckingham Palace.[75]

Iesato's mission received extensive favorable press coverage, and the JRCS Tokyo Headquarters collected and analyzed reports carried by Japanese and foreign newspapers. For example, the Japanese newspaper the *Asahi Shimbun* published an eye-catching headline that proclaimed, "Tokugawa Denies Talk of War Between Japan and the US."[76] The headline in the *Yomiuri Shimbun* proclaimed, "Pacific Ocean Should Be a Concourse of Peace." Printed in enlarged font in the article's text were forceful calls for good relations with the United States: "There is no excuse: the peaceful and friendly Japan-US relationship should be maintained" and "Eschew hyperbole and provocation."[77] A sampling of

American newspapers suggests that the U.S. media gave ample coverage to Iesato's citizen diplomacy. In Washington, DC, the *Sunday Star* ran the headline announcing Iesato's visit, "Japanese Peace Worker Soon to Visit Capital."[78] On March 1, the *Evening Star* carried a photograph of Iesato and ARC Director John Barton Payne, both looking very serious, shaking hands under the caption "Red Cross Plans Conference: Prince Tokugawa and Judge Payne Arranged Parley."[79] On March 6 in New Orleans, the headline of the *Times—Picayune* read, "Prince Tokugawa Voices 'Earnest Desire' of Japan for Peace With America," and a pull-quote in the article stated, "Japanese Statesman Brings Message of Amity."[80] In Honolulu, the *Jiji Press* headline proclaimed "Japan-US Relationship Is Strong."[81] British newspapers introduced Iesato as the "King's Visitor,"[82] and the *Morning Post* ran the headline, "Britain and Japan 'Brothers.'"[83] While welcoming Iesato as a goodwill emissary, the tone of media coverage nevertheless signaled the tension in Japan's relations with the United States and the United Kingdom in the aftermath of the Manchurian Incident.

Iesato delivered a speech at the Japan Society in London in which he expressed his sincere affection toward the United Kingdom, "Whenever I come to England, I am reminded of my first visit. It was as long ago as 1877 when I was fifteen years of age, and I stayed here for about five years as a student. During my stay a great honor was conferred upon me when I was presented to Her Majesty Queen Victoria." In response to Iesato's speech, John Allsebrook Simon, First Viscount Simon, British Foreign Secretary, emphasized the long-term friendship between Tokugawa Japan and Great Britain, citing the example of the Englishman, William Adams (1564–1620), who served as an advisor to Tokugawa Ieyasu.[84]

In the United States, Iesato held a number of press conferences and in later years remarked that he was asked the same questions by journalists and people everywhere: whether Japan and the United States or Japan and the Soviet Union would go to war. On his visit to the U.S. State Department and elsewhere, reporters asked about ongoing discussions involving legislation restricting Japanese immigration to America, another point of tension between the two countries. In a report on his tour published in the May 1934 edition of the JRCS monthly journal, he told readers he had responded diplomatically, stating his view that "The negative sentiment of people who believe that Japan and the U.S. will go to war is brought about by lack of sensitivity and misunderstandings," that as a "peace-loving man he believed war between Japan and the U.S. is avoidable," and he expressed the hope that "his visit would improve friendship between Japan and the United States." While affirming maintenance of friendly relationships with Germany and Italy, he wrote that "if the three nations, Japan, the United Kingdom, and the United States, build up a close relationship, not only Asia but the world will maintain its peace." Realistic in assessing the impact of his visit, he acknowledged that "My remarks and goodwill efforts in the United States will not have a significant impact on the current critical international affairs." Nevertheless, he held out hope that the "participants of the Tokyo International Red Cross Conference will see the real Japan, which will strengthen the amity between Japan and the rest of the world."[85] In a conversation with ARC Chairman Payne on February 28 during his visit to the United States, Iesato emphasized his "great personal interest" in promoting world peace, which he claimed "has been the tradition of my family during the three centuries it held the position as Shoguns." He also reminded Payne that his ancestor Tokugawa Iesada (1824–1858) authorized the signing of the 1854 Treaty of Peace and Amity, Japan's first international treaty of the modern era.[86]

Paradoxically, Iesato appears to have been more successful courting international support than in persuading his own government. For reasons that are not entirely clear, the government did not provide much in the way of financial support for the conference, even though Iesato met with each cabinet minister, including the Ministry of Finance, to appeal for funding.[87] In the end, only the Ministry of the Imperial Army and Imperial Navy came through, each providing 50,000 yen, a substantial amount but less than twenty-five percent of the 225,700 yen total costs of planning, logistics, sponsored activities, and accommodations.[88] The JRCS welcomed the army and navy ministries' participation as well as their financial support, in the hope involvement in the conference would encourage their adherence to the Geneva Conventions. The motives of the army and navy may have been more practical: they needed the assistance of the JRCS to treat their wounded and sick soldiers during armed conflict in accordance with the Second Geneva Convention updated in 1929 and the Hague Convention of 1907.

In the end, the cabinet made a strong show of support as Prime Minister Okada Keisuke; Yuasa Kurahei, Minister of the Imperial Household; Hirota Kōki, Minister of Foreign Affairs; Gotō Fumio, Home Minister;

Matsuda Genji, Minister of Education, Science and Culture; Hayashi Senjūrō, Army Minister; and Hasegawa Kiyoshi, Navy Vice-Minister all attended the opening ceremony.[89] Prime Minister Okada delivered a speech at the welcome reception: "I express my sincere respect and gratitude to the Red Cross and its noble spirit of the love of humanity and aids to people in need both in peacetime and wartime and mankind's welfare globally." He concluded his speech by expressing his "strong hope" that "we, the Japanese people, strive to cooperate with Great Powers in pursuit of world peace and will faithfully and tirelessly contribute to the development of mutual understanding."[90] The presence of the highest officials in Japan's government suggests Iesato had succeeded in pitching the Tokyo Conference as an instrument of soft diplomacy, especially in the aftermath of Japan's withdrawal from the League of Nations and the 1932 Shanghai Incident.

A major disappointment was that Max Huber, the president of the ICRC, did not attend the Tokyo conference. Just prior to the convening of the Tokyo conference, the ICRC informed the JRCS that Huber's absence was due to "personal reasons," citing the illness of his wife.[91] The JRCS expressed its disappointment in the strongest terms and persisted in efforts to convince Huber to attend.[92] There were likely several reasons for Huber's absence, but one factor, as discussed below, may have been political opposition to certain articles in the draft of the Tokyo Declaration relating to the protection of enemy civilians in wartime.[93]

SHOWCASING JAPANESE INTERNATIONAL HUMANITARIANISM

The conference was held October 17–29, 1934, and set a record for the number of delegates.[94] In showcasing Japan's modernity, the JRCS pulled out all the stops and spared no expense in organized exhibitions and excursions that highlighted Japan's social and economic development, including nursing education and modern industries, while also introducing Japanese culture, natural features, and history.[95] For example, delegates' wives visited JRCS hospitals, a spinning mill factory, women's prisons, and Tokyo Women's Medical Professional School, which graduated many of

Japan's female doctors.[96] The JRCS arranged excursions to famous tourist sites in Kamakura, Nikkō, Hakone, Kyoto, Osaka, Nara, Hiroshima, Kumamoto, and even Seoul and Changchun in its overseas empire. (See figures 2.6 and 2.7.) Furthermore, colonial branches of the JRCS lent assistance. The JRCS Manchurian Committee Department and the Andong Committee Department facilitated travel arrangements for seventy-five delegates from the United States, Belgium, France, the United Kingdom, Germany, India, and the LORCS, who traveled to Tokyo via Manchukuo.[97]

The JRCS also organized cultural activities and receptions to introduce delegates to the traditional arts of Kabuki, Noh, and Gagaku.[98] Iesato held a banquet at the Tokyo Kaikan, and Prime Minister Okada Keisuke hosted a dinner party at his official residence. The mayor of Tokyo also hosted a dinner party to thank participants for their support during the Great

FIGURE 2.6 Red Cross delegates arriving at Utsunomiya station to Nikkō, welcomed by crowds waving Red Cross flags.

"Visite à Nikko. Accueil fait aux délégués devant la gare de Outsunomiya: Nikkō Yūran: Utsunomiya Ekitō no Kangei," in the archival collection of the Red Cross Information Plaza, the Japanese Red Cross Society, *Dai Jūgo-kai Sekijūji Kokusai Kaigi Kinen Shashin-chō, Shōwa Jūgo nen, Nihon Sekijūjisha.*

FIGURE 2.7 Delegates visit the Buddhist Statue in Kamakura, one of several visits to Japanese religious sites.

"Daïbutsu: Kamakura Hōmen Yūran (Daibutsu)," in the archival collection of the Red Cross Information Plaza, the Japanese Red Cross Society, *Dai Jūgo-kai Sekijūji Kokusai Kaigi Kinen Shashin-chō, Shōwa Jūgo nen, Nihon Sekijūjisha*.

Kantō earthquake of 1923—a total of more than 500 guests attended. Delegates and wives visited the Great Kantō earthquake memorial near the Sumida River and paid homage to earthquake victims at the Meiji Shrine and the Yasukuni Shrine. The Iwasaki and Mitsui families hosted garden parties with demonstrations of the traditional Japanese arts of calligraphy, ink brush painting, and flower arrangement. Delegates also visited Japan Visual Arts Academy to see Japanese traditional paintings. Princess Kan'in, honorary chair of the Volunteer Nurse Women's Association, hosted a tea party to impress on delegates advances in Japanese nursing.[99] There was no end to the wining and dining of delegates.

In the context of the recent rise to power of the Nazi Party in Germany, a classical music concert celebrating the seventieth birthday of the renown German composer Richard Strauss (1864–1949) took on special significance.

Sir Klaus Pringsheim (1883–1972), from the Tokyo Academy of Music, today the Tokyo University of the Arts, conducted the orchestra at the Hibiya Public Hall.[100] Pringsheim was a German Jewish composer and conductor who had studied composition under Gustav Mahler (1860–1911).[101] He conducted two performances of a program featuring Richard Strauss's compositions not previously performed in Japan: "Thus Spoke Zarathustra, Op. 30," "Two Anthems for 16-Part Mixed Chorus, Op. 34," and "An Alpine Symphony, Op. 64."[102] The first performance on October 30 was broadcast live on radio in Berlin for Strauss's benefit, followed by a repeat performance at the closing of the conference, which received high praise in the Tokyo press.[103] Pringsheim had selected the compositions, and Strauss telegrammed him, wishing him great professional success in his new career in Asia.[104] The fact that one year earlier in 1933 the German government had adopted sweeping laws denying employment of non-Aryans in public life, including the performing arts, made JRCS's staging of Pringsheim's concert an implicit criticism of Nazism. Yet it must have been a bittersweet moment for Strauss, who was criticized at the time and after for accepting the prestigious appointment as director of the Bayreuth Festival after Arturo Toscanini (1897–1951) had resigned the directorship in protest of racist Nazi policies.[105]

After the conference, the JRCS provided memorial souvenir albums to participants with photographs that both commemorated key conference events and depicted Japanese culture, industry, natural landscape, history, and social life, including a street in Ginza ablaze with bright night lights. In showcasing the two sides of Japan in the mid-1930s, the modern and traditional, the JRCS's conference positioned Japan as a country that embraced both internationalism and non-Western traditions.

TOKYO DECLARATION OF 1934

The Tokyo conference was unprecedently diverse in terms of world representation and duration. The Fourteenth International Red Cross Conference held in Brussels in 1930 lasted just five days and unlike the Tokyo conference, few non-Western Red Cross societies or international NGOs attended. The Tokyo conference was also the largest ever held, with a total of 319 delegates.[106] Iesato acted as the chairman, and ARC director

John Barton Payne was one of seven vice-chairs.¹⁰⁷ Iesato received celebratory messages from President Roosevelt and King Haakon VII of Norway.¹⁰⁸ The general assembly of the LORCS convened concurrently, as had occurred at the Brussels conference.¹⁰⁹

The proceedings of the conference were covered extensively and favorably in the Japanese media. The *Asahi Shimbun*, Tokyo's leading national newspaper, carried daily reports and numerous photographs each day of the conference. The lead editorial in the *Asahi Shimbun* on the day the conference opened celebrated "The International Red Cross flag waving in Tokyo's beautiful autumn sky" and lauded the conference as a gathering "dedicated to furthering international cooperation" and "inspired by the universal love of the humanity, both in war and peace."¹¹⁰ The *Asahi Shimbun*'s rival, the *Yomiuri Shimbun*, even ran a lead story three days prior to the opening day under the headline "Exaltation of Peace and Philanthropy" detailing the many "truly splendid" activities the organizers had planned.¹¹¹

Perhaps the most significant achievement of the Fifteenth International Conference of the Red Cross was the unanimous adoption of the Tokyo Declaration, which included conventions on the protection of enemy civilians.¹¹² The Tokyo Declaration consisted of forty-eight resolutions, and some resolutions contained of a number of articles.¹¹³ The official name of resolution thirty-nine, commonly referenced in Western-language legal discourse as the "Tokyo Draft" is the "Draft International Convention on the Condition and Protection of Civilians of Enemy Nationality Who Are on Territory Belonging to or Occupied by a Belligerent," which was only one of the forty-eight resolutions adopted at the conference. The great majority of resolutions concerned non-war-related relief activities, reflecting the expansion of the concept of humanitarianism that the JRCS and ARC had been instrumental in promoting. These resolutions addressed the Junior Red Cross, nursing education, volunteer workers and helpers for peacetime programs, public health services, natural disaster relief activities, ambulance services for automobile accidents, mass communication, promotion of international goodwill among nations, and expansion of the Empress Shōken Fund.¹¹⁴ The eight resolutions devoted to natural disaster relief operations included the establishment of a new organization, the International Relief Union proposed by Italy.¹¹⁵ Other resolutions addressed public health and social welfare, international transport of relief supplies, deployment of sea and air ambulances, and standardization of medical supplies.[116] Drafted by the JRCS and the ARC, with input from the LORCS executive committee and numerous national Red Cross chapters, the Tokyo Declaration articulated a bold global affirmation of human dignity and the advancement of health and well-being.[117]

Among the six war-related resolutions, resolution thirty-six banned the deployment of chemical agents and aerial warfare. Resolution thirty-eight required a declaration of war in the event of hostilities between nations, thus outlawing undeclared war. Resolution thirty-nine expanded the category of enemy civilians to include those in newly occupied territories.[118] Resolution thirty-nine was drafted by the ICRC executive committee in consultation with a panel of international law scholars, and it was circulated in Geneva in August 1934, two months prior to the conference.[119] Responsibility for completing the draft fell on the ICRC's legal staff.

The Tokyo conference had four committees. The chair of the conference and vice-director of the LORCS, Lewis E. de Gielgud, nominated the ICRC and Japanese government to serve jointly as secretary of two of the four standing committees, and assigned the remaining two to the LORCS. Iesato appointed Belgian, German, British, and Siamese Red Cross representatives as temporary chairs of the four committees.[120] The draft resolutions were reviewed and voted on by delegates in seven plenary sessions. The Belgian Red Cross, which hosted the previous International Red Cross Conference, led the discussion of the articles on the protection of civilians. The committees worked quickly, completing the entire text of forty-eight resolutions in five days, after which they reconvened and unanimously adopted the document known as the Tokyo Declaration.[121]

Three years before the start of the Second Sino-Japanese War (1937–1945) and five years before World War II in Europe, the 1934 Tokyo Declaration comprehensively addressed new modes of warfare in order to enhance protections of civilians. As legal scholars have recently argued, the inclusion of peacetime protection of civilians prefigured the postwar concept of "human rights."[122] The first advance was the obligation of signatory nations to protect non-combatants from chemical gas, poison, and bacteriological weapons, both in wartime and peacetime,[123] and noted that while thirty-eight states including Japan had originally signed the 1925 Geneva Protocol prohibiting the use of chemical and bacteriological weapons, few had followed through with ratification.[124] The second area where the Tokyo Declaration broke new legal ground was in extending protection to all presumed categories of civilians, not just enemy civilians but all detainees, to include stateless individuals and denationalized persons. As the declaration noted, aerial bombing and internment could impact any group of civilians.[125] The third issue was protection of enemy civilians wherever they happened to be residing when war broke out, including those caught in newly occupied war zones.[126] The fourth was protections of POWs and enemy civilians in undeclared wars.[127] The great advancement of the Tokyo Declaration was to make enemy civilians beneficiaries of humanitarian international law in wartime.

As history would tragically show, all four issues anticipated critical humanitarian crises during World War II. In the European Holocaust, Germany exterminated millions of Jews and other "undesirables" such as Roma, Slavs, LGBTQ, and leftists, in gas chambers and forced labor camps. Both the Axis and Allied Powers indiscriminately bombed civilians. Allied firebombing assaults on Germany, whose victims included refugees from the eastern front, and Japan resulted in unprecedented civilian deaths. The Hiroshima and Nagasaki nuclear bombings not only immediately killed several hundred thousand civilians, the bombs unleashed radiation poisoning that would continue to annihilate human, animal, and plant life long after, enacting another holocaust.

Although not ratified before World War II, the Tokyo Declaration laid the foundations for the Fourth Geneva Conventions of 1949. The fourth issue, that of undeclared war, was indeed prescient, for Japan did not make a declaration of war against China in 1937, which made the Second Sino-Japanese War (1937–1945) outside the jurisdiction of the Geneva Conventions and gave Japan an excuse not to adhere to them. The JRCS faced an uphill battle with respect to aiding Chinese POWs during the Second Sino-Japanese War.[128] Moreover, undeclared war did not provide time for the evacuation of citizens of the belligerents. In fact, in World War II, many civilians found themselves stranded behind enemy lines and subjected to detainment. Although not ratified, the war-related resolutions of the Tokyo Declaration of 1934 constitute a historic landmark in international discourse on civilian human rights in wartime.

Article thirty-three of resolution thirty-nine[129] declared, "The present Convention, which bears the date of this day, is open for signature until _____, in the name of all the countries represented at the Conference." Resolution article twenty-seven urged, "The present Convention shall be ratified as soon as possible."[130] The draft was submitted to the Political Department of the Federal Council of Switzerland on August 21, 1935. The Swiss Political Department convened to circulate the proposal to France, Germany, Great Britain, and Italy. The reception was lukewarm or negative; for example, the United Kingdom representative objected the drafts were "insufficient," while the French government responded with "a firm and definite refusal."[131] As a result, on February 19, 1937, the Swiss Political Department informed the ICRC that "the auguries were insufficiently favourable."[132]

Even before the Tokyo Conference convened, the major European powers signaled their rejection of the substance of resolution thirty-nine. In fact, the draft declaration approved at the Tokyo Conference had been amended two months previously by the ICRC at a meeting in Monaco where the phrase "recognizes the great interest attaching to" was substituted for "approve the draft convention."[133] This was the first time since its founding that the international Red Cross and Red Crescent movement had been thwarted by opposition from the world powers. As a result, the convention on the protections of enemy civilians in wartime was not added to the Geneva Conventions before the outbreak of World War II.

The Fifteenth International Conference in Tokyo illustrated the challenges facing the JRCS. At a time of growing international tensions, the JRCS performed its role with skill and tact. It made a serious effort to address the RCSC's allegations of Japanese violations of the rules of war and closely cooperated with the ARC—perhaps to the displeasure of Japan's MOFA and the Imperial Japanese Army and Navy. Its commitment to furthering international humanitarianism persisted even as world tensions mounted.

In later years, Max Huber, the president of the ICRC, lauded the proceedings of the Tokyo conference as "outstandingly successful," even though he did not attend the meeting.[134] An ICRC memorandum predicted that the Tokyo conference "would expand by every means possible efforts to prevent war and encourage better understanding among nations."[135] Iesato later said to the JRCS officials, "Externally, we were facing unprecedented global crises; internally, we did not have any parallel experiences to resolve our critical situation regarding Japan. As host of the international conference, our strenuous efforts were not feeble at all. . . . We should be proud of ourselves."[136] In later years, Iesato's daughter Hoshina Yukiko recalled her father's "especially passionate" commitment to the Red Cross's mission.[137] Despite the sudden illness and the death of Iesato's only grandson, Iehide, in 1936,[138] his dedication to the JRCS and the international Red Cross and Red Crescent movement continued unabated. Iesato passed away as the age of seventy-six in 1940, before the attack on Pearl Harbor, a death likely precipitated by overwork and stress. In recognition of his exceptional contributions to humanitarian causes at home and abroad, Iesato was awarded the Grand Cordon of the Supreme Order of the Chrysanthemum shortly after his death.[139]

3

TRANSNATIONAL HUMANITARIAN MOVEMENT

The Japanese Red Cross Society and Overseas Empire

Beginning in the 1890s and continuing into World War II, the JRCS expanded overseas operations in tandem with Japanese imperialism and the worldwide Japanese diaspora. This chapter examines the JRCS chapters established in Korea and Manchuria, while chapter 4 focuses on those in Hawai'i and Brazil. Together, the four case studies evince both similarities and differences in the society's humanitarian missions, institutional goals, relations with host communities and governments, and services provided to Japanese immigrant communities. Fundraising was the paramount driver of the JRCS's overseas expansion, but the case studies show greater divergence than similarity with respect to core activities. In Korea and Manchuria, the JRCS played a vital role, through the development of local medical facilities and public health programs, in advancing colonial modernity, much as the American Red Cross (ARC) did in the U.S. empire in the same period.[1] The JRCS's role in Hawai'i and Brazil was quite different, however. In Hawai'i, a U.S. possession, the JRCS served as a networking hub for the Japanese business elite and worked to further Japan–U.S. diplomatic relations before and after strains in relations developed in the 1930s. In Brazil, however, the JRCS's primary activity was the provisioning of medical services to the Japanese immigrant community segregated from the native population and besieged by the coercive assimilation policies of the Vargas government.[2]

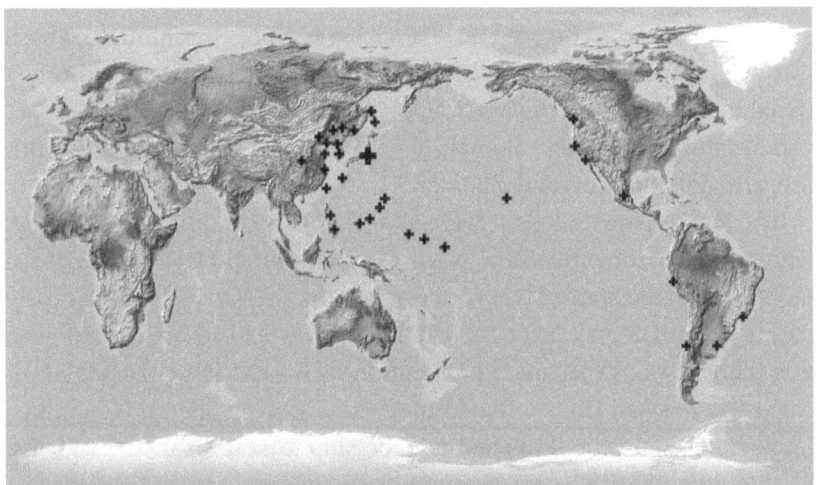

FIGURE 3.1 Overseas locations of major JRCS departments and chapters before World War II.

Author's map.

With the expansion of Japan's overseas empire, the JRCS opened chapters and branches in the new imperial territories: Pusan (1894), Taipei (1896), Liaodong (1905), the Kwantung Leased Territory (1906), Manchuria (1908), Karafuto (Sakhalin) (1909), and the South Seas Mandate (Nan'yō) (1930).[3] In addition, the JRCS established chapters and major committee departments in Vladivostok[4] and Alexandrovsk-Sakhalinsky in conjunction with the Allied Powers' 1918–1922 Siberian Intervention;[5] in the China treaty ports of Shanghai, Hankou, Tianjin, and Qingdao; in the Philippines, a U.S. possession; and in metropolitan cities in North and South America that were home to large concentrations of Japanese nationals.[6] (See figure 3.1.)

ORIGINS OF JRCS KOREA

The scale of operations, ethnic diversity, and large membership lent particular significance to JRCS activities on the Korean Peninsula. As was the case in the establishment of JRCS offices in China and Hawai'i a decade later, the opening of overseas JRCS branches in Korea was motivated both by the financial incentive to expand overseas fundraising and the institutional mission to serve the medical needs of the sizable Japanese resident community and Koraen colonial subjects through modern public health progams and hospitals and clinics.

The JRCS opened its first overseas office in Pusan in November 1894 with support from the JRCS Nagasaki Committee Department, three months after the start of the First Sino-Japanese War. Even at this early date, a total of 26,987 Japanese had already moved to Korea, and Pusan was the gateway to Japanese penetration of Korea.[7] Four years later, in August 1898 when JRCS founded the second Korean Special Committee Department in Seoul, it opened membership to non-Japanese residents. At this time, the JRCS was the only Red Cross presence in Korea. The charters of the JRCS branch offices in Korea closely paralleled those of local chapters in Japan, and their organizational structures were also similar. A total of ten branch offices were opened between 1898 and January 1905, when the JRCS established the Korean Committee Department Head Office in Seoul.[8] After the signing of the Treaty of Portsmouth on September 5, 1905, in which Russia recognized Japan's "paramount political, military, and economic interests" in Korea, the JRCS moved quickly to solidify its position. In October 1906, the JRCS convened a general assembly in Pyongyang attended by JRCS Vice-President Ozawa Takeo (1844–1926) and more than 700 members.[9] By this time, the JRCS had enrolled 7,129 dues-paying members, including 400 Korean nationals and seventy-eight Europeans and Americans.[10] The *Tokyo Asahi Shimbun* reported the general assembly to be a "thriving and great success."[11] In one of several speeches he gave before attending the meeting in Pyongyang, Ozawa noted with undisguised pride, "Our Red Cross Society is not a transplant from the West; rather, it is the product of Asian civilization."[12]

Under siege from foreign powers, the Korean government responded to the expansion of JRCS operations by founding its own Red Cross society. The Korean Kingdom ratified the Geneva Convention in January 1903, which was a precondition for joining the international Red Cross and Red Crescent movement. In October 1905, a month after the signing of the Treaty of Portsmouth but prior to formal loss of diplomatic autonomy, Emperor Gojong (1852–1919) promulgated by imperial edict the charter of the Great Korean Red Cross Society (GKRCS).[13] The GKRCS's officers were hired from the ranks of palace officials and were sent to the JRCS headquarters in Tokyo to study the administration of the Red Cross in Japan.[14] There was a lot to learn. When the GKRCS sought to educate the Korean public on the history and mission of the international Red Cross movement in an article published in the *Hwangseong Sinmun*, it mistakenly identified Florence Nightingale as the founder, not Henry Dunant, and Nightingale as being of Swiss, not British, nationality.[15] The hurried launch of the GKRCS by the Korean monarchy, it appears, was a desperate attempt to buttress its claim to sovereignty through the "soft" diplomacy of the international Red Cross and Red Crescent movement.

The Great Korean Red Cross Society (GKRCS) was short-lived. Following the conclusion of the Japan–Korea Treaty of 1905 in November of that year, Korea formally became a protectorate under the Japanese Empire, which meant losing its international status within the framework of the Geneva Convention. The monarchy, having lost what was left of its political independence, presumably on orders of the Japanese Resident General, issued Imperial Edict No. 54, dissolving the GKRCS. Furthermore, in 1908 the Japanese and Swiss governments reached an agreement that henceforth, Japan would represent Korea within the international Red Cross and Red Crescent movement. Thus, the native Korean Red Cross movement fell under the administration of the JRCS and the GKRCS was formally absorbed into the JRCS in July 1909.[16] In February of that year, Emperor Gojong symbolically sanctioned the merger by donating 200 yen to JRCS chapters in Busan, Masan, Daegu, Pyongyang, Ŭiju, and Sinŭiju; in June, Imperial Noble Consort Sunheon donated 50 yen to the JRCS Suwon Committee Department.[17]

Following the formal annexation of Korea in August 1910, the JRCS accelerated both its managerial and operational activities. By this time, more than 170,000 Japanese had settled in Korea, forming the largest concentration of overseas Japanese nationals.[18] By the end of 1910, the JRCS had enrolled 12,683 dues-paying members, including 2,072 Korean nationals and 107 foreigners, and the JRCS Korean Headquarters in Seoul organized nine provincial committee departments.[19] Now the sole Red Cross organization on the Korean Peninsula, the JRCS upgraded the status of the Korean Committee Department Head Office—renamed the JRCS Korean Headquarters in December 1910—and set up chapters and committee departments throughout the peninsula.[20] In 1915, the total number of chapters and branches in Korea reached 119,[21] and the majority of Red Cross officials and employees were colonial subjects.[22] A number of Koreans were appointed to important positions, including several heads of chapters and clinics. Koreans joined in ever-larger numbers, and by the early 1930s they comprised the majority of the membership of the JRCS Pyongyang Committee Department.[23]

RESPONDING TO THE GREAT KANTŌ EARTHQUAKE

A notable initiative of the JRCS Korean Headquarters was the provision of emergency medical treatment and material aid to resident Koreans in the greater Tokyo area injured or left destitute by the 1923 Great Kantō earthquake[24] and the ensuing massacre of Koreans. As described in chapter 1, on September 1, 1923, a magnitude 7.9 earthquake hit the Tokyo and Yokohama regions, followed by devasting firestorms and a twelve-meter tsunami that destroyed 65 percent of the housing in Tokyo and up to 90 percent in Yokohama.[25] Compounding the destruction, the earthquake unleashed a twelve-meter (thirty-nine-foot) tsunami that devastated Atami, Ōshima Island, and the Izu Peninsula south of Tokyo, triggered massive landslides, and saturated the ground soil throughout the Kantō region as far north as Ibaragi.[26] At the time, it was the largest earthquake registered in Japan in the modern era, and the death toll of 105,385 made it among the deadliest in the world in the twentieth century.[27] In the panic that followed, fueled by rumors Koreans were setting fires and poisoning wells, vigilante mobs, who in some cases were led or egged on by policemen, murdered as many as 6,000 Koreans and hundreds of Chinese mistaken for Koreans.[28]

In the midst of this humanitarian tragedy, which required mobilization of all of the JRCS's personnel and material resources, JRCS Tokyo Headquarters requested assistance from JRCS Korean Headquarters, which responded immediately by organizing a relief mission. Headed by Dr. Shiga Kiyoshi (1871–1957),[29] the vice-president of JRCS Korean Headquarters, the relief team,[30] whose eight members including Korean doctors and nurses, left Seoul on September 4 and arrived in Tokyo at midnight four days later. The medical team started its relief operations the following day, operating out of field hospitals.[31] The JRCS Korean Headquarters' response stands in sharp contrast to that of the Tokyo metropolitan government, which was slow to respond to the needs of Koreans injured and displaced from their homes and later attempted to cover up the massacre. On September 21, the Japanese governor-general of Korea, Saitō Makoto (1858–1936),[32] proposed making Aoyama Meiji Shrine Gaien Shelter the center of relief operations for Korean survivors.[33] On October 10, the JRCS relocated the JRCS Korean Headquarters' operations to Aoyama, where they established a special medical relief section dedicated to aiding Korean victims.[34] The relief teams received support from a number of JRCS chapters, especially from the JRCS Osaka Chapter.[35] The governor of Osaka was Seki Hajime (1873–1935), and Osaka Prefecture was home to nearly 40,000 Korean residents in 1922.[36] It appears that the well-established Korean population in Osaka played an important role in networking with resident Korean communities in the Kantō region, which enabled the Osaka relief teams to effectively coordinate with the JRCS Korean Headquarters.[37]

At the Aoyama Gaien Shelter, JRCS Korean Headquarters relief party employed a total of seventeen medical workers who treated 842 cases over the next three weeks. During the operation, they set up four large tent field hospitals donated by the ARC, where victims received food and medical care. The relief party dispatched medical teams that treated over 1,000 injured Koreans lodged in temporary shelters located in the greater Tokyo area. It also arranged the repatriation of resident Koreans who wished to go back to their homes in Korea and helped those who chose to stay in Japan find employment.[38] When the JRCS ended operations on October 26, 1923, the twelve Koreans still recuperating from injuries were transferred to the Manchurian Railway Temporary Hospital. Dr. Shiga and the JRCS Korean Headquarters medical relief party left Japan on November 3.[39]

Dr. Shiga received the Order of Culture in 1944 and was also awarded the Order of the Sacred Treasure, first class, on his death in 1957. However, during the Great Firebombing of Tokyo in 1945, he lost his home and most of his belongings and died impoverished, surviving on only a small pension. Dr. Shiga exemplified the spirit of universal humanitarianism that for many would entail great personal sacrifice during World War II. In an essay titled, "My Belief," published near the end of his life, he wrote, "My wish is to contribute to the welfare of humanity through

FIGURE 3.2 Dr. Shiga Kiyoshi (1871–1957). The photograph by Ken Domon (1909–1990) shows Dr. Shiga, who ended his life in great poverty, wearing eyeglasses whose frame he had taped together (Ken Domon, 1949).

Ken Domon Museum of Photography. Ken Domon, *Fūbō* (Tokyo: ARS, 1953), 18–9.

my learning. This is my only wish. Even though fifty years of my career did not amount to much, I believe that at least I could make a sacrifice of myself for humanity. This is my great consolation."[40] (See figure 3.2.)

THE JRCS AND MODERN MEDICAL PRACTICE IN KOREA

American and Canadian Korean medical missions established the first modern hospitals in Korea and introduced the first Western public health programs. As early as 1895, in response to a cholera outbreak, the Korean monarchy, with the support of Christian medical missions, established

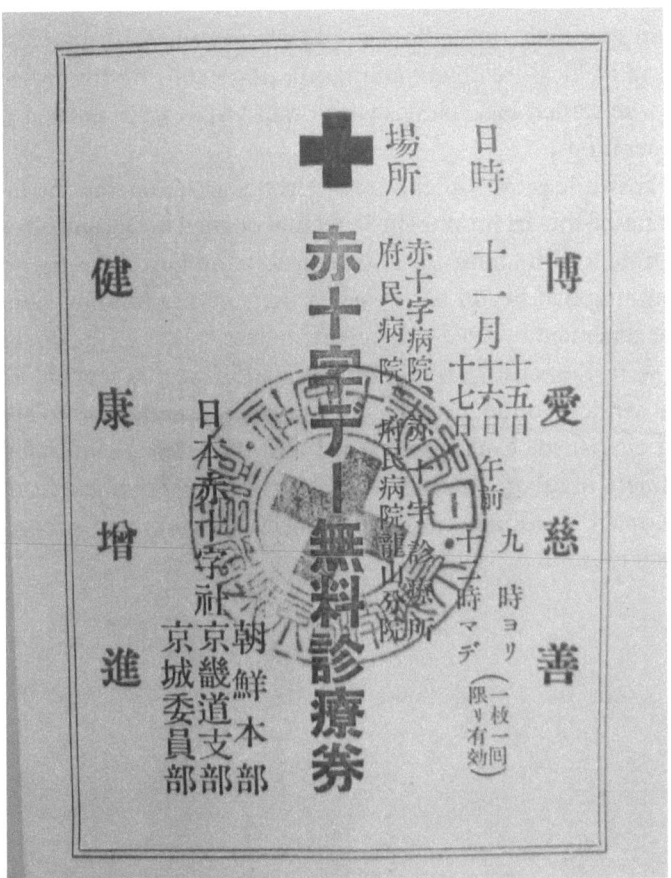

FIGURE 3.3 Voucher for free medical treatment at JRCS Korean Clinics and Hospitals (1934).

Archival collection of the Museum Meiji-mura held by the Japanese Red Cross Toyota College of Nursing, *Sekijūji Dē Ikken, Shōwa Jūni nen*, ID: B1069-4327.

the first isolation wards to combat the epidemic.[41] After Japan's annexation of the Korean Kingdom in 1910, the governor-general of Korea (GGK), the colonial governing authority, established and managed the GGK Hospital in Seoul, the Daegu Jikei Hospital, and the Pyongyang Jikei Hospital.[42] These designated medical institutions served as bases of operations for JRCS and International Red Cross programs, including tuberculosis eradication campaigns, nursing education, and midwife training.[43] (See figure 3.3.) The JRCS Korean Headquarters collaborated with the GGK in setting up a network of local clinics, linked to metropolitan hospitals, throughout the Korean Peninsula.[44] In addition to rendering medical treatment and promoting public health projects, the nurses who staffed local clinics were on call to assist in natural disaster relief operations.

The crown jewel of JRCS Korean Headquarters operations in Korea was a state-of-the-art hospital in Seoul that opened in December 1923 and at that time was the most up-to-date hospital in East Asia (figure 3.4).[45] The planning had begun two years earlier, and the funding came from revenue generated by JRCS's membership fees.[46] Half of the doctors and nurses were Koreans.[47] The hospital's mission was to provide low-cost medical services to the general public as well as services at no charge to the impoverished. It also sponsored and operated a clinic dedicated to treatment of tuberculosis patients.[48] The hospital changed its name to JRCS Korean Headquarters Hospital in March 1925 and subsequently underwent several expansions.[49]

FIGURE 3.4 The JRCS Korean Headquarters Hospital in Seoul exemplified the JRCS's contribution to modern medicine in colonial Korea.

Archival collection of the Museum Meiji-mura held by the Japanese Red Cross Toyota College of Nursing, *Chōsen-honbu Kan'nai I'inbu Sōkai, Shōwa Jūsan nen*, ID: B1085-4366.

A major accomplishment of the JRCS Korean Headquarters Hospital was to develop Korean professional nursing training.[50] The JRCS Korean Headquarters initiated a formal course of nursing training in April 1917 that enrolled both Japanese and Korean women and whose graduates would be employed in affiliated hospitals and clinics. In 1923, the hospital nursing training center admitted twenty-nine students who upon graduation were dispatched to Manchuria, Inner Mongolia, and Central China, as well as to communities within Korea itself.[51] When the JRCS Korean Headquarters Hospital opened in 1924, the medical staff included twelve Korean graduates of the JRCS's training courses.[52]

JRCS Korean Headquarters–trained nurses provided a wide range of social and medical services, including midwifery, public health, and child welfare. They served in schools and factories, organized mothers' clubs to teach modern parenting skills, and offered other maternity services.[53] In the area of medical services, the GGK, the JRCS Korean Headquarters, and Western Christian missions cooperated. As Hyaeweol Choi has noted, "American missionaries made concerted efforts to gain the trust of the Japanese colonial authorities in order to maintain and expand their missionary goals," and both looked down on traditional Korean medicine as backward and uncivilized.[54] The first professional nurses' association in Korea, the Nurses' Association of Korea (NAK), was established by missionary nurses at Severance Hospital in Seoul in 1923. In 1929, the NAK applied for membership in the Geneva-based International Council of Nurses (ICN) but was rejected on the grounds that "Korea was a colony of Japan and the ICN could not recognize both the Korean and Japanese branches."[55] The rejection created momentum for cooperation, facilitated by JRCS Tokyo Headquarters, between the NAK and Japan's professional nurses association, the Nurses' Association of Japan (NAJ). In 1932, Elizabeth Shepping, the NAK Chair, and NAJ Chair Hagiwara Take (1873–1936)[56] engineered the merging of the two organizations to form the Nurses' Association of Imperial Japan in 1933,[57] which was immediately granted ICN membership.[58] Following the merger, enrollment of Korean women in nursing programs increased dramatically. Missionary hospitals had restricted nurses' training programs to Christian converts, and friction over onerous working conditions, low pay, and contentious relations with supervisors caused Korean nurses to launch major strikes at mission hospitals in 1921, 1924, and 1926.[59] In the 1920s and increasingly after 1930, the missionary medical mission, which was chronically underfunded, faced diminishing funding and was forced to close numerous facilities.[60] With international recognition and secure funding from JRCS Korean Headquarters, training of Korean nurses increased more than fourfold, from 182 in 1930 to 780 in 1940. Over the same period, the ratio of Japanese to Korean nurses fell sharply, from 1:5 in 1930 to 1:1.5 in 1940.[61]

As the preceding discussion has shown, the JRCS in Korea exemplified the progressive, and at the same time patronizing, side of Japan's colonization policy of assimilation (*dōka seisaku*) whose goal was to raise "backward" Korea to equal standing with Japan through modernizing social institutions and economic development. The JRCS Korean Headquarters opened membership to Korean nationals, built hospitals and clinics, and provided extensive social services not only in the major cities but also in provincial cities and towns. The creed of the international Red Cross and Red Crescent movement, dramatically manifested in Dr. Shiga's mission to aid victims of the 1923 Great Kantō earthquake, posited the equality of nationalities and races in membership and relief missions. Here we see a major difference between the JRCS's policies and Japan's colonial assimilationist ideology premised on the presumed inferiority of colonial subjects. The fact that Korean nationals were awarded numerous special JRCS medals and other honors in recognition of their service suggests acceptance as equals. For instance, in 1933, four Korean members received the highest JRCS service medal and seventy-eight were entered on the honor role.[62]

The rapid growth in Korean membership and nurses' training programs may be evidence that Korean nationals were more likely to be accepted as equals and afforded opportunities to rise according to their ability than in the colonial administration. In addition, as nurses, medical aids, and leaders of local chapters, JRCS employment and membership afforded Korean women the opportunity to gain professional training and enter the public sphere.[63] In fact, JRCS Korean Headquarters' membership rose dramatically, from 10,587 in 1908, most of whom were Japanese imperial subjects,[64] to 133,469 in 1936, by which time Koreans comprised 66 percent of the membership and occupied positions as senior managers, medical staff, and fundraisers.[65]

In general, the period between the violent suppression of the March 1 Movement, and the Kwangtung Army's seizure of Manchuria (1931–1932) was largely a period of peace and stability in Korea and Northeast Asia.

An exception was the Allied intervention in the Russian civil war known as the Siberian Intervention (1918–1922) that followed the 1917 Bolshevik Revolution, and the ensuing flight of White (anti-Bolshevik) Russians into Manchuria and northern Korea. In response, the JRCS Korean Headquarters and the JRCS Manchurian Committee Headquarters dispatchd medical missions to Vladivostok. Following the withdrawal of Japanese armed forces from Russia's Maritime Provinces in October 1922, the JRCS Korean Headquarters aided more than 62,000 Russian refugees who had been displaced to Wonsan in a nine-month operation that lasted into 1923.[66]

THE JRCS KOREAN HEADQUARTERS AFTER THE 1931 MANCHURIAN INCIDENT

Peace in Northeast Asia came to an abrupt end on September 18, 1931, when the Japanese army launched an offensive to seize Manchuria. The JRCS Korean Headquarters deployed forty-five medical relief workers during the fighting in Manchuria and later in Shanghai, where Chinese and Japanese forces also clashed in the First Shanghai Incident from late January to early March 1932.[67] The May 1933 issue of *Dōhō*,[68] the monthly journal of the JRCS Nurses' Association, published firsthand testimonies of medical staff that recorded medical treatment administered to wounded Chinese civilians and soldiers. In fact, rendering medical treatment to Chinese civilians became a major focus of JRCS operations from this time on. Miyazaki Tsutako, one of the nurses from the JRCS Manchurian Committee Headquarters, recorded her surprise at an encounter with a patient she assumed from his appearance was a local civilian: "He knocked on the door before entering our clinic, which I found curious because it was not the habit of Manchurians to knock before entering. When I treated the infection on this patient's leg, he spoke fluent Japanese. Upon discovering he was Japanese, we both burst into laughter." The incident Miyazaki narrates shows that some Japanese civilians wounded in the fighting pretended to be Chinese in the mistaken belief the JRCS exclusively aided Chinese civilians.[69] This is not to say JRCS did not also assist the Japanese army. JRCS nurses worked cooperatively with nurses hired directly by the Imperial Japanese Army (IJA). Furthermore, as Red Cross volunteers, the JRCS Korean Sinŭiju Chapter collaborated with the Women's Patriotic Association and donated more than 6,500 comfort bags to IJA stationed in Mukden in 1933.[70]

During the Pacific War (1941–1945), Korean membership soared, comprising 82 percent of the total membership of the JRCS Korean Headquarters in 1942, which reached 4.5 million in 1945. Three thousand four hundred and twenty-one Koreans were awarded JRCS medals in recognition of exemplary service.[71] Furthermore, the income generated by the JRCS Korean Headquarters was the highest of any single chapter of the JRCS between 1936 and 1945: over 34 million yen comprising 16 percent of the JRCS income over this period.[72] As these data show, the rise in membership fees played a crucial role in sustaining JRCS's wartime humanitarian operations to the benefit of both military and civilian war victims.[73]

The JRCS in Korea mirrored the ideology of the assimilation of ethnicities and nationalities into Japanese imperial subjecthood that was the cornerstone of Japanese colonialism. Like the national Red Cross societies of Western imperial powers, the JRCS was both a humanitarian movement and an agent of colonial modernity. As the preceding discussion has shown, ordinary Koreans flocked to join the JRCS, where they received professional training and rose to positions of responsibility, and the society provided vital medical and social services to local communities. With the onset of full-scale war following the Marco Polo Bridge Incident of July 1937, the double-edged sword of the JRCS Korean Headquarters was manifest in the following pronouncement of the JRCS Pyongyang Committee Department during the 1938 general assembly: "The great ideal of the Red Cross transcends national borders and is based on the universal principles of humanity of philanthropism and benevolence" and then linked the JRCS's "great humanitarian mission" to patriotic "support of the fatherland."[74] In fact, from this time on, calls to "support the fatherland" appear frequently in JRCS publications.[75]

JRCS MANCHURIA: A MULTINATIONAL ORGANIZATION

JRCS activities in Manchuria originated with the provision of medical services to both civilian victims of the Russo-Japanese War (1904–1905) and sick and wounded Russian and Japanese combatants. Following the Japanese capture of Port Arthur and occupation of the Liaodong Peninsula in January 1905, in April the JRCS established the JRCS Liaodong Committee Headquarters and based its medical operations in Dalian until the end of the year.[76] An imperial war fought to determine which power would dominate Manchuria and Korea, the Russo-Japanese War saw the opposing forces each mobilize armies of over one million men and sustain huge numbers of casualties. During the war, military officers occupied a number of top Red Cross positions.[77] Over the course of the war, the JRCS organised 152 relief parties and deployed a total of 5,170 relief workers to the battlefields, medical ships, and military medical facilities in Japan.[78] Throughout the war, JRCS doctors and nurses treated wounded and sick Russian soldiers and Chinese civilians, in addition to Japanese soldiers.[79]

The activities of the JRCS in Manchuria expanded considerably after the signing of the Treaty of Portsmouth in September 1905, by which Russia ceded to Japan the Kwantung Leased Territory and railway rights in south Manchuria. The JRCS established chapters and opened hospitals and clinics within the South Manchuria Railway zone. Soon the JRCS upgraded its organization structure, founding the Kwantung Leased Territory Committee Department in December 1905, whose jurisdiction extended to Japanese concessions throughout Manchuria.[80]

In September 1906, the society convened meetings to recruit members in major cities including Dalian, Yingkou, Liaoyang, and Tieling. The JRCS Kwantung Leased Territory Committee Department had already obtained 8,147 members at that time.[81] Major initiatives included renovating and refurbishing the Russian Red Cross hospital in Lüshun and opening a new hospital in Mukden in December 1906.[82]

In March 1908, the JRCS Tokyo office made the JRCS Manchurian General Committee Department organizationally independent from the Kwantung Leased Territory Committee Department. Twelve municipal committee departments were formed,[83] and by 1909, JRCS membership totaled 22,236, nearly evenly divided between Japanese who had settled in Manchuria and native residents.[84]

Almost immediately, the JRCS Manchurian General Committee Department confronted a major public crisis with the outbreak of the bubonic plague. The pandemic started in south Manchuria in October

1910 and gradually spread to the north. The Manchurian General Committee responded by mounting intensive pandemic relief operations that extended into northern Manchuria. In January 1910, the JRCS set up an office in Dalian and later that month moved operations to Mukden, which became the operational headquarters of the epidemic prevention campaign. Ōshima Yoshimasa (1860–1926), superintendent-general of the police agency of the governor-general of Kwantung, directed the campaign. At the height of the pandemic in February 1911, the JRCS estimated that at least 200 people died every day in Changchun alone.

Ironically, railroad development and the accompanying urbanization, hallmarks of modern economic development, contributed to the spread of the bubonic plague from its origins in rural southern Manchuria. JRCS officials observed that railroad passengers from infected Chinese villages were vectors of transmission of bubonic bacteria and enlisted the support of South Manchuria Railway management to enforce public health measures, which included denying passage to second- and third-class Chinese travelers. In Harbin, the Japanese relief operations obtained the support of local law enforcement, the Qing Police Agency, in restricting the movement of local people. Some of the public health measures involved harsh restrictions on individuals' rights. The JRCS and the governor-general of Kwantung also set up detention facilities and clinics in many localities, including Dalian, Lüshun, Mukden, and Changchun.

When fully implemented, the JRCS Special Relief Regulations for the Bubonic Plague Pandemic established protocols for the handling of plague bacilli and for inspections on trains, ships, and in ports, which could lead to quarantine. It organized the Special Relief Party No. 1 in February 1911, consisting of twenty-six doctors, nurses, and an administrator trained in infectious diseases, while additional nurses stood ready to be called into service.[85] The JRCS deployed more doctors and nurses to local clinics to treat patients and administered vaccinations, focusing on essential workers. Chinese coolies and vagrants were put in quarantine, where they received daily medical checkups.

The JRCS also mounted an eradication campaign, which promoted sanitizing protocols in restaurants and public places, disinfection of hands after touching bills and coins, and involved the temporary closing of theaters and other venues where people congregated. It also distributed

15,000 leaflets to raise public awareness. By February 1911, the JRCS had treated 1,426 infected patients in south Manchuria.[86] Flowing from the Red Cross's humanitarian mandate to save lives and aid those in need, the rapid response of the JRCS to the public health crisis was seen as politically useful by colonial authorities. As the governor-general of the Kwantung Leased Territory, Ōshima Yoshimasa, argued in a letter to the Japanese Army surgeon inspector general, Baron Ishiguro Tadanori (1845–1941),[87] "Saving people who suffer from the pandemic is the original mission of the Japanese Red Cross Society and a great opportunity for the JRCS to gain the trust of the Qing Chinese people."[88]

The vigorous response of the JRCS to the bubonic plague pandemic was the organization's most visible, but not its only, contribution to advancing public health in Manchuria. In addition to modern hospitals in the metropolitan centers, it set up clinics in rural areas to improve public health of the local population and Japanese settlers. By 1922, the JRCS had established twenty local clinics, and its public health initiatives included a tuberculosis eradication campaign. The JRCS also instituted ambulance services, home medical care, school nursing, and maternal care programs. From 1922 to 1937, a total of 8,087 nurses were dispatched to clinics and outlying villages. Among the JRCS's most ambitious programs were the opening of sanitoriums and summer camps for children suffering from common childhood diseases of tuberculosis, asthma, and anemia. JRCS records reveal that 32,263 children received medical treatment in sanatoriums in Ryujuton, Lüshun, and summer seaside resorts at Xingcheng and Shanhaiguan.[89]

As in colonial Korea, the JRCS in Manchuria expanded in tandem with Japanese immigration and settlement, economic development, and military presence. Before the 1931 Manchurian Incident, Japanese military forces stationed in Manchuria consisted of the 10,000-strong division of the Kwangtung Army, which took its name from the Kwangtung Lease Territory, and six independent military police battalions stationed within the South Manchuria Railway zone. Many of the 230,000 Japanese living in Manchuria before 1931 were either merchants and entrepreneurs or employees of the South Manchuria Railway Company, which was the engine of modern economic development and employed thousands of managers, engineers, scientists, technicians, and office workers, who with their families congregated in Manchuria's largest cities, Dalian and

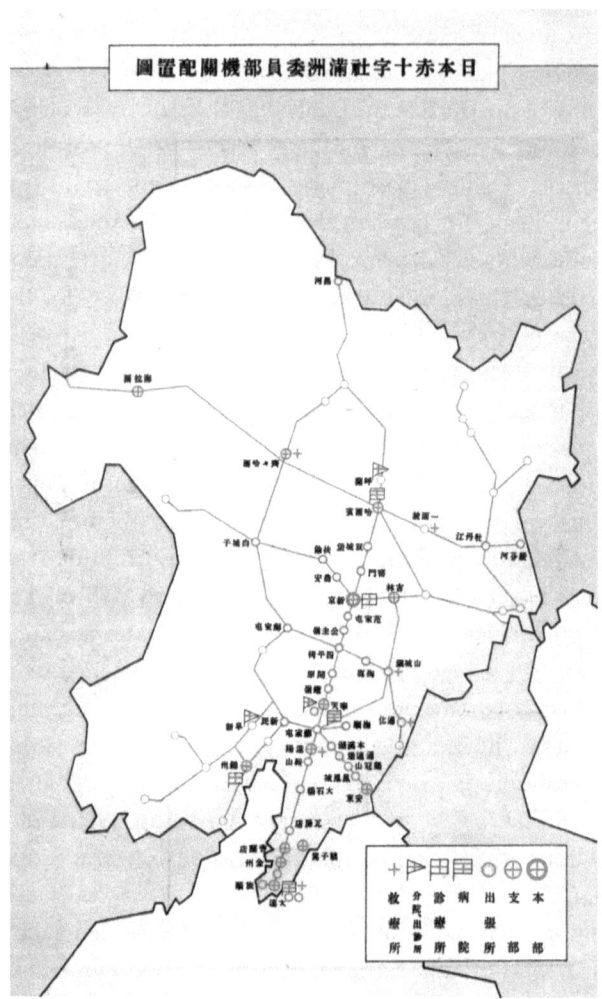

FIGURE 3.5 Location of the JRCS chapters, hospitals, clinics, and other facilities in Manchuria.

Archival collection of the Red Cross Information Plaza, the Japanese Red Cross Society, Tashiro Senzō, *Nihon Sekijūjisha Manshū Iinbu shi* (Dalian: Nihon Sekijūjisha Kantōshū Iin-honbu, 1938), 28.

Harbin. (See figure 3.5.)[90] In March 1913, in response to the growing Japanese population and to accelerate nursing education, the JRCS Manchurian Committee Department amended its charter and upgraded and renamed itself the JRCS Manchurian Committee Headquarters.[91] At that

FIGURE 3.6 JRCS emergency relief party organized at Fenghuangchen in Andong, Liaoning, Qing Dynasty (1912).

Archival collection of the Red Cross Information Plaza, the Japanese Red Cross Society, P-002937A, *Senji Kyūgo-Rinji Kyūgo: Shinkoku Hōōjō ni Rinji Kyūgosho, Senkyūhyaku-jūn nen Meiji Yonjū nen Ni gatsu.*

time, the Society had 32,474 members, of which 14,695 were natives of Manchuria and sixty-two were non-Japanese foreigners.[92] By the 1920s, the department had become a multinational organization. (See figure 3.6.) Its membership included many Westerners. The largest contingent was the 765 Russians, followed by twenty-five British subjects, fifteen Americans, and forty-five members of various European nationalities,[93] in addition to 329 Chinese and five Mongolian nationals.[94] Registered at this time were 31,021 Japanese and 28,290 identified as "Manchurian," presumably Chinese native to Manchuria regardless of whether they were of Han or Manchu ethnicity, while the category "Chinese" was reserved for recent arrivals from China proper.[95]

The Siberian Intervention opened a new chapter in JRCS operations, whose focus became aid to Russian refugees fleeing the advancing Red Army. After Bolshevik forces took control of Vladivostok in October 1922, many Russians sought refuge in Wonsan, northeast Korea; some attempted to reach Harbin. Chinese police in Mukden and Changchun, however, ordered they be detained in the Mukden Manchuria Railway West Coolie Camp and hotels in Changchun. During their internment, health conditions deteriorated, leading the JRCS Manchurian Committee Headquarters to deploy relief parties to assist the nearly 12,000 refugees between November 1922 and August 1923.[96]

In September 1931, the Kwangtung Army launched a major offensive to seize and occupy all of Manchuria.[97] On September 18, the day the Kwangtung Army began its offensive, the JRCS Mukden Hospital put out an emergency call to all medical workers and administrators to prepare stretchers and medical kits, and protected already-hospitalized patients. The timing of the JRCS response shows they were primed to launch wartime relief operations. Elsewhere, the JRCS Manchurian Committee Headquarters organised the JRCS Emergency Relief Party No. 1, consisting of twenty-four members, of whom twenty-one were female nurses, and deployed them to the Liaoyang Garrison Hospital in a mission that lasted a year.[98] Subsequently, the JRCS Manchurian Committee Headquarters dispatched relief teams to hospitals and emergency medical relief aid stations throughout Manchuria.[99] One month later, on October 15, the JRCS Tokyo Headquarters received a request from the chief of staff of the Kwantung Army to treat severely injured Chinese soldiers. In its first operation, the JRCS Mukden Hospital emergency relief party received twenty-seven soldiers. For the duration of the fighting, which lasted until mid-February 1932, JRCS treated 5,711 wounded soldiers of whom 3,649 were Chinese soldiers.[100]

Civilians were among the victims of the fighting, and the poor were treated free of charge.[101] During October 1931, the JRCS Teiling Chapter, headed by a Korean doctor, Yi Kyŏmgu, treated 1,075 refugees and sick and wounded soldiers. The JRCS Fenghuangchen Patrol Medical Relief Party in Andong[102] hired Korean medical workers headed by Yi Ch'anguk, a graduate of Chiba Medical College,[103] who administered medical care to 562 destitute Koreans. Another Korean doctor, Kwan Kakchang, treated 16,714 patients in total in Jinzhou and alongside the Anfeng Line.[104]

The JRCS Manchurian Committee Headquarters also developed peacetime relief activities. For instance, the department supported the 1923 Great Kantō earthquake relief effort, organized the JRCS Volunteer Nursing Women's Association, contributed to the development of the Junior Red Cross movement, and sponsored events such as National Red Cross Day to popularize the movement throughout Manchuria.[105] In the largest natural disaster relief operation in Manchuria, in July 1932 it responded to severe flooding known as the North Manchuria Great Flood Disaster that damaged two-thirds of housing in Harbin, a city of 350,000. In the course of this operation, several hundred thousand people were evacuated and around 30,000 were listed missing. The JRCS Manchurian Committee Headquarters treated 57,424 victims in total in an operation that lasted four months.[106]

The Kwangtung Army officially terminated military operations on February 18, 1932. One month later, the occupied territory was renamed Manchukuo and declared an independent republic, though in fact, it was a puppet state. Technically a foreign national Red Cross society, the JRCS Manchurian Committee Headquarters continued to operate as an overseas chapter of the JRCS both in the Kwantung Leased Territory and in the rest of Manchuria. In 1937, it had established chapters in all major cities;[107] twenty-seven branch societies; Red Cross hospitals in Mukden, Dalian, and Harbin; and thirteen additional clinics.[108]

As noted earlier, the JRCS Manchurian Committee Headquarters resisted pressure to dissolve after the Manchukuo government, in an effort to enhance its claim to national sovereignty, established the Manchukuo Red Cross Society (MRCS). By that time it had become truly international, with less than half of its due-paying members Japanese.[109] The largest nationality represented were the 70,474 Manchurian Chinese,[110] followed by 1,706 Russians, 114 Americans, ninety-one British, thirty-two Germans, twenty-two French, and sixteen Polish, in addition to smaller numbers of Swedes, Danes, Greeks, Norwegians, Austrians, Italians, Portuguese, Dutch, Swiss, Serbs, Czechs, Slovaks, Turks, Iranians, and Indians. Some members even hailed from the Caucasus and Baltic states such as Armenia, Estonia, Latvia, and Lithuania. Together with Chinese residents, foreigners comprised 52 percent of the membership.[111] Although records do not indicate why people joined the JRCS Manchurian Committee Headquarters, one can speculate that its formal independence from the Kwangtung Army enhanced its appeal.

A multinational organization whose institutional mission included peacetime relief activities, the JRCS Manchuria Headquarters occupied a liminal position between Japan's formal and informal empire on the Asian continent. The distinction was not always clear. In February 1933, for instance, the Harbin Association for Korean Residents appealed to JRCS Headquarters for economic assistance and public health care. In this petition, the spokesman, after diplomatically expressing gratitude for Japan's role in Manchukuo's economic development and political advancement, asked for the establishment of a Red Cross hospital to serve the large, mostly impoverished Korean immigrant community. The establishment of the hospital was necessary, he argued, because having a modern hospital was "the hallmark of civilization."[112]

Most of the JRCS's overseas branches provided medical services exclusively to Japanese imperial subjects to avoid interference with the operations of the national Red Cross society in that country. In Manchuria, however, there was no established national Red Cross movement until 1938, and JRCS Manchuria functioned as the primary health care provider for foreign nationals as well as native Chinese through its extensive network of hospitals and clinics.[113] According to the JRCS records, between 1935 and 1937 the JRCS Harbin Hospital alone treated 141,791 foreign patients in addition to 282,949 Japanese patients.[114]

The July 1937 Marco Polo Bridge Incident marked the beginning of all-out war between China and Japan, and the JRCS shifted its focus to wartime relief operations. Even after the establishment of the MRCS in 1938,[115] the JRCS Manchurian Headquarters continued to operate in Manchuria. As late as the 1939 Battles of Khalkhyn Gol (1939), JRCS Relief Party No. 179, deployed by the JRCS Manchurian Committee Headquarters,[116] treated wounded Soviet POWs at the Hailar Military Hospital in Inner Mongolia and performed a number of major surgical operations.[117] In addition, JRCS nurses treated approximately 800 wounded Japanese soldiers in North Manchuria, many of whom had sustained severe injuries.[118]

The determination of Manchukuo authorities to establish a "national" Red Cross society prompted the vice-chairperson of the JRCS Manchurian Committee Headquarters, Saitō Tateki, to appeal to the JRCS Tokyo Headquarters to support its institutional independence.[119] Subsequently, the two Red Cross organizations functioned as competing entities, and the JRCS struggled to expand its operations and to increase its membership. In 1938, the JRCS Manchurian Committee Headquarters merged with the JRCS Kwantung Leased Territory Committee Department, although it kept its head office and administration in Hsinking.[120] The MRCS also had its headquarters in Hsinking. There were now two Red Cross societies operating in Manchuria. The JRCS Manchurian Committee Headquarters continued to enlist new members, and its membership rose from 138,826 in 1937 to 216,634 in 1945. The increased revenue helped to sustain the JRCS's relief operations through the end of the Pacific War.[121]

The case studies examined here show that the JRCS's humanitarian work was integral to Japan's imperial assimilation policies in Korea and Manchuria. Japan's overseas humanitarian movement embodied in the JRCS created multiethnic and multinational organizations that mobilized the Japanese immigrant community, engaged with local governing authorities, and enlisted the native populations in both short-term crisis management and long-term development. Initially, the JRCS Korean and Manchurian Headquarters' public health and modern medical facilities principally benefited the Japanese settler population. Nevertheless, an evidence of the professional opportunities the JRCS opened to Korean colonial subjects is seen in the changing ratio of Japanese to Korean nurses. In 1910 the 220 Japanese licenced nurses vastly outnumbered the mere seventeen Koreans, but by 1940 the ranks were more equal at 1,120 to 780.[122] We should keep in mind that critical scholarship on colonial medicine has shown that the introduction of modern medicine in a colonial setting "can serve as tools of social control, as labels for deviance, and as a rationale for the legitimation of status relationships."[123] Nor is there any doubt that in general, Japan like other "colonizing powers took advantage of technological know-how to extend their geographic and political control and maximize profits through economic development. Medical services were extended first to preserve the health of the colonizers, including colonial officials, troops and developers and to limit illness among workers, included settlers."[124] Nevertheless, we should not lose sight of the fact that the introduction and institutionalization of modern public health measures and medical technology by JRCS overseas branches dramatically advanced the health and welfare of colonial subjects as is evident in the data on changes in life expectancy. Life expectancy, recognized as the single most important indicator of physical health and well-being, nearly doubled in colonial Korea, rising from 23.5 years between 1906 and 1910 to 46.64 in 1942. The infant mortality rate declined from 18.54 in 1932 to 12.08 in 1938.[125]

4

BEYOND EMPIRE

The Japanese Red Cross Society in Hawai'i and Brazil

JRCS HAWAI'I: TRANS-PACIFIC MOVEMENT

At the end of the nineteenth century, large numbers of Japanese left Japan to establish new lives in the Asia Pacific region. By 1920, over 100,000 Japanese nationals had immigrated to Hawai'i, where they made up 40 percent of the population; an equal number settled in North America, mostly on the Pacific coast; and smaller communities appeared in the cities of Western colonies throughout Southeast Asia and even as far west as British India. The JRCS followed close behind, establishing Special Committee Departments in Honolulu (1905), San Francisco (1910), and Los Angeles (1916) by World War I and later in Vancouver (1925), Manila (1925), Davao (1926), Mexico City (1936), Lima (1936), São Paulo (1936), Buenos Aires (1936), and Santiago (1936).[1]

As noted in the previous chapter, the primary driver of the JRCS's overseas expansion was fundraising. There were, however, salient differences among the JRCS's overseas branches in terms of a primary humanitarian mission, institutional goals, relations with host communities and governments, and services provided to the Japanese immigrant communities. In Korea and Manchuria, as we have seen, the JRCS focused on establishing modern hospitals, clinics, and public health initiatives in cooperation with the Japanese colonial administration. In the case of Hawai'i, however, modern medicine and public health practices preceded the arrival of the JRCS. Hawai'i had been governed by the white settler population since 1893 under the "Bayonet Constitution" and directly as a U.S. territory after annexation in 1898. While it lagged behind the continental United States, a modern medical infrastructure was in place. Geopolitically, the United States and Japan enjoyed friendly relations until Japan's seizure of Manchuria in the early 1930s; before that, their respective imperialisms in Asia, while not without tensions, were largely complementary. These factors shaped the JRCS's mission in Hawai'i, which was threefold: fundraising in support of the Japanese headquarters; networking with Japanese community leaders and the white settler population; and performing soft diplomacy to advance Japan-U.S. friendship and cooperation in the Asia Pacific region.

Large numbers of Japanese began to arrive in Hawai'i after the conclusion of the Immigration Treaty between the Japanese Empire and the Hawaiian Kingdom in 1886, which authorized sending contract immigrant laborers.[2] When the United States annexed the Hawaiian Kingdom, the Japanese population numbered 66,095 and comprised 40 percent of the entire population by the 1910s.[3] Contract laborers made up the largest class of Japanese who settled in Hawai'i before World War I, but arrivals included small businessmen, skilled workers, professionals, government officials, and managers of companies affiliated with Japan's largest industrial conglomerates. By 1941, approximately 231,200 Japanese had immigrated to Hawai'i at some point. Approximately one-third would return to Japan before World War II. As of 1940, 157,905 Japanese were settled in Hawai'i.[4]

Several characteristics of the Japanese population in Hawai'i distinguished it from the equally large immigrant Japanese communities in the continental United States and the sizable immigrant community in Brazil, which is examined later in this chapter. In Hawai'i, the Japanese were the largest ethnic group; in North and South America, they remained a small minority. Due to ease of travel between the Hawaiian islands and Japan, the majority of *Issei* or first-generation immigrants maintained close kinship, commercial, and cultural ties to Japan; saw themselves as patriotic imperial subjects; and took pride in Japan's "great power" status and expanding empire. While Japanese in Hawai'i faced discrimination from the white settler population who comprised the political, business, and cultural elite, they attended public schools and encountered fewer barriers to entry into the middle class than their counterparts in North and South America, where Japanese comprised less than 1 percent of the total population. In addition, Hawai'i's small population and geographic isolation were conducive to elite cooperation across ethnicities in the civil society sphere. These factors, it will be seen, conditioned JRCS Hawai'i's role as a transnational civil society organization.

Planning for the program of the JRCS Hawai'i Special Committee Department began in December 1906 with the goal of raising funds to support post Russo-Japanese War relief efforts. A planning document prepared by the JRCS and sent to the Trade Bureau of the Ministry of Foreign Affairs (MOFA) between late 1906 and spring of 1907 reported, "the number of Japanese emigrating to Hawai'i has been increasing year by year. . . . With the exception of Manchuria and Korea, Hawai'i has the largest JRCS membership." The authors emphasized the fundraising potential: 1,000 JRCS members, each contributing $12.50 in membership fees to the society.[5] It was an easy sell. In April 1907, the JRCS formally inaugurated the Hawai'i Special Committee Department.[6]

To galvanize support, Tokyo Headquarters asked Japan's Consulate-General of Japan in Honolulu to serve as the first JRCS commissioner in Hawai'i. Prominent members of the Japanese community rushed to join. Ishii Isakichi was representative of JRCS's Hawai'i leadership. An active member of the JRCS Hiroshima Chapter before immigrating to Hawai'i, Ishii stood at the center of Honolulu's civic and business community. He headed the local wartime relief campaign during the Russo-Japanese War;[7] operated a pharmacy and a labor brokerage firm in Honolulu; and served for a time as director of the Japanese Honolulu Chamber of Commerce.[8]

Saitō Toyoko, Director of the Honolulu Patriotic Women's Association, was among socially prominent Japanese women in Honolulu who helped to organize the local JRCS chapter.[9] During the Russo-Japanese War, Saito enlisted several American women friends who had connections to Japan as special members. Anita Newcomb McGee (1864–1940), an American Red Cross (ARC) nurse had headed a six-month medical support mission in Hiroshima in 1904,[10] and Boston-born Maggie Francis Maroney, later a Christian missionary in Hawai'i, had become friends with Ogasawara Naganari, a Japanese Navy captain, during his studies in the United States.[11] During the war, the Honolulu Japanese Patriotic Women's Association organized successful fundraising drives to support sick and wounded Japanese soldiers, to which Maroney, who became an honorary member of the JRCS in 1895, liberally contributed. When she died in 1914, the *Nippu Jiji* published a tribute to her work.[12]

The JRCS Hawaiʻi office opened two months after the conclusion of the February 1907 Gentlemen's Agreement between Japan and the United States, by which Japan agreed not to issue travel documents to common laborers seeking passage to the United States. The agreement did allow Japanese to immigrate to the United States for purposes of family unification, business, and study. For the next two decades, Japanese immigrants continued to arrive in Hawaiʻi and the Japanese population in Hawaiʻi hovered around 40 percent up to the Pacific War.[13]

The ARC did not establish a permanent chapter in Hawaiʻi until 1917, ten years after the opening of the JRCS Hawaiʻi Department. Thus, during its first decade, JRCS Hawaiʻi was the sole Red Cross society on the islands and saw itself and was seen by the general population as international in orientation rather than a Japanese outpost.[14] The JRCS hired both Japanese and non-Japanese nationals as staff and opened membership to Hawaiʻi residents of all nationalities. As of April 1907, the JRCS Hawaiʻi Special Committee Department had sixty-two foreign national members comprising a small but not insignificant 4 percent of the total membership.[15] Americans constituted three-quarters of the special members, followed by Chinese. Most of the Americans were employed in sugar-related industries where Japanese constituted the majority of the work force.[16]

The JRCS Hawaiʻi Special Committee Department solicited financial support from prominent members of the Japanese business community and professional classes. Mukōda Shōsuke and Yasuda Kazuyoshi, businessmen who two years earlier had founded the Sekishin-kai (Red Heart Association) to support Russo-Japanese War relief operations, headed up the membership drive.[17] Another early enlistee was Kishi Kantarō, the director of the Yokohama Specie Bank Hawaiʻi Branch Office, whose influence within the business community greatly aided fundraising.[18] Another key member was Mōri Iga, who had served as a JRCS doctor during the First Sino-Japanese War and during the Russo-Japanese War directed a successful fundraising campaign to support sick and wounded soldiers. In addition to his own substantial contribution, he secured donations from thirty-three Chinese living in Honolulu.[19] It is indicative of the cooperative, noncompetitive relationship between the JRCS and the ARC that Mōri became an active and esteemed member of the ARC Hawaiʻi

Chapter. Years later, the ARC expressed its appreciation in a letter to the JRCS Tokyo Headquarters, praising Mōri as an "honored member" and in language that today might sound condescending as a "leading representative of the Japanese race in Honolulu and active in many worthy causes. We commend him to you."[20]

The JRCS was careful to cultivate cooperative relations with the ARC. Three years after the founding of the Hawai'i Special Committee Department, JRCS headquarters amended its protocols to affirm that the purpose of the overseas branches was to increase Japanese membership, not to enlist the host country's citizens or other foreign nationals. Cooperation between the JRCS and the ARC reached new heights during World War I. Japan had declared war on Germany in August 1914 at the request of Great Britain, and the United States entered the war on the side of the Allied Powers in December 1917. The next year, JRCS headquarters reciprocated the ARC's support of its U.S. special departments by endorsing the establishment of ARC offices in Tokyo, Yokohama, Kobe, and Seoul.[21] Moroi Rokurō (1872–1910),[22] the chair of the JRCS Hawai'i and Consulate-General of Japan, concurrently served on the steering committee of the ARC Hawai'i Chapter.[23] During the war, he threw himself into both the JRCS and ARC's membership drives and fundraising campaigns. The *Honolulu Star-Bulletin* approvingly reported on Moroi's public appeal to his countrymen, in which he urged "All subjects of the Emperor of Japan residing in Hawaii" to demonstrate their "patriotic spirit" by donating to both the ARC and JRCS.[24] Not to be outdone, on May 7, 1918, the Japanese-language *Maui Shinbun* urged readers to become ARC members, reasoning, "The Red Cross transcends nationalities and races. It is a celebrated humanitarian organization, founded on an ethos of benevolence and humanitarianism." "How," the editorial asked, can "loyal Imperial Subjects in Hawaii" not support "this great movement." Collaboration between the JRCS and the ARC in Hawai'i is further illustrated by a Japanese-language appeal published by the ARC Hawai'i Chapter in the *Maui Shinbun* urging readers to "Donate to the Red Cross."[25] (See figures 4.1 and 4.2.)

Delegations traveling between Japan and North America frequently scheduled stopovers in Honolulu, which provided the opportunity for the practice of soft diplomacy in support of Japan-U.S. relations. In December 1930, JRCS leaders capitalized on the occasion of JRCS president Tokugawa Iesato's stop in Honolulu on his return from San Francisco to convene the

FIGURE 4.1 "Let's all donate." The ARC Hawai'i Chapter utilized Japanese-language appeals in local Japanese newspapers, here shown in the *Maui Shinbun*, for funds in support of its World War I relief operations.

"Shokun wa Susu'nnde Shukkin seyo." *Maui Shinbun*, May 7, 1918, 5, the Hoji Shinbun Digital Collection, Hoover Institution Library & Archives.

Fourth JRCS Hawai'i General Assembly in his presence.[26] In anticipation of his visit to Hawai'i, the *Nippu Jiji*, a Japanese-English language newspaper later known as the *Hawaii Times*, introduced Iesato as "the Last of the Shoguns" and a founder of the Pan-Pacific Association of Japan in 1920.[27]

FIGURE 4.2 Japanese women living in Hawai'i who joined the ARC as nurses and nurse aides. Their families were representative of Hawai'i's Japanese elite. The women's own names were not recorded. Their husbands were, respectively, starting from the back left, George Ikeda, 442nd Regimental Combat Team (https://442sd.org/george-ikeda/); Herbert Takaki, medical doctor (https://www.findagrave.com/memorial/121239199/herbert-suguru-takaki); Hayami Yamasaki, who was interned during World War II (https://www.ancientfaces.com/person/hayami-yamasaki-birth-1901-death-1992/90404728); Noboru Asahina; Wilfred C. Tsukiyama, an attorney, territorial senator, and chief justice of the Supreme Court of Hawai'i (https://en.wikipedia.org/wiki/Wilfred_Tsukiyama); Yasutaro Soga, an editor and publisher of the *Nippu Jiji* newspaper (https://encyclopedia.densho.org/Yasutaro_Soga/); Daizo Sumida, co-owner of Marumasa Soy Sauce, later known as Diamond Shoya, who was interned during World War II (https://en.wikipedia.org/wiki/Daizo_Sumida); Masayuki Tokioka, a Japanese businessman and philanthropist in Hawai'i (https://en.wikipedia.org/wiki/Masayuki_Tokioka); Edward N. Yamasaki, a veteran of the 442nd Regimental Combat Team (https://www.staradvertiser.com/2017/05/05/hawaii-news/wwii-veteran-of-the-444nd-wrote-battle-memoir/); Shujiro Takakuwa, a member of the Japanese Cultural Center of Hawai'i, who later became an internee (https://interneedirectory.jcch.com/jp/internee/furuya-kumaji-suikei); and Chiyo Iida, co-owner of S. M. Iida Ltd. (https://obits.staradvertiser.com/2013/12/14/chiyo-iida/).

"Scenery-Hawaii: Japanese Women Aid Red Cross," Dennis M. Ogawa Nippu Jiji Photograph Collection, the Hawaii Times Photo Archives Foundation.

On the day of his visit, the *Nippu Jiji* headline read, "Prince Lauds P-P Movement: Tokugawa Expresses Hope That Peace Will Be Furthered." During the reception, Iesato was quoted as saying, "It is most fitting that Honolulu is the center of the Pan-Pacific movement, for this city constitutes the crossroads of the Pacific."[28] At this time, JRCS's Hawai'i membership numbered 15,805, making it one of its largest foreign departments[29] and equal in size to the ARC Hawai'i Chapter.[30] When Iesato died in 1940, the Hawai'i Japanese-language press published special tributes extolling his efforts to promote peace between Japan and the United States.[31] Iesato was an icon for Japanese immigrants in Hawai'i, symbolizing both their Japanese roots and Japanese-American friendship. Indeed, English-language editions of Japanese newspapers in the United States referred to the JRCS as the "Imperial Japanese Red Cross Society," a term not commonly used at this time in Japan itself, and an indicator of overseas Japanese pride in the JRCS's international humanitarian presence.[32]

The centerpiece of the JRCS Hawai'i Special Committee Department's community activism was the founding in 1932 of the Honolulu Japanese Nursing Home for the Elderly at a cost of more than 62,000 yen. (See figure 4.3.) Funding came from both Hawai'i and Japan, where Prince Takamatsu was a major benefactor. The nursing home's primary purpose was to provide end-of-life care; as of December 1935, there were fifty-two Japanese residents in hospice care.[33] It also functioned as a community center for Japanese seniors in Honolulu; among other activities were heritage excursions.[34] On one such event, nursing home residents, accompanied by two JRCS nurses, visited the Honolulu Izumo Shrine, where they prayed for good health and world peace, enjoyed a lavish banquet hosted by the local Izumo Shrine Women's Association, and viewed patriotic Japanese films.[35] More ambitious community service projects of the Honolulu Special Department included tours to Japan that strengthened ties with JRCS headquarters. The 1928 tour, for example, included a visit to the JRCS General Assembly in Tokyo in May, which was attended by the Empress Nagako (Kōjun).[36]

Following the attack on Pearl Harbor, JRCS offices in Hawai'i and North America were closed early in 1942, whereupon the majority of former JRCS members threw their support to the ARC for the duration of the Pacific War (1941–1945).[37] For these Japanese Americans, the national affiliation of Red Cross chapters was not as important as its ethos of international humanitarianism that transcended wartime nationalism.

FIGURE 4.3 Japanese nursing home in Hawai'i (1930–1941).

"Scenery-Hawaii: Japanese Nursing Home," Dennis M. Ogawa Nippu Jiji Photograph Collection, the Hawaii Times Photo Archives Foundation. Hoji Shinbun Digital Collection, *Scenery-Hawaii: Japanese Nursing Home*, ID: SH1307.011. Hoover Institution Library & Archives, Stanford University, 1930–1941.

JRCS BRAZIL: BASTION OF JAPANESE IDENTITY

The first Japanese immigrants to Brazil arrived at the end of the nineteenth century, but it was after World War I that Latin America, and Brazil in particular, became the primary destination of Japanese immigration to the Western Hemisphere. The U.S. 1924 Immigration Act barred further Japanese immigration to U.S. territory, and Canada did likewise in 1928. Australia and New Zealand had closed their doors to Japanese and other Asian immigrants before World War I, which left Latin America the only continental destination point for Japanese emigration outside Japan's own empire. Nearly a quarter million Japanese immigrated to Central and South America before World War II, of whom two-thirds settled in Brazil before 1941.[38]

Japan and Brazil established diplomatic relations in 1895 with the signing of the Treaty of Amity, Commerce, and Navigation under which the Japanese government actively managed subsequent immigration in partnership with private companies. (See figure 4.4.) In Japan, a semigovernmental corporation, the Brazilian Settlement Company, arranged transportation to Brazil and the employment of immigrants upon arrival.[39] In sharp contrast to Hawai'i, the great majority of Japanese immigrants in Brazil worked and lived in enclave communities. During the peak period of immigration following World War I, Japanese made up almost half of new immigrants to Brazil. Even so, in absolute numbers, Japanese immigrants never exceeded 0.5 percent of Brazil's population, constituting a sliver of the total population of this vast and ethnically diverse nation.[40]

The largest Japanese communities settled in the state of São Paulo. Founded in 1917 by the consolidation of four smaller companies, the Overseas Enterprise Company Limited[41] contracted with the state government of São Paulo to purchase land for settlement of enclave immigrant communities that would supply laborers to coffee plantations.[42] The company established its first colony in Iguape and steadily expanded to the western region of the state, following the railroad linking Juquiá, Paulista, Noroeste, and Sorocabana.[43] By the end of the 1920s, the Japanese coffee and cotton-producing colonies extended to Bauru, Ribeirao Preto, Santos, and Rio de Janeiro.[44]

The great majority of Japanese who settled in Brazil before World War II had been born and raised in Japan. Living in enclave communities,

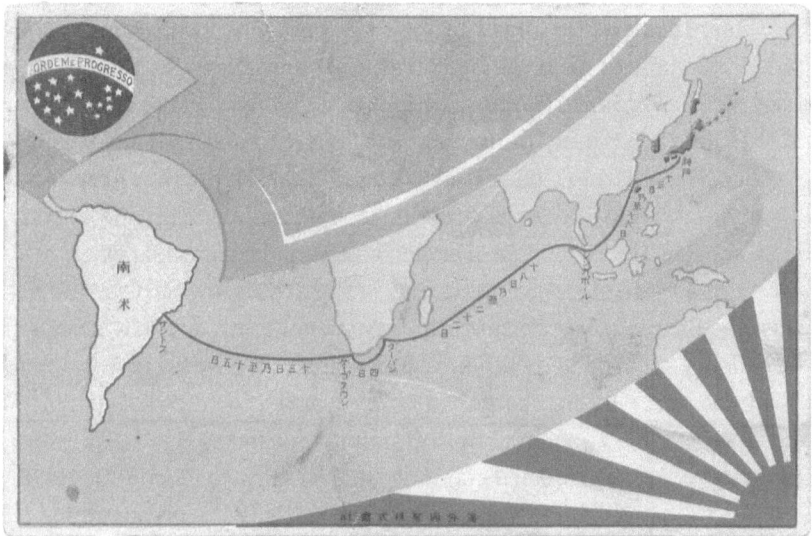

FIGURE 4.4 Postcard by the Overseas Enterprise Company Limited promoting immigration to Brazil (*Kaigai Kōgyō Kabushiki Gaisha*), (1920–1939). Founded in July 1917, the company was merged with the Brazilian Settlement Company in April 1919 and assumed management of Iguape Colony (National Diet Library of Japan, "Establishment of Emigration and Settlement Companies," accessed March 11, 2022, https://www.ndl.go.jp/brasil/e/s3/s3_3.html).
Archival collection of the Historical Museum of Japanese Immigration in Brazil.

their children attended Japanese-language schools funded by the Japanese government, which reinforced their isolation and retention of native language and cultural practices in daily life. By law and sentiment, they remained imperial subjects. Excluded from mainstream Brazilian society, they depended on the Brazil Settlement Company to provide medical care and implement public health programs.

Two decades before the JRCS established the São Paulo Special Overseas Committee Department, the Brazil Settlement Company sponsored a medical mission to Brazil headed by Dr. Kitajima Kenzō (1876–1923), a former JRCS medical doctor whose speciality was tropical diseases. Born in Fukui Prefecture and a graduate of Aichi Medical College,[45] he served as a nurse during the First Sino-Japanese War and as a doctor during the Boxer Rebellion and the Russo-Japanese War, when he received a prestigious award for distinguished service on the JRCS medical ship *Kōsai-maru*.[46] Dr. Kitajima arrived in Brazil in 1913. His selfless work in Brazil exemplified the spirit of overseas Japanese humanitarianism. Stationed in the Katsura and Registro regions of the Iguape colony,[47] where his patients included both Japanese immigrants and indigenous Brazilians, Kitajima introduced sanitation control to the local Brazilian community. After identifying hookworm as the cause of chronic malnutrition and anemia, he launched a highly successful campaign to eradicate this parasite.

Kitajima earned the gratitude and trust of those he served. Indeed, when the Brazilian Settlement Company sought to expand its holdings at the expense of the local population, it was told, "We would give our land to Dr. Kitajima without charge but never ever sell to you. Dr. Kitajima is our God!" When a malaria epidemic broke out in Juquiá in April 1923, Kitajima personally directed the campaign; tragically, he contracted the disease and his condition became incurable. His last words recorded by his son were, "Once human begins are born to this world, we all have to die. Death is inevitable. . . . As I worked as a Red Cross doctor for decades, treating wounded soldiers at the sea during the Russo-Japanese War, and working as a private doctor for ordinary people, I have witnessed a large number of deaths of humankind. . . . My thoughts about death are not that much different from those of ordinary people. . . . I want to die peacefully as my father did." Kitajima passed away in September 1923.[48] When he died, the Japanese-language newspaper *Burajiru Jihō* published a tribute to his community service that noted, among other personal details, that he loved reading Leo Tolstoy (1828–1910), the renowned Russian author who became a pacificist in his later life.[49]

In the 1920s, the official Japanese medical association in Brazil, the Dōjinkai Corporation, began planning for construction of a modern hospital in São Paulo. In 1926, land was purchased for the building site on Santa Cruz Avenue in São Paulo.[50] Local fundraising for hospital construction began in earnest in 1931 with the founding of the League for the Construction of São Paulo Japanese Hospital at the initiative of Uchiyama Iwatarō (1890–1971), the consul general of Japan's São Paulo embassy.[51] The Kwantung Army's seizure of Manchuria in 1931 and Japan's withdrwal from the League of Nations in the following year had strained relations with the United States and Great Britain, and the Foreign Ministry viewed the São Paulo Hospital as an exercise in humanitarian diplomacy.

The Japanese Brazilian community raised 100,000 yen, a substantial sum, but the hospital was a huge undertaking and the majority of the funding came from Japan. Civic organizations contributed 400,000 yen, the Japanese government contributed 250,000 yen, and the Japanese imperial family donated 50,000 yen.[52] In March 1935, the MOFA established the Association for the Patronage of the São Paulo Japanese Hospital Construction chaired by former Prime Minister Saitō Makoto (1856–1936).[53]

By the time the JRCS São Paulo Special Committee Department was established in 1936, Japanese in Brazil were well acquainted with the organization's worldwide reputation as a leader in humanitarian relief. In the 1920s and 1930s, Japanese-language newspapers in Brazil had reported extensively on the JRCS's natural-disaster relief operations, including those following the 1923 Great Kantō earthquake and natural disasters in Korea and Manchuria; the convening of the Second Oriental Red Cross Conference in Tokyo of 1926; and the opening of the state-of-the-art Red Cross Museum on Medical Science and Health in Tokyo, one of the world's largest medical museums.[54] An article on the Fifteenth International Conference of the Red Cross convened in Tokyo in 1934 pointedly reminded readers the Japanese Red Cross movement was international and global in orientation and the organizers had invited delegates from five continents.[55]

In the mid-1930s, President Vargas's government aggressively promoted assimilation laws that banned public use of immigrants' native language, dress, and cultural practices. While inclusive of all immigrants, the policy was enforced with particular rigor on the Japanese population. Eager to bolster Japan's prestige in Latin America, JRCS headquarters made the building of the Japanese Santa Cruz Hospital in São Paulo, which projected both international humanitarianism and Japan's scientific and industrial modernity, its signature project.

When the Third Pan American Red Cross Conference convened in Rio de Janeiro in September 1935, the Japanese government sent Uchiyama Iwatarō, the consul general of Japan's São Paulo embassy to delivered a pledge of support from Tokugawa Iesato to the assembled delegates.[56] The previous year in its capacity as host of the Fifteenth International Conference of the Red Cross, JRCS Tokyo Headquarters had pushed through an agenda prioritizing public health and natural disaster relief. Delegates to the Rio de Janeiro Pan American Red Cross Conference endorsed the Tokyo Declaration and spoke of the JRCS in glowing terms.[57] Noting that the JRCS was the world's largest national Red Cross society after the ARC, Central and South American delegates praised the JRCS's record not only of short-term disaster relief but promotion of long-term development of public health and social service programs, specifically citing its work on behalf of tuberculosis eradication, poverty alleviation, and the Junior Red Cross."[58] Impressed with the JRCS's overseas departments' track record of developing strong grassroots support in local communities, delegates to the Rio de Janeiro conference voted to invite the JRCS to open offices in Central and South America. Uchiyama subsequently received requests for JRCS liaison offices from Red Cross societies in Mexico, Peru, Brazil, Argentine, and Chile.[59]

Japanese-language newspapers in Brazil proudly reported on these developments. For example, on June 17, 1936 the *Nippon Shimbun* ran an article under the headline "Our (Japanese) Red Cross Branches Out Abroad: Committee Departments Are Opened Everywhere in Central and Latin America."[60] According to the report, the initiative for establishing the JRCS's Latin American chapters came from the host countries that had sought "practical assistance" from the JRCS, "the world's second most powerful national Red Cross society." Eager to dispel the notion of Japanese cultural imperialism, the article reported "JRCS Headquarters authorized special committee departments only after considering the merits of each request." The opening of the JRCS São Paulo department, the article concluded, "will strengthen the International Red Cross movement through the Japanese residing in Brazil."[61] The headline of the article carried in the *Burajiru Jihō* proclaimed, "Japanese Red Cross Society Extends Philanthropic Aid" and described the outreach to Brazil as focusing on public health and social development.[62]

The JRCS Foreign Special Committee Department in São Paulo opened in June 1936, the same year that special committee departments were established in Mexico City, Lima, Buenos Aires, and Santiago.[63] JRCS president Tokugawa Iesato led the expansion of JRCS operations in Latin America, which the Japanese government supported as a soft diplomacy initiative. At the request of the host countries, the Japanese counsel, Ichige Kōzō (1894–1945), who was serving as the head of the JRCS São Paulo department and minister plenipotentiary, became the first director of the JRCS Central and Latin American departments. Commissioned by Tokugawa Iesato, Ichige took charge of rushing to complete the São Paulo Japanese

Hospital. The JRCS São Paulo Special Committee Department recruited members from the Japanese community and cooperated with the Brazilian Red Cross in what developed into a community grassroots movement.[64]

Construction of the Hospital Santa Cruz began in August 1936, and the hospital opened its doors in April 1939. The crown jewel in JRCS's Latin America soft diplomacy campaign, it was the largest and most advanced hospital in Latin America at the time. The total ground area was 14,595.800 square meters. The building had six floors, accommodating seventy-six wards and 200 beds. In addition to internal medicine, specialty departments included surgery, ophthalmology, otolaryngology, dermatology, urology, obstetrics and gynecology, pediatrics, radiology, and physiotherapy staffed by Japanese nurses and doctors who had previously obtained Brazilian medical licenses. (See figure 4.5.) Between 1939

FIGURE 4.5 The Hospital Santa Cruz, also known as the Japanese Hospital, was opened in 1939.

"100 Years of Japanese Emigration to Brazil," National Diet Library of Japan. Aoyagi, Ikutarō, *Burajiru ni Okeru Nipponjin Hatten-shi, Jō-kan: Nikkei Imin Shiryōshuū, Nambei-hen San, Dai Njūkyū-kan* (Tokyo: Burajiru ni Okeru Nipponjin Hatten-shi Kankō I'inkai, 1952).

and 1940, the hospital served 2,205 outpatients and 101 inpatients. Impoverished patients received vouchers issued by the Brazil Dōjinkai Corporation. The hospital provided free face-to-face consultations. It also issued public health advisories as a public service. Between 1939 and 1940, 136 patients were treated at no charge.[65] Brazil broke off diplomatic relations with Japan on January 28, 1942, shortly after the United States entered the war against the Axis Powers, and seized the São Paulo Santa Cruz Hospital as an enemy asset. It was finally returned to the Japanese Brazilian community in 1990.[66]

After the eruption of the Second Sino-Japanese War in 1937, Japanese-language newspapers in Brazil doubled their efforts to promote fundraising and membership recruitment in support of the wartime relief activities of the JRCS Tokyo Headquarters. An article published in the São Paulo *Seishū Shimpō* in 1939 boasted that the entire Japanese colony in Bauru had become JRCS members and praised the JRCS as a society of *chū to ai*, faith and love.[67] The Japanese community's support of JRCS was repaid during World War II. When the Allied Powers interned Japanese as enemy aliens, the JRCS donated large sums, 380,000 yen in total, in aid; 150,000 yen was earmarked for Japanese internees in Brazil[68] and elsewhere in Latin America and 230,000 yen for Japanese held in Canada, the United States, Oceania, and India.[69]

Brazil broke off diplomatic relations with Japan early in 1942.[70] As a consequence, the JRCS São Paulo Special Committee Department and offices in Central and Latin America were closed.[71] When Japan surrendered in 1945, some Japanese immigrants in Brazil refused to believe that Japan had lost the war. Cut off from Japanese-language media under the strict assimilation policy implemented by President Vargas, an ultra-nationalist faction of the Japanese community became convinced their very survival in Brazil hinged on Japan's victory. In July 1945, they formed the *Shindō Renmei*, the "League of the Way of Emperor's Subject" and summoned members to assemble in São Paulo, believing they would welcome emissaries from Japan announcing victory. Calling themselves the *kachi-gumi* or "victory faction," by late September more than 2,000 had set up camp in São Paulo. They only came to accept the reality of Japan's surrender when the official announcement of Japanese defeat was released by the MOFA of Japan through the ICRC, the Argentine Red Cross, and the Brazilian Red Cross.[72]

The case studies of Hawai'i and Brazil show how the JRCS adapted to the particular needs of the Japanese diasporic community and calibrated activities in support of diplomatic relations between Japan and the host countries. Japanese immigration to Hawai'i began in the late nineteenth century, and the Japanese were soon the largest ethnic group on the Hawaiian islands. Although they encountered discrimination at all levels of society, from plantation workers to businessmen, they were an integral part of the islands' economy and society. Fundraising was the initial impetus for JRCS's expansion to Hawai'i and until the outbreak of World War II, the JRCS and the ARC worked in concert in Hawai'i. Americans and Japanese even joined each other's organizations.

The JRCS faced very different conditions in Brazil. Large-scale Japanese immigration to Latin America only began after World War I. Brazil soon became the primary destination of Japanese immigration to the Western Hemisphere. Nearly two-thirds of the quarter million Japanese who immigrated to Central and South America before 1941 settled in Brazil.[73] However, Japanese constituted a small minority of Brazil's population and Japanese immigrants lived in enclave communities with limited social contact with other Brazilians. While the JRCS São Paulo Special Committee Department contributed generoualy to JRCS Tokyo Headquarters' general budget, the impetus behind JRCS's expansion into Latin America in the mid-1930s was diplomatic: to cultivate friendly relations with host governments at a time when relations with the United States and Great Britain had become increasingly adversarial. The signature project, the São Paulo Japanese Hospital, was designed to generate good will and enhance Japan's prestige by providing up-to-date medical services to both Japanese immigrants and native Brazilians.

5

THE JAPANESE RED CROSS SOCIETY AND WORLD WAR II

Civilian Casualties, Internees, and Prisoners of War

The massive humanitarian crises experienced by POWs and civilian internees starkly illustrate the horrendous human costs of World War II in Asia. With the exception of Sarah Kovner's recent revisionist history of Allied prisoners of war during the Pacific War, English-language scholarship principally relies on the records of the Swiss-based International Committee of the Red Cross (ICRC), memoirs of Allied POWs, and the findings of the International Military Tribunal for the Far East and the other war crimes trials conducted by the victors throughout the Pacific War theater. These accounts, and to a lesser extent Japanese-language scholarship, either omit discussion of JRCS humanitarian relief activities or represent the JRCS as complicit in the Japanese military's war crimes, including those relating to the treatment of Allied POWs.[1]

This chapter brings to light the activities of the JRCS, which, while severely restricted by the wartime state, attempted wherever possible to carry out the Red Cross mission by administering humanitarian relief to Allied POWs, civilian internees, and forced laborers, as well as to Japanese POWs and civilians interned by the Allied Powers. To this end, the JRCS seized every opportunity available to partner with the ICRC and allied national Red Cross societies. To the extent permitted by Japan's wartime authorities and to the extent resources allowed, the JRCS administered to the needs of civilians in accordance with the Tokyo Declaration of 1934, known as the Draft International Convention on the Condition and Protection of Civilians of

Enemy Nationality Who Are on Territory Belonging to or Occupied by a Belligerent.[2] In other words, this chapter argues that while subject to powerful institutional constraints imposed by the government, the JRCS did not entirely lose its autonomy. Even in the context of the ascendancy of militarism and total war, transnational networks continued to function. In some instances, we shall see that the JRCS acted on its humanitarian mandate without the knowledge of the military authorities.

The discussion that follows is divided broadly into two sections: the Second Sino-Japanese War (1937–1945) and the Pacific War fought between the Allied Powers in the Pacific and the Japanese Empire (1941–1945). A major obstacle the JRCS faced in the Second Sino-Japanese War was that the Japanese government regarded the war as a noninternational armed conflict—outside the jurisdiction of the Geneva Conventions. In fact, neither Japan nor China declared war until December 1941, which obstructed the JRCS's access to the many Chinese soldiers taken prisoner, as the Japanese government denied them POW protections accorded to belligerents under the Geneva Conventions. Nevertheless, the JRCS engaged in negotiations with the army and navy in its effort to make them respect provisions of the 1929 Geneva Convention on Prisoners of War. The JRCS Shanghai Special Expeditionary Relief Corps (SSERC) of 1937 is a case in point.

THE JRCS IN THE SECOND SINO-JAPANESE WAR: SHANGHAI AND NANJING, 1937–1938

Historians generally date the start of World War II in Asia to fighting that broke out in the vicinity of Beijing in July 1937. What began as local scrimmages between the Imperial Japanese Army (IJA) and Nationalist Chinese Army units quickly escalated when both sides declared general mobilizations. On July 11, the IJA General Staff ordered reinforcements sent from Korea and Manchuria, and the Nationalist Government responded in kind. By July 20, Japanese troop strength in and around Beijing numbered 180,000, and after overcoming determined resistance, the IJA occupied Beijing on July 29 and Tianjin by July 31.[3] At this point, the fighting had been limited to north China, and in early August Japan opened negotiations with Chiang Kai-shek's government in Nanjing with the goal of reaching a ceasefire. However, on August 9, the Kwantung Army launched a new offensive in Chahar Province, Inner Mongolia, and established the Mongol United Autonomous Government on October 27.[4]

Simultaneously in South China, on August 9, 1937, a Japanese naval officer was shot in Shanghai, initiating the Battle of Shanghai, which was waged between August and November of 1937. Characterized by fierce fighting that mobilized multi-division armies on both sides, the Battle of Shanghai inaugurated Japan's full-scale invasion of China. The JRCS mobilized on an unprecedented scale in response to the size and intensity of military operations. In July and August of 1937, the Medical Relief Department of the JRCS, which provided medical aid in support of the IJA, dispatched a total of 149 relief parties to China, of which fifty parties were assigned to medical ships. In total, 3,573 Red Cross relief workers were deployed in 1937. The medical relief teams were organized by JRCS chapters and special departments, including the JRCS Korean Headquarters, the Taiwan Chapter, the Kwantung Leased Territory Committee Department, and the Manchurian Committee Department.[5] Because neither country declared war, the IJA did not authorize the JRCS teams to administer medical aid to Chinese soldiers, though, as we shall see in Shanghai, the JRCS tested these limits.

INVESTIGATING WAR CRIMES: THE JRCS SPECIAL EXPEDITIONARY RELIEF CORPS IN SHANGHAI, SEPTEMBER 1937 TO MARCH 1938

Planning for the SSERC to be attached to the Imperial Japanese Navy Shanghai Special Military Corps, which began sometime before August 28, 1937, accelerated after August 29, when the Red Cross Society of China (RCSC) sent an urgent telegram to the ICRC Geneva Headquarters requesting an official inquiry into reports of Japanese violations of international law. The telegram was forwarded to JRCS headquarters the following day and on August 30, the JRCS Tokyo Headquarters shared this information with the vice-minister of the Foreign Ministry of Japan, Horiuchi Kensuke (1886–1979), the vice-minister of the IJA, Umezu Yoshijirō (1882–1949), and the vice-minister of the Imperial Japanese Navy (IJN), Yamamoto Isoroku (1884–1943).[6]

Responsibility for organizing medical teams attached to military units fell to the JRCS Headquarters Medical Relief Department. Under the circumstances of alleged war crimes, however, the Investigations Department took charge. Fully staffed, the SSERC consisted of thirty-two members with deep international experience. The director was Dr. Kageyama Sadaka, at the time head of the Surgical Department of the JRCS Tokyo Hospital. A career JRCS physician, Kageyama graduated from the Medical College of the University of Tokyo in 1913 and joined the JRCS in 1914. During World War I, he was deployed for a year to the United States, Great Britain, France, Italy, and Russia. After the war, he attended the 1924 International Conference of the Red Cross in Paris.[7] Chief Nurse Makita Kise (1890–1971) had studied in the United States for eighteen years, and all members of the corps could speak at least one foreign language, most commonly English but also German, French, Cantonese, and Mandarin, making them well-equipped to communicate with all parties once on the ground in Shanghai.[8] As later noted by Kageyama, the SSERC had two major missions: "One was to uphold Red Cross humanitarianism by providing impartial medical care to refugees and civilian war victims without discrimination as to races and nationalities." The second was to mediate between ICRC representative Colonel Charles de Watteville in talks with Japanese diplomatic and military authorities in Shanghai.[9] As seen below, however, the appointment of Okamoto Suemasa, Japan's Shanghai Counsel-General, as Chairman of the SSERC, meant that decision-making authority was now vested in officials of the wartime state.

The ICRC Geneva Headquarters responded to the RCSC telegram by dispatching de Watteville to Shanghai.[10] Upon arrival in Shanghai on September 22, de Watteville immediately met with representatives of the RCSC.[11] Two days later, he held his first meeting with the Japanese side. In preparation for the meeting with de Watteville, the SSERC officers convened the first of several meetings on September 19 with representatives of Japan's Ministry of Foreign Affairs (MOFA), the IJA, and the IJN to draft a joint report that included alleged Chinese violations of the Geneva Conventions, the situation of Chinese POWs in Japanese hands, protections afforded to Red Cross medical workers, and missing persons.[12]

De Watteville held his first official meeting with Japanese military authorities in Shanghai on September 24. Kageyama Sadaka, Seki Masayuki, a pharmacist, and Atsumi Tetsuzō,[13] the SSERC interpreter, acted as mediators in the talks, which included Shanghai Consul-General Okamoto Suemasa and Consul Wajima Eiji representing MOFA; IJA officer Kimura Matsujirō, Lieutenant Colonel Infantry; IJA Lieutenant Colonel Surgeon Hirose; IJN Surgeon Colonel Surgeon Yasuyama Kōdō;[14] and IJA Lieutenant Colonel Matsubara Akio. Okamoto opened the meeting by citing Chinese violations: use of unconventional weapons, indiscriminate firing, and attacks on JRCS medical corps and field hospitals.[15] After noting Consul Okamoto's report, de Watteville broached a plan, reached in behind-the-scenes meetings with Kageyama, to mount a joint RCSC–JRCS medical operation: a field hospital to be attached to the Zhongshan Medical College Hospital in Shanghai's Nanshi District.[16] In responding to the proposal, Okamoto expressed reservations and commented that "the fierce street fighting in and around the Nanshi District would discourage Japanese civilians from seeking medical care in Nanshi; the proposed field hospital would serve only Chinese civilians, which is not fair."[17] Talks were adjourned at that point.

On September 25, Okamoto visited de Watteville at the Park Hotel Shanghai for a follow-up discussion of his proposal for the joint operation. De Watteville apparently believed it was still possible to reach an agreement and had invited a team of RCSC officials to accompany him to the hotel and wait in an adjacent meeting room. However, the negotiations did not go well as the IJA raised further objections. Okamoto pointed out that the Nanshi District was a strategic point for Japanese military operations, which, he argued, made it unsafe for international aid workers.[18] Many Chinese civilians who had sought refuge in the International Sector were suffering from infectious diseases, including cholera, and the army feared for the health of their own troops in the event of an epidemic outbreak.[19] The army's major objection, however, may have been that guerrillas would be among the Chinese civilians seeking treatment for war wounds. Japan's undeclared war and brutal prosecution of the war in China incited deep hatred among Chinese civilians who formed guerrilla bands. The IJA struggled to distinguish between Nationalist Chinese soldiers and civilian irregulars whose guerrilla operations caused numerous Japanese casualties and created a vicious circle in which civilians became targets of the Japanese forces. (See figure 5.1.) Provision of medical aid to Chinese guerrillas, IJA reasoned, would only feed the insurgency and provide an advantage to Chinese military

FIGURE 5.1 Photo taken by the JRCS Relief Party stationed on the JRCS medical ship *Taisan-maru* during the Battle of Shanghai depicting Chinese anti-Japanese slogans, "Swear to Resist Japan to the Death" and "Resolutely Boycott Japanese Products."

Archival collection of the Red Cross Information Plaza, the Japanese Red Cross Society, *Shina Jihen Jūgun Kinen Dai Ku Byōin-sen Taisan-maru Aburaya Butai, Shōwa Jūsan-nen Ni-gatsu Nijūshichi-nichi, Daijōchin Fukin*. ID: PA-000003-017A.

operations. The IJA further protested that in supporting the plan, the JRCS was taking the side of de Watteville and the Chinese, which they pointed out contravened the Red Cross's founding principle of strict neutrality. In the end, the plan was shelved and de Watteville postponed plans to proceed to Tokyo for further discussions at JRCS headquarters in Tokyo. Instead, he left Shanghai for Nanjing, Nationalist China's capital. By the time he arrived in Tokyo in late November, the IJA was preparing to assault Nanjing, and cooperation had become a distant dream. When the plan came to nought, the JRCS was criticized on the Japanese side for supporting the Chinese at the same time that the international humanitarian community began to harbor suspicions about its independence from the Japanese military.[20]

On the ground in Shanghai, the SSERC implemented a policy of treating all hospitalized Chinese as civilians. As the Japanese government had ratified the First and Second Geneva Conventions,[21] the categorizing of the sick and wounded Chinese as civilians, whom they estimated to number around 5,000, allowed the JRCS to administer medical aid to Chinese who were unacknowledged POWs.[22] The great majority of Chinese injured in the battle would have been treated by the RCSC. Despite opposition from the IJA, SSERC officers aided de Watteville's investigations by providing escort when on September 26 he inspected the IJN medical ship *Asahi-maru* and on October 14 in visits to the IJN POW camp in Shanghai and the IJA medical ship *Harupin-maru*.[23]

In addition to classifying all wounded Chinese as civilians, the SSERC was able to administer aid to the forty-seven Chinese soldiers who were officially accorded POW status by the Japanese army.[24] There is no explanation in the JRCS archives why these forty-seven Chinese soldiers were recognized as POWs, but we can infer from this fact that the society had to accept the Japanese army's highly restrictive legal interpretation of POW status. The archive does, however, contain detailed JRCS records not only on the status of the POWs' health and medical treatment, but their daily activities recorded by the hour, including clothing, meals, recreation, and psychological state. The reports noted the occurrence of illness and injuries sustained and commented that most Chinese POWs were not from the educated classes and initially behaved aggressively—perhaps out of fear. However, once they realized that they were being treated humanely, they became calm and started to respect the rules of the camp. The report, which concluded that the Chinese were mild and obedient by nature and grateful for the kindness shown to them, was highly patronizing, even as it showed concern for the POWs' welfare.[25]

De Watteville's mission in Shanghai, which would prove to be the last of the ICRC's large-scale international humanitarian operations in the Asia Pacific theater until 1945, involved complex maneuvering among the parties to the international relief network in Shanghai.[26] Throughout the five-month deployment to Shanghai,[27] SSERC officials carried out inspections of battle sites, monitored the work of the RCSC, and dated and reported in detail on every Japanese military operation, including the number of causalities.[28] Some entries were gruesome. Kageyama wrote in his postwar memoir that "after the fierce fight on 18 October, fragments of enemy soldiers' skulls lay scattered about and we collected seven items to document the scene."[29] One photograph taken by SSERC officials shows a great cloud of smoke rising into the sky after a Japanese aerial bombing and a number of dead bodies of Chinese civilians lying on the streets. Another photograph shows the wall of a building honeycombed by large bullet holes, suggesting a fierce firefight.[30] The JRCS relief team in Shanghai attached fifty-four photos to accompany the reports on de Watteville's investigations it sent to JRCS Tokyo Headquarters.[31]

The JRCS's failed efforts to work jointly with the ICRC and the RCSC illustrate the limits of transnational efforts to render impartial relief in the context of Japan's war in China. After the Battle of Shanghai, Red Cross relief missions in the Second Sino-Japanese War came to be organized separately: the RCSC treating Chinese war victims and the JRCS assisting wounded Japanese. The JRCS faced increasing difficulty gaining access to Chinese war victims, including POWs, which, in turn, led the ICRC to question its credibility and neutrality. Shimazu Tadatsugu (1903–1990), vice-president of the JRCS and chair of the JRCS War Prisoners' Relief Committee Department (WPRCD), remembered that "the JRCS made various efforts to combat prejudice against the Japanese Red Cross movement and criticisms that the JRCS did not aid war victims during the incident in Shanghai."[32] Abe Yae, one of the chief nurses of the SSERC, remembered that Atsumi, who was responsible for corresponding with the IJA, always looked "glum, morose, and sullen."[33]

JRCS AND THE NANJING MASSACRE

In striking contrast to the Battle of Shanghai, when the JRCS quickly deployed to battle sites and immediately began administering aid to Chinese war victims, the JRCS was denied access to Nanjing until after the IJA had completed the occupation of Nanjing and carried out mass killings, rapes, and other violations. According to the official record of the RCSC Nanjing Branch, the RCSC buried the bodies of 22,371 Chinese victims in the Nanjing area from January to May 1938.[34]

The first JRCS official permitted into Nanjing was Vice-President Tokugawa Kuniyuki (1886–1969),[35] who was allowed into the city January 19–23. During his stay in Nanjing, his movements were controlled by the IJA commanders. He held meetings with Prince Yasuhiko Asaka (1887–1981), who held the rank of lieutenant general,[36] and Nakajima Kesago (1881–1945),[37] the operational commander of the IJA, and visited Japanese military field hospitals. He was always escorted by doctors attached to the IJA and the IJN. In his report to the JRCS Tokyo Headquarters, he noted that the IJN had praised the JRCS's relief operations on medical ships and made passing mention to anti-Japanese graffiti and the fury aroused by IJA military operations, which drove Chinese civilians to become guerrillas in defense of their communities. He specifically mentioned the slogan "Resist the Japanese,"[38] written in large characters on the walls of public buildings in Nanjing City.[39] Nevertheless, the fact that Tokugawa Kuniyuki's report was silent on the subject of IJA atrocities is evidence that the JRCS was not able to operate independently in Nanjing.

In July 1938, six months after Kuniyuki's visit, JRCS relief parties No. 46 and No. 48, which had been stationed on a medical ship outside Nanjing, were finally allowed to enter the city and provide medical aid to sick and wounded Japanese soldiers.[40] Thus, only after military operations had completely ceased and conditions in occupied Nanjing had stabilized was the JRCS able to resume normal medical relief operations in and around Nanjing. The situation was similar in large parts of southern and eastern China, including Guangdong Province, where relief operations that included medical for aid Chinese civilians continued until August 1945.[41]

THE PACIFIC WAR, 1941–1945

JRCS WAR PRISONERS' RELIEF COMMITTEE DEPARTMENT (WPRCD)

On December 8, the day following the attack on Pearl Harbor, the American Red Cross (ARC) made enquiries to the MOFA and the JRCS through the ICRC about wartime treatment of POWs.[42] On December 11, the ICRC also made a separate request to the MOFA and to the JRCS to apply the 1929 Geneva Conventions on Prisoners of War.[43] Furthermore, on January 9,

1942, the ICRC forwarded yet another telegram from the ARC to the JRCS, which implored the JRCS and the ICRC to "take all possible steps to secure the application of the 1929 Geneva Convention" by establishing a special system to distribute aid supplies sent by the ARC to American POWs and civilian internees. Eager to comply, the JRCS forwarded the ARC's enquiry to the Army Ministry, Navy Ministry, and MOFA in a January 13 letter. However, as historians Masui Takashi and Utsumi Aiko have shown, the military ministries and the foreign ministry rejected the JRCS's recommendation, and the government's insistence on a qualified commitment to compliance carried the day.[44] The Ministry of Foreign Affairs telegrammed the ICRC of the decision on January 29. Shortly after, on February 5, the JRCS replied to the ICRC requesting that the following message be sent to the ARC: "The JRCS Headquarters will apply the law of the 1929 Geneva Convention for POWs *mutatis mutandis*.[45] To this end, we have already established the War Prisoners' Relief Committee Department at the JRCS headquarters on behalf of the ICRC as agreed to by the Japanese Government. We are ready to facilitate ICRC operations for American POWs held captive on Japanese territory."[46]

Recent scholarship on the Japanese treatment of Allied POWs has shown that the ambiguity implicit in the qualifying phrase *mutatis mutandis* opened the door to the ill-treatment of POWs by Japanese field commanders.[47] In a postwar interview, Shimazu Tadatsugu recalled that the IJA had argued that because the Japanese military code prohibited surrender, "Japanese militarists did not see it necessary to ratify the 1929 Geneva Convention while allowing for their application as circumstances permitted to enemy POWs."[48]

In reality, the JRCS International Affairs Department acted on behalf of the MOFA on POW issues during the Pacific War, and the wartime government often overruled the MOFA on policy issues.[49] On January 14, the JRCS revised the Regulations for the War Prisoners' Relief Committee Department of the Japanese Red Cross Society[50] in accordance with the Geneva Convention on Prisoners of War, which had been adopted on July 27, 1929. Soon after, the International Affairs Department of the JRCS established the WPRCD, whose responsibility was to provide medical aid and material assistance to POWs and civilian internees within Japan's formal empire in cooperation with the Central Agency for Prisoners of War of the ICRC[51] and foreign national Red Cross societies.[52] Headed by Shimazu Tadatsugu, the WPRCD consisted of seventeen members, including senior Red Cross officials and prominent scholars of the International Law of War Inoue Enji, Atsumi Tetsuzō, Matsui Keishirō, and Matsuda Michikazu, in addition to nine secretaries, five of whom were women officers.[53] (See figure 5.2.)

Furthermore, at this time the provision of aid to civilian citizens of enemy countries was not in the official mandate of the international Red Cross and Red Crescent movement. It was added to Regulations for the War Prisoners' Relief Committee Department of the Japanese Red Cross Society at the suggestion of Inoue Enji,[54] who had played a prominent role in the 1934 Tokyo Red Cross Conference in anticipation of high numbers of civilian detainees.[55] Inoue and Shimazu were influenced in this regard

FIGURE 5.2 The JRCS War Prisoners Relief Committee Department at work, 1942.

Archival collection of the Red Cross Information Plaza, the Japanese Red Cross Society, Nihon Sekijūjisha, *Hakuai: Organ de la croix-rouge janponaise*, No. 662, Juillet 1942 (Tokyo: Nihon Sekijūjisha, 1942), introduction.

by the Tokyo Declaration of 1934 and its concern for enemy civilians residing in the territory of belligerents.

The protocols of the WPRCD addressed Allied POWs and civilians held by Japan and Japanese POWs and civilian internees held by Allied Powers differently. Because the Japanese military code prohibited surrender, the WPRCD was not permitted to send aid parcels to Japanese POWs or even to civilian internees unless specifically requested by the ICRC or a foreign national Red Cross society, while foreign Red Cross societies could initiate such shipment. In other words, the IJA did not allow the WPRCD to send aid to interned Japanese soldiers and civilians unless requested to do so by the Red Cross society of the country where they were held.[56]

The regulations under which the WPRCD operated greatly limited its jurisdiction and autonomy and rendered it dependent in practice on the Prisoner of War Information Bureau. After numerous appeals, Shimazu secured an agreement to include in its operations relief for Allied civilians held in camps within the Japanese Empire. According to Shimazu's recollections, in the matter of civilian interment, for the most part the JRCS was able to operate independently of the Army Ministry.[57] However, while the IJA and IJN allowed the ICRC to maintain offices in Yokohama and Osaka, they closely monitored and limited its activities.

During the war, the JRCS organized at the request of the ICRC twenty-six tours to POW and internment camps for the ICRC to inspect conditions and treatment in Japan.[58] The JRCS also arranged for the ICRC to visit POW camps outside of Japan proper by coordinating with a number of national Red Cross societies, such as the Philippine Red Cross (PRC)[59] and the Manchukuo Red Cross Society (MRCS).[60] Meanwhile, the JRCS visited camps both inside and outside Japan on its own initiative in the early years of the war and during the war continued to donate to the ICRC's international cooperative fund.[61] JRCS inspection tours included visits to POW camps located in Zentsūji, Osaka, Tokyo, Kawasaki, and Yokohama in November 1942.[62] Early in the war, the JRCS sent material aid that included medicine, magazines, typewriters, the *Japan Times*, Bibles, and so on.[63] Generally, until late in the war, food and medical supplies in Japan were adequate to meet the basic needs of POWs held in camps in Japan and its formal colonies.

Although the JRCS WPRCD incurred criticism for "aiding the enemy" from other JRCS agencies such as the JRCS Wartime Relief Headquarters (Medical Relief Department), which deployed medical relief parties during the war,[64] it managed to maintain its wartime operations with support from both the ICRC and Allied Red Cross societies,[65] including the ARC, the British Red Cross (BRC), the Canadian Red Cross (CRC), and the South African Red Cross (SARC).[66]

According to the official accounting of JRCS headquarters, from 1937 to 1945, the total income of the society for relief activities exceeded 53 million yen.[67] Ninety percent of expenditures funded the deployment of medical relief teams in support of the IJA and IJN, the remaining 10 percent was allocated to WPRCD activities.[68]

TREATMENT OF ALLIED POWs

According to official records of the Center for Civilian Internee Rights, Inc., the association representing surviving U.S. POWs, 33,587 U.S. soldiers became POWs under the Japanese Empire and 37.3 percent of them died.[69] To put these data in prospective, the death rate of American POWs held by the Germans was 1.1 percent, and 161,000 or 0.04 percent of the 3.6 million U.S. service men deployed in the Pacific were killed in combat.[70] The mortality rate for other Allied Powers was similar. According to *The Australian Encyclopaedia, The Grolier Society of Australia, 1983* 22,376 Australians were held by the Japanese and 35.9 percent of them died. According to Utsumi, the death rate among Australian POWs was higher than the death rate among Australian soldiers who fought against the Japanese Empire on the battlefield.[71] In other words, like American soldiers deployed in the Pacific War, Australian soldiers were less likely to survive in camps than they were on the battlefield. In the European war, only Soviet POWs experienced similar mortality rates.[72]

Historian Sarah Kovner's research usefully contrasts the conditions of Allied POW camps located in Japan with those in Southeast Asian countries Japan occupied early in the war that remained battle zones. With regard to the Fukuoka POW camp, Kovner quotes a Dutch POW who described it as "the most comfortable of the places he had been held during the war."[73] Prisoners received adequate medical care and Red Cross parcels. POWs were mobilized to support Japan's war economy but initially did so voluntarily to qualify for extra food rations. Her principal findings are that "the Japanese government and military never made it policy to abuse POWs," and that the severe scarcity of food and medicine in the last phase of the war caused widespread malnutrition of Japanese civilians and soldiers.[74]

Although there are ample testimonies by Allied POWs of ill treatment by the Japanese military, the JRCS archives reveal instances of humane actions and in some cases, confidential operations. Unique requests from camp commanders included delivery of 1,200 English-language editions of the *New Testament* to the Osaka POW Camp, which were donated by the Japan Bible Association; the National Council of YMCAs of Japan contributed 100 Bibles and hymnals.[75] The WPRCD donated a gramophone with LP records to the Zentsūji POW Camp[76] and provided musical instruments such as drums and an accordion to the Hakodate POW Camp at the request by the Hakodate camp director, Lieutenant Colonel Emoto Shigeo.[77] Emoto stands out as a principled Japanese military officer. In a meeting with a director of the Prisoner of War Information Bureau of IJA, he argued, "The mission of the military on the battlefield is to defeat the enemy. But ill-treatment of POWs, once they have surrendered and capitulated, is contrary to the Japanese ethos." He raised the issue of Japanese camp guards pilfering Red Cross supplies and condemned "illicit activities" occurring "in many camps." All Red Cross parcels provided by the International Red Cross, he insisted, "must pass directly to POWs." Holding the Prisoner of War Information Bureau directly responsible, Emoto sternly warned that the "POW camps operate under the binding legal strictures of the international organizations. Because many officers and soldiers are ignorant about this, I would urge you that you should properly train and educate them. It's your responsibility."[78] It is ironic that he would be detained at the Sugamo Prison on November 22 and purged by the Supreme Commander for the Allied Powers (SCAP) at the end of the year.[79]

On occasion, the JRCS bent the rules to fulfill its humanitarian mission. Shimazu recounted how the JRCS negotiated with the ICRC to obtain the supplies of oryzalin and glucose to combat an epidemic of dysentery among predominately British prisoners in an Osaka POW camp during the autumn of 1942. The majority of the POWs in the Osaka camp were the survivors among the 1,816 British POWs who were in transit from Hong Kong to Japan on the *Lisbon-maru*, a Japanese cargo liner owned by Nippon Yusen Kabushiki Kaisha (NYK), when it was torpedoed and sunk in the South China Sea by the submarine *USS Grouper* on October 1. Eight hundred and forty-two British POWs died while 977 POWs initially survived the attack and were rescued by Japanese patrol vessels and Chinese landing ships. Nine hundred and thirty-six POWs were subsequently boarded on an IJA destroyer, the *Shinsei-maru*, for transport to Japan.[80] The large number of POWs overwhelmed sanitary facilities aboard the ship, and many POWs were diagnosed with dysentery upon arrival at the Osaka camp, where more succumbed in what developed into an epidemic. In October, the Prisoner of War Information Bureau of the IJA unofficially asked the JRCS to obtain medicine to treat these patients.[81] Under crisis conditions and at a time when Japan's own stocks of medicine were running low, the director of the Osaka camp, IJA Colonel Murata Sōtarō, turned to the JRCS headquarters Shimazu for assistance. Shimazu knew of a large shipment of medical supplies from Allied Red Cross societies stockpiled in Yokohama. Knowing that distribution of medicine was the responsibility of the ICRC, Shimazu begged Fritz Paravicini (1874–1944), the head of the Japan ICRC delegation, to release to the JRCS on an emergency basis the drugs needed to save Allied patients at the Osaka POW camp. At the time, the IJA had a strict policy of not disclosing to the ICRC the number, names, or locations of POWs held by the army, which put the JRCS and the ICRC in a bind, because according to the ICRC's own rules, national Red Cross societies were required to provide a full accounting, including the destinations, of all aid deliveries. According to Shimazu's account, at one point while making the case to Paravicini, a Swiss national, he looked him in the eye and without saying more acceded to Shimazu's firm request.[82] Immediately afterward, the Prisoner of War Information Bureau gave the green light to the JRCS, which distributed 1,000 oryzalin injections, 500 doses of glucose, and 300 yen in script for immediate delivery to the Osaka camp.[83] Many Allied POWs' lives were saved, and Shimazu recorded his personal gratitude to Paravicini in his memoir.[84]

As Kovner's research has shown, conditions in Japan's POW camps in Korea were tolerable. Living quarters were decent, and work details, which were voluntary and not particularly onerous, were welcomed as a diversion from the boredom of camp life and earned POWs extra food rations.[85] The relatively good conditions in these camps, according to historian Utsumi, may be attributable to their function as "model" camps designed to reassure Allied governments, as almost all the camp's POWs were white. Utsumi also points to the attitudes of camp commanders towards Allied POWs, which varied from respect to contempt, and as evidence of the former, quotes remarks of Colonel Noguchi Yuzuru, who reassured his charges of his "deep admiration for their loyalty and high sense of duty" and expressed his sympathy for all who had no choice but to surrender.[86]

In December 1942 the ICRC visited Allied POW camps in Korea, which were administered by the JRCS Korean Headquarters. In anticipation of the inspection the JRCS organized a shipment of English-language books. The JRCS provided a long list of books in advance of the visit. The books requested by POWs included Bibles, works of Shakespeare, and in addition books on Japanese tea ceremony, art and architecture, poetry, history, Jūdō, Ainu traditions, travel magazines, Japanese language textbooks, and medical texts. The ICRC delivered the books and sent a report on the environment and health condition of each detainee, such as their weight, to the JRCS following the inspection.[87]

Aid packages from various Allied national Red Cross societies earmarked for distribution to POW camps in Japan arrived irregularly aboard Red Cross society medical ships. In December 1942, the society received a large aid shipment of assorted goods, including toiletry articles, soap, cigarettes, and jam donated by the American, Canadian, and South African Red Cross societies, which were delivered to local JRCS chapters in Kobe, Hiroshima, and Nagasaki for distribution.[88] Upon delivery, the JRCS received official receipts from the military police, who were responsible for the actual distribution in the camps, and forwarded copies of the receipts to the ICRC.[89]

The transnational operations of the Red Cross functioned well in Allied POW camps and detention centers in Japan. Nagasaki City hosted several of the largest Allied POW and civilian internment camps in Japan proper and became a focal point for the JRCS and the ICRC's efforts due to the large numbers and diverse nationalities and occupations of detainees. For instance, in 1943, the JRCS WPRCD sent donations of books, canned food, porridge, cocoa, soup, sugar, and Yorkshire pudding with roast beef to fifteen Catholic missionaries in the Nagasaki detention camp. Shimazu personally made several visits to these camps in 1943 and 1944, and the ICRC also conducted a number of inspections at Nagasaki.[90] A Japanese camp guard later testified that the JRCS delivered blankets, shoes, sanitation goods, nutritional supplements, butter, cheese, corned beef, milk, biscuits, and cigarettes during the war. In one single delivery, he estimated, the JRCS provided around 500 boxes of goods to the Nagasaki POW camp. Allied POWs who survived the atomic bomb later confirmed they received Red Cross letters and ARC aid packages, and more than 1,400 BRC parcels had been distributed during the war.[91]

Throughout the war the JRCS coordinated with the ICRC and Allied national Red Cross societies to ensure aid deliveries. In 1943, the BRC shipped relief goods to the JRCS on British Red Cross cargo ships, which were dispatched to camps not only within the empire but to Shanghai, Hong Kong, Java, Indochina, Thailand, Burma, Malaya, Singapore, Sumatra, and Borneo. Ninety-five percent of British aid was distributed to POW camps in Southeast Asia, where the majority of British prisoners were detained.[92] Relief packages that arrived in 1943 from the ARC and CRC were sent to camps in Singapore, Manila, Hong Kong, Shanghai, and Yokohama under the direct supervision of the ICRC, which confirmed the deliveries in detailed reports to the JRCS.[93]

At the request of the ARC, the JRCS negotiated with the Japanese government to expedite the distribution of aid packages stockpiled in Vladivostok to American POWs and civilian internees in Japan.[94] The Soviet Union, a neutral power in the Pacific War until the last days of the war, transshipped Allied Red Cross packages bound for Japan. The operation required the cooperation of all parties, including their armed forces, to ensure the safe delivery. In a reciprocal gesture, the U.S. government pledged safe passage of Japanese medical ships delivering JRCS aid packages to Japanese detainees in the United States.[95] The 1944 Vladivostok operation was among the most successful examples of international collaboration in relief operations during the war. Once a month, the Japanese government sent a ship to Vladivostok, where it paid all the dues, rates, taxes, and other public charges.

Testimonies regarding the delivery of Red Cross parcels paint a mixed picture. For example, an Australian POW held in Singapore remembered that a Japanese sergeant lent him a gramophone and a set of American records and regularly delivered Red Cross aid packages to his team.[96] However, a British survivor of a Japanese jungle POW camp later charged, "the Jap refused to issue the Red Cross supplies as they said it [sic] was to be kept for an emergency."[97] British POWs held in the Changi POW camp testified in a postwar criminal investigation that while the camp received many aid deliveries, the Japanese camp guards opened each parcel and pilfered items before distributing to POWs.[98] Theft was not limited to guards, however: an Australian POW detained in Nagasaki confessed that POWs themselves stole special Red Cross Christmas treats from their mates.[99] Particularly in the last year of the war when food shortages became acute, the illicit behavior of Japanese and Korean camp guards, who themselves were near starvation, is not surprising. The theft of Red Cross food parcels occurred most frequently in jungle camps in Southeast Asia, which suffered from extreme food shortages and tropical diseases.

When the opportunity arose, the JRCS seized opportunities to visit Allied POW camps in China and Southeast Asia occupied by Japan early in the war. For example, in 1943, a group consisting of Shimazu and ten nurses visited a number of camps in Shanghai, Hong Kong, the Philippines, Vietnam, and Singapore over the course of a month.[100] Nakagawa Nozomu (1875–1964), a vice-president of the JRCS, also visited POW camps in China, in Guangdong and North China, in addition to camps in Manchuria jointly organized by the JRCS and the Manchukuo Red Cross Society (MRCS).[101] In 1944, the JRCS sent a detailed report on civilian internees at the Mukden camp and the Siping camp to the ICRC, which listed the number of internees and their nationalities, occupations, and ages. Occupations ranged from diplomats to business managers, missionaries, and merchants. Nationalities and ethnic backgrounds were also diverse: Americans, British, Canadians, Belgians, Dutch, Armenians, and Slavs.[102] The JRCS sent Red Cross relief supplies to camps in Manchukuo through the MRCS in 1943 and again in 1945.[103] The 1945 relief operation was subsidized by the South Manchuria Railway, which transported the aid free of charge.[104]

Communication between the JRCS and the Kwantung Army, which was the actual governing authority in Manchuria, worsened toward the end of the war, and the IJA increasingly restricted JRCS's disclosures of the number of Allied POWs and the sites of camps to the ICRC. The JRCS received many enquiries from the United States via the ICRC about American POWs, but in most cases, they were only able to reply, "we are still verifying with the Imperial Japanese Army and Navy."[105] Geography was another limiting factor. By 1942, the IJA held over 250,000 Allied POWs in camps scattered over a vast area stretching from New Zealand and Australia to the south, India to the west, and Manchukuo and Siberia to the north.[106] The simple reality was that neither the JRCS nor the ICRC could possibly inspect all the camps.

There were numerous well-documented incidents of Allied attacks on Japanese Red Cross medical ships transporting aid parcels that were registered under the Geneva Conventions, which significantly aggravated supply problems. The *Asahi-maru*, a Red Cross medical ship registered with the ICRC, was bombed by the British on March 26, 1942. Three weeks later, on April 13, the JRCS lodged an official complaint to the BRC through the ICRC. However, British and American attacks on Japanese Red Cross medical ships continued, which the JRCS took as a sign of Allied disregard of the Geneva Conventions.[107] A notorious incident was the November 27, 1943, attack on the Japanese Red Cross ship *Buenos Aires-maru*,[108] carrying Red Cross parcels, 1,129 sick and wounded Japanese soldiers, 165 medical aid workers, and 128 sailors. The ship was sunk by the United States in the Bismarck Sea off the coast of Papua New Guinea.[109] Ultimately, 1,264 people were rescued in what was the worst case amongst the attacks on the JRCS medical ships registered with the Red Cross.

The JRCS informed the U.S. government of the attack on behalf of the Japanese government in a letter sent through the Swiss government, the protecting power, on December 7, 1943. The letter stated, "the weather being very clear at the time of the attack, it was absolutely and perfectly possible to recognize these markings [special Red Cross markings] from the low altitude of about 1,000 meters with the sun at the back."[110] On December 22, 1943, the Japanese government formally accused the U.S. government of violating the Geneva Conventions and lodged an emergency appeal through the ICRC to the national Red Cross societies around the world, which began, "In response to a crime against humanity, we make this emergency appeal." The text stated, "We, the Japanese government lodge the most grievous complaint to the U.S. government.

We ask that the U.S. government acknowledge its regrets for such acts and immediately, thoroughly, and impartially investigate and punish the responsible commander. We request guarantees the U.S. government will ensure that its military never again commits such illegal acts and rectify its military operations."[111]

The JRCS recorded in detail at least ten attacks on medical ships between the start of the war and 1943, including the date, time, latitude, weather, angle of attacks, damage, loss of aid goods, and casualties. The U.S. government did not respond to the accusations until April 27, 1944. The U.S. reply, forwarded to Japan by the ICRC, denied violation of the Geneva Conventions with respect to the cited six cases, claiming they had been "accidental" or never occurred at all.[112] Throughout the war, the Japanese government requested the assistance of both Allied and neutral national Red Cross societies[113] to stop Allied attacks on Japanese Red Cross vessels. However, attacks continued until the end of the war.[114]

In addition to attacking the Red Cross medical ships, Allied forces attacked a number of Japanese military vessels not registered with the International Red Cross and Red Crescent that were transporting Allied POWs, causing considerable loss of life.[115] Shimazu and other historians have observed that after the *Buenos Aires-maru* incident, Japanese treatment of Allied POWs became harsher. Furthermore, the JRCS was increasingly pressured by the government to lodge complaints when Japanese military ships transporting Allied POWs were attacked. The ships had not registered with the ICRC, and some disguised themselves by painting fake Red Cross insignia on black hulls without adding the white background. Despite government pressure, the JRCS did not recognize these military ships as official Red Cross relief ships and did not file official complaints in these cases. Many Allied POWs were killed in the attacks.[116]

Early in the war, on February 5, 1942, the Washington, DC newspaper the *Evening Star* falsely reported that the *USS Mactan*, an American Red Cross medical ship, was attacked by the Japanese. The headline read, "Hospital Ship Bombed by Japanese After Leaving Philippines."[117] The ARC acted as a mediator in registering the JRCS's ensuing denial.[118] As the fighting intensified, violations of various kinds multiplied, including misuse of the Red Cross insignia, which had the effect of undermining the authority of the Red Cross in general. Belligerents became increasingly suspicious that Red Cross medical ships were secretly carrying weapons and serving as troop transports and that battlefield hospitals were being used as shields, making attacks on Red Cross ships and hospitals a global phenomenon.

TREATMENT OF CIVILIAN INTERNEES AND INTERNATIONAL EXCHANGE RELIEF OPERATIONS

The JRCS's relief operations for civilian internees are not well known. Civilian detainees in Japan included diplomats, businessmen, missionaries, students and university professors, musicians, journalists, and a group of Australian nurses, in addition to stateless individuals and denationalized persons.[119] In cases of special need, the JRCS WPRCD provided financial support to enemy civilian internees held in Japan and to Japanese citizens interred abroad. Aid to foreign internees, which was supported by the Home Ministry,[120] included free medical care at the JRCS hospitals and financial assistance following childbirth. Depending on circumstances, monthly financial support could be as much as 50 yen for adults and 30 yen for minors.[121] From April 1942 to October 1943, the JRCS's expenditures exceeded 25,000 yen.[122] The JRCS even assisted a Greek man of uncertain nationality who was declared an illegal alien due to the possession of an invalid passport.[123]

In the early years of the war, between 1942 and 1943, the JRCS successfully assisted a number of enemy alien repatriation operations. A notable repatriation operation involving Japan, the United States, and the United Kingdom took place in Portugal's colonial port cities: Lourenço Marques, now Maputo, and Mozambique in July 1942. A second alien repatriation operation mounted by Japan and the United States was carried out in Goa in October 1943. The Japanese cruise ship *Asama-maru* initially boarded detainees held in Japan, Manchukuo, and Korea. After leaving Yokohama, it made frequent port stops, including Hong Kong, Saigon, and Singapore. A second passenger ship, the Italian-flagged *Conte Verde*, carried detainees from China. The nationalities of detainees included Canadian, Mexican, Panamanian, Nicaraguan, Brazilian, Peruvian, Bolivian, Paraguayan, and

Ecuadorian. The American Red Cross charted the Swedish-flagged *M.S. Gripsholm* to transport the Japanese detainees. Altogether, approximately 3,000 civilians were delivered to Lourenço Marques.[124]

The Japan–Great Britain repatriation operation in August 1942, at Lourenço Marques, was the largest during the war. The Japanese ships, the *Tatsuta-maru* and the *Kamakura-maru*,[125] departed from Yokohama and made port calls at Shanghai, Saigon, and Singapore. The two vessels repatriated civilians and diplomats from Britain, the Netherlands, Greece, Belgium, Egypt, Australia, and Norway. The British operated three vessels, the *El Nil*, the *City of Paris*, and the *City of Canterbury*. The *El Nil* departed from Liverpool carrying Japanese internees from Europe;[126] the *City of Paris* left Mumbai, India, carrying Japanese diplomats who had assembled from the Middle East and North Africa,[127] and Japanese internees from South Asia; the *City of Canterbury* departed from Melbourne, Australia, transporting Japanese internees from Oceania.[128] Great Britain repatriated around 3,000 Japanese,[129] Japan approximately 1,800 people.[130]

After the Battle of Midway in June 1942, both Japan and the United States became concerned about the possible leaks of military intelligence when internees were repatriated.[131] As a result, the repatriation missions became difficult to carry out. In 1943 the only exchanges involved Americans, Canadians, and Latin Americans interned in Japan, and Japanese Americans who had opted for repatriation to Japan. Totaling 3,000 persons, the operation was conducted at extreme risk. In fact, by this time both the *Tatsuta-maru* and the *Kamakura-maru*, used in the 1942 Japanese and British repatriation missions, had been sunk by the Allies.[132]

The national Red Cross societies that formed the international Red Cross and Red Crescent humanitarian relief network piggybacked on the exchange operations to send Red Cross aid parcels to POWs and civilian internees still held by belligerents (figure 5.3). Because the JRCS was only permitted to send aid to Japanese abroad upon request from a foreign national Red Cross society, it seized upon the repatriation operations to deliver food parcels, gift packages from relatives, and Red Cross messages to Japanese held in Allied Powers internment camps. The JRCS also delivered Red Cross messages from Allied POWs and civilians to relatives in their home countries.[133] The ARC and BRC similarly sent Red Cross aid packages and messages to Japan.

FIGURE 5.3 Red Cross aid parcels stockpiled for delivery to Japanese civilians interned by the Allied Powers, 1942. JRCS War Prisoners Relief Committee Department (WPRCD) was ready to deliver aid parcels to Japanese civilian internees overseas.

Archival collection of the Red Cross Information Plaza, the Japanese Red Cross Society, Nihon Sekijūjisha, *Hakuai: Organ de la croix-rouge janponaise, No. 662, Juillet 1942*, introduction.

In 1943 Shimazu himself oversaw deliveries to Allied POWs held in the Japanese POW camps in Southeast Asia.[134] Shimazu recalled that the ships bearing the white Red Cross insignia traveled at high speed, zigzagging in zones where submarines were numerous, and radioed their location every day at noon to minimize the risks of attack. (See figure 5.4.) Swiss officials were on board to guaranty no military-related cargo or personnel traveled on the ships.[135]

The JRCS partnered with a Japan-based sister organization, the Committee for Provisions for Compatriots Residing in Hostile Countries,[136] in collecting donations of goods for Japanese interned abroad. Endorsed by the MOFA,[137] a number of Japanese banks and corporations, including the Yokohama Specie Bank, Mitsui & Co., Ltd., and NYK[138] raised more than 104,400 yen in 1943 and 1944.[139] The ICRC and the ARC assisted delivery. For example, in conjunction with the repatriation operation at Lourenço Marques in 1942, the JRCS sent 10,000 packs of Japanese tea to Japanese civilians interned in the United States, Britain, Canada, and Central and Latin America through the ICRC.[140] The deliveries were warmly welcomed, as evident in letters of appreciation sent to the JRCS. A letter in 1943 received from the Japanese-American internment camp in Santa Fe,

FIGURE 5.4 *Teia-maru* showing the white cross insignias in 1943. The JRCS hospital ship the *Teia-maru* was torpedoed and sunk on August 18, 1945, near Laoag, Luzon, the Philippines.

Collection of War Memorial Maritime Museum, Japan. War Memorial Maritime Museum, *Senbotsu-sen Shashin-shū* (Kobe: All Japan Seamen's Union, 2001), 59.

New Mexico thanked the JRCS for fifty-seven cases of Japanese green tea received at the camp.[141] "We, the internees, wish to express our wholehearted appreciation for your sincere thoughtfulness and support."[142] (See figure 5.5.)

RED CROSS MESSAGES

In addition to comforting Japanese interned abroad with familiar foods and daily amenities, beginning in October 1942, the JRCS WPRCD provided a measure of psychological assurance as to the health and well-being of families separated by the war by delivering messages from next of kin, which exceeded the Red Cross original mandate.[143] During World War I, only POWs were included in the Red Cross's "restoration of family links" operations. During the Pacific War, however, the JRCS coordinated

FIGURE 5.5 "One day the Red Cross delivered a supply of Japanese soy sauce to the mess hall. Old people and young alike showed their gratitude by falling to their knees, hands held in praying attitude and heads bowed." Painting and caption by Henry Sugimoto. The large banner reads, "Comfort Parcels for Interned Japanese from the Home Country."

"Gift to the Japanese in Camp from Japan," Collection of Wakayama City Museum. Sugimoto, Henry, and Kubo Sadajirō, ed., *Kiroku-kaiga: Hokubei Nihonjin no Shūyōjo* (Tokyo: Soubunsha, 1981), 37.

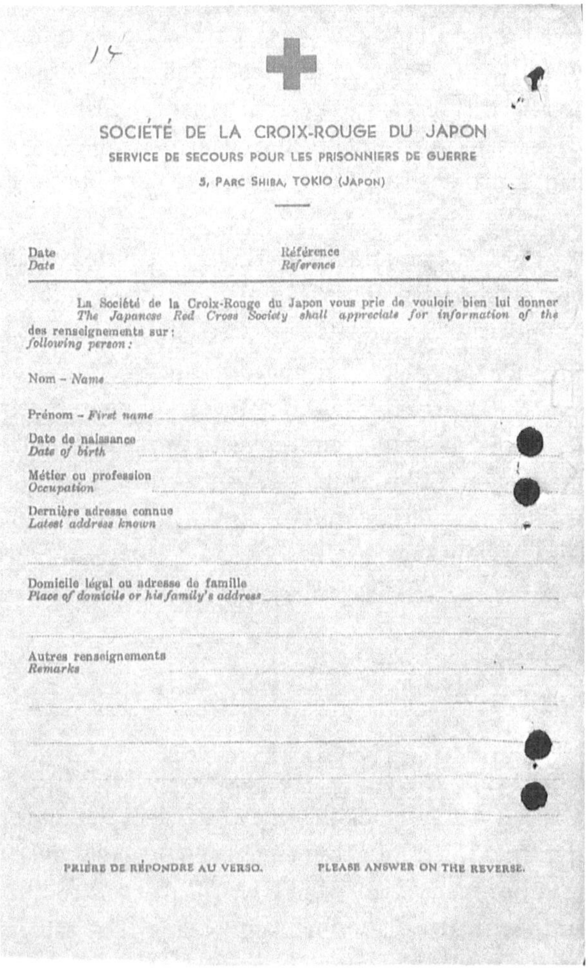

14

SOCIÉTÉ DE LA CROIX-ROUGE DU JAPON

SERVICE DE SECOURS POUR LES PRISONNIERS DE GUERRE

5, PARC SHIBA, TOKIO (JAPON)

Date
Date

Référence
Reference

La Société de la Croix-Rouge du Japon vous prie de vouloir bien lui donner des renseignements sur :
The Japanese Red Cross Society shall appreciate for information of the following person:

Nom - *Name*

Prénom - *First name*

Date de naissance
Date of birth

Métier ou profession
Occupation

Dernière adresse connue
Latest address known

Domicile légal ou adresse de famille
Place of domicile or his family's address

Autres renseignements
Remarks

PRIÈRE DE RÉPONDRE AU VERSO. PLEASE ANSWER ON THE REVERSE.

FIGURE 5.6 Blank JRCS message card.

Archival collection of Japanese Red Cross Society International Department, *Furyo* · *Hi-yokuryūsha Kyūjutsu Kanren Bunsho, Seiri bangō Ni.*

with the ICRC Central Agency for Prisoners of War to expand the service to include next of kin and mounted a large-scale effort to deliver Red Cross messages that continued until the end of the war (figure 5.6).

To this end, the JRCS obtained the support of the Ministry of Communications.[144] The number of tracings and Red Cross messages to internees and POWs delivered by the WPRCD totaled a staggering 364,960 cases between 1942 and 1945, of which 195,600 messages were delivered to Allied POWs and foreigners detained in Japan.[145] The society also provided this service to Asian detainees and laborers in Japan.[146] As Shimazu recalled in an interview in later years, no one at the JRCS had expected that the activities of the WPRCD would become such a large operation.[147]

The task was so demanding that WPRCD enlisted additional personnel to process the large number of requests. In 1944, the department hired thirty-one women students who were studying English literature at Japan Women's University.[148] Shimazu recalled that they assisted in a range of tasks relating to POWs and detainees and were especially helpful with translation. Many were volunteers who worked beyond the official hours at the office in Tokyo.[149] This recruitment was supported by the Ministry of Education of Japan in junction with student labor mobilization.[150] Thus, during the war, the JRCS's international relief activities were to a large extent staffed by volunteers from Japan's leading women's universities.

TREATMENT OF JAPANESE POWs

During the war, whenever possible the JRCS delivered aid to Japanese POWs held by the Allies. Because being taken prisoner violated military policy,[151] the government imposed restrictions that obstructed the JRCS's efforts to address their needs. What unfolded at the Featherston POW camp in New Zealand is illustrative in this regard.

On January 5, 1944, the JRCS received a confidential request for assistance from the ICRC that was prompted by a riot of Japanese POWs nearly a year earlier on February 25, 1943, known as the Featherston Incident,[152] following an ICRC inspection in mid-December of that year.[153] The ICRC reported that the 803 Japanese POWs housed in the camp, who included eight Japanese naval officers, were generally in good physical health and camp discipline was satisfactory. POWs who chose to perform labor were paid and conditions were satisfactory. The pressing issue, however, was their precarious psychological state. According to the report, many Japanese POWs felt ashamed, having failed to sacrifice their lives for the Empire of Japan, and were anxious how they would be received upon repatriation at the end of the war. Many of the POWs saw themselves as disgraced by having survived the war as POWs and feared possibly being blamed by neighbors and family members for Japan's defeat. The ICRC emphasized to the JRCS that there were many indications that Japanese POWs wished to commit suicide in detention;[154] ironically, they experienced humane treatment as humiliating, which only added to their sense of shame, emotional scars, and psychological distress. As a remedy, the ICRC asked the JRCS to send musical instruments, accompanied by sheet music, Japanese-language books on a variety of subjects, and traditional Japanese food items. For its part, the ICRC made arrangements for the Japanese POWs to engage in handicrafts, sketching, sculpting, painting, and needlework to heal their feelings of guilt and relieve the solitude of camp life.[155]

After Japan's surrender, the JRCS assisted SCAP, the U.S. occupation authority, in the repatriation and resettlement of Japanese POWs, soldiers, and civilians, upon their return. The society provided medical treatment to forced laborers from China and Korea and reunited Japanese orphans left behind on the Asian continent with their families. Family tracing continued to occupy the JRCS well into the occupation period, as many Japanese living in the overseas empire and war zones, having been displaced, scattered, gone missing, or captured, lost their links with their families, partners, and friends in the vast Asia Pacific war theatre. The JRCS assisted with the return of the remains of the war dead for burial and the repatriation of former Japanese colonial subjects to their home countries.[156] In its work to restore these human links, the JRCS cooperated with the national Red Cross societies of the Allied Powers, not only the ARC but also the RCSC and the Union of Red Cross and Red Crescent Societies of the USSR known as the Soviet Red Cross (SRC). By no means did the operations of the JRCS WPRCD end in 1945.

Under severe restrictions set by the Japanese wartime state and the IJA, JRCS humanitarian workers exerted every effort to administer to the humanitarian needs of soldiers and civilians amid the extreme violence of total war. No belligerent in World War II totally respected the rules of war, including ensuring the safety of Red Cross workers. Nevertheless, the JRCS did what it could to fulfill the Red Cross mandate by networking with the ICRC and national Red Cross societies. The operations examined in this chapter reveal striving for institutional independence and embrace of humanitarianism even within the wartime Japanese state, which was the most that could be expected in the age of total war.

6

NUCLEAR EMERGENCY

Japanese Red Cross Society Nurses in Hiroshima
and Nagasaki, August 1945

Testimonies preserved in the archives of the Japanese Red Cross Society narrate the colossal challenges faced by Red Cross personnel who carried out humanitarian aid in the immediate aftermath of the atomic bombings of Hiroshima and Nagasaki. One nurse testified to her resolute commitment to the JRCS's ideals and mission:

> When I eventually managed to find the emergency pack in which I usually packed my nursing shoes, and put them on [to negotiate a floor covered with glass fragments], I thought, "I am the new hope of a Red Cross nurse.... Yes, I am a Red Cross nurse." I felt a sudden shiver run up my spine—it ignited my fury. And I believed, "I will do it. I should do it." ... I was not aware that my legs were lacerated by glass fragments, so I carried the wounded regardless; lent my shoulder to assist their toileting; held survivors and stamped out burning embers. I carried out my relief activities without rest.... We did not take a rest or sleep at all but nobody complained of their fate. We strongly believed that our humanitarian mission should be fully accomplished without hesitation. We worked tirelessly and desperately.[1]
>
> —Gojō Mieko

Scores of JRCS nurses worked under dangerous and potentially deadly conditions after the Hiroshima and Nagasaki bombings in fulfilling their calling as medical professionals and the Red Cross's mission of the impartial provision of medical relief in wartime. In Hiroshima and Nagasaki, aid workers were exposed to the nuclear attacks, trapped by falling debris, and performed their duties even after sustaining severe injuries and while themselves experiencing radiation sickness. Their heroic efforts to aid victims included ministering to Allied POWs, colonial subjects, and foreign nationals. Many JRCS nurses subsequently died of radiation sickness, and some were driven to suicide in days or weeks immediately following the bombing or in ensuing decades, succumbing to what the medical profession later identified as post-traumatic stress disorder (PTSD). Their willingness to perform their duties in the face of the well-understood dangers of radiation poisoning and amid administrative and civic chaos demonstrates the extent to which Red Cross workers had internalized their professional mission as medical aid-givers and as exemplars of humanitarian professionalism.

HISTORICAL BACKGROUND OF PROFESSIONALISM IN JAPANESE RED CROSS NURSING

The sacrifices of JRCS nurses began well before the atomic bombing of Hiroshima and Nagasaki. Between July 1937 and August 1945, the JRCS dispatched a total of 960 relief parties to overseas battlefields and medical ships and deployed medical workers to hospitals throughout the Japanese archipelago to treat civilian victims of Allied air raids. More than 33,000 JRCS medical personnel were mobilized: 324 doctors, 31,450 nurses, and several thousand support staff.[2] A total of 1,187 died in the line of duty.[3] They lost their lives as a result of bombings, shootings, starvation, and infectious diseases.[4] The psychological stress was relentless. Red Cross nurses saw mounds of dead bodies everywhere, were stranded in jungles, saw fellow medics shot dead in front of their eyes, donned gas masks in training for chemical warfare, were forced to tie hand grenades around their waist as suicide belts with orders not to surrender, witnessed Japanese soldiers killing each other, were ordered by military commanders to kill the wounded who had become a burden to military operations, were given potassium cyanide to commit suicide themselves to avoid becoming victims of sexual violence, starved to death even while eating everything they could lay their hands on, contracted life-threatening diseases, became refugees when the war ended, faced the horror of rape, were taken captive by Allied armed forces, and, in some cases, detained for decades. They endured countless heart-wrenching fates as they experienced almost every variety of the universal cruelties of war.[5]

The JRCS nurses who performed so heroically in the aftermath of the nuclear bombings were the product of a half-century history of the development of professional nursing in Japan. The European model of female nursing education had been introduced by Heinrich von Siebold (1852–1908)[6] at the Philanthropic Society[7] General Assembly in Tokyo in 1880, and the society subsequently commissioned Shibata Shōkei (1850–1910)[8] to investigate Red Cross activities in Europe.[9] Due to the halo effect of the patronage of the imperial family, JRCS nurses attained an elevated status in Japanese society that distinguished them from other cohorts of Japanese nurses, such as the military nurses[10] who were directly hired by the Japanese army and navy during the Pacific War.

In addition to establishing nursing schools in cooperation with JRCS chapters in Japan's overseas empire, the society supported nursing training at the international level. As early as 1909, JRCS delegations attended meetings of the International Council of Nurses (ICN), and in the 1930s frequently participated in the annual International Nursing Training program.[11] JRCS nurses developed professional networks with nurses around the world while also acting as goodwill ambassadors for Japan in the international arena and reporting back on new trends in nursing in the United Kingdom and the United States.[12] In an article published in the September 1933 bulletin of the League of Red Cross Societies (LORCS), Inoue Enji, the director general of the JRCS Investigation Department, proudly announced that the JRCS employed more than 7,000 nurses and each year produced a further 1,500 graduates of nursing schools affiliated with twenty-three JRCS hospitals in Japan.[13] As discussed in chapter 1, during World War I, JRCS nurses, who would achieve international renown, were deployed to Russia, France, and Britain, where they provided vital support to national Red Cross societies whose nursing staff had been overwhelmed by the carnage of trench warfare. In recognition of the JRCS's contribution to the wartime relief, JRCS nurse Hagiwara Take (1873–1936)[14] became one of the first recipients of the Florence Nightingale Medal in 1920, and ever since then Japan has remained the most prolific producer of Nightingale Medal recipients worldwide.[15]

Initially, male nurses predominated within the JRCS. Male nurses were sent to medical ships during World War I and were deployed on medical missions to Vladivostok during the Siberian Intervention (1918–1922).[16] Their major roles in battlefield relief operations were carrying the wounded from the battlefield to hospitals and assisting with surgical operations. In most cases, wounded soldiers in military field hospitals underwent surgery without anesthesia. Male nurses held down patients during operations, making physical strength essential. By the end of World War I, however, the increased availability of anesthesias allowed the recruitment of women into the nursing profession to increase, and female nurses soon predominated; by the 1930s, the great majority of nurses were female, as Japanese men were drafted into military service.[17] In 1938, as the government prepared for total war, it amended the Military Service Law and the National Mobilization Law.[18] As imperial subjects, male Red Cross workers had no choice but to leave the JRCS and enter the armed forces of the Empire of Japan.

QUASI-MILITARY NURSING TRAINING

In 1898, the society formalized its remit, issuing "Principles of Japanese Red Cross Society Nurses," whose cardinal precepts reflected the gender-polarized world of prewar Japan. A decade later, one sees the initial signs of the society's evolution toward the more rigorous, almost militaristically disciplined training that would reach its apogee in World War II. During World War II, these precepts were enshrined as "Ten Fundamental Principles for Relief Workers" (*kyūgoin jukkun*):[19]

  I. Be humane and show great kindness.
  II. Be devoted and loyal to your work and colleagues.
  III. Be patient and forbearing.
  IV. Be faithful and self-controlled.
  V. Be humble and prudent.
  VI. Be disciplined and follow rules.

VII. Be brave and keep calm.
VIII. Be active and attentive.
IX. Be modest and honest.
X. Be gentle in demeanor and proper in person and attire.[20]

The society intensified training after the eruption of the Second Sino-Japanese War in 1937. The program now included skills explicitly attuned to the battlefield, including chemical warfare drills wearing gas masks, carrying stretchers, training in self-defense, conserving resources, observing confidentiality, practicing military saluting, giving and obeying orders, and parade ground marching drills.[21] The curriculum was built upon the "Ten Fundamental Principles for Relief Workers," with the aim not just of adding skill sets but also preparing nurses psychologically for the dangers and carnage of modern warfare. Intensive preparation for what they would encounter under fire enabled them to not panic in the heat of battle or buckle under physical duress, but to carry out their duties without hesitation as female soldiers whose duty was to save peoples' lives. For the JRCS nurses, Florence Nightingale now exemplified a disciplined soldier who acted bravely in the face of the horrors of the battlefield, as when extracting bullets from soldiers' open wounds. It was this professionalized spirit that was most exemplified in the JRCS's emergency responses at Hiroshima and Nagasaki.

According to the official history of the military medic system published after World War II by the Japan Ground Self-Defense Force Medical School, the JRCS's major responsibilities were dispatching aid workers to military forces and tending to POWs.[22] In 1939, the Ministry of the Army categorized JRCS medical workers as civilians in military employ.[23] The change in classification enhanced their legal protections, for as civilians they were formally separated from the Japanese military and could not be targeted in battle or held responsible for Japanese military violations. To further distinguish Red Cross JRCS staff from military personnel, the Ministry of the Army ordered the JRCS to create its own set of ranks for medical staff serving on the battlefield, which points to a degree of institutional autonomy.

Some international observers were alarmed by the new look of JRCS nurses. Dispatched to Shanghai during the fierce fighting between Japanese and Chinese armies in the autumn of 1937, International Committee of the Red Cross (ICRC) delegate and legal officer Colonel Charles de Watteville criticized what he characterized as the martial demeanor of Red Cross nurses when he met with Okamoto Suemasa (1892–1967), Japan's Consul General at Shanghai and acting director of JRCS Shanghai.[24] However, Kageyama Sadaka, chair of the JRCS Shanghai Special Expeditionary Relief Corps (SSERC) and himself a surgeon, countered this criticism by arguing that because of the strict quasi-military training, medical relief workers were highly disciplined and performed well, and in extreme situations, which enabled them to fulfill the Red Cross's humanitarian mission, even in the heat of fierce battles.[25]

During World War II, JRCS nurses contributed personal essays on their experiences to their professional association's journal, *Dōhō*. These essays reveal both their embrace of Red Cross humanitarian norms and the particular appeal of wartime nursing with its attendant risks to these women as an escape from the confines of middle-class gender norms. In the December 1937 issue, Inada Yuki, the director of nursing at the JRCS Headquarters Hospital described the emotions that accompanied her decision to make Red Cross nursing her career in wartime: "When I found out that the Red Cross was opening recruitment of nurses, I was really excited. I thought that even though I am a woman, I can serve on the frontline." The message was layered but unambiguous. Like her male peers in military service, Inada put her life at risk in choosing wartime nursing, yet felt compelled to reassure readers that "as an art of compassion, morality and tenderness," nursing was a profession consistent with traditional Japanese humanitarian norms.[26] She insisted that nursing was not at all a humble calling but, on the contrary, noble work demonstrating the universal love of humanity fully in accordance with the Geneva Conventions.[27] These values are redolent in the tanka poem recited by a candidate for promotion to head nurse at a ceremony attended by Empress Nagako on the eve of the Pacific War.

> I pray, I will not
> Will not spend my life in vain
> Following the path before me, I
> Walk on, walk on with resolve
> With a heart so pure and clear[28]

Within the context of World War II, the reformulated ethos of Nightingale-ism prescribed a moral code for the conduct of wartime relief, whose mandate of unflinching conduct in the face of mortal danger paralleled soldiers' code of military discipline. Nightingale-ism and related principles exerted a profound impact on trained nurses, who strove to faithfully perform their duties with the discipline and self-sacrifice of military personnel in combat situations.[29] (See figure 6.1.)

The rigorous training and ethos of JRCS nurses contrasted sharply with that of ordinary army and navy nurses, who were hired directly by the Japanese army and navy and trained in military hospitals outside the JRCS system. These military nurses were mobilized during World War II on the basis of a number of military protocols, such as the "Regulations of the Employment of Chief Nurses and Nurses"[30] set by the army.[31] Through this more lax regime, female secondary school students with only a moderate level of education were able to obtain nursing licenses without having to take the nursing examinations.[32] Nurses hired by the navy, likewise, were deployed to hospitals at naval rear bases in Japan.[33] The number of military nurses rose sharply from 3,500 in 1937 to 20,500 by 1945, 5,000 more than the number of JRCS nurses.[34] There were three categories of Japanese military nurses: full-time nurses, temporary nurses, and replacement nurses. Full-time nurses were hired during peacetime and were assigned to military hospitals; temporary nurses were hired to provide wartime medical treatment; and finally, replacement nurses were hired to fill vacancies in the ranks of military medics. Their maximum monthly wage was 55 yen, while the salaries of JRCS relief nurses ranged from 50 to 70 yen in 1939.[35] In addition, the JRCS nurses received a 3-yen-and-60-sen daily allowance in wartime.[36]

The working conditions of the military nurses differed from JRCS nurses assigned to support the armed forces. Testimonies of military nurses are very rare compared to those of the better-educated JRCS nurses, but those that exist are suggestive of differences in mentality. One former army nurse remembered her wartime experience in the postwar period, "We were driven by our fierce patriotism. We devoted ourselves to our country. In order to win the war, we sacrificed ourselves—gave our whole souls and bodies to the state. . . . I pray for my colleagues who are enshrined at Yasukuni Shrine."[37] Another nurse remembered that when

FIGURE 6.1 Predeployment ceremony in which JRCS nurses affirmed the Red Cross's humanitarian creed of saving lives and upholding the principles of the Geneva Conventions.

Shussei, photo by Ken Domon, 1938. Ken Domon Museum of Photography.

she learned of the defeat of Japan in August 1945, she was horrified and engulfed in grief.[38]

In general, military nurses were not exposed to extreme risks, and the testimonies that do exist tend to couch their battlefield experiences in the language of misfortune—they tell of their own misery and suffering, expressing anger and regret rather than pride in their professionalism or solidarity with patients. One former army nurse confessed to moments of great fear and despair while serving under fire: "I was terrified, and just spent my days in inconsolable grief. . . . Life in the field was unspeakably miserable. Our hospital was occupied by enemy forces. . . . The whole thing seemed just pointless."[39]

With the deployment of nurses to battlefields, the JRCS amended its protocols to reflect the new reality. In 1938, the "Regulations of the Japanese Red Cross Society" (*Nihon Sekijūjisha Jōrei*)[40] was amended by Imperial Edict No. 635 and renamed the "Mandate of the Japanese Red Cross Society" (*Nihon Sekijūjisha Rei*).[41] The society's official purpose thereafter became the provision and training of relief medical workers for the military. Now, quite explicitly, JRCS relief workers, dispatched to wartime operations, were placed in a military line of command and duty-bound to obey the orders of their military commanders.[42] Obeying peremptory commands and adhering to strict regulations were deemed crucial to minimizing the risk aid workers faced, surrounded by extreme violence in their work. At the same time, the JRCS was motivated by internationally established legal principles, and the 1938 amendment was instituted both in accordance with the 1906 Geneva Convention for the Amelioration of the Condition of the Wounded and Sick in Armed Forces in the Field and the Hague Convention of 1907 concerning maritime warfare—both of which had helped shape the 1922 "Wartime Relief Regulations of the Japanese Red Cross Society" (*Nihon Sekijūjisha Senji Kyūgo Kisoku*).[43] As such, the society's World War II relief operations were conducted on the basis of the reconciliation of Japanese imperial domestic law and international law; its nurses saw themselves as medical professionals providing services for victims while subject to the authority of military commands in battlefield situations to sustain their security.

Due to the demand for medical relief workers created by the full-scale invasion of China that began in the summer of 1937, the JRCS accelerated its nursing training program and in 1940 began to classify female nurses into two ranks. The *kō* (甲)-class nurse had to be between the ages of seventeen and twenty-five to enter nursing school and complete a three-year course of training; *Otsu* (乙)-class nurses, who had to be between fourteen and twenty years old, had only two years of training.[44] This change indicated that the JRCS was seeking to fill its ranks in anticipation of the wider war. To further expedite dispatching nurses to the battlefield, in 1942 the society shortened the mandatory training of *kō* class nurses from three to two years.[45] It also took the unprecedented step of hiring temporary relief nurses (*rinji kyūgo kangofu*)[46] who had not graduated from JRCS nursing schools. Temporary nurses were only required to complete a three-month internship at JRCS hospitals before embarking on their mission.[47] Due to this drastic change, the refined culture of Japanese Red Cross nurses was deemphasized, at the same time that their training increasingly focused on the honing of practical nursing skills. This, ironically, allowed nurses to thrust themselves into great danger during and in the aftermath of the nuclear bombings, while the idea of treating victims without discrimination became a conditioned reflex.

HIROSHIMA NUCLEAR BOMBING HUMANITARIAN RELIEF ACTIVITIES

Perhaps the most extraordinary humanitarian operations during the Pacific War unfolded in the aftermath of the 1945 Hiroshima and Nagasaki nuclear bombings. At 8:15 A.M. on August 6, 1945, the U.S. army dropped a nuclear bomb above the city of Hiroshima that detonated 580 meters above Shima Hospital, which was located close to the Hiroshima Prefectural Commercial Exhibition Hall—today known as the Atomic Bomb Dome. It detonated with a brilliant flash that looked like burning magnesium. The explosion released radioactive gamma rays and neutrons,[48] as well as toxic uranium that together exposed 350,000 people to high levels of radiation. By the end of December 1945, an estimated 140,000 had died. The dead included Japanese colonial subjects from Korea, Taiwan, and mainland China; students from China and Southeast Asia; German priests, Russian shop owners and musicians, and American POWs.[49]

The JRCS Hiroshima Chapter building was located 222 meters from ground zero.[50] It was completely destroyed, leaving just a skeleton and an outer wall. None of the fifteen JRCS staff working in the office that morning survived. The entire JRCS Hiroshima Chapter's administration was wiped out in a flash.

At that time, Hiroshima City had four main hospitals: the Hiroshima First Army Hospital, the Hiroshima Second Army Hospital, the Mitaki Branch Hospital, and the Hiroshima Red Cross Hospital, and all had Red Cross medical staff. The Hiroshima First Army Hospital, which was located 450 meters from the hypocenter, and the Hiroshima Second Army Hospital, situated one kilometer from the hypocenter, were destroyed in an instant, and almost all medical staff and military patients are believed to have perished. In the Hiroshima Red Cross Hospital, which stood 1.5 kilometers from ground zero, the nuclear blast destroyed the inside of the building, leaving only an outer wall.[51] Dr. Takeuchi Ken, the director of the hospital, lost consciousness after suffering eight fractures, and fifty-one hospital workers were killed. Eighty-five percent of hospital workers were critically injured, and many of their relatives were also killed or missing.[52] Under these extreme conditions, the few surviving JRCS nurses and doctors administered to victims at temporary emergency stations in the city after escaping from debris, even though most were injured and soon began to experience symptoms of radiation sickness.[53] (See figure 6.2.)

TESTIMONIES OF JRCS NURSES

Chief nurse Yukinaga Masae recorded her observations of the immediate aftermath of the atomic blast in a report dated September 4, 1945:

> The nursing residential hall was totally destroyed by fire due to the bombing on the morning of 6 August 1945. The hospital was wholly destroyed. Some patients and three-quarters of the nurses were injured by fire and flying glass fragments, which were caused by the atomic blast. . . . Thirteen nurses sustained embedded glass fragments, while an additional three nurses suffered severe burns.[54]

However, the reality was even worse than Yukinaga's official report. According to the JRCS records, forty-six nurses were killed on the day of the bombing, while five nurses suffered critical injuries.[55] Twenty-five nursing students were also killed in their dormitory.[56] In the ensuing

FIGURE 6.2 Makeshift clinics for A-bomb casualties along the Ōta River in Hiroshima, August 9, 1945 (Kawahara 1945).

Kawahara Yotsugi, "Ōtagawa Teibō ni Mōkerareta Rinji Kyūgosho, ID: SA018-1," courtesy of the Hiroshima Peace Memorial Museum.

chaos, Yukinaga could not record the scene in detail. It seems miraculous, in fact, that any official reports from that day survived. A former nursing student who was on duty that day, wrote, "I will never forget that extraordinary scene as long as I live." They were called upon to cremate a mound of corpses, including hospital staff and nursing students,[57] at the same time that they administered first aid to countless numbers of victims. They spent sleepless days washing patients' clothes in the river, disinfecting gauzes, and stocking food.[58] Furthermore, in order to protect the hospital from the fires still burning in the surrounding area, they extinguished burning embers with wet brooms. Testimonies from nurses who survived the blast graphically documented the scene.

> When I went to the lavatory, I saw a sudden, bright flash of bluish-white light from a small window. In a second, I thought that I was

dead—crushed by falling debris I was thrown to the ground with a great crash. . . . Mounds of victims, including soldiers and civilians, were lain out like pigs at the river bank of the hospital.[59]

—Kawakami Hatsue

The agonizing screams roused me to consciousness after going into shock. All the nurses were injured but we made an all-out effort to continue rescuing military patients buried under the debris. Our white gowns soon turned red with blood.[60]

—Yamamoto Tsuyako

Many nurses suffered facial and jaw fractures, abrasive wounds, cuts on their legs, and severe bruising. However, they continued to rescue their patients without treating themselves.[61]

—Yukinaga Masae

While escorting patients from the hospital to the emergency shelter, I observed a line of people walking to the north. The eyeballs of some victims had dropped from their sockets, while all the skin on the legs of others peeled off like sheets of paper. How unspeakably cruel it was.[62]

—Hirano Shigeru

One mother, whose whole body was completely covered with blood and whose skull was partially exposed, brought her baby to me. She said, "please look after my baby . . ." However, I realized that unbeknownst to the mother her baby had already died, which in her desperate effort to bring her baby to our hospital she could not see. I took her dead baby from her arms. Finally, the mother seemed relieved, and she died miserably in front of me.[63]

—Yamamoto Tsuyako

On the day of the nuclear bombing in Hiroshima, a number of nursing students were enlisted to assist with relief operations due to the shortage of trained medical staff. Most were living in the nurses' dormitory.[64] Kinutani Oshie,[65] a nursing instructor in Hiroshima who was awarded the Florence Nightingale Medal in 1959, describes the scene as follows (see also figure 6.3):

I saw a flash in the chief nurse's room, and I was buried under falling debris. But I was not pinned down and managed to crawl out from under the rubble. In the darkness, I saw students were running around, and heard voices of those buried pleading for help and screaming in great pain. Aroused to consciousness . . . I saw a student who was trapped under rubble up to her neck, while others had sustained injuries to their forehead and were bleeding massively. But there was nothing I could do to help. I saw a student who could not escape because her legs were entangled in debris. It was utter misery. I gathered together the students who were not injured or not seriously injured, and attempted to rescue as many survivors as possible. I thought that we must not abandon any victims. . . . There were students on the verge of death when we rescued them. Although we gave them first aid treatment, some of them died anyway. There were survivors, who were severely injured and were not able to walk without assistance whom we carried by stretcher to the grounds outside the main building. Around four or five o'clock we led survivors who were able to walk on their own there too. The ground was fully covered with thousands of victims. An unending stream of victims on stretchers arrived at the ground but they died one after another. It was truly the picture of hell.[66]

—Kunitani Oshie

Many nurses wrote about the horror of nuclear bomb syndrome and their fear of falling victim to radiation sickness as in the days following the blast they saw so many people who showed no external signs of injury developing high (42°C) fevers and exhibiting the symptoms of cerebral palsy. Subsequently, these people suffered from purplish subcutaneous hemorrhages, bleeding, and rapid decrease in the level of white blood cells, and then they died. In Yukinaga's case, in later life her white blood cell count remained lower than 3,000 and her weight less than 40 kg. She had to take medicine for the rest of her life.[67] Yukinaga described the pervasiveness of radiation diseases, both in her official working report and in later personal testimony:

> The cause of the real horror of the atomic bombing is not only seen in the moment of the blast but also in the fact that many victims continued to be plagued by disease. . . . We see many people, who were not injured at

FIGURE 6.3 Dead bodies laid out on the West Parade Grounds on August 8 (Takahashi Masaaki).

Takahashi Masaaki, "*Nishi Renpei-jō*, ID: NG208-05", August 8, 1945 (Collection of Hiroshima Peace Memorial Museum).

all, suddenly get sick and die, which sends shivers down our spines as we think we might soon suffer the same fate.[68]

These testimonies show that nurses' actions transcended the official mandate of humanitarian relief missions in the unprecedented horror of the atomic holocaust. In the face of total administrative chaos and in the absence of official orders, nurses who survived the blast instantly commenced humanitarian relief under the most horrific conditions and despite their own injuries. According to Dr. Shigetō Fumio, the JRCS medical staff did not slacken their efforts, even as they recognized the dangers to themselves of radiation sickness.[69] In an interview some years later, Dr. Shigetō confirmed that Japanese scientists already had knowledge of nuclear fission in 1945, and many Red Cross doctors knew that even a small amount of uranium the size of a matchbox could create a deadly

FIGURE 6.4 X-ray film exposed by radiation at the Hiroshima Red Cross Hospital (1945).

Theodore S. Needels, "Genbaku no Hōshasen ni yori Kuroku Kankō shita Ekkusu-sen Firumu, ID: 0103-0037," (Collection of Hiroshima Peace Memorial Museum).

explosive.[70] Moreover, unused X-ray film in the Hiroshima Red Cross Hospital that had not been stored in zinc cases appeared to have been exposed by the bomb's blinding flash, a chemical reaction which led the medical staff to infer the bomb was a nuclear weapon (figure 6.4).[71] Doctors believed that any state that had developed such deadly toxic weapons must have also developed a medical treatment program to counter their effects. They had hoped to receive medical support from the Supreme Commander for the Allied Powers (SCAP) immediately following Japan's surrender, but the first supplies weren't shipped out until September 8.[72]

THE ICRC MISSION IN THE AFTERMATH OF THE HIROSHIMA NUCLEAR BOMBING

The ICRC sent Marcel Junod (1904–1961) to Japan to succeed Fritz Paravicini, the head of the ICRC Tokyo Delegation, who died in Japan in 1944. By coincidence, Junod arrived at his post in Tokyo on August 9, 1945, the day of the Nagasaki nuclear bombing, and met with the JRCS president, Tokugawa Kuniyuki (1886–1969), in an air raid shelter at the JRCS headquarters.[73] Junod's original mission was to inspect Allied POW camps in Japan and later, following Japan's surrender, he would work to repatriate Japanese citizens and POWs left behind in Manchuria, Korea, and Siberia.[74] However, Junod's and the ICRC staff's mission immediately shifted to nuclear bomb relief. Between August 23 and September 15, Fritz Bilfinger, an ICRC officer sent to inspect detention camps in western Japan, was able to visit Hiroshima on August 29–30 and telegrammed the ICRC office in Tokyo on August 30, describing the condition of the city.[75] He informed them of the utter destruction of Hiroshima, describing it as "conditions beyond description," and also explained that an enormous number of people were suffering from acute leukemia and fatal visceral damage, many of whom had already died.[76] Soon after, Junod initiated negotiations with the Allied Occupation authorities, which resulted in the delivery of aid kits the following month.

On September 8, SCAP offered to send fifteen tons of medicine and medical kits, including penicillin, dried plasma, glucose, Ringers Lactate solution, sulphonamide, DDT, cresol, alcohol, nutritional supplements, tablets, bandages, and surgical appliances to Hiroshima.[77] Three tons of medicine, including penicillin, disappeared while in transit from Iwakuni. Ultimately, twelve tons of medical aid kits were distributed to forty-two hospitals, including the Red Cross and temporary aid stations in Hiroshima on September 8, 1945.[78]

AMERICAN POWs AND THE HIROSHIMA ATOMIC BOMBING

Hiroshima City did not have official POW camps, but several nuclear bomb survivors testified to seeing an American POW falling face down on the Aioi Bridge a few days after the bombing.[79] Two American soldiers, Captain Tomas C. Cartwright[80] and his copilot, Durden W. Looper, had been captured when their B-24, the *Lonesome Lady*, was shot down by Japanese fighter planes on July 28.[81] They were sent to the Chūgoku Military District Headquarters where they joined six previously captured

American airmen, including Sergeants Charles O. Baumgartner and Julius Molnar, whose B-24, the *Taloa*, had also been shot down on July 28 off the coast of Kure, a major Imperial Japanese Navy (IJN) base, in Hiroshima Prefecture. The headquarters were located underground, beneath Hiroshima Castle,[82] which was 700 meters away from the hypocenter.[83] During interrogation at the Hiroshima district headquarters, either Bumgartner or Molnar—the document simply states "an American POW"—reportedly cried out, "I am scared. I am scared." A Japanese military interrogator asked him what he was scared of, assuming perhaps he was frightened of being a POW. However, the soldier answered, "No! I am not scared of being a POW." Rather, "Hiroshima City will be attacked by an enormously powerful weapon very soon, which can annihilate this city. It means that if I am here, I will be killed!"[84]

On the day of bombing, Ōsako Ichirō,[85] a correspondent of the *Chūgoku Shimbun* newspaper, chanced upon an almost naked American POW lying prostrate at the site of the detention; everything in the vicinity had been completely destroyed. The white American soldier was lying face down at the front of the entrance to the headquarters. He was wearing only underpants, and his wrists were tied behind his back by a wire. Ōsako approached the soldier and asked him in English, "Hello. Are you a Yankee? Where are you from?" Nearing death, he opened his eyes slightly, but he did not say anything.[86] Today, the Hiroshima Prefectural History Record estimates that eleven American POWs had been detained at the Chūgoku Military District Headquarters on the day of the nuclear bombing,[87] while Hiroshima local historian Mori Shigeaki concluded that twelve POWs were killed.[88]

A quarter century later, former American airman T. C. Cartwright wrote of his experiences as a POW at the time of the Hiroshima bombing in his memoir *A Date with the Lonesome Lady: A Hiroshima POW Returns*, in which he expressed feelings of guilt at having survived the war while many fellow airmen were killed by the bombing. It happened by chance. His life was spared because, just prior to the bombing, he was moved from Hiroshima to Tokyo for further interrogation.[89] In later years, interviewed by the *Asahi Shimbun*, a Japanese newspaper, he expressed empathy for all victims of the Hiroshima atomic bomb: "The pain of the people of Hiroshima is my pain."[90]

THE JRCS RESPONSE TO THE NUCLEAR BOMBING OF NAGASAKI

It is generally believed that at the time the first nuclear bomb was dropped on Hiroshima, Nagasaki City was in a totally defenseless state. However, after the attack on Hiroshima, Japanese authorities made a number of attempts to predict which city would be the next to be targeted. As seen above, American POWs were a source of military intelligence, and Kokura, Niigata, Kyoto, and Nagasaki were assumed to be the most likely targets.[91] It appears that Nagano Wakamatsu, the director general of the JRCS Nagasaki Chapter and the governor of Nagasaki Prefecture, attempted a mass evacuation of the city.[92] Multiple survivors of the bombing recalled hearing an emergency radio broadcast on the day of the attack warning, "Attention to all Nagasaki citizens: Evacuate immediately!"[93] Before becoming governor, Nagano had worked at the Home Ministry and served in various posts, including chief of the Special Higher Police (*Tokkō*) and head of the General Affairs Bureau in the Air Defense Headquarters.[94]

According to Nagano's testimony, on the evening on August 8, the day before his city was bombed, Okazaki Takejirō, a member of the Nagasaki prefectural assembly and president of the *Nagasaki Min'yū Shimbun* newspaper, rushed into his office to report on the shocking aftermath of the bombing of Hiroshima, which he witnessed on his return from Tokyo. After conversing with Okazaki, Nagano held urgent discussions with the director general of the Nagasaki police.[95] He concluded that Nagasaki City was the next target, reasoning that it had not been damaged by previous air raids, just as Hiroshima had escaped attack prior to the nuclear bombing.[96] He upgraded Nagasaki City's status to "state of extreme emergency" and considered ordering the immediate evacuation of the city's 300,000 citizens. Aware the IJA might oppose evacuation as a form of "defeatism," the next morning Nagano convened an emergency meeting with local authorities, including the army and journalists, to prepare to issue an emergency evacuation advisory.[97] However, the atomic bomb was dropped on Nagasaki City at 11:02 A.M., right at the start of the meeting. Nagano described the extraordinary moment as follows:

> When I said "Okay, everyone . . ." to start the emergency meeting, Mr. Koura, Mayor of Sasebo City, entered the room, . . . and said to me, "The

events in Hiroshima are hellish." . . . I said, "Yes, that is why we are having this meeting now . . ." . . . Just then, suddenly, all the lights in the shelter went out.[98] The interior of the bomb shelter was exposed to a very bright flash, and I heard an extreme thundering noise. I think that was the moment the bomb exploded. . . . The sound of the blast and the shock wave took a few seconds to reach our shelter.[99] I went out of the shelter and saw the Urakami district (behind Mt. Kompira) was fully covered by enormous black smoke. I did not see fire, but the great quantity of smoke told me that a tremendous fire was burning there. I also saw smoke, like a cloud, rising up and reaching the sky.[100]

According to this and other statements, Nagano concluded that the bright flash followed by a roaring sound and great fire indicated the bomb was of the same general type as used in Hiroshima.[101] He also speculated that the United States still held several nuclear weapons and was ready to attack other Japanese cities. Nagano immediately sent the first of eight telegrams to the Home Ministry reporting on the urgent state of affairs in Nagasaki. The Home Ministry passed this information to the Supreme War Council, which had convened to discuss possible surrender.[102]

Due to Nagano's decision to convene the emergency meeting at the air raid shelter, which was shielded from the immediate blast by Mt. Kompira, the leadership structure of the city remained intact, as did the shelter's telecommunications. Unlike Hiroshima, Nagasaki City maintained its administration and communication system purely by chance, which put Nagasaki in the relatively advantageous position of being able to organize rescue operations despite unimaginable destruction. The Tateyama air raid shelter became the general headquarters of humanitarian relief activities after the crisis meeting, with Nagano himself commanding aid operations.

On the day following the bombing, Nagano drafted an emergency telegram to the JRCS headquarters calling for an on-site inspection of Nagasaki by the ICRC. He advised JRCS headquarters that the nuclear bombing appeared to be a clear violation of the Geneva Conventions and urged the ICRC to investigate conditions in Nagasaki, as at this time the city was facing an intense humanitarian crisis unaided. He wrote:[103]

> The atomic bomb that was used on Nagasaki City on the 9th of August caused immense damage. Most victims were noncombatants. Furthermore, some victims, who do not have severe injuries,

have started to vomit bile and suffer terrible bouts of diarrhea with each passing hour. The fatality rate is extremely high. From this, we can acknowledge that the damage caused by this bombing was much greater than that caused by poison gas. Therefore, I strongly urge you to open negotiations with the ICRC in order to conduct an urgent on-site inspection as soon as possible.

> For the Attention of: President, Japanese Red Cross Society
> From: Nagano Wakamatsu, Director General
> Japanese Red Cross Society Nagasaki Chapter

In judging the ICRC's response to the atomic bombing of Japan, it is important to observe that in his initial communication, by characterizing the effects of radiation as "much greater than that caused by poison gas," Nagano challenged ICRC headquarters to acknowledge the atomic bomb as a new and terrible violation of the International Law of War. Nagano did not ask for humanitarian assistance but rather justice.[104] In his request for an impromptu on-site inspection by the ICRC, he called upon it to fulfill its responsibilities to the international community in its role as the defender of its founding principles. There is no record of how ICRC headquarters responded to Nagano's appeal or even whether information that reached the ICRC in Geneva prompted discussion of the legality of the atomic bomb. The ICRC neither conducted an investigation nor appealed to SCAP to send humanitarian aid to Nagasaki. Hugh V. Clarke, an Australian POW, wrote in his memoir that a Swedish Red Cross worker visited the POW camp in Nagasaki after the bombing.[105] At this time SCAP was doing everything possible to suppress information on the nuclear bombing of Hiroshima and Nagasaki, and it is not known whether the ICRC even asked SCAP to investigate.[106]

HUMANITARIAN RELIEF ACTIVITIES FOLLOWING THE NAGASAKI NUCLEAR BOMBING

Some accounts of the Nagasaki bombing assume that most medical workers did not survive, since Nagasaki Medical College, which was clearly marked with the Red Cross insignia, was located 700 meters from ground zero and was obliterated. It is estimated that most medical workers—around 890 staff, students, and patients—were killed, which included survivors who died of acute radiation syndrome within two weeks of the attack.[107] This indicates that the power of the plutonium used in the Nagasaki nuclear bombing was greater than the uranium-type bomb deployed at Hiroshima. It is instructive that the U.S. Strategic Bombing Survey[108] misrepresented basic facts relating to the JRCS Nagasaki Chapter, claiming that it did not manage hospitals or aid stations in Nagasaki Prefecture before the bombing and hence were able to do little in terms of nuclear bomb relief operations. The report even stated the JRCS was not well organized in Japan at that time, in contrast to the American Red Cross (ARC), which is why the JRCS did not provide aid to the *hibakusha* nuclear victims.[109]

The reality was entirely different. The JRCS Nagasaki Chapter Clinic, which was located in the suburbs of the city, carried out emergency treatment in the immediate aftermath of the nuclear explosion.[110] Furthermore, Nagano, who was in command of relief operations, activated his network of JRCS contacts and was able to mount extensive relief efforts just a few hours after the bombing. Some relief teams approached ground zero to carry out first aid for survivors the very day of the bombing[111] and established emergency aid stations and makeshift hospitals at a number of places, such as Shinkōzen Primary School.[112] During the war, the JRCS dispatched Red Cross doctors and nurses to several hospitals in Nagasaki Prefecture.[113] Those who worked at the Sasebo Naval Hospital and the Isahaya Branch Naval Hospital—today known as the Red Cross Isahaya Atomic Bomb Hospital—which stood twenty-five kilometers from ground zero, carried out intensive medical relief operations.[114] The JRCS also sent staff to several major hospitals in Nagasaki Prefecture, such as the Ōmura Naval Hospital,[115] about twenty kilometers from Nagasaki City, to treat victims.

By midnight on the evening of the bombing, the Japanese National Railway had restored rail service in the nuclear bomb zone and ran four trains, which people called relief trains. One train passed close to ground zero just three hours after the bomb exploded; the area was still in full blaze.[116] The speedy repair of infrastructure allowed the JRCS to deliver medical aid kits to the hypocenter. According to a manuscript prepared by the JRCS Nagasaki Chapter, the JRCS treated approximately 2,500 victims within days of the bombing. Sixty-five medical staff on August 14 and 107 workers on August 15 joined these emergency relief activities, and they administered aid to a further 172 victims by August 15. By August 16, the total number of aid workers reached 199.¹¹⁷ Almost all JRCS chapters in Southern and Western Japan sent relief teams and staff to Nagasaki during the initial phase of aid operations.¹¹⁸ The level of radiation remained high, as plutonium is much more toxic than uranium. Medical records of the Ōmura Naval Hospital state that the case-fatality rate of nuclear bomb diseases was 100 percent as of September 10, 1945.¹¹⁹ However, JRCS workers persisted with their mission, and many would lose their lives days, months, or years later due to radiation illness. (See figure 6.5.)

TESTIMONIES OF JRCS NURSES AND ALLIED POWs DURING THE AFTERMATH OF THE NAGASAKI NUCLEAR BOMBING

A number of JRCS records contain testimonies from JRCS relief nurses who entered the nuclear bomb zone just a few hours after the bombing. Many of them even left their wounded or dead families to respond to the official JRCS call for humanitarian services. These workers testified to the grim reality of the relief operation. Staff were distressed at the sight of a stream of trucks heaped with dead bodies as though they were disposing of rubbish. They carried out autopsies by candlelight, seeing the eyeball of a dead person shining in the darkness; they saw victims whose faces were burned so severely that it was impossible to distinguish between the front and the back of their heads, and treated mouths and ear canals full of maggots. Some nursing students lost consciousness when they witnessed such dreadful scenes. Other nurses saw victims become deranged; the dead included suicide victims. While they continued to carry out their humanitarian activities at emergency aid stations, tens of thousands of dead bodies were cremated nearby.¹²⁰ Photographs of the initial nuclear bomb emergency aid operations captured nurses wearing the navy blue JRCS dress uniform with long sleeves, indicating that they did not even have time to change into white nursing gowns. The passages from the nurses' memoirs vividly convey the horror they encountered:

> A Korean male victim was constantly screaming in the Korean language, "*Aigō! Aigō!*" begging for medical aid. He grasped our legs and the hems of our clothes when we passed by.¹²¹
>
> —Onishima Eiko

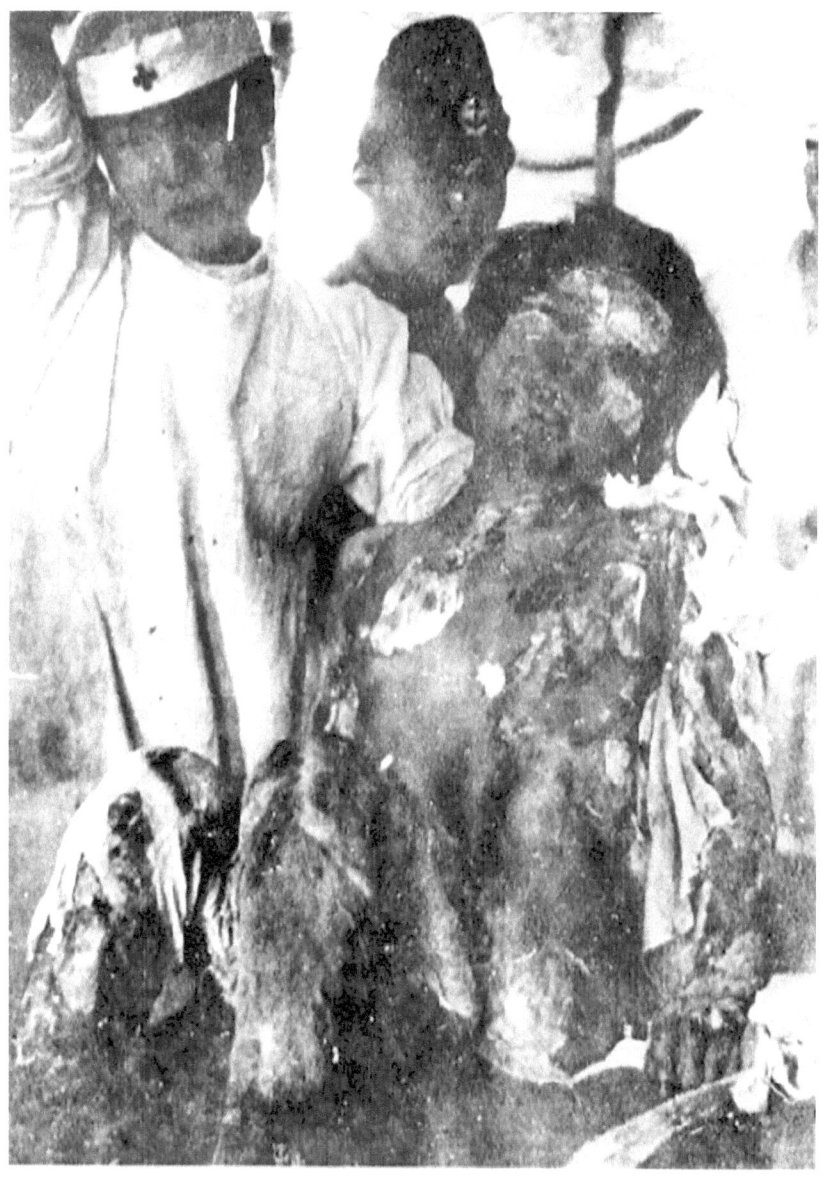

FIGURE 6.5 Red Cross nurse in Nagasaki with severly burned school girl A-bomb victim, August 10, 1945 (Shiotsuki 1945).

Shiotsuki, Masao, *Ōmura Kaigun Byōin*, ID: 6-06-01-01-0013. Nagasaki Atomic Bomb Museum, 1945.

The massive iron pole of the Mitsubishi Shipyard was ominously arched like a big wave. A foreign soldier (POW) was giving first aid to survivors using a stretcher.[122]

—Matsumoto Retsuko

Due to the terrible stink . . . I could not eat for several days. Some victims, whose conditions were relatively fine until yesterday, suddenly died (due to acute radiation syndrome). Every day I repeatedly sent off bodies of the dead transported by hand-drawn carts with a small wooden box to a place for cremation.[123]

—Hirano Mitsuko

I saw a baby screaming and suckling his or her dead mother's breast. The mother, whose eyes were closed, was still embracing her screaming baby in her arms. I didn't know which was worse—to die or to be alive at this moment.[124]

—Yamashita Fujie

We panicked because a woman, who was burned over her whole body, started to have birth pains. . . . Soldiers helped us to boil water and called out, "the hot water is ready!" When I heard the first birth cry, I was deeply moved. It was a truly fantastic thing to bring forth a new living being under such dreadful conditions. . . . I will never forget it as the only inspiring moment while I served.[125]

—Tagawa Sumiko

According to an official Nagasaki City record, the bomb targeted the industrial zone and detonated some 500 or 600 meters above the Urakami district. The district was widely known to be one of East Asia's major Roman Catholic holy places. In other words, Nagasaki City, which had been exposed to Western civilization for centuries, became ground zero. At the time there were around 20,000 Catholics in the city,[126] including Catholic missionaries from Europe and North America.[127] In addition, many Japanese colonial subjects and non-Japanese nationals were exposed to the bombing. The official record of Nagasaki City estimates that 12,000 to 13,000 Koreans and 650 Chinese were exposed to the blast, and that many of the 700 Allied POWs detained in Nagasaki were killed, injured, or subsequently suffered from radiation sickness. Approximately fifty Catholic missionaries—Americans, Canadians, French, and Polish—were exposed to radiation; it is not known how many survived. Eighteen Taiwanese perished.[128] Some Catholic missionaries based in Nagasaki—including Zenon Żebrowski (1891–1982)—who had been detained in neighboring prefectures, including Ōita and Kumamoto, survived and returned to Nagasaki a week after the bombing to aid children orphaned in the attack.[129] Today, the official record of the Nagasaki City Atomic Bomb Records Preservation Committee states, "73,884 people were killed and 74,909 injured, and 17,358 of the deaths were confirmed by post-mortem examination soon after the bombing."[130]

Nagasaki City had two large Allied POW camps. (See figure 6.6.) One was the Nagasaki Mitsubishi Dockyard Branch Camp: Fukuoka 14-B, which was located 1.7 kilometers away from ground zero;[131] the other was the Fukuoka 2-B in Kōyagi-jima, today known as Kōyagi-chō, which

FIGURE 6.6 Allied POWs at Fukuoka 2-B Camp in Nagasaki, December 25, 1943 (Matsuda 1943).

Matsuda Hiromichi, "Fukuoka furyo shūyōjo daini-bunsho no horyo tachi, 1943 (Allied POWs at Fukuoka 2-B Camp in Nagasaki), ID: Matsuda Hiromichi File No. 9," the Research Committee for Photographic Records of Nagasaki Atomic Bombing, Nagasaki Foundation for the Promotion of Peace.

was ten kilometers away from the hypocenter.¹³² According to IJA camp guard Tajima Jidayū, the Red Cross insignia was clearly visible on the concrete roof of the Mitsubishi Dockyard POW camp on the day of the bombing.¹³³

At least one Allied POW held in Nagasaki witnessed the atomic bomb before detonation while it was still in the air. Australian POW Sergeant Jack Johnson later testified,

> I saw what seemed to be three white parachutes in triangular formation at an elevation of about sixty degrees. Suddenly, there was a brilliant flash like a photographer's magnesium flash. Instinctively I dropped to the ground beside a kerbing at the side of the alleyway. Then came the blast with a deafening bang and I felt as though I had been kicked in the guts.¹³⁴

Many Allied POWs were killed or injured in the Nagasaki bombing. Australian POW Sergeant Peter McGrath-Kerr reported he was "knocked unconscious for five days, suffered from amnesia, and sustained five broken ribs and various cuts and bruises on my hands and legs."¹³⁵ There is some uncertainty as to the number of Allied POW fatalities. The Nagasaki City official history estimates that at least 200 POWs at Fukuoka B-14 were in the blast area, including 160 Dutch and Indonesians, sixteen British, and twenty-four Australian detainees.¹³⁶ Dutch POW C. Valcke testified, "We pulled out a number of dead bodies of our mates from under the debris. All of us were injured."¹³⁷ Australian POW Bombardier Hugh V. Clarke's reaction may have been typical: "I could not imagine what evil holocaust could have wrought such a catastrophe."¹³⁸ Like a number of the survivors, Dutch POW R. Solti testified that the common fate of POWs and Japanese civilians as victims of the atomic bomb aroused in them the humanitarian impulse to go to the aid of Japanese survivors.

> I became more conscious of my good health, and started to think about the victims from the bottom of my heart. I realized that I must help them. All of my hostile feelings against the Japanese people were completely banished. I perceived that me and the people of Nagasaki were in the same boat (under the nuclear bombing). We (POWs) carried victims who could not walk to the top of a hill on stretchers.¹³⁹

In addition to the number of deaths, POWs experienced psychological and physical aftereffects. British POW Staff Sergeant Ronald E. Bryer, who recalled cremating around twenty bodies each day, later wrote in a letter to Tajima, a former camp guard:

> The hillsides and the fields teemed with people fleeing the holocaust. Soldiers, prisoners and Japanese convicts. Everybody helping everyone else to stay alive, with nationality and status forgotten. Just human beings, all of us, struggling to survive.[140]

Once back in England, Bryer was shocked to discover how poorly informed his countrymen were of the Nagasaki nuclear bombing: "I felt no one really believed what I had to say."[141] There was a universality to the atomic bomb's victimization regardless of nationality that ushered in the grim new reality of the potential annihilation of the human species. Although Nagasaki City did not receive the ICRC's official international humanitarian aid in the wake of the crisis, its situation, compared to that of Hiroshima, at least was ameliorated by the quick implementation of well-organized humanitarian relief, the immediate restoration of infrastructure initiated by Nagano, and the vigorous aid operations of JRCS workers and citizens.

The individual heroism exhibited by JRCS medical personnel in responding to the horrors of the Hiroshima and Nagasaki nuclear bombings reveals a humanitarian ethos that went well beyond the JRCS's institutional role of delivering medical aid and relief in the service of the wartime state. The "humanitarian professionalism" of the JRCS ethos became fused with a desire for peace and rejection of the violence of war. The great peril and horror JRCS workers encountered at Hiroshima and Nagasaki became a transformative experience for JRCS aid workers as professionals dedicated to following at whatever personal cost "the way of humanity" (*jindō*). Their field experience demonstrated the extent to which Red Cross workers had internalized their professional mission as medical aid-givers, and eventually emerged as exemplars of the humanitarian relief ideal. Ultimately, it transformed them from mere medical aid personnel to exemplars of humanitarianism (*jindō*).

CONCLUSION

Kamo no Chōmei (1155–1216), a poet and essayist in medieval Kyoto, began his short essay, *Hōjōki*, as follows:

> The flow of the river never ceases,
> And the water never stays the same.
> Bubbles float on the surface of pools,
> Bursting, re-forming, never lingering.
> They're like the people in this world and their dwellings.[1]

In the late twelfth and early thirteenth centuries, catastrophic wars, earthquakes, tsunamis, violent storms, conflagrations, famine, and epidemic diseases, among other disasters, devastated Japan's premodern capital, Kyoto. In a tumultuous age, people witnessed unending tragedy, were consumed by anguish, and fell into deep despair. Kamo no Chōmei responded by bearing witness to human misery and came to terms with the eschatological aspects of human existence through meditation on the Buddhist concept of impermanence (*mujō*).[2]

Kamo no Chōmei's essay reminds us that human suffering is timeless and universal and that human lives are ephemeral. Yet even as he bore witness to the hell of the contemporary world, he recorded acts of kindness and self-sacrifice by ordinary people that enabled community survival in an age of great turmoil. Kamo no Chōmei asked the reader, "Where to find peace?," "What is the meaning of life?," and "How do we find meaning in our lives?" The *Hōjōki* stands as one of the great meditations on the human condition; over the ages and continuing into the modern period, at times of great danger and uncertainty, Japanese have found solace in its pages. During the Pacific War, Japanese soldiers read *Hōjōki* on the battlefield; as did Japanese civilians in Manchuria at the end of the war as they fled the Soviet invasion; as did, more recently, the Japanese who lost loved ones and were driven from their homes by the Tohoku 2011 triple disaster of earthquake, tsunami, and nuclear reactor meltdown.

As narrated in chapter 1, a melding of new and traditional humanitarian discourses fueled the dynamic development of the JRCS from its founding to World War II: both the idealism of universal compassion for war victims embodied in Henry Dunant's ICRC creed and traditional notions of *ōyake* (public duty),[3] and *jindō* (the way of humanity) inspired participation. People from all social strata joined the Japanese Red Cross Society; on the eve of World War I, the JRCS could boast of having the largest membership among the national societies of the international Red Cross and Red Crescent movement. Moreover, in contrast to the American Red Cross (ARC) and Europe's national Red Cross societies, membership did not decline when the carnage of the "war to end all wars" ground to a halt.[4] As seen in chapter 1, non-war-related JRCS missions sustained participation as local elites and community members embraced the Red Cross movement as a vehicle of mutual aid in coping with natural disasters and public health crises, most notably in response to the twin crises of the 1918 Spanish flu pandemic and the 1923 Great Kantō Earthquake.

Like all of the other international Red Cross and Red Crescent national societies at this time, the JRCS was a semigovernmental organization. No national Red Cross or Red Crescent society saw itself, or was seen by its government, as a nongovernmental organization in the contemporary meaning of that term, as exemplified by Doctors Without Borders/Médecins Sans Frontières and Amnesty International that are committed to the principle of absolute political independence and neutrality in world affairs. The characterization of the JRCS as a creature of the imperial family and the Meiji oligarchs and a statist outlier within the Red Cross movement commonly found in the English-language literature is premised on a false dichotomy between the JRCS and Western national Red Cross societies. As observed in the introduction, when the United States acquired an overseas empire in 1898, the ARC, according to U.S. historian Charles Hurd, transformed into a "quasi-official organization" operating under U.S. congressional charter.[5] The 1900 ARC charter, in the words of historian Julia Irwin, "created a unique private-public partnership." Revised in 1905 when Secretary of War William Howard Taft assumed the presidency, the new charter "gave the US Government far more authority over the ARC."[6] It is true that government officials occupied the top leadership positions in the JRCS and the society benefited greatly from the patronage of the imperial family. However, these organizational features were consistent with what historian John F. Hutchinson identifies as the international Red Cross and Red Crescent movement's essential "political economy."[7] For example, following the reorganization of the British Red Cross (BRC) after the Boer War (1899–1902), Queen Alexandra (1844–1925) became BRC president in 1905, and from 1908, it operated under royal charter. Belgium's queen, Elizabeth of Bavaria (1876–1965), served as honorary president of the Belgium Red Cross, and Maria Alexandrovna (1824–1880), empress of Russia, was instrumental in the foundation of the Russian Red Cross. In the United States, prominent political figures and captains of industry occpuied the highest offices.

On the international level, the JRCS was held in high regard within the international Red Cross and Red Crescent movement for its promotion of peacetime public health and disaster relief, sponsorship of the international Junior Red Cross movement, and role in founding the LORCS. As seen in chapter 2, during the period of Taishō democracy the JRCS leadership gained a measure of institutional autonomy evident in Ninagawa's criticism of Japan's withdrawal from the League of Nations; the JRCS's cooperation with the Red Cross Society of China (RCSC) in investigating alleged Imperial Japanese Army (IJA) war crimes during the First Shanghai Incident (1932); and the passage of the Tokyo Declaration at the Tokyo International Red Cross Conference of 1934.

The establishment and subsequent growth of the Red Cross movment in Japan after the Meiji Restoration is best understood as a revival of traditional Japanese humanitarianism in the mode of modern patriotic humanitarianism. It should not be surprising that after the great powers of the West imposed extraterritoriality and deprived Japan of tariff autonomy in the mid-nineteenth century, infringements on sovereignty that only ended after Japan demonstrated its modern military might in the First

Sino-Japanese War, nationalism contributed to the growth of the JRCS's membership. Moreover, scholars now recognize that historically nationalism and internationalism have not operated as oppositional forces. As modern Europe historian Patricia Clavin observes of internationalism in the interwar period, "in practice the history of internationalism was as much about recognizing and strengthening the power of the state as it was about challenging it to behave in new ways."[8] Japan historians Dick Stegewerns and Jessamyn R. Abel have pointed to a similar interplay of nationalism and internationalism in Japan before World War II.[9] There is nothing aberrant in the fact that many Japanese viewed participation in the Japanese Red Cross movement as a way of elevating Japan's prestige in the international community.

The middle chapters of the book explored the transnational phase of the JRCS when the society established special overseas departments both in Japan's continental empire and in cities in the Asia-Pacific region and North and South America that hosted large Japanese immigrant communities. In following the flag of Japanese imperialism, the JRCS emulated Western Red Cross societies: the BRC in the British Empire, the Dutch Red Cross in Indonesia, and the ARC in the Philippines, where the ARC opened its Manilia office in 1905, hard on the heels of the U.S. subjugation of the First Philippine Republic.[10] During the three decades beginning with the suppression of the Boxer Rebellion and ending after the Manchuria Incident, a period when Japanese, American, and British imperial interests in Asia were for the most part complementary, the JRCS, ARC, and BRC assisted one another and launched joint efforts, as during the Allied Siberian Intervention, 1918–1922.[11] Although systematic comparison of the ARC's and JRCS's support of their countries' respective overseas empires warrants book-length study, the most striking organizational divergence may have been in gender, not geopolitics: American women were active at every level of the ARC while, with the exception of nursing, men occupied all the leadership positions in the JRCS.

Even in the context of World War II when millions upon millions of soldiers and civilians died, the nuclear bombing of Hiroshima and Nagasaki created unprecented humanitarian crises. Atomic radiation poisoned all living creatures and the environment: insects, animals, flora, and even the soil itself. It was a hell that defied description. Nevertheless, the JRCS's professional staff in Hiroshima and Nagasaki instinctively strove to carry out their humanitarian mission on the ground. In addition to being subjected to extraordinary physical demands, they bore the psychological burden of knowing that for many atomic bomb victims, the most they could do was to help people die peacefully. Their heroic actions showed how, even when institutionally subordinate to the wartime state, the JRCS's professional staff faithfully carried out the society's humanitarian mission. The humanitarian actions of individual relief workers under conditions of extreme privation and personal risk restored a measure of human dignity under the most gruesome circumstances. Their responses made these medical aid providers exemplars of humanitarianism.

APPENDIX 1

RESOLUTIONS OF THE XVTH
INTERNATIONAL RED CROSS CONFERENCE

Resolutions
of the XVth International Red Cross Conference

I. Approval of I. R. C. C. Report.

The Fifteenth International Red Cross Conference,
Having taken cognizance of the general report of the International Red Cross Committee,
Notes with satisfaction the care with which the Committee has carried out the mandates entrusted to it,
Gives general approval to the initiatives taken by the Committee,
And confirms the mandates given to the Committee by the previous Conferences.

II. Competition for Medical Personnel.

The Fifteenth International Red Cross Conference,
Considering the difficulty of arranging for an International Competition for Medical and Auxiliary Personnel,
And considering the extraordinary expenses which have had to be borne by the International Red Cross Committee during the last financial year,
Assigns to the International Committee, without reserve, the capital sum together with interest to date, which was allocated to the International Red Cross Committee in 1927 from the Empress Shōken Fund for the organization of a Competition for Medical and Auxiliary Personnel.

III. I. R. C. C. Foundation.

The Fifteenth International Red Cross Conference,
In view of the report submitted to it by the Council of the International Red Cross Committee Foundation,
Gives full approval to the constitution of this Foundation, which was formed on May 1st, 1931,
And invites the Governments which are parties to the Geneva Convention to follow the example of the Swiss Confederation and to grant to the Foundation subventions sufficient to bring the total fund up to the figure of three million Swiss francs.

IV. Nominations to Council of Foundation.

The Fifteenth International Red Cross Conference,
Confirms up to the time of the meeting of the Sixteenth International Red Cross Conference the Standing Commission's nominations of the Marquis de Casa Valdés and Mr. Goldschmidt to represent the national Red Cross Societies on the Council of the International Red Cross Committee Foundation.

V. Approval of League's Report.

The Fifteenth International Red Cross Conference,
Noting with satisfaction that the League of Red Cross Societies has continued to follow a policy conducive to the continued development of Red Cross work nationally and internationally, and has thereby contributed to make the work which the Red Cross does for the alleviation of human suffering an asset of ever-growing importance to humanity,
And considering the great moral value, in such critical times as those through which the world is now passing, of regular contact and co-operation between the leaders of the Red Cross movement in all countries,
Approves the general report of the League,
Expresses to the Board of Governors of the League its earnest thanks, and expresses the hope that the League will continue, as in the past, to be a source of constant inspiration and stimulus to its Member Societies.

VI. Extension of Junior Red Cross

The Fifteenth International Red Cross Conference,
Expressing its satisfaction with the development of the Junior Red Cross, which is playing an increasingly important part in the physical and moral training of boys and girls and constitutes a valuable pledge for the future of the Red Cross movement throughout the world,
Considering that the creation of a Junior Section in each national Red Cross Society is the first step which should be taken in establishing the Junior Red Cross and that each such Section should aim at enrolling all primary and secondary school pupils in the country,
Considering also that most national Societies now have Junior Sections, and that they have been able to judge of the value of the activities of these Sections for the Red Cross as a whole.
Recommends that the national Societies support and extend the activities of their Junior Sections by all the means at their disposal, and that Societies which have not already done so, organize Junior Sections without delay, in conformity with the directions given in the XIVth Circular of the International Red Cross Committee and the League of Red Cross Societies, basing themselves upon the experience of other Societies and upon the advice of the League Secretariat.

VII. Propaganda.

The Fifteenth International Red Cross Conference,
Urges that the Secretariat of the League of Red Cross Societies should continue to compile and issue propaganda material of every practical kind and recommend it to all Red Cross Societies, with due consideration to local conditions in each country.

VIII. Junior Red Cross and Health.

The Fifteenth International Red Cross Conference,
Recognizing that Junior Red Cross members, inspired by the ideals of the Red Cross, are learning to regard the cultivation of good health as a form of practical good citizenship by which they are enabled to render service to their country and to others throughout the world,
Recommends that the national Red Cross Societies endeavour to preserve and further the moral or spiritual basis of these activities, so that the Junior Red Cross may continue to render its unique service to the health of the world.

IX. Red Cross Book for Children.

The Fifteenth International Red Cross Conference,
In consideration of the proposal made by the Swedish Delegation at the Tenth International Conference,
And taking into account the preliminary studies already carried out by the International Red Cross Committee and the League of Red Cross Societies, with a view to the preparation of a booklet designed to acquaint boys and girls with the Geneva Convention and with the nature and activities of the Red Cross,
Requests the International Committee and the League of Red Cross Societies to prepare a booklet suited to children between the ages of ten and fourteen years, explaining the principles upon which the Geneva Convention is founded, and also describing essential facts about the Red Cross movement, its history and its accomplishments,
And further requests the International Committee and the League of Red Cross Societies to provide the national Red Cross Societies with such material as will eventually enable them to supply the educational authorities in their respective countries with a chapter on the Red Cross designed for insertion in school text-books;

X. International Understanding through J. R. C.

The Fifteenth International Red Cross Conference,
Realizing the value of the contribution made by the Junior Sections of national Red Cross Societies to the realization of the ideas expressed in the XXVth

---

APPENDIX 1 IFRC Archives. "League of Red Cross Societies Monthly Bulletin Vol. XV, No. 12, December 1934."

Resolution of the Fourteenth International Red Cross Conference, relating to the Red Cross as a factor in promoting international friendship,

Noting with appreciation the resolution voted by the LIAISON COMMITTEE OF MAJOR INTERNATIONAL ORGANIZATIONS giving credit to the Junior Red Cross which, through the cordial and co-operative relations which it establishes between the boys and girls in different countries, serves the cause of better international understanding,

Urges the national Societies to encourage their Junior Sections to extend their activities in this field, in the same spirit of racial, political and religious neutrality.

XI. Red Cross Work for Ex-Juniors.

The Fifteenth International Red Cross Conference,

Considering that, in the highest interest of the Red Cross it is important that boys and girls leaving Junior groups should not be lost to the Red Cross movement, but should continue to give active co-operation in Red Cross work,

And considering the resolution on this subject already adopted by the Board of Governors of the League of Red Cross Societies at its Thirteenth Meeting in 1932,

Noting in particular the encouraging experiences of certain national Red Cross Societies since that date in organizing former Juniors (in auxiliary councils and other volunteer groups) in University, business, industry and other walks of life, for the purpose of acting as counsellors of Junior Red Cross groups, as active Red Cross workers or as promoters of Junior Red Cross membership in schools not yet enrolled,

Recommends that national Red Cross Societies continue such experiments, striving to impress upon the minds of former Juniors that they are not only welcomed but needed by the Red Cross to help in meeting the increasingly grave problems which confront it in the modern world,

And further expresses the conviction that, if invited to do so on leaving school, former leaders of Junior Red Cross groups will show initiative in helping their national Societies to find a programme of activities calculated to hold their interest.

XII. Juniors at Conferences.

The Fifteenth International Red Cross Conference,

Noting with interest the excellent results obtained from the participation of Junior delegates in the Annual Convention of the American Red Cross,

Expresses the hope that this proceeding, the success of which has been more marked every year, may be adopted by other Societies, and may be extended to the international field on the occasion of future regional and International Red Cross Conferences.

XIII. Nightingale Medal.

The Fifteenth International Red Cross Conference approves the following rules regarding the award of the Florence Nightingale Medal.

QUALIFICATIONS

1. The Florence Nightingale Medal may be awarded:

(a) To fully trained certificated nurses who have distinguished themselves in an exceptional manner by great devotion to sick or injured patients in time of war or of peace;

(b) To fully trained certificated matrons and to fully trained nurse organizers who have rendered exceptional service to the sick or injured in the direction or organization of institutions;

(c) To voluntary aids, properly enrolled in Red Cross service, who have distinguished themselves in an exceptional manner by great devotion to the sick or injured in time of war or public disaster;

(d) To nurses and voluntary aids in any of the above categories who have fallen on the Field of Honour.

DISTRIBUTION AND AWARD OF MEDALS

2. Medals will be distributed every two years.

3. Not more than thirty-six Medals may be distributed on each occasion. No minimum is laid down.

4. The privilege of presenting names is reserved exclusively to the Central Committees of national Red Cross Societies. No obligation rests, however, upon any Central Committee to present a name or names for each distribution of Medals.

5. The names proposed must be sent in so as to reach the International Red Cross Committee before March 1st of the year in which a distribution is made, so that the list may be published in time for May 12th, the birthday of Florence Nightingale.

6. The Medals are awarded by the International Red Cross Committee at its discretion.

7. The International Red Cross Committee will communicate its decisions by circular to the Central Committees of the national Societies in time for announcement by May 12th, and will forward to them as soon as possible the Medals and Diplomas to be presented to the recipients.

8. The recipients will be given their Medals in each country either by the Head of the State or by the President of the Central Committee of the national Red Cross Society, directly or indirectly. This ceremony will be carried out with the solemnity appropriate to the importance of the distinction.

FINAL CLAUSE

9. The statutes of the Florence Nightingale Medal Fund voted in Washington in 1912 remain valid, with the modifications resolved upon by subsequent Conferences.

The rules hitherto in force also remain valid except in so far as they are invalidated by the present rules.

XIV. Wearing of Nightingale Medal.

The Fifteenth International Red Cross Conference,

In order to emphasize the value and high standing of the Florence Nightingale Medal,

Invites national Red Cross Societies to study, in collaboration with their respective Governments, proposals for rules regarding the wearing of this Medal by those to whom it is awarded, for the purpose of stressing its outstanding value.

XV. Nurses in Disaster Relief.

The Fifteenth International Red Cross Conference,

In view of the report submitted by the League of Red Cross Societies on the rôle of nurses and voluntary aids in times of calamity,

Considering the importance of that rôle,

Recommends to the national Red Cross Societies

(1) To provide for the collaboration of competent, fully trained, certificated nurses in all permanent relief organizations dealing with the victims of disaster,

(2) To establish and keep up to date a roll of all the available nursing personnel in each country,

(3) To organize an efficient working plan for the recruiting and rapid mobilization of nurses and voluntary aids.

XVI. Training of Nurses.

The Fifteenth International Red Cross Conference,

Having studied the report submitted to it by the International Red Cross Committee,

Approves fully the conclusions of the said report concerning the training of nurses and voluntary aids for emergency service in times of war or disaster,

And expresses the hope that a conference of qualified experts may be held as soon as possible to study the principles of disaster relief nursing services.

XVII. Activities of Voluntary Aids.

The Fifteenth International Red Cross Conference, In order to derive fuller benefit from the co-operation of trained nurses and voluntary aids, Asks the League of Red Cross Societies and the International Red Cross Committee to make a further study of the practical activities of voluntary aids in normal times, from the point of view of all Red Cross workers.

XVIII. Utility of Voluntary Aids.

The Fifteenth International Red Cross Conference, Stressing the importance of the work done by voluntary aids in the past,
Urges those Red Cross Societies which have not as yet included them in their organization to consider the possibility of so doing.

XIX. International Relief Union.

The Fifteenth International Red Cross Conference, Noting with keen satisfaction that the International Relief Union has now been fully constituted, and that the General Council of the Union held its inaugural meeting at Geneva in July 1933,
Having taken cognizance of the report of the International Relief Union,
Addresses its thanks to the Executive Committee of the Union for this clear statement of its views of the rôle of national Societies and of the International Red Cross bodies in the working of the Union, and to Colonel Draudt for the valuable supplementary information he has supplied,
Expresses its satisfaction with the action taken by the International Red Cross Committee and the League of Red Cross Societies in defining, by agreements satisfactory to all concerned, the responsibilities assumed by them on the Union's behalf,
Expresses the hope that the national Red Cross Societies of countries whose Governments are members of the Union will find it possible to establish analogous agreements on the national plane with their respective Governments,
And, regretting the absence of Senator Ciraolo, promoter of the Union and President of the Executive Committee, addresses to him cordial congratulations on the progress made, with the effective support of Signor Mussolini, Head of the Italian Government, towards the realization of his generous conception.

XX. Regional Conferences.

The Fifteenth International Red Cross Conference, Noting with approval that during the past four years the number of national Red Cross Societies and the aggregate of their membership have continued to show progressive increase,
Expresses its appreciation to all who have contributed to strengthen the movement by their leadership both in the national and in the international field,
Expresses the hope that this development will continue, and in particular that the Red Cross Societies of countries possessing overseas dependencies or administering Mandated Territories will continue to give special attention to the possibilities which the Red Cross offers as a means of protecting the health and improving the conditions of subject populations,
Requests the International Red Cross Committee to study jointly with the Secretariat of the League of Red Cross Societies the question of Red Cross development in Territories under Mandate, and to transmit to the national Societies concerned their recommendations regarding the lines upon which Red Cross development in such territories can best be stimulated,
And, recognizing that regional Red Cross Conferences are of outstanding value during a period characterized by an important evolution in Red Cross work, which is occurring as the result of changes in social and economic conditions, expresses the hope that the League of Red Cross Societies will go forward with its regular programme of regional conferences in close consultation with the national Societies concerned in each case.

XXI. Third Pan-American Conference.

The Fifteenth International Red Cross Conference, Noting with keen satisfaction the recommendation adopted by the Seventh American International Conference held at Montevideo in December 1933, to the effect that Governments should give their support to their respective national Red Cross Societies especially in respect to their educational work and their health and relief work;
Congratulating the Brazilian Government and the Brazilian Red Cross, and also the League of Red Cross Societies, on the decision taken to assemble the Third Pan-American Conference at Rio de Janeiro in 1935 under the auspices of the League;
Expresses the hope that the success of this Conference may be assured, through the effective participation of all the national Societies of the Americas and the active co-operation of the League Secretariat.

XXII. Red Cross Truce.

The Fifteenth International Red Cross Conference, Having taken cognizance of the report of the International Commission for the Study of the Red Cross Truce, and notably of the resolution adopted by that Commission on April 14, 1933,
Thanks the members of the Commission for their report and for the careful study which they have given to this important question,
Requests the national Red Cross Societies to examine with special care the conclusions of the Commission and the possibility of associating themselves therewith,
Considering the Truce as an effective means of promoting international understanding and co-operation, expresses the hope that all national Societies which decide to adapt to the conditions prevailing in their own countries the methods successfully practised by the Czechoslovak Red Cross, will afford opportunities to representatives of the International Red Cross Committee and of the League of Red Cross Societies for following their work in this field,
And addresses to the President of the Czechoslovak Red Cross renewed congratulations on her inspiring initiative.

XXIII. The Red Cross and the Press.

The Fifteenth International Red Cross Conference, Considering the paramount importance of the press for a better understanding between the nations and the maintenance of good relations between them,
Recognizes the usefulness of the initiative taken by the Swedish Red Cross at times when the peaceful relations between the nations are threatened,
And expresses the hope that it will be possible to find a practical solution to the problems resulting from that initiative.

XIV. Prevention of War.

The Fifteenth International Red Cross Conference, Having regard to the resolutions of earlier International Red Cross Conferences, and especially to Resolutions VII of the Eleventh (Geneva) and XXV of the Fourteenth (Brussels) International Conferences, declaring that the Red Cross, without losing sight of its usual wartime and peacetime activities, must exert every effort, within the sphere of its attributions, to prevent war,
And considering that the progress made in the technique of warfare creates ever-increasing difficulties for the traditional activities of the Red Cross,
Expresses the hope that all national Red Cross Societies, while continuing, as during the past, to

APPENDIX 1 (*continued*)

spare no effort in order to safeguard the lives of millions of men, to protect other millions from suffering and privations, as well as to prevent catastrophes which threaten to destroy the intellectual and material wealth accumulated through the centuries, will amplify their action against war and in favour of a better understanding between nations by every means at their disposal.

XXV. Popular Health Instruction.

The Fifteenth International Red Cross Conference, Recognizing the importance of the health and welfare work accomplished by the national Red Cross Societies,

Taking into consideration the fact that the nature and extent of these activities are determined by national and local circumstances,

Recognizes that the usefulness of the Red Cross in this field lies largely in educating the public, in experimenting with new methods, in promoting the co-ordination of the work of governmental services and voluntary agencies, and in bridging existing gaps, using for this purpose a specially trained personnel.

XXVI. Facilities and Exemptions.

The Fifteenth International Red Cross Conference, Recalling that the Final Act of the Geneva Diplomatic Conference of 1929, in its Vth Resolution, pointed out the great desirability of all facilities and exemptions being accorded to national Red Cross Societies,

Requests national Societies to approach their respective Governments with a view to obtaining from them that, in application of this principle, the transport of relief material from one country to another through the Red Cross shall be facilitated and exempted from charges.

XXVII. Health of Seamen.

The Fifteenth International Red Cross Conference, Recommends the world-wide use of the manual published in French by the League of Red Cross Societies under the title HYGIÈNE ET MÉDECINE À BORD,

Recommends to Red Cross Societies that they endeavour to have published in the various languages translations of the League's manual, and asks them to approach the authorities in their respective countries on this subject,

Expresses the hope that the League will now give its attention to *(a)* the standardization of medical chests, and draft plans for the publication of a similar but smaller manual to be used in aerodromes, air ambulances and aeroplanes; *(b)* the standardization of chests to be used by air services;

And expresses its thanks to the League of Red Cross Societies for the results already accomplished on the initiative and with the help of the Norwegian Red Cross, in regard to the health and welfare of merchant seamen.

XXVIII. Private Information Secretariats.

The Fifteenth International Red Cross Conference, Considering the report presented by the International Red Cross Committee concerning Secretariats of Private Information in accordance with the hope expressed by Resolution XII of the Fourteenth Conference,

Considering the interest aroused by the proposal of Senator Cremonesi and the conclusive experiences of several Central Committees,

Considering also the analogy of the work done by the International Migration Service and the excellent co-operation already established between this body and several national Societies,

Encourages the national Societies which are already working in this field to continue their work on the present basis, and recommends to other Societies that they examine whether the special circumstances of their respective countries necessitate and permit of the creation (after agreement with the International Migration Service and under whatever name may appear most suitable) of services analogous to those contemplated by Senator Cremonesi.

XXIX. Disaster Relief.

The Fifteenth International Red Cross Conference, Noting with satisfaction that national Red Cross Societies are showing themselves increasingly able, thanks to systematic preparation, to play a useful rôle, in co-operation with governmental and other private bodies, in the relief of disaster sufferers,

Noting at the same time that the response of national Societies as a whole to the appeals which they receive from the International Red Cross bodies on the occasion of disasters of unusual gravity is an increasingly generous one,

And considering that preparatory work on the lines explained in the pamphlet submitted to the Conference by the Secretariat of the League of Red Cross Societies is the essential condition of efficient disaster relief work, both nationally and internationally,

Expresses its approval of the action taken by the national Societies, by the International Red Cross Committee, and by the League to improve the facilities which the Red Cross offers for disaster relief,

And formulates the hope that Red Cross Societies will continue to improve their relief organization so as to be able with ever-increasing efficiency to meet the needs of disaster sufferers in their own countries, to respond to the appeals emanating from the international Red Cross bodies on behalf of disaster sufferers elsewhere, and to keep the Secretariat of the League of Red Cross Societies fully acquainted with the development of their work in the field of disaster relief, so that it may continue to discharge its responsibilities in this field.

XXX. Highway First Aid.

The Fifteenth International Red Cross Conference, Having taken cognizance of the interesting and instructive report of the Standing International Commission on First Aid on Highways,

And noting that the Commission has carried out in every respect the mandate entrusted to it by the XIVth International Red Cross Conference,

Addresses cordial thanks to the Commission for its painstaking work and for its report,

Endorses the recommendations formulated by the Commission,

Expresses the hope that each national Red Cross Society will give special attention to the development of effective and uniform facilities for rendering first aid on highways, in close co-operation with national touring associations and automobile clubs, and will keep in close touch with the Secretariat of the League of Red Cross Societies in connexion with their further work in this field,

And expresses the hope that the League will continue to promote highway first aid activities on a uniform basis, and in this connexion will continue to benefit by the experience of those experts who, under the enlightened chairmanship of Dr. Béhague, have rendered such valuable services to the Standing International Commission.

XXXI. Road Accidents.

The Fifteenth International Red Cross Conference, Considering the importance of accurate and sufficiently detailed statistics of accidents occurring on highways,

Requests the national Red Cross Societies to collect such information, and the League Secretariat to prepare and publish these data.

APPENDIX 1 *(continued)*

XXXII. Air Ambulances.

The Fifteenth International Red Cross Conference,
Noting the continuously increasing importance attached in Red Cross and other circles to the organization of air ambulance services,
And noting with satisfaction the action taken by the League of Red Cross Societies with a view to acquainting its members with the progress made in this field,
Reiterates the recommendations embodied in Resolution XVII of the Fourteenth International Red Cross Conference, and expresses the hope that national Red Cross Societies will study from the national standpoint, and the League of Red Cross Societies from the international standpoint, the possibility:

(a) Of satisfactory agreements being concluded between Red Cross bodies, governmental and private services interested in aviation, and aero-clubs;

(b) Of establishing co-operative relations with aeroplane manufacturers in this connexion;

(c) Of organizing first-aid and training courses in order to facilitate the transport of patients by air and the administration of first aid when required in connexion with aviation work.

The Conference further expresses the hope that Governments will encourage and facilitate the use of aeroplanes by Red Cross Societies for the transport of patients, and in connexion with disaster relief work, and will continue, with the International Red Cross Committee, to study the possibility of introducing regulations and technical facilities to enable ambulance aeroplanes to cross frontiers in peacetime.

XXXIII. The Red Cross at Sea.

The Fifteenth International Red Cross Conference,
Having taken cognizance of the report of the International Red Cross Committee,
Notes the reasons which have led to the postponement of the convocation of the Commission of Experts contemplated by Resolution No. XXII of the Fourteenth International Red Cross Conference, and hopes that it will be possible to proceed to this convocation before the Sixteenth International Conference meets. The mandate given by the Fourteenth Conference to the International Red Cross Committee is renewed, and the Commission of Experts is instructed to investigate the points in regard to which it appears desirable and possible to modify the Hague Convention of 1907,
Recommends that the national Red Cross Societies concerned communicate their experiences to the International Red Cross Committee and to the League, together with any such suggestions as they may think fit,
And invites the Executive Committee of the International Relief Union and the Standing Committee of the Congresses of Military Medicine and Pharmacy to associate themselves in this study.

XXXIV. Standardization of Medical Stores.

The Fifteenth International Red Cross Conference,
Notes with keen satisfaction the work done by the Standing International Commission on the Standardization of Medical Stores in the course of its sixth, seventh, eighth and ninth sessions,
Requests the Commission to continue to keep in touch with the progress made and with new inventions which may be of such a kind as to involve changes in the previous resolutions of the Commission or to guide the Commission in its future deliberations,
Thanks the International Red Cross Committee for the care with which it has facilitated meetings of the Commission, made the necessary secretarial arrangements, and published the results of the meetings,
Expresses its gratitude to the Governments who send experts to attend the Commission, supply the necessary documentation, subsidize the International Institute for the Study of Medical Stores and contribute to its collections,
And endorses the resolutions printed in Document No. 12 submitted by the International Red Cross Committee to the Conference.

XXXV. Standing Study Commission.

The Fifteenth International Red Cross Conference,
Considering the interest of comparative studies of medical stores to Army Medical Services and to national Red Cross Societies,
Approves the modification in the statutes of the Standing International Commission on the Standardization of Medical Stores, and resolves to change the title of this Commission, which will henceforth be known as the Standing International Commission for the Study of Medical Stores,
Instructs this Commission, in addition to the work which it may undertake looking directly towards standardization, to endeavour to comply with the requests which may be addressed to it, through the intermediary of Governments, for investigations and information on particular points,
Expresses the hope that the Governments of States which are parties to the Geneva Convention, and the national Red Cross Societies which are not represented on the Commission, will promote such studies by sending in appropriate material and granting subventions,
Invites the Commission to co-operate practically for this purpose with the Standing Committee of the Congresses of Military Medicine and Pharmacy,
And instructs the Commission to modify its statutes so that they may be in conformity with the present resolution.

XXXVI. Chemical Warfare.

The Fifteenth International Red Cross Conference,
While noting that since the Fourteenth Conference the number of Governments which have ratified the Geneva Protocol of June 17th, 1925, concerning the prohibition of the use in war of asphyxiating, poisonous or similar gases, and of bacteriological methods of warfare, has considerably increased,
Recommends that the International Red Cross Committee continue its endeavours to secure the ratification of the said Protocol, or adhesion to the said Protocol, by all countries which are parties to the Geneva Convention,
Thanks the International Committee for the initiative which it has taken in order to develop in time of peace and in time of war measures for the protection of civilian populations against poisonous gas,
Expresses the hope that the International Committee will be placed in the position to continue the technical investigations which it has already undertaken in spite of the difficulties of all kinds confronting it,
Approves the activity of the Documentation Centre, and invites national Societies to give their financial assistance to the International Committee in order to contribute to the development of this centre,
Notes the conclusions of the International Commission of Jurists of 1931, and expresses the hope that the studies of this Commission will be continued with a view to finding means for the legal protection of the civilian population against the dangers of aerial warfare in its various forms.

APPENDIX 1 (*continued*)

XXXVII. Protection of Civilians.

The Fifteenth International Red Cross Conference,
Thanks the Belgian Government for the initiative which it has taken with a view to the submission to a Diplomatic Conference of the study of certain laws of war, and especially the plan for the creation of areas or towns providing adequate protection both for wounded and sick soldiers and for the civilian population,
Expresses the hope that the International Red Cross Committee and national Red Cross Societies will place themselves in communication with Governments, in order to stimulate efforts looking to the prompt execution of any measure which may tend to protect the above-mentioned elements of the population.

XXXVIII. Undeclared War.

The Fifteenth International Red Cross Conference,
Having taken cognizance of the report of the International Red Cross Committee,
Considering the regrettable consequences which might result from a too literal interpretation of the Geneva Conventions and of the Convention relative to the Treatment of Prisoners of War of July 27th, 1929, in the event of military, naval or air operations unaccompanied by a declaration of war,
Considering that these operations, whatever may be their interpretation in international law, their motives or their purposes, cause the same destruction as declared wars,
Expresses the hope that the said Conventions, which have been established for the circumstance of a declared war, will also be applied by analogy in the case of armed conflict between States without declaration of war.

XXXIX. Protection of Civilians on Enemy Territory.

The Fifteenth International Red Cross Conference,
Considering the Sixth Resolution contained in the Final Act of the Diplomatic Conference of 1929, recommending the undertaking of careful investigations with a view to the conclusion of an international convention concerning the status and protection of civilians of enemy nationality who are on the territory of a belligerent State or on territory occupied by a belligerent,
Recognizes the great interest attaching to the annexed Draft Convention concerning the fate of civilians on enemy territory or territory occupied by the enemy,
Expressly recommends this draft, subject to eventual amendments, to the attention of Governments,
And instructs the International Red Cross Committee to make all appropriate representations with a view to the conclusion of a convention at the earliest possible date.
(The Draft Convention referred to in this resolution is printed in Document No. 9 presented to the Conference by the International Red Cross Committee).

XL. Application of Geneva Convention.

The Fifteenth International Red Cross Conference,
Having taken cognizance of the collection of texts relating to the application of the Geneva Convention and to the work of national Societies in countries which are parties to this Convention (Recueil de textes relatifs a l'application de la Convention de Genève et a l'action des Sociétés nationales dans les États parties a cette Convention) prepared by the International Committee in conformity with the last paragraph of Resolution XX of the Fourteenth Conference,

Congratulates the International Committee on the fine work it has done in carrying out this mandate,
And invites the national Red Cross Societies to proceed, with the assistance of this collection, to study the legislation of their respective countries in comparison with that of other countries, with a view to drawing the attention of their respective Governments to such gaps as may exist in the national legislation and at the same time to making such changes and additions to their own statutes as may seem to them necessary.

XLI. Protection of Red Cross Property.

The Fifteenth International Red Cross Conference,
Considering that the Geneva Convention of 1929 (Article 16 paragraph 2) lays down that material belonging to relief societies, wherever it may be, shall be considered as private property,
And considering that it is desirable to settle in peacetime the important question of whether the clauses in the Geneva and Hague Conventions which protect medical stores are applicable to stores in transit by land, sea, or air,
Resolves to entrust the International Red Cross Committee with the study of this question, with a view to the submission to the Sixteenth International Red Cross Conference of a report including, if necessary, such recommendations as may appear indicated as the result of such study.

XLII. Standing Commission

The Fifteenth International Red Cross Conference,
Appoints as members of the Standing Commission for the period 1934-1938: H. E. Prince Tokugawa (Japan), H. E. General D. Ricardo Burguete y Lana (Spain), Dr. Alvaro Carlos Tourinho (Brazil), The Hon. Sir Arthur Stanley (Great Britain), and Dr. Refik Bey (Turkey),
And addresses a vote of thanks to the retiring members of the Standing Commission.

XLIII. Place and Date of XVIth Conference.

The Fifteenth International Red Cross Conference,
Resolves that the next Conference shall be held in Madrid in 1938, at a date to be determined in due course by the Spanish Red Cross in consultation with the Standing Commission of the International Red Cross.

XLIV. Increased Capital of Shôken Fund.

The Fifteenth International Red Cross Conference,
Addresses to Her Majesty the Empress of Japan and Her Majesty the Dowager Empress, the respectful expression of its profound and heartfelt gratitude for the donation which They have deigned to make with a view to increasing the capital of the Empress Shôken Fund and thus contributing to promote the humanitarian work done by the Red Cross in peacetime.

XLV. Regulations of Shôken Fund.

The Fifteenth International Red Cross Conference,
Noting the declaration of the President of the Red Cross Society of Japan,
Congratulating the International Red Cross Committee on its administration of the Empress Shôken Fund, and recognizing that the measures taken by the Committee in regard to allocations from the income of this Fund have always been in perfect conformity with the letter and spirit of the regulations governing the Fund,
Considering on the other hand Articles VIII and IX of the Statutes of the International Red Cross,
Instructs the Standing Commission to examine the modifications to be introduced into the regulations of the Empress Shôken Fund, with a view to providing for the association of the League of Red Cross Societies in the decisions relating to the allocations to be

XLVI. Vote of Thanks.

The Fifteenth International Red Cross Conference,
Begs Their Majesties the Emperor and Empress of Japan to deign to accept the homage of its respectful gratitude for the evidence of August Benevolence with which They have honoured the Conference and encouraged its work,
And expresses to H. I. H. Prince Kan-in, Honorary President of the Red Cross Society of Japan, and to H. I. H. Princess Kan-in, President of the Ladies' Volunteer Nursing Association, the respectful expression of its gratitude to Their Imperial Highnesses, and of its admiration for the splendid institutions to which They have deigned to accord Their August Patronage and Their effective support.

XLVII. Vote of Thanks.

The Fifteenth International Red Cross Conference,
Deeply touched by the very kind and friendly welcome given to it, and by the numerous attentions showered upon all delegates by the Authorities, by the Red Cross Society of Japan and by the whole Japanese people,
Expresses the assurance of its warm appreciation to all who have contributed by their hospitality, by the facilities given to delegates, and by their devoted co-operation, to ensure the success of the Conference and to make it an unforgettable memory for all who have participated in it.
The thanks of the Conference are due first and foremost:
To the Japanese Imperial Government and to the Cabinet;
To H. E. Prince Iyesato Tokugawa, President of the Red Cross Society of Japan, to Prince Kuniyuki Tokugawa and Mr. N. Nakagawa, Vice-Presidents, to the Members of the Board of Administration and of the Council of the Society,
To the Prefectural Governors, especially the Governors of Tokyo and Kanagawa;
To the Municipal Authorities, and in particular to the Mayors of Tokyo and Yokohama;
To the institutions and organizations and to private individuals who have kindly given hospitality to delegates and members of their families, especially Baron Iwasaki, Baron Mitsui, and the Yokohama Chamber of Commerce and Industry;
To General Inouye, his colleagues and subordinates at the headquarters of the Red Cross Society of Japan, to the local committees and members of the Society, in Tokyo and in the provinces, and finally to the members of the Junior Red Cross, whose enthusiasm and devotion constitute an assurance that the Red Cross Society of Japan will have a future worthy of its splendid past and of its present great development.

XLVIII. Tribute to Japan Red Cross Leaders.

The Fifteenth International Red Cross Conference,
Recognizing the eminent service rendered to the Red Cross by the illustrious founder of the Red Cross Society of Japan, the late Count Sano, and by the Presidents who have succeeded him,
Pays heartfelt tribute to the memories of Count Sano and his successors,
And expresses to Viscount Ishiguro, whose great wisdom and long experience continue to be a source of inspiration to the Society, congratulations and respectful good wishes.

Resolutions
of the Board of Governors

I

The Board of Governors of the League of Red Cross Societies,
Being desirous that the League should incorporate all national Red Cross Societies duly recognized by the International Red Cross Committee:
And noting with satisfaction that its membership of 60 Societies already includes all recognized national Red Cross bodies, with the exception of that of the U. S. S. R.;
Requests its Chairman to approach the authorized representative of the Alliance of Red Cross and Red Crescent Societies of the U. S. S. R., and to transmit through him to this body the invitation to become a member of the League.

II

The following are appointed to represent the League at the Fifteenth International Red Cross Conference:

Hon. John Barton Payne—CHAIRMAN.
Lt.-Col. P. Draudt, and Mr. S. Yamanouchi—VICE-CHAIRMEN.
Mr. Nica
Mr. Ninagawa
Mr. Ernest J. Swift—SECRETARY-GENERAL.

III

The general report of the Executive Committee for the period October 1932 to October 1934 is noted and approved.

IV

The Board of Governors addresses its congratulations and good wishes to the Iraq Red Crescent Society and the Nicaraguan Red Cross on the occasion of their formal recognition by the International Red Cross Committee and their entry into the League.

V

The Secretary-General is instructed to convey to Dame Alicia Lloyd Still, President of the Florence Nightingale International Foundation, the deep interest with which the League of Red Cross Societies will follow the Foundation's work in providing nursing facilities for post-graduate nursing education. The Board expresses the hope that national Red Cross Societies will co-operate closely with national nursing associations in the endeavour to place the Foundation upon a solid financial basis. The representatives of the League on the Grand Council and on the Committee of Management of the Foundation are instructed to give special attention, when co-

APPENDIX 1 (*continued*)

operating in working out the policies of the Foundation, to the great benefit which national Red Cross Societies may derive from the facilities provided by the Foundation.

VI

The Board of Governors notes with approval the intention of the Secretary-General to extend and develop the activities of the League Secretariat in the nursing field, and instructs him to present a programme of proposed work in this field for approval by the Executive Committee at a forthcoming meeting.

VII

The Board of Governors congratulates Senator Ciraolo, President of the Executive Committee of the International Relief Union, on the formation of the Union and on his election to the presidency. The action taken on behalf of the League in defining the limits of the responsibility undertaken by the League jointly with the International Red Cross Committee so as to provide the permanent and central services of the Union, is endorsed and approved.

VIII

The Board notes with satisfaction the action taken by the Secretariat with a view to keeping the national Red Cross Societies advised of developments in connexion with air ambulance services. The arrangements made to establish a co-operative relationship with the International Air Federation and the Permanent Committee of the International Air Ambulance Congress for this purpose are endorsed and approved.

IX

The Board expresses its deep appreciation to the President of the French Republic and H. M. the King of Norway for their action in graciously according their patronage to the Health Manual for Merchant Seamen recently published by the League of Red Cross Societies.

The gratitude of the Board is also due to Mr. T. E. Steen and to those who, in association with him, have made possible the publication of the French edition of this Manual.

X

The Board of Governors, being desirous to commemorate the happy initiative taken in 1919 by the late Mr. Henry P. Davison and those associated with him in the foundation of the League of Red Cross Societies, resolves that, until further notice, all regular meetings of the Board of Governors which are held at the headquarters of the League shall be called for May 5th, the anniversary of the League's foundation.

In particular, the fifteenth regular meeting of the Board shall be called for May 5th, 1936.

XI

The Board of Governors approves the arrangements made for holding the Third Pan-American Red Cross Conference at Rio de Janeiro in September 1935, and expresses its cordial appreciation of the action taken to this end by the Brazilian Red Cross and the Brazilian Government. Approval is also given to the proposal to organize a Near Eastern Red Cross Conference if possible at Cairo in 1936, with the participation of the three Red Crescent Societies, the Persian Red Lion and Sun, and such other national Societies as may desire to participate.

XII

The Board of Governors desires to express its gratitude to the American Red Cross for its continued support of the League's work through the generous yearly contribution which continues to represent so important a part of the League budget. Thanks are also due to the other national Societies which, in spite of difficult financial conditions, have made special efforts either by increasing their contributions or by guaranteeing their amount over a number of years.

Having regard more especially to the efforts made by the Secretariat to reduce the expenses of the League to the minimum compatible with efficiency, the Board expresses the hope that all Societies will make a corresponding effort to place their contributions upon a basis representative of the appreciation they have expressed of the services placed at their disposal by the League.

The Board of Governors expresses the hope that determined efforts will be made by the Secretary-General to secure contributions to the League for the special purposes mentioned in the Secretary-General's report, and urges that national Societies and members of the Board of Governors co-operate in these efforts.

XIII

The report of the Secretary-General is approved.

XIV

The Board of Governors, recognizing the great value of regional conferences in enabling the Red Cross Societies of adjacent countries with similar problems to compare experiences and ideas, authorizes the League Secretariat, besides proceeding with the regional conferences now scheduled, to prepare carefully matured plans for further regional conferences as and when occasion presents itself. It will be advantageous if the groups of countries participating in such conferences vary from time to time.

The Board desires to express warm thanks to Dr. Masarykova, President of the Czechoslovak Red Cross, for her excellent report.

XV

The Board of Governors, having taken cognizance of the report of Mr. de Gielgud, Under Secretary-General, notes the constructive suggestions contained in the conclusion of this report, and instructs the Secretariat to take such action as may seem advisable and possible in order to promote the extension of Red Cross organization and activity in those sections of the Far East in which Red Cross work has not yet been fully developed.

XVI

The Board of Governors,

Approves the Treasurer-General's report on the financial position of the League on June 30, 1934, and endorses in particular the action taken to safeguard the funds of the League against exchange depreciation;

Approves the expenditure of 70,000 French francs for the expenses of removal to the new headquarters;

And authorizes the Secretary-General to undertake commitments for 1935 on the basis of the budget presented, to the total amount of 2,500,000 francs.

Should the amount of the contributions received for 1935, owing to exchange fluctuations or for other reasons, fall short of the sum estimated, the Secretary-General is authorized to meet the deficit so created by drawing upon the reserve.

APPENDIX 1 (*continued*)

THE LEAGUE OF RED CROSS SOCIETIES

Chairman of the Board of Governors : Hon. John Barton PAYNE (American Red Cross).

Vice-Chairmen :
- Colonel P. DRAUDT (German Red Cross).
- Marquis de LILLERS (French Red Cross).
- Señor E. J. CONILL (Cuban Red Cross).
- Mr. S. YAMANOUCHI (Japan Red Cross).

Secretary-General : Mr. Ernest J. SWIFT.

MEMBER SOCIETIES AND THEIR REPRESENTATIVES ON THE BOARD OF GOVERNORS.

ALBANIA: *Kryqi i Kuq Shqiptar* — Tirana.

ARGENTINA: *Cruz Roja Argentina* — Cerrito 1174, Buenos Aires. — General Julio R. GARINO.*

AUSTRALIA: *Australian Red Cross Society* — Latrobe Street 42-46, Melbourne. — The Viscountess NOVAR.

AUSTRIA: *Oesterreichische Gesellschaft vom Roten Kreuze* — Milchgasse 1, Vienna. I. — Dr. Johann STEINER.

BELGIUM: *Croix-Rouge de Belgique* — 80, rue de Livourne, Brussels. — Professor Pierre NOLF.

†**BOLIVIA:** *Cruz Roja Boliviana* — La Paz.

BRAZIL: *Cruz Vermelha Brasileira* — Esplanada do Senado, Rio de Janeiro. — Major M. C. de Goes MONTEIRO.

BULGARIA: *Bĭlgarska Drougestvo Cheroen Krest* — 19, boulevard Totleben, Sofia. — Professor DANEFF.*

CANADA: *Canadian Red Cross Society* — 410 Sherbourne Street, Toronto. — Hon. G. H. FERGUSON.

CHILI: *Comité central de la Cruz Roja Chilena* — Calle Catedral 1572, Santiago. — General Luis BRIEBA.

CHINA: *The Red Cross Society of China* — 42-44 Kiukiang Road, Shanghai.

COLOMBIA: *Cruz Roja Colombiana* — Bogota. — Professor Luis F. CALDERÓN.

COSTA RICA: *Consejo Supremo de la Cruz Roja Costorricense* — Calle 5a Sur, San José. — Señor E. QUIROS AGUILAR.

CUBA: *Sociedad nacional de la Cruz Roja* — Ig. Agramonte y Av. de Bélgica, Habana. — Señor E. J. CONILL.*

CZECHOSLOVAKIA: *Ceskoslovensky Cerveny Krit* — Neklanova ul. 34, Prague. — Dr. Alice MASARYKOVA.

DANZIG: *Rotes Kreus der Freien Stadt Danzig* — Neugarten 12-16, Danzig. — Dr. KLUCK.

DENMARK: *Dansk Röde Kors* — Ved Stranden 2, Copenhagen. — Mr. J. BULOW.

DOMINICAN REPUBLIC: *Cruz Roja nacional* — Santo Domingo.

ECUADOR: *Sociedad Ecuatoriana de la Cruz Roja* — Avenida Colombia 118, Quito. — General Angel I. CHIRIBOGA.

†**EGYPT:** *Egyptian Red Crescent Society* — 34, avenue de la Reine Nazlie, Cairo. — Dr. Henry NAUS Bey.

ESTONIA: *Eesti Punane Rist* — Niguliste tän 12, Tallinn. — Dr. Hans LEESMENT.

†**FINLAND:** *Suomen Punainen Risti* — 16 Annankatu, Helsingfors. — Major M. de GRIPENBERG.

FRANCE: *Comité central de la Croix-Rouge française*, 21, rue François-I*, Paris. — Marquis de LILLERS.*

GERMANY: *Deutsches Rotes Kreuz* — Cornelius str. 4b, Berlin W. 10. — Colonel DRAUDT.*

GREAT BRITAIN: *The British Red Cross Society* — 14, Grosvenor Crescent, London, S.W. 1. — The Hon. Sir Arthur STANLEY.*

GREECE: *Ellenikos Erythros Stayros*, 41, rue Solon, Athens. — Mr. J. ATHANASAKI.

GUATEMALA: *Cruz Roja Guatemalteca* — 10 Calle Oriente, No. 32, Guatemala.

HUNGARY: *Magyar Vörös-Kereszt Egylet* — Baross utca 15 Budapest. — Mr. Elemer de SIMON.

†**ICELAND:** *Raudi Kross Islands* — Reykjavik.

INDIA: *Indian Red Cross Society* — Talkatora Road, New Delhi (in winter), Simla (in summer). — Sir Henry MONCRIEFF SMITH, Kt. C. I. E.

†**IRAQ:** *Iraq Red Crescent*. — Baghdad.

ITALY: *Croce Rossa Italiana* — Via Toscana 12, Rome. — Senator G. CIRAOLO.*

JAPAN: *The Red Cross Society of Japan* — 5 Shiba Park, Tokyo — Mr. S. YAMANOUCHI.*

LATVIA: *Latvijas Sarkandis Krusts* — Skolas iela 1, Riga. — Dr. K. BARONS.

LITHUANIA: *Lietuvos Raudonojo Kryziaus Draugijos* — Kestucio g-ve 8, Kaunas.

†**LUXEMBURG:** *Croix-Rouge du Luxembourg* — 65, rue de la Pétrusse, Luxemburg. — Mme MAYRISCH de St. HUBERT.

MEXICO: *Asociación Mexicana de la Cruz Roja* — Esq. Durango y Monterrey, Col. Roma, Mexico D. F. — Dr F. Castillo NÁJERA.

†**NETHERLANDS:** *Het Nederlandsche Roode Kruis* — Princessegracht 27, The Hague. — Mr. DONKER CURTIUS.

†**NETHERLANDS EAST INDIES:** *Croix-Rouge des Indes néerlandaises* — Weltvreden, Java. — Mr. DONKER CURTIUS.

NEW ZEALAND: *New Zealand Red Cross Society* — Dominion Headquarters, 63 Dixon Street, Wellington. — Col. J. Mac Naughton CHRISTIE, C. B. E.

†**NICARAGUA:** *Cruz Roja Nicaraguense*. — MANAGUA.

NORWAY: *Norges Röde Kors* — Grev Wedels Plass 5, Oslo. — Colonel J. MEINICH.

PANAMA: *Cruz Roja de Panamá* — Panama. — Señora Rosario G. de ARIAS.

PARAGUAY: *Comité Central de la Cruz Roja Paraguaya* — Avenida España 505, Asunción. — Dr. Andrés BARBERO.

†**PERSIA:** *Society of the Red Lion and Sun* — Teheran. — Dr. ISPAHANY.

PERU: *Sociedad Peruana de la Cruz Roja* — La Colmena N° 215-219, Casilla Postal N° 1534, Lima.— Count de MIMBELA.

POLAND: *Polski Czerwony Kryz* — Smolna 6, Warsaw. — M. Titus FILIPOWICZ.*

PORTUGAL: *Sociedade Portugueza da Cruz Vermelha* — Praça do Commercio 1, Lisbon. — Marquis de FARIA.

ROUMANIA: *Societatea nationala de Cruce Rosie* — Rue Biserica Amzei 29, Bucarest.

SALVADOR: *Consejo Supremo de la Cruz Roja Salvadoreña* — 3a Calle Poniente No. 21, San Salvador. — Dr. J. M. OLANO.

SIAM: *Sapakachad Sagan* — Chulalongkorn Memorial Hospital, Bangkok. — H. E. Phya SUBARN SOMBATI.

SOUTH AFRICA: *South African Red Cross Society* — 107-110 Exploration Bdgs. 74 Commissioner S*, Johannesburg.

SPAIN: *Cruz Roja Española* — 10 Calle de Sagasta, Madrid. — H. E. The Marquis de CASA-VALDES.

SWEDEN: *Svenska Röda Korset* — Artillerigatan 6, Stockholm. Baron E. STJERNSTEDT.*

SWITZERLAND: *Croix-Rouge suisse* — 8, Taubenstrasse, Berne. — Mr. Paul DINICHERT.

TURKEY: *Türkiye Hilâliahmer* — Yenichéhir, Ankara.

UNITED STATES: *American Red Cross* — National Headquarters : Washington, D.C. — Hon. John Barton PAYNE.*

URUGUAY: *Cruz Roja Uruguaya* — 18 de Julio, 2338. Montevideo. — Señora E. Salons de ARRILLAGA.

†**U. S. S. R.:** *Alliance of Red Cross and Red Crescent Societies of the U. S. S. R.*, Ipatievsky pereoulok, 6, Moscow.

VENEZUELA: *Sociedad Venezolana de la Cruz Roja* — Muños a Piñango 10, Caracas.

YUGOSLAVIA: *Drustvo Crvenoga Krsta Kraljenina Jugoslavije* — 19 Simina ulica, Beograd.

† Societies having no Junior membership.
* Members of the Executive Committee.

Le Gérant : B. de Rougé.

IMP. UNION, 13, RUE MÉCHAIN, PARIS

APPENDIX 1 *(continued)*

APPENDIX 2

DRAFT INTERNATIONAL CONVENTION ON THE CONDITION AND PROTECTION OF CIVILIANS, TOKYO, 1934

Draft International Convention on the Condition and Protection of Civilians of enemy nationality who are on territory belonging to or occupied by a belligerent.
Tokyo, 1934.

Chapter I

Qualification of enemy civilian (enemy alien)

Article 1.- Enemy civilians in the sense of the present Convention are persons fulfilling the two following
conditions:

a) that of not belonging to the land, maritime or air armed forces of the belligerents, as defined by international law, and in particular by Articles 1, 2 and 3 of the Regulations attached to the Fourth Hague Convention, of October 18, 1907, concerning the Laws and Customs of War on Land;

b) that of being the national of an enemy country in the territory of a belligerent, or in a territory occupied by the latter.

Chapter II

Enemy civilians in the territory of a belligerent

Section I: General Provisions

Permission to leave.

Article 2.- Subject to the provisions of Article 4, enemy civilians who may desire to leave the territory at the outset of military operations shall be granted, as rapidly as possible, the necessary authorizations, as well as all facilities compatible with such operations.

They will have the right to provide themselves with the necessary funds for their journey and to take with them at least their personal effects.

Administrative evacuation.

Article 3.- In the event of the departure of civilians being administratively organised, they shall be conducted to the frontier of their country or of the nearest neutral country.

These repatriations shall be effected with due regard to all humanitarian considerations.

The manner of such repatriations may form the subject of special agreements between belligerents.

Detention of Civilians.

Article 4.- Only civilians falling within the following categories may be held:

a) Those who are eligible for immediate mobilisation or mobilisation within a year, under the laws of their country of origin or of the country of residence;

b) those whose departure may reasonably be opposed on grounds involving the security of the Detaining Power.

In either case, appeal to the Protecting Power shall always be admitted. This Power shall have the right to demand that an inquiry be opened and the result communicated to it within three

APPENDIX 2 ICRC Database. "Treaties, States Parties and Commentaries, Draft International Convention on the Condition and Protection of Civilians of enemy nationality who are on territory belonging to or occupied by a belligerent. Tokyo, 1934." Accessed May 19, 2023. https://ihl-databases.icrc.org/en/ihl-treaties/tokyo-draft-conv-1934?activeTab=historical.

months of its request.

Detainees.

Article 5.- Those who are in preventive imprisonment or condemned to a sentence depriving them of liberty shall, on their liberation, benefit by the provisions of the present Convention.

The fact that they belong to an enemy State shall not increase the severity of the regime to which they are subjected.

Treatment of Civilians.

Article 6.- Enemy aliens who have remained in the territory, as those who have been held in application of Article 4, shall receive the treatment to which aliens are ordinarily entitled, except for measures of control or security which may be ordered, and subject to the provisions of Section III.

With these reservations, and in so far as military operations permit, they will have the possibility of carrying on their occupations.

Article 7.- Subject to the measures applied to the population in general, enemy civilians shall have the possibility of giving news of a strictly private character to next of kin, and of receiving such news.

With the same reservation they shall also have the possibility of receiving relief.

Recognized Relief Societies.

Article 8.- Enemy civilians shall have every facility for application to duly recognised Relief Societies, whose object is to act as intermediaries in welfare activities.

These Societies shall receive, for this purpose, all facilities from the authorities, within the limits compatible with military necessities.

Protection.

Article 9.- Enemy civilians shall be protected against measures of violence, insults and public curiosity.

Prohibitions.

Article 10.- Measures of reprisal directed against them are prohibited.

Article 11.- The taking of hostages is forbidden.

Section II. Enemy civilians brought into the territory of a belligerent

Newcomers.

Article 12.- Enemy civilians who for any reason may be brought into the territory of a belligerent during hostilities shall benefit by the same guarantees as those who were in the territory at the outset of military operations.

Section III. Compulsory residence and internment

General Principles.

Article 13.- Should a belligerent country judge the measures of control or security mentioned in Article 6 as inadequate, it may have recourse to compulsory residence or internment, in conformity with the provisions of the present Section.

Confinement.

Article 14.- As a general rule, the compulsory residence of enemy civilians in a specified district shall be preferred to their internment. In particular, those who are established in the territory of the belligerent shall, subject to the security of the State, be thus restricted.

Internment.

Article 15.- The internment of enemy civilians in fenced-in camps may only be ordered in one of the following cases:

a) where civilians eligible for mobilisation under the conditions set forth in Article 4 (a) of the present Convention are concerned;

b) where the security of the Detaining Power is involved;

c) where the situation of the enemy civilians renders it necessary.

Separate Camps and Health Conditions.

Article 16.- Internment camps for enemy civilians shall be separate from internment camps for prisoners of war.

These camps cannot be set up in unhealthy districts, nor where the climate would be harmful to the internees' health.

Application of PoW Convention.

Article 17.- Furthermore, the Convention of July 27, 1929, concerning the treatment of Prisoners of War is by analogy applicable to Civilian Internees.

The treatment of civilian internees shall in no case be inferior to that laid down in the said Convention.

Chapter III

Enemy civilians in territory occupied by a belligerent

Observation of the Hague Regulations.

Article 18.- The High Contracting Parties undertake to observe, as regards the condition and protection of enemy civilians in territory occupied by a belligerent, the provisions of Section III of the Regulations annexed to the Fourth Hague Convention, of 1907.

Additional Provisions.

APPENDIX 2 (*continued*)

Article 19.- The High Contracting Parties further undertake to observe the following provisions:

a) In the event of it appearing, in an exceptional case, indispensable for an occupying Power to take hostages, the latter shall always be treated humanely. Under no pretext shall they be put to death or submitted to corporal punishments;

b) Deportations outside the territory of the occupied State are forbidden, unless they are evacuations intended, on account of the extension of military operations, to ensure the security of the inhabitants;

c) Enemy civilians shall have the possibility of giving news of a strictly private character to next of kin in the interior of occupied territory and of receiving such news. The same possibility shall be granted for correspondence with the exterior, subject to the measures applied to the population of the occupying Power, in general. With the same reservation enemy civilians shall have the possibility of receiving relief.

d) Enemy civilians shall also benefit by the provisions of Article 8 of the present Convention.

Chapter IV

Section I. Execution of the Convention

Application and Execution.

Article 20.- The provisions of the present Convention shall be respected by the High Contracting Parties in all circumstances.

In the event that, in time of war, one of the belligerents should not be a party to the Convention, its provisions shall nevertheless remain obligatory between the belligerents parties thereto.

Article 21.- The text of the present Convention and of the special Conventions foreseen in Article 3 shall be posted up in all civilian internment centres and shall be communicated, at their request to those who are unable to consult it.

Article 22.- The High Contracting Powers shall exchange, through the intermediary of the Swiss Federal Council, the official translations of the present Convention, as well as the laws and regulations which they may be called upon to adopt to ensure its application.

Section II. Organisation of Control

Protecting Power, Delegates.

Article 23.- The High Contracting Parties recognise that the full execution of the present Convention implies the cooperation of Protecting Powers; they declare themselves ready to accept the good offices of these Powers.

To this end, the Protecting Powers may nominate delegates, apart from their diplomatic staff, among their own nationals or among the nationals of other neutral Powers. These delegates shall be subject to the agreement of the belligerent to which their mission accredits them.

The representatives of the Protecting Power or its accepted delegates shall be authorised to visit all places of civilian internment, without exception. They shall have access to all buildings occupied by civilian internees and be allowed to converse with them, as a general rule without witnesses, personally or by the intermediary of interpreters.

The belligerents shall facilitate to the greatest possible extent the task of the representatives or of the recognized delegates of the Protecting Power. The military authorities shall be informed of their visits.

The belligerents may agree between themselves to allow persons of the same nationality as that of the civilian internees to participate in the journeys of inspection.

Interpretation of the Convention; Conferences.

Article 24.- In case of disagreement between belligerents concerning the application of the provisions of the present Convention, the Protecting Powers shall, as far as possible, exercise their good offices with a view to settling the difference.

To this end, each of the Protecting Powers may, in particular, propose to the belligerents concerned a meeting of their representatives, possibly on properly selected neutral territory. The belligerents shall be under the obligation to take action on the proposals made to them to this effect. The Protecting Power may, if judged desirable, submit to the approval of the Powers concerned the name of a person belonging to a neutral Power, or of a personality delegated by the International Committee of the Red Cross, who shall be called upon to participate in this meeting.

International Committee of the Red Cross.

Article 25.- The above provisions do not constitute an obstacle to the humanitarian activity which the International Committee of the Red Cross may exercise for the protection of enemy civilians, with the approval of the belligerents concerned.

Section III: Final provisions

Article 26.- The present Convention, which bears the date of this day, is open for signature until ...., in the name of all the countries represented at the Conference.

Article 27.- The present Convention shall be ratified as soon as possible. The ratifications shall be deposited in Bern.
A record shall be drawn up of the deposit of each instrument of ratification and certified copies of this record shall be transmitted by the Swiss Federal Council to the Governments of all the countries in whose name the Convention has been signed or whose accession has been notified.

Article 28.- The present Convention shall come into force six months after not less than two instruments of ratification have been deposited.
Thereafter, it shall come into force for each High Contracting Party six months after the deposit of the instrument of ratification.

Article 29.- From the date of its coming into force, the present Convention shall be open for accession in the name of any country in whose name the Convention has not been signed.

Article 30.- Accessions shall be notified in writing to the Swiss Federal Council and shall take effect six months after the date on which they are received. The Swiss Federal Council shall communicate the accessions to the Governments of all the countries in whose name the Convention has been signed or whose accession has been notified.

Article 31.- A state of war shall give immediate effect to the ratifications deposited and accessions notified by the belligerent Powers before or after the beginning of hostilities. The Swiss Federal Council shall communicate by the quickest method any ratifications or accessions received from belligerent Powers.

Article 32.- Each of the High Contracting Parties shall be at liberty to denounce the present Convention. The denunciation shall not take effect until one year after the notification thereof has been made in writing to the Swiss Federal Council.

The Swiss Federal Council shall transmit the notification to the Governments of all the High Contracting Parties.
The denunciation shall have effect only in respect of the denouncing High Contracting Party.
Moreover, the denunciation shall not take effect during a war in which the denouncing Power is involved. In such a case, the present Convention shall continue to have effect, beyond the period of one year, until peace has been concluded and, in any event, until repatriation operations have been completed.

Article 33.- The Swiss Federal Council shall deposit a certified copy of the present Convention in the archives of the League of Nations. The Swiss Federal Council shall also inform the League of Nations of the ratifications, accessions and denunciations that have been notified to it.

APPENDIX 2 (*continued*)

NOTE ON SOURCES

The evidence that forms the basis of the book's revisionist narrative has been selected by the author from multiple national, local, and personal archives in Japan, Switzerland, the United States, the United Kingdom, China, Korea, and Brazil over a period of twenty years. It is the first study of the JRCS by any scholar who had unrestricted access to the privately held JRCS archives. The author gained access to the JRCS archives when employed by the Red Cross Information Plaza at the JRCS headquarters in Tokyo, cataloging and digitizing published and original documents.

Until recently, the JRCS archives in Tokyo and the outsourced JRCS Meiji-mura Museum archives housed at the JRCS Toyota College of Nursing in Toyota City were not open to researchers. Categorized as private under Japan's National Library Law, they are not part of the Japanese national archives system. Use of previously sealed documents was essential to the book as a whole and of most value in chapter 5 and chapter 6 on the JRCS activities in World War II. The JRCS Meiji-mura archives at the JRCS Toyota College of Nursing provided a wealth of primary documents on the JRCS mission in the Russo-Japanese War; preparations for the Fifteenth Tokyo International Red Cross Conference; and the JRCS's overseas activities in Europe, Hawai'i, Korea, China, Manchuria, Karafuto, and Vladivostok. Discovery of the correspondence between the JRCS, the Red Cross Society of China (RCSC), and the International Committee of the Red Cross (ICRC) relating to the 1932 Shanghai Incident revealed for the first time the JRCS's efforts to mediate between the ICRC and the Imperial Japanese Army (IJA) in response to the RCSC's allegations of violations of the rules of warfare discussed in chapter 2. The collection also yielded important documents on the JRCS's role in the founding of the League of Red Cross Societies (LORCS) in 1919 and the drafting of the 1934 Tokyo Declaration, also discussed in chapter 2.

The Red Cross Information Plaza of the JRCS headquarters in Tokyo houses the special collections of the JRCS's former Investigation Department,[1] International Affairs Department,[2] and Health Department.[3] A distinctive feature of this archive is the documentation of the activities of local chapters of the JRCS in the areas of natural disasters and social welfare relief. These documents reveal the bottom-up humanitarianism of the JRCS in its early years. A second important source in the Red Cross Information Plaza of the JRCS headquarters is the voluminous collection of oral history testimonies and memories of JRCS nurses serving during World War II, which has been used by Japanese scholars but not previously cited in English-language scholarship. Their testimonies reveal the grim reality of the battlefield humanitarian operations on the ground level.[4]

JRCS's Disaster Relief Division, Disaster Management Department, and the Social Welfare Department at the JRCS headquarters, which contain the largest single collection of primary sources on JRCS nurses, include detailed daily records of the 934 JRCS relief parties deployed during World War II.

The archives of the former JRCS International Affairs Department housed at the previously mentioned Red Cross Informational Plaza contain many documents relating to Allied POWs and civilian internees held in Japan during the Pacific War. Particularly valuable was the wartime correspondence of the JRCS with other foreign Red Cross societies and documents on the Japanese POW camp in Manchukuo and the Allied POW camp in New Zealand.

The author conducted extensive research at the archives of Japanese Red Cross Institute for Humanitarian Studies, located at the Japanese Red Cross College of Nursing in Hiroo, JRCS hospitals and local chapters in Hiroshima and Nagasaki, and private interviews with retired JRCS officials.

The American Red Cross (ARC) headquarters in Washington, DC, and the ARC Hawaiʻi Chapter rendered generous support of my research.

These collections contain rare materials on Japanese immigrant communities, including wartime correspondence with relatives in Japan not held in the National Archives and Records Administration (NARA) in Washington, DC. The British Red Cross archives granted me access to catalogued boxes of documents related to POWs held captive by Japan during World War II.

The ICRC archive in Geneva houses the largest collection of documents relating to Red Cross societies that were established outside the West. The International Federation of Red Cross and Red Crescent Societies (IFRC) archives, also in Geneva, yielded diverse sources on ground-level JRCS operations in Japan's overseas empire, the Junior Red Cross movement, and the International Council of Nurses.

The Hawaii Emigration Museum Nihojima Village archives located in Hiroshima City, the online databases of the Center for Japanese Brazilian Studies in São Paulo, the Hoover Institution, Stanford University, and the Japanese American National Museum, Los Angeles contain many documents relating to the JRCS's overseas operations in Hawai'i and Latin America. The NARA has many records of ARC and JRCS operations involving civilian internment camps during World War II. The National Archives in the United Kingdom also preserved rare oral narratives of surviving British POWs in jungle camps in Southeast Asia during World War II and their testimonies during the interrogation of the International Military Tribunal for the Far East, which was cited in chapter 5. Overall, multi-archival research brought light to local and global, national, and international historical perspectives on the Japanese Red Cross movement in the Japanese Empire and the world within a transnational historical context.

NOTES

EPIGRAPH

Tochigi Kimi, *Nihon Sekijūjisha Kangofu Dōhōkai, Dōhō Shōwa Jūroku nen Jūni gatsu gō* [Dōhō Poetry Society] (Tokyo: Nihon Sekijūjisha Kangofu Dōhōkai, 1941), 9. Originally translated into contemporary Japanese by Ono Hisako and into English by Carroll Misono, 2023.

INTRODUCTION

1. See chapter 2, 43–44.
2. The JRCS launched the Mt. Bandai relief operation in July 1888, two years after the ARC's Charleston, South Carolina, flood disaster relief operation.
3. Charles Hurd, *The Compact History of the American Red Cross: The Story of the Red Cross Volunteers and the Organization in Which They Serve* (New York: Hawthorn, 1959), 111.
4. Julia F. Irwin, *Making the World Safe: The American Red Cross and a Nation's Humanitarian Awakening* (Oxford: Oxford University Press, 2013), 30.
5. Currently named the International Federation of Red Cross and Red Crescent Societies (IFRC).
6. Yoshiya Makita, "Shokuminchi-ki Firipin ni Okeru Hoken Eisei Jigyō to Sekijūji Jindōshugi," *America Kenkyū* 56 (March 2022): 69–91.
7. Olive Checkland, *Humanitarianism and the Emperor's Japan, 1877–1977* (New York: St. Martin's, 1994). The unpublished dissertation of Gregory DePies, which makes use of Japanese-language sources, shares Checkland's presentist conceptualization. Gregory John DePies, "Humanitarian Empire: The Red Cross in Japan, 1877–1945" (PhD thesis, University of California San Diego, 2013). For the role of native religions and nationalism in the Indian Red Cross Society, see Adrian Ruprecht, "De-Centering Humanitarianism: The Red Cross and India, c. 1877–1939" (doctoral thesis, University of Cambridge, 2017),

https://doi.org/10.17863/CAM.18514, and *The Great Eastern Crisis (1875–1878) as a Global Humanitarian Movement* (Cambridge: Cambridge University Press, 2021). For the affirmation of national sovereignty of the Red Cross movement in China, see Caroline Reeves, "The Early History of the Red Cross China and Its Relation to the Red Cross Movement," in *The Red Cross Movement: Myths, Practices and Turning Points*, ed. Neville Wylie, Melanie Oppenheimer, and James Crossland (Manchester: Manchester University Press, 2020).

8. John F. Hutchinson, *Champions of Charity: War and the Red Cross* (Oxford: Westview, 1997), 203.
9. Hutchinson, *Champions of Charity*. Moynier was a cofounder of the International Committee for Relief to the Wounded, the original iteration of the ICRC. In 1864, he became the president of the Committee, and he was also a major rival of the founder, Henry Dunant. He served as the president of the ICRC for forty-six years.
10. Caroline Moorehead, *Dunant's Dream: War, Switzerland and the History of the Red Cross* (London: Carroll & Graf, 1999), 122.
11. Moorehead, *Dunant's Dream*, 122–23. The Iwakura Mission, headed by Iwakura Tomomi (1825–1883) was a Japanese diplomatic voyage to the United States, the United Kingdom, and Europe between 1871 and 1973. It brought leading Japanese politicians and students to investigate Western politics, economy, law, society, industry, technology, education, and culture. The major purpose of the mission was to introduce Japan's new government under the sovereignty of Emperor Meiji to the Western powers and to persuade government ministers that drastic reforms were needed if Japan was to preserve its sovereignty in the face of Western powers.
12. Moorehead, *Dunant's Dream*, 123.
13. Moorehead, *Dunant's Dream*, 131.
14. Hutchinson, *Champions of Charity*, 138.
15. Scholarship on the JRCS, such as that by Checkland, Kurosawa, and Käser, routinely adduces the Meiji government's desire to be accepted as "civilized" as the primary or sole explanation for Japan's pursuit of ICRC membership. As argued in chapter 1, this interpretation is narrow and reductionist. Checkland, *Humanitarianism and the Emperor's Japan*; Kurosawa Fumitaka and Kawai Toshinobu, eds., *Nihon Sekijūjisha to Jindō Enjo* (Tokyo: University of Tokyo Press, 2009); Frank Käser, "A Civilized Nation: Japan and the Red Cross 1877–1900," *European Review of History* 23, no. 1–2 (March 2016): 16–32; and DePies, "Humanitarian Empire."
16. Hutchinson, *Champions of Charity*, 206.
17. Moorehead, *Dunant's Dream*, 150–51.
18. Sho Konishi, "The Emergence of an International Humanitarian Organization in Japan: The Tokugawa Origins of the Japanese Red Cross," *American Historical Review* 114, no. 4 (October 2014): 1129–53. In Japan, Fumitaka Kurosawa and Toshinobu Kawai made the case that native humanitarian discourses predated Western contact. Kurosawa and Kawai, *Nihon Sekijūjisha to Jindō Enjo*.
19. Kosuge's critical characterization of the imperial family's role is not informed by comparisons with the role of European monarchies in national Red Cross societies. Nobuko M. Kosuge, *Nihon Sekijūjisha to Kōshitsu: Hakuai ka Hōkoku ka* (Tokyo: Yoshikawa

Kōbunkan, 2021). In the case of the British Red Cross, for example, Queen Alexandra became president in 1905 and after 1908 operated under royal charter.

20. Yamashita Mai, "Nihon Sekijūjisha ga Okonatta Heiji Kyūgo no Tenkai Katei: Ninagawa Arata ga Hatashita Yakuwari," *Social Science Series, Kyoto Sangyo University Essays*, no. 34 (March 2017): 3–24.
21. Yamashita Mai, "Senkyūhyaku hachi nen kara Senkyūhyaku Yonjū nen ni okeru Nihon Sekijūjisha no Shū'nyū Kōzō kara Mita Jigyō Tenkai," *Social Science Series 31, Kyoto Sangyo University Essays*, Kyoto Sangyo University (March 2014): 179–200.
22. Shimosawa Takashi, "Nihon Sekijūjisha Kyōdōbokin ni miru Nihonteki Bokin no Tenkai," *Shizuoka University of Art and Culture Bulletin* 16 (March 2016): 17–26. JRCS archives contain no documents explicating the relationship between JRCS's membership drives and local governing authorities, although the fact that they were linked is clear and the link strengthened with the onset of World War II. Following the outbreak of the Second Sino-Japanese War in July 1937, the JRCS accelerated membership recruitment campaigns and opened new departments under local chapters both in the home islands and colonial territories, with the goal of securing an enlarged revenue stream from membership dues. It launched two recruitment campaigns. The first, in 1937, aimed to enroll an additional 500,000 members; the second, in 1940, an additional 1,500,000 members within five years. These campaigns were great successes, which the JRCS had not expected. Thus, in 1942 it set itself the new goal of "enlisting one member per one household." As a result, there was a dramatic increase in revenue as well as membership, from 5,868,005 members in 1942 to 15,238,429 members in 1945, which included colonial subjects in overseas chapters. Nihon Sekijūjisha, ed., *Nihon Sekijūjisha Shashikō, Dai Go-kan, Shōwa jūichi nen kara Shōwa nijū nen* (Tokyo: Nihon Sekijūjisha, 1969), 361, 364, 453–54.
23. See the table and pie chart in chapter 2, 43–44.
24. Sekijūjisha, *Nihon Sekijūjisha Shashikō*, 362.
25. Glenda Sulga and Patricia Clavin, eds., *Internationalisms: A Twentieth-Century History* (Cambridge: Cambridge University Press, 2016).
26. Akira Iriye, *Global Community: The Role of International Organizations in the Making of the Contemporary World* (Berkeley: University of California Press, 2004); and Akira Iriye, *Cultural Internationalism and World Order* (Baltimore, MD: Johns Hopkins University Press, 1997).
27. Thomas W. Burkman, *Japan and the League of Nations: Empire and World Order, 1914–1938* (Honolulu: University of Hawai'i Press, 2007), 197.
28. Michael R. Auslin, *Pacific Cosmopolitans: A Cultural History of U.S.-Japan Relations* (Cambridge, MA: Harvard University Press, 2011), 146–50.
29. Michael N. Barnett, *Empire of Humanity: A History of Humanitarianism* (Ithaca, NY: Cornell University Press, 2013), 82; and Konishi, "The Emergence of an International Humanitarian Organization in Japan," 1145.
30. Indicative of the ongoing Eurocentrism of English-language scholarship is the omission of the JRCS and all other non-Western Red Cross and Red Crescent societies from Barnett's justly acclaimed global history of modern humanitarian movements. Barnett, *Empire of Humanity*.
31. Ruprecht, "De-Centering Humanitarianism."

32. Maria Framke, "Indian Humanitarianism Under Colonial Rule: Imperial Loyalty, National Self-Assertion and Anti-Colonial Emancipation," in *The Routledge Handbook of the History of Colonialism in South Asia*, ed. Harald Fischer-Tiné and Maria Framke (London: Routledge, 2021), 486–509.
33. Maria Framke and Esther Moeller, "From Local Philanthropy to Political Humanitarianism: South Asian and Egyptian Humanitarian Aid During the Period of Decolonisation," ZMO Working Papers, no. 22 (2019): 1–17.
34. Alexandra Pfeiff, "The Red Swastika Society's Humanitarian Work: A Re-Interpretation of the Red Cross in China," *New Global Studies* 10, no. 3 (2016): 373–92. Although exclusively associated with German National Socialism, the swastika originated in Buddhism as an auspicious symbol.
35. Leo van Bergen, *The Dutch East Indies Red Cross, 1870–1950: On Humanitarianism and Colonialism* (Washington, DC: Rowman & Littlefield, 2019).

1. RESPONDING TO CRISES: A PEOPLE'S HUMANITARIAN MOVEMENT

1. See Sho Konishi, "The Emergence of an International Humanitarian Organization in Japan: The Tokugawa Origins of the Japanese Red Cross," *American Historical Review* 114, no. 4 (October 2014): 1129–53.
2. Ogata Kōan was a Japanese physician and Dutch studies (*rangaku*) scholar in the late Edo period. He established the Tekijuku, a Dutch studies school in Osaka that produced a number of prominent Meiji leaders and whose guiding philosophy was service to humanity, not pursuit of fame and fortune. His philosophy had a significant influence on the development of modern Japanese medical science and its practitioners.
3. Matsudaira Norikata, also known as Ogyū Yuzuru, was the former *daimyō* of Okudono Domain in Mikawa Province and Tanoguchi Domain in Shinano Province. In the late Edo period, he held positions at the highest levels of the Tokugawa government.
4. Kuni Takeyuki, *Saga Ijin-den, 09: Sano Tsunetami, 1822–1902* (Saga: Saga Kenritsu Sagajō Honmaru Rekishi-kan, 2013), 39–42.
5. Yoshikawa Ryūko, *Nisseki no Sōshi-sha: Sano Tsunetami* (Tokyo: Yoshikawa Kōbunkan, 2001), 54–62.
6. *Shisei* 至誠.
7. Yoshikawa, *Nisseki no Sōshi-sha*, 40–41.
8. Yoshikawa, *Nisseki no Sōshi-sha*, 62.
9. Nihon Sekijūjisha, ed., *Jindō—sono Ayumi: Nihon Sekijūjisha Hyaku-nen Shi* (Tokyo: Nihon Sekijūjisha, 1979), 55–59.
10. The JRCS official history book of 1911 reported, "Due to their hostility to foreigners and xenophobia, some members of the public viewed the Philanthropic Society as blindly servile to the Christian West and held the JRCS in contempt." Nihon Sekijūjisha, ed., *Nihon Sekijūji Shashikō* (Tokyo: Nihon Sekijūjisha, 1911), 157–58.
11. *Jin* 仁.

1. RESPONDING TO CRISES 197

12. *Kunshi* 君子.
13. Nihon Sekijūjisha, ed., *Nihon Sekijūji. No. 71, March 1899* (Tokyo: Nihon Sekijūji Hakkōjo, 1899), 15.
14. Hirayama Seisai was a Japanese Shinto priest, born to a samurai family in Miharu Domain, Mutsu Province, and acted as one of the commissioners during the Tokugawa government's negotiation with Matthew C. Perry in 1854. His son, Hirayama Narinobu (1854–1929), became the fifth president of the JRCS.
15. Shimaji Mokurai was a Japanese Buddhist monk, the chief monk at Nishi Hongan-ji in Kyoto. He travelled with the Iwakura Mission (1871–1873) to Europe, Jerusalem, the Ottoman Empire, and India.
16. Nihon Sekijūjisha, *Nihon Sekijūji Shashikō*, 153–58.
17. John F. Hutchinson, *Champions of Charity: War and the Red Cross* (Oxford: Westview, 1997), 206.
18. Nihon Sekijūjisha, *Nihon Sekijūji Shashikō*, appendix, 39–45.
19. Konishi, "The Emergence of an International Humanitarian Organization in Japan," 1132–42.
20. *Hakuai* 博愛.
21. The etymology of the closely related ethical precent *jindō* (人道) references a well-traveled path or thoroughfare. *Jindō*, the modern term for humanitarianism, appears in the writing of the *rangaku* (Dutch studies) physician Ogata Kōan (1810–1863) and Meiji novelist Natsume Sōseki (1867–1916). The premodern equivalent of *jindō* was *jinrin* (人倫), meaning human ethics and morals. *Jinrin* understood in this sense appears in *The Tale of the Heike*, an epic account of the Genpei War (1180–1185) composed in the early fourteenth century, which was powerfully influenced by Buddhist precepts. On the Asian continent, *jindō* is found in Chinese Confucianism, where it is used in contrast to *tendō* (天道), conventionally translated as the way of heaven, nature, or the universe.
22. *Chūai* 忠愛.
23. Yumoto Fumihiko, ed., *Chūai* (Kyoto: Japanese Red Cross Society Kyoto Chapter, 1910).
24. See Tetsuo Najita, *Ordinary Economics in Japan: A Historical Perspective, 1750–1950* (Berkeley: University of California Press, 2009), 109–13. According to Najita, the early nineteenth-century agricultural leader, moralist, and folk hero Ninomiya Sontoku (1787–1856) popularized the notion that the labor of common farmers to produce the food that sustained social life was an expression of *jindō* that preceded religious and moral formulations of abstract morality.
25. Yaku-in and Hiden-in were major Japanese ancient humanitarian institutions founded by Empress Kōmyō in 730 that provided multiple social welfare services for ordinary people, including hospitals, free medical services to the poor, and orphanages. Takinami Sadako, *Kōmyō Kōgō: Heijōkyō ni kaketa Yume to Inori* (Tokyo: Chūkōshinsho, 2017), 91.
26. Yumoto, *Chūai*. One of the most famous Japanese poems in the *Man'yōshū* composed by Yamanoue no Okura (660?–733?) in 721, "Hinkyūmondōka," lamented the great poverty of ordinary people in his time. Yamanoue no Okura, "Hinkyūmondōka (貧窮問答歌)," in *Man'yōshū, Ichi*, trans. and ed. Nakanishi Susumu (Tokyo: Kodansha-bunko, 1996), 402–5.
27. Tsuji Zen'nosuke, ed., *Nihonjin no Hakuai* (Tokyo: Kinkōdō Shoseki, 1932).
28. *Jin'ai* 仁愛.
29. Enomoto Shigeharu, *Nihon ni okeru Jin'ai no Seishin no Kigen* (Tokyo: Taisei, 1957).

30. Nihon Sekijūjisha, ed., *Nihon Sekijūjisha Shashikō, Dai Go-kan, Shōwa jūichi nen kara Shōwa nijū nen* (Tokyo: Nihon Sekijūjisha, 1969), 362. At the end of 1915, the American Red Cross (ARC) membership was only 22,500. With the surge of war fever that swept the country when the United States entered the war in 1917, membership rose to 6.3 million by the end of 1917 and to 22 million by the end of 1918, only to decline precipitously with the war's end. Julia F. Irwin, *Making the World Safe: The American Red Cross and a Nation's Humanitarian Awakening* (Oxford: Oxford University Press, 2013), 60, 67, 165.
31. *Kinnō-ha* (勤皇派): The coalition that supported the imperial court.
32. *Sabaku-ha* (佐幕派): The coalition of former retainers of the Tokugawa shogunate who carried on armed resistance to the imperial court after January 3, 1868.
33. Nihon Sekijūjisha Shimaneken-shibu, *Nihon Sekijūjisha Shimaneken-shibu Hyaku-nen shi* (Shimane: Nihon Sekijūjisha Shimaneken-shibu, 1990), 35–36.
34. Rice, miso, and soy sauce.
35. Nihon Sekijūjisha Shimaneken-shibu, *Nihon Sekijūjisha Shimaneken-shibu Hyaku-nen shi*, 36–37.
36. Nihon Sekijūjisha Shimaneken-shibu, *Nihon Sekijūjisha Shimaneken-shibu Hyaku-nen shi*, 33–34, 48.
37. Nihon Sekijūjisha Shimaneken-shibu, *Nihon Sekijūjisha Shimaneken-shibu Hyaku-nen shi*, 33–34.
38. Nihon Sekijūjisha Hiroshimaken-shibu, ed., *Nihon Sekijūjisha Hiroshimaken-shibu Hyakunen shi: Shiryōhen* (Hiroshima: Nihon Sekijūjisha Hiroshimaken-shibu, 1991), 3–18.
39. Hara Yasutarō, a samurai from Chōshū Domain, studied at the State University of New Jersey and King's College London. A leader of the military alliance that overthrew the Tokugawa shogunate, Hara fought in the Boshin War (1868–1869) and is thought to have executed Oguri Kōzukenosuke (Tadamasa) (1827–1868), a stateman of the Tokugawa government, during the war.
40. Nihon Sekijūjisha Yamaguchiken-shibu, *Hyaku-nen no Ayumi* (Yamaguchi: Nihon Sekijūjisha Yamaguchiken-shibu, 1991), 46.
41. Nihon Sekijūjisha Yamaguchiken-shibu, *Hyaku-nen no Ayumi*, 45–65.
42. Nihon Sekijūjisha Hokkaidō-shibu, *Hokkaidō no Sekijūji sono Hyakunen* (Sapporo: Nihon Sekijūjisha Hokkaidō-shibu, 1987), 46–50.
43. Nihon Sekijūjisha Hokkaidō-shibu, *Hokkaidō no Sekijūji sono Hyakunen*, 48–49.
44. Takamatsu's refusal was undoubtedly related to his appalling experience during the Battle of Hakodate, status as former Tokugawa Loyalist, and subsequent arrest and imprisonment by the Meiji government.
45. Takamatsu was embraced and financially supported by the local community to the point that he oversaw a network of more than sixty hospitals in Tokyo in 1898. The Meiji government awarded him the Medal of Honor with Blue Ribbon in 1913 and inspired the grassroots Red Cross movement in Japan, both by his example of doctors' neutrality during battle and later in addressing poverty in modern Japanese society. Years afterward, the story of his pioneering humanitarianism was recognized at the Fifteenth International Conference of the Red Cross in Tokyo in 1934. Nihon Sekijūjisha Hokkaidō-shibu, *Hokkaidō no Sekijūji sono Hyakunen*, 49–50, 90.

1. RESPONDING TO CRISES 199

46. The First Sino-Japanese War was the first major international humanitarian relief activity for the JRCS, whose operations were organized in accordance with the Geneva Convention.
47. *Hōkoku jippei* 報国恤兵. Nihon Sekijūjisha, *Nihon Sekijūji La Croix Rouge du Nippon*. No. 25, August 1894 (Tokyo: Nihon Sekijūji Hakkōjo, 1894), 5.
48. Nihon Sekijūjisha, *Nihon Sekijūji Shashikō*, 1290.
49. Nihon Sekijūjisha, *Nihon Sekijūji Shashikō*, 1292.
50. Nihon Sekijūjisha, *Nihon Sekijūji Shashikō*, 1136–301.
51. Nihon Sekijūjisha, *Nihon Sekijūji Shashikō*, 1290.
52. Nihon Sekijūjisha, *Nihon Sekijūji Shashikō*, 1293.
53. Nihon Sekijūjisha, *Nihon Sekijūji Shashikō*, 1159–65.
54. Archival collection of the Red Cross Information Plaza, A1–159, *Shinkoku Ri Kōshō no Shaji. (Kōsho nijū-ichi nen san gatsu hajime muika) Meiji Nijū-hachi nen*.
55. There is extensive English-language scholarship on the Russo-Japanese War and the JRCS's humane treatment of Russian POWs. For example, Rotem Kowner argues that the Japanese government was very eager to be recognized in the West not only as a great power but as a civilized nation. Rotem Kowner, "Becoming an Honorary Civilized Nation: Remaking Japan's Military Image During the Russo-Japanese War, 1904–1905," *Historian* 64, no. 1 (2001): 19–38.
56. Kita Yoshito, "Jūnēbu Jōyaku Teiyakukoku-kan no Nichiro Sensō," in *Nihon Sekijūjisha to Jindō Enjo*, ed. Kurosawa Fumitaka and Kawai Toshinobu (Tokyo: University of Tokyo Press, 2009), 105.
57. Ariga Nagao was a personal advisor of the JRCS and published a number of studies on the International Law of War. He became the first Japanese candidate for the Nobel Peace Prize due to his international legal contribution during the Russo-Japanese War.
58. Ariga Nagao, *Nichiro Rikusen Kokusaihō-ron* (Tokyo: Tōkyō Kaikōsha, 1911), 220.
59. Kita, "Jūnēbu Jōyaku Teiyakukoku-kan no Nichiro Sensō," 106.
60. Nihon Sekijūjisha, *Meiji Sanjū-shichi hachi nen Sen'eki Kyūgohōkoku* (Tokyo: Nihon Sekijūjisha, 1908), 11.
61. Rikugun Daijin Kanbō, ed., *Meiji Sanjū-shichi hachi nen Sen'eki Furyo Toriatsukai Tenmatsu* (Tokyo: Yuhikaku-shobō, 1907), 23–24.
62. Nihon Sekijūjisha, *Meiji Sanjū-shichi hachi nen Seneiki Kyūgohōkoku*, 955–56.
63. Nihon Sekijūjisha, *Meiji Sanjū-shichi hachi nen Seneiki Kyūgohōkoku*, 316–20.
64. Nihon Sekijūjisha, *Meiji Sanjū-shichi hachi nen Seneiki Kyūgohōkoku*, 852–912, 957, 962. For example, the Matsuyama POW camp received 36,688 POWs in total. Nihon Sekijūjisha, *Meiji Sanjū-shichi hachi nen Seneiki Kyūgohōkoku*, 957, 989.
65. Sophia von Theill, in *Nichiro Sensō-ka no Nihon: Roshia-jin Horyo no Tsuma no Nikki*, trans. Ogiso Ryū and Ogiso Miyoko (Tokyo: Shin Jinbutsu Ōraisha, 1991), 54.
66. F. P. Kupchinsky, in *Matsuyama Horyo Shūyōjo Nikki: Roshia Shōkō no Mita Meiji Nippon*, trans. Odagawa Kenji (Tokyo: Chūōkōronsha, 1988), 129–32.
67. Kita, "Jūnēbu Jōyaku Teiyakukoku-kan no Nichiro Sensō," 110–11.
68. Kita, "Jūnēbu Jōyaku Teiyakukoku-kan no Nichiro Sensō," 115.
69. Kita, "Jūnēbu Jōyaku Teiyakukoku-kan no Nichiro Sensō," 112.

70. Nihon Sekijūjisha, ed., *Nihon Sekijūji Shashi Zokkō, Ge kan, Meiji jonjū nen kara Taishō jūichi nen* (Tokyo: Nihon Sekijūjisha, 1929), 591–622. According to historian Utsumi Aiko, a number of factors help to explain the JRCS's generally exemplary treatment of Central Power POWs. In marked contrast to the four-year long "total war" waged in Europe, Japanese military operations against German forces in East Asia were few in number and brief in duration; the number of the POWs was not high, and the Japanese government and citizens, who spontaneously welcomed POWs, were eager to secure Japan's standing as a victor and equal among the Allied Powers through its respect for the International Law of War. Utsumi Aiko, *Nihongun no Horyo Seisaku* (Tokyo: Aoki-shoten, 2005), 103.
71. Kawai Toshinobu, "Nihon Sekijūjisha no Kokusaiteki Tenkai to Heiji Jigyō," in *Nihon Sekijūjisha to Jindō Enjo*, ed. Kurosawa Fumitaka and Kawai Toshinobu (Tokyo: University of Tokyo Press, 2009), 188–89.
72. Utsumi, *Nihongun no Horyo Seisaku*, 621.
73. Kawai, "Nihon Sekijūjisha no Kokusaiteki Tenkai to Heiji Jigyō," 187–89.
74. Archival collection of the Museum Meiji-mura held by the Japanese Red Cross Toyota College of Nursing, "Bericht: des Herrn Dr. F. Paravicini, in Yokohama, über seinen Besuch der Gefangenenlager in Japan (30. Juni bis 16. Juli 1918), Internationales Komitee Vom Roten Kreuz, Dokumente, Herausgegeben Während Des, Krieges 1914–1918, Zwanzigste Folge," in *Sekijūji-kokusai-i'inkai: Zai-honnpō Doku-Ō Furyo Shisatsu Kankei, Taishō Roku nen*, ID: B1132-3130.
75. Kawai, "Nihon Sekijūjisha no Kokusaiteki Tenkai to Heiji Jigyō," 190–91.
76. Utsumi, *Nihongun no Horyo Seisaku*, 101–3.
77. Nihon Sekijūjisha, *Nihon Sekijūji Shashi Zokkō, Ge kan*, 352–77.
78. Nihon Sekijūjisha, *Jindō—sono Ayumi*, 168.
79. Kawai, "Nihon Sekijūjisha no Kokusaiteki Tenkai to Heiji Jigyō," 181–82.
80. Kawai, "Nihon Sekijūjisha no Kokusaiteki Tenkai to Heiji Jigyō," 182–84.
81. Archival collection of the Museum Meiji-mura held by the Japanese Red Cross Toyota College of Nursing, *Futsukoku Haken Kyūgohan Hōkokusho, Dai Ippen, Jimu Hōkoku* (1915), ID: 725, quoted in Kawai, "Nihon Sekijūjisha no Kokusaiteki Tenkai to Heiji Jigyō," 183.
82. Asahi Shimbun Morning ed., "Futsukoku yuki no Kangofu: Shōji Masuko," *Asahi Shimbun*, November 12, 1914, 3.
83. Asahi Shimbun Morning ed., "Kenfutsu Kangofu no Katsudō: Shanzerizē no Hana," *Asahi Shimbun*, May 14, 1915, 3.
84. Archival collection of the Museum Meiji-mura held by the Japanese Red Cross Toyota College of Nursing, *Futsukoku Haken Kyūgohan Hōkokusho, Dai Ippen, Jimu Hōkoku* (1915), ID: 725, quoted in Kawai, "Nihon Sekijūjisha no Kokusaiteki Tenkai to Heiji Jigyō," 182–84.
85. Nihon Sekijūjisha, *Nihon Sekijūji Shashi Zokkō, Ge kan*, 404.
86. Nihon Sekijūjisha, *Nihon Sekijūji Shashi Zokkō, Ge kan*, 405–32. Daniels argues that this operation was conducted as a part of the Anglo-Japanese Alliance as the Japanese women carried out their international duty for the wartime state. He focused on activities in the political discourse. Gordon Daniels, "To Succour Wounded Allies: Japanese Red Cross Nurses in England, 1915–1916," *Japan Society Proceedings*, ISSN: 0952–2050 (2008).

1. RESPONDING TO CRISES   201

87. Siberia was the place of exile for the Polish in the Russian Empire. After the agreement of the Treaty of Portsmouth in 1905, many Poles migrated to Sakhalin, where they took up long-term residence. During the Polish-Soviet War (1919–1920), some Ashkenazi Jews residing in Russia were sent to Siberia as detainees and became refugees during the civil war in Russia (1917–1923) following the Bolshevik seizure of power. The Poles in Siberia founded the Polish Rescue Committee in Vladivostok in 1919 and appealed for aid at the time of the Allied Powers' Siberian Intervention (1919–1920). The Japanese forces remained in Siberia until 1922. As the last Allied Powers Red Cross society remaining in Siberia, the JRCS became responsible for treating Polish children who had lost their families during the chaos.
88. Nihon Sekijūjisha, *Nihon Sekijūji Shashi Zokkō, Ge kan*, 829–53.
89. The eruption of Mount Bandai in 1888 was known as a major volcanic eruption in the Meiji period.
90. It is generally believed that the Johnstown flood relief operation was the first such operation. See Johnstown Area Heritage Association, "The Flood and the American Red Cross: The Flood was the First Disaster Relief Effort for the Red Cross," accessed November 27, 2022, https://www.jaha.org/attractions/johnstown-flood-museum/flood-history/the-flood-and-the-american-red-cross/. However, Barton, president of the ARC, responded to a number of previous natural disasters in the United States such as flooding of the Mississippi and Ohio Rivers in 1883 and the 1886 Charleston earthquake in South Carolina. Irwin, *Making the World Safe*, 25–26.
91. The charter of the Empress Shōken Fund stated, "The Shōken Fund assists to develop the most advanced projects and treatments carried out by the Red Cross to prevent and to eradicate tuberculosis and other fatal epidemic diseases." Nihon Sekijūjisha, ed., *Nihon Sekijūji Shashi Zokkō, Jō kan Meiji yonjū nen kara Taishō jūichi nen* (Tokyo: Nihon Sekijūjisha, 1929), 235.
92. Nihon Sekijūjisha, *Nihon Sekijūji Shashi Zokkō, Jō kan*, 233.
93. Nihon Sekijūjisha, *Jindō—sono Ayumi*, 154.
94. Nihon Sekijūjisha, *Jindō—sono Ayumi*, 180–82.
95. Nihon Sekijūjisha Kyoto-shibu, ed., *Okutango Shinsai Kyūgo-shi* (Kyoto: Nihon Sekijūjisha Kyoto-shibu, 1928).
96. Nihon Sekijūjisha, ed., *Taishō Jūni nen Kantō Daishinsai Nihon Sekijūjisha Kyūgo-shi* (Tokyo: Nihon Sekijūjisha, 1925).
97. Nihon Sekijūjisha, *Taishō Jūni nen Kantō Daishinsai Nihon Sekijūjisha Kyūgo-shi*, 181.
98. Nihon Sekijūjisha, *Jindō—sono Ayumi*, 256–57.
99. Nihon Sekijūjisha, *Nihon Sekijūji Shashi Zokkō, Jō kan*, 655–56.
100. Baron Kitasato Shibasaburō (1853–1931), known as the father of physics and bacteriology in Japan, studied under Dr. Robert Koch at the University of Berlin from 1885 to 1891 and founded Tokyo University's Institute for Study of Infectious Diseases. Among his major discoveries were the infectious agent of bubonic plague and use of antitoxin to induce passive immunity to tetanus. He was nominated for the first annual Nobel Prize in Physiology or Medicine in 1901.
101. Naikaku Tōkei-kyoku, ed., *Kokuseichōsa-hōkoku, Taishō Kyū nen, Zenkoku no Bu, Dai ikkan* (Tokyo: Naikaku Tōkei-kyoku, 1928), 1.

102. Naimushō Eisei-kyoku, ed., *Ryūkōsei Kanbō: 'Supein Kaze' Dairyūkō no Kiroku* (Tokyo: Heibonsha, 2008), 104. Historical demographer Hayami Akira has calculated deaths at 453,152 based on excess mortality. Hayami Akira, *Nihon wo Osotta Supein Infuruenza: Jinrui to Wirusu no Dai-ichiji Sekai Sensō* (Tokyo: Fujiwara-shoten, 2006), 234–40. Hence, approximately 43 percent of the Japanese population was infected.
103. The pandemic struck Europe in the chaotic conditions of the last year of World War I. "Spanish Flu," Wikipedia, accessed April 7, 2022, https://en.wikipedia.org/wiki/Spanish_flu#Europe.
104. Nihon Sekijūjisha, *Hakuai: Organ of the Japanese Red Cross Society, No. 395, March 1920* (Tokyo: Hakuai Hakkōjo, 1920), 14–15.
105. Nihon Sekijūjisha, *Nihon Sekijūjisha Shashikō, Dai Go-kan*, 362. The ARC membership was 5.7 million in 1920. Irwin, *Making the World Safe*, 165.
106. Nihon Sekijūjisha, *Hakuai: Organ of the Japanese Red Cross Society, No. 394, February 1920* (Tokyo: Hakuai Hakkōjo, 1920), 17.
107. Nihon Sekijūjisha, *Hakuai: Organ of the Japanese Red Cross Society, No. 394*, 15.
108. Nihon Sekijūjisha, *Nihon Sekijūji Shashi Zokkō, Ge kan*, 794.
109. Nihon Sekijūjisha, *Hakuai: Organ of the Japanese Red Cross Society, No. 395*, 18; Nihon Sekijūjisha, *Hakuai: Organ of the Japanese Red Cross Society, No. 396, April 1920* (Tokyo: Hakuai Hakkōjo, 1920), 14; and Nihon Sekijūjisha, *Hakuai: Organ of the Japanese Red Cross Society, No. 397, May 1920* (Tokyo: Hakuai Hakkōjo, 1920), 16.
110. Nihon Sekijūjisha, *Taishō Jūni nen Kantō Daishinsai Nihon Sekijūjisha Kyūgo-shi*, 368.
111. League of Red Cross Societies, "Teaching Health to Juniors of Japan," *The World's Health, Index to Volume VI* (January–December 1925): 66–67.
112. Nihon Sekijūjisha, *Nihon Sekijūjisha Shashikō, Dai Yon-kan*, 256–60.
113. Nihon Sekijūjisha, *Nihon Sekijūji Shashikō*, 1749–58.
114. Nihon Sekijūjisha, *Nihon Sekijūjisha Shashikō, Dai Yon-kan*, 257–58.
115. Nihon Sekijūjisha, *Nihon Sekijūji Shashi Zokkō, Jō kan*, 1445–48.
116. Nihon Sekijūjisha, *Jindō—sono Ayumi*, 183.
117. Nihon Sekijūjisha, *Jindō—sono Ayumi*, 183–84.
118. Nihon Sekijūjisha, *Jindō—sono Ayumi*, 183–86.
119. Nihon Sekijūjisha, *Jindō—sono Ayumi*, 187.
120. See Julia F. Irwin, *Catastrophic Diplomacy: US Foreign Disaster Assistance in the American Century* (Chapel Hill: University of North Carolina Press, 2023).
121. The American Red Cross Archives, *The American National Red Cross Annual Report*, June 30, 1924, 59, 61, 84, 90, 95; Nihon Sekijūjisha, *Taishō Jūni nen Kantō Daishinsai Nihon Sekijūjisha Kyūgo-shi*, 774–80; Nihon Sekijūjisha, *Nihon Sekijūjisha Shashikō, Dai Yon-kan*, 204; Nihon Sekijūjisha, *Nihon Sekijūji Shashi Zokkō, Jō kan*, 954; and Irwin, *Making the World Safe*, 189.
122. Tang Erho, a medical doctor and politician, joined the Provisional Government of the Republic of China in 1937 and later served on the North China Political Affairs Commission. Nihon Sekijūjisha, *Nihon Sekijūjisha Shashikō, Dai Yon-kan*, 204; and Nihon Sekijūjisha, *Hakuai: Shinsaigō, No. 437, October 1923* (Tokyo: Hakuai Hakkōjo, 1923), 12–13.
123. Nihon Sekijūjisha, *Jindō—sono Ayumi*, 183–87.

124. Kusama Hidesaburō, "President Wilson and the Idea of the International Red Cross," *Chiiki-kenkyū Sōsho. Dai San-kan. Eibei no Seiji Gaikō* (Nagoya: International Research Centre, Aichi Gakuin University, 2005), 8.
125. Daphne A. Reid and Patrick F. Gilbo, *Beyond Conflict: The International Federation of Red Cross and Red Crescent Societies, 1919–1994* (Geneva: International Federation of Red Cross and Red Crescent Societies, 1997).
126. Yamashita Mai, "Nihon Sekijūjisha ga Okonatta Heiji Kyūgo no Tenkai Katei: Ninagawa Arata ga Hatashita Yakuwari," *Social Science Series, Kyoto Sangyo University Essays*, no. 34 (March 2017): 3–24; Melanie Oppenheimer, "Reflections on the Easternisation of the Red Cross Movement: The Role of the Japanese Red Cross and the League of Red Cross Societies, 1907–1926," *Pacific and American Studies, Center for Pacific and American Studies (CPAS), Graduate School of Arts and Sciences, The University of Tokyo*, no. 20 (March 2020): 23–39.
127. Ninagawa Arata, *Jindō no Sekai to Nipponjin* (Tokyo: Hakuai Hakkōjo, 1936). The advocacy of Ninagawa and the JRCS headquarters were significant factors driving the revolution of modern humanitarianism. With the end of World War I, recognition of the important awareness of peacetime activities increased within the Red Cross humanitarian movement. The JRCS was at the forefront of this movement.
128. Nihon Sekijūjisha, *Nihon Sekijūji Shashi Zokkō, Ge kan*, 438–58.
129. Nihon Sekijūjisha, *Nihon Sekijūji Shashi Zokkō, Ge kan*, 448; Ninagawa, *Jindō no Sekai to Nipponjin*, 454–55.
130. Nihon Sekijūjisha, *Nihon Sekijūji Shashi Zokkō, Ge kan*, 449–50.
131. Reid and Gilbo, *Beyond Conflict*, 34.
132. Ninagawa Arata, "Jindō no Gimu to Gijutsuteki-iken no Kōkan," in *Jindō no Sekai to Nipponjin* (Tokyo: Hakuai Hakkōjo, 1936), 73–74.
133. Ninagawa, "Jindō no Gimu to Gijutsuteki-iken no Kōkan."
134. Ninagawa, *Jindō no Sekai to Nipponjin*, 318–21.

2. INTERNATIONALISM IN CRISIS: THE FIFTEENTH INTERNATIONAL CONFERENCE OF THE RED CROSS IN TOKYO, 1934

1. The International Red Cross and Red Crescent Movement was a global humanitarian network. It consisted of the International Committee of the Red Cross (ICRC), the League of Red Cross Societies (LORCS), and National Red Cross and Red Crescent Societies.
2. On May 15, 1932, young naval officers assassinated Prime Minister Inukai Tsuyoshi and attempted to kill Makino Nobuaki (1861–1949), the Lord Keeper of the Privy Seal of Japan, several political leaders, and heads of corporations in a failed coup attempt. The coup leaders were assisted by army cadets. The incident weakened Japanese democracy and the rule of law and accelerated the rise of Japanese militarism.
3. In English-language historiography, the Tokyo Declaration is commonly referred to as "the draft," short for the "Draft International Convention on the Condition and

Protection of Civilians of Enemy Nationality Who Are on Territory Belonging to or Occupied by a Belligerent" of 1934; "the draft," however, only references the thirty-ninth resolution of the Tokyo Declaration, while the Tokyo Declaration itself consisted of forty-eight resolutions. As discussed in the section "Tokyo Declaration of 1934" on pages 171–80, the greater part of the document addressed peacetime relief issues and the prevention of war. See appendices in this book.

4. See below, 50–53.
5. Nihon Sekijūjisha, ed., *Nihon Sekijūjisha Shashikō, Dai Go-kan, Shōwa jūichi nen kara Shōwa nijū nen* (Tokyo: Nihon Sekijūjisha, 1969), 362.
6. Nihon Sekijūjisha, ed., *Nihon Sekijūjisha Shashikō, Dai Yon-kan, Taishō jūni nen kara Shōwa jū nen* (Tokyo: Nihon Sekijūjisha, 1957), 107.
7. Haraguchi Daisuke, *Kizokuin Gichō: Tokugawa Iesato to Meiji Rikken-sei* (Tokyo: Yoshida Shoin, 2018), 272–73; and Higuchi Takehiko, *Dai Jūroku-dai Tokugawa Iesato—Sono Go no Tokugawa-ke to Kindai Nihon* (Tokyo: Shōdensha, 2012), 54.
8. The Taishō political crisis was a period of severe political turmoil in Japan, which began with the fall of the Saionji Kin'mochi (1849–1940) cabinet and the death of the Meiji Emperor in 1912. Japan's political parties and public opinion wanted to wrest control of the cabinet from nonelected government officials and transition to fully democratic governance where the prime minister was the leader of the majority party in parliament. See Tetsuo Najita, *Hara Kei and the Politics of Compromise, 1905–1915* (Cambridge, MA: Harvard University Press, 1967).
9. Katō Tomosaburō (1861–1923) was a career officer in the Imperial Japanese Navy and served as prime minister of Japan from 1922 to 1923. Shidehara Kijūrō (1872–1951) was a leading Japanese diplomat in the prewar period who embraced Wilsonian internationalism in the interwar period. He served as prime minister of Japan from 1945 to 1946 and supported Japan's postwar "peace" constitution.
10. Haraguchi Daisuke, "Tokugawa Iesato's Political Position Before and After the Washington Conference (1921–22)," *Kyūshū Shigaku* ISSN 04511638 (2014): 42–60; and Haraguchi, *Kizokuin Gichō*, 151–89.
11. The residence of Iesato was set on fire by a member of the National Levelers Association (*Zenkoku Suiheisha*), the predecessor of Buraku Liberation League, in September 1925. Higuchi, *Dai Jūroku-dai Tokugawa Iesato*, 115–18.
12. Tokugawa Iesato was among twenty prominent political figures and wealthy industrialists targeted for assassination in the Blood-Pledge Corps Incident, February and March 1931. Stephen S. Large, "Nationalist Extremism in Early Shōwa Japan: Inoue Nisshō and the 'Blood-Pledge Corps Incident', 1932," *Modern Asian Studies* 35, no. 3 (July 2001): 533–64; and Nakajima Takeshi, *Ketsumeidan Jiken* (Tokyo: Bungeishunjū, 2016), 405.
13. Higuchi, *Dai Jūroku-dai Tokugawa Iesato*, 96–101.
14. Higuchi, *Dai Jūroku-dai Tokugawa Iesato*, 100–101.
15. JRCS Red Cross Information Plaza Archive, "Prince Tokugawa's Address to Be Delivered at the Party to Be Given by the League of Red Cross Societies," *File No. 10. The Fourteenth International Conference of the Red Cross (1930)*.
16. Nihon Sekijūjisha, *Nihon Sekijūjisha Shashikō, Dai Yon-kan*, 111, 145–52.
17. Nihon Sekijūjisha, *Nihon Sekijūjisha Shashikō, Dai Yon-kan*, 111.

18. Inoue served as Surgeon Major Class Three in the Fifteenth Division of the Imperial Japanese Army between 1920 and 1922 and became Surgeon Major General in 1922. Nihon Sekijūjisha, *Hakuai: Organ of the Japanese Red Cross Society, No. 450, November 1924* (Tokyo: Hakuai Hakkōjo, 1924), 12; and Fukukawa Hideki, ed., *Nippon Rikugun Shōkan Jiten* (Tokyo: Fuyōshobō, 2001), 93.
19. Archival collection of the Museum Meiji-mura held by the Japanese Red Cross Toyota College of Nursing, *Dai Jūgo-kai Sekijūji Kokusai-kaigi, Shōwa Shichi-nen Dō Hachi-nen*, ID: B1096-4381.
20. Archival collection of the Museum Meiji-mura held by the Japanese Red Cross Toyota College of Nursing, *Kagakusen Jinmin Hogo Kokusai I'inkai: Shōwa Ni nen Itaru Go nen*, ID: B1731-3968.
21. Taoka Ryōichi, professor at Tohoku Imperial University, wrote a book entitled *Air Strikes and International Law* in 1937. Taoka Ryōichi, *Air Strikes and International Law* (Tokyo: Ganshōdō-shoten, 1937).
22. Nihon Sekijūjisha, *The Geneva Conventions* (Tokyo: Nihon Sekijūjisha, 1933).
23. Louise Young, "War Fever: Imperial Jingoism and the Mass Media," in *Japan's Total Empire: Manchuria and the Culture of Wartime Imperialism* (Berkeley: University of California Press, 1998), 55–114. In America and Europe, public support for the national Red Cross society also increased dramatically with the outbreak of war. For example, the ARC membership rose from 22,500 at the beginning of 1916 to 22 million adults and 11 million children by early 1919. Julia F. Irwin, *Making the World Safe: The American Red Cross and a Nation's Humanitarian Awakening* (Oxford: Oxford University Press, 2013), 66–67.
24. "Sekijūji no Shigoto wa Kokumu no Enjo de aru" [The Mission of the Red Cross Is to Support the Mission of Nation States], in *Hakuai: Organ of the Japanese Red Cross Society, No. 566, July 1934*, ed. Nihon Sekijūjisha (Tokyo: Nihon Sekijūjisha, 1934), 30.
25. Rotary International, *Twenty-First Annual Convention of Rotary International: Chicago, Illinois, U.S.A., June 23–27, 1930* (Chicago: Rotary International, 1930), 162–65, accessed December 23, 2022, http://bit.ly/2jBoLlx; and Higuchi, *Dai Jūroku-dai Tokugawa Iesato*, 109–10.
26. Nihon Sekijūjisha, *Nihon Sekijūjisha Hachi-jū-nen Shōshi* (Tokyo: Nihon Sekijūjisha, 1957), 19. In fact, the ARC sent more than seventy-eight representatives and officers, making the ARC by far the largest delegation, double even the JRCS delegation. Nihon Sekijūjisha, *Nihon Sekijūjisha Hachi-jū-nen Shōshi*, 20. The JRCS reserved seating for the ARC delegation, and John Barton Payne, the chairman of the ARC, acted as a vice-chairman during the meeting. Nihon Sekijūjisha, *Nihon Sekijūjisha Shashikō, Dai Yon-kan*, 112.
27. Archival collection of the Museum Meiji-mura held by the Japanese Red Cross Toyota College of Nursing, *Dai Jūgo-kai Sekijūji Kokusai-kaigi, Ji Shōwa Jū nen Itaru dō Jūichi nen*, ID: B1115-4400; and Nihon Sekijūjisha, *Nihon Sekijūjisha Shashikō, Dai Yon-kan*, 52. See chapter 1, 31.
28. The name of the League of Red Cross Societies was changed to the League of Red Cross and Red Crescent Societies in 1983 and the International Federation of Red Cross and Red Crescent Societies in 1991.
29. Daphne A. Reid and Patrick F. Gilbo, *Beyond Conflict: The International Federation of Red Cross and Red Crescent Societies, 1919–1994* (Geneva: International Federation of Red Cross and Red Crescent Societies, 1997), 75.

30. A range of the national societies were involved in the Junior Red Cross, including Japan, the United States, Canada, England, Italy, Czechoslovakia, Australia, Argentina, Chile, South Africa, Turkey, and Syria. Reid and Gilbo, *Beyond Conflict*, 72.
31. Nihon Sekijūjisha, *The Japan Junior Red Cross: Special Number of the Fifteenth International Red Cross Conference Tokyo, October 20–29, Vol. IX, No. 4, October 1934* (Tokyo: Nihon Sekijūjisha, 1934), 2, 26.
32. Nihon Sekijūjisha, ed., *Dai Jūgo-kai Sekijūji Kokusai Kaigishi* (Tokyo: Nihon Sekijūjisha, 1937), 333.
33. Nihon Sekijūjisha, *Dai Jūgo-kai Sekijūji Kokusai Kaigishi*, 328–68.
34. Inoue Enji, *Ōshū Taisengo no Sekijūji Heiwa-jigyō Shōnen Sekijūji* (Tokyo: Hakuai Hakkōjo, 1925), 39, 41, 57–58, 60.
35. Inoue, *Ōshū Taisengo no Sekijūji Heiwa-jigyō Shōnen Sekijūji*, 369–413.
36. Nihon Sekijūjisha, *Hakuai: Organ of the Japanese Red Cross Society, No. 562, March 1934* (Tokyo: Nihon Sekijūjisha, 1934), 30.
37. Nihon Sekijūjisha, *Nihon Sekijūjisha Shashikō, Dai Go-kan*, 282.
38. Ninagawa Arata, *Jindō no Sekai to Nipponjin* (Tokyo: Hakuai Hakkōjo, 1936), 148–49.
39. Nihon Sekijūjisha Kangofu Dōhōkai, *Dōhō Shōwa Hachi-nen Ni gatsu-gō* (Tokyo: Nihon Sekijūjisha Kangofu Dōhōkai, 1933), 1.
40. Nihon Sekijūjisha, *Nihon Sekijūjisha Shashikō, Dai Yon-kan*, 246.
41. Nihon Sekijūjisha, *Shina-jihen ni Kansuru Nihon Sekijūjisha Kyūgo Jigyō Gaiyō, 3* (Tokyo: Nihon Sekijūjisha, 1933), 5.
42. This RCSC was founded in 1912 just after the Republican (Xinhai) Revolution (1911–1912), under the significant guidance of the JRCS.
43. Archival collection of the Museum Meiji-mura held by the Japanese Red Cross Toyota College of Nursing, *Dai Jūgo-kai Sekijūji Kokusai-kaigi, Shōwa Shichi-nen Itaru dō Kyū nen: Buraun Giruguddo Kankei*, ID: B1099-4384.
44. The report said, "unable to trace them and locate them." Archival collection of the Museum Meiji-mura held by the Japanese Red Cross Toyota College of Nursing, *Dai Jūgo-kai Sekijūji Kokusai-kaigi, Shōwa Shichi-nen Itaru dō Kyū nen: Buraun Giruguddo Kankei*, ID: B1099-4384.
45. Archival collection of the Museum Meiji-mura held by the Japanese Red Cross Toyota College of Nursing, *Dai Jūgo-kai Sekijūji Kokusai-kaigi, Shōwa Shichi-nen Itaru dō Kyū nen, Shōwa Shichi-nen Itaru dō Kyū nen: Buraun Giruguddo Kankei*, ID: B1099-4384.
46. For example, at that time, the German Red Cross (GRC) was not in direct contact with the JRCS but was informed by Shigemitsu Mamoru (1887–1957), vice-minister for the Foreign Ministry of Japan, that due to the unstable political situation in Germany following Adolf Hitler's appointment as chancellor and the government's distrust, the GRC might not be able to attend. In the end, the GRC joined the conference represented by its president, Alfred Ernest Albert. Archival collection of the Museum Meiji-mura held by the Japanese Red Cross Toyota College of Nursing, *Dai Jūgo-kai Sekijūji Kokusai-kaigi, Shōwa Hachi nen Dō Kyūnen*, ID: B1100-4385; and Nihon Sekijūjisha, *Nihon Sekijūjisha Shashikō, Dai Yon-kan*, 145.

47. Archival collection of the Museum Meiji-mura held by the Japanese Red Cross Toyota College of Nursing, *Dai Jūgo-kai Sekijūji Kokusai-kaigi, Shōwa Kyū-nen*, ID: B1107-4392.
48. Archival collection of the Museum Meiji-mura held by the Japanese Red Cross Toyota College of Nursing, *Dai Jūgo-kai Sekijūji Kokusai-kaigi, Shōwa Kyū-nen*, ID: B1107-4392.
49. Archival collection of the Museum Meiji-mura held by the Japanese Red Cross Toyota College of Nursing, *Dai Jūgo-kai Sekijūji Kokusai-kaigi, Shōwa Kyū-nen*, ID: B1101-4386.
50. Archival collection of the Museum Meiji-mura held by the Japanese Red Cross Toyota College of Nursing, *Dai Jūgo-kai Sekijūji Kokusai-kaigi, Shōwa Kyū-nen*, ID: B1102-4387.
51. 馬天則.
52. Initially the director general of the RCSC, Wang Yuan (王元), was willing to participate in the conference but this was opposed by President Chiang Kai-shek, who complained that the RCSC only consisted of professional aid workers not qualified to conduct international relations and believed Chinese government diplomats should be in the delegation. Connie Chow 周琇環, ed., 國民政府時期外交部工作報告〈民國二十二年至二十六年〉[Report on the Work of the Ministry of Foreign Affairs Under the National Government, 1933–1937] (Taiwan: Academia Historica, 1999), 179; and Nihon Sekijūjisha, *Sekijūji Kokusai Kaigi Giji Gaiyō, Dai Jūgo-kai*, 42–43.
53. Nihon Sekijūjisha, *Sekijūji Kokusai Kaigi Giji Gaiyō*, 236.
54. Nihon Sekijūjisha, *Dai Jūgo-kai Sekijūji Kokusai Kaigishi*, 9.
55. Nihon Sekijūjisha, *Dai Jūgo-kai Sekijūji Kokusai Kaigishi*, 10.
56. Nihon Sekijūjisha, *Dai Jūgo-kai Sekijūji Kokusai Kaigishi*, 4–8; and the Archival Collection of the Museum Meiji-mura held by the Japanese Red Cross Toyota College of Nursing, *Dai Jūgo-kai Sekijūji Kokusai-kaigi, Shōwa Shichi-nen Itaru dō Kyū nen*, ID: B1098-4383; and Nihon Sekijūjisha, *Dai Jūgo-kai Sekijūji Kokusai Kaigishi*, 87–89.
57. Nihon Sekijūjisha, *Dai Jūgo-kai Sekijūji Kokusai Kaigishi*, 6–7.
58. Records show correspondence with a wide range of representatives such as those in Denmark, Belgium, Canada, Great Britain, France, Italy, Egypt, South Africa, Mexico, Chile, Bolivia, Nicaragua, Persia, Afghanistan, Iraq, Siam, India, the Soviet Union, Latvia, Czechoslovakia, Yugoslavia, Cuba, Haiti, and Australia, in addition to NGOs such as the Save the Children International Union, the China International Famine Relief Commission, and the Sovereign Military Order of Malta (SMOM). Archival collection of the Museum Meiji-mura held by the Japanese Red Cross Toyota College of Nursing, *Dai Jūgo-kai Sekijūji Kokusai-kaigi*.
59. Nihon Sekijūjisha, *Dai Jūgo-kai Sekijūji Kokusai Kaigishi*, 218–38.
60. Nihon Sekijūjisha, *Dai Jūgo-kai Sekijūji Kokusai Kaigishi*, 7.
61. ICRC Archives, CRi 15/I, XV Conference, Intern, De La + Rouge I, 1 à 150, du 26.5.1931 au 21.6.1934, 9; and the Archival Collection of the Museum Meiji-mura held by the Japanese Red Cross Toyota College of Nursing, *Dai Jūgo-kai Sekijūji Kokusai-kaigi*, ID: B1096-4381.
62. Shimazu Tadatsugu (1903–1990) became a vice-president of the JRCS and the director general of the JRCS Prisoners' Relief Committee Department during the Pacific War. After World War II, he served as the president of the JRCS under the Supreme Commander for the Allied Powers (SCAP) occupation.

63. Japan Center for Asian Historical Records, *Sekijūji Kokusai Kaigi Kankei Ikken, Dai Ni-kan, Ichi, Shōwa Hachi-nen, Bunkatsu ni*, REF: B04013279300 (Diplomatic Archives of the Ministry of Foreign Affairs of Japan, *Sekijūji Kokusai Kaigi Kankei Ikken, Dai Ni-kan*, REF: I-5-3-0-3_002), PDF, 92–93.
64. Nihon Sekijūjisha, *Nihon Sekijūjisha Shashikō, Dai Yon-kan*, 142.
65. Archival collection of the Museum Meiji-mura held by the Japanese Red Cross Toyota College of Nursing, *Dai Jūgo-kai Sekijūji Kokusai-kaigi, Shōwa Hachi-nen Dō Kyū-nen*, ID: B1100-4385.
66. Nihon Sekijūjisha, *Nihon Sekijūjisha Shashikō, Dai Yon-kan*, 148–49.
67. ICRC Archives, "The League of Red Cross Societies: Report on the Development of Red Cross Organization and Activity in the Far East, Based on a Study of the Work of the Red Cross in Japan, China, the Philippine Islands and the Netherlands East Indies, November 1932–February 1933," 7–8, in Cri 15/0 25, Bulletin XV Conference, Voyage XV Conf.
68. Archival collection of the Museum Meiji-mura held by the Japanese Red Cross Toyota College of Nursing, *Dai Jūgo-kai Sekijūji Kokusai-kaigi*, ID: B1102-4387.
69. "Indian Red Cross Society: Constituted Under Act XV of 1920," in the Archival Collection of the Red Cross Information Plaza, *Dai Jūgo-kai Kokusai Kaigi ni okeru Kiroku narabini Insatsubutsu*, vol. 6; and the Archival Collection of the Museum Meiji-mura held by the Japanese Red Cross Toyota College of Nursing, *Dai Jūgo-kai Sekijūji Kokusai-kaigi, Shōwa Kyū-nen*, ID: 1106-4391.
70. Nihon Sekijūjisha, *Dai Jūgo-kai Sekijūji Kokusai Kaigishi*, 521.
71. Nihon Sekijūjisha, *Nihon Sekijūjisha Shashikō, Dai Yon-kan*, 146–48.
72. "Rokoku no Renmei Kamei wo Manjōicchi de Kaketsu: Sekjūjirenmai Rijikai," *Asahi Shimbun*, October 19, 1934, 2.
73. Archival collection of the Museum Meiji-mura held by the Japanese Red Cross Toyota College of Nursing, *Sovieto Renpō Sekijūjisha yori Mimaikin Haibunkata ni Kansuru Bunsho, Shōwa Kyū-nen*, ID: B1822-4249; Nihon Sekijūjisha, *Nihon Sekijūjisha Hachi-jū-nen Shōshi*, 19. Christian Georgievich Rakovsky (1873–1941) was a representative of the Soviet RCRC. Rakovsky was a former Soviet ambassador to Great Britain and France. The Japanese government recognized that Rakovsky rejected Leon Trotsky's criticisms of Stalinism. Diplomatic Archives of the Ministry of Foreign Affairs of Japan, *Sekijūji Kokusai Kaigi Kankei Ikken, Dai Yon-kan, Bunkatsu Ichi*, REF: B04013280200, Japan Center for Asian Historical Records, *Sekijūji Kokusai Kaigi Kankei Ikken, Dai Yon-kan*, REF: I-5-3-0-3_004, PDF, 47–50.
74. Nihon Sekijūjisha, *Nihon Sekijūjisha Shashikō, Dai Yon-kan*, 112.
75. Nihon Sekijūjisha, *Nihon Sekijūjisha Shashikō, Dai Yon-kan*, 112.
76. "Nichibei-sen Ronsō wo Haigeki," *Asahi Shimbun*, February 26, 1934, 3.
77. "Taiheiyō wa Heiwa no Kidō e," *Yomiuri Shimbun*, February 26, 1934, 2.
78. "Japanese Peace Worker Soon to Visit Capital: Prince Tokugawa, Grandson of Last Shogun Ruler, Will Make Fifth Tour of U.S.," *Sunday Star*, Washington, DC, February 18, 1934, D-3.
79. "Red Cross Plans Conference: Prince Tokugawa and Judge Payne Arranged Parley," *Evening Star*, Washington, DC, March 1, 1934, A-4.

80. Archival collection of the Museum Meiji-mura held by the Japanese Red Cross Toyota College of Nursing, *Dai Jūgo-kai Sekijūji Kokusai-kaigi*, ID: B1107-4392.
81. Archival collection of the Red Cross Information Plaza, *Mansen, Karafuto, Tokubetsu-i'inbu Kankei, Ji Shōwa Hachi nen Itaru dō Jūichi nen*, ID: 4284.
82. "King's Visitors," *Gloucester Citizen*, November 2, 1933, 1.
83. "Britain and Japan 'Brothers': Prince Tokugawa and the Future," *Morning Post*, November 15, 1933, in Japan Center for Asian Historical Records, *Sekijūji Kokusai Kaigi Kankei Ikken, Dai Ni-kan, Ichi, Shōwa Hachi-nen, Bunkatsu yon*, REF: B04013279500 (Diplomatic Archives of the Ministry of Foreign Affairs of Japan, *Sekijūji Kokusai Kaigi Kankei Ikken, Dai Ni-kan*, REF: I-5-3-0-3_002), PDF, 56.
84. Diplomatic Archives of the Ministry of Foreign Affairs of Japan, *Sekijūji Kokusai Kaigi Kankei Ikken, Dai Ni-kan*, REF: I-5-3-0-3_002, PDF, 67–70. Willian Adams, known as Miura Anjin in Japanese, served Tokugawa Ieyasu and his successor Tokugawa Hidetada, from his arrival in Japan in 1600 until his death in 1620.
85. Nihon Sekijūjisha, *Hakuai: Organ of the Japanese Red Cross Society*, No. 564, May 1934 (Tokyo: Nihon Sekijūjisha, 1934), 1–2.
86. Translation of article from the ARC monthly magazine *The Red Cross Courier*, April 1934, 292, quoted in *Hakuai* under title "Tokugawa Kōshaku ni Taisuru Beikokumin no Kokoro karana Kangei," No. 566, July 1934, 10–11; and "Red Cross Plans Conference: Prince Tokugawa and Judge Payne Arranged Parley."
87. Nihon Sekijūjisha, *Dai Jūgo-kai Sekijūji Kokusai Kaigishi*, 136–40.
88. Nihon Sekijūjisha, *Dai Jūgo-kai Sekijūji Kokusai Kaigishi*, 595–97.
89. Nihon Sekijūjisha, *Dai Jūgo-kai Sekijūji Kokusai Kaigishi*, 106.
90. National Archives of Japan, *Okada Sōridaijin Aisatsu*, Dai Jūgokai Sekijūji Kokusaikaigi Sanretsusha Kangei Bansankai Yakai Shorui, Naikaku Sōridaijin Kanbō Sōmuka Shiryō, ID: A15060259900.
91. ICRC Archives, CRi 15/II, XV Conference II, 151 à 300, du 26.6.1934 au 12.11.1934, 279.
92. Archival collection of the Museum Meiji-mura held by the Japanese Red Cross Toyota College of Nursing, *Dai Jūgo-kai Sekijūji Kokusai-kaigi*, ID: B1107-4392.
93. Andre Durand, *History of the International Committee of the Red Cross: From Sarajevo to Hiroshima* (Geneva: Henry Dunant Institute, 1978), 290–92.
94. Thirty-six delegates represented Japan and its overseas empire, while several hundred delegates representing forty-five nation states and fifty-four Red Cross and Red Crescent Societies attended the meeting. The total number of participants reached 319. In place of ICRC President Max Huber, Geneva sent its vice-president. Nihon Sekijūjisha, *Dai Jūgo-kai Sekijūji Kokusai Kaigishi*, 106; Nihon Sekijūjisha, Nihon Sekijūjisha Shashikō, *Dai Yon-kan*, 111, 145.
95. Olive Checkland argues that the JRCS served as a loyal servant of Japanese imperialism, only superficially adhered to the ICRC humanitarianism, and was led by Japanese nationalists. She contends that Japan had no right to consider itself a member of the International Red Cross at all because its government had failed to adhere to the Geneva Convention of July 27, 1929, and characterizes the Tokyo Conference as a superb "propaganda exercise." Limited to English-language sources, Checkland appears unaware of

the alternative narrative presented in this chapter, derived from JRCS archives. While she holds JRCS responsible for the actions of Japan's military, she does not hold the Red Cross Societies of the other Great Powers to the same standard. Olive Checkland, *Humanitarianism and the Emperor's Japan, 1877–1977* (New York: St. Martin's, 1994), 79–92.

96. Nihon Sekijūjisha, *Nihon Sekijūjisha Shashikō, Dai Yon-kan*, 124–25.
97. Nihon Sekijūjisha, *Nihon Sekijūjisha Shashikō, Dai Yon-kan*, 128–36.
98. Nihon Sekijūjisha, *Nihon Sekijūjisha Shashikō, Dai Yon-kan*, 126.
99. Nihon Sekijūjisha, *Nihon Sekijūjisha Shashikō, Dai Yon-kan*, 125–28, 136–37.
100. Tokuji Saisho, "Art Music Letters," *Japan Times*, October 24, 1934, 8.
101. Thomas Mann (1875–1955) was his brother-in-law. During World War II, Klaus Pringsheim was put under house arrest when his son was accused of involvement in the Sorge espionage incident (1941–1942).
102. *Also sprach Zarathustra*, Op. 30; *Zwei Gesänge fur 16 stimmigen gemischten*, Op. 34; and *Eine Alpensinfonie*, Op. 64. Nihon Sekijūjisha, *Dai Jūgo-kai Sekijūji Kokusai Kaigishi*, 127; and Zaidanhōjin Geijutsu Kenkyū Shinkōzaidan© and Tokyo Art University Hyakunenshi Kankō-i'inkai, *Tokyo Art University Hyakunenshi Ensōkai-hen Dai Ni-kan* (Tokyo: Ongaku no Tomo sha Corporation, 1933), 3.
103. Zaidanhōjin Geijutsu Kenkyū Shinkōzaidan© and Tokyo Art University Hyakunenshi Kankō-i'inkai, *Tokyo Art University Hyakunenshi Ensōkai-hen Dai Ni-kan*, 311–23; and "Ueno no Gasshō ni Doitsu kara Origami: Shutorausu Okina mo Kangeki, Berurin de Kiita Sanjū nichi Yoru no Hōsō," *Asahi Shimbun*, November 1, 1934, 7.
104. Katō Shimei, *Nihon no Gensō: Geijutsuka Kurausu Puringusuhaimu no Shōgai* (Tokyo: Kangensha, 1950), 191–93.
105. Pringsheim, as a Jewish composer, expressed his anxiety and hope for the future through his performance. Indeed, Hayasaki explores the sensitive relationship between Nazi Germany and the Japanese Empire regarding the treatment of German Jews residing in Japan. She revealed that the German musicians of Jewish descent were under the surveillance of the Imperial Government of Japan in the 1930s, but they were still welcomed by the Japanese due to their great talent and performance, such as Leonid Kreutzer (1884–1953). Hayasaki Erina, *Berurin Tōkyō Monogatari: Ongaku-ka Kurausu Puringusuhaimu* (Tokyo: Ongaku no Tomo sha Corp, 1994), 225–48.
106. Nihon Sekijūjisha, *Dai Jūgo-kai Sekijūji Kokusai Kaigishi*, 104–20.
107. The chairman of the LORCS and the representatives of various national societies served as vice-chairs. Nihon Sekijūjisha, *Sekijūji Kokusai Kaigi Giji Gaiyō*, 141–42.
108. Nihon Sekijūjisha, *Sekijūji Kokusai Kaigi Giji Gaiyō*, 139–40.
109. Nihon Sekijūjisha, *Nihon Sekijūjisha Shashikō, Dai Yon-kan*, 87–89, 107–10, 177–79.
110. "The International Red Cross Flag Waving in the Beautiful Autumn Sky in Great Tokyo," *Asahi Shimbun*, October 20, 1934, 3, 5, 10, 15.
111. "The International Red Cross Conference: Splendid Opening Ceremony with the Exaltation of Peace and Philanthropy," *Yomiuri Shimbun*, October 17, 1934, 7.
112. Resolutions 37 and 39. See appendices in this book.
113. *Ketsugi* 決議.
114. The Empress Shōken Fund, one of world's largest funders of the International Red Cross and Red Crescent Movement, was initiated by JRCS President Matsukata Masayoshi

2. INTERNATIONALISM IN CRISIS 211

(1835–1924) in 1912 to support non-war-related activities of the Red Cross and Red Crescent worldwide and drew on the endowment granted by Empress Shōken initially to fund JRCS relief activities in the aftermath of the eruption of 1888 Fukushima Mount Bandai. Matsukata served as Japanese prime minister from 1891 to 1892 and as president of the JRCS from 1902 to 1912. Nihon Sekijūjisha, ed., *Nihon Sekijūji Shashi Zokkō, Jō-kan Meiji yonjū-nen kara Taishō jūichi-nen* (Tokyo: Nihon Sekijūjisha, 1929), 516–17; Fujimura Tōru, ed., *Matsukata Masayoshi Kankei Monjo, Dai Go-kan* (Tokyo: Daitōbunka Daigaku Tōyō Kenkyūjo, 1983), 209–10; and Tokutomi I'ichirō, *Kōshaku Matsukata Masayoshi Den, Kon-kan* (Tokyo: Kōshaku Matsukata Masayoshi Dennki Hensan-I'inkai, 1935), 1027–53. Romain Fathi and Melanie Oppenheimer highlighted the global impact of the Empress Shōken Fund on the international humanitarian movement and its significant financial contribution to the ICRC, which received half of the income. Romain Fathi and Melanie Oppenheimer, "The Shōken Fund and the Evolution of the Red Cross Movement," *European Review of History* 30, no. 5 (June 2023): 812–31.

115. The International Relief Union, whose mission was disaster relief, traces its origins to ideas put forth by Giovanni Attilio Ciraolo (1873–1954) in response to the Messina earthquake of 1908, and established as the International Relief Union in 1927.

116. Nihon Sekijūjisha, *Sekijūji Kokusai Kaigi Giji Gaiyō*, 323–75. The government of Benito Mussolini (1883–1945) advocated for inclusion of the International Relief Union, while the JRCS extensively participated in discussion of the Junior Red Cross and natural disaster relief operations. Nihon Sekijūjisha, *Sekijūji Kokusai Kaigi Giji Gaiyō*, 131–322. These and other initiatives appeared to represent a new direction for the Red Cross in the affirmation of human dignity and advancement of health and well-being.

117. Nihon Sekijūjisha, *Sekijūji Kokusai Kaigi Giji Gaiyō*, 131–322.

118. Nihon Sekijūjisha, *Sekijūji Kokusai Kaigi Giji Gaiyō*, 359–71.

119. "Protect de convention internationale concernant la condition et la protection des civils de nationalité ennemie qui se trouvent sur le territoire d'un belligérant ou sur un territoire occupé par lui," RICR, August 1934, 657–62, in Jean-Claude Favez, *The Red Cross and the Holocaust*, trans. John Fletcher and Beryl Fletcher (London: Cambridge University Press, 1999), 15, 307; and Durand, *History of the International Committee of the Red Cross*, 291.

120. Nihon Sekijūjisha, *Sekijūji Kokusai Kaigi Giji Gaiyō*, 161–62.

121. Nihon Sekijūjisha, *Sekijūji Kokusai Kaigi Giji Gaiyō*, 131–322.

122. Van Dijk argued the Tokyo Draft of 1934 was one of the origins of the interwar human rights movement. Boyd van Dijk, "Human Rights in War: On the Entangled Foundations of the 1949 Geneva Conventions," *American Society of International Law* 112, no. 4 (2018): 553–82; and Boyd van Dijk, *Preparing for War: The Making of the Geneva Conventions* (Oxford: Oxford University Press, 2022), 67–75.

123. Van Dijk, *Preparing for War*, 359–60.

124. The JRCS voiced criticisms of Britain's post–World War I chemical weapons production in the JRCS monthly magazine. It referred to Prime Minister David Lloyd George's justification of its chemical warfare program as a negative movement in the interwar period. Nihon Sekijūjisha, *Hakuai, No. 450*, 10.

125. Nihon Sekijūjisha, *Sekijūji Kokusai Kaigi Giji Gaiyō*, 359–60, 367–68.

126. Nihon Sekijūjisha, *Sekijūji Kokusai Kaigi Giji Gaiyō*, 361–67.

127. Nihon Sekijūjisha, *Sekijūji Kokusai Kaigi Giji Gaiyō*, 360–61.
128. After the war during the International Military Tribunal for the Far East in 1946, the Allied Powers wrestled with how to prosecute Japan's war crimes against the Chinese.
129. Resolution thirty-nine of the Tokyo Declaration is known as the Tokyo Draft in the Western legal historical discourse.
130. "Draft International Convention on the Condition and Protection of Civilians of Enemy Nationality Who Are on Territory Belonging to or Occupied by a Belligerent, Tokyo, 1934," *Treaties, States Parties and Commentaries*, ICRC, accessed December 27, 2022, https://ihl-databases.icrc.org/en/ihl-treaties/tokyo-draft-conv-1934.
131. Durand, *History of the International Committee of the Red Cross*, 291–92.
132. Durand, *History of the International Committee of the Red Cross*, 291–92. Van Dijk highlights the failure of the ICRC to support the draft version of the Tokyo Convention and the total disregard of civilian protections exhibited by the Allied Powers during World War II. Van Dijk, "Human Rights in War," 565; and van Dijk, *Preparing for War*, 64–67.
133. Durand, *History of the International Committee of the Red Cross*, 290–92.
134. Nihon Sekijūjisha, *Nihon Sekijūjisha Hachi-jū-nen Shōshi*, 20.
135. Durand, *History of the International Committee of the Red Cross*, 290.
136. Nihon Sekijūjisha, *Dai Jūgo-kai Sekijūji Kokusai Kaigishi*, 1.
137. Hoshina Yukiko, *Hana Aoi: Tokugawa-tei Omoide-banashi* (Tokyo: Mainichi Shimbunsha, 1998), 186–95.
138. Hoshina, *Hana Aoi*, 185.
139. The Supreme Order of the Chrysanthemum is the Japanese government's most prestigious award, usually reserved for members of the imperial family in prewar Japan.

3. TRANSNATIONAL HUMANITARIAN MOVEMENT: THE JAPANESE RED CROSS SOCIETY AND OVERSEAS EMPIRE

1. Julia F. Irwin, *Making the World Safe: The American Red Cross and a Nation's Humanitarian Awakening* (Oxford: Oxford University Press, 2013), 191–92.
2. Jeffrey Lesser, "Immigration and Shifting Concepts of National Identity in Brazil During the Vargas Era," *Luso-Brazilian Review* 31, no. 2, University of Wisconsin Press (Winter 1994): 23–44.
3. The South Seas Mandate (Nan'yō) included Tinian, Saipan, Palau, Pohnpei, Yap, Truk Lagoon, and Jaluit Atoll. The Society also solicited donations from Japanese living in cities around the world: Townsville, Australia; Batavia, Dutch East Indies; Mumbai, India; Berlin, Germany; Europe; and New York City, United States. Nihon Sekijūjisha, ed., *Nihon Sekijūjisha Shashikō, Dai Yon-kan, Taishō jūni nen kara Shōwa jū nen* (Tokyo: Nihon Sekijūjisha, 1957), 516–44; and the Archival Collection of the Museum Meiji-mura held by the Japanese Red Cross Toyota College of Nursing, *Man, Sen, Karafuto Tokubetsu-i'inbu Shokuin Shokkai, Ji Shōwa Go nen Itaru dō Roku nen*, ID: B1185-3868; *Zai Taunzuviiru Nihonryōjikan Kankei, Meiji Sanjū-shichi nen Itaru Yonjū nen*, ID: B1361-2396; *Zai Jawa Yokotake Heitarō Kankei Shorui, Meiji Sanjūkyū nen*, ID: B1370-2408; *Zai Munbai, Majima*,

Furugōri Kankei, Meiji Sanjū-shichi nen Itaru Yonjū nen, ID: B1385-2417; *Zai Berurin Oikawa Shigenobu Kankei, Meiji Yonjū nen*, ID: 1396-2428; and *Zai Nyūyōk Sōryōji Kankei, Meiji Sanjū-shichi nen Itaru Sanjū-kyū nen*, ID: 1356-2389.

4. Nihon Sekijūjisha, ed., *Nihon Sekijūjisha Shashikō, Dai Go-kan, Shōwa jūichi nen kara Shōwa nijū nen* (Tokyo: Nihon Sekijūjisha, 1969), 416–17.

5. Archival collection of the Museum Meiji-mura held by the Japanese Red Cross Toyota College of Nursing, *Akō Tokubetsu-i'inbu, Ji Taishō Jūni nen Itaru Jūyo nen*, ID: 1749-4022.

6. Locations of JRCS offices included Manila, Davao, Honolulu, San Francisco, Los Angeles, Vancouver, Mexico City, Lima, São Paulo, Buenos Aires, and Santiago. Nihon Sekijūjisha, *Nihon Sekijūjisha Shashikō, Dai Go-kan*, 417; and Nihon Sekijūjisha, ed., *Nihon Sekijūji Shashi Zokkō, Jō kan Meiji yonjū nen kara Taishō jūichi nen* (Tokyo: Nihon Sekijūjisha, 1929), 954, 958.

7. Since ancient times, Pusan served as Japan's gateway to the Asian continent. The Japan-Korea Treaty of 1876 established Pusan as a Japanese "treaty port" modeled on the Western powers' China treaty port system. Gaimushō Ryōji Ijū Bu, ed., *Waga Kokumin no Kaigai Hatten: Ijū Hyakunen no Ayumi Shiryō-hen* (Tokyo: Gaimushō Ryōji Ijū Bu, 1971), 148–52; and Peter Duss, *The Abacus and the Sword: The Japanese Penetration of Korea, 1895–1910* (Berkeley: University of California Press, 1995).

8. Ten branch offices were located in Seoul, Incheon, Pusan, Wonsan, Masan, Gunsan, Pyongyang, Sŏngjin (now Kimchaek), Mokpo, and Nampo. Archival collection of the Red Cross Information Plaza, *Nihon Sekijūjisha Chōsen-honbu Yōran*, 2–3.

9. In addition to Russia, Great Britain and the United States recognized Japan's claims on the Korean Peninsula following the Russo-Japanese War. Ozawa Takeo was a former lieutenant general and served as the president of the Imperial Japanese Army Academy before joining the JRCS. "Honsha Chōsen-tokuden Sekijūji Sōkai," *Tokyo Asahi Shimbun*, October 2, 1906, 4.

10. Nihon Sekijūjisha, ed., *Nihon Sekijūji Shashikō* (Tokyo: Nihon Sekijūjisha, 1911), 272.

11. "Honsha Chōsen-tokuden Sekijūji Sōkai," *Tokyo Asahi Shimbun*, October 2, 1906, 4.

12. Ozawa Takeo, *Taishō Go nen San gatsu: Nihon Sekijūjisha Fukushachō: Ozawa Danshaku Kōwa Hyakudai* (Tokyo: Hakuai Hakkōjo, 1916), 161.

13. Nihon Sekijūjisha, *Nihon Sekijūji Shashikō*, 266–73; Daikan Sekijūjisha, *Daikan Sekijūjisha Hachijū-nen Shi* (Seoul: Daikan Sekijūjisha, 1987), 40–42.

14. Nihon Sekijūjisha, *Nihon Sekijūji Shashikō*, 266–71.

15. Daikan Sekijūjisha, *Daikan Sekijūjisha Hachijū-nen Shi*, 41–42.

16. Nihon Sekijūjisha, *Nihon Sekijūji Shashikō*, 272–73; Irie Keishirō and Ōhata Tokushirō, *Jūtei: Gaikōshi Teiyō* (Tokyo: Seibundō, 1964), 146–48; Nihon Sekijūjisha, *Nihon Sekijūji Shashi Zokkō, Jō kan Meiji yonjū nen kara Taishō jūichi nen*, 596–97. Following the March 1 Incident of 1919, Korean nationalists in exile in Shanghai set up a short-lived Red Cross society. While supported by the Korean Independence Movement, it was not recognized by the ICRC. According to the records of the Republic of Korea National Red Cross, it became less active after 1923. Daikan Sekijūjisha, *Daikan Sekijūjisha Hachijū-nen Shi*, 44–46.

17. Nihon Sekijūjisha, *Nihon Sekijūji Shashi Zokkō, Jō kan Meiji yonjū nen kara Taishō jūichi nen*, 596–97.
18. Chōsen Sōtokufu, *Chōsen Sōtokufu Tōkei Nenpō, Meiji Yonjūsan nen* (Seoul: Chōsen Sōtokufu, 1912), 75.
19. Located at Mokpo, Daegu, Pusan, Masan, Pyongyang, Nampo, Sinuiju, Gunsan, and Chongjin.
20. Located at Seoul, Cheongju, Gongju, Jeonju, Gwangju, Daegu, Pusan, Haeju, Pyongyang, Sinŭiju, Chuncheon, Hamhŭng, Ranam, North and South Gyeongsang, North and South Hamgyeong, North and South Pyongan, Jeolla, South Chungcheong, Hwanghae, Gangwon-do, Gyeonggi-do, and Chongjin. Chōsen Sōtokufu, *Chōsen Sōtokufu Tōkei Nenpō, Meiji Yonjūsan nen*, 776; Nihon Sekijūjisha, *Nihon Sekijūji Shashi Zokkō, Jō kan Meiji yonjū nen kara Taishō jūichi nen*, 931–36; Archival collection of the Museum Meiji-mura held by the Japanese Red Cross Toyota College of Nursing, *Manshū, Chōsen, Karafuto-i'inbu Shain Sōkai, Taishō Jūgo nen*, ID: B1146-3175; Archival collection of the Red Cross Information Plaza, *Chōsen-honbu Kankei Shorui Nisatsu no uchi Ichi*, PDF, 191–92; Archival collection of the Red Cross Information Plaza, *Chōsen-honbu Kankei Shorui Nisatsu no uchi Ni*, PDF, 6.
21. Archival collection of the Museum Meiji-mura held by the Japanese Red Cross Toyota College of Nursing, *Manshū, Chōsen, Karafuto-i'inbu Shain Sōkai, Taishō Jūgo nen*, ID: B1146-3175.
22. Archival collection of the Museum Meiji-mura held by the Japanese Red Cross Toyota College of Nursing, *Man, Sen, Karafuto Tokubetsu-i'inbu Shokuin Shokkai, Ji Shōwa Shichi nen Itaru dō Hachi nen*, ID: B1789-4160.
23. Archival collection of the Museum Meiji-mura held by the Japanese Red Cross Toyota College of Nursing, *Man, Sen, Karafuto Tokubetsu-i'inbu Shokuin Shokkai, Ji Shōwa Shichi nen Itaru dō Hachi nen*, ID: B1789-4160.
24. See also pages 30–33 in chapter 1.
25. Saigai Kyōkun no Keishō ni Kansuru Senmonchōsakai Hōkokusho, *Hōkokusho, 1923 Kantō Daishinsai, Dai Ippen* (Tokyo: Cabinet Office, Government of Japan, 2006), 4.
26. Large areas in Tokyo, Kanagawa, Yamanashi, Shizuoka, Chiba, Saitama, and Ibaragi Prefectures were affected. Saigai Kyōkun no Keishō ni Kansuru Senmonchōsakai Hōkokusho, *Hōkokusho*, 50, 81, 93.
27. Saigai Kyōkun no Keishō ni Kansuru Senmonchōsakai Hōkokusho, *Hōkokusho*, 2.
28. Estimates of the number of victims vary greatly. A Japanese government-commissioned study reported 2,600 as the low number and 6,600 as the high number, both round numbers, and 667 Chinese killed or missing. Saigai Kyōkun no Keishō ni Kansuru Senmonchōsakai Hōkokusho, *Hōkokusho, 1923 Kantō Daishinsai, Dai Nihen* (Tokyo: Cabinet Office, Government of Japan, 2008), 218–19, 221. Kang details the mechanism of how the military, police, and vigilantes committed crimes against Korean residents in Kantō. Duk-sang Kang, *Kantō Daishinsai* (Tokyo: Chūkō-shinsho, 1975). The record of the Tokyo Metropolitan Police Department (TMPD) is mixed, as in some cases police stations provided shelter and protection from vigilante mobs to Koreans displaced from their homes. Keishichō, *Taishō Taishin Kasai-shi* (Tokyo: Keishichō, 1925), 32–33. At the

same time, some police instigated killings, and resident Koreans were not the only victims; Japanese anarchists, socialists, labor leaders, and other radicals were also targeted, most notably the anarchist Ōsugi Sakae (1885–1923) and radical feminist poet Itō Noe (1895–1923), who were executed by Amakasu Masahiko (1891–1945), in what was known as the Amakasu Incident. Amakasu was an officer in the Imperial Japanese Army (IJA) and later became the head of the Manchukuo Film Association.

29. Dr. Shiga Kiyoshi (1871–1957), a Japanese physician and bacteriologist, graduated from the Medical School of the Tokyo Imperial University in 1896 and studied under Paul Ehrlich (1854–1915) in Germany. He became world famous for the discovery of *Shigella dysenteriae* in 1897. He studied under Dr. Kitasato Shibasaburō (1853–1931), the father of Japanese infectious diseases studies, and introduced the Bacillus Calmette–Guérin vaccine to Japan in 1924.

30. Archival collection of the Museum Meiji-mura held by the Japanese Red Cross Toyota College of Nursing, *Shinsai ni Kansuru Hijōbu Kessaisho, Taishō Jūni nen Ku gatsu Itaru dō Jūsan nen Jū gatsu*, ID:1163; and Nihon Sekijūjisha, *Nihon Sekijūjisha Shashikō, Dai Yon-kan*, 292–93.

31. Nihon Sekijūjisha, ed., *Taishō Jūni nen Kantō Daishinsai Nihon Sekijūjisha Kyūgo-shi* (Tokyo: Nihon Sekijūjisha, 1925), 92, 147; Chōsensōtokufu I'in, *Chōsensōtokufu I'in Nijū nen shi* (Keijō: Chōsensōtokufu I'in, 1928), 40; and Masui Takashi, "Relief Activities of Kansai and Adjacent Local Governments During the Great Kanto Earthquake in 1923," *Journal of Humanitarian Studies* 4 (March 2015): 181.

32. Saitō Makoto (1858–1936) acted as the Japanese governor of Korea from 1919 to 1927 and from 1929 to 1931. After resigning from the Korean administration, he became the Japanese prime minister in 1932 and resigned in 1934. He was assassinated during the February 26 Incident in 1936.

33. Keishichō, *Taishō Taishin Kasai-shi*, 490–92.

34. Nihon Sekijūjisha, *Taishō Jūni nen Kantō Daishinsai Nihon Sekijūjisha Kyūgo-shi*, 147.

35. Masui, "Relief Activities of Kansai and Adjacent Local Governments During the Great Kanto Earthquake in 1923," 181.

36. Seki Hajime (1873–1935) acted as the mayor of Osaka from 1923 to 1935 and is commonly known as the "Father of Osaka" for making Osaka a world-class modern city. Masui, "Relief Activities of Kansai and Adjacent Local Governments During the Great Kanto Earthquake in 1923," 181.

37. "Resident Koreans" refers to Korean nationals who had established residence in Japan. The Osaka prefectural government provided transportation to 830 victims who wished to leave the Tokyo region and established temporary shelters and makeshift hospitals in facilities such as train stations, schools, homes of volunteers, welfare institutes, and temples. Victims who were severely injured were hospitalized at JRCS hospitals and other clinics. Masui, "Relief Activities of Kansai and Adjacent Local Governments During the Great Kanto Earthquake in 1923," 181–84.

38. Nihon Sekijūjisha, *Taishō Jūni nen Kantō Daishinsai Nihon Sekijūjisha Kyūgo-shi*, 147–48.

39. Nihon Sekijūjisha, *Taishō Jūni nen Kantō Daishinsai Nihon Sekijūjisha Kyūgo-shi*, 148.

40. Shiga Kiyoshi, *Shiga Kiyoshi: Aru Saikin Gakusha no Kaisō* (Tokyo: Nihon Tosho Center, 1997), 25.

41. Sonja M. Kim, *Imperatives of Care: Women and Medicine in Colonial Korea* (Honolulu: University of Hawai'i Press, 2019), 80.
42. Archival collection of the Red Cross Information Plaza, *Chōsen-honbu Kankei Shorui Nisatsu no uchi Ni*, PDF, 8–9, 77–95.
43. Archival collection of the Red Cross Information Plaza, *Chōsen-honbu Kankei Shorui Nisatsu no uchi Ni*.
44. Archival collection of the Museum Meiji-mura held by the Japanese Red Cross Toyota College of Nursing, *Manshū, Chōsen, Karafuto-i'inbu Shain Sōkai, Taishō Jūgo nen*, ID: B1146-3175.
45. *Nihon Sekijūjisha Chōsen Honbu Shinryōjo Dai Ikkai Nenpō, Taishō Jūgo nen*, in the Archival Collection of the Museum Meiji-mura held by the Japanese Red Cross Toyota College of Nursing, *Chōsen Honbu Byōin, Taishō Jūgo nen*, ID: 1688-3496, 1.
46. Archival collection of the Red Cross Information Plaza, *Nihon Sekijūjisha Chōsen-honbu Yōran*, 3–10.
47. Archival collection of the Red Cross Information Plaza, *Nihon Sekijūjisha Chōsen-honbu Yōran*, 14–18.
48. Archival collection of the Red Cross Information Plaza, *Nihon Sekijūjisha Chōsen-honbu Yōran*, 3–8.
49. *Nihon Sekijūjisha Chōsen Honbu Byōin Nenpō, Shōwa Jūni nen*, in the Archival Collection of the Museum Meiji-mura held by the Japanese Red Cross Toyota College of Nursing, *Chōsen-honbu Kan'na I'inbu Sōkai, Shōwa Jūsan nen*, ID: B1085-4366, 1–6.
50. In Korea, nursing had traditionally been a male profession. Christian mission hospitals established the first nurses' training programs while limiting enrollment to Korean women "of strong Christian faith." Kim, *Imperatives of Care*, 79–80, 83, 87.
51. Ogcheol Lee, "Red Cross Nursing Education in Korea: 1920–2014," *Journal of Humanitarian Studies* 4 (March 2015): 75–76; and the Archival Collection of the Red Cross Information Plaza, Nurses' Association of Korea, *Bulletin of the Nurses' Association of Korea*, no. 13 (Summer 1929): 75–76. According to Kim, two thirds of the places at GGK nurses' training programs were reserved for Japanese. Kim, *Imperatives of Care*, 85.
52. *Nihon Sekijūjisha Chōsen Honbu Shinryōjo Dai Ikkai Nenpō, Taishō Jūgo nen*, 20.
53. Archival collection of the Red Cross Information Plaza, Nurses' Association of Korea, *Bulletin of the Nurses' Association of Korea*, 20–33.
54. Hyaeweol Choi, *Gender and Mission Encounters in Korea: New Women, Old Ways* (Berkeley: University of California Press, 2009), 10.
55. Kim, *Imperatives of Care*, 93–94.
56. Hagiwara Take (1873–1936) was a leading JRCS nurse who was one of the recipients of the first Florence Nightingale Medal in 1920 due to her great contributions to natural disasters and World War I relief operations. See pages 23–25 in chapter 1.
57. Nihon Sekijūjisha, *Nihon Sekijūjisha Hachi-jū nen Shōshi* (Tokyo: Nihon Sekijūjisha, 1957), 57; and Kim, *Imperatives of Care*, 94.
58. Nihon Sekijūjisha, *Nihon Sekijūjisha Hachi-jū nen Shōshi*, 57; and Kim, *Imperatives of Care*, 94.
59. Kim, *Imperatives of Care*, 92–93.

60. Kim, *Imperatives of Care*, 101.
61. Kim, *Imperatives of Care*, 87.
62. Archival collection of the Museum Meiji-mura held by the Japanese Red Cross Toyota College of Nursing, *Chōsen-honbu Sōkai Manshū-honbu Shainshō Juten Tokugawa Fuku-shachō Shucchō Hōkoku, Shōwa Hachi nen Jūichi*, ID: 1752-4037.
63. Kim, *Imperatives of Care*, 85.
64. Nihon Sekijūjisha, *Nihon Sekijūji Shashi Zokkō, Jō kan Meiji yonjū nen kara Taishō jūichi nen*, 670.
65. Archival collection of the Museum Meiji-mura held by the Japanese Red Cross Toyota College of Nursing, *Chōsen-honbu Sōkai Manshū-honbu Shainshō Juten Tokugawa Fuku-shachō Shucchō Hōkoku, Shōwa Hachi nen Jūichi*, ID: 1752-4037; and Chōsen Sōtokufu, *Chōsen Sōtokufu Tōkei Nenpō, Shōwa Jūichi nen* (Seoul: Chōsen Sōtokufu, 1938), 336.
66. Nihon Sekijūjisha, *Nihon Sekijūjisha Shashikō, Dai Yon-kan*, 244–45.
67. Nihon Sekijūjisha, *Nihon Sekijūjisha Shashikō, Dai Yon-kan*, 251.
68. 同方.
69. Nihon Sekijūjisha Kangofu Dōhōkai, *Dōhō Shōwa Hachi nen Go gatsu gō* (Tokyo: Nihon Sekijūjisha Kangofu Dōhōkai, 1933), 25–26.
70. Comfort parcels were gift packages prepared by civilians to be sent to imperial Japanese military soldiers, typically containing goods such as toiletries, dried fruits, canned foods, and letters of encouragement. *Shagyō Genkyō-sho Shōwa Hachi nen Ni gatsu, Nihon Sekijūjisha Shingishū-shibu*, in the Archival Collection of the Museum Meiji-mura held by the Japanese Red Cross Toyota College of Nursing, *Nakagawa Fuku-shachō Manshū Chōsen Shucchō Fukumei, Shōwa Hachi nen*, ID: 1739-3982.
71. Chōsen Sōtokufu, *Chōsen Sōtokufu Tōkei Nenpō, Shōwa Jūshichi nen* (Seoul: Chōsen Sōtokufu, 1944), 243; and Nihon Sekijūjisha, *Nihon Sekijūjisha Shashikō, Dai Go-kan*, 363–64.
72. 34,010,359 yen and 29 sen out of a total JRCS general income, including general accounts, of 207,729,839 yen and 21 sen. Nihon Sekijūjisha, *Nihon Sekijūjisha Shashikō, Dai Go-kan*, 466–70.
73. We introduce these data with the caution that it is not possible to determine to what extent the rapid rise in membership and outpouring of financial contributions in the context of total war was voluntary and to what extent it was pressured. With the onset of the Pacific War, colonial policy in Korea shifted from "soft" assimilation under Governor-General Saitō to a harder, more coercive policy of assimilation. Beginning in 1937, Japanese colonial administration introduced a policy of severe cultural assimilation, *kōminka seisaku*, in Taiwan and Korea in preparation for total war. In Korea, for example, the use of written Korean was banned, and visiting Shinto shrines and adopting Japanese-sounding names were made mandatory. On the other hand, as Takashi Fujitani argues in *Race for Empire: Koreans as Japanese and Japanese as Americans During World War II*, the data on military enlistment, which show applications far outpacing acceptances, suggests a significant element of voluntarism. Takashi Fujitani, *Race for Empire: Koreans as Japanese and Japanese as Americans During World War II* (Berkeley: University of California Press, 2011), 40–49.

74. *Hōkoku jippei* 報国恤兵.
75. Archival collection of the Museum Meiji-mura held by the Japanese Red Cross Toyota College of Nursing, *Chōsen-honbu Kan'nai I'inbu Sōkai, Shōwa Jūsan nen*, ID: B1085-4366.
76. Tashiro Senzō, *Nihon Sekijūjisha Manshū-i'inbu shi* (Dalian: Nihon Sekijūjisha Kantōshū Iin-honbu, 1938), 1–2.
77. For example, Kamio Mitsuomi (1855–1927), commander of Japan's Liaodong Garrison, headed he JRCS Liaodong Committee Headquarters. Nihon Sekijūjisha, *Nihon Sekijūji Shashi Zokkō, Jō kan Meiji yonjū nen kara Taishō jūichi nen*, 936.
78. Nihon Sekijūjisha, *Nihon Sekijūji Shashikō*, 1339–40.
79. See chapter 1, 21–22.
80. Nihon Sekijūjisha, *Nihon Sekijūji Shashi Zokkō, Jō kan Meiji yonjū nen kara Taishō jūichi nen*, 937; Tashiro, *Nihon Sekijūjisha Manshū-i'inbu shi*, 5–6. Russia ceded major economic concession in China, the South Manchuria Railway, which connected Dalian to Changchun and including policing and administrative rights with a parallel railway zone.
81. Tashiro, *Nihon Sekijūjisha Manshū-i'inbu shi*, 7.
82. Tashiro, *Nihon Sekijūjisha Manshū-i'inbu shi*, 8.
83. Lüshun, Dalian, Jinzhou, Yingkou, Liaoyang, Mukden, Xinmin, Tieling, Changchun, and Ando Prefectures (currently Donggang, Jilin) in 1908, and Harbin in 1909. Tashiro, *Nihon Sekijūjisha Manshū-i'inbu shi*, 8–11.
84. Tashiro, *Nihon Sekijūjisha Manshū-i'inbu shi*, 46.
85. Male nurses predominated within the JRCS in the pre–World War I period. See chapter 6, 140.
86. Archival collection of the Museum Meiji-mura held by the Japanese Red Cross Toyota College of Nursing, *Manshū Pesuto Kankei, Meiji Yonjūyo nen Zen*, ID: B788-1054.
87. Ishiguro Tadanori (1845–1941) later served as the JRCS president from 1917 to 1920. He worked hard to promote cooperative relationships with the American Red Cross and the British Red Cross and developed the International Red Cross movement in the Asia Pacific region in the interwar years.
88. Archival collection of the Museum Meiji-mura held by the Japanese Red Cross Toyota College of Nursing, *Manshū Pesuto Kankei, Meiji Yonjūyo nen Zen*, ID: B788-1054.
89. Tashiro, *Nihon Sekijūjisha Manshū-i'inbu shi*, 125–161.
90. Louise Young, *Japan's Total Empire: Manchuria and the Culture of Wartime Imperialism* (Berkeley: University of California Press, 1998), 30–33.
91. Nihon Sekijūjisha, *Nihon Sekijūji Shashi Zokkō, Jō kan Meiji yonjū nen kara Taishō jūichi nen*, 940–44.
92. Tashiro, *Nihon Sekijūjisha Manshū-i'inbu shi*, 46.
93. Europeans included fifteen Poles, ten Germans, eight French, five Italians, two Danes, two Belgians, two Spanish, and one Greek citizen.
94. Archival collection of the Museum Meiji-mura held by the Japanese Red Cross Toyota College of Nursing, *Manshū, Chōsen, Karafuto-i'inbu Shain Sōkai*, ID: B1146-3175.
95. Tashiro, *Nihon Sekijūjisha Manshū-i'inbu shi*, 47. Japanese sources identified the resident populations of Manchuria by ethnic group and distinguished between Manchu

people (*Manshū-jin* or *Manshū-zoku*: 満洲人 or 満洲族) and Han people (*Kan-jin* or *Kanminzoku*: 漢人 or 漢民族). The JRCS sources also distinguished between Manchukuo (*Manshū-jin*: 満洲人) and Republic of China nationals (*Chūkaminkoku-jin*: 中華民国人).

96. Nihon Sekijūjisha, *Nihon Sekijūjisha Shashikō, Dai Yon-kan*, 244–45.
97. The Manchurian Incident in 1931 and the First Shanghai Incident in 1932 involved major commitments of JRCS resources at considerable cost. The total administrative and operational expenses reached 364,392 yen and 75 sen. Nihon Sekijūjisha, *Nihon Sekijūjisha Shashikō, Dai Yon-kan*, 248. During the Manchurian Incident, the Society sent six relief parties to combat zones in Manchuria as well as to hospitals in Korea and the main islands of Japan. Nihon Sekijūjisha, *Nihon Sekijūjisha Shashikō, Dai Yon-kan*, 246. The JRCS Manchurian Committee Department played a key role during the incident as a hub station. It organized the first relief parties and deployed medical workers. Tashiro, *Nihon Sekijūjisha Manshū-i'inbu shi*, 63–86.
98. Tashiro, *Nihon Sekijūjisha Manshū-i'inbu shi*, 63–67.
99. Tashiro, *Nihon Sekijūjisha Manshū-i'inbu shi*, 63–86.
100. Tashiro, *Nihon Sekijūjisha Manshū-i'inbu shi*, 71–72.
101. Nihon Sekijūjisha Kangofu Dōhōkai, *Dōhō Shōwa Hachi nen Go gatsu gō* (Tokyo: Nihon Sekijūjisha Kangofu Dōhōkai, 1933), 25.
102. Present-day Dandong.
103. Chiba Medical College is currently the School of Medicine at Chiba University. Teiji Kenjō, "Meiji kara Shōwa-ki no Chiba Igaku Sen'mon Gakkō, Chiba Ikagaigaku ni okeru Ryūgakusei no Dōkō," *Kokusai Kyōiku* 2 (March 2009): 18, accessed March 28, 2022, https://opac.ll.chiba-u.jp/da/curator/900116289/kokusaikyouiku_2_11.pdf.
104. Tashiro, *Nihon Sekijūjisha Manshū-i'inbu shi*, 75–76.
105. Tashiro, *Nihon Sekijūjisha Manshū-i'inbu shi*, 97–372. On November 15, 1934, the JRCS organized a three-day celebration of Red Cross Day, marking Japan's ratification of the Geneva Convention and to promote the 1934 Tokyo International Red Cross Conference.
106. Tashiro, *Nihon Sekijūjisha Manshū-i'inbu shi*, 113–18.
107. Ryojun, Dalian, Jinzhou, Pulandian, Hishika (modern Pikou Subdistrict), Yingkou, Liaoyang, Mukden, Donggang, Hsinking (*Shinkyō*), Jilin, Harbin, Qiqihar, Hailar and Jinzhou.
108. Tashiro, *Nihon Sekijūjisha Manshū-i'inbu shi*, 28–32.
109. Tashiro, *Nihon Sekijūjisha Manshū-i'inbu shi*, 48–50.
110. The JRCS records differentiated between Manchurian Chinese (満洲人) and Republic of China Chinese (中華民国人).
111. Tashiro, *Nihon Sekijūjisha Manshū-i'inbu shi*, 49–50.
112. *Harubin Chōsenjin Kyoryūmin-kai Seigansho*, in the Archival Collection of the Museum Meiji-mura held by the Japanese Red Cross Toyota College of Nursing, *Nakagawa Fukushachō Manshū Chōsen Shucchō Fukumei, Shōwa Hachi nen*, ID: 1739-3982.
113. Tashiro, *Nihon Sekijūjisha Manshū-i'inbu shi*, 162–94.
114. Tashiro, *Nihon Sekijūjisha Manshū-i'inbu shi*, 187.
115. Shen Chieh, *"Manshūkoku" Shakai Jigyōshi* (Kyoto: Minerva Shobō, 1996).
116. Nihon Sekijūjisha Ibarakiken-shibu, *Hyaku-nen no Ayumi* (Mito: Nihon Sekijūjisha Ibarakiken-shibu, 1988), 449.

117. Henry Dunant Study Center, ed., *Hozutsu no Ato ni: Jūgun Kangofu Kiroku Shashin-shū* (Tokyo: Medical Friend sha, 1981), 72–73.
118. Aichi Jūgun Kangofu no Kiroku Henshū-i'inkai, ed., *Aichi Jūgun Kangofu no Kiroku* (Nagoya: Nihon Sekijūjisha Aichiken-shibu, 1980), 130. The number of severe injuries of the Japanese soldiers indicated that the battle was fierce. Indeed, the Japanese Army censored accounts of the Battles of Khalkhyn Gol because of the great losses suffered.
119. Archival collection of the Red Cross Information Plaza, *Manshūkoku Sekijūjisha Sōsetsu, Ji Shō wa Jūni nen Itaru Jūsan nen*, ID: 4449, PDF, 30–31.
120. Tashiro, *Nihon Sekijūjisha Manshū-i'inbu shi*, 1–4.
121. Nihon Sekijūjisha, *Nihon Sekijūjisha Shashikō, Dai Go-kan*, 363–64.
122. Kim, *Imperatives of Care*, 87.
123. Charles E. Rosenberg and Janet Golden, *Framing Diseases: Studies in Cultural History* (New Brunswick, NJ: Rutgers University Press, 1992); and Michael Shiyung Liu, *Prescribing Colonization: The Role of Medical Practices and Policies in Japan-Ruled Taiwan, 1895–1945* (Ann Arbor, MI: Association for Asian Studies, 2009), 174.
124. Liu, *Prescribing Colonization*, 166.
125. Ishi Yoshikuni, *Kankoku no Jinkō Zōka no Bunseki* (Tokyo: Keiso, 1972), 114, 121; and Sai Kiei 崔義楹, "Chōsen Jūmin no Seimeihyō: Dai Ikkai Seimeihyō (Shōwa Gan kara Go-nen) no Hojū oyobi Dai Nikai (Sōwa Roku kara Jū-nen) Seisai Seimeihyō," in *Chōsen Igakkai Zasshi Dai Nijūkyū-kan, Dai Nijū-gō*, ed. Chōsen Igakkai (Keijo [Seoul]: Chōsen Igakkai, 1939), 2180–220.

4. BEYOND EMPIRE: THE JAPANESE RED CROSS SOCIETY IN HAWAI'I AND BRAZIL

1. Nihon Sekijūjisha, ed., *Nihon Sekijūjisha Shashikō, Dai Go-kan, Shōwa jūichi nen kara Shōwa nijū nen* (Tokyo: Nihon Sekijūjisha, 1969), 330, 417; Nihon Sekijūjisha, ed., *Nihon Sekijūji Shashi Zokkō, Jō kan Meiji yonjū nen kara Taishō jūichi nen* (Tokyo: Nihon Sekijūjisha, 1929), 954, 958; Japan Center for Asian Historical Records, *Nijū, Kaigai Tokubetsu-i'inbu Secchi*, REF: B12082304000; *Sanjūni, Kanada Bankūbaa*, REF: B12082305200; Archives of the Ministry of Foreign Affairs of Japan, *Sekijūji Kankei Zakken*, REF: B-3-11-3-14, PDF, 5–6, 16–17; Nihon Sekijūjisha, *Taishō jūyo-nen-do Jigyōnenpō* (Tokyo: Nihon Sekijūjisha, 1925), 100–101; and *Taishō jūgo-nen-do Jigyōnenpō* (Tokyo: Nihon Sekijūjisha, 1926), 118.
2. *Kan'yaku imin* 官約移民.
3. National Museum of Japanese History, "Hawai'i: 150 Years of Japanese Migration and Histories of Dream Islands," accessed October 13, 2021, https://www.rekihaku.ac.jp/english/exhibitions/project/old/191029/index.html; Gaimushō Ryōji Ijū Bu, ed., *Waga Kokumin no Kaigai Hatten: Ijū Hyakunen no Ayumi Shiryō-hen* (Tokyo: Gaimushō Ryōji Ijū Bu, 1971), 146–47; and Robert C. Schmitt, *Demographic Statistics of Hawaii: 1778–1965* (Honolulu: University of Hawai'i Press, 1968), 120.
4. Schmitt, *Demographic Statistics of Hawaii*, 120.

5. Archival collection of the Museum Meiji-mura held by the Japanese Red Cross Toyota College of Nursing, *Hawai Tokubetsu-i'inbu Kankei, Meiji Sanjūkyū nen Itaru Yonjūnen*, ID: B1346-2379.
6. Nihon Sekijūjisha, ed., *Nihon Sekijūji Shashikō* (Tokyo: Nihon Sekijūjisha, 1911), 279; and the Archival Collection of the Museum Meiji-mura held by the Japanese Red Cross Toyota College of Nursing, *Hawai Tokubetsu-i'inbu Kankei, Meiji Sanjūkyū nen Itaru Yonjūnen*, ID: B1346-2379.
7. Archival collection of the Museum Meiji-mura held by the Japanese Red Cross Toyota College of Nursing, *Hawai Tokubetsu-i'inbu Kankei, Meiji Sanjūkyū nen Itaru Yonjūnen*, ID: B1346-2379; and *Zai Hawai Ishii Isakichi Kankei, Meiji Sanjūshichi nen Itaru Yonjūnen*, ID: B1372-2410.
8. Nakajima Yumiko, *Hawai Samayoeru Rakuen: Minzoku to Kokka no Shōtotsu* (Tokyo: Tokyo Shoseki, 1993), 149–54; "Mr. Ishii in Hawaii," *Japan Times*, August 9, 1907, 3; and "Kaigai no Kotō ni Naku," *Yomiuri Shimbun*, March 23, 1908, 3.
9. The Honolulu chapter was officially activated in June 1905, at the same time as the Seattle, San Francisco, Pyongyang, Mokpo, Masan, and Shanghai chapters. Hishiki Hidekazu, ed., *Aikoku Fujinkai Yonjū-nen-shi, Furoku* (Tokyo: Aikoku Fujinkai, 1941), 7. The Patriotic Women's Association in Japan was founded in 1900 by Okumura Ihoko (1845–1907), during the Boxer Rebellion (1899–1901) with the support of Ogasawara Naganari (1867–1958) and Konoe Atsumaro (1863–1904). Its initial mission was to support bereaved families of Japanese soldiers. During the Russo-Japanese War, Japan and Great Britian were allied powers and the Japanese Patriotic Women's Association modeled its activities on the British Red Cross Volunteer Nursing Association. It gradually expanded its missions to childcare, poverty relief in rural areas, and fundraising for victims of natural disasters. In 1912, the total membership was 816,609, which included 60,783 in Taiwan, 7,773 in Korea, and 1,604 overseas. Mitsui Kōzaburō, *Aikoku Fujinkai-shi* (Tokyo: Aikoku Fujinkai Hakkōjo, 1912), 5–14, appendix, 27–29; and Hishiki Hidekazu, ed., *Aikoku Fujinkai Yonjū-nen-shi* (Tokyo: Aikoku Fujinkai, 1941).
10. The University of Tokyo Meiji Shinbun Zasshi Bunko Archives, *Aikoku Fujin, Dai gojūgo-gō Meiji Sanjūshichi nen Roku-gatsu Itsu-ka*, 3; *Nihon Sekijūji, No. 135, April 1904* (Tokyo: NihonSekijūji Hakkōjo, 1904), introduction, 17–18; and *Nihon Sekijūji, No. 146, October 1904* (Tokyo: NihonSekijūji Hakkōjo, 1904), 13.
11. Archival collection of the Museum Meiji-mura held by the Japanese Red Cross Toyota College of Nursing, *Zai Honolulu Aikoku Fujinkai Kankei, Meiji Sanjūshichi nen Dō Sanjūhachi nen*, ID: B1348-2381. According to Makita, Maroney was a member of both the JRCS and the ARC. Makita focuses on the ARC Hawai'i Chapter and notes how the international Red Cross movement in the Asia Pacific region diverged from the western European model of one national society per nation-state. Makita Yoshiya, *Jindō no Chiseigaku: Hawaii ni Okeru Sekijūji Jigyō to Jindōshugi wo Meguru Hōbunka no Hen'yō*, in *"Hō Bunkaken" to America: Nijusseiki Toransu Nashonaru Historii no Shin-shikaku*, ed. Ishii Noriko and Imano Yuko (Tokyo: Sophia University Press, 2022), 27–30, 45–47.
12. The University of Tokyo Meiji Shinbun Zasshi Bunko Archives, *Aikoku Fujin, Dai rokujūyon-gō Meiji Sanjūshichinen Jū-gatsu Hatsu-ka*, 2; "Maronii-jō Iku," *Nippu Jiji*, May 5, 1914,

4; and Ogasawa Naganari, *Shishaku Ogasawara Naganari* (Tokyo: Ogasawara Naganari Shishaku Kiju Kinen Hensan-kai, 1943), 36–37. Maroney made substantial donations through the Honolulu Patriotic Women's Association to treat sick and wounded soldiers during the Russo-Japanese War. She was born in Boston, moved to Hawai'i as a missionary, and became a member of the JRCS in 1895. "Maronii-jō Iku," *Nippu Jiji*, May 5, 1914, 4.

13. After the enactment of the Immigration Act of 1924 in the United States, the percentage of the Japanese population in Hawai'i flattened out: 41.5 percent in the 1920s, 42.7 percent in the 1930s, and 37.9 percent in the 1940s. Schmitt, *Demographic Statistics of Hawaii*.
14. There were several earlier short-lived Red Cross operations in Hawai'i: first, during the Philippine-American War (1899–1902) to treat U.S. soldiers wounded in the Philippines, and subsequent medical missions between 1907 and 1911 to combat outbreaks of bubonic plague, cholera, and typhoid epidemics. The American Red Cross, *History of the American Red Cross in Hawaii* (Honolulu: The American Red Cross, 2020), 1.
15. Total membership was 1,727. Nihon Sekijūjisha, *Nihon Sekijūji Shashikō*, 279.
16. Archival collection of the Museum Meiji-mura held by the Japanese Red Cross Toyota College of Nursing, *Hawai Tokubetsu-i'inbu Hikitsugi Shain Meibo, Meiji Yonjūsan nen*, ID: B1429-2853.
17. Archival collection of the Museum Meiji-mura held by the Japanese Red Cross Toyota College of Nursing, *Zai Hawai Mukōda, Yasuda, Kankei, Meiji Sanjūhachi nen Itaru Yonjūnen*, ID: B1387-2419. A JRCS planning document circulated to the Ministry of Foreign Affairs in 1907 reported the society collected more than 2,300 yen from more than 1,000 members in Hawai'i, which was a substantial sum at the time, approximately $3 million today. Archival collection of the Museum Meiji-mura held by the Japanese Red Cross Toyota College of Nursing, *Hawai Tokubetsu-i'inbu Kankei, Meiji Sanjūkyū nen Itaru Yonjūnen*, ID: B1346-2379; and Tadahiko Shirakawa, "Meiji kara Reiwa Nedan-shi," accessed March 7, 2022, https://coin-walk.site/J077.htm. Mukōda was a garment manufacturer and Yasuda was a coffee grower, both from Yamaguchi Prefecture. "Naka Kona Kikyōkai: Chinen-shi Kangei-kai," *Nippu Jiji*, July 17, 1937, 8; "Cōhii Hogo Undō: Dantai wo Soshiki," *Nippu Jiji*, April 1, 1937, 6; "Naka Hongan-ji Keirōkai: Kōreisha Hōmeiroku," *Hawaii Times*, June 1, 1955, 7; Yamaguchi-ken Suō Ōshima Monogatari, "Meiji Yonjū-ni nen Zai Hawai Yamaguchi-ken Jin'mei-bo," accessed February 14, 2023, https://blog.goo.ne.jp/nonta-oshima-y/e/1947c59ab640cbd987204e6393fc233c; and the Archival Collection of the Museum Meiji-mura held by the Japanese Red Cross Toyota College of Nursing, *Zai Hawai Mukōda, Yasuda, Kankei, Meiji Sanjūhachi nen Itaru Yonjū nen*, ID: B1387-2419.
18. Archival collection of the Museum Meiji-mura held by the Japanese Red Cross Toyota College of Nursing, *Zai Hawai Kishi Kantarō Kankei, Meiji Sanjūshichi nen Itaru Yonjūnen*, ID: B1375-2413; *Zai Hawai Ishii Isakichi Kankei, Meiji Sanjūshichi nen Itaru Yonjū nen*, ID: B1372-2410; and *Zai Hawai Norizuki, Onami, Hayashi Kankei, Meiji Sanjūshichi nen Itaru Yonjū nen*, ID: B1383-2415.
19. Archival collection of the Museum Meiji-mura held by the Japanese Red Cross Toyota College of Nursing, *Zai Hawai Mōri Iga Kankei, Meiji Sanjūshichi nen*, ID: B1365-2400.

20. Letter dated September 26, 1934. Archival collection of the Red Cross Information Plaza, *Mansen, Karafuto, Tokubetsu-i'inbu Kankei, Ji Shōwa Hachi nen Itaru dō Jūichi nen*, ID: 4284, PDF, 218.
21. The JRCS opened its special committee departments in San Francisco in February 1910 and in Los Angeles in November 1916, in addition to departments in Hankou in July 1905, Shanghai in November 1905, Tianjin in February 1910, and Vladivostok in September 1918. Nihon Sekijūjisha, *Nihon Sekijūji Shashi Zokkō, Jō kan Meiji yonjū nen kara Taishō jūichi nen*, 510–11, 949–54, 958.
22. During his service in Honolulu as Japan's consul general between 1916 and 1919, Moroi Rokurō authored a number of reports on the anti-Japanese movement in the Unites States and its impact on Japanese immigrants, which on the American West Coast culminated in the passage in 1920 of new restrictions on Japanese land ownership. Moroi Tadakazu, *Moroi Rokurō-kun Tsuitō Ihōroku* (Tokyo: Ko Moroi Kōshi Tsuioku I'inkai, 1941).
23. Makita Yoshiya, "Jindō, Teikoku, Shokuminchi: Dai Ichiji Sekaitaisen-ki no Ajia Taiheiyō Chiiki ni Okeru Kokusai Sekijūji Undō," *Journal of Humanitarian Studies, Japanese Red Cross Institute for Humanitarian Studies* 8 (Tokyo: Tōshindō, 2019): 52.
24. "Ask Japanese to Give Help to Red Cross Work," *Honolulu Star-Bulletin*, September 25, 1917, 8; and "Local Red Cross Membership Will Total More Than 15,750," *Honolulu Star-Bulletin*, October 2, 1917, 2.
25. "Hōkoku no Tameni Ōbo seyo," *Maui Shinbun*, May 7, 1918, 1; and "Shokun wa Susu'nnde Shukkin seyo," *Maui Shinbun*, May 7, 1918, 5. Cooperation between the JRCS and ARC was not limited to Hawai'i. Founded in 1916, JRCS's Los Angeles Special Committee Department joined with the ARC Los Angeles chapter to raise funds for war orphans, widows, medical supplies, and clothing. Nihon Sekijūjisha, *Nihon Sekijūji Shashi Zokkō, Jō kan Meiji yonjū nen kara Taishō jūichi nen*, 955–58.
26. Nihon Sekijūjisha, *Nihon Sekijūjisha Shashikō, Dai Yon-ka*, 539.
27. In 1917, the Pan-Pacific Union (PPU) was established by the Hawaiian internationalists at Honolulu, the center of the Pacific. Alexander Hume Ford initiated the movement. The purpose of the PPU to was to cultivate good relations among the Pacific Rim nations of Japan, the Unites States, Canada, Australia, New Zealand, and China. In 1920, Tokugawa Iesato founded the Pan-Pacific Association of Japan as a branch association of the international PPU. The inaugural luncheon of the association was held at the Peer Club in Tokyo, a gala event attended by more than twenty U.S. congressmen and a hundred Japanese peers, politicians, and entrepreneurs, including Japan's preeminent industrialist, Shibusawa Eiichi (1840–1931). "Ford Working for Pan-Pacific Home: Hopes to Acquire University Club by Time Prince Tokugawa Visits," *Nippu Jiji*, October 27, 1930, 8; Iimori Akiko, "Pan-Pacific Union and Japan's Attitude in the Early 1920s: A Study of the Origin of the IPR Conference," *Journal of Asia-Pacific Studies*, no. 35 (January 2019): 30–42.
28. "Prince Lauds P-P Movement: Tokugawa Expresses Hope That Peace Will Be Furthered," *Nippu Jiji*, December 5, 1930, 10.
29. Nihon Sekijūjisha, *Nihon Sekijūjisha Shashikō, Dai Yon-kan*, 539.

30. When the ARC Hawai'i Chapter was founded in 1917, approximately 16,000 people joined the organization. The American Red Cross, *History of the American Red Cross in Hawaii*, 2.
31. "Prince Iyesato Tokugawa Dies in Tokyo Today: Late Prince Tokugawa, 77, Strove for Promotion of America-Japan Relations," *Nippu Jiji*, June 5, 1940, 9.
32. The *Kashū Mainichi Shinbun*, the *Hawai Hōchi*, the *Maui Shinbun*, the *Nippu Jiji*, the *Rafu Shimpō*, the *Shin Sekai Asahi Shinbun*, and the *Yamato Shinbun*.
33. "Nihon-jin Yōrōin Zai-in-sha: Chikaku Gojūni mei to Naru," *Nippu Jiji*, December 17, 1935, 5.
34. Archival collection of the Museum Meiji-mura held by the Japanese Red Cross Toyota College of Nursing, *Manshū, Chōsen, Karafuto, Tokubetsu-i'inbu Kankei, Ji Shōwa Yo nen Itaru dō Shichi nen*, ID: B1746-4019.
35. One film depicted the life of Miyamoto Musashi, a renowned swordsman and man of letters; the other was a documentary marking the 2,600th anniversary of the founding of the Japanese state by the legendary Emperor Jimmu. "Izumo Taisha Fujin-kai Shusai: Nihon-jin Yōrōin Ian-kai," *Nippu Jiji*, December 9, 1940, 5; and Yomota Inuhiko, *Nihon Eiga-shi Hyakujū-nen* (Tokyo: Shūeisha Shinsho, 2014), 107.
36. Archival collection of the Museum Meiji-mura held by the Japanese Red Cross Toyota College of Nursing, *Mansen, Karafuto, Tokubetsu-i'inbu Kankei, Ji Taishō Jūni nen Itaru Shōwa San nen*, ID: B1681-3493; "Hawai Nihon Sekijūjishain Bokoku Kankōdan Dan'in Boshū," *Hawai Hōchi*, January 30, 1928, 4; and "Natsui Haruyoshi-shi Kikoku," *Maui Shinbun*, April 20, 1920, 3.
37. Nihon Sekijūjisha, *Nihon Sekijūjisha Shashikō, Dai Yon-kan*, 417.
38. Toake Endoh, *Exporting Japan: Politics of Emigration Toward Latin America* (Urbana: University of Illinois Press, 2009), 18. The U.S. 1924 Immigration Act severely restricted immigration to the Unites States and Hawai'i.
39. *Burajiru Takushoku-gaisha* 伯剌西爾拓殖会社.
40. Nihon Imin Hachijūnen-shi Hensan I'inkai, *Burajiru Nihon Imin Hachijūnen-shi* (São Paulo: Toppan Puresu Insatsu Shuppan Gaisha, 1991), 28–29, 32–34, 85–86, 103.
41. *Kaigai Kōgyō Kabushiki Gaisha* 海外興行株式会社.
42. Nihon Imin Hachijūnen-shi Hensan I'inkai, *Burajiru Nihon Imin Hachijūnen-shi*, 27, 34; and National Diet Library of Japan, "Establishment of Emigration and Settlement Companies," accessed January 29, 2023, https://www.ndl.go.jp/brasil/e/s3/s3_3.html.
43. Colonies were Juqueri, Cotia, Baiben, Burejao, and Birigui. Nihon Imin Hachijūnen-shi Hensan I'inkai, *Burajiru Nihon Imin Hachijūnen-shi*, 53–57; National Diet Library of Japan, "From Colonos to Independent Farmers," accessed October 28, 2021, https://www.ndl.go.jp/brasil/e/s3/s3_1.html.
44. Nihon Imin Hachijūnen-shi Hensan I'inkai, *Burajiru Nihon Imin Hachijūnen-shi*, 67, 71–77.
45. Currently Nagoya University.
46. Kitajima received the Fifth Class, Gold and Silver Rays, Order of the Rising Sun. After resigning from the JRCS in 1908, he joined Nippon Yusen Kabushiki Kaisha (NYK) and served as a doctor for Prince Kuni Yoshihiko (1873–1929) during his travels to Europe.

47. Iguape was a remote rural area in São Paulo state. Katsura Tarō (1848–1913), Japanese prime minister, Takahashi Korekiyo (1854–1936), President of the Bank of Japan, and the industrialist Shibusawa Eiichi (1840–1931), known as a father of Japanese capitalism, were among the sponsors of the Iguape colony. The colony's initial purpose was to cultivate rice for export to Japan to increase Japan's food self-sufficiency.
48. Aoyagi Ikutarō, *Burajiru ni Okeru Nipponjin Hatten-shi, Ge-kan: Nikkei Imin Shiryōshū, Nambei-hen San, Dai Sanjukkan* (Tokyo: Burajiru ni Okeru Nipponjin Hatten-shi Kankō I'inkai, 1953), 182–86.
49. "Jūnishichōchūbyō no Sensei: Kitajima Ishi no Eimin," *Burajiru Jihō*, September 21, 1923, 7.
50. The Dōjinkai Corporation of Japanese official medical institution in Brazil (*Zai Burajiru Nipponjin Dōjinkai*) was founded by the Japanese government in 1924 and was dissolved in 1942 when Brazil broke off diplomatic relations with Japan. "Zai Burajiru Nihonjin Dōjinkai," accessed March 11, 2022, https://ja.wikipedia.org/wiki/%E5%9C%A8%E3%83%96%E3%83%A9%E3%82%B8%E3%83%AB%E6%97%A5%E6%9C%AC%E4%BA%BA%E5%90%8C%E4%BB%81%E4%BC%9A; and Aoyagi, *Burajiru ni Okeru Nipponjin Hatten-shi, Ge-kan*, 169–75; and Nihon Imin Hachijūnen-shi Hensan I'inkai, *Burajiru Nihon Imin Hachijūnen-shi*, 121.
51. *San Pauro Nihon Byōin Kensetsu Kisei Dōmeikai* 聖市日本病院建設期成同盟会. Uchiyama Iwatarō (1890–1971), a councilor of Japan's São Paulo embassy, became a chair of the league. National Diet Library of Japan, "Dojinkai Corporation of Japanese Residing in Brazil and Nihon Hospital," accessed February 15, 2023, https://www.ndl.go.jp/brasil/e/column/dojinkai.html.
52. Nihon Imin Hachijūnen-shi Hensan I'inkai, *Burajiru Nihon Imin Hachijūnen-shi*, 119–21; and National Diet Library of Japan, "Dojinkai Corporation of Japanese Residing in Brazil and Nihon Hospital."
53. *Nihon Byōin Kensetsu Kōenkai* 日本病院建設後援会. Saitō Makoto (1858–1936) chaired the association; the vice-chair, Tokugawa Yorisada (1892–1954), who was one of the permanent members of the executive committees of the JRCS Tokyo Headquarters, later succeeded Saitō as chair. Aoyagi, *Burajiru ni Okeru Nipponjin Hatten-shi, Ge-kan*, 178; National Diet Library of Japan, "Dojinkai Corporation of Japanese Residing in Brazil and Nihon Hospital"; and Nihon Sekijūjisha, *Shōwa jū-ichinen-do Jigyōnenpō* (Tokyo: Nihon Sekijūjisha, 1936), 4.
54. "Rokujūgo-ko no Kyūgohan: Nihon Sekijūjisha no Sōdōin," *Burajiru Jihō*, September 21, 1923, 1; and "Nihon Sekijūji Gojū-nen Sai ni Nippon de Bankoku Sekijūi Taikai," *Burajiru Jihō*, April 30, 1926, 6.
55. "Bankoku Sekijūji Kaigi Tōkyō de Kaisai saru," *Seishū Shimpō*, October 23, 1934, 2; and "Sekijūji Taikai: Kakkoku Daihyō Zokuzoku Raichaku," *Burajiru Jihō*, October 24, 1934, 5.
56. Archival collection of Japanese Red Cross Society International Department, *Kizōtosho Kankei 154, Dai San-kai Han-bei Sekijūji Kaigi ni Kansuru Bunsho*.
57. Ernest J. Swift, "The Third Pan American Red Cross Conference," *Bulletin of the Pan American Union* 69, no. 8 (August 1935): 592–96; "Agenda of the Third Pan American Red Cross Conference," *Bulletin of the Pan American Union* 69, no. 8 (August 1935): 597–98.

226   4. BEYOND EMPIRE

58. Nihon Sekijūjisha, *Shōwa jū-nen-do Jigyōnenpō* (Tokyo: Nihon Sekijūjisha, 1935), 121; "Waga Sekijūji no Kaigai Shinshutsu: Chū-nambei Kakuchi ni I'inbu wo Secchi," *Nippon Shimbun*, June 17, 1936, 2; and "Nihon Sekijūjisha no Hakuai no Te wa Nobu," *Burajiru Jihō*, June 15, 1936, 5.
59. "Waga Sekijūji no Kaigai Shinshutsu," 2.
60. "Waga Sekijūji no Kaigai Shinshutsu," 2.
61. "Waga Sekijūji no Kaigai Shinshutsu," 2.
62. "Nihon Sekijūjisha no Hakuai no Te wa Nobu," 5.
63. Nihon Sekijūjisha, *Nihon Sekijūjisha Shashikō, Dai Go-kan*, 330. JRCS's São Paul Special Committee Department was initially planned to be established in 1925, the same year as JRCS Vancouver, but was delayed due to adverse economic conditions affecting overseas Japanese communities. Japan Center for Asian Historical Records, *Nijū, Kaigai Tokubetsu-i'inbu Secchi*, REF: B12082304000; Archives of the Ministry of Foreign Affairs of Japan, *Sekijūji Kankei Zakken*, REF: B-3-11-3-14, PDF, 8–9.
64. "Waga Sekijūji no Kaigai Shinshutsu," 2.
65. Aoyagi, *Burajiru ni Okeru Nipponjin Hatten-shi, Ge-kan*, 175–82.
66. National Diet Library of Japan, "Dojinkai Corporation of Japanese Residing in Brazil and Nihon Hospital"; and National Diet Library of Japan, "Japanese Community Situations Before and After the Outbreak of the War Between Japan and the U.S.," accessed October 12, 2021, https://www.ndl.go.jp/brasil/e/s5/s5_2.html.
67. "Chū to Ai no Nihon Skijūjisha e," *Seishū Shimpō*, February 7, 1939, 3.
68. During the war, Japanese immigrants in Brazil were forcefully displaced, and some were sent to temporary immigrant shelters or moved inland to undeveloped areas. Their assets were frozen, and some assets were not returned until the 2000s. Japanese immigrants in other Latin American countries, such as Peru, were sent to internment camps in the Unites States. National Diet Library of Japan, "Japanese Community Situations Before and After the Outbreak of the War Between Japan and the U.S."; and Takahashi Yukiharu, *Nikkei Burajiru Imin-shi* (Tokyo: San-ichi, 1993), 185–96.
69. Yoshida Shigeru, "Sangi'in Gi'in Inoue Natsue-kun Teishutsu Nihon Sekijūjisha Zaigai Shisan ni Kansuru Shitsumon ni Taisuru Tōbensho, Shitsumon Shuisho: Dai Go-kai Tokubetu Kokkai Tōbensho, Tōbensho Dai Hachijūhachi Gō, Naikaku Sankō Dai Hyaku-gō, Shōwa Nijūyo-nen Go-gatsu Nijūichi-nichi," House of Councillors, the National Diet of Japan, accessed September 2021, https://www.sangiin.go.jp/japanese/joho1/kousei/syuisyo/005/touh/t005088.htm.
70. I'ino Masako, Kimura Kenji, and Kumei Teruko, eds., *Sensō to Nihonjin Imin* (Tokyo: Toyo Shorin, 1997), 299.
71. Nihon Sekijūjisha, *Nihon Sekijūjisha Shashikō, Dai Yon-kan*, 417.
72. Takahashi, *Nikkei Burajiru Imin-shi*, 210–41. The struggle with the *Shindō Renmei*, which included assassinations and terrorist attacks, continued for a few more years. Takahashi, *Nikkei Burajiru Imin-shi*, 220; and National Diet Library of Japan, "Kachigumi and Makegumi," accessed January 5, 2024, https://www.ndl.go.jp/brasil/e/s6/s6_1.html.
73. Endoh, *Exporting Japan*, 18.

5. THE JAPANESE RED CROSS SOCIETY AND WORLD WAR II: CIVILIAN CASUALTIES, INTERNEES, AND PRISONERS OF WAR

1. In Japanese scholarship, Utsumi Aiko uses the records of the International Military Tribunal for the Far East and oral histories of Allied POWs to analyze the history of Japanese treatment of POWs from the First Sino-Japanese War to the Pacific War. Utsumi argues that race was a decisive factor in Japan's treatment of Allied POWs. Asian Allied POWs were generally treated leniently to encourage their active collaboration, while white Allied POWs were often subject to harsh treatment and suffered correspondingly high mortality rates. Utsumi Aiko, *Nihongun no Horyo Seisaku* (Tokyo: Aoki-shoten, 2005). Utilizing both ICRC and JRCS archives, Ōkawa Shirō focuses on the efforts of Dr. Paravicini as the Head of the ICRC Japan delegation and favorably evaluates his performance under severe constraints imposed by Japan's wartime government. Ōkawa Shirō, ed., *Ōbeijin-Horyo to Sekijūji katsudō—Paravichiini Hakase no Fukken* (Tokyo: Ronsō-sha, 2005); and Ōkawa Shirō, "Research on the Japanese Red Cross Society Documents Concerning the Treatment of Western Prisoners of War in Japanese Hands During World War II," *Heisei Jūhachi nendo—Heisei Jūkyū nendo: Kagaku Kenkyūhi Hojyo-kin Kiban Kenkyū Kenkyū Seika Hōkokusho* (2008). Tachikawa Kyōichi and Yadohisa Haruhiko survey treatment of POWs in the modern era and conclude that even though the JRCS did not coordinate with the ICRC on POWs during the First Sino-Japanese War and the Russo-Japanese War, the JRCS fulfilled its humanitarian mission. During World War I, the JRCS coordinated closely with the ICRC. However, during World War II, the Japanese Army imposed severe restrictions on the ICRC that made their operations very difficult. Tachikawa Kyōichi and Yadohisa Haruhiko, "Seifu oyobi Gun to ICRC tō tono Kankei—Nisshin Sensō kara Taiheiyō Sensō made—(Kōhen)," *Bōei Kenkyūjo Kiyō*, Vol. 11–2 (January 2009): 105–50, accessed May 29, 2018, http://www.nids.mod.go.jp/publication/kiyo/pdf/bulletin_j11_2_4.pdf.

Tsurumi Shunsuke (1922–2015), a leading Japanese postwar intellectual later active in the anti–Vietnam War movement in Japan, who was a student at Harvard University in 1942 and among Japanese nationals repatriated after Pearl Harbor, has written about the uncertain fate of ordinary people caught between belligerent powers. Tsurumi Shunsuke, Katō Norihiro, and Kurokawa Sō, *Nichibei Kōkansen* (Tokyo: Shinchōsha, 2006). Komiya Mayumi, who researched the experiences of Allied civilian internees in camps from Hokkaido to Kyushu, documented the experiences of widely diverse groups, including Aleut in Otaru Camp in Hokkaido, Australian nurses in Yokohama Camp, British travelers in Fukushima, and Italian diplomats in Tokyo, among others, and concluded that treatment was mostly adequate. Allied firebombing toward the end of the war was the principal cause of loss of life among internees. Komiya Mayumi, *Tekikoku-jin Yokuryū—Senji-ka no Gaikoku Minkan-jin: Rekishi Bunka Laiburari* (Tokyo: Yoshikawa Kōbun-kan, 2009). Until recently, English-language scholarship that did not use Japanese-language sources has represented Japanese cruelty towards the Allied POWs as reflective of unique Japanese traits. The most recent academic history in this vein is Olive Checkland, *Humanitarianism and the Emperor's Japan, 1877–1977* (New York: St. Martin's, 1994). John W. Dower's pathbreaking study of racism on both sides of the Pacific War challenged this school of interpretation. John W. Dower, *War Without Mercy: Race and Power in the Pacific War* (London: Faber and Faber, 1986). Most recently, Sarah Kovner's multi-archive research on Japanese POW policy presents case studies of four POW camps that show great variation in treatment and mortality rates and concludes "there was nothing inherent to Japanese culture or character that led to the occurrence of inhumane treatment." Sarah Kovner, *Prisoners of the Empire: Inside Japanese POW Camps* (Cambridge, MA: Harvard University Press, 2020), 3.

2. The Tokyo Declaration was adopted at the Fifteenth International Conference of the Red Cross in Tokyo, hosted by the JRCS in 1934.

3. The battle on July 29 was known as the Tongzhow munity, in which the troops of the Chinese collaborationist East Hebei Army killed several hundred Japanese and Korean civilians in the Japanese-controlled district of Beijing.

4. In September 1939, the Mongol United Autonomous Government was reorganized as the Mengjiang United Autonomous Government, consisting of three "autonomous" governments, Japanese, Han Chinese, and Mongolians, and was renamed the Mongolian Autonomous Federation in August 1941. It functioned as a quasi-puppet state of the Japanese Empire until 1945. Sakamoto Tsutomu, "Abuduru Iburahimu no Sairainichi to Mōkyō Seikenka no Isurāmu Seisaku," in *Nicchū Sensō to Isurāmu: Manmō-Ajia Chiiki ni okeru Tōchi Kaijū Seisaku*, ed. Sakamoto Tsutomu (Tokyo: Keio University Press, 2008), 37–49.

5. Nihon Sekijūjisha, ed., *Nihon Sekijūjisha Shashikō, Dai Go-kan, Shōwa jūichi nen kara Shōwa nijū nen* (Tokyo: Nihon Sekijūjisha, 1969), 145–47.

6. Archival collection of the Museum Meiji-mura held by the Japanese Red Cross Toyota College of Nursing, *Sekijūji-kokusai-i'inkai Shanhai Haken: Wattoviru Taisa Ikken, Shōwa jūni-nen*, ID: B1067-4324.

7. Kegayama left the JRCS in 1946 and continued as a director of the surgical department at Seibo Hospital (International Virgin Mary Hospital) in Tokyo. In 1968, he received the Pontifical Equestrian Order of St. Gregory the Great from the Roman Curia. Kageyama Sadaka, *Nihon Sekijūji Damashii: Nisseki Shanhai Haken Tokubetsu Kyūgohan no Ki* (Tokyo: Shufu no Tomo Shuppan Service Centre, 1971), 92.

8. Kageyama, *Nihon Sekijūji Damashii*, 11. Makita Kise (1890–1971) was born in Gifu Prefecture and stayed in the United States from 1915 to 1934. She worked at a hospital in Los Angeles. During the Allied Occupied period, she served the Allied authorities. She was awarded the Nightingale Medal in 1965. Toyama Prefectural School of Nursing, Midwifery and Public Health, "Makita Kise-shi no Kōseki," accessed January 31, 2023, https://www.pref.toyama.jp/branches/1277/gakuin/kise%20makita.html; Japan Nursing Association, "Toyamaken no Sengo Kango Kyōiku wo Kizuita 'Makita Kise' sann'tte Don'na Hito?," accessed January 31, 2023, https://infini.fan/reports/reports-88/; and Kageyama, *Nihon Sekijūji Damashii*, 15–17.

9. Kageyama, *Nihon Sekijūji Damashii*, 11–22.

10. Archival collection of the Red Cross Information Plaza, *Dempō Shokan Utsushi A*; ICRC Archives, CR 217, Conflict sino-japonais, Correspondance avec les Croix-Rouges (E-Z), 03.08.1937–07.08.1939, Croix-Rouge japonaise, 03.08.1937–30.03.1938, correspondence

5. THE JAPANESE RED CROSS SOCIETY AND WORLD WAR II   229

envoyée, 03.08.1937–19.12.1938, no. 5; and ICRC Archives, CR 217, Conflict sino-japonaise—Correspondance avec les Croix-Rouges Letter A-D, 07.08.1937–14.07.1939, Croix-Rouge chinoise, 14.08.1937–15.06.1939, correspondence envoyée, Correspondance reçue, 29.08.1937–27.12.1938, no. 0.

11. Archival collection of the Red Cross Information Plaza, *Suzuki Takenori Nisshi: Nihon Sekijūjisha Shanhai Haken Tokubetsu Kyūgohan*, PDF, 26.
12. The JRCS had five meetings, which were held between September 19 and October 3, 1937, in Shanghai. Japanese authorities included Shanghai Consul-General Okamoto Suemasa and Consul Wajima Eiji representing MOFA; IJA officer Kimura Matsujirō, Lieutenant Colonel Infantry; IJA Lieutenant Colonel Surgeon Hirose; IJA international law specialist Saitō Yoshihira; IJN Surgeon Colonel Yasuyama Kōdō; IJN Lieutenant Colonel Matsubara Akio; and IJN international law specialist Nobuo Jumpei. Archival collection of the Museum Meiji-mura held by the Japanese Red Cross Toyota College of Nursing, *Sekijūji-kokusai-i'inkai Shanhai Haken*, ID: B1067-4324.
13. Atsumi became one of the key officials of the JRCS War Prisoners' Relief Committee Department to treat Allied POWs during the Pacific War.
14. Yasuyama Kōdō later became the director of Ōmura Naval Hospital in Nagasaki and conducted nuclear bombing emergency relief.
15. *Unlawful Actions of the Chinese in the Light of the Geneva Conventions and the Hague Declaration*, in the Archival Collection of the Museum Meiji-mura held by the Japanese Red Cross Toyota College of Nursing, *Sekijūji-kokusai-i'inkai Shanhai Haken*, ID: B1067-4324; and Kageyama, *Nihon Sekijūji Damashii*, 36–38.
16. Kageyama, *Nihon Sekijūji Damashii*, 36–38, 148–51.
17. Kageyama, *Nihon Sekijūji Damashii*, 76.
18. Kageyama, *Nihon Sekijūji Damashii*, 38, 148–51.
19. Archival collection of the Red Cross Information Plaza, *Tsūchō Shokan Utsushi B*, PDF, 28.
20. Archival collection of the Red Cross Information Plaza, *Tsūchō Shokan Utsushi B*, PDF, 29.
21. Kageyama, *Nihon Sekijūji Damashii*, 71.
22. Kageyama, *Nihon Sekijūji Damashii*, 74.
23. Kageyama, *Nihon Sekijūji Damashii*, 38–40, 47–48.
24. "Furyo Toriatsukai Jōkyō: Treatment of Prisoners of War," in the Archival Collection of the Museum Meiji-mura held by the Japanese Red Cross Toyota College of Nursing, *Sekijūji-kokusai-i'inkai Shanhai Haken*, ID: B1067-4324.
25. "Furyo Toriatsukai Jōkyō: Treatment of Prisoners of War," in the Archival Collection of the Museum Meiji-mura held by the Japanese Red Cross Toyota College of Nursing, *Sekijūji-kokusai-i'inkai Shanhai Haken*, ID: B1067-4324.
26. Kageyama, *Nihon Sekijūji Damashii*, 11–12.
27. SSERC left Shanghai on February 9, 1938, and was disbanded on February 23. Archival collection of the Red Cross Information Plaza, *Suzuki Takenori Nisshi*, PDF, 147–49.
28. Archival collection of the Museum Meiji-mura held by the Japanese Red Cross Toyota College of Nursing, *Sekijūji-kokusai-i'inkai Shanhai Haken*, ID: B1067-4324.

29. Kageyama, *Nihon Sekijūji Damashii*, 57.
30. Kageyama, *Nihon Sekijūji Damashii*, 55; Archival collection of the Red Cross Information Plaza, *Suzuki Takenori Nisshi*, PDF, 163–65; and the Archival Collection of the Red Cross Information Plaza, *B3-24: Shinajihen Jūgun Kinen: Dai Kyū Byōinsen Taisanmaru Aburaya Butai, Shōwa Jūni nen kara Jūsan nen*.
31. Archival collection of the Museum Meiji-mura held by the Japanese Red Cross Toyota College of Nursing, *Sekijūji-kokusai-i'inkai Shanhai Haken*, ID: B1067-4324. Today, there are a number of photo albums, which are preserved in JRCS archives, showing the harsh reality in Shanghai. Archival collection of the Red Cross Information Plaza, *B3-24: Shinajihen Jūgun Kinen: Dai Kyū Byōinsen Taisan-maru Aburaya Butai, Shōwa Jūni nen kara Jūsan nen*.
32. Archival collection of the Red Cross Information Plaza, *Tsūchō Shokan Utsushi B*, PDF, 29.
33. Kageyama, *Nihon Sekijūji Damashii*, 151.
34. The report was not disclosed during the Tokyo War Crime Trial. Nankin Jiken Chōsa Kenkyūkai, ed., *Nankin Jiken Shiryōshū ② Chūgoku Kankei Shiryōhen* (Tokyo: Aoki Shoten, 1992), 263, 266, 269.
35. Tokugawa Kuniyuki became the president of the JRCS in 1940 after the sudden death of Tokugawa Iesato, JRCS president, who hosted the Fifteenth International Conference of the Red Cross in Tokyo.
36. Prince Asaka was a career officer in the Imperial Japanese Army. He was promoted to the rank of general in August 1939. During the International Military Tribunal for the Far East, SCAP interrogated Prince Asaka about his involvement in the Nanjing Massacre and he was stripped of imperial family status.
37. Nakajima Kesago was appointed commander of the IJA Sixteenth Division with the start of the Second Sino-Japanese War in 1937 and participated in the Second Shanghai Incident. He retired in September 1939 and died in October 1945 due to illness.
38. *Kōnichi* 抗日.
39. Nihon Sekijūjisha, *Hakuai: Organ of the Japanese Red Cross Society, No. 610, March 1938* (Tokyo: Nihon Sekijūjisha, 1938), 1–2.
40. Archival collection of Japanese Red Cross Society Disaster Relief Division, Disaster Management and Social Welfare Department Archive, *Kyūgohan Gyōmuhōkokusho: Nihon Sekijūjisha Dai 46 & 48 Kyūgohan, Senkyūhyaku-sanjū-hachi nen shichi gatsu nano-ka kara Senkyūhyaku-sanjū-hachi nen shichi gatsu nijū-ichi nichi*; and the Archival Collection of Japanese Red Cross Society Disaster Relief Division, Disaster Management and Social Welfare Department, *Senjikyūgohan Gyōmuhōkokusho*.
41. Archival collection of Japanese Red Cross Society Disaster Relief Division, Disaster Management and Social Welfare Department, *Senjikyūgohan Gyōmuhōkokusho*.
42. Nihon Sekijūjisha, *Nihon Sekijūjisha Hachi-jū nen Shōshi* (Tokyo: Nihon Sekijūjisha, 1957), 20; and Shimazu Tadatsugu, *Jindō no Hata no Moto-ni: Nisseki to Tomoni Sanjūgo-nen* (Tokyo: Kōdan-sha, 1965), 70.
43. Archival collection of Japanese Red Cross Society International Department, *Furyo • Hi-yokuryūsha Kyūjutsu Kanren Bunsho, Seiri bangō yon: Sekijūji-kokusai-i'inkai*

5. THE JAPANESE RED CROSS SOCIETY AND WORLD WAR II   231

kara no Denpōtō, (Shōwa Jūroku nen Jūni gatsu kara Jūshichi nen San gatsu): Furyo Jōyaku Tekiyō to Furyo Jōhōkyoku Secchi ni Kansuru Kōshin, Nisseki Shachō ate Bunsho tō: Senkyūhyaku-yonjū-ichi nen Jūni gatsu Jūichi nichi Dai Sanzen-nihyaku-nanajū-yon gō; Masui Takashi, Taiheiyō Sensō-chū no Kokusai Jindō Katsudō no Kiroku (Kaitei-ban) (Tokyo: Nihon Sekijūjisha, 1994), 3.

44. Masui Takashi, Taiheiyō Sensō-chū no Kokusai Jindō Katsudō no Kiroku (Kaitei-ban), 15–16; and Utsumi, Nihongun no Horyo Seisaku, 177–78.
45. Junyō 準用.
46. Utsumi, Nihongun no Horyo Seisaku, 176–79; Masui Takashi, Taiheiyō Sensō-chū no Kokusai Jindō Katsudō no Kiroku (Kaitei-ban), 15–16; and the Archival Collection of Japanese Red Cross Society International Department, Furyo • Hi-yokuryūsha Kyūjutsu Kanren Bunsho, Seiri bangō yon: Sekijūji-kokusai-i'inkai kara no Denpōtō, (Shōwa Jūroku nen Jūni gatsu kara Jūshichi nen San gatsu): Furyo Jōyaku Tekiuō to Furyo Jōhōkyoku Secchi ni Kansuru Kōshin, Nisseki Shachō ate Bunsho tō: Senkyūhyaku-yonjū-ni nen Ichi gatsu Kokonoka hatsu Dai Yonsen-yonhyaku-nijū-ni gō; and the Archival Collection of Japanese Red Cross Society International Department, Furyo • Hi-yokuryūsha Kyūjutsu Kanren Bunsho, Seiri bangō Go no Ichi: Senji no Katsudō Zenpan ni Kansuru Sekijūji-kokusai-i'inkai tono Kōshin, (Ichi), (Shōwa Jūyo nen Ku gatsu kara Jūhachi nen Hachi gatsu), PDF, 26–31.
47. Utsumi, Nihongun no Horyo Seisaku, 176–79.
48. Nihon Sekijūjisha, Nihon Sekijūjisha Hachi-jū nen Shōshi, 20–21.
49. Testimony of Nakagawa Nozomu (1875–1964), a politician and bureaucrat at the Home Ministry. Nakagawa served as a vice-president of the JRCS from 1932 to 1946. Nihon Sekijūjisha, Nihon Sekijūjisha Hachi-jū nen Shōshi, 20–21.
50. Nihon Sekijūjisha Furyo Kyūjutsu I'inbu Kisoku. The Regulations for the War Prisoners' Relief Committee Department of the Japanese Red Cross Society was originally created by the society in 1914, in accordance with the declaration of the Ninth International Conference of the Red Cross in 1912 in Washington, DC. Archival collection of the Red Cross Information Plaza, Furyo • Hi-yokuryūsha Kyūjutsu Kanren Bunsho, Seiri bangō San: Furyo Kyūjustu Kitei; and Nihon Sekijūjisha, ed., Nihon Sekijūji Shashi Zokkō, Ge kan Meiji yonjū nen kara Taishō jūichi nen, 597.
51. ICRC established the Central Agency for Prisoners of War in 1939. Nihon Sekijūjisha, Nihon Sekijūjisha Shashikō, Dai Go-kan, 76.
52. Nihon Sekijūjisha, Nihon Sekijūjisha Shashikō, Dai Go-kan, 217.
53. Archival collection of the Red Cross Information Plaza, Furyo • Hi-yokuryūsha Kyūjutsu Kanren Bunsho, Seiri bangō San, PDF, 9.
54. Inoue Enji was former director general of the Investigation Department of the JRCS. Inoue played a significant role in organizing JRCS operations during World War I and in securing the invitation to host the Fifteenth International Conference of the Red Cross to Tokyo (1934).
55. Archival collection of the Red Cross Information Plaza, Shimazu Meiyo-shachō Intabyū II: Teisei Genkō, PDF, 29–30; and Shimazu, Jindō no Hata no Moto-ni, 70–71.
56. Nihon Sekijūjisha, Nihon Sekijūjisha Shashikō, Dai Go-kan, 217.

232   5. THE JAPANESE RED CROSS SOCIETY AND WORLD WAR II

57. Nihon Sekijūjisha, *Nihon Sekijūjisha Hachi-jū nen Shōshi*, 20–21.
58. Nihon Sekijūjisha, *Nihon Sekijūjisha Shashikō, Dai Go-kan*, 76.
59. Archival collection of Japanese Red Cross Society International Department, *Furyo・Hi-yokuryūsha Kyūjutsu Kanren Bunsho, Seiri bangō Jū no Ichi: Furyo Kyūjutsu tō ni Kansuru Sekijūji-kokusai-i'inkai tono Kōshin, (Ichi), (Shōwa Jūshichi nen Ni gatsu kara Jūkyūnen Ni gatu): Kyūjutsu Haikyū, Kōkansen Gurripusuhorumu-gō, Teia-maru Sekisai Kyūjutsuhin, Sekijūji-kokusai-i'inkai Chūnichi-daihyō-ho Pesutarocchi ni yoru Furyo Shūyōjo (Zentsūji, Osaka-honjo, Sakurajima-bunsho, Amagasaki-bunsho, Motomachi, Ube-bunsho, Onoda-bunsho, Ōhama-bunsho, Hakodate-honjo, Kamaishi-bunsho) Shisatsu tō*.
60. Archival collection of Japanese Red Cross Society International Department, *Furyo・Hi-yokuryūsha Kyūjutsu Kanren Bunsho, Seiri bangō Ni: Shōwa Jūshichi nen San gatsu: Furyo Kyūjutsu I'inbu: Sekijūji Tsūshin, Dō-yūzei, Kōkansen Takusō: Sekijūji Tsūshin, Shūyōjo, Zatsu: d. Shūyōjo*.
61. Nihon Sekijūjisha, *Nihon Sekijūjisha Shashikō, Dai Go-kan*, 80. The JRCS donated 100,000 CHF in total to the ICRC between 1936 to 1944. Nihon Sekijūjisha, *Nihon Sekijūjisha Hachi-jū nen Shōshi*, 21.
62. Nihon Sekijūjisha, *Nihon Sekijūjisha Shashikō, Dai Go-kan*, 218; and Masui Takashi, *Taiheiyō Sensō-chū no Kokusai Jindō Katsudō no Kiroku (Kaitei-ban)*, 34.
63. Archival collection of Japanese Red Cross Society International Department, *Furyo・Hi-yokuryūsha Kyūjutsu Kanren Bunsho, Seiri bangō Jūhachi: Naigai Furyo Shūyōjo eno Buppin Kizō, (Shōwa Jūshichi nen Jū gatsu kara Jūhachi nen Shi gatsu)*, PDF, 28–66.
64. Archival collection of the Red Cross Information Plaza, *Shimazu Meiyo-shachō Intabyū II*, 30.
65. Archival collection of Japanese Red Cross Society International Department, *Furyo・Hi-yokuryūsha Kyūjutsu Kanren Bunsho, Seiri bangō Jū no Ichi*.
66. Archival collection of Japanese Red Cross Society International Department, *Furyo・Hi-yokuryūsha Kyūjutsu Kanren Bunsho, Seiri bangō Jū no Ichi*.
67. Equivalent to 24.2 billion yen in 2015.
68. The JRCS spent a total of 53,001,914 yen and 78 sen (equivalent to 24 billion yen in 2015) on its entire humanitarian relief activities, of which 48,517,344 yen and 64 sen (equivalent to 21.9 billion yen in 2015) were used to fund the medical relief department, which deployed relief parties. The remaining 10 percent of 457,909 yen and 69 sen (equivalent to 206.5 million yen in 2015) was allocated to WPRCD. Nihon Sekijūjisha, *Nihon Sekijūjisha Shashikō, Dai Go-kan*, 219; and Tadahiko Shirakawa, "Meiji kara Heisei Nedan-shi," accessed June 18, 2018, http://sirakawa.b.la9.jp/Coin/J077.htm.
69. Utsumi mostly cited Japanese records and scholarship. Utsumi, *Nihongun no Horyo Seisaku*, 3–4.
70. "Research Starters: US Military by the Numbers," National WWII Museum, New Orleans, accessed August 27, 2021, https://www.nationalww2museum.org/students-teachers/student-resources/research-starters/research-starters-us-military-numbers; and Naval History and Heritage Command, "U.S. Prisoners of War and Civilian American Citizens Captured and Interned by Japan in World War II: The Issue of Compensation by Japan," accessed April 15, 2022, https://www.history.navy.mil/research/library/online-reading

5. THE JAPANESE RED CROSS SOCIETY AND WORLD WAR II 233

-room/title-list-alphabetically/u/us-prisoners-war-civilian-american-citizens-captured.html. For recent revisionist history of Japanese treatment of Allied POWs, see Kovner, *Prisoners of the Empire*.

71. Utsumi, *Nihongun no Horyo Seisaku*, 3–4.
72. John Dower showed that Germany took 5.5 million Soviet prisoners, of whom at least 3.5 million (64 percent) were dead by mid-1944. On the other hand, 235,473 American and British prisoners were captured by Germany and only 9,348 (4 percent) did not survive, whereas 35,756 of 132,134 (27 percent) of Anglo-American POWs captive in Japanese hands died. In addition, some 60,000 to 70,000 Allied captives, mostly Australian, British, Indian, and Dutch were eventually put as forced laborers on the construction of the Burma-Siam railway. Furthermore, approximately 300,000 Asian forced laborers, including Javanese, Tamil, Malayan, Burmese, and Chinese, may have been mobilized to the Burma-Siam railway construction site. Dower, *War Without Mercy*, 47–48. Sarah Kovner also showed the average mortality rate of Allied POWs, including Britain, the Netherlands, Australia, the United States, Canada, and New Zealand, was 27 percent. The highest mortality rate was the Australians at 34 percent, whereas the lowest death rate was the Canadians at 16 percent. Kovner, *Prisoners of the Empire*, 5.
73. Kovner, *Prisoners of the Empire*, 137.
74. Kovner, *Prisoners of the Empire*, 3–4, 137–56. Japanese historian Katō Yōko attributes food shortages in Japan to poor planning throughout the Japanese Empire and specifically to the military, which drained the countryside of able-bodied workers. In contrast to wartime Germany, where caloric intake actually rose during the war, using 1933 data as a baseline, Japan suffered a 60 percent decline. Katō Yōko, *Soredemo Nihon-jin wa 'Sensō' wo Eranda* (Tokyo: Asahi Shuppan-sha, 2010), 468–71.
75. Archival collection of Japanese Red Cross Society International Department, *Furyo・Hi-yokuryūsha Kyūjutsu Kanren Bunsho, Seiri bangō Jūhachi*, PDF, 19–27.
76. Archival collection of the Red Cross Information Plaza, *Shimazu Meiyo-shachō Intabyū II*, 31.
77. Archival collection of Japanese Red Cross Society International Department, *Furyo・Hi-yokuryūsha Kyūjutsu Kanren Bunsho, Seiri bangō Jū no Ni: Furyo Kyūjutsu tō ni Kansuru Sekijūji-kokusai-i'inkai tono Kōshin, (Ni), (Shōwa Jūkyū nen Shi gatsu kara Nijūnen Roku gatsu: Pesutarocchi Daihyō ni yoru Furyo Shūyōjo (Fukuoka Dai Jūnana Bunsho, Dō Dai Jūni Bunsho, Zentsūji) Shisatsu, Zai-Man Furyo, Hi-yokuryūsha ni tsuite, Angusuto Daihyō-ho ni yoru Shūyōjo (Hakodate, Muroran, Kamaishi) Shisatsu tōtō*, PDF, 162–65. Before becoming a camp director, Emoto served as a commanding officer of Shinagawa station in Tokyo and ended up during the war as a lieutenant colonel. Yoshimura Kazuaki, *On'shi・Emoto Shigeo Den: Kakaru Shi Ariki* (Tokyo: Jihi Shuppan-bu, Kurashi no Techō-sha, 2008), 384–405.
78. Yoshimura, *On'shi・Emoto Shigeo Den*, 405–8. Emoto's fluent English and humane treatment of Allied POWs at the Hakodate camp aroused suspicions as to his loyalties, and he was demoted to a command overseeing Korean laborers at the Sorachi coal mine camp, in a remote area of Hokkaido. When war ended, POWs at Hakodate camp rioted; desperate to restore order, Emoto was called back to the Hakodate camp and negotiated

a settlement as the POWs respected and trusted him. Kono Toru, "Lieutenant Colonel Shigeo Emoto: Soldier and Teacher," *Bulletin of Tokyo Kasei University Kiyō Dai 33 Shū* 1 (October 1993): 2; and Yoshimura, *On'shi ・ Emoto Shigeo Den*, 570–83.

79. Emoto was released from prison in 1948, and he served as an interpreter and translator for the Legal Affairs Bureau of SCAP from November 1948 to early 1949. In later life he worked as an English-language instructor for a number of organizations in Japan, including the Nichibei Kaiwa Gakuin (English Language School), Yokohama YMCA, the Fuji Bank, Mitsui & Co., Ltd., and the Ministry of International Trade and Industry. He also organized his private English language school. Yoshimura, *On'shi ・ Emoto Shigeo Den*, 607–8, 667–68, 716–807.

80. Chaen Yoshio, ed., *Furyo Jōhōkyoku ・ Furyo Toriatsukai no Kiroku: Tsuki Kaigun Heigakkō 'Kokusaihō': Jūgonen Sensō Jūyō-bunken Shiriizu, Dai Hasshū* (Tokyo: Fuji Shuppan, 1992), 43–44; POW Research Network Japan, "Lisbon Maru," POW Research Network, accessed August 18, 2021, http://www.powresearch.jp/en/archive/ship/lisbon.html; Shimazu, *Jindō no Hata no Moto-ni*, 77–80; and the Archival Collection of the Red Cross Information Plaza, *Furyo ・ Hi-yokuryūsha Kyūjutsu Kanren Bunsho, Seiri bangō Jūhachi*, PDF, 1–6.

81. The IJA sent an official request to the JRCS on November 9. Archival collection of Japanese Red Cross Society International Department, *Furyo ・ Hi-yokuryūsha Kyūjutsu Kanren Bunsho, Seiri bangō Jūhachi*, PDF, 1–6; Shimazu, *Jindō no Hata no Moto-ni*, 77–80.

82. Shimazu, *Jindō no Hata no Moto-ni*, 79–80.

83. Archival collection of Japanese Red Cross Society International Department, *Furyo ・ Hi-yokuryūsha Kyūjutsu Kanren Bunsho, Seiri bangō Jūhachi*, PDF, 1–6.

84. Shimazu, *Jindō no Hata no Moto-ni*, 77–80.

85. Kovner, *Prisoners of the Empire*, 120–36.

86. Utsumi, *Nihongun no Horyo Seisaku*, 213–15.

87. Archival collection of Japanese Red Cross Society International Department, *Furyo ・ Hi-yokuryūsha Kyūjutsu Kanren Bunsho, Seiri bangō Ni: d. Shūyōjo*, PDF, 2–59. During the Pacific War (1941–1945), the JRCS Korean Headquarters was responsible for the treatment of Allied POWs held in camps on the Korean Peninsula. For example, in November 1943, it hosted Max Pestalozzi the ICRC Japan representative's eleven-day inspection of POW camps in Manchukuo. Archival collection of Japanese Red Cross Society International Department, *Sengo Shori Kankei 250, Manshū Chōsen deno Furyo no Atsukai ni kakaru Sekijūji-kokusai-i'inkai tono Tsūshinbunsho-tō*.

88. For instance, the CRC sent 1,328 cases of assorted provisions, while the ARC delivered 1,456 cases of assorted provisions, 480 toiletry cases, more than 60,000 cigarettes, and a range of other goods. Archival collection of Japanese Red Cross Society International Department, *Furyo ・ Hi-yokuryūsha Kyūjutsu Kanren Bunsho, Seiri bangō Jū no Ichi*, PDF, 24–28, 47.

89. Archival collection of Japanese Red Cross Society International Department, *Furyo ・ Hi-yokuryūsha Kyūjutsu Kanren Bunsho, Seiri bangō Jū no Ichi*, PDF, 38–47.

90. Archival collection of Japanese Red Cross Society International Department, *Furyo ・ Hi-yokuryūsha Kyūjutsu Kanren Bunsho, Seiri bangō Jū no Ichi*, 44–47; Archival collection of the Red Cross Information Plaza, *Furyo ・ Hi-yokuryūsha Kyūjutsu Kanren*

5. THE JAPANESE RED CROSS SOCIETY AND WORLD WAR II   235

Bunsho, Seiri bangō Nijūsan: Furyo Shūyōjo Shisatsu Kanren Shiryō, (Shōwa Jūhachi nen Roku gatsu kara): Furyo Kyūjutsu I'inchō Seibu Gunkanku-ka Furyo Shūyōjo Shisatsu, Honkon Nanpō Shisatsu, Shimazu Shachō no Seibu Gunkanku-ka Furyo Shūyōjo (Kumamoto, Shin-iizuka, Nagasaki, Nishi-sonogi-gun Kashii-mura, Orio, Yahata, Moji) Shisatsu ni Kansuru Shucchō Gyōmu Hōkokusho, tōtō; and the Archival Collection of Japanese Red Cross Society International Department, *Furyo • Hi-yokuryūsha Kyūjutsu Kanren Bunsho, Seiri bangō Nijūsan: Furyo Shūyōjo Shisatsu Kanren Shiryō*.

91. Tajima Jidayū and Inoue Shunji, "Renga no Kabe: Nagasaki Horyo Shūyō-jo to Gembaku no Dokyumento," in *Nihon no Gembaku Kiroku* ⑬, ed. Ienaga Saburō, Odagiri Hideo, and Kuroko Kazuo (Tokyo: Nihon Tosho Center, 1991), 104–6, 159, 203; Hugh V. Clarke, *Last Stop Nagasaki!* (London: George Allen & Unwin Australia, 1984), 75.
92. Archival collection of Japanese Red Cross Society International Department, *Furyo • Hi-yokuryūsha Kyūjutsu Kanren Bunsho, Seiri bangō Hachi*, PDF, 46.
93. Archival collection of Japanese Red Cross Society International Department, *Furyo • Hi-yokuryūsha Kyūjutsu Kanren Bunsho, Seiri bangō Hachi*, PDF, 23–24.
94. The volume of correspondence between the JRCS and the ARC via the ICRC during the war was the highest within the WPRCD operations. Archival collection of Japanese Red Cross Society International Department, *Furyo • Hi-yokuryūsha Kyūjutsu Kanren Bunsho, Seiri bangō Nijū: Sekijūji-kokusai-i'inkai tono Kōshin, (Shōwa Jūhachi nen San gatsu kara Jūky nen Jū gatsu (March 1943 to October 1944): Beikokujin Furyo Kyūjutsu (Beikoku Sekijūjisha), Nihon Kokunai Seikatsu Konkyū Gaikokujin Kyūsai, tōtō ni Kansuru ken*.
95. Archival collection of Japanese Red Cross Society International Department, *Furyo • Hi-yokuryūsha Kyūjutsu Kanren Bunsho, Seiri bangō Hachi*, PDF, 74–99.
96. Clarke, *Last Stop Nagasaki!*, 64–65.
97. The National Archives, the War Office, *Documents Relating to Prisoner of War Camps in the Far East*, no. 0103-8253.
98. The National Archives, *Allied P.O.W. Captured in the Far East*, CAG/HIST/J/8/1/3.
99. Clarke, *Last Stop Nagasaki!*, 68.
100. Archival collection of Japanese Red Cross Society International Department, *Furyo • Hi-yokuryūsha Kyūjutsu Kanren Bunsho, Seiri bangō Nijūsan*, PDF, 59; and Nihon Sekijūjisha, *Nihon Sekijūjisha Shashikō, Dai Go-kan*, 218.
101. Nihon Sekijūjisha, *Nihon Sekijūjisha Hachi-jū nen Shōshi*, 21.
102. Archival collection of Japanese Red Cross Society International Department, *Furyo • Hi-yokuryūsha Kyūjutsu Kanren Bunsho, Seiri bangō Jū no Ni*, PDF, 82–107.
103. Archival collection of Japanese Red Cross Society International Department, *Furyo • Hi-yokuryūsha Kyūjutsu Kanren Bunsho, Seiri bangō Nijūnana: Furyo matawa Hi-sentōin ate Kyūjutsu-hin Mushō Yusō, (Shōwa Jūhachi nen Jūichi gatsu kara Nijūnen Shi gatsu)*, PDF, 10–13, 35–38.
104. Archival collection of Japanese Red Cross Society International Department, *Furyo • Hi-yokuryūsha Kyūjutsu Kanren Bunsho, Seiri bangō Nijūnana: Furyo matawa Hi-sentōin ate Kyūjutsu-hin Mushō Yusō, (Shōwa Jūhachi nen Jūichi gatsu kara Nijūnen Shi gatsu)*, PDF, 53–59. In December 1944, the ICRC visited civilian internment camps in Manchukuo. This visit, arranged by the JRCS and the MRCS, was preceded by many

rounds of negotiations. Perhaps in a necessary concession, the ICRC met with officials from the Manchukuo Foreign Ministry and the Japanese Embassy to Manchukuo to discuss humanitarian issues. Archival collection of Japanese Red Cross Society International Department, *Furyo · Hi-yokuryūsha Kyūjutsu Kanren Bunsho, Seiri bangō Ni: d. Shūyōjo*, PDF, 59–78. Since the MRCS was not recognized as a National Red Cross Society, confidentiality prevailed.

105. Nihon Sekijūjisha, *Nihon Sekijūjisha Hachi-jū nen Shōshi*, 21.
106. Utsumi, *Nihongun no Horyo Seisaku*, 10.
107. Archival collection of Japanese Red Cross Society International Department, *Sonota Kokusaibu Hokan Bunsho, Seiri bangō Ni: Junēbu Jōyaku Ihan (Byōinsen Kōgeki) ni Tai-suru Kōgi-bun: a. Jōyaku Ihan*, PDF, 11–19, 51–56.
108. The Imperial Army operated at least twenty medical ships as of 1942. Rikujō Jieitai Eisei Gakkō, ed., *Daitōa Sensō Rikugun Eisei Shi. /1/ Rikugun Eisei Gai-shi*. (Tokyo: Yūkensha, 1970), 493.
109. Archival collection of Japanese Red Cross Society International Department, *Sonota Kokusaibu Hokan Bunsho, Seiri bangō Ni*, PDF, 61–70. Masui Takashi and Mori Masanao, *Shinban Sekai to Nihon no Sekijūji: Sekai-saidai no Jindō Shien Kikan no Katsudō* (Tokyo: Tōshindō, 2014), 91–92.
110. Archival collection of Japanese Red Cross Society International Department, *Sonota Kokusaibu Hokan Bunsho, Seiri bangō Ni: Junēbu Jōyaku Ihan (Byōinsen Kōgeki) ni Tai-suru Kōgi-bun: a. Jōyaku Ihan*, PDF, 68–79.
111. Archival collection of Japanese Red Cross Society International Department, *Sonota Kokusaibu Hokan Bunsho, Seiri bangō Ni: Junēbu Jōyaku Ihan (Byōinsen Kōgeki) ni Tai-suru Kōgi-bun: a. Jōyaku Ihan*, 156–60; Archival collection of the Red Cross Information Plaza, *Shimazu Meiyo-shachō Intabyū II*, 35–36.
112. The United States' reply did not address the remaining four alleged violations. Archival collection of Japanese Red Cross Society International Department, *Sonota Kokusaibu Hokan Bunsho, Seiri bangō Ni*, PDF, 22–29, 117–23.
113. The BRC, the ARC, and the Australian Red Cross.
114. The JRCS made emergency appeals to protecting powers Sweden, Switzerland, Argentina, and Portugal on behalf of the Japanese imperial government in response to Allied attacks on the Japanese Red Cross medical ships. Archival collection of Japanese Red Cross Society International Department, *Sonota Kokusaibu Hokan Bunsho, Seiri bangō Ni*.
115. Archival collection of Japanese Red Cross Society International Department, *Furyo · Hi-yokuryūsha Kyūjutsu Kanren Bunsho, Seiri bangō Jūroku: Beikoku Sekijūjisha tono Kōshin, (Shōwa Jūshichi nen Shi gatsu kara Nijū nen Shichi gatsu): Beikokujin Furyo oyobi Beikokujin Yokuryūsha ni Kansuru ken narabini Beikoku Musabetsu Bakugeki ni Kansuru ken tō*; and Kovner, *Prisoners of the Empire*.
116. Archival collection of the Red Cross Information Plaza, *Shimazu Meiyo-shachō Intabyū II*, 35–36.
117. "Hospital Ship Bombed by Japanese After Leaving Philippines," *Evening Star*, Washington, DC, February 5, 1942, 20.

118. Archival collection of the Red Cross Information Plaza, *Shimazu Meiyo-shachō Intabyū II*, 35–36; Archival collection of the Red Cross Information Plaza, *Sonota Kokusaibu Hokan Bunsho, Seiri bangō Ni*, PDF, 7–8.
119. The Otaru Detention Camp in Hokkaido held forty Aleut people who were taken from the Aleutian Islands in 1942. See Komiya, *Tekikoku-jin Yokuryū*, 123–27.
120. Archival collection of Japanese Red Cross Society International Department, *Furyo・Hi-yokuryūsha Kyūjutsu Kanren Bunsho, Seiri bangō Jūsan: Seikatsu Konkyūsha ni Kansuru Shiryō, (Shōwa Jūshichi nen Shi gatsu kara Jūkyū nen Go gatsu)*.
121. Archival collection of Japanese Red Cross Society International Department, *Furyo・Hi-yokuryūsha Kyūjutsu Kanren Bunsho, Seiri bangō Jūsan no Ichi: Seikatsu Konkyūsha ni Kansuru Shiryō*, PDF, 10–11.
122. Archival collection of Japanese Red Cross Society International Department, *Furyo・Hi-yokuryūsha Kyūjutsu Kanren Bunsho, Seiri bangō Jūsan no Ichi: Seikatsu Konkyūsha ni Kansuru Shiryō*, PDF, 33.
123. Archival collection of Japanese Red Cross Society International Department, *Furyo・Hi-yokuryūsha Kyūjutsu Kanren Bunsho, Seiri bangō Jū no Ichi*, PDF, 85–93.
124. Komiya, *Tekikoku-jin Yokuryū*, 72–74.
125. Komiya, *Tekikoku-jin Yokuryū*, 79.
126. Komiya, *Tekikoku-jin Yokuryū*, 79–82.
127. Iraq and Ethiopia. Tsurumi, Katō, and Kurokawa, *Nichibei Kōkansen*, 257.
128. Komiya, *Tekikoku-jin Yokuryū*, 79–82. In addition, Japanese diplomats and civilians residing in parts of the African continent that were territories of the British Empire, such as Egypt, Kenya, Uganda, and South Africa, were also moved by trains and airplanes to Lourenço Marques, currently Maputo in Mozambique. Tsurumi, Katō, and Kurokawa, *Nichibei Kōkansen*, 259.
129. Tsurumi, Katō, and Kurokawa, *Nichibei Kōkansen*, 257.
130. Komiya, *Tekikoku-jin Yokuryū*, 79.
131. Komiya, *Tekikoku-jin Yokuryū*, 85–90.
132. Komiya, *Tekikoku-jin Yokuryū*, 158–63.
133. Deliveries for Japanese POW camps might also have been included.
134. Nihon Sekijūjisha, *Nihon Sekijūjisha Shashikō, Dai Go-kan*, 218.
135. Shimazu, *Jindō no Hata no Moto-ni*, 90.
136. *Tekikoku Zairyū Dōhō Taisaku I'inkai* 敵国在留同胞対策委員会.
137. Nihon Sekijūjisha, *Nihon Sekijūjisha Shashikō, Dai Go-kan*, 218–19.
138. Archival collection of Japanese Red Cross Society International Department, Nihon Sekiūjisha, *Tekikoku ni okeru Hi-yokuryū Hōjin ni taisuru Imonkin Kyoshutsu Ichiran* (Tokyo: Nihon Sekiūjisha, 1942).
139. Nihon Sekijūjisha, *Nihon Sekijūjisha Shashikō, Dai Go-kan*, 218–19.
140. In a 1943 exchange operation, the JRCS sent 17,000 letters, in addition to Japanese tea, soy sauce, miso, toys for children, medicine, and books. Nihon Sekijūjisha, *Nihon Sekijūjisha Shashikō, Dai Go-kan*, 218.
141. Archival collection of Japanese Red Cross Society International Department, *Furyo・Hi-yokuryūsha Kyūjutsu Kanren Bunsho, Seiri bangō Jū no Ichi*, PDF, 52–58.

142. Archival collection of Japanese Red Cross Society International Department, *Furyo · Hi-yokuryūsha Kyūjutsu Kanren Bunsho, Seiri bangō Jū no Ichi*, PDF, 53.
143. Nihon Sekijūjisha, *Nihon Sekijūjisha Shashikō, Dai Go-kan*, 217–18; and Shimazu, *Jindō no Hata no Moto-ni*, 71.
144. Nihon Sekijūjisha, *Nihon Sekijūjisha Shashikō, Dai Go-kan*, 78, 217–19. The WPRCD created the "Outline of the Enforcement of the Red Cross Messages."
145. Nihon Sekijūjisha, *Nihon Sekijūjisha Shashikō, Dai Go-kan*, 218–19.
146. The WPRCD forwarded letters of Southeast Asian Muslims and ethnic Chinese civilian internees held at the Fukushima detention center to their families living under Japanese military occupations. Archival collection of Japanese Red Cross Society International Department, *Furyo · Hi-yokuryūsha Kyūjutsu Kanren Bunsho, Seiri bangō Jū no Ni*, PDF, 108–16.
147. Archival collection of the Red Cross Information Plaza, *Shimazu Meiyo-shachō Intabyū II*, 30–31.
148. Nihon Sekijūjisha, *Shōwa jūkyū nen-do Jigyōnenpō* (Tokyo: Nihon Sekijūjisha, 1944), 18.
149. Archival collection of the Red Cross Information Plaza, *Shimazu Meiyo-shachō Intabyū II*, 30–31.
150. Student labor mobilization in Japan began in 1938 following the outbreak of the Second Sino-Japanese War (1937–1945). At the time of Japan's defeat in August 1945, there were more than 3,400,000 student laborers. Ministry of Education, Cultures, Sports, Science, and Technology of Japan, "Gakuto Dōin," in *Gakusei Hyakunen-shi*, accessed April 18, 2022, https://www.mext.go.jp/b_menu/hakusho/html/others/detail/1317693.htm.
151. Japanese military code (*senjinkun*) instructed imperial Japanese soldiers "not to accept the shame of being a POW." Kovner, *Prisoners of the Empire*, 41.
152. During the incident, forty-eight Japanese POWs and one New Zealander were killed.
153. Archival collection of Japanese Red Cross Society International Department, *Furyo · Hi-yokuryūsha Kyūjutsu Kanren Bunsho, Seiri bangō Ni: d. Shūyōjo*, PDF, 100–108.
154. Archival collection of Japanese Red Cross Society International Department, *Furyo · Hi-yokuryūsha Kyūjutsu Kanren Bunsho, Seiri bangō Ni: d. Shūyōjo*, PDF, 100–108; and Nihon Sekijūjisha, *Nihon Sekijūjisha Shashikō, Dai Go-kan*, 77–78.
155. Nihon Sekijūjisha, *Nihon Sekijūjisha Shashikō, Dai Go-kan*, 78.
156. Nihon Sekijūjisha, ed., *Nihon Sekijūjisha Shashikō, Dai Rokkan, Shōwa nijū nen kara Shōwa sanjū nen* (Tokyo: Nihon Sekijūjisha, 1972); and Nihon Sekijūjisha, ed., *Nihon Sekijūjisha Shashikō, Dai Nana-kan, Shōwa sanjū ichi nen kara Shōwa yonjū nen* (Tokyo: Nihon Sekijūjisha, 1986).

6. NUCLEAR EMERGENCY: JAPANESE RED CROSS SOCIETY NURSES IN HIROSHIMA AND NAGASAKI, AUGUST 1945

1. Kobayashi Kiyoko, Ōhara Yasuo, and Fukiura Tadamasa, eds., *Hozutsu no Ato ni: Junshoku Jūgun Kangofu Tsuitō Ki: Memories of War-Dead Red Cross Nurses*, Vol. 1 (Tokyo: Henry Dunant Study Center, 1977), 47–52.

2. Nihon Sekijūjisha, ed., *Nihon Sekijūjisha Shashikō, Dai Go-kan, Shōwa jūichi nen kara Shōwa nijū nen* (Tokyo: Nihon Sekijūjisha, 1969), 179.
3. Nihon Sekijūjisha Kangofu Dōhōkai Ōitaken-shibu, *Ōita no Kyūgo Kang-shi* (Ōita City: Nihon Sekijūjisha Kangofu Dōhōkai Ōitaken-shibu, 1986), 99.
4. Nihon Sekijūjisha, ed., *Jindō—sono Ayumi: Nihon Sekijūjisha Hyakunen-shi* (Tokyo: Nihon Sekijūjisha, 1979), 173.
5. Kawaguchi Keiko and Kurokawa Aiko, *Jūgun Kangofu to Nihon Sekijūjisha: Sono Rekishi to Jūgun Shōgen* (Kyoto: Tosho-shuppan Bunrikaku, 2008); Jūgun Kangofu-tachi no Daitōa Sensō Kankō I'inkai, *Jūgun Kangofu-tachi no Daitōa Sensō—Watashi-tachi wa Nani wo Mita-noka* (Tokyo: Shōdensha, 2006); Kawashima Midori, Kawahara Yukari, Yamazaki Yūji, and Yoshikawa Ryūko, *Sensō to Kangofu* (Tokyo: Tosho Kankōkai, 2016); Kobayashi Kiyoko, Ōhara Yasuo, and Fukiura Tadamasa, eds., *Hozutsu no Ato ni: Junshoku Jūgun Kangofu Tsuitō Ki: Memories of War-Dead Red Cross Nurses*, Vol. 1 (Tokyo: Henry Dunant Study Center, 1977); Kobayashi Kiyoko, Tanaka Sumako, Ōhara Yasuo, and Fukiura Tadamasa, eds., *Zoku Hozutsu no Ato ni: Junshoku Jūgun Kangofu Tsuitō Ki: Memories of War-Dead Red Cross Nurses*, Vol. 2 (Tokyo: Henry Dunant Study Center, 1978); and Kobayashi Kiyoko, Tanaka Sumako, Ōhara Yasuo, and Fukiura Tadamasa, eds., *Zoku-zoku Hozutsu no Ato ni: Junshoku Jūgun Kangofu Tsuitō Ki: Memories of War-Dead Red Cross Nurses*, Vol. 3 (Tokyo: Henry Dunant Study Center, 1980).
6. Heinrich von Siebold was an antiquarian, collector, and translator working at the Austrian Embassy in Tokyo.
7. The Philanthropic Society (*Hakuai-sha*) was the precursor to the JRCS. See chapter 1, 11–14.
8. Shibata Shōkei was a Japanese chemist and pharmacist who studied organic chemistry under August Wilhelm von Hofmann at Friedrich Wilhelm University (now the Humboldt University of Berlin) and studied pharmaceutics and hygiene at Ludwig-Maximilian University of Munich in Germany.
9. Nihon Sekijūjisha Eiseibu, *Nihon Sekijūjisha Kangofu Yousei Hyakushūnen Kinenshi* (Tokyo: Nihon Sekijūjisha Eiseibu, 1992), 25. Drawing on examples of nursing in Germany at the next assembly in 1883, Shibata recommended training female nurses for wartime relief operations. Nisseki Chūō Joshi Tandai Kenkyūkai, ed., *Shashin Kiroku: Nihon Sekijūji Kango Kyōiku no Ayumi: Hakuai-sha kara Nisseki Chūō Joshi Tandai made* (Tokyo: Sōsei-shobō, 1988), 14. Accepting a number of suggestions, the JRCS appointed Hashimoto Tsunatsune (1845–1909)—the director of the Medical Department of the Imperial Japanese Army (Nihon Sekijūjisha Eiseibu, *Nihon Sekijūjisha Kangofu Yousei Hyakushūnen Kinenshi*, 10)—as the first director of the JRCS Hospital Institution for the Training of Nurses. In 1890 it accepted its first intake in preparation for wartime relief activities. Nihon Sekijūjisha, ed., *Nihon Sekijūji Shashikō* (Tokyo: Nihon Sekijūjisha, 1911), 749–93. Further transforming nursing's professional status, Princess Arisugawa created the Volunteer Nurse Women's Association in 1887 to promote JRCS wartime relief activities. In the traditional Japanese sphere, nursing was often seen as a humble, dirty, and abominable job (Nihon Sekijūjisha Kangofu Dōhōkai Ōitaken-shibu, *Ōita no Kyūgo Kang-shi*, 35); therefore, well-educated women or women from a high social class had traditionally avoided the profession.

10. *Riku-kaigun kangofu* 陸海軍看護婦.
11. Archival collection of the Red Cross Information Plaza, *Kokusai Kaigofu Kōshū, Shōwa Roku nen Itaru dō Sanjū nen*, ID: 4528; Aya Takahashi, *The Development of the Japanese Nursing Profession: Adopting and Adapting Western Influences* (London: Routledge Curzon, 2004), 117–18, 121; and the Archival Collection of the Red Cross Information Plaza, *Dai Nana Hachi-kai Bankoku Kangofu Taikai, Shōwa hachi, jūichi, jūninen, dō jūsan nen*, ID: 4558.
12. Regarding the relationships between the JRCS and the International Council of Nurses (ICN), Takahashi argued that the JRCS used the ICN as a "stage" to advertise their achievements to the international community. Takahashi, *The Development of the Japanese Nursing Profession*, 119. In other words, the JRCS portrayed their nurses as civilized modern women to the West, where Europeans and Americans were developing nursing on the basis of a Christian-based charity activity and feminist-inspired professionalism. Takahashi argued that after the JRCS nurses received worldwide acclaim for advances in logistics and care for sick and wounded soldiers, POWs, and civilians, the society no longer used the ICN for its international promotion. Takahashi, *The Development of the Japanese Nursing Profession*, 122; Tabuchi Masayo, "Koushūeisei Koushūkai no Keika ni Tsukite," in Nihon Sekijūjisha, *Hakuai: Organ of the Japanese Red Cross Society, No. 428, December 1922* (Tokyo: Hakuai Hakkōjo, 1922), 15–18; Inoue Natsue, "America ni okeru Shakai Kangofu," in Nihon Sekijūjisha Kangofu Dōhōkai, *Dōhō Shōwa Roku nen San gatsu gō* (Tokyo: Nihon Sekijūjisha Kangofu Dōhōkai, 1931), 10–12.
13. League of Red Cross Societies, *Monthly Bulletin* (September 1933): 168.
14. Hagiwara Take (1873–1936), known as the "Japanese Nightingale," was born in the village of Itsukaichi, the birthplace of the famous Itsukaichi Constitution produced during the People's Rights Movement. Her maternal grandfather, Ishikawa Tomoyasu, who graduated from an elite academy, the Shōhei-zaka Gakumonjo, of the Tokugawa Shogunate, was a doctor of Chinese medicine and influenced her career. She graduated from JRCS nursing school in 1897; was an honorary delegate of the ICN for twenty-two years; and served as the first chair of the Nursing Association of Japan. Hagiwara was awarded the Florence Nightingale Medal in recognition of her service in the 1896 Sanriku earthquake; relief operations in Russia, France, and England in World War I; and care of Polish orphans during the Siberian Intervention (1919–1920). Mori Reiko, *Kenshin: Hagiwara Take no Shōgai* (Tokyo: KK. Sanshusha, 1995).
15. Nihon Sekijūjisha, *Jindō—sono Ayumi*, 381–86.
16. Yamazaki Yūji, "Male Nurses of the Japanese Red Cross Society in the 1910s: Male Nurses in the History of Modern Nursing (6)," *Nihon Sekijūji Musashino Tanki-daigaku Kiyō, Dai Jūni-gō* (1999): 92.
17. A total of 2,071 male nurses were deployed in major wars between the First Sino-Japanese War (1894–1895) and the Siberian Intervention (1918–1922), excluding World War I (1914–1918), while the total number of female nurses was 4,154. Furthermore, the JRCS trained 1,589 male nurses and 6,969 female nurses from 1907 to 1922. Therefore, the response to the call for nurses was much higher from men than from women. Yamazaki, "Male Nurses of the Japanese Red Cross Society in the 1910s," 117. The number of male

nurses dramatically decreased, and female nurses increasingly predominated from the 1930s to 1945—the JRCS trained only eighty-nine male relief workers, including clerks, from 1943 to 1944. Nihon Sekijūjisha, *Nihon Sekijūjisha Shashikō, Dai Go-kan*, 132–33.

18. Katō Yōko, *Chōhei-sei to Kindai Nippon: 1868–1945* (Tokyo: Yoshikawa Kōbunkan, 1996).
19. Takahashi Aya argues that the JRCS's "Ten Fundamental Principles for Relief Workers" were created to promote "Nightingale-ism"—an approach employed by the Red Cross organization worldwide, which reveres Florence Nightingale as a great woman and exemplar of compassionate nursing. Takahashi contends that the principles—which form the general moral principles for all nursing practice—also apply to quasi-military settings. Under their influence, she argues, nurses were able to maintain collective morale as aid workers under strict discipline during missions in war—and this, in turn, was partly responsible for the elevated status of the society's nurses in Japanese society. Takahashi, *The Development of the Japanese Nursing Profession*, 40–49. Yoshikawa Ryūko finds similar importance in the "Ten Fundamental Principles," highlighting the testimonies of nurses who found in them a source of encouragement and pride, particularly by providing a historic link to the brave example of Red Cross workers in the extreme contexts of wartime humanitarian operations. Yoshikawa Ryūko, "Relief Activities of Red Cross Nurses Immediately After the Hiroshima Atomic Bombing (6 August 1945)," trans. Suzuki Michiko, *Journal of Humanitarian Studies* 2 (March 2013), 73, 78.
20. Translated by author.
21. Archival collection of Japanese Red Cross Society Disaster Relief Division, Disaster Management and Social Welfare Department, *Senjikyūgohan Gyōmuhōkokusho: Nihon Sekijūjisha Hyōgokenshibu, Dai Hyaku-roku Kyūgohan, Sen-kyūhyaku-yonjū nen jūni gatsu kara Sen-kyūhyaku-yonjū-roku nen hachi gatsu.*
22. Concerning the structure of relief teams on the battlefield, the JRCS requested that the Army Ministry staff relief teams consist exclusively of JRCS members to reduce the risks of working with less-well-trained military nurses in battlefield situations. The two groups of nurses wore different uniforms. For example, military nurses wore lapel pins with stars of the Japanese Imperial Army, while the JRCS nurses wore Red Cross badges and lapel pins with paulownias produced by the JRCS to exhibit their ranks. Rikujō Jieitai Eisei Gakkō, ed., *Daitōa Sensō Rikugun Eisei Shi. /1/ Rikugun Eisei Gai-shi* (Tokyo: Yūkensha, 1970), 200; Shōkei-kan Sepcial Exhibition, *Senshōbyōsha no Rōku no sobade: "Hakui no Tenshi" to yobareta Jūgunkangofu tachi*, (19 July 2017—10 September 2017); Nihon Sekijūjisha, ed., *Nihon Sekijūjisha Reikirui-Shū* (Tokyo: Nihon Sekijūjisha, 1925), 346–49.
23. *Gunzoku* 軍属. Nihon Sekijūjisha, *Nihon Sekijūjisha Shashikō, Dai Go-kan*, 113–14.
24. Kageyama Sadaka, *Nihon Sekijūji Damashii: Nisseki Shanhai Haken Tokubetsu Kyūgohan no Ki* (Tokyo: Shufu no Tomo Shuppan Service Centre, 1971), 81.
25. Kageyama, *Nihon Sekijūji Damashii*, 81.
26. *Jinjutsu* (仁述) was widely expounded by Ogata Kōan (1810–1863) as the core ethic of medical doctors. Kōan had great impact upon Japanese modern medicine and humanitarianism at both the grassroot and governmental level.
27. Nihon Sekijūjisha Kangofu Dōhōkai, *Dōhō Shōwa Jūni nen Jūni gatsu gō* (Tokyo: Nihon Sekijūjisha Kangofu Dōhōkai, 1937), 2–5.

28. Japanese poem consisting of thirty-one syllables. Tochigi Kimi, *Nihon Sekijūjisha Kangofu Dōhōkai, Dōhō Shōwa Jūroku nen Jūni gatsu gō* [Dōhō Poetry Society] (Tokyo: Nihon Sekijūjisha Kangofu Dōhōkai, 1941), 9. Originally translated into contemporary Japanese by Ono Hisako and into English by Carroll Misono, 2023. Reprinted with permission.
29. Ueno, Kawaguchi, and Kurokawa critically assess both JRCS and military nurses for supporting Japanese militarism. Ueno fails to distinguish the JRCS nurses from military nurses, who were directly hired by the Imperial Japanese Army and Navy outside the system of the JRCS, in commenting that becoming a military nurse was a route for women to be worshiped at the Yasukuni Shrine. Ueno asserts that JRCS nurses provided frontline support to the military, fostered nationalism, and bore war responsibility. Ueno Chizuko, *Nationalism and Gender* (Melbourne: Trans Pacific, 2004), 21; and Kawaguchi and Kurokawa, *Jūgun Kangofu to Nihon Sekijūjisha*.
30. *Kangofuchō oyobi Kangofu Saiyō Kisoku* 看護婦長及看護婦採用規則. "Regulations of the Employment of Chief Nurses and Nurses" had been created for recruiting JRCS nurses by the army; however, in 1923 it was amended to recruit ordinary nurses.
31. Rikujō Jieitai Eisei Gakkō Shūshinkai, ed., *Rikugun Eisei Seido-shi* (Tokyo: Hara Shobō, 1990), 493–505.
32. Rikujō Jieitai Eisei Gakkō Shūshinkai, *Rikugun Eisei Seido-shi*, 493.
33. Kawaguchi Keiko and Kurokawa Akiko, *Jūgun Kangofu to Nihon Sekijūjisha*, 72.
34. JRCS nurses reached 15,368 in 1945. Rikujō Jieitai Eisei Gakkō Shūshinkai, *Rikugun Eisei Seido-shi*, 494.
35. Rikujō Jieitai Eisei Gakkō, *Daitōa Sensō Rikugun Eisei Shi. /1/ Rikugun Eisei Gai-shi*, 490.
36. Rikujō Jieitai Eisei Gakkō, *Daitōa Sensō Rikugun Eisei Shi*, 200.
37. Yuri Hanae, ed., *Jūgun Kaisō no Ki* (Tokyo: Moto Riku-Kaigun Jūgun Kangofu no Kai, 1982), introduction.
38. Yuri, *Jūgun Kaisō no Ki*, 17.
39. Yuri, *Jūgun Kaisō no Ki*, 16–17.
40. *Nihon Sekijūjisha Jōrei* 日本赤十字社条例.
41. *Nihon Sekijūjisha Rei* 日本赤十字社令.
42. Nihon Sekijūjisha, *Nihon Sekijūjisha Shashikō, Dai Go-kan*, 112–13.
43. Nihon Sekijūjisha, *Nihon Sekijūjisha Shashikō, Dai Go-kan*, 143–45.
44. Nihon Sekijūjisha, *Nihon Sekijūjisha Shashikō, Dai Go-kan*, 123; Nihon Sekijūjisha Eiseibu, *Nihon Sekijūjisha Kangofu Yousei Hyakushūnen Kinenshi*, 35.
45. Nihon Sekijūjisha, *Nihon Sekijūjisha Shashikō, Dai Go-kan*, 132; Nisseki Chūō Joshi Tandai Kenkyūkai, *Shashin Kiroku*, 86.
46. *Rinji kyūgo kangofu* 臨時救護看護婦.
47. Nihon Sekijūjisha, ed., *Nihon Sekijūjisha Shashikō, Dai Go-kan*, 130–31. Yamashita Mai has studied changes in the curricula, and far from diminishing trainee nurses' medical or battlefield preparedness, she found the streamlining omitted courses in the liberal arts, such as history, education, psychology, and music—traditionally seen as important means through which the society's ideal nurse could demonstrate her humanity. Yamashita Mai, *Kangofu no Rekishi: Yorisou Senmonshoku no Tanjō* (Tokyo: Yoshikawa Kōbunkan, 2017), 49.

48. Nihon Sekijūjisha Hiroshimaken-shibu, ed., *Nihon Sekijūjisha Hiroshimaken-shibu Hyaku-nen shi: Shiryōhen* (Hiroshima: Nihon Sekijūjisha Hiroshimaken-shibu, 1991), 86.
49. The City of Hiroshima, "Shisha-sū ni Tsuite," accessed January 4, 2021, https://www.city.hiroshima.lg.jp/soshiki/48/9400.html; Othman Putih, *Waga Kokoro no Hiroshima: Maraya kara Kita Nanpō Tokubetsu Ryūgakusei*, trans. Onozawa Jun et al. (Tokyo: Keisō Shobō, 1997); and *Hiroshima Genbaku Sensai-shi Dai Ikkan*, 168–81.
50. The United States Strategic Bombing Survey, *Nagasaki Hibaku Gojusshūnen Kinen: Beikoku Senryaku Bakugeki Chōsa Hōkokusho*, trans. Nagasaki International Cultural Centre and Bilingual Group Co. (Nagasaki: Fujikihakueisha, 1996), 392.
51. Yoshikawa Ryūko, "Relief Activities of Red Cross Nurses Immediately After the Hiroshima Atomic Bombing," 69.
52. Shigetō Fumio, "Genshi Bakudan Saigai Kyūgo no Keiken," in *Kyūgo no Kōshūroku: Shōwa sanjūsan-nen go-gatsu* (Tokyo: Japanese Red Cross Society, 1958), 25.
53. Yoshikawa, "Relief Activities of Red Cross Nurses Immediately After the Hiroshima Atomic Bombing," 69.
54. "Working Report of Wartime Relief Parties," the Archival Collection of Japanese Red Cross Society Disaster Relief Division, Disaster Management and Social Welfare Department, *Senjikyūgohan Gyōmuhōkokusho: Nihon Sekijūjisha Hyōgokenshibu, Dai Hyakuroku Kyūgohan, Sen-kyūhyaku-yonjū nen jūni gatsu kara Sen-kyūhyaku-yonjū-roku nen hachi gatsu*, ID: 51-039, PDF, 404–5.
55. Nihon Sekijūjisha Hiroshimaken-shibu, *Nihon Sekijūjisha Hiroshimaken-shibu Hyaku-nen shi*, 86–87.
56. Shigetō Fumio, "Genshi Bakudan Saigai Kyūgo no Keiken," 25.
57. Yoshikawa, "Relief Activities of Red Cross Nurses Immediately After the Hiroshima Atomic Bombing," 74.
58. Yoshikawa, "Relief Activities of Red Cross Nurses Immediately After the Hiroshima Atomic Bombing," 76.
59. Nihon Sekijūjisha Kangofu Dōhōkai Hiroshimaken-shibu, ed., *Chinkon no Fu: Nihon Sekijūjisha Hiroshimaken-shibu Senji Kyūgo-shi* (Hiroshima: Nihon Sekijūjisha Kangofu Dōhōkai Hiroshimaken-shibu, 1981), 24.
60. Yukinaga Masae, *Kinoko-gumo Nisseki Jūgun Kangofu no Shuki* (Tokyo: All Publishing, 1984), 128–29.
61. Yukinaga, *Kinoko-gumo Nisseki Jūgun Kangofu no Shuki*, 113–14.
62. Nihon Sekijūjisha Kangofu Dōhōkai Hiroshimaken-shibu, *Chinkon no Fu*, 117.
63. Yukinaga, *Kinoko-gumo Nisseki Jūgun Kangofu no Shuki*, 129.
64. Yoshikawa, "Relief Activities of Red Cross Nurses Immediately After the Hiroshima Atomic Bombing," 73.
65. Maiden name: Taniguchi.
66. Nihon Sekijūjisha Kangofu Dōhōkai Hiroshimaken-shibu, *Chinkon no Fu*, 137–38.
67. Yoshikawa, "Relief Activities of Red Cross Nurses Immediately After the Hiroshima Atomic Bombing," 76.
68. September 1, 1945. Archival collection of Japanese Red Cross Society Disaster Relief Division, Disaster Management and Social Welfare Department, *Senjikyūgohan*

Gyōmuhōkokusho: Nihon Sekijūjisha Hyōgokenshibu, Dai Hyaku-roku Kyūgohan; and Yukinaga, *Kinoko-gumo Nisseki Jūgun Kangofu no Shuki*, 157.

69. In the postwar period, Dr. Shigetō served as the president of the Hiroshima Red Cross Hospital and Atomic-bomb Survivors Hospital. He contributed to medical treatment for *hibakusha* and conducted studies about the physical effects of radiation.
70. Nihon Sekijūjisha Hiroshimaken-shibu, *Nihon Sekijūjisha Hiroshimaken-shibu Hyaku-nen shi: Shiryōhen*, 410.
71. "Genbaku no Hōshasen ni yori Kuroku Kankō shita Ekkusu-sen Firumu, ID: 0103-0037," Hiroshima Peace Memorial Museum Peace Database, accessed January 4, 2021, https://hpmm-db.jp/list/detail/?cate=artifact&search_type=detail&data_id=19364.
72. Shiina Masae, *Genbaku Hanzai: Hibakusha wa Naze Hōchi Saretaka* (Tokyo: Ōtsuki-shoten, 1985), 34.
73. Nihon Sekijūjisha, *Nihon Sekijūjisha Hachi-jū nen Shōshi* (Tokyo: Nihon Sekijūjisha, 1957), 72.
74. In fact, after the war the JRCS would make an all-out effort through numerous channels to make contact with the Union of Red Cross and Red Crescent Societies of the USSR and the Red Cross Society of China. Nihon Sekijūjisha, *Nihon Sekijūjisha Hachi-jū nen Shōshi*, 72.
75. ICRC Archives, B G 003 51-3, G3/51, "Diary to the Report: Report on the Evacuation of POW & CI in the Hiroshima Sector, September 17, 1945," Correspondence entre le siège et Marcel Junod, 03/01/1945–12/04/1946.
76. ICRC Archives, A CL 16.06.02 Appendix 3, "Report on the Effects of the Atomic Bomb at Hiroshima"; ICRC Archives, B G 003 51-4, G3/51, "Report by Marcel Junod on 9 November, 1945," *Letters reçues de Marcel Junod (don't rapports n*3?, 4–9) (après mai 1946, voir G8 76: 24.04.1945–05.11.1947)*.
77. Shiina, *Genbaku Hanzai*, 55–56.
78. Shiina, *Genbaku Hanzai*, 36.
79. Mori Shigeaki, *Genbaku de Shinda Beihei-hishi* (Tokyo: Kōbun-sha, 2008), 35–37.
80. Cartwright was the author of *A Date with the Lonesome Lady: A Hiroshima POW Returns* (Fort Worth, TX: Eakin, 2002).
81. On July 28, a total of twenty-two fighter planes were shot down, including two B-24 bombers: *Lonesome Lady* and *Taola*. Mori, *Genbaku de Shinda Beihei-hishi*, 67.
82. Hiroshima Castle was constructed by daimyō Mōri Terumoto (1553–1625) in 1589 and was designated a National Treasure in 1931.
83. Mori, *Genbaku de Shinda Beihei-hishi*, 63–77.
84. Mori, *Genbaku de Shinda Beihei-hishi*, 88–90; and Hiroshima City Office, ed., *Hiroshima Genbaku Sensai-shi Dai Ikkan: Sōsetsu* (Hiroshima: Hiroshima City Office, 1971), 176.
85. Ōsako was working with the International Committee of the Red Cross (ICRC) during their mission in Japan.
86. Hiroshima City Office, ed., *Hiroshima Genbaku Sensai-shi Dai Nikan: Kakusetsu* (Hiroshima: Hiroshima City Office, 1971), 176–77, 183.
87. Hiroshima Prefecture, ed., *Hiroshima Ken-shi, Kindai Ni* (Hiroshima: Hiroshima Prefecture, 1981), 1040–41.

6. NUCLEAR EMERGENCY   245

88. Mori, *Genbaku de Shinda Beihei-hishi*, 238.
89. Cartwright visited Hiroshima in October 1999 on what he called a "pilgrimage," where he met with local historian Mori Shigeaki, whose research on the Hiroshima atomic bombing was commended by the U.S. government when President Obama visited Hiroshima in 2016. Cartwright, *A Date with the Lonesome Lady*; and Mori, *Genbaku de Shinda Beihei-hishi*.
90. T. C. Cartwright, "Hiroshima no Hito no Itami wa Watashi no Itami," *Asahi Shimbun*, October 8, 1999.
91. Kuroki Yūji, *Genbaku Tōka wa Yokoku sarete-ita! Dai-go Kōkū Jōhō Rentai Jōhōshitsu Kinmusha no Kiroku* (Tokyo: Kōjin-sha, 1992). Kokura City was close to the Yawata Steel Works, which was a key supplier of munitions to the military. Niigata City carried out a mass emergency evacuation on August 11, 1945, following an emergency order of Hatakeda Shōfuku, the governor of Niigata Prefecture on August 10. Fearing a nuclear attack and perhaps distrusting the government, many residents began to evacuate on their own initiative. Once underway, the evacuation took a few days to complete, rendering Niigata City "like a ghost town." The Niigata government issued emergency rice rations and assigned host families who lacked accommodations in the countryside. Hatakeda issued the order on his own authority despite resistance from the Home Ministry. Niigatashi-shi Hensan Kindaishibukai, ed., *Niigatashi-shi Shiryō-hen Nana: Kindai San* (Niigata City: Niigata City, 1994), 206–10.
92. Nagano's dual role as JRCS director and prefectural governor was a part of wartime mobilization. It was common for prefectural governors to serve as director general of JRCS chapters.
93. Nagasaki Atomic Bomb Museum, ed., *Nagasaki Genbaku Sensai-shi, Dai Ikkan: Sōsetsu-hen Kaitei-ban* (Nagasaki: Fujiki Hakuei-sha, 2006), 218.
94. Watanabe Sawako, *Matsu* (Tokyo: Watanabe Sawako, 1974).
95. Matsuki Hidefumi and Yaku Yasuhiro, *Genbaku Tōka Mokusatsu sareta Gokuhi Jōhō* (Tokyo: NHK Publishing, 2012), 201–2.
96. Nagasaki-ken Keisatsu Shi Henshū I'inkai, ed., *Nagasaki-ken Keisatsu Shi, Ge-kan* (Nagasaki: Nagasaki-ken Keisatsu Honbu, 1979), 852–53.
97. Nagasaki City—Peace and Atomic Bomb, "Nagasakiken Bōkū Honbu Ato: Tateyama Bōkūgō," accessed April 5, 2023, https://nagasakipeace.jp/visit/insti/tateyama.html; and Nagasaki-ken Keisatsu Shi Henshū I'inkai, *Nagasaki-ken Keisatsu Shi, Ge-kan*, 853.
98. Nagasaki-ken Keisatsu Shi Henshū I'inkai, *Nagasaki-ken Keisatsu Shi, Ge-kan*, 853–54.
99. Nagasaki Broadcasting Company, "Hibakusha no Shōgen Dai Jūyon kai," accessed January 4, 2021, http://archive.fo/QXJcm.
100. Nagasaki-ken Keisatsu Shi Henshū I'inkai, *Nagasaki-ken Keisatsu Shi, Ge-kan*, 854.
101. Nagasaki Atomic Bomb Museum, *Nagasaki Genbaku Sensai-shi, Dai Ikkan: Sōsetsu-hen Kaitei-ban*, 220–21.
102. Nagasaki Atomic Bomb Museum, *Nagasaki Genbaku Sensai-shi, Dai Ikkan*, 224–28; and Kojima Noboru, *Tennō*, 5 (Tokyo: Kazetto Shuppan, 2007), 191–94.
103. Yasuyama Kōdō, *Kanzen-ban: Nagasaki Genbaku no Kiroku* (Tokyo: Tokyo Tosho Shuppan-kai, 2007), 63–67.

104. Nagano specifically requested that the ICRC conduct an investigation to determine the legality of the atomic bomb. However, ICRC Tokyo representative Marcel Junod only authorized sending medical aid to Hiroshima.
105. Hugh V. Clarke, *Last Stop Nagasaki!* (London: George Allen & Unwin Australia, 1984), 105.
106. Michael Barnett cites the example of the ICRC's refusal to investigate allegations of the use of poison gas by the Italian Army in the conquest of Ethiopia as evidence of the ICRC's Eurocentric bias and violation of its own principles. Michael N. Barnett, *Empire of Humanity: A History of Humanitarianism* (Ithaca, NY: Cornell University Press, 2013), 92–93.
107. Shirabe Raisuke, ed., *Genbaku Omoide no Shukishū: Wasurenagusa, Dai Go gō (Saishū-hen)* (Nagasaki: Kyū-Nagasaki Ika Daigaku Genbaku Gisei Gakuto Izokukai, 1974), 3; Nagasaki City—Peace and Atomic Bomb, "Nagasaki Ikadaigaku Tō," accessed April 5, 2023, https://nagasakipeace.jp/search/about_abm/gallery/ikadai.html; Nagasaki Atomic Bomb Museum, "Kyū Nagasaki Ika Daigaku Monchū," accessed April 5, 2023, https://hibakuikou-map.jp/bombed-remains/ikou04/; and Nagasaki Shiyakusho Sōmubu Chōsa Tōkeika, ed., *Nagasaki Shisei Rokujū-go-nen Shi, Kō-hen* (Nagasaki: Nagasaki Shiyakusho Sōmubu Chōsa Tōkeika, 1959), 486–87.
108. The United States Strategic Bombing Survey, *Nagasaki Hibaku Gojusshūnen Kinen*, 293.
109. A *hibakusha* is a person who suffered the effects of nuclear bombs.
110. Nagasaki Atomic Bomb Museum, *Nagasaki Genbaku Sensai-shi, Dai Ikkan: Sōsetsu-hen Kaitei-ban*, 498.
111. Nihon Sekijūjisha Nagasakiken-shibu, *Hyaku-nen no Ayumi* (Nagasaki: Nihon Sekijūjisha Nagasakiken-shibu, 1988), 16–19.
112. Nagasaki City—Peace and Atomic Bomb, "Rescue and Relief Activities," accessed April 5, 2023, https://nagasakipeace.jp/part_2_09.html.
113. Nihon Sekijūjisha Nagasakiken-shibu, *Hyaku-nen no Ayumi*, 16–19.
114. Yamaguchi Tadayoshi, "Bakushin-chi kara 25km Hanareta Isayaya de Mokugeki shita 'Iki-jigoku' no Wasure-enu Kioku," accessed January 6, 2024, https://www.city.isahaya.nagasaki.jp/soshiki/7/2141.html.
115. Nihon Sekijūjisha Nagasakiken-shibu, *Hyaku-nen no Ayumi*, 18.
116. Personal paper written in 2013, held by Tasaki Hiroshi. Tasaki Hiroshi, "Haiki deno Hibakusha Kyūgo to Niji-hibaku no Taiken," accessed May 29, 2016, http://www.geocities.jp/sasebun/shiru/3taikenhibaku.pdf.
117. Nihon Sekijūjisha Nagasakiken-shibu, *Hyaku-nen no Ayumi*, 16–18.
118. Nihon Sekijūjisha Nagasakiken-shibu, *Hyaku-nen no Ayumi*, 18; and Yoshikawa, "Relief Activities of Red Cross Nurses Immediately After the Hiroshima Atomic Bombing," 70.
119. Yasuyama, *Kanzen-ban*, 111.
120. Nihon Sekijūjisha Nagasakiken-shibu, ed., *Senkō no Kage de: Genbaku Hibakusha Kyūgo Sekijūji Kangofu no Shuki* (Nagasaki: Nihon Sekijūjisha Nagasakiken-shibu, 1980).
121. Nihon Sekijūjisha Nagasakiken-shibu, *Senkō no Kage de*, 70.
122. Nihon Sekijūjisha Nagasakiken-shibu, *Senkō no Kage de*, 103–4.
123. Nihon Sekijūjisha Nagasakiken-shibu, *Senkō no Kage de*, 65.
124. Nihon Sekijūjisha Nagasakiken-shibu, *Senkō no Kage de*, 59.

125. Nihon Sekijūjisha Nagasakiken-shibu, *Senkō no Kage de*, 63.
126. Nagasaki City—Peace and Atomic Bomb, "1945.8.9 at 11:02 A.M. August 9, 1945," accessed April 5, 2023, https://nagasakipeace.jp/en/search/record/photo/part_2_01.html#:~:text =August%209%2C%201945%20Bockscar%2C%20the,Nagasaki%20was%20overcast%20 that%20morning.
127. Nagasaki-shi Genbaku Hibaku Taisaku-bu, ed., *Nagasaki Genbaku Hibaku Gojū-nen Shi* (Nagasaki: Nagasaki-shi Genbaku Hibaku Taisaku-bu, 1996), 291–92.
128. Nagasaki-shi Genbaku Hibaku Taisaku-bu, *Nagasaki Genbaku Hibaku Gojū-nen Shi*, 287–96.
129. Nagasaki-shi Genbaku Hibaku Taisaku-bu, *Nagasaki Genbaku Hibaku Gojū-nen Shi*, 292.
130. Nagasaki City—Peace and Atomic Bomb, "1945.8.9 at 11:02 A.M. August 9, 1945."
131. Nagasaki City—Peace and Atomic Bomb, "Mitsubishi Zōsen Saiwai-machi Kōjō," accessed June 13, 2018, http://nagasakipeace.jp/japanese/atomic/record/gallery/saiwaimachi.html.
132. Nagasaki-shi Genbaku Hibaku Taisaku-bu, *Nagasaki Genbaku Hibaku Gojū-nen Shi*, 296.
133. Tajima Jidayū, a former Japanese camp guard, who was also a private first class (PFC) of the Japanese Imperial Army, transcribed the memories of Allied POWs who were bombed and wrote about aid goods provided by the JRCS and its issuance of Red Cross messages in his book entitled, *Renga no Kabe: Nagasaki Horyo Shūyō-jo to Genbaku no Dokyumento* (Tokyo: Gendai-shi Shuppan-kai Hakkō, 1980). He was moved by witnessing the tragic deaths of Allied POWs, who lost their lives without the presence of their families and partners during the nuclear bombing. Due to the attack, Tajima himself became disabled and suffered from bad eyesight and illness brought about by radiation-related diseases. Tajima Jidayū and Inoue Shunji, "Renga no Kabe: Nagasaki Horyo Shūyō-jo to Genbaku no Dokyumento," in *Nihon no Genbaku Kiroku 13*, ed. Ienaga Saburō, Odagiri Hideo, and Kuroko Kazuo (Tokyo: Nihon Tosho Center, 1991), 124.
134. Clarke, *Last Stop Nagasaki!*, 99–100.
135. Clarke, *Last Stop Nagasaki!*, 96–97.
136. Nagasaki-shi Genbaku Hibaku Taisaku-bu, *Nagasaki Genbaku Hibaku Gojū-nen Shi*, 295.
137. Tajima and Inoue, "Renga no Kabe," 132.
138. Clarke, *Last Stop Nagasaki!*, 124. Dutch surviving POW Hugh V. Clarke's memoir narrates his experience of the Nagasaki nuclear bombing, his postwar relationships with a Japanese Catholic priest and former camp guards, and the heroic work of atomic bomb victim and Buddhist medical doctor Akizuki Tatsuichiro. Clarke's visit to Nagasaki to meet Japanese survivors in August 1983 proved to be cathartic. Clarke, *Last Stop Nagasaki!*
139. Clarke, *Last Stop Nagasaki!*, 206. Australian POW Sergeant Bert Miller remembered that "he spent two days rescuing civilians and children from the fires raging through-out the devastated city and scavenging for food and water." Clarke, *Last Stop Nagasaki!*, 101.
140. Nagasaki-shi Genbaku Hibaku Taisaku-bu, *Nagasaki Genbaku Hibaku Gojū-nen Shi*, 294–96; Ronald E. Bryer, *White Ghosts of Nagasaki* (North Yorkshire, England: Ronald E. Bryer, 1997), 114; and Tajima and Inoue, "Renga no Kabe," 155–56. British surviving POW

Ronald E. Bryer's memoir, *White Ghosts of Nagasaki*, recounts his experience of the Nagasaki nuclear bombing and his lifelong friendship with Tajima Jidayū, a former Japanese POW camp guard. Bryer was an official guest at the Nagasaki Peace Memorial Service on August 9, 1979, by Nagasaki City and the first Allied POW to attend the peace ceremony in Nagasaki. He met with the Nagasaki mayor and with friends he had made while interned in Nagasaki Mitsubishi shipyard. Tajima and Inoue, "Renga no Kabe," 64–65.

141. Bryer, *White Ghosts of Nagasaki*, 123.

CONCLUSION

1. Kamo no Chōmei, *Hōjōki*, trans. Asami Kazuhiko (Tokyo: Chikuma-shobō, 2011); and Kamo no Chōmei, *Hōjōki: A Hermit's Hut as Metaphor*, trans. Matthew Stavros (Japan: Vicus Lusorum, 2020), 1–2.
2. *Mujō* 無常.
3. *Ōyake* 公. Murakami Yōichirō, *Shiru wo Manabu: Aratamete Gakumon no Susume* (Tokyo: Kawade Shobō Shinsha, 2011), 140–41.
4. Nihon Sekijūjisha, ed., *Nihon Sekijūjisha Shashikō, Dai Go-kan, Shōwa jūichi nen kara Shōwa nijū nen* (Tokyo: Nihon Sekijūjisha, 1969), 362. The American Red Cross (ARC) experienced explosive growth during World War I. According to Irwin, by 1919 ARC's membership included 22 million adults and 11 million children. Julia F. Irwin, *Making the World Safe: The America Red Cross and a Nation's Humanitarian Awakening* (Oxford: Oxford University Press, 2013), 67.
5. Charles Hurd, *The Compact History of the American Red Cross: The Story of the Red Cross Volunteers and the Organization in Which They Serve* (New York: Hawthorn, 1959), 111.
6. Irwin, *Making the World Safe*, 30.
7. John F. Hutchinson, *Champions of Charity: War and the Red Cross* (Oxford: Westview, 1997), 2.
8. Patricia Clavin, "International Organizations," in *The Cambridge History of the Second World War: Volume II Politics and Ideology*, ed. Richard Bosworth and Joseph Maiolo (London: Cambridge University Press, 2015), 142.
9. Dick Stegewerns, *Nationalism and Internationalism in Imperial Japan: Autonomy, Asian Brotherhood, or World Citizenship?* (London: Routledge Curzon, 2003), 4; and Jessamyn R. Abel, *The International Minimum: Creativity and Contradiction in Japan's Global Engagement, 1933–1964* (Honolulu: University of Hawai'i Press, 2015), 8–9.
10. Dorothy S. Albertson, *The History of the American National Red Cross: Volume XXXIV, The History of the Red Cross in the Philippine Islands* (Washington, DC: American National Red Cross, 1950), iii.
11. Shemo cites Irwin in arguing that the ARC frequently spread American influence along with humanitarian aid, and in the case of the Siberian Intervention "hoped to mold a citizenry that was fit to withstand the presumed threat of Bolshevism and anarchy." Connie Shemo, "Imperialism, Race, and Rescue: Transformation in the Woman's Foreign Mission Movement After World War I," *Diplomatic History* 43, no. 2 (April 2019): 266.

NOTE ON SOURCES

1. *Chōsa-bu* 調査部.
2. *Gaiji-bu* 外事部.
3. *Eisei-bu* 衛生部.
4. Michiko Suzuki, "The Japanese Red Cross Society's Emergency Responses in Hiroshima and Nagasaki, 1945," *Social Science Japan Journal* (July 2021): 347–67, https://doi.org/10.1093/ssjj/jyab026.

BIBLIOGRAPHY

ARCHIVES REFERENCED

BRAZIL

Center for Japanese-Brazilian Studies (CJBS), https://cenb.org.br/articles/index_en.
Historical Museum of Japanese Immigration in Brazil (HMJIB), https://www.bunkyo.org.br/br/museu-historico/.

JAPAN

Diplomatic Archives of the Ministry of Foreign Affairs of Japan (MOFA), Tokyo.
Chiran Peace Museum (CPM), Kagoshima.
Hawaii Emigration Museum Nihojima Village (HEMNV), Hiroshima.
Himeyuri Peace Museum (HPM), Okinawa.
Hiroshima Red Cross Hospital & Atomic-bomb Survivors Hospital Library (HRCH ASHL), Hiroshima.
Japanese Red Cross Institute for Humanitarian Studies Archives (JRC IHS), Tokyo.
Japanese Red Cross Society Nurse Association Dohokai Archives (JRCS NAD), Tokyo.
Japan Center for Asian Historical Records (JACAR), https://www.jacar.go.jp/english/index.html.
Japan Ground Self Defense Force Medical Service School Shōkokan Archives (JGSDF MSSS), Tokyo.
Maizuru Repatriation Memorial Museum Library (MRMML), Kyoto.
Meiji-mura Museum Japanese Red Cross Archives (MM JRC), Toyota.
Museum of Japanese Emigration to Hawaii (MJEH), Yamaguchi.
Nagasaki City Library (NCL), Nagasaki.
Nagasaki Atomic Bomb Museum (NABM), Nagasaki.

Nagasaki Foundation for the Promotion of Peace (NFPP), Nagasaki.
National Archives of Japan (NAJ), Tokyo.
National Diet Library (NDL), Tokyo.
National Institute for Defense Studies Archives (NIDS), Tokyo.
National Showa Memorial Museum (NSMM), Tokyo.
Shokei-kan: Historical Materials Hall for the Wounded and Sick Retired Soldiers, etc., Japan.
The All Japan Federation of Karafuto Library (AJFKL), Tokyo.
The Hiroshima Peace Memorial Museum Archives (HPMM), Hiroshima.
The International Research Center for Japanese Studies Library (IRCJSL), Kyoto.
The Japanese Red Cross College of Nursing Archives (JRCS CN), Tokyo.
The Japanese Red Cross Institute for Humanitarian Studies (JRCIHS), Tokyo.
The Japanese Red Cross Society Disaster Relief Division Disaster Management and Social Welfare Department Archives (JRCS DRD DM SWD), Tokyo.
The Japanese Red Cross Society Hiroshima Chapter Archives (JRCS HC), Hiroshima.
The Japanese Red Cross Society International Department Archives (JRCS ID), Tokyo.
The Japanese Red Cross Society Nagasaki Chapter Archives (JRCS NC), Nagasaki.
The Japanese Red Cross Society Red Cross Information Plaza Archives (JRCS RCIP), Tokyo.
The Japanese Red Cross Toyota College of Nursing Library (JRCS TCN L), Toyota.
The Ken Domon Museum of Photography (KDMP), Yamagata.
The University of Tokyo Libraries (UTL), Tokyo.
The University of Tokyo Meiji Shinbun Zasshi Bunko (UTMSZB), Tokyo.
Wakayama City Museum (WCM), Wakayama.
War Memorial Maritime Museum (WMMM), Kobe.
Yushima Seidō Shibunkai Archives, Tokyo.

SWITZERLAND

International Committee of the Red Cross Archives (ICRC), Geneva.
International Federation of Red Cross and Red Crescent Societies Archives (IFRC), Geneva.

UNITED KINGDOM

British Red Cross Archives (BRC), London.
Imperial War Museum (IWM), London.
National Archives (BNA), London.
The British Library (BL), London.

UNITED STATES

American Red Cross Archives (ARC), Washington, DC, https://www.redcross.org/about-us/who-we-are/history.html.
American Red Cross of Hawaii Headquarters Archives (ARC H), Honolulu, https://www.redcross.org/local/hawaii/about-us.html.

The Hawaiian Historical Society Library (HHSL), Honolulu, https://www.hawaiianhistory.org/research/library/.

The *Hawaii Times* Photo Archives, Honolulu.

The Hoover Institution on War, Revolution, and Peace at Stanford University, California, https://www.hoover.org/.

The Japanese American National Museum (JANM), California, https://www.janm.org/.

The National WWII Museum (NWWM), New Orleans, https://www.nationalww2museum.org/.

The University of Hawai'i Manoa Library (UHML), Honolulu, https://manoa.hawaii.edu/library/.

National Archives and Records Administration (NARA), Washington, DC, https://www.archives.gov/.

Poster House, New York, https://posterhouse.org/.

PUBLISHED PRIMARY SOURCES

Aichi Jūgun Kangofu no Kiroku Henshū-i'inkai あいち従軍看護婦の記録編集委員会, ed. *Aichi Jūgun Kangofu no Kiroku* あいち従軍看護婦の記録 [The Record of Aichi Military Nurses]. Nagoya: Nihon Sekijūjisha Aichiken-shibu, 1980.

Albertson, Dorothy S. *The History of the American National Red Cross: Volume XXXIV, The History of the Red Cross in the Philippine Islands*. Washington, DC: American National Red Cross, 1950.

Aoyagi, Ikutarō 青柳郁太郎. *Burajiru ni Okeru Nipponjin Hatten-shi, Ge-kan: Nikkei Imin Shiryōshū, Nambei-hen San, Dai Sanjukkan* ブラジルに於ける日本人発展史 下巻：日系移民資料集 南米編3 第３０巻 [The Development of the History of the Japanese Immigrants in Brazil, Vol. 2: Collection of Documents on Japanese Immigrants, Latin America 3, Vol. 30]. Tokyo: Burajiru ni Okeru Nipponjin Hatten-shi Kankō I'inkai, 1953.

———. *Burajiru ni Okeru Nipponjin Hatten-shi, Jō-kan: Nikkei Imin Shiryōshū, Nambei-hen San, Dai Nijūkyū-kan* ブラジルに於ける日本人発展史 上巻：日系移民資料集 南米編3 第２９巻 [The Development of the History of the Japanese Immigrants in Brazil, Vol. 1: Collection of Documents on Japanese Immigrants, Latin America 3, Vol. 29]. Tokyo: Burajiru ni Okeru Nipponjin Hatten-shi Kankō I'inkai, 1952.

Burajiru Jihōsha, ed. *Burajiru Nenkan 1933 nen* 伯剌西爾年鑑 １９３３年 [Brazil Book of the Year, 1933]. Sao Paulo: Burajiru Jihōsha, 1933.

Chōsen Sōtokufu 朝鮮総督府. *Chōsen Sōtokufu Tōkei Nenpō, Meiji Yonjūsan nen* 朝鮮総督府統計年報 （明治四十三年） [Annual Report of the Governor-General of Chōsen, 1910]. Seoul: Chōsen Sōtokufu, 1912.

———. [1936]. Seoul: Chōsen Sōtokufu, 1938.

———. [1940]. Seoul: Chōsen Sōtokufu, 1942.

———. [1942]. Seoul: Chōsen Sōtokufu, 1944.

Chōsensōtokufu I'in 朝鮮総督府医院. *Chōsensōtokufu I'in Nijū-nen Shi* 朝鮮総督府医院二十年史 [The Twenty-Year History of the Medical Institute of the Governor-General of Korea]. Keijō: Chōsensōtokufu I'in, 1928.

Daikan Sekijūjisha 大韓赤十字社. *Daikan Sekijūjisha Hachijū-nen Shi* 大韓赤十字社八十年史 [The Eighty-Year History of the Korean Red Cross Society]. Seoul: Daikan Sekijūjisha, 1987.

Gaimushō Ryōji Ijū Bu, ed. *Waga Kokumin no Kaigai Hatten: Ijū Hyakunen no Ayumi Hon-pen* わが国民の海外発展：移住百年の歩み（本編）[The Overseas Development of the Japanese People: The 100 Year History of Immigration, Overview]. Tokyo: Gaimushō Ryōji Ijū Bu, 1971.

———. [Sources]. Tokyo: Gaimushō Ryōji Ijū Bu, 1971.

Hibaku Kenzōbutsu wo Kangaeru Kai 被爆建造物を考える会. *Hiroshima no Hibaku Kenzōbutsu—Hibaku 45 Shūnen Chōsa Hōkokusho* 広島の被爆建造物—被爆４５周年調査報告書 [Hiroshima's Atomic Bombed Buildings: The Forty-Five Year Anniversary, Research Paper]. Hiroshima: Asahi Newspaper Hiroshima Branch, 1990.

Hishiki Hidekazu 飛鋪秀一, ed. *Aikoku Fujinkai Yonjū-nen-shi* 愛国婦人会四十年史 [The Forty-Year History of the Patriotic Women's Association of Japan]. Tokyo: Aikoku Fujinkai, 1941.

———. *Aikoku Fujinkai Yonjū-nen-shi, Furoku* 愛国婦人会四十年史：附録 [The Forty-Year History of Patriotic Women's Association of Japan: Appendix]. Tokyo: Aikoku Fujinkai, 1941.

Hiroshima City Office, ed. *Hiroshima Genbaku Sensai-shi Dai Ikkan: Sōsetsu* 広島原爆戦災誌 第一巻 総説 [The History of the Hiroshima Atomic Bombing, Vol. 1: Overview]. Hiroshima: Hiroshima City Office, 1971.

———. [Vol. 2: Section 1, Aftermath of the Hiroshima Atomic Bombing]. Hiroshima: Hiroshima City Office, 1971.

Hiroshima Genbaku Iryō-shi Hensan-i'inkai 広島原爆医療史編纂委員会, ed. *Hiroshima Genbaku Iryō-shi* 広島原爆医療史 [Medical History of the Hiroshima Atomic Bombing]. Hiroshima: Zaidan-hōjin Hiroshima Genbaku Shōgai Taisaku Kyōgikai, 1961.

Hiroshima Prefecture, ed. *Hiroshima Ken-shi, Kindai Ni* 広島県史 近代２ [The History of Hiroshima Prefecture: Modern 2]. Hiroshima: Hiroshima Prefecture, 1981.

Hiroshima Sekijūji Kango Sen'mon Gakkō: Nihon Sekijisha Kangofu Dōhōkai Hiroshimaken-shibu 広島赤十字看護専門学校 日本赤十字社看護婦同方会広島県支部. *Hiroshima Sekijūji Kango Semmon Gakkō Gojū-nen Shi* 広島赤十字看護専門学校５０年史 [The 50-Year History of the Hiroshima Red Cross Nursing College]. Hiroshima: Hiroshima Sekijūji Kango Semmon Gakkō, 1990.

International Red Cross Committee for Central China. *A Review of Activities from September 1937 to March 1939*.

Inoue, Enji 井上円治. *Ōshū Taisengo no Sekijūji Heiwa-jigyō Shōnen Sekijūji* 欧州大戦後の赤十字平和事業少年赤十字 [Junior Red Cross: Red Cross Peace Program After the First World War]. Tokyo: Hakuai Hakkōjo, 1925.

Inoue, Natsue 井上なつゑ. "America ni okeru Shakai Kangofu." In Nihon Sekijūjisha Kangofu Dōhōkai 日本赤十字社看護婦同方会. *Dōhō Shōwa Roku nen San gatsu gō* 同方 昭和六年三月号 [Japanese Red Cross Nurse Association Magazine, June 1931], 10–2. Tokyo: Nihon Sekijūjisha Kangofu Dōhōkai, 1931.

Japanese Red Cross Society Hiroshima Red Cross Hospital & Atomic-bomb Survivors Hospital. *Peace Education: Toward a Peaceful World Free of Nuclear Weapons*. The Hiroshima International Center. Hiroshima: Hiroshima Red Cross Hospital & Atomic-bomb Survivors Hospital Social Division, 2011.

Keishichō 警視庁. *Taishō Taishin Kasai-shi* 大正大震火災誌 [The Record of the Taishō Great Earthquake and Fire]. Tokyo: Keishichō, 1925.

Kōseishō Imu-kyoku 厚生省医務局. *Nihon Kango Seido-shi Nen'pyō* 日本看護制度史年表 [The Chronological Table of the History of the Japanese Nursing System]. Tokyo: Kōseishō Imu-kyoku, 1960.

League of Red Cross Societies. "Teaching Health to Juniors of Japan." *The World's Health, Index to Volume VI* (January–December 1925): 66–67.

Manshūkokushi Hensan Kankōkai 満洲国史編纂刊行会. *Manshūkokushi Kakuron* 満洲国史：各論 [Detailed History of Manchukuo]. Tokyo: Man'mō Dōhō Engokai, 1971.

———. [Overview of the History of Manchukuo]. Tokyo: Man'mō Dōhō Engokai, 1971.

Manshūkoku Sekijūjisha 満洲国赤十字社. *Jin'ai: Jūni-gatsu-gō* 仁愛 1 2 月号 [Jin'ai, December]. Manchūkuo: Manshūkoku Sekijūjisha, 1944.

———. [Jin'ai, February 1941]. Manchūkuo: Manshūkoku Sekijūjisha, 1941.

———. [Jin'ai, February and March]. Manchūkuo: Manshūkoku Sekijūjisha, 1945.

———. [Jin'ai, Inaugural Edition, 1939]. Manchūkuo: Manshūkoku Sekijūjisha, 1939.

———. [Jin'ai, April 1939]. Manchūkuo: Manshūkoku Sekijūjisha, 1939.

———. [Jin'ai, January]. Manchūkuo: Manshūkoku Sekijūjisha, 1941.

———. [Jin'ai, July]. Manchūkuo: Manshūkoku Sekijūjisha, 1941.

———. [Jin'ai, March]. Manchūkuo: Manshūkoku Sekijūjisha, 1942.

Manshūkoku Sekijūjisha Hōten Byōin 満洲国赤十字社奉天病院. *Sekiyō, Dai Nana-gō, Kōtoku Roku-nen Shichi-gatsu Tuitachi* 赤陽 第七号 康徳六年七月一日 [Sekiyō, Vol. 7, July 1, 1939]. Mukden: Manchukuo Red Cross Society Mukden Hospital, 1939.

Matsuyama Sekijūji-byōin 松山赤十字病院編, ed. *Matsuyama Sekijūji-byōin Nanajū-nen Shi* 松山赤十字病院七十年史 [The Seventy-Year History of Matsuyama Red Cross Hospital]. Matuyama: Matsuyama Sekijūji-byōin, 1982.

Mitsui Kōzaburō 三井光三郎. *Aikoku Fujinkai-shi* 愛国婦人会史 [The History of Patriotic Women's Association of Japan]. Tokyo: Aikoku Fujinkai Hakkōjo, 1912.

Moroi, Tadakazu 諸井忠一. *Moroi Rokurō-kun Tsuitō Ihōroku* 諸井六郎君追悼遺芳録 [Tribute and Works by Moroi Rokurō]. Tokyo: Ko Moroi Kōshi Tsuioku I'inkai, 1941.

Nagasaki Atomic Bomb Museum, ed. *Nagasaki Genbaku Sensai-shi, Dai Ikkan: Sōsetsu-hen Kaiteiban* 長崎原爆戦災誌 第 1 巻（総説編 改訂版） [The History of the Nagasaki Atomic Bombing, Vol. 1: Overview, Revised Edition]. Nagasaki: Fujiki Hakuei-sha, 2006.

Nagasaki-ken Keisatsu Shi Henshū I'inkai 長崎県警察史編集委員会編, ed. *Nagasaki-ken Keisatsu Shi, Ge-kan* 長崎県警察史 下巻 [The History of Nagasaki Prefecture Police, Vol. 2]. Nagasaki: Nagasaki-ken Keisatsu Honbu, 1979.

Nagasaki Peace Institute 長崎平和研究所. "Nagasaki no Genbaku Higai Gaiyō to Shishōsha no Kazu 長崎の原爆被害概要と死傷者の数" [Overview of the Nagasaki Atomic Bombing and Death Toll]. http://www.nagasaki-heiwa.org/n5/A5.html. Accessed March 28, 2015.

Nagasaki-shi 長崎市編, ed. *Nagasaki Genbaku Sensai-shi, Dai Go-kan: Shiryō hen* 長崎原爆戦災誌 第5巻（資料編） [The History of the Nagasaki Atomic Bombing, Vol. 5: Sources]. Nagasaki: Nagasaki Kokusai Bunka Kaikan, 1983.

———. [Vol. 3: Region, Before and After the End of the War]. Nagasaki: Nagasaki Kokusai Bunka Kaikan, 1983.

———. [Vol. 4: Academic Research]. Nagasaki: Nagasaki Kokusai Bunka Kaikan, 1984.

Nagasaki-shi Genbaku Hibaku Taisaku-bu 長崎市原爆被爆対策部編, ed. *Nagasaki Genbaku Hibaku Gojū-nen Shi* 長崎原爆被爆５０年史 [Fifty Years the Nagasaki Atomic Bombing]. Nagasaki: Nagasaki-shi Genbaku Hibaku Taisaku-bu, 1996.

Naikaku Tōkei-kyoku 内閣統計局編, ed. *Kokuseichōsa-hōkoku, Taishō Kyū nen, Zenkoku no Bu, Dai ikkan* 国政調査報告 大正９年 全国の部 第１巻 [The Report of the National Census, 1920, National, Vol. 1]. Tokyo: Naikaku Tōkei-kyoku, 1928.

Naimushō Eisei-kyoku 内務省衛生局編, ed. *Ryūkōsei Kanbō: 'Supein Kaze' Dairyūkō no Kiroku* 流行性感冒——「スペイン風邪」大流行の記録 [The Flu Pandemic: The Record of the Spanish Flu]. Tokyo: Heibonsha, 2008.

National Archives of Japan. Furyo Jōhōkyoku. *Furyo Jōhōkyoku no Gyōmu ni Tsuite* 俘虜情報局ノ業務ニ就テ [Works of the Prisoners of War Information Bureau]. Tokyo: Furyo Jōhōkyoku, 1941.

——. *Okada Sōridaijin Aisatsu* 岡田総理大臣挨拶 [Speech Note by Prime Ministaer Okada], Dai Jūgokai Sekijūji Kokusaikaigi Sanretsusha Kangei Bansankai Yakai Shorui, Naikaku Sōridaijin Kanbō Sōmuka Shiryō. ID: A15060259900.

Nihon Imin Hachijūnen-shi Hensan I'inkai 日本移民八十年史編纂委員会. *Burajiru Nihon Imin Hachijūnen-shi* ブラジル日本移民八十年史 [The Eighty-Year History of the Japanese Immigrants in Brazil]. São Paulo: Toppan Puresu Insatsu Shuppan Gaisha, 1991.

Nihon Sekijūjisha 日本赤十字社編, ed. *Dai Jūgo-kai Sekijūji Kokusai Kaigishi* 第十五回赤十字国際会議誌 [The Records of the Fifteenth International Conference of the Red Cross]. Tokyo: Nihon Sekijūjisha, 1937.

——. *Dai Jūrokkai Sekijūji Kokusai Kaigi Haken Iin Hōkoku* 第十六回赤十字国際会議派遣委員報告 [The Report on the Sixteenth International Conference of the Red Cross]. Tokyo: Nihon Sekijūjisha, 1940.

——. *Eisei Nippon no Kaiko: Kigen Nisen-roppyaku-nen Hōshuku Kinen* 衛生日本の回顧：紀元２６００年奉祝記念 [Reflections on Hygiene and Sanitation in Japan: Celebration for the 2,600-Year Anniversary of Emperor Jinmu's Accession]. Tokyo: Dai-nippon Shuppan, 1941.

——. *Fukkoku-ban Dōhō Shōwa Hachi nen* 復刻版 同方 昭和八年 [Reprint Edition: Japanese Red Cross Nurse Association Magazine, 1933]. Tokyo: Nihon Sekijūjisha, 2014.

——. [1932]. Tokyo: Nihon Sekijūjisha, 2014.

——. [1928]. Tokyo: Nihon Sekijūjisha, 2014.

——. *Genkō: Nihon Sekijūjisha Reikirui-shū* 現行 日本赤十字社例規類集 [JRCS Regulations: The Latest Edition]. Tokyo: Hakuai Hakkōjo, 1919.

——. *Hakuai: Organ de la croix-rouge janponaise, No. 662, Juillet 1942* 博愛 第６６２号. Tokyo: Nihon Sekijūjisha, 1942.

——. *No. 622, March 1939* 博愛 第６２２号. Tokyo: Nihon Sekijūjisha, 1939.

——. *No. 620, January 1939* 博愛 第６２０号. Tokyo: Nihon Sekijūjisha, 1939.

——. *No. 610, March 1938* 博愛 第６１０号. Tokyo: Nihon Sekijūjisha, 1938.

——. *No. 609, February 1938* 博愛 第６０９号. Tokyo: Nihon Sekijūjisha, 1938.

——. *No. 608, January 1938* 博愛 第６０８号. Tokyo: Nihon Sekijūjisha, 1938.

——. *No. 566, July 1934* 博愛 第５６６号. Tokyo: Nihon Sekijūjisha, 1934.

——. *No. 564, May 1934* 博愛 第５６４号. Tokyo: Nihon Sekijūjisha, 1934.

——. *No. 562, March 1934* 博愛 第５６２号. Tokyo: Nihon Sekijūjisha, 1934.

———. *No. 520, September 1930* 博愛 第５２０号. Tokyo: Nihon Sekijūjisha, 1930.
———. *No. 450, November 1924* 博愛 第４５０号. Tokyo: Hakuai Hakkōjo, 1924.
———. *No. 437, November 1923* 博愛: 震災號 第４３７号. Tokyo: Hakuai Hakkōjo, 1923.
———. *No. 398, June 1920* 博愛 第３９８号. Tokyo: Hakuai Hakkōjo, 1920.
———. *No. 397, May 1920* 博愛 第３９７号. Tokyo: Hakuai Hakkōjo, 1920.
———. *No. 396, April 1920* 博愛 第３９６号. Tokyo: Hakuai Hakkōjo, 1920.
———. *No. 395, March 1920* 博愛 第３９５号. Tokyo: Hakuai Hakkōjo, 1920.
———. *No. 394, February 1920* 博愛 第３９４号. Tokyo: Hakuai Hakkōjo, 1920.
———. *Ihōroku: Junshoku Kyūgoin* 遺芳録 殉職救護員 [Memorial and Tribute to Relief Workers Who Died on Duty]. Tokyo: Nihon Sekijūjisha, 1957.
———. *Jindō—sono Ayumi: Nihon Sekijūjisha Hyaku-nen Shi* 人道－その歩み：日本赤十字社百年史 [The Advance of Humanitarianism: Centennial History of the Japanese Red Cross Society]. Tokyo: Nihon Sekijūjisha, 1979.
———. *Kango-gaku Kyōiku Katei* 看護学教育課程 [Textbook for Nursing Education Science]. Tokyo: Nihon Sekijūjisha, 1896.
———. *Kōshu Kango Kyōtei, Jō-kan* 甲種看護教程上巻 [Training Textbook for *Kō* Class Nursing, Vol. 1]. Tokyo: Nihon Sekijūjihakkōjo, 1910.
———. *Kōshu Kango Kyōtei, Ge-kan* 甲種看護教程下巻 [Training Textbook for *Kō* Class Nursing, Vol. 2]. Tokyo: Nihon Sekijūji Hakkōjo, 1910.
———. *Kyūgoin Seito Kyōiku Shiryō* 救護員生徒教育資料 [Documents for Nursing Students' Education]. Tokyo: Nihon Sekijūjisha, 1911.
———. *Nihon Sekijūjisha Kyūgo Kangofuchō・Kangofu Meibo* 日本赤十字社救護看護婦長・看護婦名簿 [Registers of Japanese Red Cross Society's Chief Nurses and Nurses]. Tokyo: Nihon Sekijūjisha, 1942.
———. *Nihon Sekijūji* 日本赤十字 *La Croix Rouge du Nippon. No. 291. January 1912* [Organ of the Japanese Red Cross Society, No. 291, January 1912]. Tokyo: Nihon Sekijūji Hakkōjo, 1912.
———. [No. 146, April 1904]. Tokyo: Nihon Sekijūji Hakkōjo, 1904.
———. [No. 135, October 1904]. Tokyo: Nihon Sekijūji Hakkōjo, 1904.
———. [No. 71, March 1899]. Tokyo: Nihon Sekijūji Hakkōjo, 1899.
———. [No. 25, August 1894]. Tokyo: Nihon Sekijūji Hakkōjo, 1894.
———. *Otsushu Kango Kyōtei* 乙種看護教程 [Training Textbook for *Otsu* Class Nursing]. Tokyo: Nihon Sekijūji Hakkōjo, 1910.
———. *Shina-jihen ni Kansuru Nihon Sekijūjisha Kyūgo Jigyō Gaiyō* 支那事変に関する日本赤十字社救護事業概要 [Summary of the Japanese Red Cross Society Relief Activities During the Manchurian Incident]. Tokyo: Nihon Sekijūjisha, 1932.
———. *Shina-jihen ni Kansuru Nihon Sekijūjisha Kyūgo Jigyō Gaiyō, 3* 支那事変に関する日本赤十字社救護事業概要（三）[The Summary of the Japanese Red Cross Society Relief Activities During the Manchurian Incident, Vol. 3]. Tokyo: Nihon Sekijūjisha, 1933.
———. *Nihon Sekijūjisha Reikirui-Shū* 日本赤十字社例規類集 [The Regulations of the Japanese Red Cross Society]. Tokyo: Nihon Sekijūjisha, 1925.
———. *Meiji Sanjū-san nen Shinkoku jihen Nihon Sekijūjisha Kyūgo Kiyō* 明治三十三年清国事変日本赤十字社救護紀要 [The Report on the Relief Activities During the First Sino-Japanese War]. Tokyo: Nihon Sekijūjisha, 1902.

———. *Meiji Sanjū-shichi hachi nen Sen'eki Kyūgohōkoku* 明治三十七八年戦役救護報告 [The Record of Russo-Japanese War Relief Activities]. Tokyo: Nihon Sekijūjisha, 1908.

———. *Nihon Sekijūji Shashikō* 日本赤十字社史稿 [The History of the Japanese Red Cross Society, Vol. 1]. Tokyo: Nihon Sekijūjisha, 1911.

———. *Nihon Sekijūjisha Shashikō, Dai Hakkan, Shōwa yonjūichi-nen kara Shōwa gojū-nen* 日本赤十字社社史稿 第8巻 昭和41年－昭和50年 [The History of the Japanese Red Cross Society, Vol. 8, 1966–1975]. Tokyo: Nihon Sekijūjisha, 1988.

———. [Vol. 7, 1956–1965]. Tokyo: Nihon Sekijūjisha, 1986.

———. [Vol. 6, 1946–1955]. Tokyo: Nihon Sekijūjisha, 1972.

———. [Vol. 5, 1936–1945]. Tokyo: Nihon Sekijūjisha, 1969.

———. [Vol. 4, 1926–1935]. Tokyo: Nihon Sekijūjisha, 1957.

———. [Vol. 3, 1908–1922]. Tokyo: Nihon Sekijūjisha, 1929.

Nihon Sekijūjisha 日本赤十字社編, ed. *Nihon Sekijūji Shashi Zokkō, Jō-kan Meiji yonjū-nen kara Taishō jūichi-nen* 日本赤十字社史続稿 上巻 明治41年－大正11年 [The History of the Japanese Red Cross Society, Vol. 2, 1908–1922]. Tokyo: Nihon Sekijūjisha, 1929.

———. *Nihon Sekijūjisha Hachijū-nen Shōshi* 日本赤十字社八十年小史 [A Brief History of Eighty Years of the Japanese Red Cross Society]. Tokyo: Nihon Sekijūjisha, 1957.

———. *Sekijūji Kokusai Kaigi Giji Gaiyō, Dai Jūgo-kai* 赤十字国際会議議事概要 第15回 [The Minutes of the Fifteenth International Conference of the Red Cross]. Tokyo: Nihon Sekijūjisha, 1936.

———. *Sekijūji Kokusai Kaigi ni Kansuru Gaikokujin no Shoken, Dai Jūgo-kai* 第15回赤十字国際会議に関する外国人の所見．第15回 [Views of Foreigners Regarding the Fifteenth International Conference of the Red Cross]. Tokyo: Nihon Sekijūjisha, 1935.

———. *Shōwa jūkyū-nen-do Jigyōnenpō* 昭和十九年度事業年報 [Annual Report of the Japanese Red Cross Society, 1944]. Tokyo: Nihon Sekijūjisha, 1944.

———. [1943]. Tokyo: Nihon Sekijūjisha, 1943.

———. [1942]. Tokyo: Nihon Sekijūjisha, 1942.

———. [1935]. Tokyo: Nihon Sekijūjisha, 1936.

———. [1935]. Tokyo: Nihon Sekijūjisha, 1935.

———. [1926]. Tokyo: Nihon Sekijūjisha, 1926.

———. [1925]. Tokyo: Nihon Sekijūjisha, 1925.

———. *Sekijūji no Ugoki* 赤十字の動き [The Activities of the Red Cross]. Tokyo: Nihon Sekijūjisha, 1984.

———. *Tairiku Kaihatsu Eisei-ten Gō* 大陸開発衛生展號 [Exhibition on the Development of Public Health in the Continent]. Tokyo: Nihon Sekijūjisha, 1939.

———. *Taishō Jūni nen Kantō Daishinsai Nihon Sekijūjisha Kyūgo-shi* 大正十二年関東大震災日本赤十字社救護誌 [The Record of the Japanese Red Cross Society Relief Activities for the Great Kantō Earthquake, 1923]. Tokyo: Nihon Sekijūjisha, 1925.

———. *The Geneva Conventions* 赤十字諸規約. Tokyo: Nihon Sekijūjisha, 1933.

———. *The Japan Junior Red Cross: Special Number of the Fifteenth International Red Cross Conference Tokyo, October 20–29, Vol. IX, No. 4, October 1934* 少年赤十字 第九巻 第四号. Tokyo: Nihon Sekijūjisha, 1934.

Nihon Sekijūjisha Aichi-shibu 日本赤十字社愛知支部. *Sekijūjiki no Moto ni* 赤十字旗の下に [Under the Flag of the Red Cross]. Nagoya: Nihon Sekijūjisha Aichiken-shibu, 1941.

Nihon Sekijūjisha Chibaken-shibu 日本赤十字社千葉県支部. *Kiri no Hana: Senji Kyūgo Taiken Kirokushū* 桐の華：戦時救護体験記録集 [Paulownia Flowers: Records of Wartime Relief Experiences]. Chiba: Nihon Sekijiūjisha Chiba-ken Shibu Kangofu Dōsōkai, 1992.

Nihon Sekijūjisha Eiseibu 日本赤十字社衛生部. *Nihon Sekijūjisha Kangofu Yousei Hyakushūnen Kinenshi* 日本赤十字社看護婦養成百周年記念誌 [Centenary Memorial Magazine for Japanese Red Cross Society Nursing Education]. Tokyo: Nihon Sekijūjisha Eiseibu, 1992.

Nihon Sekijūjisha Ehimeken-shibu 日本赤十字社愛媛県支部編, ed. *Nisseki Ehimeken-shibu Hyaku-nen Shi* 日本赤十字社愛媛県支部百年史 [The 100-Year History of the Japanese Red Cross Society Ehime Chapter]. Ehime: Nihon Sekijūjisha Ehimeken-shibu, 1989.

Nihon Sekijūjisha Genshiryoku Hōshanō Shōgai Taisaku I'inkai 日本赤十字社原子力放射能障害対策委員会. *Nihon Sekijūjisha Genbaku Byōin Shinryō Kiroku, sono-ichi* 日本赤十字社原爆病院診療記録. 其の1 [The Medical Records of Japanese Red Cross Atomic Bomb Hospitals, Vol. 1]. Tokyo: Nihon Sekijūjisha Genshiryoku Hōshanō Shōgai Taisaku I'inkai, 1959.

Nihon Sekijūjisha Hiroshimaken Shibu 日本赤十字社広島県支部. *Nanajsshū-nen Kinen-shi Genkō 2 Genshi-bakudan Hibaku* 70周年記念誌原稿 2. 原子爆弾被爆 [Seventieth Anniversary Edition, the Detonation of the Atomic Bomb, Section 2].

Nihon Sekijūjisha Hyōgo-shibu 日本赤十字社兵庫支部. *Ai wa Kagayaku* 愛は輝く [Shining Love]. Kōbe: Nihon Sekijūjisha Hyōgo-shibu, 1940.

Nihon Sekijūjisha Ishikawaken-shibu 日本赤十字社石川県支部編, ed. *Kagayaku Sekijūji* 輝く赤十字 [Illustrious Red Cross]. Kanazawa: Nihon Sekijūjisha Ishikawaken-shibu, 1941.

Nihon Sekijūjisha Kangofu Dōhōkai 日本赤十字社看護婦同方会. *Dōhō Shōwa Sanjū nen Shi gatsu gō* 同方 昭和十三年 四月号 [Japanese Red Cross Nurse Association Magazine, April 1938]. Tokyo: Nihon Sekijūjisha Kangofu Dōhōkai, 1938.

———. [December 1941]. Tokyo: Nihon Sekijūjisha Kangofu Dōhōkai, 1941.

———. [December 1937]. Tokyo: Nihon Sekijūjisha Kangofu Dōhōkai, 1937.

———. [February 1933]. Tokyo: Nihon Sekijūjisha Kangofu Dōhōkai, 1933.

———. [January 1933]. Tokyo: Nihon Sekijūjisha Kangofu Dōhōkai, 1933.

———. [May 1933]. Tokyo: Nihon Sekijūjisha Kangofu Dōhōkai, 1933.

———. [March 1932]. Tokyo: Nihon Sekijūjisha Kangofu Dōhōkai, 1932.

———. *Dōhō, Special Number Issued in Commemoration of the Late Miss Take Hagiwara, Superintendent of Nurses of the Japanese Central Red Cross Hospital and President of the Nurses' Association of the Japanese Empire, Shōwa Jūni nen Roku gatsu* 同方 昭和十二年 六月 萩原タケ子記念号 [Japanese Red Cross Nurse Association Magazine, June 1937]. Tokyo: Nihon Sekijūjisha Kangofu Dōhōkai, 1937.

Nihon Sekijūjisha Kangofu Dōhōkai Hiroshimaken-shibu 日本赤十字社看護婦同方会広島県支部編, ed. *Chinkon no Fu: Nihon Sekijūjisha Hiroshimaken-shibu Senji Kyūgo-shi* 鎮魂の譜 日本赤十字社広島県支部戦時救護史 [Notes of the Requiem: The History of the Japanese Red Cross Society Hiroshima Chapter Wartime Relief Activities]. Hiroshima: Nihon Sekijūjisha Kangofu Dōhōkai Hiroshimaken-shibu, 1981.

Nihon Sekijūjisha Kangofu Dōhōkai Miyagiken-shibu 日本赤十字社看護婦同方会 宮城県支部, ed. *Michi Nihon Sekijūjisha Miyagiken-shibu: Jūgun Kangofu no Kiroku* 道 日本赤十字社宮城県支部：従軍看護婦の記録 [The Path of Japanese Red Cross Society Miyagi Chapter: The Record of Military Nurses]. Sendai: Nihon Sekijūjisha Kangofu Dōhōkai Miyagiken-shibu, 1984.

Nihon Sekijūjisha Kangofu Dōhōkai Ōitaken-shibu 日本赤十字社看護婦同方会大分県支部. *Ōita no Kyūgo Kango-shi* 大分の救護看護史 [The History of Relief Nursing in Ōita]. Ōita City: Nihon Sekijūjisha Kangofu Dōhōkai Ōitaken-shibu, 1986.

Nihon Sekijūjisha Kangoshi Dōhōkai 日本赤十字社看護師同方会. *Hakuai no Michi Eien naru Ayumi: Furōrensu Naichingēru Kishō ni Kagayaku Hitobito: Dai Ikkai—Dai Yonjukkai* 博愛の道永遠なる歩み：フローレンス・ナイチンゲール記章に輝く人々：第１回－第４０回 [Unending Pursuit of Philanthropy: Recipients of the Florence Nightingale Medal (The First to the Fortieth Award)]. Tokyo: Nihon Sekijūjisha Kangoshi Dōhōkai, 2006.

Nihon Sekijūjisha Kikaku Kōhō-shitsu 日本赤十字社企画広報室編, ed. *Nihon Sekijūjisha Sōritsu Hyaku-nijusshūnen Kinenten: Kinenten Katarogu Sen-happyaku nanajūnana kara Nisen-ni* 日本赤十字社創立１２５周年記念展：記念展カタログ　１８７７－２００２ [Special Exhibition of the 125th Anniversary of the Japanese Red Cross Society: Catalogue 1877-2002]. Tokyo: Nihon Sekijūjisha, 2002.

Nihon Sekijūjisha Hiroshimaken-shibu 日本赤十字社広島県支部編, ed. *Nihon Sekijūjisha Hiroshimaken-shibu Hyaku-nen shi: Shiryōhen* 日本赤十字社広島県支部百年史：資料編 [Centennial History of the Japanese Red Cross Society Hiroshima Chapter: Records]. Hiroshima: Nihon Sekijūjisha Hiroshimaken-shibu, 1991.

———. *Sekijūji Monogatari: Nihon Sekijūjisha Hiroshima-ken Shibu Hyakunen no Ayumi* 赤十字物語：日本赤十字社広島県支部百年の歩み [The Story of the Red Cross: Centennial History of the Japanese Red Cross Society Hiroshima Chapter]. Hiroshima: Nihon Sekijūjisha Hiroshimaken-shibu, 1989.

Nihon Sekijūjisha Hokkaido-shibu 日本赤十字社北海道支部. *Hokkaidō no Sekijūji sono Hyakunen* 北海道の赤十字 その百年 [Centennial History of the Japanese Red Cross Society Hokkaido Chapter]. Sapporo: Nihon Sekijūjisha Hokkaido-shibu, 1987.

Nihon Sekijūjisha Hyōgoken-shibu 日本赤十字社兵庫県支部編, ed. *Hyōgo no Sekijūji Hyakunen Shi* ひょうごの赤十字百年史 [Centennial History of the Japanese Red Cross Society Hyōgo Chapter]. Kōbe: Nihon Sekijūjisha Hyōgoken-shibu, 1991.

Nihon Sekijūjisha Ibarakiken-shibu 日本赤十字社茨城県支部. *Hyaku-nen no Ayumi* 百年のあゆみ [Centennial History of the Japanese Red Cross Society Ibaraki Chapter]. Mito: Nihon Sekijūjisha Ibarakiken-shibu, 1988.

Nihon Sekijūjisha Kanagawaken-shibu 日本赤十字社神奈川県支部. *Hyaku-nen no Ayumi* １００年のあゆみ [Centennial History of the Japanese Red Cross Society Kanagawa Chapter]. Yokohama: Nihon Sekijūjisha Kanagawaken-shibu, 1989.

Nihon Sekijūjisha Kumamotoken-shibu 日本赤十字社熊本県支部. *Nihon Sekijūjisha Kumamotoken-shibu: Jigyō-hen* 日本赤十字社熊本県支部史：事業編 [The History of the Japanese Red Cross Society Kumamoto Chapter: Activities]. Kumamoto: Nihon Sekijūjisha Kumamotoken-shibu, 1991.

Nihon Sekijūjisha Kumamotoken-shibu 日本赤十字社熊本県支部. *Nihon Sekijūjisha Kumamotoken-shibu: Sōsetsu-hen* 日本赤十字社熊本県支部史：総説編 [The History of the Japanese Red Cross Society Kumamoto Chapter: Overview]. Kumamoto: Nihon Sekijūjisha Kumamotoken-shibu, 1991.

Nihon Sekijūjisha Kyoto-shibu 日本赤十字社京都支部編纂, ed. *Okutango Shinsai Kyūgo-shi* 奥丹後震災救護誌 [The Record of Relief Activities for the Kita Tango Earthquake]. Kyoto: Nihon Sekijūjisha Kyoto-shibu, 1928.

Nihon Sekijūjisha Nagasaki Genbaku Byōin 日本赤十字社長崎原爆病院. *Genshi Bakudan Shōgaishō ni Kansuru Chōsa Kenkyū Itaku Jigyō Hōkokusho: Heisei nijūni nendo* 原子爆弾障害症に関する調査研究委託事業報告書：平成２２年度 [The Research Project Report on Atomic Bomb Diseases, 2010]. Nagasakai: Nihon Sekijūjisha Nagasaki Genbaku Byōin, 2011.

Nihon Sekijūjisha Nagasakiken-shibu 日本赤十字社長崎県支部. *Hyaku-nen no Ayumi* 百年のあゆみ [Centennial History of the Japanese Red Cross Society Nagasaki Chapter]. Nagasaki: Nihon Sekijūjisha Nagasakiken-shibu, 1988.

———. *Senkō no Kage de: Genbaku Hibakusha Kyūgo Sekijūji Kangofu no Shuki* 閃光の影で—原爆被爆者救護赤十字看護婦の手記—[The Shadow of a Flash: Memoirs of the Atomic Bombing Relief Activities]. Nagasaki: Nihon Sekijūjisha Nagasakiken-shibu, 1980.

Nihon Sekijūjisha Okinawaken-shibu 日本赤十字社沖縄県支部. *Hyaku-nen no Ayumi* 百年のあゆみ [Centennial History of the Japanese Red Cross Society Okinawa Chapter]. Naha: Nihon Sekijūjisha Okinawaken-shibu, 1991.

Nihon Sekijūjisha Shimaneken-shibu 日本赤十字社島根県支部. *Nihon Sekijūjisha Shimaneken-shibu Hyaku-nen shi* 日本赤十字社島根県支部百年史 [Centennial History of the Japanese Red Cross Society Shimane Chapter]. Shimane: Nihon Sekijūjisha Shimaneken-shibu, 1990.

Nihon Sekijūjisha Yamaguchiken-shibu 日本赤十字社山口県支部. *Hyaku-nen no Ayumi* 百年のあゆみ [The 100 Year History of the Japanese Red Cross Society Yamaguchi Chapter]. Yamaguchi: Nihon Sekijūjisha Yamaguchiken-shibu, 1991.

Niigata City. *Tsūshi-hen Yon Kindai Ge* 通史編 4 近代 下 [General History, Vol. 4-2]. Niigata: Niigata City, 1997.

Niigatashi-shi Hensan Kindaishibukai 新潟市史編さん近代史部会 編, ed. *Niigatashi-shi Shiryō-hen Nana: Kindai San* 新潟市史 資料編 7 近代 3 [The History of Niigata City: Sources, Vol. 7, Modern 3]. Niigata City: Niigata City, 1994.

Nisseki Gifu Senji Kyūgo no Kiroku Henshū-i'inkai 日赤岐阜戦時救護の記録編集委員会, ed. *Nisseki Gifu Senji Kyūgo no Kiroku* 日赤岐阜戦時救護の記録 [The Record of the Wartime Relief Activities of the Japanese Red Cross Society Gifu Chapter]. Gifu: Nihon Sekijūjisha Gifuken-shibu, 1982.

Nisseki Ishikawa Jūgun Kangofu no Kiroku Hensan-i'inkai 日赤石川従軍看護婦の記録編纂委員会, ed. *Nisseki Ishikawa Jūgun Kangofu no Kiroku* 日赤石川従軍看護婦の記録 [The Record of Military Nurses of the Japanese Red Cross Society Ishikawa Chapter]. Kanazawa: Nihon Sekijūjisha Ishikawaken-shibu, 1974.

Ogasawa Naganari 小笠原長生. *Shishaku Ogasawara Naganari* 子爵小笠原長生 [Viscount Ogasawara Naganari]. Tokyo: Ogasawara Naganari Shishaku Kiju Kinen Hensan-kai, 1943.

Okinawa Sekijūjisha 沖縄赤十字社. *Hakuai: Okinawa no Sekijūji* 博愛：沖縄の赤十字 [Philanthropy: The Red Cross in Okinawa]. Naha: Okinawa Sekijūjisha, 1968.

Okinawa Sekijūjisha 沖縄赤十字社. *Senkyūhyaku-nanajūichi nen-do Jigyōgaiyō 1971* 年度事業概要 [Annual Report of the Okinawan Red Cross Society, 1971]. Naha: Okinawa Sekijūjisha, 1971.

Osaka-fu 大阪府編, ed. *Kantōchihō Shinsai Kyūenshi* 関東地方震災救援誌 [The Record of the Relief Activities for the Earthquake in Kantō]. Osaka: Osaka-fu, 1924.

Ozawa, Takeo 小澤武雄. *Taishō Go nen San gatsu: Nihon Sekijūjisha Fukushachō: Ozawa Danshaku Kōwa Haykudai* 大正五年三月 日本赤十字社副社長 小澤男爵講話百題 [One Hundred Speech Notes by the Japanese Red Cross Society Vice-President, Baron Ozawa, March 1916]. Tokyo: Hakuai Hakkōjo, 1916.

Rikugun Daijin Kanbō 陸軍大臣官房, ed. *Meiji Sanjū-shichi hachi nen Sen'eki Furyo Toriatsukai Tenmatsu* 明治三十七八年戦役俘虜取扱顛末 [The Record of Treatment of Prisoners of War During the Russo-Japanese War]. Tokyo: Yuhikaku-shobō, 1907.

Saigai Kyōkun no Keishō ni Kansuru Senmonchōsakai Hōkokusho 災害教訓の継承に関する専門調査会報告書. *Hōkokusho, 1923 Kantō Daishinsai, Dai Ippen* １９２３関東大震災 報告書 第一編 [Report on 1923 Great Kantō Earthquake, Vol. 1]. Tokyo: Cabinet Office, Government of Japan, 2006.

———. [Vol. 2]. Tokyo: Cabinet Office, Government of Japan, 2008.

Shigetō, Fumio 重藤文夫. "Genshi Bakudan Saigai Kyūgo no Keiken 原子爆弾災害救護の経験" [The Experience of Nuclear Bombing Relief Activities]. In *Kyūgo no Kōshūroku: Shōwa sanjūsan-nen go-gatsu* 救護の講習録：昭和三十三年五月 [The Records of Medical Relief Training, May 1958]. Tokyo: Japanese Red Cross Society, 1958.

Tashiro, Senzō 田代仙蔵. *Nihon Sekijūjisha Manshū-i'inbu shi* 日本赤十字社満洲委員部史 [The History of the Manchurian Committee Department of the Japanese Red Cross Society]. Dalian: Nihon Sekijūjisha Kantōshū Iin-honbu, 1938.

The American Red Cross Archives. *The American National Red Cross Annual Report*, June 30. Washington, DC: The American National Red Cross, 1919.

———. June 30, 1920.

———. June 30, 1921.

———. June 30, 1922.

———. June 30, 1923.

———. June 30, 1924.

———. June 30, 1925.

———. 1926–1927.

———. 1928–1929.

———. 1929–1930.

———. *The Red Cross Courier*, April 1934. Washington, DC: The American National Red Cross, 1934.

The American Red Cross Library. *History of the American Red Cross in Hawaii*. Honolulu: The American Red Cross, 2020.

The Japanese Red Cross Society. *Materials Relating to the History of Relief Work in Japan*. Tokyo: The Japanese Red Cross Society, 1934.

The Red Cross Home Journal. *Hiroshima Nagasaki Genbaku Shiryō Kōkai-ten Owaru* 広島、長崎原爆資料公開展終る [Report on Public Exhibition of Documents About Hiroshima and Nagasaki Atomic Bombings]. Tokyo: Japanese Red Cross Society, 1954.

The United States Strategic Bombing Survey. *Nagasaki Hibaku Gojusshūnen Kinen: Beikoku Senryaku Bakugeki Chōsa Hōkokusho* 長崎被爆５０周年記念：米国戦略爆撃調査報告書 [The Fiftieth Memorial of the Nagasaki Atomic Bombing: The United States Strategic Bombing Survey]. Translated by Nagasaki International Cultural Centre and Bilingual Group Co. Nagasaki: Fujikihakueisha, 1996.

Yuan, Yingqi 顧英奇, ed. 中国红十字会九十周年 *90 Years of the Chinese Red Cross*. Beijing: The Editorial Committee of the Ninety-Year Anniversary of the Red Cross Society of China, 1994.

Yuri, Hanae 油利花枝, ed. *Jūgun Kaisō no Ki* 従軍回想の記 [Memoirs of Army and Navy Nurses]. Tokyo: Moto Riku-Kaigun Jūgun Kangofu no Kai, 1982.

Zhang, Yufa 張玉法, ed. 中華民國紅十字會百年會史, 1904–2003 [Centennial History of the Red Cross Society of the Republic of China, 1904–2003]. Taipei: The Association of the Red Cross Society of the Republic of China, 2004.

SECONDARY SOURCES

Abel, Jessamyn R. *The International Minimum: Creativity and Contradiction in Japan's Global Engagement, 1933–1964.* Honolulu: University of Hawai'i Press, 2015.

Adachi, Nobuko, ed. *Japanese Diasporas: Unsung Pasts, Conflicting Presents, and Uncertain Futures.* London: Routledge, 2006.

"Agenda of the Third Pan American Red Cross Conference." *Bulletin of the Pan American Union* 69, no. 8 (August 1935): 597–98.

Ambaras, David R. *Japan's Imperial Underworlds: Intimate Encounters at the Borders of Empire.* London: Cambridge University Press, 2018.

Ambrosius, Lloyd E. *Wilsonian Statecraft: Theory and Practice of Liberal Internationalism During World War I.* The United States: Scholarly Resources Inc., 1991.

Anderson, Marine S. *In Close Association: Local Activist Networks in the Making of Japanese Modernity, 1868–1920.* Cambridge, MA: Harvard University Press, 2022.

Aoki, Hisa 青木ヒサ. *Dai Ni ji Kōkansen: Teia-maru no Hōkoku* 第二次・交換船：帝亜丸の報告 [The Second Prison of War Exchange Repatriation Voyage: Report from Teia-maru]. Tokyo: Maeda Shobō, 1944.

Ariga, Nagao 有賀長雄. *Nichiro Rikusen Kokusaihō-ron* 日露陸戦国際法論 [Theory of the International Law for Land Warfare in the Russo-Japanese War]. Tokyo: Tōkyō Kaikōsha, 1911.

Asano Tamanoi, Mariko, ed. *Crossed Histories: Manchuria in the Age of Empire.* Honolulu: University of Hawai'i Press, 2005.

Auslin, Michael R. *Pacific Cosmopolitans: A Cultural History of U.S.-Japan Relations.* Cambridge, MA: Harvard University Press, 2011.

———. *Negotiating with Imperialism: The Unequal Treaties and the Culture of Japanese Diplomacy.* Cambridge, MA: Harvard University Press, 2004.

Aydin, Cemil. *The Politics of Anti-Westernism in Asia: Visions of World Order in Pan-Islamic and Pan-Asian Thought*. New York: Columbia University Press, 2019.

Azuma, Eiichiro. *Between Two Empires: Race, History, and Transnationalism in Japanese America*. London: Oxford University Press, 2005.

Barnett, Michael N. *Empire of Humanity: A History of Humanitarianism*. Ithaca, NY: Cornell University Press, 2013.

Barnhart, Michael A. *Japan Prepares for Total War: The Search for Economic Security, 1919–1941*. Ithaca, NY: Cornell University Press, 1987.

Barshay, Andrew E. *State and Intellectual in Imperial Japan: The Public Man in Crisis*. Berkeley: University of California Press, 2021.

Beasley, William G. *Japanese Imperialism, 1894–1945*. London: Clarendon, 1987.

Bix, Herbert P. *Hirohito and the Making of Modern Japan*. New York: HarperCollins, 2000.

Benthall, Jonathan, and Jerome Bellion-Jourdan. *The Charitable Crescent: Politics of Aid in the Muslim World*. London: I. B. Tauris, 2003.

Bentley, Michael, ed. *Companion to Historiography*. London: Routledge, 1997.

Berry, Nicholas O. *War and the Red Cross: The Unspoken Mission*. London: Basingstoke Macmillan, 1997.

Bōeihōmu-shimbunsha 防衛ホーム新聞社. *Shōkokan—Shirarezaru Gun'i Igaku no Kiseki* 彰古館一知られざる軍医医学の軌跡 [Shōkokan Museum: Unknown Story of Military Doctor Medicine]. Tokyo: Bōeihōmu-shimbunsha, 2009.

Boister, Neil, and Robert Cryer. *The Tokyo International Tribunal: A Reappraisal*. Oxford: Oxford University Press, 2008.

Brackman, Arnold C. *The Other Nuremberg: The Untold Story of the Tokyo War Crimes Trials*. London: William Collins, 1989.

Bugnion, François. "The International Committee of the Red Cross and Nuclear Weapons: From Hiroshima to the Dawn of the 21st Century." *International Review of the Red Cross* 87, no. 859 (2005): 511–24.

Burke, Peter. *Eyewitnessing: The Uses of Images as Historical Evidence*. London: Reaktion, 2001.

Burkman, Thomas W. *Japan and the League of Nations: Empire and World Order, 1914–1938*. Honolulu: University of Hawai'i Press, 2007.

Bush, Lewis William. *Okawaisōni—Tokyo Horyo Shūyōjo no Eihei-kiroku* おかわいそうにー東京捕虜収容所の英兵記録 [Clutch of Circumstance]. Translated by Akashi Yōji 明石洋二. Tokyo: Bumgei-shunjū-shinsha, 1956.

Brecher, Puck W. *Honored and Dishonored Guests: Westerners in Wartime Japan*. London: Harvard University Asia Center, 2017.

Bryer, Ronald E. *White Ghosts of Nagasaki*. North Yorkshire, England: Ronald E. Bryer, 1997.

Cambon, Kenneth M. D. *Guest of Hirohito* ゲスト オブ ヒロヒト：新潟俘虜収容所1941–1945 [Guest of Hirohito: Niigata POW Camp, 1941–1945]. Translated by Mori Masaaki 森正昭. Tokyo: Tsukiji Shokan, 1995.

Caprio, Mark E. *Japanese Assimilation Policies in Colonial Korea, 1910–1945*. Seattle: University of Washington Press, 2009.

Carr, Edward Hallett. *The Twenty Year's Crisis, 1919–1939: An Introduction to the Study of International Relations*. London: Palgrave, 2001.

Cartwright, T. C. *A Date with the Lonesome Lady: A Hiroshima POW Returns*. Fort Worth, TX: Eakin, 2002.

———. "Hiroshima no Hito no Itami wa Watashi no Itami 広島の人の痛みは私の痛み" [Hiroshima's Pain Is My Pain]. *Asahi Shimbun*, October 8, 1999.

Cartwright, T. C., and Mori, S. (trans.). *A Date with the Lonesome Lady: A Hiroshima POW Returns* 爆撃機 ロンサムレディー号：被爆死したアメリカ兵. Translated by Mori Shigeaki 森重昭. Tokyo: NHK Publishing, 2004.

Chaen, Yoshio 茶園義男, ed. *Furyo Jōhōkyoku・Furyo Toriatsukai no Kiroku: Tsuki Kaigun Heigakkō 'Kokusaihō': Jūgonen Sensō Jūyō-bunken Shiriizu, Dai Hasshū* 俘虜情報局・俘虜取扱の記録（付）海軍兵学校『国際法』：十五年戦争重要文献シリーズ 第8集 [Prisoners of War Information Bureau: The Record of POW Treatment, Imperial Japanese Naval Academy "International Law," Important Records of the Fifteen Years' War, Vol. 8]. Tokyo: Fuji Shuppan, 1992.

———. *Furyo ni Kansuru Sho-hōki Ruishū: Jūgonen Sensō Gokuhi Shiryōshū, Dai Jūisshū* 俘虜ニ関スル諸法規類聚：十五年戦争極秘資料集 第十一集 [The Classified Regulations of POW Treatment: Confidential Documents of the Fifteen Years War, Vol. 11]. Tokyo: Fuji Shuppan, 1998.

Chatani, Sayaka. *Nation-Empire: Ideology and Rural Youth Mobilization in Japan and Its Colonies*. Ithaca, NY: Cornell University Press, 2018.

Checkland, Olive. *Humanitarianism and the Emperor's Japan, 1877–1977*. New York: St. Martin's, 1994.

Choi, Hyaeweol. *Gender and Mission Encounters in Korea: New Women, Old Ways*. Berkeley: University of California Press, 2009.

Chung, Soojin. "Woman's Work for Woman: The Controversial Role of Female Missionaries in Korea, 1885–1945." *Fides et Historia* 52, no. 2 (Summer/Fall 2020): 17–27.

Clancey, Gregory K. *Earthquake Nation: The Cultural Politics of Japanese Seismicity*. Berkeley: California University Press, 2006.

Clarke, Hugh V. *Last Stop Nagasaki!* London: George Allen & Unwin Australia, 1984.

———. *Nagasaki Furyo Shūyō-jo* 長崎俘虜収容所 [Nagasaki POW Camp]. Translated by Sonoda Kenji 園田健二. Tokyo: Nagasaki Bunken-sha, 1988.

Clavin, Patricia. "International Organizations." In *The Cambridge History of the Second World War: Volume II Politics and Ideology*, edited by Richard Bosworth and Joseph Maiolo, 139–161. London: Cambridge University Press, 2015.

Collins, Sandra. *The 1940 Tokyo Olympic Games: The Missing Olympics: Japan, the Asian Olympics, and the Olympic Movement*. London: Routledge, 2008.

Connaughton, Richard M. *The War of the Rising Sun and the Tumbling Bear—A Military History of the Russo-Japanese War, 1904-5*. London: Routledge, 1988.

Connie Chow 周琇環, ed. 國民政府時期外交部工作報告〈民國二十二年至二十六年〉 [Report on the Work of the Ministry of Foreign Affairs Under the National Government, 1933–1937]. Taiwan: Academia Historica, 1999.

Conrad, Sebastian. *The Quest for the Lost Nation: Writing History in Germany and Japan in the American Century*. Translated by Alan Nothnagle. Berkeley: University of California Press, 2010.

Cook, Theodore Failor, and Cook Hayuko Taya. *Japan at War: An Oral History*. London: Phoenix, 2000.

Daniels, Gordon. "To Succour Wounded Allies: Japanese Red Cross Nurses in England, 1915–1916." *Japan Society Proceedings*, ISSN: 0952–2050 (2008).

Davidann, Jon T. *The Limits of Westernization: American and East Asian Intellectuals Create Modernity, 1860–1960*. London: Routledge, 2020.

DePies, Gregory John. "Humanitarian Empire: The Red Cross in Japan, 1877–1945." PhD thesis, University of California San Diego, 2013.

De Saint-Exupery, Antonie. *Hoshi no Ōjisama* 星の王子さま [The Little Prince]. Translated by Naitō Arō 内藤濯. Tokyo: Iwanami Shoten, 2017.

Dewey, John. "The Reflex Arc Concept in Psychology." *Psychological Review* 3 (1896): 357–70.

Dittrich, Viviane E., Kerstin von Lingen, Philipp Osten, and Jolana Makraiová, eds. *The Tokyo Tribunal: Perspectives on Law, History and Memory*. Brussels: Torkel Opsahl Academic, 2020.

Doak, Kevin Michael. *A History of Nationalism in Japan: Placing the People*. Leiden: Brill, 2007.

——. "What Is a Nation and Who Belongs? National Narratives and the Ethnic Imagination in Twentieth-Century Japan." *American Historical Review* 102, no. 2 (1997): 283–309.

Domon, Ken 土門拳. *Fūbō* 風貌 [Face with History]. Tokyo: ARS, 1953.

Dower, John W. *Cultures of War: Peal Harbor, Hiroshima, 9–11, IRAQ*. New York: W. W. Norton/New Press, 2010.

——. *Embracing Defeat: Japan in the Wake of World War II*. London: Penguin, 1999.

——. *Japan in War & Peace: Selected Essays*. New York: New Press, 1993.

——. *War Without Mercy: Race and Power in the Pacific War*. London: Faber and Faber, 1986.

Duara, Prasenjit. *Sovereignty and Authenticity: Manchukuo and the East Asian Modern*. Lanham, MD: Rowman & Littlefield, 2003.

Dudden, Alexis. *Japan's Colonization of Korea: Discourse and Power*. Honolulu: University of Hawai'i Press, 2005.

Durand, Andre. *History of the International Committee of the Red Cross: From Sarajevo to Hiroshima*. Geneva: Henry Dunant Institute, 1978.

Duss, Peter. *The Abacus and the Sword: The Japanese Penetration of Korea, 1895–1910*. Berkeley: University of California Press, 1995.

Eccleston, Bernard. *State and Society in Post-War Japan*. Oxford: Polity, 1989.

Eckert, Carter J. *Offspring of Empire: The Koch'ang Kims and the Colonial Origins of Korean Capitalism, 1876–1945*. Seattle: University of Washington Press, 1991.

Endō, Takeo 遠藤健男. *Manshū no Fubuki Manshūkoku Sekijūjisha Chamusu Sekijūjibyōin no Saigo* 満州のふぶき 満州国赤十字社 佳木斯赤十字病院の最後 [Snowstorm in Manchuria: The Manchukuo Red Cross Society, the End of Jiamusi Red Cross Hospital]. Osaka: Sankei Group, 2001.

Endoh, Toake. *Exporting Japan: Politics of Emigration Toward Latin America*. Urbana: University of Illinois Press, 2009.

Enomoto, Shigeharu 榎本重治. *Nihon ni okeru Jin'ai no Seishin no Kigen* 日本における仁愛の精神の起源 [The Birth of Humanitarian Ideas in Japan]. Tokyo: Taisei, 1957.

Fathi, Romain, and Melanie Oppenheimer. "The Shôken Fund and the Evolution of the Red Cross Movement." *European Review of History* 30, no. 5 (June 2023): 812–31.

Favez, Jean-Claude. *The Red Cross and the Holocaust*. Translated by John Fletcher and Beryl Fletcher. London: Cambridge University Press, 1999.

Fibiona, Indra, Siska Nurazizah Lestari, and Ahmad Muhajir. "Uniting in Humanity: The Role of Indonesian Red Cross, 1870–1960." *Indian Historical Studies* 4, no. 1 (2020): 74–83. DOI: 10.14710/ihis.v4i1.8071.

Fletcher-Cooke, John. *The Emperor's Guest, 1942–1945*. London: Leo Cooper, 1972.

Hagakure Kenkyūkai 葉隠研究会. *Hagakure Kenkyū, yonjūkyū gō* 葉隠研究 四十九号 [Hagakure Research, Vol. 49]. Saga: Hagakure Kenkyūkai, 2003.

Forsythe, David P. *Humanitarian Politics: The International Committee of the Red Cross*. Baltimore, MD: Johns Hopkins University Press, 1977.

Forsythe, David P., and Barbra Ann J. Rieffer-Flanagan. *The International Committee of the Red Cross: A Neutral Humanitarian Actor (Global Institutions)*. London: Routledge, 2007.

Fowcus, Harold, "The Fifteenth International Red Cross Conference at Tokyo, October 20–29, 1934." *Journal of the Royal Army Medical Corps* LXIV, no. 3 (March 1935): 145–52.

Framke, Maria. "Indian Humanitarianism Under Colonial Rule: Imperial Loyalty, National Self-Assertion and Anti-Colonial Emancipation." In *The Routledge Handbook of the History of Colonialism in South Asia*, edited by Harald Fischer-Tiné and Maria Framke, 486–509. London: Routledge, 2021.

Framke, Maria, and Esther Moeller. "From Local Philanthropy to Political Humanitarianism: South Asian and Egyptian Humanitarian Aid During the Period of Decolonisation." ZMO Working Papers, no. 22 (2019): 1–17.

Francks, Penelope. *The Japanese Consumer: An Alternative Economic History of Modern Japan*. London: Cambridge University Press, 2009.

———. *Rural Economic Development in Japan: From the Nineteenth Century to the Pacific War*. London: Routledge, 2007.

Fujii, Jun 藤井淳. *Kūkai no Shisōteki Tenkai no Kenkyū* 空海の思想的展開の研究 [Kūkai: The Development of His Philosophy]. Tokyo: Transview, 2008.

Fujimura, Tōru 藤村通, ed. *Matsukata Masayoshi Kankei Monjo, Dai Go-kan* 松方正義関係文書 第五巻 [Documents Related to Matsukata Masayoshi]. Tokyo: Daitōbunka Daigaku Tōyō Kenkyūjo, 1983.

Fujita, Hisakazu 藤田久一. *Kaku ni Tachi-mukau Kokusaihō: Genten kara no Kenshō* 核に立ち向かう国際法：原点からの検証 [Nuclear Weapons' Challenge to International Law: A Fundamental Analysis]. Kyoto: Houritsubunka-sha, 2011.

———. *International Regulation of the Use of Nuclear Weapons*. Oasaka: Kansai University Press, 1988.

Fujitani, Takashi. *Race for Empire: Koreans as Japanese and Japanese as Americans During World War II*. Berkeley: University of California Press, 2011.

Fujiwara, Akira 藤原彰 ed. *Nankin-jiken wo Dou-miruka: Nicchūbei Kenkyūsha ni yoru Kenshō* 南京事件をどうみるか：日・中・米研究者による検証 [How to Interpret the Nanjing Massacre: Analysis by Japanese, Chinese and American Scholars]. Tōkyō: Aoki-shoten, 1998.

———. *Nankin no Nihon-gun: Nankin Daigyakusatsu to sono Haikei* 南京の日本軍：南京大虐殺とその背景 [The Japanese Army in Nanjing: The Background to the Nanjing Massacre]. Tokyo: Ōtsuki-shoten, 1997.

Fukuda, Tetsuko 福田哲子. *Biruma no Fūtaku: Nisseki Jūgun Kangofu ga Mita Biruma Saigo no Hi* ビルマの風鐸：日赤従軍看護婦が見たビルマの最後の日 [Wind Chimes in Burma: Japanese Red Cross Military Nurses on their Last Day in Burma]. Tokyo: Sōbunsha, 1995.

Fukukawa, Hideki 福川秀樹 ed. *Nippon Rikugun Shōkan Jiten* 日本陸軍将官辞典 [Dictionary of Imperial Japanese Imperial Army Officers]. Tokyo: Fuyōshobō, 2001.

Funakoshi, Ioko 舟越五百子. "15 nen Sensō ni okeru Nihon Sekijūjisha no Kango Kyōiku—Kyūgo Kangofu Yōsei no Shisō Tōsei— １５年戦争下における日本赤十字社の看護教育－救護看護婦養成課程の思想統制－" [Japanese Red Cross Society Nursing Education During the Fifteen Years War: The Role of Mindfulness in Relief Nursing Education]. *Tōhoku Daigaku Daigaguin Kyōikugaku Kenkyūka, Kenkyū Nenpō, Dai Gojūnana shū, Dai Ichi-gō* 東北大学大学院教育学研究科研究年報 第５７集 第１号 (2008).

Fussell, Paul. *Thank God for the Atom Bomb and Other Essays*. London: Summit, 1988.

Gailey, Harry A. *Bougainville, 1943–1945: The Forgotten Campaign*. Lexington: University Press of Kentucky, 1991.

Garon, Sheldon M. "From Meiji to Heisei." In *The State and Civil Society in Japan*, edited by Frank J. Schwartz and Susan J. Pharr, 42–62. London: Cambridge University Press, 2003.

——. *Molding Japanese Minds: The State in Everyday Life*. Princeton, NJ: Princeton University Press, 1997.

Gerteis, Christopher. *Gender Struggles: Wage-Earning Women and Male-Dominated Unions in Postwar Japan*. Cambridge, MA: Harvard University Press, 2009.

Gerteis, Christopher, and Timothy S. George. *Japan Since 1945: From Postwar to Post-Bubble*. London: Bloomsbury, 2013.

Gluck, Carol. *Japan's Modern Myths: Ideology in the Late Meiji Period*. Princeton, NJ: Princeton University Press, 1987.

Gluck, Carol, and Stephen R. Graubard, eds. *Showa: The Japan of Hirohito*. New York: W. W. Norton, 1992.

Gordon, Andrew. *A Modern History of Japan: From Tokugawa Times to the Present*. Oxford: Oxford University Press, 2003.

——. *Postwar Japan as History*. Berkeley: University of California Press, 1993.

——. *The Wages of Affluence: Labor and Management in Postwar Japan*. Cambridge, MA: Harvard University Press, 1998.

Hacker, Barton, and Margaret Vining. *A Companion to Women's Military History (History of Warfare)*. London: Brill Academic, 2012.

Haraguchi, Daisuke 原口大輔. *Kizokuin Gichō: Tokugawa Iesato to Meiji Rikken-sei* 貴族院議長・徳川家達と明治立憲制 [The Chairmen of the Japanese House of Peers: Focus on Prince Tokugawa Iesato, the Sixteenth Head of the Tokugawa Family]. Tokyo: Yoshida Shoin, 2018.

——. "Tokugawa Iesato's Political Position Before and After the Washington Conference (1921–22) ワシントン会議前後の徳川家達とその政治的位置." *Kyūshū Shigaku* 九州史学 ISSN 04511638 (2014): 42–60.

Harootunian, Harry. *History's Disquiet: Modernity, Cultural Practice, and the Question of Everyday Life*. New York: Columbia University Press, 2002.

——. *Overcome by Modernity: History, Culture, and Community in Interwar Japan*. Princeton, NJ: Princeton University Press, 2001.

——. *Uneven Moments: Reflections on Japan's Modern History*. New York: Columbia University Press, 2019.

Hardacre, Helen. *Shinto and the State, 1868–1988*. Princeton, NJ: Princeton University Press, 1989.

Hardie, Robert. *The Burma—Siam Railway: The Secret Diary of Dr. Robert Hardie, 1942–45*. London: Imperial War Museum, 1984.
Harrison, Harietta. "Popular Responses to the Atomic Bomb in China, 1945–1966." *Past & Present* 218, suppl_8 (January 1, 2013): 98–116.
Hasegawa, Tsuyoshi. *Racing the Enemy: Stalin, Truman, and the Surrender of Japan*. Cambridge, MA: Belknap Press of Harvard University Press, 2005.
Hatano, Sumio. *One Hundred-Fifty Years of Japanese Foreign Relations: From 1868 to 2018*. Tokyo: Japan Publishing Industry Foundation for Culture (JPIC), 2022.
———. *The Pacific War and Japan's Diplomacy in Asia*. Tokyo: Japan Publishing Industry Foundation for Culture (JPIC), 2021.
Hayashi, Eidai 林えいだい. *Nippon Furyo Shūyō-jo—Sukkechi Shashin-kiroku* にっぽん俘虜収容所ースケッチ写真記録 [POW Camps in Japan: Sketches and Photographs]. Tokyo: Akashi-shoten, 1991.
Hayami, Akira 速水融. *Nihon wo Osotta Supein Infuruenza: Jin'rui to Wirusu no Dai-ichiji Sekai Sensō* 日本を襲ったスペイン・インフルエンザ：人類とウィルスの第一次世界戦争 [The Spanish Flu Pandemic in Japan: The First World War Epidemic and the Human Race]. Tokyo: Fujiwara-shoten, 2006.
Hayasaki, Erina 早崎えりな. *Berurin Tōkyō Monogatari: Ongaku-ka Kurausu Puringusuhaimu* ベルリン東京物語：音楽家クラウス・プリングスハイム [Berlin and Tokyo: The Story of Musician Klaus Pringsheim]. Tokyo: Ongaku no Tomo sha Corp, 1994.
Hein, Laura E., and Mark Selden, eds. *Living with the Bomb: American and Japanese Cultural Conflicts in the Nuclear Age*. London: M. E. Sharpe, 1997.
Henry Dunant Study Center, ed. *Hozutsu no Ato ni: Jūgun Kangofu Kiroku Shashin-shū* 「ほづつのあとに」従軍看護婦記録写真集 [The Aftermath of Gunfire: Photo Album of Red Cross Nurses]. Tokyo: Medical Friend sha, 1981.
Higuchi, Takehiko 樋口雄彦. *Dai Jūroku-dai Tokugawa Iesato—Sono Go no Tokugawa-ke to Kindai Nihon* 第十六代 徳川家達—その後の徳川家と近代日本 [The Tokugawa Family in Modern Japan: Its Sixteenth Head Tokugawa Iesato]. Tokyo: Shōdensha, 2012.
Himeyuri Peace Museum. *Okinawa Rikugun Byōin Kangofu-tachi no Okinawa-sen: Nisengo nen Himeyuri Heiwa Kinen Shiryōkan Kikaku-ten* 沖縄陸軍病院看護婦たちの沖縄戦：２００５年ひめゆり平和祈念資料館企画展 [Nurses at the Okinawa Military Hospital During the Battle of Okinawa: 2005 Himeyuri Peace Memorial Museum Special Exhibition]. Naha: Okinawaken Jyoshi・Ichikō Himeyuri Dōsōkai Himeyuri Heiwa Kinen Shiryō Kan, 2005.
Hiroshima shi Genbaku Taiken-ki Kankō-kai 広島市原爆体験記刊行会編, ed. *Genbaku Taiken-ki* 原爆体験記 [The Record of Experiences of the Atomic Bombing]. Tokyo: Asahi-sensho, 1975.
Hiruma Kishida, Yuka. *Kenkoku University and the Experience of Pan-Asianism: Education in the Japanese Empire*. London: Bloomsbury Academic, 2020.
Hofmann, Reto. *The Fascist Effect: Japan and Italy, 1915–1952*. Ithaca, NY: Cornell University Press, 2015.
Holmes, Linda Goetz. *Guests of the Emperor: The Secret History of Japan's Mukden POW Camp*. London: Naval Institute Press, 2010.
Hoshina, Yukiko 保科順子. *Hana-aoi: Tokugawa-tei Omoide-banashi* 花葵：徳川邸おもいで話 [Flower *Aoi*: Memories of the Tokugawa Palace]. Tokyo: Mainichi Shimbunsha, 1998.

Hora, Tomio 洞富雄. *Nicchū Sensō Daizangyaku-jiken Shiryōshū, Dai Ni-Kan* 日中戦争南京大残虐事件資料集 第二巻 [Records of the Nanjing Massacre During the Second Sino-Japanese War, Vol. 2]. Tokyo: Aoki-shoten, 1985.

———. *Nicchū Sensō Shi Shiryō 8: Nankin Jiken I* 日中戦争史資料 8：南京事件 I [Documents on the History of the Second Sino-Japanese War, Vol. 8: Nanjing Incident, I]. Tokyo: Kawade Shobō Shinsha, 1973.

———. *Nicchū Sensō Shi Shiryō 9: Nankin Jiken II* 日中戦争史資料 9：南京事件 I [Documents on the History of the Second Sino-Japanese War, Vol. 9: Nanjing Incident, II]. Tokyo: Kawade Shobō Shinsha, 1973.

Hurd, Charles. *The Compact History of the American Red Cross: The Story of the Red Cross Volunteers and the Organization in Which They Serve*. New York: Hawthorn, 1959.

Hutchinson, John F. *Champions of Charity: War and the Red Cross*. Oxford: Westview, 1997.

Ibuse, Masuji 井伏鱒二. *Kuroi Ame* 黒い雨 [Black Rain]. Tokyo: Shinchosha Bunko, 1970.

Iimori, Akiko 飯森明子. "初期汎太平洋同盟（PPU）と日本の対応：IPRへの日本の原点 Pan-Pacific Union and Japan's Attitude in the Early 1920s: A Study of the Origin of the IPR Conference." *Journal of Asia-Pacific Studies*, no. 35 (January 2019): 30–42.

———. "Sekijūji Kokusai Kaigi to Tōkyō Shōchi Mondai 赤十字国際会議と東京招致問題" [The International Conference of the Red Cross and Issues Regarding the Invitation to Tokyo]. *Tokiwa Kokusai Kiyō* 常盤国際紀要. ISSN. 13430645 (2002): 51–71.

I'ino, Masako 飯野正子, Kimura Kenji 木村健二, and Kumei Teruko 粂井輝, eds. *Sensō to Nihonjin Imin* 戦争と日本人移民 [War and Japanese Immigrants]. Tokyo: Toyo Shorin, 1997.

Inochi no Tō Shukishū Hensan-i'inkai いのちの塔手記集編纂委員会編, ed. *Inochi no Tō: Hiroshima Sekijūji, Genbaku-byōin eno Shōgen* いのちの塔 広島赤十字・原爆病院への証言 [Monument to Life: Testimonies of Workers from Hiroshima Red Cross Hospital & Atomic-bomb Survivors Hospital]. Hiroshima: Chūgoku-shimbunsha, 1992.

Iokibe, Makoto 五百旗頭真. *Daisaigai no Jidai: Sandai Shinsai kara Kangaeru* 大災害の時代：三大震災から考える [The Era of Great Disasters: Japan and Its Three Major Earthquakes]. Tokyo: Iwanami Shoten, 2023.

Ishi, Yoshikuni 石南国. *Kankoku no Jinkō Zōka no Bunseki* 韓国の人口増加の分析 [Analysis of Population Growth in Korea]. Tokyo: Keiso, 1972.

Irie, Akira 入江昭. *Rekishi wo Manabu toiukoto* 歴史を学ぶということ [What Is Studying History?]. Tokyo: Kodansha, 2005.

———. *Rekishika ga Miru Gendai Sekai* 歴史家が見る現代世界 [Historians' Views on the Contemporary World]. Tokyo: Kodansha, 2014.

Irie, Keishirō 入江啓四郎, and Ōhata Tokushirō 大畑篤四郎. *Jūtei: Gaikōshi Teiyō* 重訂 外交史提要 [Synopsis of Diplomatic History]. Tokyo: Seibundō, 1964.

Iriye, Akira. *Cultural Internationalism and World Order*. Baltimore, MD: Johns Hopkins University Press, 1997.

———. *Global and Transnational History: The Past, Present, and Future*. New York: Palgrave Macmillan, 2013.

———. *Global Community: The Role of International Organizations in the Making of the Contemporary World*. Berkeley: University of California Press, 2004.

Irwin, Julia F. *Catastrophic Diplomacy: US Foreign Disaster Assistance in the American Century*. Chapel Hill: University of North Carolina Press, 2023.

———. *Making the World Safe: The America Red Cross and a Nation's Humanitarian Awakening*. Oxford: Oxford University Press, 2013.

Isami, Tomoyuki 勇知之, and Nihon Sekijūjisha 日本赤十字社. *Seinan Sensō to Hakuaisha Sōsetsu Hiwa: Nihon Sekijūjisha Hasshō Monogatari* 西南戦争と博愛社創設秘話：日本赤十字社発祥物語 [The Satsuma Rebellion and the Secret History of the Hakuaisha Foundation: The Story of the Foundation of the Japanese Red Cross Society]. Kumamoto: Nihon Sekijūjisha Kumamotoken-shibu, 2010.

Ishibiki, Michi 石引ミチ. *Jūgun Kangofu: Nisseki Kyūgohan Hitō Haisōki* 従軍看護婦：日赤救護班比島敗走記 [Military Nurses: The Japanese Red Cross Medical Teams from the Philippines]. Tokyo: Gendaishi Shuppankai, Tokuma Shoten, 1979.

Iwasaki, Nobuhiko 岩崎信彦, Ueda Tadakazu 上田惟一, Hirohara Moriaki 広原盛明, Ajisaka Manabu 鯵坂学, Takagi Masao 高木正朗, and Yoshihara Naoki 吉原直樹, eds. *Zōhoban Chōnaikai no Kenkyū* 増補版：町内会の研究 [Expanded Edition: Chōnaikai Studies]. Tokyo: Ochanomizu-shobō, 2013.

Iwasawa Yūji 岩沢雄司, ed. *International Law Documents, 2018* 国際法条約集 2018年版. Tokyo: Yūhikaku, 2018.

Japanese Red Cross Institute for Humanitarian Studies, ed. *Journal of Humanitarian Studies* 2 (March 2013). Tokyo: Japanese Red Cross Institute for Humanitarian Studies, 2013.

———. Vol. 4. Tokyo: Japanese Red Cross Institute for Humanitarian Studies, 2015.

Jien 慈円. *Gukanshō: Zen Gendaigo-yaku* 愚管抄：全現代語訳 [Theory of History: Jottings of a Fool: An Interpretation of Present Times]. Translated by Ōsumi Kazuo 大隅和雄. Tokyo: Kodansha Gakujutu-bunko.

Jūgun Kangofu-tachi no Daitōa Sensō Kankō I'inkai 従軍看護婦たちの大東亜戦争刊行委員会. *Jūgun Kangofu-tachi no Daitōa Sensō—Watashi-tachi wa Nani wo Mita-noka* 従軍看護婦たちの大東亜戦争—私たちは何を見たか [Military Nurses in the Pacific War: What We Saw]. Tokyo: Shōdensha, 2006.

Junod, Marcel. "Dr. Junod's Report on 9 November 1945." Translated by Ōkawa Shirō 大川四郎. *Journal of Humanitarian Studies* 2 (March 2013): 146–56.

———. *Warrior Without Weapons*. London: Alden, 1951.

Kageyama, Sadaka 陰山寀. *Nihon Sekijūji Damashii: Nisseki Shanhai Haken Tokubetsu Kyūgohan no Ki* 日本赤十字魂：日赤上海派遣特別救護班の記 [Spirit of the Red Cross: The Record of the Japanese Red Cross Society Shanghai Special Expeditionary Relief Corps]. Tokyo: Shufu no Tomo Shuppan Service Centre, 1971.

Kamino, Tomoya 上野友也. *Sensō to Jindō Shien: Sensō no Hisai wo meguru Jindō no Seiji* 戦争と人道支援：戦争の被災をめぐる人道の政治 [War and Humanitarian Assistance: The Politics of Humanitarian Aid to War Victims]. Sendai: Tohoku University Press, 2002.

Kamo no Chōmei 鴨長明. *Hōjōki* 方丈記 [An Account of My Ten Foot Square Hut]. Translated by Asami Kazuhiko 浅見和彦. Tokyo: Chikuma-shobō, 2011.

———. *Hōjōki: A Hermit's Hut as Metaphor*. Translated by Matthew Stavros. Japan: Vicus Lusorum, 2020.

Kang, Duk-sang. *Kantō Daishinsai* 関東大震災 [Great Kantō Earthquake]. Tokyo: Chūkō-shinsho, 1975.

Kang, Duk-sang. *Kantō Daishinsai: Gyakusatsu no Kioku* 関東大震災：虐殺の記憶 [Great Kantō Earthquake: Recalling the Massacre]. Tokyo: Seikyūbunkasha, 2003.

Katō, Michiko 加藤三千子. *Hakui no Fūgetsuka: Passhigu Kahan: Nihon Sekijūji Jūgun Kangofu Kaisōki* 白衣の風月花：パッシグ河畔: 日本赤十字従軍看護婦回想記 [Flourence in White Vestments: Pasig City: Memoirs of Japanese Red Cross Military Nurses]. Tokyo: Hyūman Dokyumentosha, 1990.

Katō, Shimei 加藤子明. *Nihon no Gensō: Geijutsuka Kurausu Puringusuhaimu no Shōgai* 日本の幻想 芸術家クラウス・プリングスハイムの生涯 [Japan's Fantasy: The Life of an Artist, Klaus Pringsheim]. Tokyo: Kangensha, 1950.

Katō, Yōko 加藤陽子. *Chōhei-sei to Kindai Nippon: 1868–1945* 徴兵制と近代日本：1868–1945 [Conscription and Modern Japan, 1868–1945]. Tokyo: Yoshikawa Kōbunkan, 1996.

———. *Manshū Jihen kara Nicchū Sensō e—Shirīzu Nihon Kin-gendaishi (5)* 満州事変から日中戦争へーシリーズ日本近現代史〈5〉 [From the Manchurian Incident to the Second Sino-Japanese War: Japanese Modern and Contemporary History, Vol. 5]. Tokyo: Iwanami Shoten, 2007.

———. *Sensō no Nihon Kin'gendai-shi: Tōdai-shiki Lessun! Seikanron kara Taiheiyō Sensō made* 戦争の日本近現代史 東大式レッスン！征韓論から太平洋戦争まで [Japanese Modern and Contemporary Wartime History: University of Tokyo Style Lectures! From Advocacy of the Invasion of Korea to the Pacific War]. Tokyo: Kodansha, 2002.

———. *Soredemo Nihon-jin wa 'Sensō' wo Eranda* それでも、日本人は「戦争」を選んだ [Despite Everything, Japanese Chose War]. Tokyo: Asahi Shuppan-sha, 2010.

Kameyama, Michiko 亀山美知子. *Kindai Nihon Kangoshi: I, Nihon Sekijūjisha to Kango* 近代日本の看護史: 日本赤十字社と看護 [History of Nursing in Modern Japan: Vol. 1, the Japanese Red Cross Society and Nurses]. Tokyo: Domesu, 1984.

Käser, Frank. "A Civilized Nation: Japan and the Red Cross 1877–1900." *European Review of History* 23, no. 1–2 (March 2016): 16–32.

Kawai, Toshinobu 河合利修. "Nihon Sekijūjisha no Kokusaiteki Tenkai to Heiji Jigyō 日本赤十字社の国際的展開と平時事業" [The International Development and Peacetime Activities of the Japanese Red Cross Society]. In *Nihon Sekijūjisha to Jindō Enjo* 日本赤十字社と人道援助 [The Japanese Red Cross Society and Humanitarian Assistance], edited by Kurosawa Fumitaka 黒沢貴文 and Kawai Toshinobu 河合利修, 227–68. Tokyo: University of Tokyo Press, 2009.

Kawaguchi, Keiko 川口啓子, and Kurokawa Akiko 黒川章子. *Jūgun Kangofu to Nihon Sekijūjisha: Sono Rekishi to Jūgun Shōgen* 従軍看護婦と日本赤十字社：その歴史と従軍証言 [Military Nurses and the Japanese Red Cross Society: History and Testimonies]. Kyoto: Tosho-shuppan Bunrikaku, 2008.

Kawashima, Midori 川嶋みどり, Kawahara Yukari 川原由佳里, Yamazaki Yūji 山崎裕二, and Yoshikawa Ryūko 吉川龍子. *Sensō to Kangofu* 戦争と看護婦 [Wars and Nurses]. Tokyo: Tosho Kankōkai, 2016.

Kawahara, Yukari 川原由佳里. "Biruma-sen ni okeru Nihon Sekijūjisha Kyūgo Kangofu no Katsudō (1): Nichijō no Eisei-shien no Seido to Jittai ni Shōten wo Atete ビルマ戦における日本赤十字社救護看護婦の活動（1）：日常の衛生支援の制度と実態に焦点をあてて" [Activities of Japanese Red Cross Society Relief Nurses During the Burma Campaign, Vol. 1: System and Reality of Daily Medical Assistance]. *Heisei 25, 26 nendo, Gakkōhōjin Nihon Sekijūjigakuen: Sekijūji to Kango · Kaigo ni Kansuru Kenkyūjosei: Kenkyū Hōkokusho*

平成２５，２６年度「学校法人日本赤十字学園 赤十字と看護・介護に関する研究助成」研究報告書 (March 2015): 28–43.

———. "125-Year History of the Japanese Red Cross Nursing Education." *Journal of Humanitarian Studies* 4 (March 2015): 93–101. Tokyo: Japanese Red Cross Institute for Humanitarian Studies.

Kawahara, Yukari 川原由佳里, Yamazaki Yūji 山崎裕二, Takano Tomomi 鷹野朋実, Yoshikawa Ryūko 吉川龍子, and Kawashima Midori 川嶋みどり. "Dainiji Sekaitaisen ni okeru Nihon Sekijūjisha no Kyūgohan no Katsudō 第二次世界大戦における日本赤十字社救護班の活動" [The Relief Activities of the Japanese Red Cross Society's Medical Parties During the Second World War]. *Heisei 25, 26 nendo, Gakkōhōjin Nihon Sekijūjigakuen: Sekijūji to Kango・Kaigo ni Kansuru Kenkyūjosei: Kenkyū Hōkokusho* 平成２５，２６年度「学校法人日本赤十字学園 赤十字と看護・介護に関する研究助成」研究報告書 (March 2015).

Keene, Donald and Shiba Ryotaro. *The People and Culture of Japan: Conversation Between Donald Keene and Shiba Ryotaro*. Translated by Tony Gonzalez. Tokyo: Japan Publishing Industry Foundation for Culture, 2016.

Kenjō, Teiji 見城 悌治. "Meiji kara Shōwa-ki no Chiba Igaku Sen'mon Gakkō, Chiba Ikagaigaku ni okeru Ryūgakusei no Dōkō 明治〜昭和期の千葉医学専門学校・千葉医科大学における留学生の動向" [The History of Foreign Students at Chiba Medical College and Chiba Medical University from Meiji to Early Showa Period]. *Kokusai Kyōiku* 2 (March 2009): 11–62. Accessed March 28, 2022. https://opac.ll.chiba-u.jp/da/curator/900116289/kokusaikyouiku_2_11.pdf.

Kita, Yoshito 喜多義人. "Junēbu Jōyaku Teiyakukoku-kan no Nichiro Sensō ジュネーブ条約締約国間の日露戦争" [The Geneva Conventions and the Russo-Japanese]. In *Nihon Sekijūjisha to Jindō Enjo* 日本赤十字社と人道援助 [The Japanese Red Cross Society and Humanitarian Assistance], edited by Kurosawa Fumitaka 黒沢貴文 and Kawai Toshinobu 河合利修, 105–39. Tokyo: University of Tokyo Press, 2009.

Kim, Sonja M. *Imperatives of Care: Women and Medicine in Colonial Korea*. Honolulu: University of Hawai'i Press, 2019.

Komiya, Mayumi 小宮まゆみ. *Tekikoku-jin Yokuryū—Senji-ka no Gaikoku Minkan-jin: Rekishi Bunka Laiburari* 敵国人抑留―戦時下の外国民間人（歴史ライブラリー） [Enemy Internees: Foreign Civilians During the War (History Library)]. Tokyo: Yoshikawa Kōbunkan, 2009.

Kobayashi, Kiyoko 小林清子, Ōhara Yasuo 大原康男, and Fukiura Tadamasa 吹浦忠正, eds. *Hozutsu no Ato ni: Junshoku Jūgun Kangofu Tsuitō Ki: Memories of War-Dead Red Cross Nurses*, Vol. 1 ほづつのあとに 殉職従軍看護婦追悼記 [The Aftermath of Gunfire: Memorializing Red Cross Nurses Who Died in War, Vol. 1]. Tokyo: Henry Dunant Study Center, 1977.

Kobayashi, Kiyoko 小林清子, Tanaka Sumako 田中須磨子, Ōhara Yasuo 大原康男, and Fukiura Tadamasa 吹浦忠正, eds. *Zoku Hozutsu no Ato ni: Junshoku Jūgun Kangofu Tsuitō Ki: Memories of War-Dead Red Cross Nurses*, Vol. 2 続 ほづつのあとに 殉職従軍看護婦追悼記 [The Aftermath of Gunfire: Memorializing Red Cross Nurses Who Died in War, Vol. 2]. Tokyo: Henry Dunant Study Center, 1978.

———. *Zoku-zoku Hozutsu no Ato ni: Junshoku Jūgun Kangofu Tsuitō Ki: Memories of War-Dead Red Cross Nurses*, Vol. 3 続々 ほづつのあとに 殉職従軍看護婦追悼記 [The Aftermath of Gunfire: Memorializing Red Cross Nurses Who Died in War, Vol. 3]. Tokyo: Henry Dunant Study Center, 1980.

Kojima, Noboru 児島襄. *Tennō, 5* 天皇 5 [Emperor, Vol. 5]. Tokyo: Kazetto Shuppan, 2007.

Konishi, Sho. "The Emergence of an International Humanitarian Organization in Japan: The Tokugawa Origins of the Japanese Red Cross." *American Historical Review* 114, no. 4 (October 2014): 1129–53.

Kono, Toru. "Lieutenant Colonel Shigeo Emoto: Soldier and Teacher." *Bulletin of Tokyo Kasei University Kiyō Dai 33 Shū* 1 (October 1993): 1–18.

Konoe, Fumimaro. *The Memoirs of Prince Fumimaro Konoye*. Tokyo: Okuyama, 1946.

Korson, George. *At His Side: The Story of the American Red Cross Overseas in World War II*. New York: Coward-McCann, 1945.

Kosuge, Nobuko M. "Prompt and Utter Destruction: The Nagasaki Disaster and the Initial Medical Relief." *International Review of the Red Cross* 866, no. 89 (2007): 279–303.

Kosuge, Nobuko 小菅信子. *Nihon Sekijūjisha to Kōshitsu: Hakuai ka Hōkoku ka* 日本赤十字社と皇室：博愛か報国か [Japanese Red Cross Society and the Imperial Family: Benevolence or Patriotic Services]. Tokyo: Yoshikawa Kōbunkan, 2021.

Kovner, Sarah. *Prisoners of the Empire: Inside Japanese POW Camps*. Cambridge, MA: Harvard University Press, 2020.

Kowner, Rotem. "Becoming an Honorary Civilized Nation: Remaking Japan's Military Image During the Russo-Japanese War, 1904–1905." *Historian* 64, no. 1 (2001): 19–38.

Kratoska, Paul H., ed. *Asian Labor in the Wartime Japanese Empire: Unknown History*. London: East Gate, 2005.

Kuba, Chie 久場千恵. *Kanashii Tsuioku Sekijūji Kyūgo Kangofu Jūnanasai no Okianawa-sen, Ima Heiwa wo Motomete* 悲しい追憶 赤十字救護看護婦十七歳の沖縄戦、今平和を求めて [Sorrowful Memories: Seventeen-Year-Old Red Cross Nurses in the Battle of Okinawa]. Okinawa: Nanyō-Bunko, 2004.

Kuni, Takeyuki 國雄行. *Saga Ijin-den, 09: Sano Tsunetami, 1822–1902* 佐賀偉人伝, 09: 佐野常民, 1822–1902 [The Biography of Sano Tsunetami]. Saga: Saga Kenritsu Sagajō Honmaru Rekishi-kan, 2013.

Kupchinsky, F. P. In *Matsuyama Horyo Shūyōjo Nikki: Roshia Shōkō no Mita Meiji Nippon* 松山捕虜収容所日記：ロシア将校の見た明治日本 [Diary from the Matsuyama POW Camp: A Russian Military Officer in Meiji Japan]. Translated by Odagawa Kenji 小田川研二. Tokyo: Chūōkōronsha, 1988.

Kuroki, Yūji 黒木雄司. *Genbaku Tōka wa Yokoku sarete-ita! Dai-go Kōkū Jōhō Rentai Jōhōshitsu Kinmusha no Kiroku* 原爆投下は予告されていた！第五航空情報連隊情報室勤務者の記録 [The Atomic Bombing Was Expected: The Record of an Officer of the Fifth Air Intelligence Regiment Information Office]. Tokyo: Kōjin-sha, 1992.

Kurosawa, Fumitaka 黒沢貴文. "Kindai Nihon to Sekijūji 近代日本と赤十字" [Modern Japan and the Red Cross]. In *Nihon Sekijūjisha to Jindō Enyo* 日本赤十字社と人道援助 [The Japanese Red Cross Society and Humanitarian Assistance], edited by Kurosawa Fumitaka 黒沢貴文 and Kawai Toshinobu 河合利修, 1–36. Tokyo: University of Tokyo Press, 2009.

Kurosawa, Fumitaka 黒沢文貴, and Kawai Toshinobu 河合利修, eds. *Nihon Sekijūjisha to Jindō Enjo* 日本赤十字社と人道援助 [The Japanese Red Cross Society and Humanitarian Assistance]. Tokyo: University of Tokyo Press, 2009.

Kusama, Hidesaburō 草間秀三郎. *Aa, Hakuai-maru: Sekijūji Byōin sen no Saigo* ああ、博愛丸—赤十字病院船の最期 [Oh, Hakuai Maru: The Last Moments of a Red Cross Medical Ship]. Tokyo: Nippon Tosho Kankōkai, 2013.

———. "President Wilson and the Idea of the International Red Cross ウィルソン大統領と国際赤十字構想." *Chiiki-kenkyū Sōsho. Dai San-kan. Eibei no Seiji Gaikō* 地域研究叢書 第3巻「英米の政治外交」 [Area Studies Library, Vol. 3, "Political Diplomacy of the UK and the US"]. Nagoya: International Research Centre, Aichi Gakuin University, 2005.

Kushner, Barak, and Muminov Sherzod. eds. *The Dismantling of Japan's Empire in East Asia: Deimperialization, Postwar Legitimation and Imperial Afterlife.* London: Routledge, 2017.

Large, Stephen S. "Nationalist Extremism in Early Shōwa Japan: Inoue Nisshō and the 'Blood-Pledge Corps Incident', 1932." *Modern Asian Studies* 35, no. 3 (July 2001): 533–64.

Lee, Ogcheol. "Red Cross Nursing Education in Korea: 1920–2014." *Journal of Humanitarian Studies* 4 (March 2015): 75–79.

Lesser, Jeffrey. "Immigration and Shifting Concepts of National Identity in Brazil During the Vargas Era." *Luso-Brazilian Review* 31, no. 2, University of Wisconsin Press (Winter 1994): 23–44.

———. *Negotiating National Identity: Immigrants, Minorities, and the Struggle for Ethnicity in Brazil.* Durham, NC: Duke University Press, 1999.

Lincicome, Mark. *Imperial Subjects as Global Citizens: Nationalism, Internationalism, and Education in Japan.* Lanham, MD: Lexington Books, 2009.

Liu, Michael Shiyung. *Prescribing Colonization: The Role of Medical Practices and Policies in Japan-Ruled Taiwan, 1895–1945.* Ann Arbor, MI: Association for Asian Studies, 2009.

Loye, Dominique, and Coupland Robin. "International Assistance for Victims of Use of Nuclear, Radiological, Biological and Chemical Weapons: Time for a Reality Check?" *International Review of the Red Cross* 91, no. 874 (June 2009): 329–40.

———. "Who Will Assist the Victims of Use of Nuclear, Radiological, Biological and Chemical Weapons—and How?" *International Review of the Red Cross* 89, no. 866 (June 2007): 329–44.

MacCarthy, Aidan. *A Doctor's War.* London: Grub Street, 2006.

Mahon, Michael. *Foucault's Nietzschean Genealogy: Truth, Power, and the Subject.* Albany, NY: State University of New York Press, 1992.

Makita, Yoshiya 牧田義也. *Jindō no Chiseigaku: Hawaii ni Okeru Sekijūji Jigyō to Jindōshugi wo Meguru Hōbunka no Hen'yō* 人道の地政学：ハワイにおける赤十字事業と人道主義をめぐる法文化の変容 [Geopolitics of Humanitarianism: Changes of Legal Culture with the Red Cross Operations and Humanitarianism in Hawai'i]. In *"Hō Bunkaken" to America: Nijusseiki Toransu Nashonaru Historii no Shin-shikaku* 「法—文化圏」とアメリカ：２０世紀トランスナショナル・ヒストリーの新視角 [Twentieth-Century Transnational America: The Formation and the Transformation of Legal-Cultural Spheres], edited by Ishii Noriko 石井紀子 and Imano Yuko 今野裕子, 25–58. Tokyo: Sophia University Press, 2022.

———. "Jindō, Teikoku, Shokuminchi: Dai Ichiji Sekaitaisen-ki no Ajia Taiheiyō Chiiki ni Okeru Kokusai Sekijūji Undō 人道・帝国・植民地：第一次世界大戦のアジア太平洋地域に

おける国際赤十字運動" [Humanitarianism, Empire and Colonization: The International Red Cross Movement in the Asia-Pacific Region During the First World War]. *Journal of Humanitarian Studies, Japanese Red Cross Institute for Humanitarian Studies* 8 (Tokyo: Tōshindō, 2019): 50–60.

———. "Shokuminchi-ki Firipin ni Okeru Hoken Eisei Jigyō to Sekijūji Jindōshugi 植民地期フィリピンにおける保健衛生事業と赤十字人道主義" [Public Health and the Red Cross Humanitarianism in the Colonial Philippines]. *America Kenkyū* アメリカ研究 [Japanese Journal of American Studies] 56 (March 2022): 69–91.

———. "The Ambivalent Enterprise: Medical Activities of the Red Cross Society of Japan in the Northeastern Region of China During the Russo-Japanese War." In *Entangled Histories: The Transcultural Past of Northeast China*, edited by Dan Ben-Canaan, Frank Grüner, and Ines Prodöhl, 189–203. Heidelberg: Springer, 2014.

Manela, Erez. *The Wilsonian Moment: Self-Determination and the International Origins of Anticolonial Nationalism*. Oxford: Oxford University Press, 2007.

Maruhama, Eriko 丸浜江里子. *Gensuibaku Shomei Undō no Tanjō: Tōkyō Suginami no Jūmin Pawā to Suimyaku* 原水爆署名運動の誕生：東京・杉並の住民パワーと水脈 [The Birth of Hydrogen Bomb Ban Petition Movement: Wellspring of the Power of the People of Suginami District, Tokyo]. Tokyo: Yushisha, 2021.

Maruyama, Masao. *Thought and Behaviour in Modern Japanese Politics*. London: Oxford University Press, 1963.

Masamura, Kimihiro 正村公宏. *Sengo-shi Jō* 戦後史 上 [Post-War History, Vol. 1]. Tokyo: Chikuma shobō, 1990.

———. [Vol. 2]. Tokyo: Chikuma shobō, 1990.

Masui, Takashi 桝居孝. "Relief Activities of Kansai and Adjacent Local Governments During the Great Kanto Earthquake in 1923 関東大震災の被災者に対する関西諸府県及び近隣県の救援活動—大阪府と日本赤十字社の当時の記録からの一考察." *Journal of Humanitarian Studies* 4 (March 2015): 172–87.

———. *Taiheiyō Sensō-chū no Kokusai Jindō Katsudō no Kiroku (Kaitei-ban)* 太平洋戦争中の国際人道活動の記録（改訂版）[The Record of International Relief Activities During the Pacific War (Revised Edition)]. Tokyo: Nihon Sekijūjisha, 1994.

———. *Sekai to Nihon no Sekijūji* 世界と日本の赤十字 [The Red Cross in the World and Japan]. Tokyo: Taimusu, 1999.

Masui, Takashi 桝居孝, and Mori Masanao 森正尚. *Shinban Sekai to Nihon no Sekijūji: Sekaisaidai no Jindō Shien Kikan no Katsudō* 新版 世界と日本の赤十字-世界最大の人道支援機関の活動 [The Red Cross in the World and Japan: The Activities of the World's Largest Humanitarian Organization: New Edition]. Tokyo: Tōshindō, 2014.

Matsui, Yoshirō 松井芳郎, Saburi Haruo 佐分晴夫, Sakamoto Shigeki 坂元茂樹, Obata Kaoru 小畑郁, Matsuda Takeo 松田竹男, Tanaka Norio 田中則夫, Okada Izumi 岡田泉, and Yakushiji Kimio 薬師寺公夫. *Kokusaihō Dai Go-han* 国際法 第5版 [International Law, Vol. 5]. Tokyo: Yūhikaku, 2012.

Matsuki, Hidefumi 松木秀文, and Yaku Yasuhiro 夜久恭裕. *Genbaku Tōka Mokusatsu sareta Gokuhi Jōhō* 原爆投下 黙殺された極秘情報 [Atomic Bombing: Secret Information Was Pigeonholed]. Tokyo: NHK Publishing, 2012.

Mazlish, Bruce. *The Idea of Humanity in a Global Era.* New York: Palgrave Macmillan, 2009.
McCormack, Gavan. *The Emptiness of Japanese Affluence: Revised Edition.* New York: East Gate, 2001.
Michino, Gregory F. *Death on the Hellships: Prisoners at Sea in the Pacific War.* Annapolis, MD: Naval Institute Press, 2001.
Miller, Ian J. *The Nature of the Beasts: Empire and Exhibition at Tokyo Imperial Zoo.* Berkeley: University of California Press, 2013.
Minohara, Tosh, Hon Tze-Ki, and Dawley Evan, eds. *The Decade of the Great War: Japan and the Wider World in the 1910s.* Leiden: Brill, 2014.
Mita, Chiyoko 三田千代子. "Burajiru ni Okeru Kokumin-kokka no Keisei to Nihon Imin ブラジルにおける国民国家の形成と日本人移民" [Brazil Nation-Building and Japanese Immigrants]. In *Sensō to Nihon-jin Imin* 戦争と日本人移民 [War and Japanese Immigrants], edited by I'ino Masako 飯野正子, Kimura Kenji 木村健二, and Kumei Teruko 粂井輝子, 285–308. Tokyo: Toyo Shorin, 1997.
Miyabe, Ichizō 宮部一三. *Hakui no Tenshi: Biruma Saizensen, Jūgun Kangofu Shitō no Shuki* 白衣の天使：ビルマ最前線 従軍看護婦死闘の手記 [Angels in White: Memories of the Battlefield Nurses in Burma]. Tokyo: Soubunsha, 1982.
———. *Shindemo Horyo ni Naranaide: Biruma Nisseki Wakayama Jūgun Kangofu no Higeki* 死んでも捕虜にならないで：ビルマ・日赤和歌山従軍看護婦の悲劇 [Die Rather Than Be Taken Captive: Japanese Red Cross Society Nurses from Wakayama Chapter in Burma During the Pacific War]. Tokyo: Soubunsha, 1996.
Miyashita, Miyoko 宮下美代子. *Ashita naki shunjū: Hachirogun to Kōdō wo Tomoni shite* 晨なき春秋：八路軍と行動を共にして [Medical Service for the Eighth Route Army]. Tokyo Nihon Kango Kyōkai Shuppankai, 1979.
Miyoshi, Masao. *Off Center: Power and Culture Relations Between Japan and the United States.* Cambridge, MA: Harvard University Press, 1998.
Miyoshi, Masao, and Harry Harootunian, eds. *Postmodernism and Japan.* Durham, NC: Duke University Press, 1989.
Mizui, Kiyoko 水井潔子, and Mizui Katsura 水井桂. *Jūgun Kangofu Monogatari—Nisseki Kangofu no Mita Chūgoku Sensen* 従軍看護婦物語―日赤看護婦の見た中国戦線 [The Story of Military Nurses: Japanese Red Cross Nurses in the Second Sino-Japanese War]. Tokyo: Kōjinsha, 2007.
Moeller, Esther. "The Suez Crisis of 1956 as a Moment of Transnational Humanitarian Engagement." *European Review of History* 23, nos. 1–2 (January 2016): 136–53.
Molony, Barbara, and Kathleen S. Uno. *Gendering Modern Japanese History.* Cambridge, MA: Harvard University Press, 2005.
Moore, Aaron William. *Writing War: Soldiers Record the Japanese Empire.* Cambridge, MA: Harvard University Press, 2013.
Moorehead, Caroline. *Dunant's Dream: War, Switzerland and the History of the Red Cross.* London: Carroll & Graf, 1999.
Mori, Shigeaki 森重昭. *Genbaku de Shinda Beihei-hishi* 原爆で死んだ米兵秘史 [The Secret History of American POW Atomic Bomb Victims]. Tokyo: Kōbun-sha, 2008.
Mori, Shigeaki 森重昭, Mori Kyoko 森佳代子, Soejima Hideki 副島秀樹, eds. *Genbaku no Higeki ni Kokkyō wa Nai: Hibakusha・Mori Shigeaki Chōsa to Irei no Hansei* 原爆の悲劇に

国境はない：被爆者・森重昭 調査と慰霊の半生 [Global Tragedy of Atomic Bombing: Atomic Bomb Victim Mori Shigeaki a Life of Inquiry and Consoling]. Tokyo: Asahi Shimbun Shuppan, 2023.

Mori, Reiko 森禮子. *Kenshin: Hagiwara Take no Shōgai* 献身：萩原タケの生涯 [Dedication: Biography of Hagiwara Take]. Tokyo: KK. Sanshusha, 1995.

Moto Nisseki Jūgun Kangofu no Kai 元日赤従軍看護婦の会, ed. *Nihon Sekijūji Jūgun Kangofu: Senjō ni Sasageta Seishun* 日本赤十字従軍看護婦：戦場に捧げた青春 [Japanese Red Cross Society Nurses on the Battlefield]. Tokyo: Moto Nisseki Jūgun Kangofu no Kai, 1985.

——. [Vol. 2]. Tokyo: Moto Nisseki Jūgun Kangofu no Kai, 1988.

Moriya, Misa 守屋ミサ. *Jūgun Kangofu no Mita Byōin-sen—Hiroshima-: Aru Yōgo-kyōyu no Gen-taiken* 従軍看護婦の見た病院船・ヒロシマ ある養護教諭の原体験 [A Military Nurse on a Medical Ship: Experience of a School Nurse]. Tokyo: Nōsan Gyoson Bunka Kyōkai, 1998.

Murakami, Yōichirō 村上陽一郎. *Shiru wo Manabu: Aratamete Gakumon no Susume* 知るを学ぶ：あらためて学問のすすめ [Acquiring Knowledge: Revival of an Encouragement of Learning]. Tokyo: Kawade Shobō Shinsha, 2011.

Myers, Ramon H., and Mark R. Peattie, eds. *The Japanese Colonial Empire, 1895–1945*. Princeton, NJ: Princeton University Press, 1984.

Nagai, Hitoshi 永井均, ed. *Sensō Hanzai Chōsa Shiryō: Furyo Kankei Chōsa Chūō-i'inkai Chōsa Hōkokusho Tsuzuri* 戦争犯罪調査資料：俘虜関係調査中央委員会調査報告書綴 [War Crime Investigation Documents: Investigation Reports by the Central Committee of the POWs Related Investigation]. Tokyo: Azuma Shuppan, 1995.

Nagasaki Shiyakusho Sōmubu Chōsa Tōkeika 長崎市役所総務部調査統計課, ed. *Nagasaki Shisei Rokujū-go-nen Shi, Kō-hen* 長崎市政六十五年史 後編 [Sixty-Five Year History of the Nagasaki City Government, Vol. 3]. Nagasaki: Nagasaki Shiyakusho Sōmubu Chōsa Tōkeika, 1959.

Najita, Tetsuo. *Hara Kei in the Politics of Compromise, 1905–1915*. Cambridge, MA: Harvard University Press, 1967.

——. *Ordinary Economics in Japan: A Historical Perspective, 1750–1950 (Twentieth Century Japan: The Emergence of a World Power)*. Berkeley: University of California Press, 2009.

——. *Sōgofujo no Keizai: Mujinkō Hōtoku no Minshū Shisō-shi* 相互扶助の経済：無尽講・報徳の民衆思想史 [Ordinary Economics in Japan: A Historical Perspective, 1750–1950]. Translated by Igarashi Akio 五十嵐暁郎 and Fukui Masako 福井昌子. Tokyo: Misuzu-shobō, 2015.

Najita, Tetsuo, and Victor J. Koschmann, ed. *Conflict in Modern Japanese History: The Neglected Tradition*. Ithaca, NY: Cornell East Asia Series, 2010.

Nakagaki, Noriko 中垣紀子, ed. *Daiichiji Sekai Taisengo ni okeru Nihon Sekijūjisha no Pōrando Sensai Koji Kyūsai Katsudō ni Kansuru Kenkyū Hōkokusho* 「第一次世界大戦後における日本赤十字社のポーランド戦災孤児救済活動」に関する研究報告書 [Research Report on "Relief Activities for Polish Orphans by the Japanese Red Cross Society After the First World War"]. Toyota: Nihon Sekijūji Toyota Kango Daigaku, 2008.

Nakajima, Takeshi 中島岳志. *Ketsumeidan Jiken* 血盟団事件 [Blood-Pledge Corps Incident]. Tokyo: Bungeishunjū, 2016.

Nakajima, Yumiko. *Hawai Samayoeru Rakuen: Minzoku to Kokka no Shōtotsu* ハワイ・さまよ える楽園：民族と国家の衝突 [Sojourn in Hawai'i Paradise: Collision Between Race and State]. Tokyo: Tokyo Shoseki, 1993.

Nakakita, Kōji 中北浩爾. *Keizai Fukkō to Sengo Seiji: Nihon Shakaitō 1945–1951 nen* 経済復興 と戦後政治：日本社会党１９４５－１９５１年 [Economic Revival and Post-War Politics: The Japan Socialist Party, 1945–1951]. Tokyo: University of Tokyo Press, 1998.

Nankin Jiken Chōsa Kenkyūkai 南京事件調査研究会, ed. *Nankin Jiken Shiryōshū* ① *Chūgoku Kankei Shiryōhen* 南京事件資料集 ① アメリカ関係資料編 [Documents for the Nanjing Incident, Vol. 1, Documents by America]. Tokyo: Aoki Shoten, 1992.

——. *Nankin Jiken Shiryōshū* ② *Chūgoku Kankei Shiryōhen* 南京事件資料集 ② 中国関係資料編 [Documents for the Nanjing Incident, Vol. 2, Documents by China]. Tokyo: Aoki Shoten, 1992.

Nietzsche, Freidrich. *Thus Spoke Zarathustra*. Translated by Thomas Common. London: Dover Thrift Editions, 1999.

Nihon Kango Kyōkai 日本看護協会. *Kindai Nihon Kango Sōgō Nenpyō* 近代日本看護総合年 表 [Chronology of Nursing in Modern Japan]. Tokyo: Nihon Kango Kyōkai, 1986.

Nihon Kango Rekishi Gakkai 日本看護歴史学会, ed. *Nihon no Kango no Ayumi: Rekishi wo Tsukuru Anata e* 日本の看護のあゆみ 歴史をつくるあなたへ [The History of Japanese Nursing: To You Who Make History]. Tokyo: Japanese Nursing Association, 2014.

Ninagawa, Arata 蜷川新. "Jindō no Gimu to Gijutsuteki-iken no Kōkan 人道の義務と技術的 意見の交換" [Discussion on Humanitarian Duty and Its Technologies]. In *Jindō no Sekai to Nipponjin*, 73–86. Tokyo: Hakuai Hakkōjo, 1936.

——. *Jindō-heiwa no Shito Sekijūji* 人道平和の使徒赤十字 [An Apostle of Humanitarian Peace: The Red Cross]. Tokyo: Zen-nihon Sekijūji Jūgyōin Kumiai Regō-kai, 1955.

——. "Jindō-kokumin toshite no Nipponjin 人道国民としての日本人" [The Japanese as a Humanitarian People]. In *Jindō no Sekai to Nipponjin*, 318–21. Tokyo: Hakuai Hakkōjo, 1936.

——. *Jindō no Sekai to Nipponjin* 人道の世界と日本人 [The Humanitarian World and the Japanese People]. Tokyo: Hakuai Hakkōjo, 1936.

——. *Jindō no Shisetsu* 人道の使節 [The Ambassador of Humanitarians]. Tokyo: Teikoku Bunka Kyōkai, 1928.

Ninkovich, Frank. *The Wilsonian Century: U.S. Foreign Policy since 1900*. Chicago: University of Chicago Press, 1999.

Nisseki Chūō Joshi Tandai Kenkyūkai 日赤女子中央短大研究会編, ed. *Shashin Kiroku: Nihon Sekijūji Kango Kyōiku no Ayumi: Hakuai-sha kara Nisseki Chūō Joshi Tandai made* 写真記 録：日本赤十字看護教育のあゆみ：博愛社から日赤中央女子短大まで [Photo Collection: Nursing Education of the Japanese Red Cross Society from Hakuaisha to Japanese Red Cross Central Junior College for Women]. Tokyo: Sōsei-shobō, 1988.

Nisseki Kyōdō Kenkyū Purojekuto 日赤共同研究プロジェクト. *Nihon Sekijūjisha no Sugao* 日本 赤十字社の素顔 [The True Face of the Japanese Red Cross Society]. Tokyo: Akebi Shobō, 2003.

Noguchi, Tai のぐちたい. *Tatakai no hakui wa tōku: Nihon Sekijūjisha kyūgo kangofu no jūgunki* 戦いの白衣は遠く：日本赤十字社救護看護婦の従軍記 [Japanese Red Cross Army Nurses]. Tokyo: Hokufū Shobō, 1985.

Ōe, Kenzaburō 大江健三郎. *Hiroshima Nōto* ヒロシマ・ノート [Hiroshima Notes]. Tokyo: Iwanami Shoten, 1965.

———. *Kaku-jidai no Sōzō-ryoku* 核時代の想像力 [The Power of Imagination in the Nuclear Age]. Tokyo: Shinchō-sensho, 2007.

Ogata, Sadako 緒方貞子. *Manshūjihen to Seisaku no Keisei Katei* 満州事変と政策の形成過程 [The Manchurian Incident: The Policy Formation Process]. Tokyo: Genshobō, 1966.

Ōishi, Matashichi 大石又七. *Bikini-jiken no Shinjitsu: Inochi no Kiro de* ビキニ事件の真実 いのちの岐路で [The Reality of the Bikini Incident: A Turning Point in My Life]. Tokyo: Misuzu-shobō, 2003.

Ōkawa, Shirō 大川四郎, ed. *Ōbeijin-Horyo to Sekijūji katsudō—Paravichiini Hakase no Fukken* 欧米人捕虜と赤十字活動ーパラヴィチーニ博士の復権 [European and American POWs and the Activities of the Red Cross: The Rehabilitation of Dr. Paravicini]. Tokyo: Ronsōsha, 2005.

———. *Research on the Japanese Red Cross Society Documents Concerning the Treatment of Western Prisoners of War in Japanese Hands During World War II (Taiheiyō Sensōchū no Nihon Kokunai ni okeru Ōbeijin-Horyo no Shogū ni Kansuru Nihon Sekijūjisha Bunsho no Kenkyū)* 太平洋戦争中の日本国内における欧米人捕虜の処遇に関する日本赤十字社文書の研究. Heisei Jūhachi nendo—Heisei Jūkyū nendo: Kagaku Kenkyūhi Hojyo-kin Kiban Kenkyū Kenkyū Seika Hōkokusho 平成18年度〜平成19年度科学研究費補助金 基盤研究 研究成果報告書 (2008).

Ōmori, Fumiko 大森文子. *Ōmori Fumiko ga Kenbun shita Kango no Rekishi* 大森文子が見聞した看護の歴史 [Ōmori Fumiko and Nursing History]. Tokyo: Japanese Nursing Association, 2003.

Ong, Charlson. *The Philippine National Red Cross 50 Years of Courage and Commitment*. Hong Kong: Philippine National Red Cross and GMA Foundation, 1997.

Oppenheimer, Melanie. "Reflections on the Easternisation of the Red Cross Movement: The Role of the Japanese Red Cross and the League of Red Cross Societies, 1907–1926." *Pacific and American Studies, Center for Pacific and American Studies (CPAS), Graduate School of Arts and Sciences, The University of Tokyo*, no. 20 (March 2020): 23–39.

Orr, James Joseph. *The Victims as Hero: Ideologies of Peace and National Identity in Postwar Japan*. Honolulu: University of Hawai'i Press, 2001.

Ōsako, Ichirō 大佐古一郎. *Dokutā Junō: Buki naki Yūsha* ドクター・ジュノー 武器なき勇者 [Dr. Junod: Warrior Without Weapons]. Tokyo: Shinchosha-bunko, 1981.

———. *Hiroshima Shōwa Nijū-nen* 広島 昭和二十年 [Hiroshima in 1945]. Tokyo: Chūkō-shinsho, 1975.

O'Sullivan, Kevin, Matthew Hilton, and Juliano Fiori. "Humanitarianisms in Context." *European Review of History* 23 (2016): 1–2, 1–15.

Otaka, Takeshi 小高健. "The Institute for Infectious Diseases Under the Jurisdiction of the Ministry of Home Affairs 内務省所管伝染病研究所." *Journal of the Japanese Society for the History of Medicine* 35, no. 4 (October 30, 1989): 373–407.

———. "The Kessei Yakuin, Serum Institute of the Imperial Government of Japan 血清薬院." *Journal of the Japanese Society for the History of Medicine* 34, no. 3 (July 30, 1988): 386–413.

Ōtake, Yasuko 大嶽康子. *Byōinsen: Yasen byōin* 病院船：野戦病院 [Medical Ships and Battlefield Hospitals]. Tokyo: Nihon Kango Kyōkai Shuppankai, 1979.

Ōtani, Wataru 大谷渡. *Kangofu-tachi no Nanpō Sensen: Teikoku no Rakujitsu wo Seotte* 看護婦たちの南方戦線：帝国の落日を背負って [Nurses on the Southern Battlefield: The Fall of an Empire]. Osaka: Tōhō-shuppan, 2011.

Peace Museum of Saitama Prefecture. "Senji Kyūgo-Nisseki Kangofu-tachi no Kiseki Tenji-Zuroku" 戦時救護—日赤看護婦たちの軌跡 展示図録 [Illustrated Book: Wartime Relief and Japanese Red Cross Nurses], 2007.

Peattie, M. R. "Japanese Colonial Empire, 1895–1945." In *The Cambridge History of Japan*, Vol. 6: *The Twentieth Century*, edited by Peter Duus, 217–70. London: Cambridge University Press, 1989.

Pictet, Jean S. *Red Cross and Peace*. Geneva: International Committee of the Red Cross, 1951.

———. *Red Cross Principles*. Geneva: International Committee of the Red Cross, 1956.

Putih, Othman. *Waga Kokoro no Hiroshima: Maraya kara Kita Nanpō Tokubetsu Ryūgakusei* わが心のヒロシマ：マラヤから来た南方特別留学生 [Hiroshima in My Heart: Students from Malaya]. Translated by Onozawa Jun et al. 小野沢純 他. Tokyo: Keisō Shobō, 1997.

Pfeiff, Alexandra. "The Red Swastika Society's Humanitarian Work: A Re-Interpretation of the Red Cross in China." *New Global Studies* 10, no. 3 (2016): 373–92.

———. "Two Adoptions of the Red Cross: The Chinese Red Cross and the Red Swastika Society from 1904–1949." Doctoral thesis, European University Institute, January 2018.

Reeves, Caroline. "The Early History of the Red Cross China and Its Relation to the Red Cross Movement." In *The Red Cross Movement: Myths, Practices and Turning Points*, edited by Neville Wylie, Melanie Oppenheimer, and James Crossland. Manchester: Manchester University Press, 2020.

Reid, Daphne A., and Patrick F. Gilbo. *Beyond Conflict: The International Federation of Red Cross and Red Crescent Societies, 1919–1994*. Geneva: International Federation of Red Cross and Red Crescent Societies, 1997.

Richardson, Teresa Eden Pearce-Serocold. *In Japanese Hospitals During War-Time: Fifteen Months with the Red Cross Society of Japan (April 1904 to July 1905)*. Edinburgh: W. Blackwood, 1905.

Rikujō Jieitai Eisei Gakkō 陸上自衛隊衛生学校, ed. *Daitōa Sensō Rikugun Eisei Shi. /1/ Rikugun Eisei Gai-shi*. 大東亜戦争 陸軍衛生史／１／陸軍衛生概史 [The Pacific War: The History of Military Medics, Vol. 1, the General History of Military Medics]. Tokyo: Yūkensha, 1970.

Rikujō Jieitai Eisei Gakkō Shūshinkai 陸上自衛隊衛生学校修親会, ed. *Rikugun Eisei Seido-shi* 陸軍衛生制度史 [The History of the Military Medic System]. Tokyo: Hara-shobō, 1990.

Rosenberg, Charles E., and Janet Golden. *Framing Diseases: Studies in Cultural History*. New Brunswick, NJ: Rutgers University Press, 1992.

Rotary International. *Twenty-First Annual Convention of Rotary International: Chicago, Illinois, U.S.A., June 23–27, 1930*. Chicago: Rotary International, 1930. Accessed December 23, 2022. http://bit.ly/2jBoLlx.

Ruoff, Kenneth James. *The People's Emperor Democracy and the Japanese Monarchy, 1945–1995*. Cambridge, MA: Harvard University Press, 2001.

Ruprecht, Adrian. "The Great Eastern Crisis (1875–1878) as a Global Humanitarian Movement." *Journal of Global History* 16, no. 2 (2021): 159–84.

———. "De-Centering Humanitarianism: The Red Cross and India, c. 1877–1939." Doctoral thesis, University of Cambridge, 2017. https://doi.org/10.17863/CAM.18514.

Sakamoto, Tsutomu 坂本勉. "Abuduru Iburahimu no Sairainichi to Mōkyō Seikenka no Isurāmu Seisaku アブデュルレシト・イブラヒムの再来日と蒙疆政権下のイスラーム政策" [Return of Abdurresid Ibrahim to Japan and Muslim Policy of Under Mengjiang United Autonomous Government]. In *Nicchū Sensō to Isurāmu: Manmō-Ajia Chiiki ni okeru Tōchi Kaijū Seisaku* 日中戦争とイスラーム：満蒙・アジア地域における統治・懐柔政策 [Second Sino-Japanese War and Muslims: Governance and Pacification Policy in Manchuria in Mongolia], edited by Sakamoto Tsutomu 坂本勉, 1–82. Tokyo: Keio University Press, 2008.

———, ed. *Nicchū Sensō to Isurāmu: Manmō-Ajia Chiiki ni okeru Tōchi Kaijū Seisaku* 日中戦争とイスラーム：満蒙・アジア地域における統治・懐柔政策 [Second Sino-Japanese War and Muslims: Governance and Pacification Policy in Manchuria in Mongolia]. Tokyo: Keio University Press, 2008.

Sakamoto Yūichi 坂本悠一, ed. *Asahi Shimbun Gaichi-ban II, 6* 朝日新聞外地版 II 6 [Asahi Shimbun: Overseas Territories Edition II, Vol. 6]. Tōkyō: Yumani Shobō, 2012.

Sai, Kiei 崔羲楹. "Chōsen Jūmin no Seimeihyō: Dai Ikkai Seimeihyō (Shōwa Gan kara Go-nen) no Hojū oyobi Dai Nikai (Sōwa Roku kara Jū-nen) Seisai Seimeihyō 朝鮮住民ノ生命表：第一回生命表（昭和元—五年）ノ補充及ビ第二回（昭和六—十年）精細生命表" [Korean Life Tables, First Survey (1926–1930) and Second Survey (1931–1935)]. In *Chōsen Igakkai Zasshi Dai Nijūkyū-kan, Dai Nijū-gō* 朝鮮医学会雑誌 第二十九巻第十二號 [Journal of the Korean Medical Association, Vol. 29 No. 12], edited by Chōsen Igakkai, 2180–220. Keijo (Seoul): Chōsen Igakkai, 1939.

Saitō, Yutaka 斉藤豊. "Nankin-jiken to Kokusaihō-ihan 南京事件と国際法違反" [The Nanjing Massacre and the Violation of the International Law of War]. In *Nankin-jiken wo Doumiruka: Nicchūbei Kenkyūsha ni yoru Kenshō* 南京事件をどうみるか：日・中・米研究者による検証 [How to Interpret the Nanjing Massacre: Analysis by Japanese, Chinese and American Scholars], edited by Fujiwara Akira, 82–98. Tokyo: Aoki Shoten, 1998.

Sasaki, Kōji 佐々木剛二. *Imin to Toku: Nikkei Burajiru Chishikijin no Rekishi Minzokushi* 移民と徳：日系ブラジル知識人の歴史民族誌 [Immigrants and Morality: Race and Intellectual History of Japanese Immigrants in Brazil]. Nagoya: Nagoya University Press, 2020.

Sartre, Jean-Paul. *Being and Nothingness: An Essay on Phenomenological Ontology*. London: Routledge, 1989.

———. *Existentialism and Humanism*. London: Eyre Methuen, 1948.

Schmitt, Robert C. *Demographic Statistics of Hawaii: 1778–1965*. Honolulu: University of Hawai'i Press, 1968.

Schonberger, Howard B. *Aftermath of War: Americans and the Remaking of Japan, 1945–1952*. London: Kent State University Press, 1989.

Selden, Kyoko, and Mark Selden, eds. *The Atomic Bomb: Voices from Hiroshima and Nagasak*. London: East Gate, M. E. Sharpe, 1989.

Seraphim, Franziska. *War Memory and Social Politics in Japan, 1945–2005*. Cambridge, MA: Harvard University Press, 2006.

Shemo, Connie. "Imperialism, Race, and Rescue: Transformation in the Woman's Foreign Mission Movement After World War I." *Diplomatic History* 43, no. 2 (April 2019): 265–81.

Shen, Chieh 沈潔. *"Manshūkoku" Shakai Jigyōshi* 「満洲国」社会事業史 ["Manchukuo" The History of Social Service]. Kyoto: Minerva Shobō, 1996.

Shibata, Shingo 芝田進午. "Nagasaki no Rekishi to Genzai 長崎の歴史と現在" [The History of Nagasaki and the Present Time]. In *Sensō to Heiwa no Riron* 戦争と平和の理論 [Theory of War and Peace], edited by Shibata, Shingo 芝田進午, 32–47. Tokyo: Keisōshobō, 1992.

Shiga, Kiyoshi 志賀潔. *Shiga Kiyoshi: Aru Saikin Gakusha no Kaisō* 志賀潔：或る細菌学者の回想 [Shiga Kiyoshi: Reflections of a Bacteriologist]. Tokyo: Nihon Tosho Center, 1997.

Shigemitsu, Mamoru 重光葵. *Gaikō Kaisō-roku* 外交回想録 [A Diplomatic Memoir]. Tokyo: Chūkō-bunko, 2011.

Shigetō, Fumio 重藤文夫, and Ōe Kenzaburō 大江健三郎. *Taiwa Genbakugo no Ningen* 対話 原爆後の人間 [Dialogue: Humankind After the Atomic Bombings]. Tokyo: Shinchō-sensho, 1971.

Shiina, Masae 椎名麻紗枝. *Genbaku Hanzai: Hibakusha wa Naze Hōchi Saretaka* 原爆犯罪：被爆者はなぜ放置されたか [The Atomic Bombing Crime: Why Were Victims Neglected?]. Tokyo: Ōtsuki-shoten, 1985.

Shimazu, Tadatsugu 島津忠承. *Jindō no Hata no Moto-ni: Nisseki to Tomoni Sanjūgo-nen* 人道の旗のもとに：日赤とともに３５年 [Under a Humanitarian Flag: My Thirty-Five Years with the Japanese Red Cross Society]. Tokyo: Kodansha, 1965.

Shimosawa, Takashi 下澤嶽. "Nihon Sekijūjisha Kyōdōbokin ni miru Nihonteki Bokin no Tenkai 日本赤十字社、共同募金にみる日本的募金の展開" [The Development of Japanese Fundraising System Through the Experience of the Japanese Red Cross Society and the Community Chest]. *Shizuoka University of Art and Culture Bulletin* 16 (March 2016): 17–26.

Shin, Di-Wook, and Michael Robinson, eds. *Colonial Modernity in Korea*. Cambridge, MA: Harvard Asia Center, 1999.

Shinozaki, Moritoshi 篠崎守利. "Chūgoku Kōjūji-kai to Shin Matsumin Hatsu no Hyōshō Mondai 中国紅十字会と清末民初の標章問題" [The Chinese Red Cross Society and Symbolizing the People the Late Qing]. In *Sensō・Saigai to Kindai Higashi Ajia no Minshū Shūkyō* 戦争・災害と近代東アジアの民衆宗教 [War, Disaster and Folk Religion in Modern East Asia], edited by Takeuchi Fusaji 武内房司, 134–156. Tokyo: Yūshisha, 2014.

Shirabe Raisuke 調来助, ed. *Genbaku Omoide no Shukishū: Wasurenagusa, Dai Go gō (Saishū-hen)* 原爆思い出の手記集：忘れな草 第５号（最終編）[Memories of Atomic Bomb Survivors: Forget Me Not, Vol. 5 (Last Edition)]. Nagasaki: Kyū-Nagasaki Ika Daigaku Genbaku Gisei Gakuto Izokukai, 1974.

Shirane, Seiji. *Imperial Gateway: Colonial Taiwan and Japan's Expansion in South China and Southeast Asia, 1895–1945*. Ithaca, NY: Cornell University Press, 2022.

Shirato, Hitoyasu 白戸仁康. *Hokkaidō no Horyo Shūyōjo: Mou-hitotsu no Sensō Sekinin* 北海道の捕虜収容所：もう一つの戦争責任 [POW Camps in Hokkaido: Another War Responsibility]. Hokkaido: Hokkaido Shimbun, 2008.

Shōkei-kan Sepcial Exhition. *Senshōbyōsha no Rōku no sobade: "Hakui no Tenshi" to yobareta Jūgunkangofu tachi, (19 July 2017–10 September 2017)* 戦傷病者の労苦のそばで：「白衣の天使」と呼ばれてた従軍看護婦たち（2017.7.19–2017.10.9）[At the Side of the Sick and Wounded: Military Nurses as "Angels in White"].

Stanlaw, James. "Japanese Emigration and Immigration: From the Meiji to the Modern." In *Japanese Diasporas: Unsung Pasts, Conflicting Presents, and Uncertain Futures*, edited by Nobuko Adachi, 35–51. London: Routledge, 2006.

Stegewerns, Dick. *Nationalism and Internationalism in Imperial Japan: Autonomy, Asian Brotherhood, or World Citizenship?* London: Routledge Curzon, 2003.

Stephan, John J. *Hawaii Under the Rising Sun*. Honolulu: University of Hawai'i Press, 1984.

———. *The Russian Far East: A History*. Stanford, CA: Stanford University Press, 1996.

Sugimoto, Henry 杉本ヘンリー, and Kubo Sadajirō 久保貞次郎, ed. *Kiroku-kaiga: Hokubei Nihonjin no Shūyōjo* 記録絵画：北米日本人の収容所 [Painting: Recording North American Japanese in Detention Camps in Painting]. Tokyo: Soubunsha, 1981.

Sulga, Glenda, and Patricia Clavin, eds. *Internationalisms: A Twentieth-Century History*. Cambridge: Cambridge University Press, 2016.

Suzuki, Michiko. "History of Disaster, Recovery, and Humanitarianism: The Japanese Red Cross Society in the Modern World, 1877–1945." PhD thesis, SOAS University of London, 2019.

———. "The Emergence of Modern Humanitarian Activities: The Evolution of Japanese Red Cross Movement from Local to Global." *Tokyo Fuchu International Studies Journal* 8, no. 1, Tokyo University of Foreign Studies (May 2020): 59–105.

———. "The Japanese Red Cross Society's Emergency Responses in Hiroshima and Nagasaki, 1945." *Social Science Japan Journal* (July 2021): 374–67. https://doi.org/10.1093/ssjj/jyab026.

Suzuki, Michiko 鈴木路子. "Nihon Sekijūjisha no Kinkyū Jindō-shien no Rekishi ni Tsuite 日本赤十字社の原爆緊急人道支援の歴史について" [History of the Japanese Red Cross Society Nuclear Bombing Emergency Humanitarian Relief Activities in Hiroshima and Nagasaki, 1945]. *Journal of Humanitarian Studies, Japanese Red Cross Institute for Humanitarian Studies* 6. Tokyo: Tōshindō, 2017, 200–220.

Swift, Ernest J. "The Third Pan American Red Cross Conference." *Bulletin of the Pan American Union* 69, no. 8 (August 1935): 592–96.

Tabuchi Masayo, "Koushūeisei Koushūkai no Keika ni Tsukite 公衆衛生講習会の経過に就きて" [The Report on International Public Health Nursing Conference]. In Nihon Sekijūjisha 日本赤十字社. *Hakuai: Organ of the Japanese Red Cross Society, No. 428, December 1922* 博愛 第４２８号, 15–18. Tokyo: Hakuai Hakkōjo, 1922.

Tachikawa, Kyōichi 立川京一. "Kyūgun ni okeru Horyo no Toriatsukai—Taiheiyō Sensō no Jōkyō wo Chūshin-ni—旧軍における捕虜の取り扱いー太平洋戦争の状況を中心にー" [POW Treatment by the Japanese Army During the Pacific War]. *Bōei Kenkyūjo Kiyō*, Vol. 10-1 防衛研究所紀要第10巻第1号 (September 2007): 99–142. Accessed May 29, 2018. www.nids.mod.go.jp/publication/kiyo/pdf/bulletin_j10_1_3.pdf.

Tachikawa, Kyōichi 立川京一, and Yadohisa Haruhiko 宿久晴彦. "Seifu oyobi Gun to ICRC tō tono Kankei—Nisshin Sensō kara Taiheiyō Sensō made—(Kōhen) 政府及び軍とＩＣＲＣ等との関係ー日清戦争から太平洋戦争までー（前編）" [The Relations Between the Government and Army, and the ICRC: From the First Sino-Japanese War to the Pacific War, Vol. 1]. *Bōei Kenkyūjo Kiyō*, Vol. 11-1 防衛研究所紀要第11巻第1号 (November 2008): 69–125. Accessed May 29, 2018. www.nids.mod.go.jp/publication/kiyo/pdf/bulletin_j11_1_4.pdf.

———. [Vol. 2], *Bōei Kenkyūjo Kiyō*, Vol. 11-2 防衛研究所紀要第11巻第2号 (January 2009): 105–50. Accessed May 29, 2018. http://www.nids.mod.go.jp/publication/kiyo/pdf/bulletin_j11_2_4.pdf.

Tajima, Jidayū 田島治太夫, and Inoue Shunji 井上俊治. *Renga no Kabe: Nagasaki Horyo Shūyō-jo to Genbaku no Dokyumento* 煉瓦の壁 長崎捕虜収容所と原爆のドキュメント [The Brick Wall: The Documentary of Nagasaki POW Camps and the Atomic Bombing]. Tokyo: Gendai-shi Shuppan-kai Hakkō, 1980. In *Nihon no Genbaku Kiroku 13* 日本の原爆記録 13 [The Japanese Record of the Atomic Bombing, Vol. 13], edited by Ienaga Saburō 家永三郎, Odagiri Hideo 小田切秀雄, and Kuroko Kazuo 黒古一夫, 8–219. Tokyo: Nihon Tosho Center, 1991.

Takahashi, Aya. *The Development of the Japanese Nursing Profession: Adopting and Adapting Western Influences*. London: Routledge Curzon, 2004.

Takahashi, Yukiharu. *Nikkei Burajiru Imin-shi* 日系ブラジル移民史 [The History of Japanese Immigrants in Brazil]. Tokyo: San-ichi, 1993.

Takayama, Jun 高山純. *Edojidai Hawai Hyōryūki: 'Iban Hyōryū Kikokuroku' no Kenshō* 江戸時代ハワイ漂流記：「夷蛮漂流帰国録」の検証 [Castaway in Hawai'i During the Edo Period: Examination on "The Records on Experience of Castaway in Hawai'i"]. Tokyo: San-ichi, 1997.

Takemae, Eiji. *The Allied Occupation of Japan*. London: Continuum, 2002.

Takeuchi, Nobuo 竹内信夫. *Kūkai no Shisō* 空海の思想 [Thoughts of Kūkai]. Tokyo: Chikuma-shobō, 2014.

Takinami, Sadako 瀧浪貞子. *Kōmyō Kōgō: Heijōkyō ni kaketa Yume to Inori* 光明皇后：平城京にかけた夢と祈り [Empress Kōgō: Deam, Faith, and Prayer for the Imperial Capital, Heijōkyō]. Tokyo: Chūkōshinsho, 2017.

Tanaka, Mikiko 田中美樹子. "Japanese Organization of National General Mobilization and Neighbor Groups *(Tonarigumi)* in the Pacific War: Reorganization of Neighborhood Groups 戦時下における「新体制」と隣組：地域組織の再編成." *The Ōtani Philosophical Society, Ōtani University, The Philosophical Studies*, no. 50 (2003): 73–85.

Tanaka, Yuki. *Japan's Comfort Women: Sexual Slavery and Prostitution During World War II and the US Occupation*. London: Routledge, 2002.

Tanaka, Yuki, and John W. Dower. *Hidden Horrors: Japanese War Crimes in World War II*. Boulder, CO: Westview, 1996.

Taoka, Ryōichi 田岡良一. *Air Strikes and International Law* 空襲と国際法. Tokyo: Ganshōdō-shoten, 1937.

The City of Hiroshima. *The War of the Hiroshima Atomic Bombing Journal*. Hiroshima: City of Hiroshima, 1971.

Tokutomi, I'ichirō 徳富猪一郎. *Kōshaku Matsukata Masayoshi Den, Kon-kan* 公爵松方正義伝・坤巻 [Biography of Prince Matsukata Masayoshi, Vol. 2]. Tokyo: Kōshaku Matsukata Masayoshi Dennki Hensan-I'inkai, 1935.

Tomida, Hiroko, and Gordon Daniels. "Medical Ambassadors: Japanese Red Cross Nurses in Britain, 1915–1916." Shakai Inobēshon Kenkyū 社会イノベーション研究 (June 2018): 99–122. Accessed April 25, 2022. http://www.seijo.ac.jp/pdf/fasiv/4-1/tomida&daniels.pdf.

Tosh, John. *The Pursuit of History: Aims, Methods and New Directions in the Study of Modern History*. London: Longman, 2002.

Tsuji, Zen'nosuke 辻善之助, ed. *Nihonjin no Hakuai* 日本人の博愛 [The Humanitarian Ideas of the Japanese]. Translated by Masao Nagasawa. Tokyo: Kinkōdō Shoseki, 1932.

———. *Kōshitsu to Nihon Seishin* 皇室と日本精神 [Imperial Family and Japanese Spirit]. Tokyo: Direct Publishing.

Tsurumi, Shunsuke 鶴見俊介, Katō Norihiro 加藤典洋, and Kurokawa Sō 黒川創. *Nichibei Kōkansen* 日米交換船 [Japan-U.S. Prisoner of War Exchange Repatriation Voyage]. Tokyo: Shinchosha, 2006.

Ueda, Tadakazu 上田惟一. "Dai San-setsu: Jūgonen Sensō to Kōkyōkumiai・Chōnaikai 第三節 十五年戦争と公共組合・町内会" [Section 3: Community Associations and Chōnaikai During the Fifteen Years War]. In *Zōhoban Chōnaikai no Kenkyū* 増補版：町内会の研究 [Expanded Edition: Chōnaikai Studies], edited by Iwasaki Nobuhiko 岩崎信彦, Ueda Tadakazu 上田惟一, Hirohara Moriaki 広原盛明, Ajisaka Manabu 鯵坂学, Takagi Masao 高木正朗, and Yoshihara Naoki 吉原直樹, 95–103. Tokyo: Ochanomizu-shobō, 2013.

Uchiyama, Hatsu 内山ハツ, ed. *Dōkoku no Hitō Jūgun-ki: Nisseki Dai Sanbyaku-ni Kyūgohan Nagasakiken-shibu Kikō Bunshū* 慟哭の比島従軍記：日赤第３０２救護班長崎県支部寄稿文集 [On the Battlefield in the Philippines: Collected Essays of the Japanese Red Cross Society Nagasaki Chapter Relief Party No. 302]. Nagasaki: Nisseki Kyūgohan Nagasakiken-shibu, 1994.

Ueno, Chizuko. *Nationalism and Gender*. Translated by Beverley Anne Yamamoto. Melbourne: Trans Pacific, 2004.

Upham, Frank K. *Law and Social Change in Postwar Japan*. Cambridge, MA: Harvard University Press, 1987.

Utsumi, Aiko 内海愛子. *Furyo Toriatsukai ni Kansuru Shogaikoku kara no Kōgishū: Jūgonen Sensō Gokuhi Shiryōshū, Dai Jūroku-shū* 俘虜取扱に関する諸外国からの抗議集：十五年戦争極秘資料集 第十六集 [Complaints from Foreign Countries Regarding POW Treatment: Confidential Documents of the Fifteen Years War, Vol. 16]. Tokyo: Fuji Shuppan, 1989.

———. *Nihongun no Horyo Seisaku* 日本軍の捕虜政策 [POW Treatment Policy of the Japanese Imperial Army]. Tokyo: Aoki-shoten, 2005.

van Bergen, Leo. *The Dutch East Indies Red Cross, 1870–1950: On Humanitarianism and Colonialism*. Washington, DC: Rowman & Littlefield, 2019.

van Dijk, Boyd. *Preparing for War: The Making of the Geneva Conventions*. Oxford: Oxford University Press, 2022.

———. "Human Rights in War: On the Entangled Foundations of the 1949 Geneva Conventions." *American Society of International Law* 112, no. 4 (2018): 553–82.

von Lingen, Kerstin, ed. *Debating Collaboration and Complicity in War Crimes Trials in Asia, 1945–1956*. London: Palgrave Macmillan, 2017.

———. *Transcultural Justice at the Tokyo Tribunal: The Allied Struggle for Justice, 1946–48*. Leiden: Brill, 2018.

von Theill, Sophia. In *Nichiro Sensō-ka no Nihon: Roshia-jin Horyo no Tsuma no Nikki* 日露戦争下の日本：ロシア軍人捕虜の妻の日記 [Japan During the Russo-Japanese War: The Diary of a Wife of a Russian POW]. Translated by Ogiso Ryū 小木曽龍 and Ogiso Miyoko 小木曽美代子. Tokyo: Shin Jinbutsu Ōraisha, 1991.

Wakakuwa, Midori 若桑みどり. *Sensō ga Tsukuru Josei Zō* 戦争がつくる女性像 [The Images of Women Created by War]. Tokyo: Chikuma-shobō, 1995.

Wang, Yangming 王陽明. *Denshūroku* 伝習録 [Instructions for Practical Living]. Translated by Mizoguchi Yūzō 溝口雄三. Tokyo: Chūōkōron-shinsha, 2005.

War Memorial Maritime Museum 戦没した船と海員の資料館. *Senbotsu-sen Shashin-shū* 戦没船写真集 [Photographs of Sunken Warships: War Memorial Maritime Museum]. Kobe: All Japan Seamen's Union, 2001.

Watanabe, Sawako. *Matsu* 松 [The Pine Tree]. Tokyo: Watanabe Sawako, 1974.

White, Hayden. *Metahistory: The Historical Imagination in Nineteenth-Century Europe*. Baltimore, MD: Johns Hopkins University Press, 1973.

White, Hayden. *Tropics of Discourse: Essays in Cultural Criticism*. Baltimore, MD: Johns Hopkins University Press, 1978.

Wilmshurst, Elizabeth, and Susan Breau, eds. *Perspective on the ICRC Study on Customary International Humanitarian Law*. New York: Cambridge University Press, 2007.

Wilson, Sandra, Robert Cribb, Beatrice Trefalt, and Dean Aszkielowicz. *Japanese War Criminals: The Politics of Justice After the Second World War*. New York: Columbia University Press, 2017.

Wylie, Neville, Melanie Oppenheimer, and James Crossland, eds. *The Red Cross Movement: Myths, Practices and Turning Points*. Manchester: Manchester University Press, 2020.

Yamanoue no Okura 山上憶良. "Hinkyūmondōka 貧窮問答歌" [Dialogue on Poverty]. In *Man'yōshū*, Vol. 1 万葉集（一） [Collection of Ten Thousand Leaves, Vol. 1]. Translated and edited by Nakanishi Susumu 中西進, 402–5. Tokyo: Kodansha-bunko, 1996.

Yamashita, Mai 山下麻衣. "Senkyūhyaku hachi nen kara Senkyūhyaku Yonjū nen ni okeru Nihon Sekijūjisha no Shū'nyū Kōzō kara Mita Jigyō Tenkai 1908年から1940年における日本赤十字社の収入構造から見た事業展開" [Analysis of Japanese Red Cross Society (JRCS) Finances from 1908 to 1940 in Terms of Its Revenue Structure]. *Social Science Series 31, Kyoto Sangyo University Essays*, Kyoto Sangyo University (March 2014): 179–200.

———. *Kangofu no Rekishi: Yorisou Senmonshoku no Tanjō* 看護婦の歴史：寄り添う専門職の誕生 [The History of Nurses: The Birth of the Care Professional]. Tokyo: Yoshikawa Kōbunkan, 2017.

———. "Nihon Sekijūjisha ga Okonatta Heiji Kyūgo no Tenkai Katei: Ninagawa Arata ga Hatashita Yakuwari 日本赤十字社がおこなった平時救護の展開過程：蜷川新が果たした役割" [The Development of Japanese Red Cross Society (JRCS) Peacetime Relief Efforts: The Role Played by Ninagawa Arata]. *Social Science Series, Kyoto Sangyo University Essays*, no. 34 (March 2017): 3–24.

———. *Rekishi no naka no Shōgaisha* 歴史のなかの障害者 [The Disabled in History]. Tokyo: Hosei University Press, 2012.

Yamazaki, James N., and Louis B. Fleming. *Children of the Atomic Bomb: An American Physician's Memoir of Nagasaki, Hiroshima, and the Marshall Islands*. Durham, NC: Duke University Press, 1995.

Yamazaki, Yūji 山崎裕二. "Male Nurses of the Japanese Red Cross Society in the 1910s: Male Nurses in the History of Modern Nursing (6) 1910年代における日本赤十字社の救護看護人：近代看護師のなかの男性看護者（6）." *Nihon Sekijūji Musashino Tanki-daigaku Kiyō, Dai Jūni-gō* (1999): 92–122.

Yanai, Kiyoshi 柳井潔. *Kokō no Hana: Biruma Jūgun Tokushi Kangofu no Sokuseki* 孤高の華—ビルマ従軍特志看護婦の足跡 [Distant Flowers: The Story of Military Volunteer Nurses in Burma]. Tokyo: Kantō Shuppan, 1970.

Yasuyama, Kōdō 泰山弘道. *Kanzen-ban: Nagasaki Genbaku no Kiroku* 完全版 長崎原爆の記録 [Complete Edition: The Record of the Nagasaki Atomic Bombing]. Tokyo: Tokyo Tosho Shuppan-kai, 2007.

Yellen, Jeremy A. *The Greater East Asia Co-Prosperity Sphere: When Total Empire Met Total War*. Ithaca, NY: Cornell University Press, 2023.

Yomota, Inuhiko 四方田犬彦. *Nihon Eiga-shi Hyakujū-nen* 日本映画史１１０年 [One Hundred and Ten-Year History of Japanese Films]. Tokyo: Shūeisha Shinsho, 2014.

Yoneyama, Lisa. *Hiroshima Traces: Time, Space, and the Dialectics of Memory*. Berkeley: University of California Press, 1999.

Yosano, Shigeru 与謝野秀. *Ichi Gaikōkan no Omoide no Yōroppa* 一外交官の思い出のヨーロッパ [Memoir of a Diplomat in Europe]. Tokyo: Chikuma-shobō, 1981.

Yoshida, Yutaka 吉田裕. *Tennō no Guntai to Nankin-jiken* 天皇の軍隊と南京事件 [The Emperor's Army and the Nanjin Incident]. Tokyo: Aoki-shoten, 1986.

———. *Ajia, Taiheiyō Sensō—Shiriiizu Nihon Kin-gendaishi (6)* アジア・太平洋戦争―シリーズ日本近現代史〈6〉 [The Asia-Pacific War: Japanese Modern and Contemporary History, Vol. 6]. Tokyo: Iwanami Shoten, 2007.

Yoshihara, Naoki 吉原直樹. "Dai San-setsu: Ōsaka ni okeru Nihon Sekijūji Hōshidan Seiritsu no Hitokoma 第三節 大阪における日本赤十字奉仕団成立の一齣" [Section 3: The Foundation of the Japanese Red Cross Society Volunteer Corps in Ōsaka]. In *Zōho-ban Chōnaikai no Kenkyū* 増補版：町内会の研究 [Expanded Edition: Chōnaikai Studies], edited by Iwasaki Nobuhiko 岩崎信彦, Ueda Tadakazu 上田惟一, Hirohara Moriaki 広原盛明, Ajisaka Manabu 鯵坂学, Takagi Masao 髙木正朗, and Yoshihara Naoki 吉原直樹, 143–69. Tokyo: Ochanomizu-shobō, 2013.

———. *Sengo Kaikaku to Chiiki Jūmin Soshiki: Senryōka no Toshi Chōnaikai* 戦後改革と地域住民組織：占領下の都市町内会 [Post-War Restoration and Local Community Organizations: Chōnaikai in Urban Areas under the SCAP Occupation]. Tokyo: Minervashobo, 1989.

Yoshikawa, Ryūko 吉川龍子. *Nisseki no Sōshi-sha: Sano Tsunetami* 日赤の創始者：佐野常民 [Sano Tsunetami, the Founder of the Japanese Red Cross Society]. Tokyo: Yoshikawa Kōbunkan, 2001.

———. "Relief Activities of Red Cross Nurses Immediately After the Hiroshima Atomic Bombing (6 August 1945)." Translated by Suzuki Michiko 鈴木路子. *Journal of Humanitarian Studies* 2 (March 2013): 64–79.

Yoshimura, Kazuaki 吉村和嘉. *On'shi・Emoto Shigeo Den: Kakaru Shi Ariki* 恩師・江本茂夫傳 かかる師ありき [My Esteemed Professor, Dr. Enomoto Shigeo]. Tokyo: Jihi Shuppan-bu, Kurashi no Techō-sha, 2008.

Young, Louise. *Japan's Total Empire: Manchuria and the Culture of Wartime Imperialism*. Berkeley: University of California Press, 1998.

Yow, Valerie Raleigh. *Recording Oral History: A Guide for the Humanities and Social Sciences*. Oxford: Altamira, 2005.

Yukinaga, Masae 雪永政枝. *Kango Jinmei Jiten* 看護人名辞典 [Biographical Dictionary of Nurses]. Tokyo: Igaku-shoin, 1968.

———. *Kinoko-gumo Nisseki Jūgun Kangofu no Shuki* きのこ雲 日赤従軍看護婦の手記 [The Mushroom Cloud: Memoirs of the Japanese Red Cross Military Nurses]. Tokyo: All Publishing, 1984.

Yumoto, Fumihiko 湯本文彦, ed. *Chūai* 忠愛 [Faith and Love]. Kyoto: Japanese Red Society Kyoto Chapter, 1910.

Zaidanhōjin Geijutsu Kenkyū Shinkōzaidan © and Tokyo Art University Hyakunenshi Kankō-i'inkai 財団法人芸術研究振興財団©, 東京芸術大学百年史刊行委員会. *Tokyo Art University Hyakunenshi Ensōkai-hen Dai Ni-kan* 東京芸術大学百年史演奏会篇第二巻 [Centennial History of Tokyo University of the Arts: Performances, Vol. 2]. Tokyo: Ongaku no Tomo sha Corporation, 1933.

NEWSPAPERS AND MAGAZINES

Asahi Shimbun. "Chōsenjin Hyōshō: Nyūji wo Sewashita Tei no Tsuma to Musume 朝鮮人表彰 乳児を世話した鄭の妻と娘" [Koreans Win Prize for Infant Care: Chung's Wife and Daughter]. *Asahi Shimbun*, November 12, 1923, 2.

———. "Hakketsubyō no Muryō Chiryō: Tōkyō ni iru Genbaku Kanja ni 白血病の無料治療 東京にいる原爆患者に" [Free Medical Treatment of Leukemia for Atomic Bomb Patients]. *Asahi Shimbun*, November 27, 1954, 7.

———. "Kichō na Shiryō Ichidōni Genbaku Shiryō Kōkaiten Hiraku 貴重な資料一堂に 原爆資料公開展開く" [Exhibition of Invaluable Atomic Bombing Documents Opens to the Public]. *Asahi Shimbun*, November 26, 1954, 7.

———. "Manshūkoku Shōnin wa Izure Jitsugen: Nikaragua Fukudaitōryō Dan 滿洲國承認は何れ實現：ニカラグア副大統領談" [Manchukuo Will be Recognized as a State Soon: Nicaraguan Vice-President]. *Asahi Shimbun*, October 7, 1934, 1.

———. "Nichibei-sen Ronsō wo Haigeki 日米戰論争を排撃" [Refutation of Talk of War Between Japan and America]. *Asahi Shimbun*, February 26, 1934, 3.

———. "Rokoku no Renmei Kanyū wo Manjōicchi de Kaketsu: Sekjūjirenmai Rijikai 露國の聯盟加入を滿場一致で可決 赤十字連聯理事會" [The Board of Directors of the LORCS Unanimously Accept USSR Membership]. *Asahi Shimbun*, October 19, 1934, 2.

———. "Ueno no Gasshō ni Doitsu kara Origami: Shutorausu Okina mo Kangeki, Berurin de Kiita Sanjū nichi Yoru no Hōsō 上野の合唱に獨逸から折り紙 シュトラウス翁も感激 伯林で聞いた卅日夜の放送" [Origami from Germany: In Berlin, Strauss Was Moved Listening to the Nightime Concert Broadcast from Ueno on the 30th]. *Asahi Shimbun*, November 1, 1934, 7.

Asahi Shimbun Morning ed., "Futsukoku yuki no Kangofu: Shōji Masuko 佛國行の看護婦 庄司ます子" [A Japanese Nurse in France: Shōji Masuko]. *Asahi Shimbun*, November 12, 1914.

———. "Kenfutsu Kangofu no Katsudō: Shanzerizē no Hana 遣佛看護婦の活動 シャンゼリゼーの花" [The Activities of Japanese Nurses in France: The Flowers of Champs-Élysées]. *Asahi Shimbun*, May 14, 1915.

Burajiru Jihō. "Jūnishichōchūbyō no Sensei: Kitajima Ishi no Eimin 十二指腸蟲病の先生 北島醫師の永眠" [The Doctor of Hookworm Disease]. *Burajiru Jihō*, September 21, 1923, 7.

———. "Kimpin no Kizō 金品の寄贈" [Donations of Money and Supplies]. *Burajiru Jihō*, July 25, 1932, 1.

———. "Nihon Sekijūji Gojū-nen Sai ni Nippon de Bankoku Sekijūi Taikai 日本赤十字五十年祭に日本で萬國赤十字社大會" [The Japanese Red Cross Hosts Fiftieth Anniversary International Red Cross Conference in Japan]. *Burajiru Jihō*, April 30, 1926, 6.

———. "Nihon Sekijūjisha no Hakuai no Te wa Nobu 日本赤十字社の博愛の手は伸ぶ" [Japanese Red Cross Society Extends Philanthropic Aid]. *Burajiru Jihō*, June 15, 1936, 5.
———. "Rokujūgo-ko no Kyūgohan: Nihon Sekijūjisha no Sōdōin 六十五個の救護班：日本赤十字社の總動員" [Sixty-Five Relief Parties: The Japanese Red Cross Socity in Full Mobilization]. *Burajiru Jihō*, September 21, 1923, 1.
———. "Sekijūji e!!! 赤十字へ！！！" [Let's Donate to the Red Cross!!!]. *Burajiru Jihō*, August 15, 1932, 2.
———. "Sekijūji e Kimpin Kizō: Netsu ga Agaru 赤十字へ金品寄贈 熱が上る" [Raising Money and Collecting Supplies: Donations to the Red Cross]. *Burajiru Jihō*, July 25, 1932, 3.
———. "Sekijūji Taikai: Kakkoku Daihyō Zokuzoku Raichaku 赤十字大會各國代表続々来着" [Delegations to the Red Cross Conference Arriving in Japan]. *Burajiru Jihō*, October 24, 1934, 5.
Evening Star. "Red Cross Plans Conference: Prince Tokugawa and Judge Payne Arranged Parley." *Evening Star*, Washington, DC, March 1, 1934, A-4.
Gloucester Citizen. "King's Visitors." *Gloucester Citizen*, November 2, 1933, 1.
Hawai Hōchi. "Hawai Nihon Sekijūjishain Bokoku Kankōdan Dan'in Boshū 布哇日本赤十字社員 母國觀光團々員募集" [JRCS Hawai'i Recruits Members for the Japan Tour]. *Hawai Hōchi*, January 30, 1928, 4.
———. "Sekijūjihonbu wa Hawai Shibu wo shite Shiberia ni Daiichi Yasen Byōin wo Tsukuraseyo Gokengen 赤十字本部は布哇支部をして西比利亞に第一野戰病院を作らせよご建言" [American Red Cross Headquarters Instructs Hawaii Branch Society by Headquarters to Establish the First Field Hospital in Siberia]. *Hawai Hōchii*, July 24, 1918, 1.
Hawaii Times. "Naka Hongan-ji Keirōkai: Kōreisha Hōmeiroku コナ本願寺敬老會：高齢者芳名録" [Kona Hongan-ji Temple Senior Association: Visitors' Book]. *Hawaii Times*, June 1, 1955, 7.
Honolulu Star-Bulletin. "Ask Japanese to Give Help to Red Cross Work." *Honolulu Star-Bulletin*, September 25, 1917, 8.
———. "Local Red Cross Membership Will Total More Than 15,750." *Honolulu Star-Bulletin*, October 2, 1917, 2.
Hwangseong Sinmun. "Daikan Sekijūjisha Kōfu Shushi-sho 大韓赤十字社公布趣旨書" [The Aim of the Great Korean Red Cross Society]. *Hwangseong Sinmun*, February 12, 1906, 3.
Japan Times. "Mr. Ishii in Hawaii." *Japan Times*, August 9, 1907, 3.
Maui Shinbun. "Hōkoku no Tameni Ōbo seyo 報國の爲めに應募せよ" [Join the Red Cross to Support the Fatherland]. *Maui Shinbun*, May 7, 1918, 1.
———. "Natsui Haruyoshi-shi Kikoku 夏井春吉氏歸國" [Mr. Haruyoshi Natsui Returns to Japan]. *Maui Shinbun*, April 20, 1920, 3.
———. "Shoku wa Susu'nnde Shukkin seyo 諸君は進んで出金せよ" [Donate to the Red Cross]. *Maui Shinbun*, May 7, 1918, 5.
Nippon Shimbun. "Waga Sekijūji no Kaigai Shinshutsu: Chū-nambei Kakuchi ni I'inbu wo Secchi 我赤十字の海外進出：中南米各地に委員部を設置" [Our Red Cross Goes Abroad: Committee Departments Opened Throughout Central and Latin America]. *Nippon Shimbun*, June 17, 1936, 2.
Nippu Jiji. "Cōhii Hogo Undō: Dantai wo Soshiki 珈琲保護運動期成：團體を組織" [Coffee Industry Protection Association: Foundation of the Association]. *Nippu Jiji*, April 1, 1937, 6.

———. "Ford Working for Pan-Pacific Home: Hopes to Acquire University Club by Time Prince Tokugawa Visits." *Nippu Jiji*, October 27, 1930, 8.

———. "Izumo Taisha Fujin-kai Shusai: Nihon-jin Yōrōin Ian-kai 出雲大社婦人會主催：日本人養老院慰安會" [Izumo Shrine Women's Association Event: Japanese Nursing Home Excursion to Japan]. *Nippu Jiji*, December 9, 1940, 5.

———. "Maronii-jō Iku マロニ嬢逝く" [Mrs. Maroney Passed Away]. *Nippu Jiji*, May 5, 1914, 4.

———. "Naka Kona Kikyōkai: Chinen-shi Kangei-kai 中コナ基教会 智念師觀迎會" [Kona Christian Church Welcoming Clergy]. *Nippu Jiji*, July 17, 1937, 8.

———. "Nihon-jin Yōrōin Zai-in-sha: Chikaku Gojūni mei to Naru 日本人養老院在院者：近く五十二名となる" [Japanese Nursing Home Soon to House Fifty-Two Residents]. *Nippu Jiji*, December 17, 1935, 5.

———. "Prince Iyesato Tokugawa Dies in Tokyo Today: Late Prince Tokugawa, 77, Strove for Promotion of America-Japan Relations." *Nippu Jiji*, June 5, 1940, 9.

———. "Prince Lauds P-P Movement: Tokugawa Expresses Hope That Peace Will Be Furthered." *Nippu Jiji*, December 5, 1930, 10.

Osaka Mainichi. "Kantō Shinsai Gahō, Dai San shū 関東震災画報 第三輯" [Earthquake Pictorial Edition, Part Three]. Tokyo: Osaka Mainichi, 1923.

Seishū Shimpō. "Bankoku Sekijūji Kaigi Tōkyō de Kaisai saru 万國赤十字會議 東京で開催さる" [The International Red Cross Conference Convenes in Tokyo]. *Seishū Shimpō*, October 23, 1934, 2.

———. "Chū to Ai no Nihon Skijūjisha e 忠と愛の日本赤十字社へ" [Joining the Japanese Red Cross Society: Faith and Love]. *Seishū Shimpō*, February 7, 1939, 3.

———. "Heiwa wa Kodomo kara: Umi wo Koete 'Jidō' Akushu 平和は子供から：海を越へて「學童」の握手" [Children Work for Peace: Shaking Hands Across the Seas]. *Seishū Shimpō*, October 19, 1934, 3.

———. "Jūgo Butai no Nekkan: Hakui no Tenshi mo Sanka 銃後部隊の熱汗 白衣の天使も參加" [Desperate Activities of the Home Front Forces: White Angels Also Join]. *Seishū Shimpō*, November 13, 1938, 4.

———. "Sekijūji Byōin wa Shōbyōsha Shūyō ni Miteru 赤十字病院は傷病者収容に充てる" [The Red Cross Hospital Is full of Sick and Wounded]. *Seishū Shimpō*, January 17, 1938, 2.

Sunday Star. "Japanese Peace Worker Soon to Visit Capital: Prince Tokugawa, Grandson of Last Shogun Ruler, Will Make Fifth Tour of U.S." *Sunday Star*, Washington, DC, February 18, 1934, D-3.

Time. "China, Japan & France." *Time*, April 1, 1927. Retrieved April 11, 2011.

Tokuji, Saisho. "Art Music Letters." *Japan Times*, October 24, 1934, 8.

Tokyo Asahi Shimbun. "Nichiman Sekijūjisha Kyōtei 日満赤十字社協定" [The Agreement Between the Japanese Red Cross Society and the Manchukuo Red Cross Society]. *Asahi Shimbun*, July 23, 1938, 1.

Yomiuri Shimbun. "Kaigai no Kotō ni Naku 海外の孤島に泣く" [Lamentations on a Remote Island]. *Yomiuri Shimbun*, March 23, 1908, 3.

———. "Taiheiyō wa Heiwa no Kidō e 太平洋は平和の軌道へ" [Movement Towards Peace in the Pacific]. *Yomiuri Shimbun*, February 26, 1934, 2.

WEBSITES AND DATABASES

American Red Cross of Hawaii. "Our History." Accessed August 30, 2021. https://www.redcross.org/local/hawaii/about-us.html#:~:text=Officially%20chartered%20as%20a%20chapter,during%20the%20Spanish%20American%20War.

Bugnion, François. *International Committee of the Red Cross and the Protection of War Victims. Geneva: International Committee of the Red Cross.* Geneva: International Committee of the Red Cross, 2003. Accessed May 29, 2018. https://www.icrc.org/en/publication/0503-international-committee-red-cross-and-protection-war-victims.

Fukubayashi, Tōru. "POW Camps in Japan Proper." *POW Research Network Japan.* Accessed May 22, 2018. http://www.powresearch.jp/en/archive/camplist/index.html#fukuoka.

Hayashi, Shigeo. *Yamazato no Oka yori Mita Bakushinchi kara Dai-ichi Byōin madeno Panorama* 山里の丘より見た爆心地から第1病院までのパノラマ [HilltopPanoramaView—Ground Zero to the First Hospital], ID: 6-12-00-00-0004. Nagasaki Atomic Bomb Museum, 1945.

Himeyuri Peace Museum. Accessed May 31, 2012. http://www.himeyuri.or.jp/.

Hoji Shinbun Digital Collection. *Scenery-Hawaii: Japanese Nursing Home* 日本人養老院, ID: SH1307.011. Hoover Institution Library & Archives, Stanford University, 1930–1941.

———. *Scenery-Hawaii: Japanese Women Aid Red Cross* 赤十字入りした日本人女性, ID: SH1704.009. Hoover Institution Library & Archives, Stanford University, 1930–1941.

House of Councillors, the National Diet of Japan. "Shitsumon Shuisho: Dai Go-kai Kokkai (Tokubetsu-kai), Tōbensho, Tōbensho Dai Hachi-jū Hachi-gō 質問主意書 第5回国会（特別会）答弁書 答弁書第八十八号 内閣参甲第一〇〇号 昭和二十四年五月二十一日" [Summary of Questions: The Fifth Session (Special Meeting) Answer No. 88-100, May 21, 1949]. Accessed May 29, 2018. http://www.sangiin.go.jp/japanese/joho1/kousei/syuisyo/005/touh/t005088.htm.

Hiroshima Genbaku Sensai-shi 広島原爆戦災誌 [The History of the Hiroshima Atomic Bombing]. Hiroshima Peace Memorial Museum Peace Database, 1971. Accessed April 25, 2022. https://hpmm-db.jp/book/.

Hiroshima Peace Memorial Museum. Accessed April 25, 2022. https://hpmmuseum.jp/.

Hiroshima Peace Memorial Museum Peace Database. "Film Exposed by Atomic Radiation, ID: 0103-0037." Accessed April 25, 2022. https://hpmm-db.jp/list/detail/?cate=artifact&search_type=detail&data_id=19364.

ICRC. "Convention Relative to the Treatment of Prisoners of War. Geneva, 27 July 1929." Accessed January 9, 2024. https://ihl-databases.icrc.org/en/ihl-treaties/gc-pow-1929.

———. *Convention (II) for the Amelioration of the Condition of Wounded, Sick and Shipwrecked Members of Armed Forces at Sea. Geneva, 12 August 1949.* Geneva: ICRC. Accessed April 26, 2022. https://ihl-databases.icrc.org/ihl/full/GCII-commentary#:~:text=Convention%20(II)%20for%20the%20Amelioration,Geneva%2C%2012%20August%201949.&text=With%20this%20Convention%2C%20the%20protection,time%20in%20a%20Geneva%20Convention.

———. "Draft International Convention on the Condition and Protection of Civilians of Enemy Nationality Who Are on Territory Belonging to or Occupied by a Belligerent. Tokyo, 1934." *Treaties, States Parties and Commentaries.* Accessed December 27, 2022. https://ihl-databases.icrc.org/en/ihl-treaties/tokyo-draft-conv-1934.

———. *Protocols Additional to the Geneva Conventions of 12 August 1949*. Geneva: ICRC. Accessed April 26, 2022. https://www.icrc.org/en/doc/assets/files/other/icrc_002_0321.pdf.

———. *Rules of International Humanitarian Law and Other Rules Relating to the Conduct of Hostilities*. Geneva: ICRC, 2005.

———. *The Geneva Conventions of 12 August 1949*. Geneva: ICRC. Accessed April 26, 2022. https://www.icrc.org/en/doc/assets/files/publications/icrc-002-0173.pdf.

Japan Nursing Association. "Toyamaken no Sengo Kango Kyōiku wo Kizuita 'Makita Kise' sann'tte Don'na Hito? 富山県の戦後看護教育を築いた「牧田きせ」さんってどんな人？" [Who Is Makita Kise? Devoted to Nursing Education in Postwar Japan]. Accessed January 31, 2023. https://infini.fan/reports/reports-88/.

Johnstown Area Heritage Association. "The Flood and the American Red Cross: The Flood Was the First Disaster Relief Effort for the Red Cross." Accessed November 27, 2022. https://www.jaha.org/attractions/johnstown-flood-museum/flood-history/the-flood-and-the-american-red-cross/.

Kawahara, Yotsugi 川原四儀. "Ōtagawa Teibō ni Mōkerareta Rinji Kyūgosho, 9 August 1945 太田川堤防に設けられた臨時救護所（1945年8月9日）" [Field Hospitals on Ōta River Bank, 9 August 1945]. Hiroshima Peace Memorial Museum. Accessed June 12, 2021. http://hpmmuseum.jp/modules/exhibition/index.php?action=ItemView&item_id=116&lang=eng.

Konoe, Tadateru. "The Legacy of Hiroshima: A World Without Nuclear Weapons." 2010 World Summit of Nobel Peace Laureates. Accessed May 22, 2018. http://www.jrc.or.jp/vcms_lf/kokusai_HiroshimaspeechENG_111108.pdf.

Livejournal, "Japanese Red Cross Society Hospital in Vladivostok." Accessed October 28, 2021. https://yaromirr.livejournal.com/6528.html.

Ministry of Education, Cultures, Sports, Science, and Technology of Japan. "Gakuto Dōin 学徒動員" [Students Mobilization]. In *Gakusei Hyakunen-shi* 学制百年史 [The 100 Year History of the Education System]. Accessed April 18, 2022. https://www.mext.go.jp/b_menu/hakusho/html/others/detail/1317693.htm.

Miyasaka, Ippei 宮坂一平. "Senchi ni Sasageta Seishun: Moto Nisseki Jūgun Kangofu no Shōgen: Sekijūji no Seishun 戦地にささげた青春 元日赤従軍看護婦の証言 赤十字の精神" [Testimony of Japanese Red Cross Society Nurses on the Battlefield: The Spirit of the Red Cross]. Accessed June 18, 2018. http://www.jiji.com/jc/v4?id=jrcnurse0013.

Nagasaki Atomic Bomb Museum. "Kyū Nagasaki Ika Daigaku Monchū 旧長崎医科大学門柱" [Gate of Nagasaki Medical College]. Accessed April 5, 2023. https://hibakuikou-map.jp/bombed-remains/ikou04/.

Nagasaki Broadcasting Company. "Hibakusha no Shōgen Dai Jūyon kai 被爆者の証言第１４回" [The Voice of Hibakusha, No. 14]. Accessed March 30, 2017. http://archive.fo/QXJcm.

Nagasaki City—Peace and Atomic Bomb. Accessed March 29, 2018. http://nagasakipeace.jp/index_e.html.

———. "Mitsubishi Zōsen Saiwai-machi Kōjō 三菱造船幸町工場" [Mitsusbish Shipbuilding Saiwai-machi Factory]. Accessed June 13, 2018. http://nagasakipeace.jp/japanese/atomic/record/gallery/saiwaimachi.html.

———. "Nagasakiken Bōkū Honbu Ato: Tateyama Bōkūgō 長崎県防空本部跡：立山防空壕" [Tateyama Air Defence Headquarters: Tateyama Air Raid Shelter]. Accessed April 5, 2023. https://nagasakipeace.jp/visit/insti/tateyama.html.

———. "Nagasaki Ikadaigaku Tō 長崎医科大学等" [Nagasaki Medical College and Others]. Accessed April 5, 2023. https://nagasakipeace.jp/search/about_abm/gallery/ikadai.html.

———. "Rescue and Relief Activities." Accessed April 5, 2023. https://nagasakipeace.jp/part_2_09.html.

———. "1945.8.9 at 11:02 A.M. August 9, 1945." Accessed April 5, 2023. https://nagasakipeace.jp/en/search/record/photo/part_2_01.html#:~:text=August%209%2C%201945%20Bockscar%2C%20the,Nagasaki%20was%20overcast%20that%20morning.

Naval History and Heritage Command. "U.S. Prisoners of War and Civilian American Citizens Captured and Interned by Japan in World War II: The Issue of Compensation by Japan." Accessed April 15, 2022. https://www.history.navy.mil/research/library/online-reading-room/title-list-alphabetically/u/us-prisoners-war-civilian-american-citizens-captured.html.

National Diet Library of Japan. "Dojinkai Corporation of Japanese Residing in Brazil and Nihon Hospital." Accessed February 15, 2023. https://www.ndl.go.jp/brasil/e/column/dojinkai.html.

———. "Establishment of Emigration and Settlement Companies." Accessed January 29, 2023. https://www.ndl.go.jp/brasil/e/s3/s3_3.html.

———. "From Colonos to Independent Farmers." Accessed October 28, 2021. https://www.ndl.go.jp/brasil/e/s3/s3_1.html.

———. "Japanese Community Situations Before and After the Outbreak of the War Between Japan and the U.S." Accessed October 12, 2021. https://www.ndl.go.jp/brasil/e/s5/s5_2.html.

———. "Kachigumi and Makegumi." Accessed January 5, 2024. https://www.ndl.go.jp/brasil/e/s6/s6_1.html.

National Museum of Japanese History, "Hawai'i: 150 Years of Japanese Migration and Histories of Dream Islands." Accessed October 13, 2021. https://www.rekihaku.ac.jp/english/exhibitions/project/old/191029/index.html.

Needels, Theodore S. "Genbaku no Hōshasen ni yori Kuroku Kankō shita Ekkusu-sen Firumu 原爆の放射線により黒く感光したX線フィルム [X-ray Film Exposed by Radiation]. ID: 0103-0037," Hiroshima Peace Memorial Museum Peace Database. https://hpmm-db.jp/list/detail/?cate=artifact&search_type=detail&data_id=19364.

Okinawa Prefectural Peace Memorial Museum. Accessed May 22, 2018. http://www.himeyuri.or.jp/EN/info.html.

POW Research Network Japan. "Fukuoka Dai Ni Bunsho (Kōyagi Kawanami Zōsen 福岡第２分所（香焼・川南造船）" [Fukuoka 2b POW Camp: Kōyagi Kawanam Shipbuilding]. Last modified April 2009. Accessed May 29, 2018. http://www.powresearch.jp/jp/pdf_j/powlist/fukuoka/fukuoka_2b_kawanami_j.pdf.

———. "Fukuoka Dai Jūyon Bunsho (Nagasaki Mitsubishi Zōsen) 福岡第１４分所（長崎三菱造船）" [Fukuoka 14b POW Camp: Nagasaki Mitsubishi Shipbuilding]. Last modified June 2012. Accessed May 29, 2018. http://www.powresearch.jp/jp/pdf_j/powlist/fukuoka/fukuoka_14b_nagasaki_j.pdf.

———. "Lisbon Maru." Accessed August 18, 2021. http://www.powresearch.jp/en/archive/ship/lisbon.html.

Sasamoto, Taeko 笹本妙子. "Fukuoka Dai Jūyon Bunsho (Nagasaki-shi Saiwai-cho) 福岡第１４分所（長崎市幸町）." POW Research Network Japan. Accessed May 21, 2014. http://www.powresearch.jp/jp/pdf_j/research/fk14_saiwai_j.pdf.

Shiotsuki, Masao 塩月正雄. *Ōmura Kaigun Byōin* 大村海軍病院 [Ōmura Naval Hospital], ID: 6-06-01-01-0013. Nagasaki Atomic Bomb Museum, 1945.

Shirakawa, Tadahiko しらかわただひこ. "Meiji kara Heisei Nedan-shi 明治〜平成 値段史" [Monetary Value in the Meiji and Taishō Periods]. Accessed March 7, 2022. https://coin-walk.site/J077.htm.

Takahashi Masaaki 高橋正明. "Nishi Renpei-jō, August 8, 1945 西練兵場（1945年8月8日）" [West Parade Grounds]. ID: NG208-05. Hiroshima Peace Memorial Museum Database. Accessed April 26, 2022. https://hpmm-db.jp/list/detail/?cate=picture&search_type=detail&data_id=52746W.

The City of Hiroshima. "Shisha-sū ni Tsuite 死者数について" [Concerning the Number of Victims]. Accessed April 26, 2022. https://www.city.hiroshima.lg.jp/soshiki/48/9400.html.

———. "*Hiroshima Dai Ni Rikugun Byōin Ato* 広島第二陸軍病院跡 The Remains of the Hiroshima Second Army Hospital." Accessed April 26, 2022. https://www.city.hiroshima.lg.jp/soshiki/48/9277.html.

The Japanese Red Cross Society. "About Japanese Red Cross: History." Accessed April 12, 2022. https://www.jrc.or.jp/english/about/history/.

———. "*Hatsu no Saigai kyūgo Katsudō: Bandai-san Funka* 初の災害救護活動〜磐梯山噴火" [The First Natural Disaster Relief Activity: The Eruption of Mount Bandai]. Accessed May 21, 2014. http://www.jrc.or.jp/vcms_lf/plaza_volume1_100715.pdf.

"Posters of the Japanese Red Cross Society," Poster House. Accessed March 25, 2022. https://posterhouse.org/blog/posters-of-the-japan-red-cross-society/.

———. *Sekijūji to Kakuheiki* 赤十字と核兵器 [The Red Cross and Nuclear Weapons]. Accessed April 26, 2022. http://www.jrc.or.jp/activity/international/results/150206_002974.html.

———. "*Tenji Shōkai*, Vol. 1.10, *Nisen-jūichi nen Shichi gatsu Tsuitachi: Pōrando Koji Kyūsai* 展示紹介Ｖｏｌ．１０，２０１１．７．１：ポーランド孤児救済" [Introduction to the Exhibition, Vol. 1.10: Relief Activities for Polish Orphans]. Accessed July 16, 2014. http://www.jrc.or.jp/plaza/l3/l4/Vcms4_00002334.html.

The National Archives. Accessed May 29, 2018. http://www.archives.gov/.

The National WWII Museum, New Orleans, "Research Starters: US Military by the Numbers." Accessed August 27, 2021. https://www.nationalww2museum.org/students-teachers/student-resources/research-starters/research-starters-us-military-numbers.

The Nihon Keizai Shimbun. "Nagoya no Josei Kangoshi ga Jushō: Naichingēru Kishō 名古屋の女性看護師が受賞：ナイチンゲール紀章" [Nurses in Nagoya Awarded the Nightingale Medal]. *The Nihon Keizai Shimbun* 日本経済新聞, May 13, 2017. Accessed June 18, 2018. http://www.nikkei.com/article/DGXLASFD13H2Q_T10C17A5CN0000/.

Toyama Prefectural School of Nursing, Midwifery and Public Health. "Makita Kise-shi no Kōseki 牧田きせ氏の功績" [Contributions of Makita Kise]. Accessed January 31, 2023. https://www.pref.toyama.jp/branches/1277/gakuin/kise%20makita.html.

Ward, Roweba. "The Asia-Pacific War and the Failed Second Anglo-Japanese Civilian Exchange, 1942–45 アジア太平洋戦争と実現しなかった第二次日英残留民間人の交換." *Asia-Pacific Journal: Japan Focus*. Accessed May 29, 2018. http://www.japanfocus.org/-Rowena-Ward/4301.

Yamaguchi-ken Suō Ōshima Monogatari 山口県周防大島物語. "Meiji Yonjū-ni nen Zai Hawai Yamaguchi-ken Jin'mei-bo 明治４２年在ハワイ山口県人名簿" [The Lists of Japanese

Immigrants from Yamaguchi Prefecture to Hawai'i, as of 1909]. Accessed February 14, 2023. https://blog.goo.ne.jp/nonta-oshima-y/e/1947c59ab640cbd987204e6393fc233c.

2018 Kizuna Hawaii. "1860—Kairin-Maru & Powhatan." Accessed October 8, 2021. https://kizuna hawaii.com/timeline/kanrin-maru/.

PERSONAL DOCUMENTS AND CONFERENCE PAPERS

Aoki, Toshiyuki 青木歳幸. "Generality of Humanithropy by Tsunetami Sano 佐野常民の博愛思想とその系譜." Paper presented at *The Ninth International Symposium on History of Indigenous Knowledge (ISHIK2019), Hohhot, China, August 17, 2019*.

Ōe, Kenzaburō 大江健三郎. "Hiroshima no Heiwa Shisō wo Tsutaeru, Dai Ikkai Kōenkai 広島の平和思想を伝える 第１回講演会" [The Peace Ideology of Hiroshima No. 1]. Lecture Organized by the Hiroshima Peace Culture Centre of Hiroshima City, Hiroshima, October 2, 2010.

Tasaki, Hiroshi 田崎浩. "Haiki deno Hibakusha Kyūgo to Niji-hibaku no Taiken 早岐での被爆者救護活動と二次被爆の体験" [Experience of Atomic Bombing Relief Activities and Indirect Exposure in Haiki]. Accessed May 29, 2016. http://www.geocities.jp/sasebun/shiru/3taikenhibaku.pdf.

Tomonaga, Masao 朝長万左男. "Humanitarian Impact of Nuclear Weapons." Accessed April 26, 2022. http://www.regjeringen.no/upload/UD/Vedlegg/Hum/hum_tomonaga.pdf.

U.S. Army Center of Military History. Accessed May 22, 2018. http://www.history.army.mil/.

U.S. Strategic Bombing Survey. "The Effects of the Atomic Bombings of Hiroshima and Nagasaki, June 19, 1946. President's Secretary's File, Truman Papers." Accessed February 11, 2020. https://www.trumanlibrary.gov/library/research-files/u-s-strategic-bombing-survey-effects-atomic-bombings-hiroshima-and-nagasaki.

Yamaguchi, Tadayoshi 山口忠喜. "Bakushin-chi kara nijū-go kiro-mētoru Hanareta Isayaya de Mokugeki shita 'Iki-jigoku' no Wasure-enu Kioku 爆心地から２５ｋｍ離れた諫早で目撃した「生き地獄」の忘れえぬ記憶" [Indelible Memories of "Living Hell": What I Saw in Isahaya, 25 km from the Hypocenter]. Accessed January 6, 2024. https://www.city.isahaya.nagasaki.jp/soshiki/7/2141.html.

ARCHIVAL DOCUMENTS

Diplomatic Archives of the Ministry of Foreign Affairs of Japan, Tokyo, Japan. *Sekijūji Kokusai Kaigi Kankei Ikken, Dai Ni-kan* 赤十字国際会議関係一件 第二巻 [Documents Related to the International Conference of the Red Cross, Vol. 2]. REF: I-5-3-0-3_002.

———. REF: I-5-3-0-3_002.

———. [Vol. 4]. REF: I-5-3-0-3_004.

———. *Sekijūji Kankei Zakken* 赤十字社関係雑件 [Documents Related to the Red Cross Society]. REF: B-3-11-3-14.

BIBLIOGRAPHY 297

ICRC Archives, Geneva, Switzerland. B G 003 51-3, G3/51. "Diary to the Report: Report on the Evacuation of POW & CI in the Hiroshima Sector, September 17, 1945." Correspondence entre le siège et Marcel Junod, 03/01/1945–12/04/1946.

———. B G 003 51-4, G3/51. "Report by Marcel Junod on 9 November, 1945." *Letters reçues de Marcel Junod (don't rapports n*3?, 4–9) (après mai 1946, voir G8 76: 24.04.1945–05.11.1947).*

———. A CL 16.06.02 Appendix 3, "Report on the Effects of the Atomic Bomb at Hiroshima."

———. CR 00/91-263, Croix-Rouge de Madchoukouo, 1–23, 01.12.1934–14.02.1950.

———. CR 217, Conflict sino-japonais, Correspondance avec les Croix-Rouges (E-Z), 03.08.1937–07.08.1939, Croix-Rouge japonaise, 03.08.1937–30.03.1938, correspondence envoyée, 03.08.1937–19.12.1938, no. 5.

———. CR 217, Conflict sino-japonaise—Correspondance avec les Croix-Rouges Letter A-D, 07.08.1937–14.07.1939, Croix-Rouge américaine, 07.08.1937–05.01.1939.

———. Croix-Roue britannique, 31.08.1937–10.12.1938.

———. Croix-Rouge chinoise, 14.08.1937–15.06.1939.

———. Correspondence envoyée, Correspondance reçue, 29.08.1937–27.12.1938. No. 0.

———. CRi 15/I, XV Conference, Intern, De La + Rouge I, 1 à 150, du 26.5.1931 au 21.6.1934.

———. CRi 15/II, XV Conference II, 151 à 300, du 26.6.1934 au 12.11.1934.

———. CRi 15/0 25, Bulletin XV Conference, Voyage XV Conf.

ICRC Database. "Treaties, States Parties and Commentaries, Draft International Convention on the Condition and Protection of Civilians of Enemy Nationality Who Are on Territory Belonging to or Occupied by a Belligerent, Tokyo, 1934." Accessed May 19, 2023. https://ihl-databases.icrc.org/en/ihl-treaties/tokyo-draft-conv-1934?activeTab=historical.

IFRC Archives. "League of Red Cross Societies Monthly Bulletin Vo. XV No. 9 September 1933."

———. "Regulations of the XVth International Red Cross Conference." League of Red Cross Societies Monthly Bulletin Vol. XV No. 12, December 1934: 232–40.

Japan Center for Asian Historical Records, Tokyo, Japan. *Sekijūji Kokusai Kaigi Kankei Ikken, Dai Ni-kan, Ichi, Shōwa hachi-nen, Bunkatsu Ichii* 赤十字国際会議関係一件 第二巻 １．昭和八年 分割１．[Documents Relating to the International Conference of the Red Cross, Vol. 2–1, 1933, Part 1]. REF: B04013279200.

———. [Part 2]. REF: B04013279300.

———. [Part 4]. REF: B04013279500.

———. [Vol. 4, Part 1]. REF: B04013280200.

———. *Nijū, Kaigai Tokubetsu-i'inbu Secchi* 20. 海外特別委員部設置 [20. Foundation of Foreign Committee Departments]. REF: B12082304000.

———. *Sanjūni, Kanada Bankūbaa* 32. 加奈太晩香坡 [Vancouver, Canada]. REF: B12082305200.

Matsuda, Hiromichi 松田弘道. "Fukuoka Furyo Shūyōjo Daini-bunsho no Horyo Tachi 福岡俘虜収容所第２分所の捕虜たち" [Allied POWs at Fukuoka 2-B Camp in Nagasaki]. ID: Matsuda Hiromichi File No. 9, 25 December 1943. The Research Committee for Photographic Records of Nagasaki Atomic Bombing, Nagasaki Foundation for the Promotion of Peace.

Meiji-Mura Museum Japanese Red Cross Archives, Toyota College of Nursing, Toyota-City, Japan. *Akō Tokubetsu-i'inbu, Ji Taishō Jūni nen Itaru Jūyo nen* 亜港特別委員部 自大正十二年 至十四年 [Alexandrovsk-Sakhalinsky Special Committee Department, 1923–1925]. ID: 1749-4022.

———. "Bericht: des Herrn Dr. F. Paravicini, in Yokohama, über seinen Besuch der Gefangenenlager in Japan (30. Juni bis 16. Juli 1918), Internationales Komitee Vom Roten Kreuz, Dokumente, Herausgegeben Während Des, Krieges 1914–1918, Zwanzigste Folge ジュネーブ赤十字国際委員会代表ドクトル パラヴィチニ 在日本俘虜収容所視察報告書" [The Report on POW Detention Visits by Dr. Paravicini, ICRC Japan Delegation]. In *Sekijūji-kokusai-i'inkai: Zai-honnpō Doku-Ō Furyo Shisatsu Kankei, Taishō Roku nen* 赤十字国際委員會 在本邦独墺俘虜視察関係 大正六年 [International Committe of the Red Cross: Documents Related to German and Austrian POW Detention Visits, 1917]. ID: B1132-3130.

———. *Chōsen-honbu Kan'nai I'inbu Sōkai, Shōwa Jūsan nen* 朝鮮本部 管内 委員部總會 昭和十三年 [The General Assembly at the Korean Headquarters, Branches, and Committee Departments, 1938]. ID: B1085-4366.

———. *Chōsen-honbu Sōkai Manshū-honbu Shainshō Juten Tokugawa Fuku-shachō Shucchō Hōkoku, Shōwa Hachi nen Jūichi* 朝鮮本部總會 満州本部社員章授典 徳川副社長出張報告 昭和八年十一月 [Report on Vice-President Tokugawa's Visit to JRCS Korean Headquarters General Assembly, and the Medals Award Ceremony for Membership of JRCS Manchurian Committee Department, November 1933]. ID: 1752-4037.

———. *Chūshihōmen Imon Shisatsu Hōkoku: Furoku, Shashinchō, Kitagawa Shokutaku Hōkoku, Shōwa jūyo nen go gatsu* 中支方面慰問視察報告 附録 写真帖 北川嘱託報告 昭和十四年五月 [Report of the Investigation in Central China, Photo Album by Office Kitagawa, May 1939]. ID: B1213-4513.

———. *Dai Jūgo-kai Sekijūji Kokusai-kaigi, Shōwa Shichi-nen Itaru dō Kyū nen* 第十五回赤十字國際會議 自昭和七年 至と九年 [The Fifteenth International Red Cross Conference, 1931–1934]. ID: B1098-4383.

———. [1932]. ID: B1097-4382.

———. [1933–1934]. ID: B1100-4385.

———. [1932–1933]. ID: B1096-4381.

———. [1934]. ID: B1101-4386.

———. ID: B1102-4387.

———. ID:1106-4391.

———. ID: B1107-4392.

———. [1935–1936]. ID: B1115-4400.

———. [Documents Related to Brown and Gielgud: The Fifteenth International Red Cross Conference, 1932–1934]. ID: B1099-4384.

———. *Eikoku Sekijūjisha Senji Jigyō Hōkokusho* 英国赤十字社 戦時事業調査報告書 [Research Report on the Wartime Relief Activities of the British Red Cross]. (1916). ID: 636-735.

———. *Harubin Chōsenjin Kyoryūmin-kai Seigansho* 哈爾浜朝鮮人居留民會請願書 [Petition by the Association for Korean Residents in Harbin]. In *Nakagawa Fuku-shachō Manshū Chōsen Shucchō Fukumei, Shōwa Hachi nen* 中川副社長満洲朝鮮出張復命 昭和八年 [Report on Vice-President Nakagawa's Visit to Manchuria and Korea, 1933]. ID: 1739-3982.

———. *Hawai Tokubetsu-i'inbu Hikitsugi Shain Meibo, Meiji Yonjūsan nen* 布哇特別委員部 引継社員名簿 昭和四十年四月 [Membership List of the Hawai'i Special Committee Department, April 1907]. ID: B1429-2853.

——. *Hawai Tokubetsu-i'inbu Kankei, Meiji Sanjūkyū nen Itaru Yonjūnen* 布哇特別委員部 明治三十九年 至四十年 [Documents Relating to Hawai'i Special Committee Department, 1906–1907]. ID: B1346-2379.

——. *Kagakusen Jinmin Hogo Kokusai I'inkai: Shōwa Ni nen Itaru Go nen* 化學戰人民保護國際委員会 昭和二年至五年 [International Committee for Protection of Civilians from Chemical Warfare, 1927–1930]. ID: B1731-3968.

——. *Manshū Pesuto Kankei, Meiji Yonjūyo nen Zen* 満洲ペスト関係 明治四十四年全 [Documents Related to the Plague Pandemic in Manchuria, 1911]. ID: B788-1054.

——. *Mansen, Karafuto, Tokubetsu-i'inbu Kankei, Ji Taishō Jūni nen Itaru Shōwa San nen* 満鮮、樺太 特別委員部関係自大正十二年 至昭和三年 [File on the Special Committee Departments in Manchuria, Korea, and Karafuto, 1923–1928]. ID: B1681-3493.

——. *Man, Sen, Karafuto Tokubetsu-i'inbu Shokuin Shokkai, Ji Shōwa Go nen Itaru dō Roku nen* 満、鮮、樺太 特別委員部 職員嘱解 自昭和五年 至同六年 [Staff Recruitment and Dismissal Records at the Special Committee Departments in Manchuria, Korea, and Karafuto, 1930–1931]. ID: B1185-3868.

——. [1932–1933]. ID: B1789-4160.

——. *Manshū, Chōsen, Karafuto-i'inbu Shain Sōkai, Taishō Jūichi nen* 満州、朝鮮 樺太委員部 社員総会 大正十一年 [The General Assembly at the Special Committee Departments in Manchuria, Korea, and Karafuto, 1922]. ID: B1146-3175.

——. *Manshū, Chōsen, Karafuto, Tokubetsu-i'inbu Kankei, Ji Shōwa Yo nen Itaru dō Shichi nen* 満洲、朝鮮、樺太 特別委員部 関係 自昭和四年 至同七年 [Documents About the Special Committee Departments in Manchuria, Korea, and Karafuto, 1929–1932]. ID: B1746-4019.

——. *Nakagawa Fuku-shachō Manshū Shōsen Shuchō Fukumei, Shōwa Hachi nen* 中川副社長満洲朝鮮出張復命 昭和八年 [Report on Vice-President Nakagawa's Visit to Manchuria and Korea, 1933]. ID: 1739-3982.

——. *Nihon Sekijūjisha Chōsen Honbu Byōin Nenpō, Shōwa Jūni nen* 日本赤十字社朝鮮本部病院年報（昭和十二年） [Annual Report of the Japanese Red Cross Society Korean Headquarters Hospital, 1937]. In *Chōsen-honbu Kan'nai I'inbu Sōkai, Shōwa Jūsan nen* 朝鮮本部 管内 委員部總會 昭和十三年 [The General Assembly at the Korean Headquarters, Branches, and Committee Departments, 1938]. ID: B1085-4366.

——. *Nihon Sekijūjisha Chōsen Honbu Shinryōjo Dai Ikkai Nenpō, Taishō Jūgo nen* 日本赤十字社朝鮮本部診療所第一回年報（大正十三年） [The First Annual Report of the Japanese Red Cross Society Korean Headquarters Clinic, 1924]. In *Chōsen Honbu Byōin, Taishō Jūgo nen* 朝鮮本部病院 大正十五年 [Japanese Red Cross Society Korean Headquarters Hospital, 1926]. ID: 1688-3496.

——. *Ōshū Senran: Futsukoku Haken Kyūgohan Hōkokusho, Hōkoku Dai Jūsan-gō* 欧州戦乱 佛國派遣救護班報告書 報告第十三号 [The European Great War: Report on the Japanese Red Cross Society Relief Parties to France, Vol. 13]. (1915). ID: 725.

——. *Sekijūji-kokusai-i'inkai Shanhai Haken: Wattoviru Taisa Ikken, Shōwa Jūni nen* 赤十字國際委員会上海派遣 ワットヴィル大佐一件 昭和十二年 [The Deployment of the International Committee of the Red Cross to Shanghai: The Case of Colonel Watteville 1937]. ID: B1067-4324.

———. *Shagyō Genkyō-sho Shōwa Hachi nen Ni gatsu, Nihon Sekijūjisha Shingishū-shibu* 社業現況書昭和八年二月日本赤十字社新義州支部 [Report on JRCS Sinŭiju Chapter, February 1933]. In *Nakagawa Fuku-shachō Manshū Chōsen Shucchō Fukumei, Shōwa Hachi nen* 中川副社長満洲朝鮮出張復命 昭和八年 [Report on Vice-President Nakagawa's Visit to Manchuria and Korea, 1933]. ID: 1739-3982.

———. *Shinsai ni Kansuru Hijōbu Kessaisho, Taishō Jūni nen Ku gatsu Itaru dō Jūsan nen Jū gatsu* 震災ニ関スル非常部決裁書 自大正十二年九月 至同十三年十月 [Documentation Approval for the Disaster by the Emergency Department, September 1923–October 1924]. ID:1163.

———. *Sovieto Renpō Sekijūjisha yori Mimaikin Haibunkata ni Kansuru Bunsho, Shōwa Kyū-nen* ソヴィエト聯邦赤十字社ヨリ見舞金配分方ニ関スル文書 昭和九年 [Documents Related to Donations by the Union of Red Cross and Red Crescent Societies of the USSR]. ID: B1822-4249.

———. *Zai Berurin Oikawa Shigenobu Kankei, Meiji Yonjū nen* 在伯林老川茂信関係 明治四十年 [Documents Related to Oikawa Shigenobu in Berlin, 1907]. ID: 1396-2428.

———. *Zai Hawai Ishii Isakichi Kankei, Meiji Sanjūshichi nen Itaru Yonjūnen* 在布哇石井勇吉関係 明治三十七年 至四十年 [Documents Related to Ishii Yūkichi, 1904–1907]. ID: B1372-2410.

———. *Zai Hawai Kishi Kantarō Kankei, Meiji Sanjūshichi nen Itaru Yonjūnen* 在布哇岸幹太郎関係 明治三十七年 至四十年 [Documents Related to Kishi Kantarō, 1904–1907]. ID: B1375-2413.

———. *Zai Hawai Mōri Iga Kankei, Meiji Sanjūshichi nen* 在布哇毛利伊賀関係 明治三十七年 [Documents Related to Ishii Yūkichi, 1904]. ID: B1365-2400.

———. *Zai Hawai Mukōda, Yasuda, Kankei, Meiji Sanjūhachi nen Itaru Yonjūnen* 在布哇向田、安田、関係 明治三十八年 至四十年 [Documents Related to Mukōda and Ysuda, 1905–1907]. ID: B1387-2419.

———. *Zai Hawai Norizuki, Onami, Hayashi Kankei, Meiji Sanjūshichi nen Itaru Yonjū nen* 在布哇法月、尾浪、林関係 明治三十七年 至四十年 [Documents Related to Ishii Yūkichi, 1904–1907]. ID: B1383-2415.

———. *Zai Honolulu Aikoku Fujinkai Kankei, Meiji Sanjūshichi nen Dō Sanjūhachi nen* 在ホノルル愛國婦人會関係 明治三十七年 同三十八年 [Documents Related to Patriotic Women's Association in Honolulu, 1904–1905]. ID: B1348-2381.

———. *Zai Jawa Yokotake Heitarō Kankei Shorui, Meiji Sanjūkyū nen* 在爪哇横竹平太郎関係 明治三十九年 [Documents Related to Yokotake Heitarō, 1906]. ID: B1370-2408.

———. *Zai Munbai, Majima, Furugōri Kankei, Meiji Sanjū-shichi nen Itaru Yonjū nen* 在孟買間島、古郡関係 明治三十七年 至四十年 [Documents Related to Majima and Furugōri in Mumbai, 1904–1907]. ID: B1385-2417.

———. *Zai Nyūyōk Sōryōji Kankei, Meiji Sanjū-shichi nen Itaru Sanjū-kyū nen* 在紐育日本総領事関係 明治三十七年 至三十九年 [Documents Related to the General-Consulate of Japan in New York, 1904–1906]. ID: 1356-2389.

———. *Zai Taunzuviiru Nihonryōjikan Kankei, Meiji Sanjū-shichi nen Itaru Yonjū nen* 在タウンズヴ井ール日本領事館関係 明治三十七年 至四十年 [Documents Related to the Consulate of Japan in Townsville, 1904–1907]. ID: B1361-2396.

Museum of Japanese Immigrants in Brazil Archive, Sao Paolo, Brazil. *Postcard by Foreign Business Company*.

The Japanese Red Cross Society Disaster Relief Division, Disaster Management and Social Welfare Department Archives, Tokyo, Japan. *Kyūgohan Gyōmuhōkokusho: Nihon Sekijūjisha Dai Yonjūroku, Yonjūhachi Kyūgohan, Senkyūhyaku-sanjūhachi-nen shichi-gatsu nano-ka kara Senkyūhyaku-sanjūhachi-nen shichi-gatsu nijūichi-nichi* 業務報告書：日本赤十字社第４６，４８救護班（１９３８年７月７日—１９３８年７月２１日）[Working Reports of Wartime Relief Parties: Japanese Red Cross Society, Relief Party No. 46 and No. 48 (July 7, 1938–July 21, 1938)].

———. *Senjikyūgohan Gyōmuhōkokusho* 戦時救護班業務報告書 [Working Reports of Wartime Relief Parties].

———. *Senjikyūgohan Gyōmuhōkokusho: Nihon Sekijūjisha Hokkaidōshibu, Dai Ryoppyaku-nijūhachi Kyūgohan, Sen-kyūhyaku-jonjūyo-nen kara Sen-kyūhyaku-yonjūgo-nen jū-gatsu* 戦時救護班業務報告書：日本赤十字社北海道支部第６２８救護班（１９４４年７月—１９４５年１０月）[Working Reports of Wartime Relief Parties: Japanese Red Cross Society Hokkaido Chapter, Relief Party No. 628 (July 1944–October 1945)].

———. [Japanese Red Cross Society Hyōgo Chapter, Relief Party No. 106 (December 1940–August 1946)].

———. *Senjikyūgohan Gyōmuhōkokusho: Nihon Sekijūjisha Hyōgokenshibu, Dai Hyaku-yonjū Kyūgohan, Senkyūhyaku-sanjūshichi-nen ku-gatsu kara Senkyūhyaku-yonjū-nen jūni-gatsu* 戦時救護班業務報告書：日本赤十字社兵庫県支部第１４０救護班（１９３７年９月—１９４０年１２月）[Working Reports of Wartime Relief Parties: Japanese Red Cross Society Hyōgo Chapter, Relief Party No. 140 (September 1937–December 1940)].

The Japanese Red Cross Society International Department Archives, Tokyo, Japan. *Furyo ni Kansuru Sho-hōki Ruishū* 俘虜ニ関スル諸法規類集 [Collection of the Conventions on POW Treatment]. Tokyo: Furyo Jōhōkyoku [Prisoner of War Information Bureau], 1946.

———. *Furyo Toriatsukai no Kiroku, (Shōwa sanjū-nen jūni-gatsu)* 俘虜取扱の記録（昭和三十年十二月）[Records of POW Treatment]. Tokyo: Furyo Jōhōkyoku, 1955.

———. *Kizōtosho Kankei 154, Dai San-kai Han-bei Sekijūji Kaigi ni Kansuru Bunsho* 第三回汎米赤十字会議ニ関スル文書 [Documents Related to the Third Pan American Red Cross Conference].

———. *Sengo Shori Kankei 250, Manshū Chōsen deno Furyo no Atsukai ni kakaru Sekijūji-kokusai-i'inkai tono Tsūshinbunsho-tō* 戦後処理関係２５０：満州・朝鮮での俘虜の扱いに係る赤十字国際委員会との通信文書等 [Documents Related to Allied Occupation Period, No. 250: Correspondence with the ICRC Regarding POW Treatment in Manchukuo and Korea].

———. *Furyo・Hi-yokuryūsha Kyūjutsu Kanren Bunsho, Seiri bangō Ichi: Furyo oyobi Hinan'min Kankei Tsuzuri, Chōsa-bu* 俘虜・被抑留者救恤関連文書 整理番号-０１：俘虜及避難民関係綴 調査部 [Documents Related to the Treatment of POWs and Civilian Internees, No. 1: Documents Related to POWs and Refugees, the Investigation Department].

———. *Seiri bangō Go no Ichi: Senji no Katsudō Zenpan ni Kansuru Sekijūji-kokusai-i'inkai tono Kōshin, (Ichi), (Shōwa Jūyo nen Ku gatsu kara Jūhachi nen Hachi gatsu)* 俘虜・被抑留者救恤関連文書 整理番号-０５-１：戦時の活動全般に関する赤十字国際委員会との交

信（一）（昭和14年9月〜18年8月）[Documents Related to the Treatment of POWs and Civilian Internees, No. 5-1: Correspondence with the International Committee of the Red Cross Related to Wartime Activities, Vol. 1, (September 1939 to August 1943)].

———. *Seiri bangō Hachi: Sekijūji-kokusai-i'inkai tono Kōshin, (Shōwa jūroku-nen jūni-gatsu kara nijūni-nen ichi-gatsu): Furyo, Zai-yokuryūtekikokujin no Kyūjutsu ni Kansuru ken, Shanhai Sekijūji-kokusai-i'inkai Egure Daihyō karano Gyōmu Hōkoku, Urajiosutokku Keiyu Beikoku-jin Furyo narabi Hi-yokuryūsha ate Kyūjutsuhin oyobi Tsūshin no Yusō, Chūnichi-daihyō-sha no Shogū tō ni Kansuru ken Hoka* 俘虜・被抑留者救恤関連文書 整理番号-０８：赤十字国際委員会との交信（昭和16年12月〜22年1月）：俘虜・在留敵国人俘虜の救恤に関する件、在上海赤十字国際委員会エグレ代表からの業務報告、ウラジオストック経由米国人俘虜並被抑留者宛救恤品及通信の輸送、駐日代表者の処遇等に関する件ほか [Documents Related to the Treatment of POWs and Civilian Internees, No. 8: Correspondence with the International Committee of the Red Cross (December 1941 to January 1947): POW and Enemy Civilian Treatment; the Report from Egle, the Head of Shanghai Office, the International Committee of the Red Cross; Parcels and Messages for American POWs Transported from Vladivostok and Civilian Internees; the Head of the Japan Delegation, the International Committee of the Red Cross, etc.].

———. *Seiri bangō Jūhachi: Naigai Furyo Shūyōjo eno Buppin Kizō, (Shōwa jūshichi-nen jū-gatsu kara jūhachi-nen shi-gatsu)* 俘虜・被抑留者救恤関連文書 整理番号-１８：内外俘虜収容所への物品寄贈。（昭和17年10月〜18年4月）[Documents Related to the Treatment of POWs and Civilian Internees, No. 18: Relief Parcels for POW Camps Inside and Outside the Main Islands of Japan (October 1942 to April 1943)].

———. *Seiri bangō Jū no Ni: Furyo Kyūjutsu tō ni Kansuru Sekijūji-kokusai-i'inkai tono Kōshin, (Ni), (Shōwa jūkyū-nen shi-gatsu kara nijū-nen roku-gatsu: Pesutarocchi Daihyō ni yoru Furyo Shūyōjo (Fukuoka Dai Jūnana Bunsho, Dō Dai Jūni Bunsho, Zentsūji) Shisatsu, Zai-Man Furyo, Hi-yokuryūsha ni tsuite, Angusuto Daihyō-ho ni yoru Shūyōjo (Hakodate, Muroran, Kamaishi) Shisatsu tōtō* 俘虜・被抑留者救恤関連文書 整理番号-１０-２：俘虜救恤等に関する赤十字国際委員会との交信（二）（昭和19年4月〜20年6月）：ペスタロッツィ代表による俘虜収容所（福岡第１７分所・同第１２分所、善通寺）視察、在満俘虜・被抑留者について、アングスト代表補による収容所（函館、室蘭、釜石）視察、等々 [Documents Related to the Treatment of POWs and Civilian Internees, No. 10-2: Correspondence with the International Committee of the Red Cross Regarding POW Treatment, Vol. 1 (April 1944 to June 1945): Protection Visits by Pestalozzi to POW Camps (Fukuoka 17 and 12, Zentsūji); POWs and Civilian Internees in Manchukuo; Protection Visits of Angst, Assistant Delegate, to POW Camps (Hakodate, Muroran, Kamaishi), etc.].

———. *Seiri bangō Jū no Ichi: Furyo Kyūjutsu tō ni Kansuru Sekijūji-kokusai-i'inkai tono Kōshin, (Ichi), (Shōwa jūshichi-nen ni-gatsu kara jūkyū-nen ni-gatu): Kyūjutsu Haikyū, Kōkansen Gurripusuhorumu-gō, Teia-maru Sekisai Kyūjutsuhin, Sekijūji-kokusai-i'inkai Chūnichi-daihyō-ho Pesutarocchi ni yoru Furyo Shūyōjo (Zentsūji, Ōsaka-honjo, Sakurajima-bunsho, Amagasaki-bunsho, Motomachi, Ube-bunsho, Onoda-bunsho, Ōhama-bunsho, Hakodate-honjo, Kamaishi-bunsho) Shisatsu tō* 俘虜・被抑留者救恤関連文書 整理番号-１０-１：俘虜救恤等に関する赤十字国際委員会との交信（一）（昭和17年2月〜19年2月）：救恤品配

給、交換船グリップスホルム号・帝亜丸積載救恤品、赤十字国際委員会駐日代表補ペスタロッツィによる俘虜収容所（善通寺、大阪本所、桜島分所、尼ケ崎分所、元町、宇部分所、小野田分所、大濱分所、函館本所、釜石分所）視察等 [Documents Related to the Treatment of POWs and Civilian Internees, No. 10-1: Correspondence with the International Committee of the Red Cross Regarding POW Treatment, Vol. 1 (February 1942 to February 1944): Aid Parcels on M.S. Gripsholm and Teia Maru; Protection Visits by Pestalozzi, Delegate of Japan Delegation, the International Committee of the Red Cross, to Zentsūji, Ōsaka-honjo, Sakurajima-bunsho, Amagasaki-bunsho, Motomachi, Ube-bunsho, Onoda-bunsho, Ōhama-bunsho, Hakodate-honjo, and Kamaishi-bunsho POW Camps].

———. *Seiri bangō Jūroku: Beikoku Sekijūjisha tono Kōshin, (Shōwa jūshichi-nen shi-gatsu kara nijū-nen shichi-gatsu): Beikokujin Furyo oyobi Beikokujin Yokuryūsha ni Kansuru ken narabini Beikoku Musabetsu Bakugeki ni Kansuru ken tō* 俘虜・被抑留者救恤関連文書 整理番号-１６：米国赤十字社との交信（昭和17年4月〜20年7月）：米国人俘虜及び米国人抑留者に関する件並びに米国無差別爆撃に関する件等 [Documents Related to the Treatment of POWs and Civilian Internees, No. 16: American POWs and Civilian Internees; Indiscriminate US Air Raids (April 1942 to July 1945)].

———. *Seiri bangō Jūsan: Seikatsu Konkyūsha ni Kansuru Shiryō, (Shōwa jūshichi-nen shi-gatsu kara jūkyū-nen go-gatsu)* 俘虜・被抑留者救恤関連文書 整理番号-１３：生活困窮者の救済に関する資料．（昭和17年4月〜19年5月） [Documents Related to the Treatment of POWs and Civilian Internees, No. 13: Documents Related to Poverty Relief Activities (April 1942 to May 1944)].

———. *Seiri bangō Jūsan no Ichi: Seikatsu Konkyūsha ni Kansuru Shiryō* 俘虜・被抑留者救恤関連文書 整理番号-１３-１：生活困窮者の救済に関する資料 [Documents Related to the Treatment of POWs and Civilian Internees, No. 13-1: Documents Related to Poverty Relief Activities].

———. *Seiri bangō Ni: Shōwa jūshichi-nen san-gatsu: Furyo Kyūjutsu-i'inbu: Sekijūji Tsūshin, Dō-yūzei, Kōkansen Takusō: Sekijūji Tsūshin, Shūyōjo, Zatsu* 俘虜・被抑留者救恤関連文書 整理番号-０２：昭和十七年三月 俘虜救恤委員部：赤十字通信・同郵税・交換船託送、赤十字通信・収容所・雑 [Documents Related to the Treatment of POWs and Civilian Internees, No. 2: Red Cross Messages, Postage Fees, and Shipment; Red Cross Messages and Camps, etc., March 1942].

———. *Seiri bangō Nijū: Sekijūji-kokusai-i'inkai tono Kōshin, (Shōwa jūhachi-nen san-gatsu kara jūkyū-nen jū-gatsu (March 1943 to October 1944): Beikokujin Furyo Kyūjutsu (Beikoku Sekijūjisha), Nihon Kokunai Seikatsu Konkyū Gaikokujin Kyūsai, tōtō ni Kansuru ken* 俘虜・被抑留者救恤関連文書 整理番号-２０：赤十字国際委員会との交信（昭和18年3月〜19年10月）：米国人俘虜救恤（米国赤十字社）、日本国内生活困窮外国人救済、等々に関する件 [Documents Related to the Treatment of POWs and Civilian Internees, No. 20: Correspondences with the International Committee of the Red Cross (March 1943 to October 1944): American POW Treatment (The American Red Cross); Poverty Relief Activities for Foreign Civilians, etc.].

———. *Seiri bangō Nijūnana: Furyo matawa Hi-sentōin ate Kyūjutsu-hin Mushō Yusō, (Shōwa jūhachi-nen jūichi-gatsu kara nijū-nen shi-gatsu)* 俘虜・被抑留者救恤関連文書 整理

番号-２７：俘虜又ハ抑留非戦闘員宛救恤品無償運送．（昭和18年11月〜20年4月）[Documents Related to the Treatment of POWs and Civilian Internees, No. 26: The Transportation of Charity Parcels for POWs and Civilian Internees (November 1943 to April 1945)].

——. *Seiri bangō Nijūsan: Furyo Shūyōjo Shisatsu Kanren Shiryō, (Shōwa jūhachi-nen roku-gatsu kara): Furyo Kyūjutsu I'inchō Seibu Gunkanku-ka Furyo Shūyōjo Shisatsu, Honkon Nanpō Shisatsu, Shimazu Shachō no Seibu Gunkanku-ka Furyo Shūyōjo (Kumamoto, Shin-iizuka, Nagasaki, Nishi-sonogi-gun Kashii-mura, Orio, Yahata, Moji) Shisatsu ni Kansuru Shucchō Gyōmu Hōkokusho, tōtō* 俘虜・被抑留者救恤関連文書 整理番号-２３：俘虜収容所視察関係資料（昭和18年6月〜）：俘虜救恤委員長西部軍管下俘虜収容所視察・香港南方出張視察、島津副社長の西部軍管下俘虜収容所（熊本、新飯塚、長崎、西彼杵群香椎村、折尾、八幡、門司）視察に関する出張業務報告書、等々 [Documents Related to the Treatment of POWs and Civilian Internees, No. 23: Documents Related to Protection Visits to POW Camps (from June 1943): Reports on Protection Visits by Shimazu to POW Camps in Hong Kong, South East Asia, and Western Military District (*Kumamoto, Shin-i'izuka, Nagasaki, Nishi-sonogi-gun Kashii-mura, Orio, Yahata, Moji*)].

——. *Seiri Bangō Roku: Shina Jihen ni Okeru Waga Seiryoku Han'inai no Risaimin Kyūgo ni Tsuite* 俘虜・被抑留者救恤関連文書 整理番号-０６：支那事変に於ける我勢力範囲内の罹災民救護に就て [Documents Related to the Treatment of POWs and Civilian Internees, No. 6: Medical Relief for Victims of the Second Sino-Japanese War in the Occupied Territories of Japan].

——. *Seiri bangō San: Furyo Kyūjustu Kitei* 俘虜・被抑留者救恤関連文書 整理番号-０３：俘虜救恤員規定 [Documents Related to the Treatment of POWs and Civilian Internees, No. 3: The Regulations for War Prisoners Relief].

——. *Seiri bangō yon: Sekijūji-kokusai-i'inkai kara no Denpōtō, (Shōwa jūroku-nen jūni-gatsu kara jūshichi-nen san-gatsu): Furyo Jōyaku Tekiyō to Furyo Jōhōkyoku Secchi ni Kansuru Kōshin, Nisseki Shachō ate Bunsho tō: Senkyūhyaku-yonjū-ni nen Ichi gatsu Kokonoka hatsu Dai Yonsen-yonhyaku-nijūni-gō* 俘虜・被抑留者救恤関連文書　整理番号-０４：赤十字国際委員会からの電報等（昭和16年12月〜17年3月）：俘虜条約適用と俘虜情報局設置に関する交信、日赤社長宛文書等：一九四二年一月九日発 第四四二二号 [Documents Related to the Treatment of POWs and Civilian Internees, No. 4: Telegrams from the International Committee of the Red Cross (December 1941 to March 1942): Application to the Treaty for POW Treatment and the Foundation of the Prisoner of War Information Bureau, Letters to the Japanese Red Cross Society President, etc. 9 January 1942, No. 4422].

——. *Sonota Kokusaibu Hokan Bunsho, Seiri bangō Ni: Junēbu Jōyaku Ihan (Byōinsen Kōgeki) ni Taisuru Kōgi-bun: a. Jōyaku Ihan* その他国際部保管文書 整理番号-０２：ジュネーヴ条約違反（病院船攻撃）に対する抗議文：a. 条約違反 [Documents Held by the International Department, No. 2: Complaint Letter Regarding Violations of the Geneva Conventions (Attacks on Red Cross Medical Ships): a. Violations of the Treaty].

——. *Soren Yokuryū Nihonjin Hikiage ni kanshi Renraku, Renmei・I'inkai: Gaiji-bu, Shōwa Nijū-ichi nen Jū gatsu* ソ連抑留日本人 引揚に関し連絡 連盟・委員会：外事部 昭和二十一年十月 [Documents Related to Japanese Internees in the Soviet Union (The Leagues of

Red Cross Societies, the International Committee of the Red Cross, and the International Department of the Japanese Red Cross Society), October 1946].

The Japanese Red Cross Society Red Cross Information Plaza Archives, Tokyo Japan. A1–159, *Shinkoku Ri Kōshō no Shaji (Kōsho nijū-ichi nen san gatsu hajime muika) Meiji Nijū-hachi nen*Ａ１－１５９清国李鴻章の謝辞（光緒二十一年三月初六日）明治28年 [A Thank-You Letter from Li Hongzhang, 1895].

———. *Beikoku Sekijūji Dokutoru Piitā Satsuei: Nihon Shinsai Shashin (Zen Hyaku Sanjū-nana yō)* 米国赤十字ドクトル、ピーター撮影：日本震災写真（全百三十七葉）[Photographs of Japanese Earthquake by Dr. Peter: 137 Photographs]. ID: PH-000005-044.

———. *B3-24: Shinajihen Jūgun Kinen: Dai Kyū Byōinsen Taisan-maru Aburaya Butai, Shōwa Jūni nen kara Jūsan nen* Ｂ３－２４ 支那事変従軍記念 第九病院船泰山丸油谷部隊 昭和12年〜13年 [Photo Album: The Deployment the Medical Ship No. 9 Taisan-maru and Aburaya Corps to the Second Sino-Japanese War, 1937–1938].

———. *Chōsen-honbu Kankei Shorui Nisatsu no uchi Ichi* 朝鮮本部関係書類二冊の内一 [Documents About the Korean Headquarters, Vol. 1].

———. [Vol. 2].

———. *C-2207A Nichiro Sensō (Meiji Sanjūshichi・hachi nen Sen'neki) Kanja Yusōchuū no Kinenshashin nen* Ｃ２－２２０７ 日露戦争（明治３７・８年戦役）患者輸送中の記念写真 [Memorial Photo of Patients During the Transportation].

———. *Dai Jūgo-kai Sekijūji Kokusai Kaigi ni Okeru Kiroku narabini Insatsubutsu San* 第十五回国際会議ニ於ケル記録並ニ印刷物 三 [Printed Materials for the Fifteenth International Conference].

———. [Vol. 6].

———. *Dai Jūgo-kai Sekijūji Kokusai Kaigi Kinen Shashin-chō, Shōwa Jūgo nen, Nihon Sekijūjisha* 第十五回赤十字國際會議記念寫眞帳 昭和九年十月 日本赤十字社 [The Memorial Album of the Fifteenth International Conference of the Red Cross, the Japanese Red Cross Society, October 1934].

———. *Dai Nana Hachi-kai Bankoku Kangofu Taikai, Shōwa hachi, jūichi, jūninen, dō jūsan nen* 第七八回萬國看護婦大會 昭和八、十一、十二年 同十三年 [The Seventh and Eighth International Nursing Conferences, 1933, 1936, 1937, and 1938]. ID: 4558.

———. *Dempō Shokan Utsushi A* 電報 書翰 写 A [Shimazu Notes: A].

———. *Tsūchō Shokan Utsushi B* 通牒 書翰 写 B [Shimazu Notes: B].

———. ICRC: *Report on the Activity of the International Committee of the Red Cross for the Indemnification of Former Allied Prisoners of War in Japanese Hands: Article 16 of the Peace Treaty of 8 September 1951 Between the Allied Powers and Japan.* Geneva: ICRC, 1971.

———. *Kokusai Kangofu Kōshū, Shōwa Roku-nen Itaru dō Sanjū-nen* 國際看護婦講習 自昭和六年 至同十三年 [International Nursing Education Course, 1931–1938]. ID: 4528.

———. Nihon Sekiūjisha 日本赤十字社. *Tekikoku ni okeru Hi-yokuryū Hōjin ni taisuru Imonkin Kyoshutsu Ichiran* 敵國に於ける被抑留邦人に對する慰問金醵出一覽 [Lists of Donation for Japanese Civilian Internees in Enemy Countries]. Tokyo: Nihon Sekiūjisha, 1942.

———. *Mansen, Karafuto, Tokubetsu-i'inbu Kankei, Ji Shōwa Hachi nen Itaru dō Jūichi nen* 満鮮、樺太 特別委員部関係自昭和八年 至同十一年 [File on the Special Committee Departments in Manchuria, Korea, and Karafuto, 1933–1937]. ID: 4284.

———. *Manshūkoku Sekijūjisha Sōsetsu, Ji Shō wa Jūni nen Itaru Jūsan nen* 満洲国赤十字社創設 自昭和十二年 至十三年 [The Foundation of the Manchukuo Red Cross Society, 1937–1938]. ID: 4449.

———. *Manshūkoku Sekijūjisha Sōritsu Kinen Shukuten: Tokugawa Fuku-shachō Shucchō Hōkoku Sono ni no ni* 満州国赤十字社創立記念祝典 徳川副社長出張報告 共二ノ二 [Official Trip Report by Vice-President Tokugawa on the Foundation Ceremony of the Manchukuo Red Cross Society, Vol. 2-2]. ID: 4450.

———. *Mori Hideomi Kanren Shiryō* 森秀臣関連史料 [Documents Related to Mori Hideomi].

———. *Nihon Sekijūjisha Chōsen-honbu Yōran* 日本赤十字社朝鮮本部要覧 [Outline of the Japanese Red Cross Society Korean Headquarters].

———. Nurses' Association of Korea. *Bulletin of the Nurses' Association of Korea*, no. 13 (Summer 1929).

———. Photograph: JRCS Taiwan Chapter 1921 (1) & (2).

———. "Prince Tokugawa's Address to Be Delivered at the Party to Be Given by the League of Red Cross Societies." File No. 10. The Fourteenth International Conference of the Red Cross (1930).

———. P-002937A, *Senji Kyūgo-Rinji Kyūgo: Shinkoku Hōōjō ni Rinji Kyūgosho, 1912 Senkyūhyaku-jūni nen Meiji Yonjū nen Ni gatsu, Manshū-i'inbu* 戦時救護 臨時救護 清国鳳凰上に臨時救護所 １９１２年（明治４５年２月）満州委員部 [Wartime Relief-Emergency Relief: Emergency Relief Station at Fenghuangchen in Qing Dynasty, February 1912, Manchurian Committee Department].

———. *Rieki Daihyōkoku no Shūyōjo Shisatsu Hōmon Yōkyū Kaisū oyobi Yōkyū Shutsugan Shorui no Utsushi narabini Yōkyū Shutsugan no Juri oyobi Kyoka ni Kansuru Kiroku* 利益代表国ノ収容所視察訪問要求回数及要求出願書類ノ写並二要求出願ノ受理及許可ニ関スル記録 [Records of Inspections of POW Camps by Protecting Powers]. Tokyo: Furyo Jōhō-kyoku [Prisoner of War Information Bureau], 1945.

———. *Shimazu Meiyo-shachō Intabyū II: Teisei Genkō* 島津名誉社長インタビューII（訂正原稿） *The Interview of Honorable President Shimazu II (Edited Version)*.

———. *Suzuki Takenori Nisshi: Nihon Sekijūjisha Shanhai Haken Tokubetsu Kyūgohan* 鈴木武徳日誌：日本赤十字社上海派遣特別救護班 [The Diary of Suzuki Takenori: The Japanese Red Cross Society Shanghai Special Expeditionary Relief Corps].

The National Archives, London. *Allied P.O.W. Captured in the Far East*, CAG/HIST/J/8/1/3.

———. The War Office, *Documents Relating to Prisoner of War Camps in the Far East*, no. 0103-8253.

The University of Tokyo Meiji Shinbun Zasshi Bunko Archives. *Aikoku Fujin, Dai gojūgo-gō Meiji Sanjūshichi-nen Roku-gatsu Itsu-ka* 愛國婦人第五十五號 明治三十七年六月五日 [Patriotic Women, No. 55, June 5, 1904].

———. [No. 56, June 20, 1904].

———. [No. 64, October 20, 1904].

INDEX

The 1854 Treaty of Peace and Amity, 58
The 1867 Paris International Exposition, 12, 19
The 1873 Vienna International Exposition, 12
The 1906 Geneva Convention for the Amelioration of the Condition of the Wounded and Sick in Armed Forces in the Field, 145
The 1924 International Conference of the Red Cross in Paris, 111
The 1930 Brussels International Red Cross Conference, 38
The 1949 Fourth Geneva Convention's provisions on the Protection of Civilian Persons in Time of War, 38. *See also* Geneva Conventions; Tokyo Declaration of 1934

Abe Yae, 115
Adams, William, 57, 209n84
Afghanistan, 40, 207n58
Africa, 7–8, 36, 41, 129, 237n128
Aichi Medical College, 101
aid parcels, 49, 119, 121, 124–126, 129, *130*
Ainu, 123

Akizuki Tatsuichiro: Buddhist medical doctor, 247
Albert, Alfred Ernest, 206n46
Aleutian Islands, 227, 237n119
Alexandrovna, Maria, 167
Alexandrovsk-Sakhalinsky, 69
Allied civilian internees, 10, 123, 227
Allied Occupation, 153, 228n8
Allied Powers, 24, 65, 69, 79, 95, 106, 108, 109, 119–121, 126–127, 129, *130*, 135, 200n70, 201n87, 212n128, 212n132, 221n9, 228n8, 236n114
Allied POWs, 10, 23, 108, 117, 119, 120–124, 126–127, 129–130, 134, 138, 153, 159–164, *162*, 190, 227n1, 229n13, 233n70, 233n72, 233n78, 234n87, 247n133
Amakasu Incident: Amakasu Masahiko, 215n28
America-Japan Society (AJS), 6–7
American POWs, 117, 120, 124, 126, 147, 153–154, 155
American Red Cross (ARC), 2, 24, 27, 38, 68, 93, 103, 116, 127, 129, 158, 166, 190, 198n30, 218n87, 222n14, 224n30, 248n4; ARC Philippines Chapter, 55–56

Amnesty International, 166
Ando (Donggang), 218n83
Anglo-Japanese Alliance, 25, 200n86
anti-Japanese graffiti, 116; *Kōnichi*, 230n38
anti–Vietnam War movement, 227
Aoyama Meiji Shrine Gaien Shelter, 73
ARC Hawai'i Chapter, 95, 98, 221n11, 224n30
ARC Los Angeles Chapter, 223n25
ARC nurse, 93
Argentina, 48, 104, 206n30, 236n114
Argentine Red Cross, 106
Ariga Nagao, 21, 22, 199n57, 199n58
Armenia, 87
Army Ministry, 117, 119, 241n22
Asahi-maru, 114, 126
Asahina, Noboru, 97
Asahi Shimbun, 56, 63, 70, 154
Ashkenazi Jews, 201n87
Asian Allied POWs, 227n1
Asian forced laborers, 134, 233n72
Asia Pacific, 1, 9, 54, 91, 92, 114, 168, 218n87, 221n11
Asia Pacific war theatre, 135
assimilation, 9, 68, 78, 80, 89, 103, 106, 217n73; Japan's colonial assimilationist policy, 78
Association of the Promoting Establishment of São Paulo Japanese Hospital, 103
Atami, 72
Atomic Bomb Dome. *See* Hiroshima Prefectural Commercial Exhibition Hall
atomic bombing, 10, 147, 150–151, 153–154, 157, 168–169, 241n19, 245n89, 247n138
Atsumi Tetsuzō, 111, 118
Australia, 48, 100, 120, 126, 129, 207n58, 212n3, 223n27, 233n72
Australian nurses, 128, 227n1
Australian POWs, 120, 125, 157, 163, 247n139
Austria, 21, 87, 239n6
Axis Powers, 65, 106

Bandō POW Camp, 23; Beethoven's Ninth Symphony, 23; POWs created a local market and established a range of facilities in the community, 23
Bank of Japan, 225n47
Barton, Clara, 26; Flooding of the Mississippi and Ohio Rivers in 1883 and the 1886 Charleston South Carolina, 201n90
Batavia, 212n3
battlefield humanitarian operations, 19, 128, 140, 190
Battle of Hakodate, 19, 198n44
Battle of Midway, 129
Battle of Shanghai, 110, *113*, 115
Battles of Khalkhyn Gol, 88, 220n118; Hailar Military Hospital, 88; JRCS Relief Party No. 179, 88
Baumgartner, Charles O., 154
Bauru, 100, 106
Bayonet Constitution, 92
Beijing, 31–32, 109, 228n3
Belgium, 34, 60, 64, 125, 129, 167, 207n58, 218n93
Belgium Red Cross, 167
belligerents, 63, 65, 109, 119, 128, 129, 135–136, 203n3, 212n130, 227n1
benevolence, 13, 17, 20, 26, 80, 95
Berlin, 62, 212n3
Bilfinger, Fritz, 153
Bismarck Sea, 126
Blood-Pledge Corps Incident. *See* Inoue Nisshō
Boer War, 167
Bolivia, 128, 207n58
Bolshevik Revolution. *See* Siberian Intervention
Bombing of civilians, 10, 65, 137–139, 146, 164
Borneo, 124
Boshin War, 198n39
Boxer Rebellion, 20, 101, 168, 221n9
Brazil, 9, 68, 92, 100–107, *101*, 128, 189, 212n2, 225n50, 225n51, 225n52, 225n53, 226n66, 226n68
Brazilian Red Cross, 105, 106
Brazilian Settlement Company, 100, 102

Britain, 2, 15, 34, 54, 55, 57, 64, 71, 87, 121, 124–125, 256, 129, 130, 139, 168, 209n83, 227n1, 233n72
British India, 8, 55, 91
British POWs, 121, 122, 124, 125, 164, 191, 233n72
British Red Cross (BRC), 24, 25, 120, 124, 167, 191, 194n19, 218n87, 221n9; British Red Cross (BRC) nurses, 25; Netley Hospital, 24
British Red Cross Volunteer Nursing Association, 221n9
Brown, Sydney H., 50
Brussels, 38, 40, 62–63
Bryer, Ronald E., 164, 247n140
bubonic plague, 81–83, 201n100, 222n14; use of antitoxin to induce passive immunity to tetanus, 201n100
Buddhism, 16, 196n34, 196n34, 197n21
Buenos Aires, 91, 104, 126, 127, 213n6
Buenos Aires-maru, 126, 127
Burajiru Jihō, 102, 104, 225n49, 225n54, 225n55
Burakumin, 39
Burma, 124, 233n72
Burma-Siam railway, 233n72
Bushidō, 16

California, 31
Canada, 48, 74, 100, 106, 125, 128–129, 130, 162, 206n30, 207n58, 223n27, 233n72
Canadian Red Cross (CRC), 30, 48, 120
Cantonese, 111
Cape Town, 24
Cartwright, Tomas C., 153–154, 245n89
Catholic missionaries, 124, 161, 162, 247n138
Caucasus and Baltic states, 87
Central and Latin America, 100, 104, 106, 107, 130
Central and Latin American Red Cross Societies, 130
Chahar Province, 110
Changchun, 60, 82, 86, 218n80, 218n83
Changi POW camp, 125

chemical gas, poison, and bacteriological weapons, 41, 65, 138, 141, 211n124
Cheongju, 214n20
Chiang Kai-shek, 50, 109, 115, 207n52
Chicago, 31, 42
children, 25, 30, 45–49, 47, 48, 83, 101, 162, 201n87, 205n23, 207n58, 247n139, 248n4
Chile, 30, 48, 104, 206n30, 207n58
China, 8, 21–22, 28–30, 31–32, 32, 38, 42, 49–50, 53, 65, 69, 70, 72, 77, 79–83, 85–88, 94, 109–116, 122, 125, 128, 135, 142, 145, 147, 161, 189, 193n7, 202n122, 207n52, 208n67, 213n7, 238n146
China International Famine Relief Commission, 207n58
China treaty port system, 213n7
Chinese collaborationist East Hebei Army, 228n3
Chinese Confucianism, 197n21; *tendō*, 197n21; the way of heaven, nature, or the universe, 197n21
Chinese Hawaiians, 94
Chinese medicine, 240n14
Chinese POWs, 20, 65, 111, 114
Chinese Red Cross. *See* Red Cross Society of China (RCSC)
Chinese Red Swastika Society, 8; Chinese Red Cross movement, 8, 30; Chinese religious society, 8; *Daoyuan*, 8
Chinese soldiers, 86, 109–110, 112, 114
Chinese war victims, 115
cholera, 27, 74–75, 112, 222n14
chōnaikai: village associations, 5
Chongjin, 214n19, 214n20
Chōshū Domain, 198n39
Christianity, 7, 16, 93; Christian-based charity, 7, 240n12; Western values, 1
chūai, 197, 197n23, 197n26; "faith and love," 16
Chūgoku Military District Headquarters, 153–154; District Headquarters in Hiroshima, 154
Chūgoku Shimbun, 154
Chuncheon, 214n20

Ciraolo, Giovanni Attilio, 211
City of Canterbury, 129
City of Paris, 129
civic organizations, 6, 103
civilian casualties, 108–136
civilian internees, 10, 108, 117–119, 123–125, 128–131, 190–191, 227n1, 235n104, 238n146
civil society, 2, 13, 17–18, 40, 45–46, 93
Clarke, Hugh V., 157, 163, 235n91, 247n138
Clive, Robert, 55
Colombian Red Cross, 30
colonial subjects, 48, 70, 72, 76, 78, 83, 89, 90, 135, 138, 146, 161
Committee for Provisions for Compatriots Residing in Hostile Countries, 130
Confucianism, 5, 16, 197n21
Conte Verde, 128
Coolidge, Calvin, U.S. President, 30
crime against humanity, 127
Crown Prince Hirohito, 40
Cuba, 40, 207n58
Czechoslovakia, 87, 206n30, 207n58

Daegu, 71, 75, 214n19, 214n20
daimyō, 40, 196n3
Dalian, 81–82, 83, 87, 218n80
Davao, 91, 213n6
Davison, Henry P., 34
de Gielgud, Lewis E., 41, 53, 64
denationalized persons, 65, 128
Denmark, 15, 87, 207n58, 218n93
de Watteville, Charles, 111–115, 142
disaster relief operation, 30, 39, 193n2
diseases, 42, 82–83, 101, 112, 125, 138–139, 148, 150, 159, 165, 201n91, 201n100, 215n29, 247n133
divergence, 68, 168
Doctors Without Borders/Médecins Sans Frontières, 166
Dōjinkai Corporation, 102, 106, 225n50, 225n51, 225n52, 225n53, 226n66
Domon Ken, *74, 144*

Draft International Convention on the Condition and Protection of Civilians of Enemy Nationality Who are on Territory Belonging to or Occupied by a Belligerent of 1934. *See* Tokyo Declaration of 1934
Dunant, Henry, 71, 194n9
Dutch East Indies, 21, 212n3
Dutch East Indies Red Cross (NIRK), 8, 21, 196n35, 247n138
Dutch POW, 120, 163
Dutch studies (*Rangaku*), 196n2, 197n21

earthquakes, 26, 28, 30–32, 31, 32, 39–40, 45, 61, 72–74, 78, 87, 103, 165–166, 201n90, 211n115, 215n31, 215n35, 215n36, 215n37, 240n14
East Asia, 21, 36, 76, 161, 200n70
Ecuador, 129
Edo Period, 16, 196n2, 196n3; Tokugawa era, 16
Edward VIII, 56
Egypt, 129, 207n58, 237n128
Egyptian Red Crescent, 8
Ehrlich, Paul, 215n29
El Nil, 129
emergency aid stations, 30, 158, 147, 149, 158, 159
emergency appeal, 126–127, 236n114
emergency evacuation, 155, 245n91
Emoto Shigeo, 121; Legal Affairs Bureau of SCAP, 234n79
Emperor Gojong, 70–71
Emperor Meiji, 15, 194n11, 204n8
Empress Kōmyō, 16, 197n25; imperial charities, 16; Yaku-in and Hiden-in, 16, 197n25
Empress Nagako, 98, 142
Empress Shōken, 15; Empress Shōken Fund, 63, 201n91, 210–211n114
England, 2, 5, 25, 39, 52, 54, 57, 96, 98, 108, 111, 121, 123, 134, 154, 164, 166, 190, 195n30, 199n55, 200n86, 206n30, 209n95, 227n1, 233n78, 234n79, 240n14

INDEX 311

Enomoto Shigeharu, 16, 197n29
epidemic diseases, 165, 201n91
Estonia, 87
Ethiopia, 36, 237n127, 246n106
ethos, 35, 95, 98, 121, 143, 164
Eurocentrism in Red Cross historiography, 3–4; Christiandom, 3; Christian humanitarianism's altruism, 7; civilized races, 3; compassion and volunteerism, 7; Eurocentric chauvinism, 3; Eurocentric narrative, 7; non-Western countries, 3; non-Western humanitarianism in the pre-WWII period, 3; Western centrism, 2; Westernization, 7
Europe, 3–4, 19, 23, 25, 27, 33–36, 41, 64–66, 70, 85, 120, 129, 139, 161, 168, 189, 194n11, 194n19, 197n15, 200n70, 202n103, 205n23, 212n3, 218n93, 221n11, 224n46, 240n12
Evening Post, 52
Evening Star, 57, 127, 208n79, 236n117
exchange operations, 129, 237n140

famine, 16, 28, 165
Far East, 108, 191, 208n67, 212n128, 227n1, 230n36
Featherston POW camp, 134
February 1907 Gentlemen's Agreement between Japan and the United States, 94; family unification, 94; travel documents, 94
Federal Council of Switzerland, Political Department, 66
field hospitals, 19, 22, 73, 112, 116, 128, 140
Fifteenth International Red Cross Conference of Tokyo in 1934, 45, 53; 1934 Tokyo International Red Cross Conference, 1, 219n105; adopt English as an official language, alongside French, 54; Fifteenth Congress, 44; largest international humanitarian congress of the interwar period, 36; legal protections of civilians in wartime, 1; Tokyo Conference, 53–59

First Shanghai Incident. *See* Shanghai Incident of 1932
First Sino-Japanese War, 9, 13, 20–21, 70, 94, 101, 199n46, 227n1, 240n17; peace negotiations, 21; Shimonoseki, 21
Florence Nightingale, 71, 141, 241n19
Florence Nightingale Medal, 139, 149, 216n56, 240n14
forced labours, 23, 65, 108, 135, 233n72
foreign nationals, 87, 88, 94–95, 118, 119, 134, 129, 138, 161
Fourth Geneva Convention of 1949, 9
France, 21, 23–25, 34, 48, 54, 60, 66, 87, 111, 139, 162, 207n58, 208n73, 218n93, 240n14; Minister of War and National Defense, 24
French Red Cross (FRC), 24, 30
Friedrich Wilhelm University (now the Humboldt University of Berlin), 239n8
Fukui City, 26
Fukui Prefecture, 101
Fukuoka, 19, 23, 120, 162, *162*, 163
Fukuoka POW camps, 120; Fukuoka 2-B Camp, *162*; Fukuoka 14-B. *See* Nagasaki Mitsubishi Dockyard Branch Camp
Fukushima, 26, 27, 166, 211n114, 227n1, 238n146
Fyodorovna, Maria, 23

Gagaku, 60
Gangwon-do, 214
gas chambers, 65
gender, 140, 142, 168, 215n28, 240n12; exception of nursing, men occupied all leadership positions in the JRCS, 168
Geneva, 1, 3, 22, 38, 54, 64, 65, 77, 157, 191, 209n94
Geneva Conventions, 3–4, 9, 11–12, 14, 18, 21–22, 38, 41, 50, *51*, 58–59, 65–66, 70–71, 109, 111, 114, 116, 126–127, 142, *144*, 145, 156; the 1864 Geneva Convention, 12; the 1906 Amelioration of the Condition of the Wounded and Sick in Armies in the Field, 21; the 1925 Geneva Protocol

Geneva Conventions (*continued*)
  prohibitions on the use of chemical and biological weapons, 38; the 1929 Geneva Conventions, 116; The 1949 Fourth Geneva Convention's provisions on the Protection of Civilian Persons in Time of War, 38; First and Second Geneva Conventions, 114; the Second Geneva Convention, 21, 58; Second Geneva Convention updated in 1929, 58
Genpei War, 197
George, David Lloyd, 211n24; chemical warfare program, 211
George V, King, 25
German POWs, 23
German Red Cross (GRC), 206n46
Germany, 9, 15, 21, 30, 48, 58, 60, 62, 65–66, 95, 206n46, 210n105, 212n3, 215n29, 233n72, 233n74, 239n8, 239n9; National Socialism, 9, 196n34
Ginza, 62
globalization, 6
Goa, India, 128
Gongju, 214n20
Gotō Fumio, 58
governor-general of Kwantung, 82
Grand Duchess Maria Pavlovna, 23
Grand Duchess Xenia Alexandrovna, 23
Grassroots movements of the Red Cross in Japan: broad popular acceptance, 17; built upon local self-improvement initiatives, 17; orientation toward disaster relief and community improvement, 17; poverty, hunger, orphans, epidemics, medical services, and public health in local communities, 17; rapid growth in membership and activities, 17; the tumult of rapid industrialization and social change, 17. *See* Japanese Red Cross Society (JRCS)
Great Britain, 15, 54–55, 57, 66, 95, 102, 107, 111, 129, 207n58, 208n73, 213n9
Great Depression, 9, 49

Great Kantō earthquake, 26, 30–32, *31*, *32*, 39–40, 61, 72–74, 78, 86, 103, 166, 215n31; appeal from President Calvin Coolidge to provide $5 million of aid, 31; ARC's Japanese relief fund ultimately reached $11,631,302.63, 31; bilateral assistance to multilateral international humanitarian cooperation, 33
Great Korean Red Cross Society (GKRCS), 71
Great Powers, 9, 36, 59, 92, 167, 210n95
Greece, 30, 87, 128, 129, 218n93
Greek Red Cross, 48
ground zero, 147, 158, 161, 163
Guangdong, 116
guerrillas, 112, 116
Gunsan, 213n8, 214n19
Gwangju, 214n20
Gyeonggi-do, 214n20

Haakon VII, 63
Haeju, 214n20
Hagiwara Take, 77, 139, 216n56, 240n14; Japanese Nightingale, 240n14
Hague Conventions, 59, 145; Hague Convention of 1907, 59, 145; Second Hague Conference of 1907, 21
Haiti, 207n58
Haiti Red Cross Society, 55
Hakodate POW Camp, 121
Hakone, 60
hakuai, 15, 18, 41, 209n86
Hakuai-sha. *See* Japanese Red Cross Society (JRCS)
Hamhŭng, 214n20
Hankou, 69, 223n21
Han or Manchu ethnicity, 85
Hara Takashi (Kei), 204n8
Hara Yasutarō, 18, 198n39; the State University of New Jersey and King's College, London, 198n39; Yamaguchi Prefecture, 18, 222n17; Yamaguchi Red Cross Society (YRCS), 19
Harbin, 82, 84, 85, 87–88, 218n83

Harbin Association for Korean Residents, 88
Harupin-maru, 114
Hasegawa Kiyoshi, 59
Hashimoto Tsunatsune, 239n9
Hatakeda Shōfuku, 245n91; emergency order, 245n91
Hawai'i, 9, 68, 70, 91–100, 107, 189–191, 192, 222n13, 222n17, 223n25, 224n38
Hawaiian-Japanese Labor Convention of 1886, 92
Hayashi Senjūrō, 59
Heian Japan, 15, 16
hibakusha, xi, 158, 244n69, 246n109
Hirano Mitsuko, 161
Hirano Shigeru, 149
Hirayama Seisai, 13, 197n14
Hirose, 112, 229n12
Hiroshima, 10, 18–20, 60, 65, 93, 123, 137–138, 141, 146–149, *148*, 151–158, 164, 168, 190–191
Hiroshima and Nagasaki atomic bombings, 10, 137–138, 139, 146–164; annihilate human, animal, and plant life long after, 65; atomic radiation poisoned all living creatures and the environment, including insects, animals, flora, and even the soil itself, 168; it was a hell that defied description, 168
Hiroshima Castle, 154, 244n82
Hiroshima Army Hospitals, 147
Hiroshima Philanthropic Society. *See* Nagase Tokihira
Hiroshima Philanthropic Women's Association, 18
Hiroshima Prefectural Commercial Exhibition Hall, 146
Hiroshima Prefecture, 18, 154
Hiroshima Red Cross Hospital, 18, 147, 152, 152, 244n69
Hirota Kōki, 58
Historiographical Institute of the University of Tokyo, 16
Hitler, Adolph, 36, 206n46

Hōjōki. *See* Kamo no Chōmei
Hokkaido, 19–20, 227n1, 233n78
Home Ministry, 55, 128, 155, 156, 231n49, 245n91
Hong Kong, 122, 124–125, 128
Honolulu, 24, 57, 91, 93–95, 98, 213n6, 221n9, 223n22
Honolulu Izumo Shrine, 98; Izumo Shrine Women's Association, 98
Honolulu Japanese Nursing Home, 98
Honolulu Japanese Patriotic Women's Association, 93
Honolulu Star-Bulletin, 95, 223n24
Horiuchi Kensuke, 110
Hsinking, 89, 219n107
Huber, Max, 50, 59, 67, 209n94
human dignity, 64, 166, 169, 211n116
humanitarian: aid, 8, 10, 12, 41–42, 137, 157, 164, 248n11; crises, 6, 16, 35, 65, 108, 156, 168; diplomacy, 9, 50–53, 66, 102; internationalism, 35, 36, 42, 45; mission, 19, 22, 33, 35, 44, 49, 56, 68, 80, 91, 108, 121, 137, 142, 146–154, 169, 190, 227n1, 241n19; professionalism, 10, 138, 164; relief activities, 108, 146–154, 156, 157–159, 232n68; studies, 190
humanitarianism (*jindō*), 10, 15, 23, 26, 28, 31, 33, 35, 83, 109, 164, 166, 169
humanity, 12, 15, 34, 35, 59, 63, 73–74, 80, 127, 142, 164, 166, 196n2
human rights, 64, 66, 211n122
Hwanghae, 214n20
hypocenter, 147, 154, 158, 163

Ichige Kōzō, 104
ICN. *See* International Council of Nurses (ICN)
ICRC. *See* International Committee of the Red Cross (ICRC)
ICRC Central Agency for Prisoners of War, 117, 133, 231n51
ICRC delegation, 122
ICRC executive committee, 64
ICRC mission, 15, 152–153

ICRC Tokyo Delegation, 152
idealism, 35, 38, 166
ideals, 6, 42, 137
Iguape, 100, 102, 225n47
Iguape Colony, 101, 102, 225n47
Iida, Chiyo, 97; S. M. Iida Ltd., 97
Ikeda, George, 97
Immigration Act of 1924, 222n13
Imperial Court Museum, 16
Imperial Edict No. 54, 71
imperial family, 1, 5, 11–17, 25, 27, 35, 53, 103, 139, 166, 167, 194n19, 212n139, 230n36; the patronage of, 5; very close tied to the imperial regime, 4
imperialism, 2, 19, 68, 92, 104, 168, 209n95
Imperial Japanese Army (IJA), 18, 22, 50, 66, 79, 80, 109–117, 119–122, 125–126, 135, 155, 163, 167, 190, 204n18, 213n9, 215n28
Imperial Japanese Navy (IJN), 21, 50, 110, 111, 112, 114, 116, 119, 120, 154, 204n9
Imperial Japanese Red Cross Society, 98
Imperial Rescript on Education, 4
imperial subjects, 78, 80, 88, 92, 95, 101, 140
Inada Yuki, 142
Incheon, 22, 213n8
independence, 8, 52, 54, 71, 87, 88, 113, 136, 166
India, 7, 8, 48, 55, 60, 91, 106, 126, 129, 197n15, 207n58, 212n3
Indian Ocean earthquake and tsunami, 30, 40
Indian Red Cross Society, 8, 55, 193n7
Indigenous Brazilians, 102
Indochina, 124
infant mortality, 90
infectious diseases, 42, 82, 112, 138, 215n29
Inner Mongolia, 77, 88, 110
Inoue Enji, 41, 42, 47, 48–49, 55, 118–119, 139, 231n54
Inoue Nisshō, 204n12; Blood-Pledge Corps Incident, 204n12; Buraku Liberation League, 204n11; National Levelers Association, 204n11

international armed conflicts, 12, 20, 109
International Committee of the Red Cross (ICRC), 10, 26, 12, 108, 115, 136, 141–142, 203n1, 244n85
International Committee on Intellectual Cooperation, 6
international community, 54, 55, 56, 157, 168, 240n12
international cooperation, 33, 36, 38, 39, 42, 63
International Council of Nurses (ICN), 77, 139, 191, 240n12
international exchange relief operations, 128–131, 237n140
International Federation of Red Cross and Red Crescent Societies (IFRC), 33, 46, 191, 193n5
international humanitarianism, 1, 20, 28, 32, 38–40, 42, 49–50, 59–62, 67, 98, 103, 113, 164
internationalism, 5, 6–7, 35, 36–67, 54–56, 124, 139, 157, 168, 240n12
international law, 16, 21–22, 35, 36, 38, 49–50, 64–65, 110, 145, 229n12
international law of war, 21, 38, 41, 118, 157, 199n57, 200n70
International Military Tribunal for the Far East, 108, 191, 227n1, 230n36
International Nursing Training programme, 139
international organizations, 1, 6, 41, 54, 121
International Red Cross and Red Crescent Movement, 1, 8, 30, 38, 40, 45, 46, 50, 52, 56, 66, 67, 70, 71, 78, 104, 118, 139, 166–167, 211n114, 221n11
International Relief Union, 64, 211n115, 211n116
internment camp, 65, 86, 119, 123, 129, 191, 226n68, 235n104
Inukai Tsuyoshi, 36, 203n2
Investigation Department. *See* JRCS Investigation Department
Iran, 7, 40, 87
Iraqi Red Crescent Society, 55, 207n58, 237n127
Isahaya Branch Naval Hospital, 158

Ishiguro Tadanori, 83, 218n87
Ishii Isakichi, 93; Japanese Honolulu Chamber of Commerce, 93
Ishikawa Tomoyasu, 240n14
Italian Red Cross (IRC), 30
Italy, 15, 30, 34, 36, 58, 64, 66, 87, 111, 206n30, 207n58, 227n1, 218n92
Itō Noe, 215n28
Itsukaichi Constitution, 240n14
Iwakuni, 153
Iwakura Mission, 3, 194n11, 197n15
Iwasaki and Mitsui families, 61
Izu Peninsula, 72

Japan Bible Association, 121
Japanese-American friendship, 98
Japanese Americans, 98, 129, 168
Japanese Army. *See* Imperial Japanese Army (IJA)
Japanese Association in China, 53
Japanese Brazilian community, 103, 106
Japanese Buddhism, 16
Japanese camp guards, 121, 124, 125, 247n133
Japanese Christians, 14
Japanese civilian internees, 10, 124, 129, *130*
Japanese civilians, 10, 80, 112, 121, 128, 130, *130*, 153, 163, 166
Japanese colonial subjects, 135, 146, 161
Japanese Cultural Center of Hawai'i, *97*
Japanese culture, 16, 60–62, 121, 123, 228n1
Japanese emigration, 9, 68, 100, 107, 191
Japanese Empire, 16, 44, 49, 69, 71, 77, 92, 109, 119, 120, 135, 139, 167–168, 191, 210n105, 228n104, 233n74
Japanese government, 18, 27, 31, 53, 64, 66, 100–101, 103, 104, 109, 114, 117, 121, 124, 126–127, 199n55, 200n70, 208n73, 212n139, 214n28, 225n50
Japanese governor-general of Korea, 73
Japanese immigrant communities, 9, 10, 68, 89, 91, *97*, 168, 191
Japanese immigration, xv, 57, 83, 89, 91–94, 98, 100, 102, 106–107, 223n22, 226n68

Japanese Imperial domestic law, 145
Japanese Imperial family. *See* imperial family
Japanese military operations, 112, 114, 200n70
Japanese National Railway, 158; relief trains, 158
Japanese nationals, 33, 69, 71, 91, 161, 227n1
Japanese Navy. *See* Imperial Japanese Navy (IJN)
Japanese nursing, 62, *99*
Japanese orphans, 135
Japanese Patriotic Women's Association, 93, 221n9
Japanese POWs, 10, 108, 119, 130, 134–135, 190, 228n1, 248n140; disgraced by having survived, 135; engage in handicrafts, sketching, sculpturing, painting, and needlework, 135; feelings of guilt, 135; sense of shame, emotional scars, and psychological distress, 135; wished to commit suicide, 135
Japanese Prewar Internationalism, 6–7
Japanese Red Cross movement, 103, 115, 168, 191
Japanese Red Cross Society (JRCS): advancing modern medical care and public health, 1; bottom-up, local initiatives, 4; civil society organization, 17, 40, 45, 93; humanitarian practices, 1; indigenous humanitarian movement, 1; Japanese humanitarian traditions, 1; local needs, 4, 5, 18; membership, 5, 24, 27, 42, *43*, *44*, 81, 93; ordinary Japanese people's communitarianism and patriotism, 6; a people's humanitarian movement, 11; pioneering programmes of natural disaster relief and poverty mitigation, 4; responding to local needs and building on community values, 4; responding to local humanitarian crises, 6; semi-governmental organizations, 2; strong grassroots vector, 1; a top-down movement directed by the Meiji government, 11; top-down organization, 1; transnational organization, 1

Japanese Santa Cruz Hospital in São Paulo (Hospital Santa Cruz, also known as the Japanese Hospital), 103, *105*, 106
Japanese society, 4, 7, 15, 16, 139, 198n45, 241n19
Japanese soldiers, 42, 81, 88, 93, 116, 119, 126, 138, 166, 220n118, 221n9
Japan-Great Britain repatriation operation, 129
Japan Ground Self-Defense Force Medical School, 141
Japan-Korea Treaty of 1905, 71, 213n7
Japan's National Library Law, 189
Japan Society, London, 57
Japan's São Paulo Embassy, 102, 103, 225n51
Japan Times, 119
Japan Visual Arts Academy, 61
Japan Women's University, 134
Java, 124, 233n72
Jeolla, 214n20
Jiji Press, 57
Jilin, 219n107
jindō, 26, 164, 166, 194n15, 197n21, 197n24; the way of humanity, 164
jinrin, 197n21; human ethics and morals, 197n21
Jinzhou, 86, 218n83, 219n107
Johnson, Jack, 163
Johnstown Flood, 26, 201n90
JRCS Andong Committee Department, 60
JRCS Brazil, 9, 100–107
JRCS doctors, 21, 81, 94
JRCS ethos, 35, 164
JRCS Fenghuangchen Patrol Medical Relief Party, 86
JRCS Foreign Special Committee Department, 104
JRCS Fukushima Chapter, 27
JRCS general assembly, 26, 98
JRCS Hawai'i, 9, 93–94, 91–99; establishing modern hospitals, clinics and public health initiatives, 91; facilitated diplomatic relations with the United States, 9; Fourth JRCS Hawai'i General Assembly, 96; organizational bridge between local Japanese and American elites, 9; transnational civil society organization, 93
JRCS Headquarters, 5, 24, 26, 27, 42, *43*, *44*, 49, 54, 71, 81, 88, 93, 95, 98, 103, 104, 110, 111, 113, 117, 120, 122, 145, 153, 156, 167, 189, 190, 203n127
JRCS Headquarters Hospital, 32, 75–76, 142
JRCS Headquarters Medical Relief Department, 111
JRCS Hiroshima Chapter, 18, 93, 146–147
JRCS Hokkaido Chapter, 20
JRCS Hospital Institution for the Training of Nurses, 239n9
JRCS hospitals, 60, 139, 146, 190, 215n37
JRCS inspection tours, 119
JRCS International Affairs Department, 117, 190
JRCS Investigation Department, 41, 111, 139, 190, 231n54
JRCS Iwate Chapter, 27–28
JRCS Korean Headquarters, 70–80, 110, 123, 234n87; development of local medical facilities and public health, in advancing colonial modernity, 9
JRCS Korean Sinŭiju Chapter, 79–80
JRCS Kwantung Leased Territory Committee Department, 81, 89, 110
JRCS Liaodong Committee Headquarters, 81, 218n77
JRCS Manchurian Committee Department, 60, 79, 84–89, 110, 219n97
JRCS medical ship, 102, *113*, 124, 126
JRCS Nagasaki Committee Department, 70, 155, 158
JRCS Nurses, 10, 22, 24, *25*, 28, 79, 88, 98, 115, 137–139, 140–143, *144*, 146–152, 159–164, 190, 240n12, 241n22, 242n30; exemplars of the humanitarian relief ideal, 10, 164; Paris mission, 24; quasi-military, 140–146
JRCS Osaka Chapter, 73

JRCS Pyongyang Committee Department, 72, 80
JRCS Saitama Chapter, 28
JRCS São Paulo Special Committee Department, 103, 105, 106, 107; Central and Latin American departments, 104; JRCS's Latin American chapters, 104
JRCS Shanghai Special Expeditionary Relief Corps (SSERC), 51, 109–111, 114–115, 142, 229n27; impartial medical care to refugees and civilian war victims without discrimination as to races and nationalities, 111; uphold Red Cross humanitarianism, 111
JRCS's Latin America soft diplomacy campaign, 105
JRCS's Los Angeles Special Committee Department, 223n25
JRCS Special Overseas Committee Department, 101
JRCS Special Relief Regulations for Bubonic Plague Pandemic, 82; JRCS Emergency Relief Party No. 1, 86; lead to quarantine, on trains, ships and in ports, 82
JRCS Taiwan Chapter, 110
JRCS Teiling Chapter, 86
JRCS Tochigi Chapter, 27
JRCS Tokyo Headquarters, 30, 56, 72, 77, 86, 88, 93, 95, 103, 106, 107, 110, 115, 116, 225n53
JRCS Vancouver, 226n63
JRCS Volunteer Nursing Women's Association, 86
JRCS War Prisoners' Relief Committee Department (WPRCD), 115, 116–120, 121, 128, 130, 131, 134–135, 232n68, 235n94, 238n144, 238n 146; delivered blankets, shoes, sanitation goods, nutritional supplements, butter, cheese, corned beef, milk, biscuits, and cigarettes, 124; Regulations for the War Prisoners' Relief Committee Department of the Japanese Red Cross Society, 117, 118, 231n50; sent donations of books, canned food, porridge, cocoa, soup, sugar, and Yorkshire pudding with roast beef to fifteen Catholic missionaries in the Nagasaki detention camp, 123–124
JRCS Wartime Relief Headquarters, 120
JRCS WPRCD. See JRCS War Prisoners' Relief Committee Department (WPRCD)
JRCS Yamaguchi Chapter, 19
Judo, 123
Junior Red Cross, 28, 29, 45–49, 63, 87, 104, 167, 191, 206n30, 211n116; International Junior Red Cross Exhibition, 47–48; International Junior Red Cross Movement, 48–49, 167; seventeen posters promoting daily hygiene about public health campaigns, 28
Junod, Marcel, 152–153
Juquiá, 100, 102

Kachi-gumi "victory faction," 106
Kageyama Sadaka, 111, 142, 228n7
Kamakura, 16, 60, 61
Kamakura-maru, 129
Kamio Mitsuomi, 218n77
Kamo no Chōmei, 165; the Buddhist concept of impermanence (*mujō*), 165; The flow of the river never ceases, 165; *Hōjōki*, 165–166; human misery, 165; human suffering is universal and that human lives are ephemeral, 165
Karafuto. See Sakhalin
Katō Tomosaburō, 39
Katsura and Registro regions, 102
Katsura Tarō, 225n47
Kawahara Yotsugi, 148
Kawakami Hatsue, 149
Kawasaki, 119
Kenya, 237n128
Kimura Matsujirō, 112, 229n12
kindness and self-sacrifice, 165
Kinutani Oshie, 149
Kishi Kantarō, 94

Kitajima Kenzō, 101; identifying hookworm as the cause of chronic malnutrition and anemia, 102; medical mission specialising in tropical diseases, 101; received the 5th Class, Gold and Silver Rays, the Order of the Rising Sun, 224n46
Kitasato Shibasaburō, 27, 215n29
Kita Tango Earthquake, 26
Kobe, 95, 123
Koch, Robert, 201n100
Kokura, 20, 155, 245n91
Konoe Atsumaro, 221n9
Korea, 9, 20–22, 48, 68, 69–81, 83, 85, 89, 90, 91, 93, 103, 109, 122, 123, 128, 135, 146, 153, 189, 216n50; Christian mission hospitals, 213n16, 215n37, 216n50; colonial, 76, 83, 90
Korean doctor, 72, 86
Korean Kingdom, 70, 75
Korean laborers, 233n78
Korean language, 161; *Aigō!*, 161
Korean nationals, 70, 71, 78, 80, 88, 215n37
Korean Red Cross movement, 70–71
Kōsai-maru, 102
Koteda Yasusada. See Shimane Red Cross Society (SRCS)
Kreutzer, Leonid, 210n105
Kūkai, 15; Buddhist injunction to overcome egoism, 15; convey universal love of nature, humanity, and the universe, 15; *Shōryō-shū*, 15
Kumamoto, 12, 60, 162
Kunitani Oshie, 150
Kure, 154
Kwangtung Army, 78, 83, 86, 87
Kwan Kakchang, 86
Kwantung Leased Territory, 69, 81, 83, 87
Kwantung Leased Territory Committee Department. See JRCS Kwantung Leased Territory Committee Department
Kyoto, 60, 155, 165
Kyushu, 19, 227

Laoag, 131
Latin America, 100, 103–107, 129, 130, 191
Latvia, 87, 207n58
League for the Construction of São Paulo Japanese Hospital, 102
League of Nations, 6, 9, 34, 36, 41, 53, 59, 102, 167; Japan's withdrawal, 9, 49, 59, 167
League of Red Cross Societies (LORCS), 2, 9, 26, 28, 30, 33–35, 39, 41–42, 45–46, 49, 53, 56, 60, 63–64, 139, 167, *172*, 190, 203n1, 205n28; Foundation of the League of Red Cross Societies, 9
Levelers Association, 39
LGBTQ, 65
Liaodong, 69, 81, 218n77
Liaoyang, 81, 86
life expectancy, 90
Li Hongzhang, 21
Lima, 91, 104, 213n6
Lincoln, Abraham, 7
Lisbon-maru, 122
London, 24, 25, 57
Lonesome Lady, 153, 154
Looper, Durden W., 153
Los Angeles, 91, 191, 216n6, 223n21
Lourenço Marques, 128–130, 237n128
Ludwig-Maximilian University of Munich, 239n8
Lüshun, 22, 81, 82, 83, 218n83
Lüshunkou, 22
Luzon, *131*

Maggie Francis Maroney, 93
Mahler, Gustav, 62
Makita Kise, 111, 228n8
Malaya, 124, 133, 233n72
male nurses, 140, 218n85, 240n17
Manchukuo, 36, 54–55, 60, 87, 88, 125, 126, 128, 190
Manchukuo Film Association, 215n28
Manchukuo Red Cross Society (MRCS), 87, 119, 125

INDEX 319

Manchuria, 9, 20–22, 36, 48, 54, 68–69, 77, 79, 80–89, 91–93, 102–103, 109, 125, 126, 153, 166, 168, 189
Manchurian Committee Department. See JRCS Manchurian Committee Department
Manchurian General Committee, 81–82
Manchurian Incident, 6, 9, 42, 57, 79–80, 83, 219n97
Manchurian Railway Temporary Hospital, 73
Manila, 91, 124, 213n6
Mann, Thomas, 210n101
Maputo. See Lourenço Marques
March 1 Movement, 78
Marco Polo Bridge Incident, 80, 88
Masan, 71, 213n8, 214n19, 221n9
Ma Tianzhe, 53
Matsubara Akio, 112, 229n12
Matsuda Genji, 59
Matsudaira Norikata, 11, 196n3; Okudono Domain, 196n3
Matsuda Michikazu, 118
Matsue Benevolent Love Society, 17; Oki Islands, 17; Onoze fire of 1884, 17
Matsui Keishirō, 118
Matsukata Masayosho, 211n114
Matsumoto Retsuko, 161
Matsuyama, 20, 22, 199n64
Maui Shinbun, 95, 96, 223n25
McGee, Anita Newcomb, 93
McGrath-Kerr, Peter, 163
medical care, 2, 16, 18, 20–22, 24, 27–28, 30, 42, 72, 74–76, 83, 86, 101, 111–112, 120, 128, 135, 143, 152, 244n69
Medical Department of the Imperial Japanese Army, 239n9
medical missions, 23, 74, 78, 79, 101, 138, 140, 145, 222n14
Medical Relief Department. See JRCS Wartime Relief Headquarters
medical relief teams, 20–21, 26, 30, 110, 120
medical ship. See JRCS medical ship

medical workers, 22–23, 26, 27, 28, 32, 49, 73, 79, 86, 111, 138, 141, 145, 157–158, 219n97
medieval Japan, 165
Meiji Emperor. See Emperor Meiji
Meiji government, 11–13, 19–20, 166, 194n15
Meiji period, 23, 27, 201n89
Meiji Shrine, 61, 73
Melbourne, 129
Mengjiang United Autonomous Government, 228n4
Messina earthquake of 1908, 211n115
Mexico/Mexico City, 91, 104, 128, 131, 207n58, 213n6
Middle East, 7–8, 36, 41, 46, 129
militarism, 38, 49, 53, 54, 109, 203n2, 242n29
Military Corps, 110
military discipline, 143
military hospitals, 20, 50, 88, 143
military intelligence, 129, 155
military nurses, 139, 143, 145, 241n22, 242n29
military operations, 52, 87, 110, 112, 114, 116, 127, 138, 200n70
military police, 83, 123, 214n28
Military Service Law, 140
Ministry of Army: Army Ministry, 58, 117, 119, 141
Ministry of Communications, 133
Ministry of Education of Japan, 134
Ministry of Foreign Affairs of Japan (MOFA), 52, 55, 66, 93, 103, 106, 111–112, 116–117, 130, 229n12
Ministry of Foreign Affairs of the Republic of China in Nanjing, 53
Ministry of Imperial Army, 58
Ministry of Imperial Navy, 58
missionaries, 6, 77, 124, 125, 128, 161–162
Mitaki Branch Hospital, 147
Mitsui & Co., Ltd., 130, 161, 234n79, 248n140
Miyamoto Musashi, 224n35
Miyazaki Tsutako, 79
modern warfare, 41, 141
MOFA. See Ministry of Foreign Affairs of Japan (MOFA)

Mokpo, 213n8, 214n19, 221n9
Molnar, Julius, 154
Mongolian Autonomous Federation, 85, 110, 228n4
Mōri Iga, 94
Mori Shigeaki, 154, 244n79, 245n89
Mōri Terumoto, 244n82
Morning Post, 57
Moroi Rokurō, 95, 223n22
Mount Bandai, 26, 201n89, 211n114; eruption, 26
Moynier, Gustave, 3, 194n9
Mozambique, 128, 237n128
MRCS. *See* Manchukuo Red Cross Society (MRCS)
M.S. Gripsholm, 129
Mt. Kompira, 156
mujō. *See* Kamo no Chōmei
Mukden, 80, 81, 82, 85–86, 87, 125, 218n83
Mukden Manchuria Railway West Coolie Camp, 86
Mukōda Shōsuke, 94
Mumbai, 129, 212n3
Murata Sōtarō, 122
musicians, 121, 128, 135, 147, 210n105
Muslim, 8

Nagano Wakamatsu, 155, 157
Nagasaki, 10, 27, 65, 123–125, 137–138, 141, 146, 155–164
Nagasaki City, 123, 155–156, 158, 161–164, 245n97; state of extreme emergency, 155
Nagasaki City Atomic Bomb Records Preservation Committee, 162
Nagasaki detention camp, 124
Nagasaki Medical College, 157
Nagasaki Min'yū Shimbun, 155
Nagasaki Mitsubishi Dockyard Branch Camp, 162; Kōyagi-chō, 162–163; Kōyagi-jima, 162–163; Mitsubishi Dockyard POW camp, 163
Nagasaki Peace Memorial Service, 248n140
Nagasaki Prefecture, 155, 158

Nagase Tokihira, 18; community medical care, 18; Hiroshima garrison of the Imperial Japanese Army, 18; Hiroshima Red Cross Hospital, 18; Philanthropic (*Hakuai*) Hospital, 18
Nagoya, 20
Nagoya University. *See* Aichi Medical College
Nakagawa Nozomu, 125, 231n49
Nakajima Kesago, 116, 230n37
Nampo, 213n8, 214n19
Nanjing, 53, 109, 113, 115–116
Nanjing massacre, 115–116
Nanshi District, Shanghai, 112
Nara, 60, 191
nationalism, 5, 8, 9, 16, 42, 44, 98, 168, 193n7, 242n29
Nationalist Chinese Army, 109, 112
National Mobilization Law, 140
National Red Cross Day, 87
national Red Cross societies, 1, 4, 2, 6, 7, 15, 17, 21, 26, 33, 38, 46, 48, 49, 54, 56, 80, 87, 88, 104, 108, 117, 119, 122, 123, 124, 126, 127, 129, 166, 194n19, 205n23
National Red Cross Society. *See* national Red Cross societies
native Japanese humanitarianism, 16
Natsume Sōseki, 197n21
natural disaster relief, 4, 26, 30–33, 39, 46, 54, 63–64, 76, 87, 103, 211n116; earthquakes, 26, 28, 30–32, *31*, *32*, 39–40, 45, 61, 72–74, 78, 87, 103, 165–166, 201n90, 211n115, 215n31, 215n35, 215n36, 215n37, 240n14; floods, 26, 30; great fires, 26; tsunamis, 26, 165; typhoons, 26
Nazi Germany, 36, 62, 210n105
Needels, Theodore S., 152
Netherlands, 8, 19, 48, 87, 125, 129, 163, 196n2, 208n67, 233n72, 247n138
neutrality, 8, 12, 19, 40, 49, 54, 113, 115, 124, 127, 166, 198n45
New Testament, 121
New York, 34
New Zealand, 48, 100, 126, 134, 190, 223n27

Nicaraguan Red Cross, 55, 128
Nightingale-ism, 143
Niigata, 155, 245n91
Nikkō, 60, *60*
Ninagawa Arata, 5, 33–35, 49, 167, 194n20, 203n126; the humanitarian league of peoples, 34; the political league of peoples, 34
Ninomiya Sontoku, 197n24
Nippon Shimbun, 104
Nippon Yusen Kabushiki Kaisha (NYK), 54, 122, 224n46
Nippu Jiji, 94, 96, 97–99, 221–222n112
Nobel Prize, 201n100
Nobuo Jumpei, 229n12
Noguchi Yuzuru, 123
nongovernmental organizations (NGOs), 2, 6, 45
Noroeste, 100
North Africa, 129
North America, 91, 95, 98, 161
North and South America, 1, 36, 41, 69, 92, 168
North and South Gyeongsang, 214n20
North and South Pyongan, 214n20
North China, 109, 125
Northeast China, 42, 49
North Korea, 79
North Manchuria Great Flood Disaster, 87
Norway, 63, 87, 129
nuclear bombings, 65, 137–139, 146, 151, 158–159, 164, 245n91
nuclear bomb syndrome, 150, 159
Nurses' Association of Imperial Japan, 77
Nurses Association of Japan (NAJ), 77
Nurses' Association of Korea (NAK), 77
nursing education, 18, 46, 59, 63, 75, 77, 84, 139, 140, 145

Obama, Barack, U.S. President, 245n89
Oceania, 41, 106, 129
Ogasawara Naganari, 93, 221n9
Ogata Kōan, 11, 18, 19, 196n2; Tekijuku, a Dutch studies school in Osaka, 196n2

Oguri Kōzukenosuke (Tadamasa), 198n39
Ogyū Yuzuru. *See* Matsudaira Norikata
Ōita, 23, 162
Okada Keisuke, 58, 59, 60
Okamoto Suemasa, 111, 112, 142
Okazaki Takejirō, 155
Okumura Ihoko, 221n9
Ōmura Naval Hospital, 158, 159, 229n14
oral history, 190
oryzalin, 121, 122
Osaka, 11, 18–19, 25, 60, 73, 119, 121–122
Osaka POW Camp, 121–122; oryzalin and glucose, to treat an epidemic of dysentery among predominately British, 121
Osaka prefectural government, 215n37
Ōsako Ichirō, 154
Ōshima Island, 72
Ōshima Yoshimasa, 82, 83
Ōsugi Sakae, 215n28
Otaru Camp, 227n1, 237n119
Ottoman Empire, 4, 7, 15, 197n15
Overseas Enterprise Company Limited, 100, *101*
ōyake, 166
Oyster Bay Long Island, 34
Ozawa Takeo, 70, 213n9

Pacific, 57, 91, 92, 94, 98, 109, 114
pacificism, 45, 102
Pacific War, 10, 36, 80, 89, 94, 98, 108, 109, 116–135, 139, 142, 146, 166, 190, 207n62
Panama, 128
Pan American Red Cross Conference. *See* Third Pan American Red Cross Conference
Pan-Pacific Association of Japan, 96, 223n27; Peer Club in Tokyo, 223n27; U.S. congressmen, 223n27
Pan-Pacific movement, 98, 223n27
Papua New Guinea, 126
Paraguay, 128
Paravicini, Fritz, 122, 152–153

Paris, 12, 19, 24, 56, 111, 129
patriotic humanitarianism, 35, 40–45, 50, 167; elevating Japan's prestige in the international community, 168
patriotic service (*hōkoku jippei*), 20
Patriotic Women's Association, 28
patriotism, 6, 20, 42, 143
patronage, 5, 11, 16, 103, 139, 167
Paulista, 100
Payne, John Barton, 45, 57, 58, 63, 205n26
peace, 21, 34, 36, 38, 39, 44, 45, 47, 49, 57, 58, 59, 63, 79, 98, 164, 166, 204n9, 248n140
peacetime relief activities, 5, 9, 26–28, 87, 88; peacetime activities, 45, 203n127; poverty relief, epidemic disease treatment, care of orphans, and public health services, 26
Pearl Harbor, 67, 98, 116, 227n1
People's Rights Movement, 240n14
Peru, 48, 104, 128, 226n68
Pestalozzi, Max, 234n87
Philanthropic Society, 5, 11–15, 18–20, 139, 196n10, 239n7
Philippine-American War, 222n14
Philippines, 119, 125, 127, 168, 222n14
plutonium, 158, 159
Poincaré, Raymond, 24
poison gas, 157, 246n106
Poland, 25, 48, 240n14, 201n87, 218n93
Polish-Soviet War, 25, 201n87
Port Arthur, 81
post-traumatic stress disorder (PTSD), 138
post-war period, 16
potassium cyanide, 138–139
poverty, 4–6, 16–17, 26, 104
POW camps, 23, 114, 119–125, 130, 134, 153, 157, 162, 163, 190, 234n87
POWs, 22–23, 65, 108, 114, 115, 116, 117, 119–127, 129–131, 134–135, 147, 164
Prince Kan'in Kotohito, 32
Prince Komatsu Akihito, 13, 15
Prince Kuni Yoshihiko, 224n46
Princess Arisugawa, 239n9
Prince Takamatsu, 98

Prince Tokugawa Iesato, 6–7, 57
Prince Yasuhiko Asaka, 116
Principles of Japanese Red Cross Society Nurses, 140
Pringsheim, Klaus, 62; German Jewish, 62; Hibiya Public Hall, 62; Tokyo Academy of Music, 62; Tokyo University of the Arts, 62
Prisoner of War Information Bureau, 119, 121–122
professionalism, 8, 10, 21, 25, 138–140, 145, 164
professional nurses, 27, 77; died in the line of duty, 28, 138
professionals, 35, 92, 138, 145, 164
public. *See ōyake*
public health crises, 27, 166
Pusan, 69, 70, 213n7, 213n8, 214n19, 214n20
Pyongyang, 70, 71, 72, 75, 80, 213n8
Pyongyang Jikei Hospital, 75

Qing Chinese, 83
Qingdao, 69
Qing Police Agency, 82
Queen Alexandra, 167, 194n19
Queen Victoria, 57

radiation, 65, 138, 146–148, 150–152, 157–159, 161–162, 168, 244n69
radiation diseases, 150, 247n133; acute leukemia and fatal visceral damage, 153; bad eyesight and illness, 247n133; high (42-degree) fevers and exhibiting the symptoms of cerebral palsy, 150; purplish subcutaneous haemorrhages, bleeding, rapid decrease in the level of white blood cells, and then they died, 150; radiation illness, 159; radiation-related diseases, 148; radiation sickness, 138, 147, 150, 162
Rakovsky, Christian Georgievich, 208n73
Ranam, 214n20
RCSC. *See* Red Cross Society of China (RCSC)
RCSC Nanjing Branch, 115
Red Crescent Alliance, 55
Red Cross emblem, 7, 13, 15, 50

Red Cross Isahaya Atomic Bomb Hospital.
  See Isahaya Branch Naval Hospital
Red Cross messages, 22, 129, 131–134, 247n133
Red Cross Museum on Medical Science and
  Health in Tokyo, 103
Red Cross parcels, 121, 124–125
Red Cross Society of China, Beijing, 31–32
Red Cross Society of China (RCSC), 8,
  30, 31, 38, 50–53, 66, 110–112, 114–115,
  135, 167, 189–190, 206n42, 207n52; local
  philanthropic activities in China, 8;
  new arrival of the Western Red Cross
  movement, 8; Red Cross Societies
  transported to Asia narrowly served the
  metropole, 8
Red Cross Society of China (Shanghai), 32, 51
Red Lion and Sun Society of Persia, 55
refugees, 25, 65, 79, 86, 111, 139, 201n87
Regimental Combat Team, 97
Regulations of the Employment of Chief
  Nurses and Nurses, 143, 242n30
relief operations, 20, 26–33, 42, 72–73, 140,
  145, 149, 158; international exchange,
  128–131; Japanese, 82; JRCS's, 26–33, 41,
  86–89, 103, 116; natural disaster, 26, 28,
  30–33, 64; pandemic, 27–28, 82; Russo-
  Japanese War, 94
resident-Koreans, 72, 73, 215n37
Ribeirao Preto, 100
Rio de Janeiro, 100, 103–104
Roma, 65
Roosevelt, Franklin Delano, 56, 63
Roosevelt, Theodore, 34
Russia, 21, 23, 30, 70, 79, 80–81, 85–87, 111,
  139, 167
Russian Red Cross (RRC), 22, 81, 167
Russian refugees, 79, 86
Russo-Japanese War, 5, 9, 21–23, 32, 80–81,
  93–94, 101–102, 199n57, 213n9, 221n9,
  227n1; donated 2,000 blankets and 1,500
  sets of undershirts, nightclothes, and
  obi, 22; rural Japanese communities, 23;
  Russian POWs, 22; siege of Port Arthur, 21

Ruth, Babe, 7
Ryujuton, 83

Saigon, 128–129
Saitō Makoto, 73, 103, 215n32, 225n53
Saitō Tateki, 88
Saitō Toyoko, 93
Saitō Yoshihira, 229n12
Sakhalin, 69, 201n87
samurai, 11, 16, 18–19, 197n14
San Francisco, 91, 95
San Francisco earthquake, 28
Sano Tsunetami, 11, 19
Sanriku earthquake, 26, 240n14
Santa Fe, 130–131
Santiago, 91, 104
São Paulo, 91, 100–107, 191
São Paulo Santa Cruz Hospital. *See* Japanese
  Santa Cruz Hospital in São Paulo
Sasebo Naval Hospital, 158
Satsuma Rebellion, 12–13, 18
Save the Children International Union, 207n58
SCAP. *See* Supreme Commander for the
  Allied Powers (SCAP)
Seattle, 221n9
Second Oriental Red Cross Conference in
  Tokyo, 103
Second Sino-Japanese War, 64–65, 106, 109,
  115, 141, 195n22, 238n150; anti-Japanese
  slogan, 113; Resist the Japanese, fight for
  our lives, 116
Seishū Shimpō, 106
Seki Hajime, 73, 215n36
Seki Masayuki, 111
Sekishin-kai (Red Heart Association), 94
Seoul, 60, 70–72, 75–77, 95
Serum Institute, 27
sexual violence, 139
Shakespeare, 123
Shanghai, 20, 30, 32, 49–52, 59, 69, 79,
  109–115, 124–125, 129, 141–142, 167, 190
Shanghai Incident of 1932, 49–53, 59, 79,
  167, 190, 219n97; Chapei (Zhabei), 51;

Shanghai Incident of 1932 (*continued*)
Chinese Red Cross ambulances, 51; JRCS' cooperation with the Red Cross Society of China (RCSC) in investigating alleged Imperial Japanese Army (IJA)'s war crimes, 167; JRCS Extra Relief Party No. 13, 50; Kaiding District in a bamboo garden near Mo Lo Shiang, 52
Shanghai Military Logistics Hospital, 50
Shanhaiguan, 83
Shepping, Elizabeth, 77
Shibata Shōkei, 139, 239n8
Shibusawa Eiichi, 223n27, 225n47
Shidehara Kijūrō, 39, 204n9
Shiga Kiyoshi, 72, 73, 74, 215n29; Awarded the Order of the Sacred Treasure, 1st class, 73; Bacillus Calmette–Guerin vaccine, 215n29; *Shigella dysenteriae*, 215n29
Shigemitsu Mamoru, 206n46
Shima Hospital, 146
Shimaji Mokurai, 14, 197n15
Shimane Prefecture, 17–19, 22
Shimane Red Cross Society (SRCS), 18; JRCS Shimane Chapter, 18; to provide emotional support to families bereaved, 18; raise funds to establish a war memorial and hold memorial services, 18
Shimazu Tadatsugu, 55, 115, 117–119, 121–122, 124, 125, 127, 130, 134, 207n62
Shindō Renmei, "the League of the Way of Emperor's Subject," 106, 226n72
Shinkōzen Primary School, 158
Shinsei-maru, 122
Shinto, 13, 16, 197n14
Shizuoka, 22–23
Shōhei-zaka Gakumonjo, 240
Siam, 7, 64, 207n58
Siberia, 25, 126, 153, 201n87
Siberian Intervention, 69, 79, 85, 140, 201n87, 240n14
Singapore, 124–125, 128–129
Sinŭiju, 71, 79–80
Slavs, 65, 87, 125

soft diplomacy, 53, 59, 71, 92, 95, 104–105
Soga, Yasutaro, 97
Solti, R., 163
Sŏngjin (Kimchaek), 213n8
Sorachi coal mine camp, 233n78
Sorocabana, 100
South Africa, 207n58, 237n128
South African Red Cross (SARC), 120
South Asia, 8, 129
South China Sea, 122
Southeast Asia, 91, 120, 124–125, 130, 147, 191
South Manchuria Railway Co., Ltd., 54, 82, 83
South Seas Mandate (*Nan'yō*), 69, 212n3
Sovereign Military Order of Malta (SMOM), 207n58
Soviet prisoners, 88, 120, 233n72
Soviet Red Cross (SRC). *See* Union of Red Cross and Red Crescent Societies of the USSR (Soviet RCRC)
Soviet Union, 48, 57, 124, 166, 208n73
Spanish flu pandemic, 9, 27, 166
Special Committee Departments in Honolulu, 91
Special Higher Police (*Tokkō*), 155
SSERC. *See* JRCS Shanghai Special Expeditionary Relief Corps (SSERC)
stateless individuals, 65, 128
State of São Paulo, 100, 102, 104
Statistics Bureau of the imperial Japanese government, 27
St. Petersburg, 23
Strauss, Richard, 61, 62; An Alpine Symphony, Bayreuth Festival, Op. 64, 62; Thus Spoke Zarathustra, Op. 30, 62; Two Anthems for 16-Part Mixed Chorus, Op. 34, 62
student labor mobilization, 134, 238n150
Suez Canal, 24
Sugamo Prison, 121
Sugimoto, Henry, 132
Sumatra, 124
Sumida, Daizo, 97
Sumida River, 61
Sunday Star, 57

INDEX 325

Supreme Commander for the Allied Powers (SCAP), 121, 152, 207n62; offered to send fifteen tons of medicine and medical kits, including penicillin, dried plasma, glucose, Ringers Lactate solution, sulphonamide, DDT, cresol, alcohol, nutritional supplements tablets, bandages, and surgical appliances to Hiroshima, 153
Supreme Court of Hawai'i, 97
Supreme War Council, 156
surrender, 106, 117, 119, 121, 123, 135, 138, 152–153, 156
Swiss Political Department. *See* Federal Council of Switzerland, Political Department
Switzerland, 3, 7, 34, 54, 71, 87, 108, 122, 126, 126, 130, 189
Syria, 206n30

Taft, William Howard, 2, 167
Tagawa Sumiko, 161
Taipei, 20, 69
Taisan-maru, 113
Taishō democracy, 35, 39, 167, 204n8
Taiwan, 20, 27–28, 146, 217n73
Taiwan Chapter. *See* JRCS Taiwan Chapter
Tajima Jidayū, 163, 247n133
Takahashi Korekiyo, 225n47
Takahashi Masaaki, 151
Takaki, Herbert, 97
Takakuwa, Shujiro, 97
Takamatsu Ryōun, 19; *Dōaisha*, 20; former Tokugawa Loyalist, 198n44; Medal of Honor with Blue Ribbon in 1913, 198n45
Takeuchi Ken, 147
Takioka, Masayuki, 97
The Tale of the Heike, 197
Taloa, 154
Tamil, 233
Tang Erho, 32, 202n122
Tateyama air raid shelter, 156
Tatsuta-maru, 129

Teia-maru, 131
temporary relief nurses (*rinji kyūgo kangofu*), 143, 146
Tenth International Conference of the Red Cross, 22; Washington Declaration, 22
Thailand, 15, 124
Third Pan American Red Cross Conference, 103
Tianjin, 69, 109
Tieling, 81, 218n83
Times—Picayune, 57
Tohoku 2011 triple disaster of earthquake, tsunami, and the Fukushima nuclear reactor meltdown the Japanese who lost loved ones and were driven from their homes, 166
Tokugawa Family, 9, 38, 39
Tokugawa government, 19, 39–40, 57, 196n3, 197n14, 198n31, 198n39
Tokugawa Iesada, 58
Tokugawa Iesato, 6–7, 9, 38–40, 42, 44–45, 53–54, 56–59, 61, 63–64, 67, 95–96, 98, 103–104; ameliorate the suffering of human beings in need, 54; Disaster Charity Association, 40; Eton College, 39; Grand Cordon of the Supreme Order of the Chrysanthemum, 67; LORCS' Standing Committee, 39, 64; Nobleman Association, 40; Saiseikai Imperial Gift Foundation, 39; served as honorary Chair of the House of Peers from 1903 to 1933, 39; shogunate, 39–40; *Shōgun-sama*, 40; Tokyo Jikei Association, 39
Tokugawa Ieyasu, 57, 209n84
Tokugawa Kuniyuki, 116, 153, 230n35
Tokugawa Yoshihisa, 34
Tokushima, 23
Tokyo, 9, 15, 20, 25–27, 30, 36, 38–41, 45–46, 52, 61–62, 72–74, 103, 113, 153–155, 198n45
Tokyo Declaration of 1934, 9, 38, 41, 45, 59, 62–67, 103, 108, 119, 167, 190, 203n3, 228n2; the 1949 Fourth Geneva Convention's provisions on the Protection

Tokyo Declaration of 1934 (*continued*) of Civilian Persons in Time of War, 38; ambulance services for automobile accidents, 63; civilians of enemies residing in the territory of belligerents, 119; dissemination of information, 63; Draft International Convention on the Condition and Protection of Civilians of Enemy Nationality Who are on Territory Belonging to or Occupied by a Belligerent of 1934, 134n3; the foundation of the Fourth Geneva Convention of 1949, 9; mass communications, 63; natural disaster relief activities, 32, 54, 63; nursing education, 46, 59, 63, 84, 139; promotion of international goodwill among nations, 63; public health services, 26, 63; resolution thirty-nine, 63–64, 66, 212n129; Tokyo Draft, 63, 211n122, 212n128; volunteer workers and helpers for peacetime programmes, 63; wartime and peacetime protection of civilians, 9. *See also* Geneva Conventions

Tokyo Draft. *See* Geneva Conventions; Tokyo Declaration of 1934

Tokyo Imperial University, 215n29

Tokyo International Red Cross Conference. *See* Fifteenth International Red Cross Conference of Tokyo in 1934

Tokyo Kaikan, 60

Tokyo metropolitan government, 73

Tokyo Metropolitan Police Department (TMPD), 214n28

Tokyo University's Institute for Study of Infectious Diseases, 201n100

Tokyo War Crime Trial. *See* International Military Tribunal for the Far East

Tokyo Women's Medical Professional School, 59–60

Tolstoy, Leo, 102

Tongzhow munity, 228n3

Toscanini, Arturo, 62

total war, 41, 109, 135–136, 140, 200n70, 217n73

Toyota City, 189

Trade Bureau of the Ministry of Foreign Affairs, 93

transnational humanitarian movement, 9, 68–90; transnational activities, 46; transnational networks, 109

Trans-Pacific movement, 91–99

Treaty of Amity, Commerce and Navigation, 100

Treaty of Portsmouth, 70, 81, 201n87

Trotsky, Leon, 102, 208n73

Tsar Nicholas II, 23

Tsuji Zen'nosuke, 16; commemoration ceremonies for the war dead of enemies in the aftermath of battles, 16

Tsukiyama, Wilfred C., 97

tuberculosis (TB), 27; eradication campaign, 75, 83, 104

Turkey, 30, 87, 206n30

Turkish Red Crescent Society, 4, 55

Uchiyama Iwatarō, 102–104, 225n51

Uganda, 237n128

ultra-nationalists, 106

Umezu Yoshijirō, 110

Union of Red Cross and Red Crescent Societies of the USSR (Soviet RCRC), 30, 55–56, 135, 244n74

United Kingdom (UK), 23–25, 39, 48, 56–58, 60, 66, 128, 139, 189, 191, 194n11

United States (U.S.), 2, 6–7, 9, 33, 34, 39, 44–46, 48, 54, 56–58, 60, 92–95, 98, 102, 106–107, 111, 124–130, 139, 156, 166–167, 189, 194n11, 198n30, 201n90, 213n9, 228n8, 233n72, 236n112

United States Strategic Bombing Survey, 263

University of Berlin, 201n100

University of Tokyo, 16, 111

Urakami district, 156, 161

uranium, 146, 151–152, 159

U.S. 1924 Immigration Act (Immigration Act of 1924), 100, 222n13, 224n38

U.S. government, 2, 31, 124, 126–127, 167, 245n89
U.S.-Japan cooperation, 34
USS Grouper, 122
USS Mactan, 127
U.S. soldiers, 120, 222n14
USSR embassy, 56
U.S. State Department, 57
Utsunomiya, 60

Valcke, C., 163
Vancouver, 91, 213n6
Vargas, Getúlio, Brazilian President, 103, 106; assimilation laws that banned public use of immigrants' native language, dress, and cultural practices, 103
victimization, 164
victims, 26, 28, 30, 33, 50, 52, 61, 65, 73, 78, 80–81, 86–87, 111, 115, 138–139, 145–150, 154, 156, 158–161, 163–164, 166, 169, 214–215n28, 215n37
Vietnam, 125
village associations (*chōnaikai*), 5
Vladivostok, 25, 69, 85, 124, 140, 189, 201n87, 223n21
Volunteer Nurse Women's Association, 61, 239n9
Volunteer Nursing Association, 28
von Hofmann, August Wilhelm, 239n8
von Siebold, Heinrich, 139

Wajima Eiji, 112, 229n12
Wang Yuan, 207n52
War Council of the ARC, 34
war crimes, 108, 110–111, 167
War Prisoners' Relief Committee Department (WPRCD). *See* JRCS War Prisoners' Relief Committee Department (WPRCD)
wartime mobilization, 109, 140, 245n92
wartime relief activities, 16, 32, 33, 106, 139, 239n9
Wartime Relief Regulations of the Japanese Red Cross Society, 145

Washington, DC, 56–57, 127, 190–191, 231n50
Washington Declaration, 22
Washington Naval Treaty Conference in 1922, 39
West Assault course, 7
Western-centered humanitarian enlightenment, 34
Western Hemisphere, 100, 107
Western National Red Cross Societies, 7, 33, 166
White Cross insignias, 130, 131
Wilson, Woodrow, 33, 34
Women's Patriotic Association, 80
Wonsan, 79, 86, 213n8
World War I, 1, 6, 9, 22–23, 24, 25, 25, 33, 34, 36, 38, 41, 91–92, 95, 96, 100, 107, 111, 131, 139, 140, 166, 202n103, 203n127, 211n124, 216n56, 227n1, 240n14, 240n17, 248n4; Allied soldiers from the Battles of Arras, Champagne, and Verdun between 1915 and 1916, 24; Trans-Siberian Railway, 23
World War II, 2, 5–6, 8, 26, 40, 49, 64–66, 68, 73, 92, 100, 106–109, 135, 140–143, 145, 166, 168, 189–191, 207n62
WPRCD. *See* JRCS War Prisoners' Relief Committee Department (WPRCD)

Xingcheng, 83
Xinmin, 218n83

Yamaguchi Red Cross Society (YRCS). *See* Hara Yasutarō
Yamamoto Gombei, 39
Yamamoto Isoroku, 110
Yamamoto Tsuyako, 149
Yamanoue no Okura, 197n26; Hinkyūmondōka, 197n26; *Man'yōshū*, 197n26; Nara period, 197n26
Yamasaki, Edward N., 97
Yamasaki, Hayami, 97
Yamashita Fujie, 161
Yasuda Kazuyoshi, 94

Yasukuni Shrine, 61, 143, 242n29
Yasuyama Kōdō, 112, 229n12, 229n14
Yawata Steel Works, 245n91
Yellow River floods, 28–30
Yi Ch'anguk, 86; Chiba Medical College, 86
Yi Kyŏmgu, 86
Yingkou, 81, 218n83
YMCA, 121
Yokohama, 30, 39–40, 72, 95, 119, 122, 124, 128–130
Yokohama Camp, 227n1
Yokohama Specie Bank, 94, 130
Yomiuri Shimbun, 56, 63
Yuasa Kurahei, 58
Yugoslavia, 207n58

Yukinaga Masae, 147–148, 149, 150–151; Working Report of Wartime Relief Parties, 243n54
Yumoto Fumihiko, 15; all strata of Japanese society, 16; praxis of native Japanese humanitarianism, 16; "public" response to poverty, hunger, and famine in the Edo Period, 16; the revival of ancient Japanese tradition, 16; from rich to poor and from samurai to merchant, 16

Żebrowski, Zenon, 162
Zentsūji, 119, 121
Zentsūji POW Camp, 121
Zhongshan Medical College Hospital, 112

GPSR Authorized Representative: Easy Access System Europe, Mustamäe tee
50, 10621 Tallinn, Estonia, gpsr.requests@easproject.com

www.ingramcontent.com/pod-product-compliance
Lightning Source LLC
Chambersburg PA
CBHW031231290426
44109CB00012B/253